NEW IMMIGRANT LITERATURES
IN THE UNITED STATES

New Immigrant Literatures in the United States

A Sourcebook to Our Multicultural Literary Heritage

EDITED BY
Alpana Sharma Knippling

Emmanuel S. Nelson, Advisory Editor

Greenwood Press
Westport, Connecticut • London

Library of Congress Cataloging-in-Publication Data

New immigrant literatures in the United States : a sourcebook to our
  multicultural literary heritage / edited by Alpana Sharma Knippling.
     p.   cm.
  Includes bibliographical references and index.
  ISBN 0–313–28968–9 (alk. paper)
    1. American literature—Minority authors—History and criticism.
  2. American literature—Foreign authors—History and criticism.
  3. Immigrants—United States—Intellectual life. 4. Minorities—
United States—Intellectual life. 5. Ethnic groups in literature.
  6. Immigrants in literature. 7. Ethnicity in literature.
  I. Knippling, Alpana Sharma.
  PS153.M56N475   1996
  810.9'920693—dc20   95–45211

British Library Cataloguing in Publication Data is available.

Library of Congress Catalog Card Number: 95–45211
ISBN: 0–313–28968–9

First published in 1996

Greenwood Press, 88 Post Road West, Westport, CT 06881
An imprint of Greenwood Publishing Group, Inc.

Printed in the United States of America

The paper used in this book complies with the
Permanent Paper Standard issued by the National
Information Standards Organization (Z39.48–1984).

10 9 8 7 6 5 4 3 2

Contents

II. Caribbean-American Literatures

III. European-American Literatures

IV. Mexican-American Literatures

Preface

Alpana Sharma Knippling

This book constitutes a critical introduction to the new immigrant literatures of the United States. By "new" is meant post-World War II, although all the chapters begin with, or refer to, the historical circumstances of the first generation's immigration to the United States, whether this occurred in the nineteenth century or the twentieth. It may, perhaps, be unnecessary to point out that two historical groups that do not fall within the definition of this book's title are the Native American and African-American ones. The former group lays claim to the origins of this country and is indigenous to it, while the latter group suffered a brutal and forced immigration that deserves a separate and fuller treatment. All other significant racial and ethnic groups and their literatures are represented in this book, although some exclusions were unavoidable, given the immense scope of the project and the plain lack of qualified contributors despite all efforts to locate them. Hence, while the book deplores the lack of treatment of Vietnamese-American and German-American literatures (among others), it is hoped that future scholarship in these areas will redress this lack.

In addition to constituting a critical introduction to post-World War II literatures, the book aims especially at representing hitherto marginalized literatures, specifically the Asian-, Caribbean-, and Mexican-American ones. Participating in this aim, many of the chapters also include discussion of new immigrant women's writing, perhaps the least known and most obviously "gendered" subgenre in the field of immigrant literature. The individual chapters themselves achieve a fine balance between the needs of a reference chapter written for general readers and the needs of a critical and interpretive chapter written for scholars and researchers in fields as diverse as multicultural literature, diasporic literature, critical and cultural studies, comparative literature, and ethnic and multi-ethnic studies. As such, it is hoped that, with both its bibliographical and critical components, the book will address a wide range of needs in the class-room and the library equally.

Contributors have provided an introductory section that conveys the historical and cultural background to the literature in question. Most contributors have also incorporated one or more of the following sections and, in some instances, a combination of these: Literary-Cultural History, Dominant Concerns, Major Authors, Early and Recent Efforts, Prevailing Genres, and Conclusion. In some cases, contributors found it necessary to invent their own sections, thus impart-ing to the book a genuine multiplicity and heterogeneity that mirror the very multiplicity and heterogeneity of new immigrant culture in the United States. In fact, each of the chapters is unique and announces its uniqueness in the way that it is structured. An exemplary instance is Fred Gardaphe's chapter, titled "Italian/American Literature." By discarding the ubiquitous hyphen, Gardaphe follows in the tradition of scholars in his field who think that hyphenation neg-atively emphasizes ethnicity and a minority status over a viable American cul-tural identity. A somewhat similar rationale has been introduced in the field of Asian-American literature according to which hyphenation institutes unequal power relations; the Filipino American essay, for instance, eschews hyphenation altogether. We should extend a similar skepticism to other chapters in the book in which hyphenation should emerge as a problematic idea; here, one thinks almost automatically of the much contested coinage, "Mexican-American."

Two additional comments: most of the chapters focus on writing in English, although many of them make references to non-English writings, and some, like the Pakistani-American chapter and the Chinese-American chapter, include dis-cussions of these; second, on more than one occasion, contributors have included prose/nonfiction/autobiographical texts in their primary bibliography in cases where these texts appeared to constitute a significant part of the corpus of the immigrant "literature" in question.

This book would not have been possible without the expert counsel and guid-ance of Emmanuel Nelson. Not only in his official capacity as advisory editor for Greenwood Publishing Group's multivolume project on ethnic and post-colonial literatures but also in his unofficial capacity as fellow scholar, colleague, and friend, he aided the project every step of the way, from suggesting names of potential contributors to advising me on matters of format. I wish to thank him for his numerous helpful interventions and advice. At Greenwood, I would like to thank former senior editor of humanities Marilyn Brownstein, associate editor of acquisitions George F. Butler, coordinating editor Maureen Melino and production editor Kim Hastings for all their expert and prompt guidance. My research assistant, Emily Carlson, did an excellent job of proofreading the man-uscript, and I thank her for all the hours she put into this project. Thanks also to colleague Ralph Grajeda for his help and advice. Last but not least, I would like to thank my husband, Jim Knippling, who patiently read my many drafts, helped clarify my writing, and kept the home fire burning.

Introduction

Alpana Sharma Knippling

When the *Golden Venture,* a ship smuggling Chinese men and women into the United States, was grounded in June 1993, it provoked a resurgence of the national debate about U.S. immigration policy and, in the pages of popular American newsmagazines, the pros and cons of allowing immigrants, whether legal or illegal, into the United States. So far, the cons seem to outweigh the pros. *Time*'s coverage of the ill-fated *Golden Venture* event portrayed the Chinese immigrants as having voluntarily subjected themselves to bestial conditions, "crammed into the filthy hold of a ship for months at sea" (Church 26). It went on to render Mexican illegal immigrants in almost rodentlike language, as "sneak[ing], run[ning], and tunnel[ing] across the frontier in numbers far greater than the border patrol can possibly control" (26). The ambiguous victory of Proposition 187 in November 1994 in California, which favors the withdrawal of state-level aid from illegal immigrants, certainly reflects many American people's growing disenchantment with what they perceive as an open-door, welfare-state image of the United States. According to a July 1993 poll taken by *Newsweek,* while 59 percent of Americans consider immigration a good thing for the country in the past, compared to 31 percent who think it was bad, 60 percent believe that today immigration is not good, compared to only 20 percent who believe it is still good; further, only 20 percent think that the United States is still a "melting pot" (Thomas and Murr 19). Pessimism about the national economy, coupled with an impatience at the apparent ease with which immigrants can cross the U.S. border and take up minimum-wage jobs that most Americans would shun, makes immigration a volatile topic, a devil's cocktail, indeed, of controversy and debate. A fitting subject for such debate and a case in point is the radical Islamic cleric Sheik Omar Abdel-Rahman, whose name,

Newsweek reports, was on a State Department watch list for Islamic radicals, yet who had been let into the country four times before his green card (permanent resident-alien status) was revoked in 1992 (Turque et al. 25).

As we stand at the brink of the twenty-first century, the timeliness of a national debate about U.S. immigration policy should not blind us to the fact that demeaning representations of immigrants in popular culture have existed since at least the mid-nineteenth century. Interestingly, *Time*'s imagery, which depicts Chinese and Mexican immigrants as a kind of infestation or plague invading the sacrosanct shores of America, uncannily echoes E. L. Doctorow's fictitious description, in his novel *Ragtime,* of immigrants, primarily Italian and East European, headed to Ellis Island at the turn of the century. These immigrants are viewed through the lens of the American character, Father, who is leaving American shores to undertake an exploration of the North Pole with members of Peary's expedition. Father, a patriot and a manufacturer of flags and fireworks, perceives the immigrants with a kind of shudder or dread:

[The transatlantic vessel's] decks were packed with people. Thousands of male heads in derbies. Thousands of female heads covered with shawls. It was a rag ship with a million eyes staring at him. Father, a normally resolute person, suddenly foundered in his soul. A weird despair seized him. The wind came up, the sky had turned overcast. . . . He watched the ship till he could see it no longer. Yet aboard her were only more customers, for the immigrant population set great store by the American flag. (15–16)

Doctorow's Chapter 3 describes the living conditions of turn-of-the-century immigrants in New York City in a way that refuses the sentimental and nostalgic invitation of a Norman Rockwell painting. At the same time, what it also resists is the knee-jerk, unthinking stereotyping of the tenement, hand-to-mouth existence of many early immigrants in the metropolis. Doctorow's description, deliberately unromantic and gritty, takes a critical distance on stereotyping by unpacking its historical apparatus. The Italian and Eastern European immigrants he describes are taken, on arrival, to Ellis Island, where they are tagged, bathed, renamed, and separated from some members of their families—"old folks, people with bad eyes, riffraff, and . . . those who looked insolent" (17)—who end up on return voyages. The immigrants who stay are hated by New Yorkers because they are "filthy and illiterate":

They stank of fish and garlic. They had running sores. They had no honor and worked for next to nothing. They stole. They drank. They raped their own daughters. They killed each other casually. Among those who despised them the most were the second-generation Irish, whose fathers had been guilty of the same crimes. (17–18)

By delving into the stockpile of racist immigrant imagery, Doctorow shows it for what it is: an exploitative strategy for the elite to maintain both cultural superiority and economic monopoly. The objects of derision, the immigrants, constitute the very labor for an expanding American capitalism and, through this capitalist economy, a growing pride in American citizenship among Americans and, by extension, immigrants themselves. Father's manufacturing of flags and fireworks, which the immigrants "set great store" by and which, in all likelihood, they themselves will labor to produce, is the perfect emblem of this curious marriage of capitalism and patriotism. Later chapters of *Ragtime* discuss the absorption of immigrants into the cheap labor market, including their participation in Henry Ford's breakthrough invention, the assembly line, which replaced the principle of heterogeneity with that of mechanization.

What this discussion of historical-literary representations of immigration should suggest so far is a picture of a society increasingly driven toward homogeneity, continuously setting itself on the track of socioeconomic betterment, even as it is founded on the labor of others perhaps less privileged but themselves more or less aligned to the same track. In this sense, the United States is always caught in the process of remaking itself, although what is being remade is at once abstract (a field of meanings, values, and possibilities) and concrete (an endlessly and identically replicable commodity, such as a Ford car).

Still, the similarities between Doctorow's turn-of-the-century immigration and the picture of immigration today end after a point. Most of the legal immigrants entering the country today are of non-European descent and, as many of the Asian immigrant chapters included in this volume bear out, are subjected to a harsher treatment in American public culture, owing to their visible racial otherness. Over 80 percent of new immigrants are people of color. The state of California is 40 percent immigrant, and perhaps nowhere else is race such an urgent and explosive subject. But it took the violent racial unrest in the wake of the first Rodney King verdict in 1992 to alert many of us to the conflicts between African Americans and Korean Americans, which, if they were not tragic enough in themselves, were exploited in the media to the point of provoking angry criticism from the Korean-American quarter. Repeated local television airing of two videotapes in tandem—one showing the beating of Rodney King by policemen, the other showing the shooting of Latasha Harlins by shopkeeper Soon Ja Du—prompted a Korean-American newspaper to say:

Our complaint is directed to the constant refrain of "the Korean-born grocer killing a black teenager," which couldn't help but sow the seeds of racial hatred . . . [and make us wonder]: was there any conspiracy among the . . . white-dominated media to pit one ethnic group against another and sit back and watch them destroy one another? (quoted in Kim 30)

Corroborating this view of a kind of unofficial, neoimperialist divide-and-rule policy were other Korean Americans, according to whom "while headlines like 'Irish American businessman jailed' or 'Jewish shopkeeper arrested' are unimaginable, the *Los Angeles Times* titled its article 'Korean Grocer Who Killed

Black Teen Gets Probation.' To be complete . . . the title should have added that the judge was white'' (quoted in Kim 30).

Hence, we may safely say that while immigration has always been part and parcel of American history, new global macroeconomic factors ranging from population growth to expanded telecommunications have effected a surge of migration to the United States, which, while it is still lower than the peak surge of 1900–1920, has made for a newly charged hostility directed at immigrants of color. It is not surprising, then, that the European modes of assimilation so prevalent in the earlier decades of this century have been replaced by Asian, Caribbean, and Mexican modes of difference, even resistance. Among these groups, cultural difference is, at best, celebrated and, at the least, held in tension with the impulse to assimilate. As Shan Qiang He puts it in his chapter, ''Chinese-American Literature'':

The word ''immigrant'' has a verbal felicity. Its literal meaning, ''moving into,'' has the connotation of ''settling down'' and ''reaching the destination of assimilation,'' whereby the word itself will be put under erasure. This seems to be the manifest destiny of European immigrants in America. However, that destination of assimilation always moves a little beyond the reach of Chinese immigrants, ''strangers from a different shore.''(43)

One consequence of changes in the racial and cultural makeup of new U.S. immigrants has been the widespread dissemination of unfounded and contradictory knowledge about immigration and the U.S. economy. Contrary to the myth of immigrants' depleting the national economy, studies often quoted by pro-immigrationists show that the long-term benefits of immigration vastly outnumber short-term costs. For instance, the unskilled labor of immigrants complements the skilled labor of United States-born workers, thus increasing the economic stability of the general population; what is more, in their lifetime, immigrants pay more in taxes ($85 billion) than they receive in government benefits ($24 billion); finally, immigrants earn more than native-born Americans, and an increase in their population leads to an increase in new jobs (for more facts and figures, see Mills 21–22). Of course, it must be said that experts favoring restriction on immigration see things differently. Still, it is worth noting that the current flow of immigrants to the United States is considerably lower than the 1900–1920 peak: whereas immigrants were 1 percent of the population then, they constitute only one-third of 1 percent today.

Coupled with popular misinformation is a plain lack of information about the history of certain immigrant groups in the country. For this reason, some of the chapters in this volume, such as the Filipino, Korean, Dominican, and Sephardic Jewish ones, will redress an imbalance of knowledge about new, emerging, previously underrepresented, or marginalized immigrant literatures. Still other chapters in the volume will productively historicize and problematize the very concept of immigration in unexpected ways. It may surprise some general readers to learn that the Chinese were here from the mid-1800s onward, that the competition they offered gold miners in the Sierra Nevada led to their lynching and torturing and that they went on to build many of the country's transcontinental railroads; that Japanese Americans were put in concentration camps during World War II, leading to the generational divide between the issei and the nisei; that before the restrictive immigration law of 1924, there was an Indian diaspora in the States largely owing to British imperialism in India; that part of the United States was once half of Mexico, annexed by the United States as a result of the Mexican-American War (1846–1848) and sealed by the Guadalupe Hidalgo Treaty of 1848, which gave Mexicans the choice either to move to what was left of Mexico or to remain in the ceded territory and become U.S. citizens; and that U.S. citizenship was bestowed on Puerto Ricans as a result of the colonial history of the United States in Puerto Rico dating back to the 1898 Spanish-American War.

The cultural changes embodied in the figure of the new immigrant did not occur without certain crucial changes in the legal history of immigration. Briefly described, this history includes the effects of a number of arcane and tortuously convoluted immigration acts and reforms, the most significant of which is the Immigration and Nationality Act Amendments of 1965; the following account has been summarized from Mills (15–19).

The Chinese Exclusion Act of 1882 had ensured the trend toward a predominantly white immigrant body, further bolstered by a provision in the 1924 Johnson-Reed Act that, in effect, excluded the Japanese as well. According to the 1924 act, no more than 150,000 non-Western immigrants could enter the country per year; the law's quota divisions worked in favor of the British and Northern European groups. Subsequently, there was a considerable drop in immigration. Compared to the 23.5 million people who came to the United States from 1880 to 1920, the period from 1921 to 1930 yielded only 4 million, and the decade of the 1940s saw just 1 million. The McCarran-Walter Immigration and Nationality Act of 1952 did not really change this figure significantly, although it removed the racial barriers to naturalization and, by extension, immigration. But it wasn't until the new amendments of 1965, passed in the progressive spirit of the 1960s, that the country began to see an upsurge in the number of non-Western immigrants. Unprecedented and far-reaching in its effects, the 1965 bill did not identify immigrants by race, allowing up to 20,000 people from any single country and admitting only 120,000 immigrants of a total of 290,000 from the Western Hemisphere. The key idea behind the bill was family reunification—80 percent of the numerically limited visas were for close relatives of American citizens and residents—but an unforeseen loophole inadvertently allowed the parents, spouses, and offspring of any adult American citizen to enter the country regardless of numerical restrictions. As a result, non-Western immigration brought the total number of immigrants to a number matched only by the statistics seen at the turn of the century.

Subsequently, two immigration laws were created to check the increase of immigrants to the United States. There is general agreement among immigration experts that these laws have ended up creating quite the opposite effect. The first one, the 1986 Immigration Reform and Control Act (IRCA), granted amnesty to illegal immigrants who entered the country before 1982, on one hand, and, on the other, made employers punishable for hiring illegal aliens. As a result of IRCA, 2.6 million illegal immigrants accepted amnesty, but it did not prove impossible for employers, if they so chose, to avoid the restrictions. After the first two years, illegal immigration began to rise again. Current estimates show that 500,000 illegal immigrants enter the country each year. In like manner, the Immigration Act of 1990 has increased immigration. An attempt to offset the 1965 law's family reunification loophole, which had the effect of admitting more immigrants with large extended families, the 1990 law intended to build a stronger economy out of immigration: there would be 10,000 visas for people willing to invest $1 million in a new business that hired at least ten employees. However, the law was passed without a corresponding reduction in the number of immigrants entering the country as part of the family reunification policy. Consequently, instead of reducing immigration, it increased to 140,000 the number of immigrants admitted on the basis of their job skills or talents.

Unintended and unprecedented effects of immigration laws call attention not only to the shifting exigencies and contradictions typifying current U.S. legislative history vis-à-vis the new immigration but also to larger transnational informational flows whose digital revolution is already rendering the print revolution of the twentieth century old-fashioned and obsolete. In this context, it is entirely symptomatic that our critical language revels in, and thus reveals, the ironies of all our "post-" words: post-modernism, post-nationalism, post-colonialism/coloniality, post-feminism, post-literacy, post-Marxism, post-cold war, and so on. To evoke the figure of the new immigrant at this epochal moment, hence, is ultimately to gesture beyond national concerns that adjudicate, but that cannot by themselves contain, the economy of the new immigration. It seems, at present, unlikely that we will use the term "post-immigration" to describe the changes that are already with us; in fact, it does not seem far-fetched to predict the implementation of new immigration laws in the next century as a way to counter some of those changes. Yet we must invent a critical apparatus that will link the new immigration and the production of new literary forms to questions of transnational and transcultural changes: for instance, the role of new media networks in mediating and determining immigrants' relation to nation, diaspora, homeland; the new fragmentations and collectivities that attach to gender and class formations when these are transported from the home country to the new one; and how, or whether, *immigrant* cultural productions differ from *diasporic* ones. It is emerging questions such as these and others that Arjun Appadurai has studied in his recent work (1990, 1993), leading him to formulate a properly global cultural analysis that asks us to reimagine the links between "flows" as diverse as "persons, technologies, finance, information, and ideology" (Appadurai 337).

But for now, we can safely say that immigration in the United States does not carry the same face as it did at the turn of the century. The real question seems to be whether, or when, the country will catch up with its new face. This volume is but a humble realization of that attractive possibility.

WORKS CITED

Appadurai, Arjun. "Disjuncture and Difference in the Global Cultural Economy." *Public Culture* 2.2 (Spring 1990): 1–24. Rpt. in *Colonial Discourse and Post-Colonial Theory: A Reader.* Ed. Patrick Williams and Laura Chrisman. New York: Columbia UP, 1994. 324–339.

———. "Patriotism and Its Futures." *Public Culture* 5.3 (Spring 1993): 411–429.

Church, George J. "Send Back Your Tired, Your Poor . . ." *Time,* June 21, 1993: 26–27.

Doctorow, E. L. *Ragtime.* 1975. New York: Bantam, 1981.

Kim, Elaine H. "The Color of Money." *Asian American Quarterly: A. Magazine* 2.1 (1992): 30–31.

Mills, Nicolaus, ed. "Introduction: The Era of the *Golden Venture.*" *Arguing Immigration: Are New Immigrants a Wealth of Diversity . . . or a Crushing Burden?* New York: Touchstone, 1994. 11–27.

Thomas, Rich, and Andrew Murr. "The Economic Cost of Immigration." *Newsweek,* August 9, 1993: 18–19.

Turque, Bill, et al. "Why Our Borders Are Out of Control." *Newsweek,* August 9, 1993: 25.

I
ASIAN-AMERICAN LITERATURES

1

Arab-American Literature
Evelyn Shakir

INTRODUCTION

As we approach the end of the twentieth century, Arab-American literature shows every sign of coming into its own. One by one, new writers are surfacing, new voices are sounding. It is an exciting moment for those of us who have been waiting a long time for poems and stories that make myth of (and so make real) our experience and that of our immigrant ancestors.

At the same time, a few scholars have begun paying attention to the body of work, scant though it may be, produced by earlier generations of Arab-American writers. It is now possible to see that over the last eighty or ninety years, Arab-American literature has developed in three distinct stages—early, middle, and recent—each of them responsive to the political currents of its day.

LITERARY-CULTURAL HISTORY

There was a time when poets and writers were the boast of the Arab-American community. In the early decades of this century, a brotherhood of émigré writers in New York City, experimenting with English but generally doing their best work in Arabic, produced poetry (and sometimes fiction) of such originality that it breathed new life into Arabic literature back home, setting it on a road that would eventually lead to modernism.[1] Even today, these writers are celebrated

An earlier, slightly different version of this chapter, under the title "Coming of Age: Arab American Literature," appeared in *Ethnic Forum* 13.2/14.1 (1993–1994): 63–80.

in the Arab world, and their achievements generously acknowledged, but in America, from which safe haven they once looked east to challenge literary convention, religious authority, and Ottoman domination of Arab lands, they are virtually unknown.

The reason is not hard to find. What these authors wrote in Arabic is inaccessible to most Americans; what they wrote in English is, for the most part, long out of print. Still, one pioneer writer does live on in memory and imagination.

Strange as it may seem to American literati, the leader of the New York school was none other than Gibran Kahlil Gibran, whose *Prophet,* originally written in English, has been translated into over twenty languages and remains the best-selling book in the history of Alfred A. Knopf. As an Arab American, I grew up believing that Gibran was universally admired. But when I got to college, I soon learned that my professors, for whom poetry and preaching did not mix, considered him a charlatan. It was not a judgment I could carry home with me.

My parents had known and loved Gibran during his Boston days (before he moved to New York); one uncle had even married a Gibran cousin. Both families were part of the first wave of Arabic-speaking immigrants to America, a movement that started in the 1880s, crested just before World War I, then petered out in the late 1920s and 1930s, by which time over 100,000 natives of Greater Syria (modern-day Syria, Lebanon, Jordan, and Israel/Palestine) had come to stay. Usually Christian, often unschooled, typically poor, they had somehow learned to look beyond their mountain villages—beyond even Beirut, Damascus, and Jerusalem—toward an ''Ameerka'' that dangled opportunities too good to be passed up.

Gibran's mother saw her chance. In 1895, flat out of patience with a husband who could be relied on neither to support his family nor to conduct himself with honor, she brought her children to Boston. Gradually, the boy's talent as an artist attracted the attention of Yankee patrons, who helped finance his studies in Beirut and then in Paris and encouraged both his art and poetry. Later, in New York, he organized and was president of a pen league for Arab writers and helped found an Arab arts magazine.[2] But by the end of his life, Gibran himself was writing almost exclusively in English and, in the process, providing a textbook example of successful negotiation between ethnic writer and mainstream American reader.

In attempting to portray themselves or their community, American writers of Arab heritage have never had a blank canvas to work on. In Gibran's day, ''Orientalist'' bias dating back to the Crusades had already left a nearly indelible smear; later, the Arab–Israeli conflict (as reported in the American media) would fill in its own ugly detail. How, then, to introduce oneself to an audience with its own ideas about the culture in which one is rooted, ideas usually unflattering, sometimes patronizing, and occasionally wildly romantic.

Gibran's strategy was to play along with audience expectations, not, of course, the hard-core stereotype of the lascivious Oriental infidel, but another stock role apparently as congenial to him as it was seductive to his audience. In *The Prophet,* he takes on the persona of Almustafa ("The Chosen"), an Eastern oracle whose aphorisms transcend the teachings of any sect but whose biblical cadences, syntax, and diction place him in the company of Jesus. At the same time, a brooding photo of the author (on the back of the book jacket) encourages readers to confuse Gibran himself with Almustafa, as does the blurb below announcing that Gibran "was born in Lebanon, a land that has produced many prophets."

This implicit claim that the Arab homeland is a fountainhead of wisdom and spirituality (repeated by some Arab-American writers down to our own day) has never dispelled the suspicion with which actual immigrants from the Arab world have been viewed and with which Gibran was probably all too familiar. In 1899, just four years after his arrival in Boston, that city's Associated Charities reported, "Next to the Chinese, who can never be in any real sense Americans, the Syrians [i.e., Lebanese and Syrians] are the most foreign of all our foreigners. . . . and out of the nationalities would be distinguished for nothing whatever excepting as curiosities" (Woods 46).

For several decades, such assessments persisted. Certainly, they were still current in 1914, the year a prominent Arab-American autobiographer resorted, as Gibran had, to a religious discourse, but of a different sort.[3] *A Far Journey* by the Lebanese-born pastor Abraham Rihbany, while crammed with biblical allusion, is neither prophetic in tone nor hortatory in intent. Instead, it employs the neighbor-next-door voice of a good-humored Protestant minister explicating a text on a Sunday morning—except that it is his own life the Reverend Rihbany is laying out, placing it at every turn in the context of biblical narrative. He tells, for instance, how family and friends brought presents at his birth, as did the "Wise Men of old," and how "they sang and were exceeding glad, because unto them a child was born, a son was given" (4).

As this rhetoric suggests, Rihbany draws the boundaries of his society so as to include the Jews of Palestine, which he knew as a part of Greater Syria. Thus, he is able to turn the landscape of home into a Sunday school pastoral and to claim the Christ as one of his own. "Whatever else Jesus was," Rihbany later wrote, "as regards his modes of thought and life and his method of teaching, he was a Syrian of the Syrians. According to authentic history Jesus never saw any other country than Palestine" (*Syrian Christ* 4).

A Far Journey, with its strong sense of audience and its eagerness to instruct, continued Rihbany's early career as a lecturer on the Orient. That desire to serve as mediator between Arab and American societies also characterized Ameen Rihani, who was twelve years old in 1888, the year he accompanied his father to the United States. A member of Gibran's circle, Rihani wrote essays on his homeland for leading American journals and published over two dozen books (half in English, half in Arabic), including several volumes of poetry (Orfalea and Elmusa 3). But his most ambitious and most interesting work (at least in English) remains the *Book of Khalid* (1911), with illustrations by Kahlil Gibran.

Like *Candide*, *Khalid* is a satire in which a young dreamer, exiled from home, undergoes a string of disillusioning experiences that teach him a sober view of life. It is clear from the start that Rihani has Voltaire in mind. Just as Candide, caught kissing the baron's daughter (rumored to be his cousin), is set upon by the baron and literally kicked out of the "terrestrial paradise" of Westphalia, so—in a cockeyed echo of that scene—Khalid, in love with *his* cousin, is beaten from the door by *her* father, whereupon he sets out on a journey not away from, but in search of, "the Paradise of the World." His destination is America (45).

But America turns out to be no paradise. The very passage here is a "via dolorosa" in which Khalid is exploited by a series of sharpers eager to bleed him of every cent. Once arrived in New York, he slowly achieves an intellectual awakening, but at a price. His experiments with atheism, free love, and politics—exciting at first, embittering at last—drive him back to Syria, where he finds people and institutions are no less venal than in the United States. Only in the pine forests of Lebanon does he heal, soul and body. There, the modest resolution at which Candide arrives—"let's cultivate our garden"—is echoed in a hermit's invitation—"Come, let us till and cultivate the vineyard together" (247). But Khalid is not ready to retreat from the world. He craves the sweetness of human intercourse and finds it, briefly, with a few dear friends, whose death or departure leaves him empty-handed at the end.

In reading Rihani, it is not just *Candide* that comes to mind. *Khalid* is a sampler of voices and genres borrowed from a crowd of European and American authors. Next to Voltaire, Carlyle is the most obvious model, and among Americans, Emerson and Whitman. Each of these men is referred to in the book, as are many others with whom Rihani enters into brief or extended dialogue, among them Dickens, Tennyson, Balzac, Shakespeare, Paine, Arnold, Montaigne, Epictetus, Swinburne, Diderot, Pascal, Ibsen, Homer, Marx, Spencer, and Rousseau.

Implicit in all this name-dropping is the claim that here is an "Oriental" who can run with Western writers, who can match their erudition and imitate their tone, their wordplay, the particular flavor of their philosophical flights. On the basis of that boast (more than on any association with the Holy Land), Rihani demands respect for himself and, by implication, for his people.

The first generation of Arab-American writers (as might be expected of immigrants in an age of rampant xenophobia) dressed carefully for their encounter with the American public, putting on the guise of prophet, preacher, or man of letters. They could not hide their foreignness, but they could make it respectable. Their American-born children—those who came of age in the 1930s, 1940s, and 1950s—costumed themselves as "regular Americans" and hoped to pass, which may be why they produced so little literature. Aside from a few volumes of poetry, there are only two books of interest and one chapter of a third.

Vance Bourjaily's autobiographical novel, *Confessions of a Spent Youth*

(1960), devotes just one chapter to ethnic matters.[4] In that chapter we learn that Bourjaily's hero, Quince, has been brought up "not so much to conceal as to ignore" his Lebanese background, in large part because his father, "busy being an American," seems eager to dismiss the past (238). Consequently, the little that Quince knows about the Arab world he has picked up outside home. Predictably, it carries an anti-Arab bias—"We seemed to be on the wrong side in the Crusades" (239) and "My views [on Palestine] were vaguely Zionist" (247).

Even when World War II takes Quince to the Middle East, he views it through the lens of European literature. In Aden he sees naked laborers supervised by men with whips: "I think of Rimbaud and of the legend that it was into such an antique port, to become such an overseer that he disappeared . . . I feel his whip in my hand" (239). Later, in Suez, Quince masquerades as a native. The prank allies him with Europeans like Richard Burton and E. W. Lane, who also donned Arab gear, and speaks again to his lack of identification with Arab people.

Yet by the time Quince completes a brief visit to his ancestral village, he has succumbed to the fantasy that all sanity and possibility of wholeness reside in the peasant culture his father and grandmother left behind. Had they stayed put, he might have been as "simple and steadfast and proud" as his Lebanese cousins, instead of a modern American, "uselessly complicated and discontent" (272).

Confessions appeared in 1960, as did *Which Way to Mecca, Jack?,* a comic autobiography by William Peter Blatty (best known as the author of the *Exorcist*). Unlike Bourjaily, Blatty grew up immersed in his Lebanese ethnicity and eager to escape it. In childhood, the other kids would taunt him, "So wotta you, a camel?" (18); later, when he wanted to be an actor, Hollywood dismissed him as too "biblical." (Rihbany would not have understood how his best credential could become an ethnic slur.) In *Mecca,* Blatty jokes away painful memories by burlesquing himself, his background, and—above all—his overbearing mother, a Saladin of an immigrant who can hardly make a move or say a word without humiliating him. In front of girls he is trying to impress, she brags, "My God, my Will-yam he *never dirty his diaper!*" (11).

After a two-year stint for the U.S. Information Agency in Lebanon, Blatty feels better about his background but is still angry at Hollywood. "I've got to make them accept me," he tells a friend (189). With the friend's connivance, he disguises himself as an Arabian prince with four "mothers" at home and forty or so brothers. "In my country," he explains, "we do not count girl shildren [*sic*]" (200). Hollywood swallows it all. Lionized by the likes of George Gobel, Dick Powell, and June Allyson, Blatty has the last laugh, or so he claims. Still, it is clear that Hollywood has embraced not William Blatty, Arab American, but Prince Khairallah el Aswad el Xeer, a personification of its own romantic (and essentially Orientalist) fantasies about the East. To win the favor of an industry that trades in images, he has had to turn himself into a cartoon Arab.

Eugene Paul Nassar's memoir, *Wind of the Land,* published twenty years later and made up of two extended prose poems, provides yet another version of growing up Lebanese-American. But to move from Blatty to Nassar is to cross a great psychological divide. In place of slapstick, we have lyricism; instead of resentment, celebration. Unlike Blatty, Nassar has never yearned to distance himself from his ethnicity, much less his immigrant parents and their friends. In their values, he finds nearly everything he needs (literature provides the rest) to nourish his spirit and explain his life.

As Nassar tells it, evil enters the Lebanese community only as the second generation presumes to correct its parents or, worse, abandons them to a lonely existence in which contact with grandchildren is a special event (sometimes just photos in the mail) rather than the daily bread of life. Implicitly rejecting the American ethos that mental health requires breaking away from parents into independent existence (and that clinging to home is tantamount to neurosis), Nassar finds fulfillment only insofar as he feels at one with those who have come before him. "And he *was* his father (he hoped); otherwise he was only himself and that was not enough" (70).

Some years ago, when I began searching for Arab-American literature, I was pleased to discover the writers I have mentioned and a few others. But, given the hundred-year history of Arabs in America, it was a slim and unbalanced diet on which to feast. The writings of the first generation, though surely interesting and often amusing, seemed dated and did not speak directly enough to my own experience. The second-generation writers were closer to the mark, yet each in his own way fell short of what I needed.

Bourjaily did introduce the Arab–Israeli conflict (something I was concerned about), if only to show that young Quince perceived it—as he did everything else about the Middle East—in terms dictated by the West. It was a response I could understand. Not until I got to college was I free—even in my own mind—to question American policies in the Middle East. On another subject, Bourjaily was less satisfying. *Confessions*—even in its one chapter on the Middle East—remained a resolutely male book, a 1950s-style bildungsroman, in which women exist to serve men's fantasies.

I could sympathize with the embarrassments William Peter Blatty endured. I, too, had grown up in an era when anything "foreign" (family, food, church, language) was, by definition, second-class. Under such circumstances, his broad humor was as good a marketing tool as any, but it was also a betrayal. I found it hard to feel good about a book jacket featuring a voluptuous belly dancer or a blurb inviting readers to buy this "wacky best-seller about the adventures of an American sheik."

After Blatty, Nassar was a delight. He treated his characters with respect and made poetry of their lives. In his pages, I was on familiar terrain. I ran into folktales that had helped shape my own sense of humor, endearments that had come my way; I recognized my parents' own definition of honor, my mother's relaxed way with the deity. But I wondered at what was left out. How had Nassar avoided the hostility of bigots, the galling dictates of parents bred in a different culture, frustration (if nothing else) at events in the Middle East? These, too, were things I needed to read about.

DOMINANT CONCERNS IN RECENT LITERATURE

The Emergence of an Arab Identity

Gradually, I became aware that there were a few poets moving about in rooms I wanted investigated. I first discovered them in a twenty-page booklet called *Wrapping the Grape Leaves: A Sheaf of Contemporary Arab-American Poets* (1982), edited by Gregory Orfalea. Though it contained only eleven poems, it was a landmark publication, testifying to a sea change in Arab Americans' sense of themselves.

Since World War II, some half a million Arabs have again made their way to the United States, no longer just from the Levant but also from Egypt, Iraq, and, to a lesser extent, northern Africa and the Arabian peninsula. As likely to be Muslim as Christian, they have often been better educated and more politically aware than their predecessors. Some have come as students and decided to stay, often after marrying American wives. Others are refugees from war, state terrorism, or military occupation.

These new immigrants have helped rekindle a sense of ethnicity in the established community and promoted a sense of kinship with the Arab world in general, not just one corner of it, thus raising an old question, What should people in the Arabic-speaking community call themselves? For years, "Syrian" (i.e., people of Greater Syria) was the term of choice, even though most of those to whom it applied were, in fact, from present-day Lebanon. Then, as new political boundaries were established, and American relations with modern Syria deteriorated, many early immigrants and their descendants found it both more accurate and more politically comfortable to call themselves "Lebanese." Finally, in 1967, after the humiliating defeat of Arab armies in the Six-Day War with Israel (and influenced by the thinking of recent immigrants), more and more members of the community started calling themselves "Arab," a statement of solidarity with a people who were being savaged in the American media.

It was analogous to the decision made in the 1960s by the descendants of African slaves to call themselves "black," taking on with pride what had been a term of derision. Another sign of the times was the establishment of national organizations like the American-Arab Anti-Discrimination Committee, which, within a year of its founding, had published *Wrapping the Grape Leaves.*

Six years later, that little collection had given birth to a full-scale anthology, *Grape Leaves: A Century of Arab American Poetry.* Also edited by Orfalea, this time in partnership with Sharif Elmusa, and published by the University of Utah Press, *Grape Leaves* announced a body of literature the existence of which came as news to most American scholars. The twenty poets represented in the volume range from early immigrants like Gibran and Rihani to young American-born writers who came of age after the 1967 war. Not all the poems included have an explicit ethnic dimension, but those that do, ring with fresh images, words, and preoccupations. For instance, I can think of nothing in American poetry quite like the highway scene in "After the Funeral of Assam Hamady," a poem by Sam Hamod (whose Lebanese-born father was a Muslim imam).

In the poem, Hamod recalls driving at ninety miles an hour across South Dakota, bringing his father, grandfather, and their friend back from a funeral in Iowa. Suddenly, his grandfather clutches Hamod's arm and orders, "Stop!" It is sunset, time to pray. Hamod, who wants no part of this performance, stays in the car while the older men unroll a Navajo blanket, try to figure out which way is east, and then "face what must surely be South." As they raise their voices in prayer, autos whiz by, an old woman gawks, and the son—out of the car now but still embarrassed—stands guard. "*Allahu sumud,*" they pray, "*lum yuulud wa'alum uulud*"[5] (166, 168).

Arabic—foreign and undecipherable—noses its way (without shame) into the poem, asking forgiveness of father, grandfather, and friend.

> . . . I am standing here now
> trying so hard to join them
> on that old prayer blanket—
> as if the pain behind my eyes
> could be absolution. (169)

Responding to the Arab–Israeli Conflict

Guilt, regret, walking the line between this culture and that, between holding on and letting go—these are the abiding concerns of many ethnic literatures. For Arab Americans, what gives the drama edge and rivets attention is the Middle East quarrel between Arabs and Israelis. That is their defining subject.

One sees it, for instance, in the work of the accomplished poet Naomi Shihab Nye. On one hand, Nye is the least parochial of poets. She writes loving poems about Greeks, Pakistanis, Hondurans and about the Mexican neighbors in her San Antonio neighborhood. What's more, she knows that "ethnics" have no lock on tradition. At an ethnic fair in Texas, she overhears a young man wishing that he, too, had a heritage. "And the tall American trees," comments Nye, "were dangling their thick branches right down over his head" ("Speaking Arabic" 462).

On the other hand, Nye's Arab ancestry is of central importance in her life and in one body of her poems, perhaps because she is not that far removed from her origins. At midcentury, her Palestinian father (whose family had lost its home in the 1948 war with Israel) came to this country to attend college, married an American, and stayed to build a life here. Once, however, like many other Palestinian émigrés, he took his family back home for a year. That was in 1966, when Naomi was fourteen. Ever since, her extended family in Palestine have kept their hold on her memory and affections. "Sitti, Sitti," she writes, addressing her grandmother, "can anyone know how often they are thought of? It might be too heavy to hold" ("Pins" 460).

Grandmother, uncles, aunts, their children, their neighbors—all now live under occupation. When Nye goes back to visit, she is subjected to sharp questioning by Israeli crossing guards. Their voices hard, they want to know if she plans to speak to anybody.

> I wanted to say No, I have come all this way for a silent reunion.
> But they held my passport in their hands. ("Olive Jar" 104)

For Arab Americans who visit or just think about the Middle East, impotence, anger, and shame often go hand in hand. After the Gulf War, Nye cannot bring herself to bake her annual flag cake, "the one with strawberries for stripes and blueberries for states and white mountain frosting puffing up proudly between" ("Trouble with Stars and Stripes" 20). On the West Bank, Israeli soldiers explode tear gas outside her grandmother's house; the canisters are marked "Made in Pennsylvania" ("An Old Painful Story" 6).

American-made warplanes and bombs featured prominently in the 1982 Israeli invasion of Lebanon, which opened the way to the massacre of hundreds of Palestinian civilians by a right-wing Lebanese militia. The slaughter at Sabra and Shatila refugee camps is the subject of "Blood," Nye's most powerful poem on the Middle East. After early stanzas in which—lightheartedly, whimsically—she and her father establish their credentials as "true" Arabs, the poem cracks open in grief.

> Who calls anyone "civilized"?
> Where can the crying heart graze?
> What does a true Arab do now? ("Blood" 31)

Yet Nye's poetry and essays are lined with hope and studded with emblems of endurance: her grandmother, 104 years old, hands tattooed with birds; the lemon tree her grandmother tends like an obsession (in the dead of winter, it dreams of lemons); the yellow glove Nye lost in a stream one childhood winter but found again in June, "draped on a twig. A muddy survivor. A quiet flag" ("Double Vision" 72; "Yellow Glove" 28–29).

Beyond Romanticism

Elmaz Abinader comes from a family of survivors, people who lived through the mass starvation and pestilence that carried off tens of thousands of Lebanese during World War I. In her book *Children of the Roojme* (1991), Abinader tells her family's story, drawing upon 2,000 pages of diaries, journals, and letters written by her father and grandfather and upon conversations with her mother and aunt. From this raw material she fashions a world as real as imagination can make it—an offering to her ancestors.

But it is not an easy gift. The world Abinader reconstructs is shot through with hardship, horror, and bitter grievance. Many Arab-American writers tend to idealize the old-world culture, as embodied in family and community. Abinader takes a harder look and sees that human nature is everywhere the same. Beset by war's miseries, families give way—a half-crazed mother abandons her children, cousins compete for food. Other mothers—as if driven by primitive instinct—perform feats of bitter heroism. Abinader's grandmother Mayme (her husband in America) crawls miles on her belly, risking discovery by highwaymen and soldiers, a few small bags of food tied under her dress.

Her face turned hot and red and the bags skimmed the ground. Their weight pulled on her stomach, her arms, and her breasts; her face scraped shrubs and her knees absorbed tiny rocks. . . . She would feed her daughters. In spite. (151)

Years earlier, at the birth of her first daughter, Mayme had lifted her arms in joy, but the other women had seen nothing to celebrate.

The midwife did not stay. Each neighbor retreated, backed out the door. *What a shame,* they said, not sorry, half expecting it. *Barren eighteen years and only a girl.* Her husband would leave her now, they guessed. (156)

Abinader broaches a sensitive subject. Patriarchy in the Arab world is not a matter to which most Arab-American writers before her have attended. The tendency instead has been to focus on strong, wise mothers and grandmothers who are nobody's pawns and who often sum up what is truest and best in their culture.[6] But Abinader worries about women as victims, as does the Palestinian-American writer Diana Abu-Jaber, whose *Arabian Jazz* (1993)—a freewheeling and exuberant novel—casts a skeptical eye on both Arab and American societies.

Jazz centers on Matoussem Ramoud, a widowed Palestinian immigrant from Jordan; his two daughters, Jem and Melvina; and his sister Fatima (a literary descendant of Blatty's mother). Megaphonic, self-dramatizing, impossible, Fatima campaigns to marry off her nieces to any Arab man in sight. In the novel's most farcical scene, she scouts up a prospective groom, whose mother clutches Jem's jaw and orders her to open wide. "How can I know my daughter-in-law," she explains, "before I know her teeth?" (64). And so it goes. As if intent on desentimentalizing Arab-American literature, Abu-Jaber quickly establishes the Arab world as a breeding ground for grotesques and buffoons.

When the novel moves beyond farce, dark memories intrude—and demons of guilt. As a little girl, Fatima was forced to bury alive one newborn sister after another, so that her brother, Matoussem, would have enough to eat.

Although Abu-Jaber is a decidedly talented writer with a wonderful ear for immigrant dialect, her book will offend many Arab Americans, for the same reason that Philip Roth is anathema to so many Jews. It is bad enough to be stereotyped by others, but to be played for a laugh (or worse) by one's own can be especially enraging. Still, there is a countermovement to this novel. Deep into her story, in scenes as bold-faced as those that lampooned Arab zanies, Abu-Jaber trains her sights on mainstream American bigots. The woman for whom Jem works offers to save her from her background:

"Your father and all his kind aren't any better than Negroes . . . [but] you can come under my wing. . . . We'll try putting some pink lipstick on you, maybe lightening your hair, make you *American.* . . . I'll scrub all the scum right off you." (294–295)

Later, at a Labor Day picnic, the Ramoud family shares its meal with two young hikers. After an hour of lunch, conversation, and music, Matoussem reveals he is from Jordan. "*Arabs,*" one boy says to the other, "Jesus fucking Christ. And we ate their *food*" (361).

This kick in the teeth, brutal under any circumstances, is more so, given Matoussem Ramoud's gentle, trusting nature and his infatuation with America. That romance is acted out in his happy marriage to an Irish-American woman (who dies on a visit to Jordan) and his happy obsession with jazz, the quintessential American art form into which he drums the rhythms of home.

But Jem has a harder time reconciling the disparate elements of her life. At one point, tired of trying to please people "who don't like Arabs," she flirts with the notion of marrying her sardonic cousin Nassir and returning with him to Jordan. Nassir (in America to pursue a post-doctorate at Harvard) tries to disabuse her of her fantasies by insisting that the Middle East is neither "unique" nor "magical." His assertion flies in the face of Arab-American romanticism, calling to mind, instead, the skepticism of Ameen Rihani and the frankness of Elmaz Abinader.

Yet Nassir (who seems to speak for the author) understands Jem's complaint.

"To be the first generation in this country, with another culture always looming over you, you [Jem and her sister] are the ones who are born homeless, bedouins, not your immigrant parents. . . . You're torn in two. You get two looks at the world. You may never have a perfect fit, but you see far more than most ever do. Why not accept it?" (330)

Jazz may not achieve a perfect fit of its sundry parts, but in its two or more looks, it mirrors the two or more minds of many second-generation Arab Americans.

Like Abu-Jaber, the Lebanese-American writer Joseph Geha is an ethnic iconoclast. In *Through and Through,* a collection of artful short fiction, Geha quizzes those elements of their identity that Arab Americans have been most proud of. "Monkey Business," for instance, features an imported bride from Lebanon who tells of conversations with the Virgin, claims to have raised a goat from the dead, and—at an American wake—tries to resurrect the deceased. Geha's story spoofs pride of association with the Holy Land, in the first place by embodying its mystery in a delusional psychotic, but then by looking askance at the "practical" immigrants who, had they lived in Jesus' day, would probably have dismissed his miracles, too, as "bad business."

The title story, "Through and Through," manhandles another Arab-American point of pride, the legendary immigrant ancestor, hardworking, honest, successful. Like that legend, the narrator of the story comes to America determined to do well, by which he means—in parody of the Arab preoccupation with honor— to make a name for himself, as a gangster. Even at that he fails, gets mixed up in a murder, and flees to the Middle East, where he hides out for fifty years. But it is not the Middle East of Arab-American myth, just the American underworld all over again. "A handful of family syndicates ran the whole place [Lebanon] with defined territories, bosses, and soldiers" (122).

Though the narrator of "Through and Through" claims to be a spiritual person and wears a sliver of the true cross around his neck for luck, he has no soul and no hankering to reform. On the road to Damascus, he is astonished not by God but by the attempt to imagine the millions of particles of "flaked off flesh, saliva, lint, sodium, dandruff, dead mouth tissue" shed on the thoroughfare over its 5,000-year history (115). Decades later, on his way back to Toledo, he stops to view a storage tank on which the image of Jesus has reportedly been sighted. The narrator sees only Al Capone and, at the end, dead through and through, confesses only to the name John Doe.

Like other characters in Geha's stories, John Doe confuses religion with magic, and spirituality with superstition. In "Holy Toledo," an ignorant immigrant woman (living in Detroit) governs her life by old-country taboos, never eating from a yellow dish or leaving a slipper "upside down with its sole stepping on God's face" (89). Above all, she puts her faith in her most prized possession, an amulet against the evil eye. But in truth, hers is the evil eye, blighting the lives of her young grandchildren (their mother dead, their father gone) with her claim to be in pain and dying. As for the evil eye *she* dreads, it turns out to be the clear gaze of anyone who sees through her posturings. "You're not sick," her grandson tells her, breaking her spell (96). Of course, he is punished, but already he and his sister are making plans to run away to "America," thus completing the work of emigration begun two generations earlier. They will find freedom in Boston, Chicago, or "Holy Toledo" (holier than the claustrophobic world they leave behind) but will also pay the price of exile, "the rest of their lives lost in the American homesickness" (98).

The question facing the children as they prepare for flight is what to pack and what to leave behind. Sometimes the temptation is to leave everything behind. Geha has described most of his youth and young adulthood as "an attempt to escape from my Arab roots.'' He was ashamed of his parents' accents, wanted to eat only American food, refused to dance the Arab *dabke,* would not write about his family and community. ''To include such material would be to identify myself with exactly what I'd been avoiding all my life'' (''Where I'm From'' 58, 61).

In the story ''Almost Thirty,'' Geha's change of heart is allegorized when the narrator, alone and suicidal, returns home to heal. Later, in its most emblematic moment, the story suggests that it is possible to be, in one person, both American and (in Geha's words) ''one of my people.'' At a family picnic, Cousin George, who has never danced to either Arabic or American music, does ''a wonderful thing.'' He throws down the egg salad sandwich his ''American'' wife has prepared, stands up with her, and advances on the *dabke,* as do the narrator and his wife, another ''American.'' First, the four practice a bit on the side, stumbling and laughing.

Then, with our arms locked, we broke into the dance and joined it. The snake [of dancers] became a circle, things got dizzy, we were stamping. ''Crazy Americans,'' Aunt Afifie said as we spun past her. (47)

CONCLUSION

At first, Arab-American writers, living in a society frankly suspicious of ''Orientals,'' tried to prove that they and their compatriots were not so alien, after all. For a long time after that, as open disparagement of particular ethnic groups yielded ground to a general understanding that ethnicity itself was in bad taste, Arab Americans fell silent. Most recently, with ethnicity in fashion at home and Arabs in trouble abroad, Arab Americans have been entering into spirited political debate with one another and with the public at large.

In literature, a number of people have spoken up at once, eager to join the conversation, to tell what they know about family and nation. Women, in particular, have found their tongue. For anyone wanting to listen in, there is much to learn and to enjoy. For Arab Americans, there is something more. To borrow Dr. Johnson's pronouncement about biography, the new Arab-American literature gives us ''what comes near to ourselves, what we can turn to use.''[7] Its usefulness is exactly commensurate with its evolving capacity to move beyond self-consciousness and sentimentality to a place of sure footing and from there to contrive stories, characters, and idiom that we recognize, to address issues that we care about—above all, to make art of *our* experience, too.

NOTES

1. Though these writers of the *Mahjar* (Emigration) broke rigid conventions of Arabic poetry, they were not modernists in the American and European sense. For inspiration,

they looked to the nineteenth-century Romantics and Transcendentalists, not to Eliot, Pound, and Yeats.

2. Arab critics differ in their estimate of Gibran's talent and achievements, many preferring his prose to his poetry, some arguing that his urge to philosophize sidetracked his lyric gifts. What seems most clear is his significance for other writers who were inspired by his poetic doctrines, his experimental style, or the sheer force of his personality. The critic Salma Jayyusi has gone so far as to call Gibran "the single most important influence on Arabic poetry and literature during the first half of this century" (4).

3. Comments on Rihbany draw on my article "Mother's Milk: Women in Arab American Autobiography."

4. Comments on Bourjaily draw on my article "Pretending to Be Arab." Comments on Nassar draw on my article "Starting Anew." For a further discussion of Bourjaily, Blatty, and Nassar, see also my article "Arab Mothers, American Sons."

5. "God [is] the Everlasting Refuge, / who has not begotten and has not been begotten." Translation from Arthur J. Arberry, *The Koran Interpreted* (Oxford: Oxford UP, 1982).

6. In this connection, see my article "Mother's Milk."

7. See *Boswell's Journal of a Tour to the Hebrides with Samuel Johnson, LLD,* ed. Frederick A. Pottle and Charles H. Bennett (New York: Literary Guild, 1936), p. 55.

SELECTED PRIMARY BIBLIOGRAPHY

Abinader, Elmaz. *Children of the Roojme.* New York: Norton, 1991.

Abu-Jaber, Diana. *Arabian Jazz.* New York: Harcourt, 1993.

Adnan, Etel. *The Indian Never Had a Horse and Other Poems.* Sausalito, CA: Post-Apollo, 1985.

———. *Sitt Marie Rose.* Trans. Georgina Kleege. Sausalito, CA: Post-Apollo, 1982.

And Not Surrender: American Poets on Lebanon. Ed. Kamal Boullata. Washington, DC: Arab-American Cultural Foundation, 1982.

Awad, Joseph. *The Neon Distances.* Francestown, NH: Golden Quill, 1980.

———. *Shenandoah Long Ago.* Richmond, VA: Poet's, 1990.

Blatty, William Peter. *I'll Tell Them I Remember You.* New York: Norton, 1973.

———. *Which Way to Mecca, Jack?* New York: Lancer, 1960.

Bourjaily, Vance. *Confessions of a Spent Youth.* New York: Dial, 1960.

Geha, Joseph. *Through and Through: Toledo Stories.* St. Paul: Graywolf P, 1990.

———. "Where I'm From—Originally." *Townships.* Ed. Michael Martone. Iowa City: U of Iowa P, 1992. 56–66.

Gibran, Gibran Kahlil. *Jesus the Son of Man.* New York: Knopf, 1928.

———. *The Madman.* New York: Knopf, 1918.

———. *The Prophet.* New York: Knopf, 1923.

Hamod, H. S. (Sam). "After the Funeral of Assam Hamady." *Dying with the Wrong Name, New and Selected Poems 1968–1979.* Rpt. in Orfalea and Elmusa. 165–169.

———. *Dying with the Wrong Name, New and Selected Poems, 1968–1979.* New York: Anthe, 1980.

Hazo, Samuel. *Blood Rights.* Pittsburgh: U of Pittsburgh P, 1968.

Joseph, Lawrence. *Curriculum Vitae.* Pittsburgh: U of Pittsburgh P, 1988.

Milhem, D. H. *Rest in Love.* New York: Dovetail, 1975.

Nassar, Eugene Paul. *Wind of the Land.* Belmont, MA: Association of Arab-American University Graduates, 1979.

Nye, Naomi Shihab. "Blood." *Yellow Glove.* Portland: Breitenbush Publications, 1986. 31.

————. *Different Ways to Pray.* Portland, OR: Breitenbush Publications, 1980.

————. "Double Vision in a New Old World." *American Way* (January 1993): 68+.

————. "An Old Painful Story." *San Antonio Express-News Magazine,* May 2, 1993: 6–9.

————. "Olive Jar." *A Quartet: Texas Poets in Concert.* Denton: U of North Texas P, 1990. 104.

————. "Pins." *Michigan Quarterly Review* 31.4 (Fall 1992): 460–461.

————. "Speaking Arabic." *Michigan Quarterly Review* 31.4 (Fall 1992): 462.

————. "Trouble with Stars and Stripes." *Mint.* Rockport, NY: State Street P Chapbooks, 1991. 20.

————. "Yellow Glove." *Yellow Glove.* Portland, OR: Breitenbush Publications, 1986. 28–29.

Orfalea, Gregory. *The Capital of Solitude.* Greenfield Center, NY: Greenfield Review, 1988.

————. ed. *Wrapping the Grape Leaves: A Sheaf of Contemporary Arab-American Poets.* Washington, DC: American-Arab Anti-Discrimination Committee, 1982.

Orfalea, Gregory, and Sharif Elmusa, eds. *Grape Leaves: A Century of Arab American Poetry.* Salt Lake City: U of Utah P, 1988.

Rihani, Ameen. *The Book of Khalid.* 1911. Beirut: Rihani House, 1973.

Rihbany, Abraham. *A Far Journey.* Boston: Houghton, 1914.

————. *The Syrian Christ.* Boston: Houghton, 1916.

Rizk, Saloom. *Syrian Yankee.* Garden City, NY: Doubleday, 1943.

Williams, David. *Traveling Mercies.* Cambridge, MA: Alice James, 1993.

SELECTED SECONDARY BIBLIOGRAPHY

Gibran, Jean, and Kahlil Gibran. *Gibran.* Boston: New York Graphic Society, 1974.

Hooglund, Eric, ed. *Crossing the Waters: Arabic-Speaking Immigrants to the United States before 1940.* Washington, DC: Smithsonian, 1987.

Jayyusi, Salma, ed. *Modern Arabic Poetry, An Anthology.* New York: Columbia UP, 1987.

Naff, Alixa. *Becoming American: The Early Arab Immigrant Experience.* Carbondale: Southern Illinois UP, 1985.

Orfalea, Gregory. *Before the Flames: A Quest for the History of Arab Americans.* Austin: U of Texas P, 1988.

————. "Doomed by Our Blood to Care: The Poetry of Naomi Shihab Nye." *Paintbrush* 18. 35 (Spring 1991): 56–66.

————. "On Arab Americans: A Bibliographic Essay." *American Studies International* 27. 2 (October 1989): 26–41.

————. *U.S.–Arab Relations: The Literary Dimension.* Washington, DC: National Council on U.S.–Arab Relations, 1984.

Ostle, Robin. "The Literature of the *Mahjar.*" *The Lebanese in the World.* Ed. Albert
    Hourani and Nadim Shehadi. London: Centre for Lebanese Studies, 1992. 209–
    225.
Shakir, Evelyn. "Arab Mothers, American Sons: Women in Arab American Autobiog-
    raphy." *MELUS* 17. 3 (Fall 1991–1992): 5–15.
———. "Coming of Age: Arab American Literature." *Ethnic Forum* 13–14. 2, 1 (1993–
    1994): 63–80.
———. "Mother's Milk: Women in Arab American Autobiography." *MELUS* 15.4
    (Winter 1988): 39–50.
———. "Pretending to Be Arab: Role Playing in Vance Bourjaily's 'Fractional Man.' "
    MELUS 9.1 (Spring 1982): 7–21.
———. "Starting Anew: Arab-American Poetry." *Ethnic Forum* 3 (Fall 1983): 23–36.
Woods, Robert. *City Wilderness.* Boston: Houghton, 1898.
Zoghby, Mary. "Memory, Image, and Identity in Arab American Poetry." *Paintbrush*
    18.35 (Spring 1991): 21–28.

2
Armenian-American Literature
Khachig Tololyan

INTRODUCTION

Ethnics aspire to inclusion in the larger polity even as they struggle for exclusion on their own terms, for the right to draw and patrol communal boundaries of their choice, to nurture and maintain certain differences, to build identities rather than to have collective subject positions assigned to them by the dominant culture. This paradox of desiring not the full inclusion that is assimilation but an exclusion of their own is central to their collective lives, which improve as the opportunities afforded by full participation in the heterogeneity of mainstream economic, political, cultural, and sexual life become available. Ethnics seek participation as citizens in the political culture of the host land, in part, to earn the right to represent their homelands; and they seek to participate in the cultural production of the host land, in part, to acquire the ability to construct and circulate representations of themselves, rather than to be represented by others. Inevitably, the self-representations they create are haunted by the paradoxes of simultaneously seeking sameness and difference, inclusion and exclusion.

An analogous anxiety of exclusion also lingers at the margins of this overview of the literary production of Armenian Americans. Any overview becomes possible only through a series of exclusions. Some of these are common to all panoramic enterprises: not all works in a given category can be included, sampled, and analyzed. Other exclusions are peculiar to certain ethnic formations,

I am grateful to Professor Lorne Shirinian (Department of Literature, Royal Canadian Military College) for his ideas and bibliographical assistance and to Professor Ellen Rooney (Department of English, Brown University) for her critical reading of an earlier draft.

because of the specificity, particularity, even idiosyncrasy of their patterns of cultural production. In the case of the Armenian Americans, whose ranks include both ethnic and diasporic populations, these patterns emerge from the highly unusual history of the Armenian people.

LITERARY-CULTURAL HISTORY

Armenians are an ancient West Asian people who speak a singular Indo-European language related to Hittite (now extinct), old Greek, and old Persian. Historical Armenia was a land of some 110,000 square miles in eastern Anatolia and the southwestern Transcaucasus. Though known to neighboring peoples first as Urartu, then as Armenia, the land is Haiastan or Hyasdan in Armenian, and the people Hye (pronounced "high"). Intermittently ruled by one of four major native dynastic kingdoms or by neighboring states from the seventh century B.C. to the eleventh century A.D., Armenia was then invaded, conquered, settled, colonized, and divided among three empires: the Ottoman Turkish, Persian, and Russian. Since the eleventh century, war and oppression, along with the search for economic opportunity, have driven waves of Armenians into individual migrancy and collective diaspora. Beginning in the sixteenth century, the increasingly wealthy and sophisticated Armenian merchant diasporas produced most of Armenian literary culture: the first Armenian book was printed in Venice in 1512; the first Armenian newspaper was published in Madras, India, in 1794; until World War I, most Armenian novels, poems, and plays were published in primary intrastate diasporas[1] such as those of Istanbul, Turkey, and Tbilisi, the capital of Georgia. By 1914, nearly half of the Armenians in the world lived not in their homeland but in diasporan communities, many of them centuries old. Some of these diasporas were established as long ago as the twelfth century (Crimea), the fourteenth (Poland), the fifteenth (Istanbul), the seventeenth (Iran, India) and the nineteenth (Egypt); others were created by survivors of the genocide of 1915–1918. During World War I, in a prefiguration of what the Nazi Reich would do to Jews during World War II, the Ottoman Turkish state governed by the regime of the "Young Turks" used the opportunity provided by the militarization of society and the distraction of the West to carry out the first genocide of the twentieth century, killing 1.5 out of the 2 million Armenian subjects of the empire. The new diasporas created in the wake of this genocide (Lebanon, Syria, Greece, France, and, to some extent, the United States) are marked by the trauma of their inception.

The American ethnodiasporan[2] community has a complex history. Though "John Martin the Armenian" arrived in the Virginia colony in 1618, significant Armenian migration to the United States began in the nineteenth century. In the 1830s, American Protestant missionaries began to convert some Armenians from their ancient faith, the Armenian Apostolic branch of Christianity, and to teach them English. The first English-speaking Protestant converts immigrated between 1839 and 1880. After 1880, news of America the bountiful provided the "pull" needed for Armenian Apostolic immigrants in larger numbers, while the search for economic opportunity and the many Turkish massacres preceding the genocide provided the "push"; the mail, the telegraph, and the steamship provided the means and facilitation. By 1891, there were enough Armenian factory workers in Worcester, Massachusetts, to necessitate the construction of the first Armenian Apostolic church in America. During the 1890s, 12,000 immigrants arrived, most fleeing massacres, and in the first decade of the twentieth century their numbers continued to climb: just under 10,000 arrived in 1913 alone. These figures are small compared to other migrations—from Italy, say—and they constituted a small proportion of the more than 4,000,000 Armenians living worldwide in 1914. Yet they had a special significance for the areas of Turkish-dominated Armenia from which the majority of migrants came: some regions (Kharpert, Marsovan, Bitlis, Aintab) steadily lost a high percentage of their youth to migration. Because of their shared origins, the communities they created in America were tight-knit and resistant to rapid assimilation. (A similar phenomenon is known to students of other migrations.) On the eve of World War I, there were 60,000 Armenians in the United States, 1.5 percent of all Armenians in the world. By 1924 (when changes in American law drastically limited migration), there were nearly 100,000. Virtually all of the 40,000 newcomers were traumatized survivors of the genocide: orphans, frequently victims of rape and witnesses to the slaughter of their families.

This community of immigrants and survivors was knit together between the two world wars, receiving newcomers in very small numbers and—given the depression—climbing the economic ladder very slowly. Like the rest of white America, its movement into the middle class gathered momentum in the post-1945 American peace, which also brought in some 20,000 Armenian refugees, half soldiers in the Soviet army who had been captured by Germany and released by the Allies and who feared to return to the USSR and the rest rendered homeless by the war. Old Armenian political divisions sharpened during this entire period, especially after the United States recognized the USSR in 1933, and emissaries from Soviet Armenia gained entry into the community. These political divisions created a civil war of words—and in one notable case led to the assassination of a bishop in church—that is woven into the texts of the period. The arguments, which were largely incomprehensible to children born in America, accentuated the sense that the adults were haunted by alien passions, alternately threatening and trivial but always inaccessible. These political concerns, mapped onto generational divisions, endured and grew more complicated when the post-1965 immigration ushered in new politicized groups who have been slow to assimilate into the existing ethnic community. They have, in fact, shaken it by renewing the diasporan challenge to ethnicity, energizing some and alienating other third-generation Armenian-American ethnics, including readers and practitioners of literature.

Around 85,000 Armenians came from the USSR between 1972 and 1989. (Like Jewish and Cuban emigrants from communist states, they were treated by the United States as political refugees, though the majority came in search of a better economic life.) Another 100,000 came as refugees from the civil war in Lebanon (1975–1991): virtually all are Armenophone, and many are intensely politicized. Around 75,000 have come from Iran, both before and after the Khomeini revolution of 1978–1979. As a result of these migrations, the Armenian-American community now numbers around 750,000 (12 percent of the world's Armenians), is multiply politicized, more Armenophone than at any point since World War II, oriented toward business and the professions, and—since the 1991 collapse of the USSR and the rise of the independent Republic of Armenia—in a crisis of self-examination whose literary effects cannot yet be assessed.[3] There are twenty-six functioning ethnic elementary and secondary Armenian day schools, endowed chairs of Armenian studies in major universities, over 100 Apostolic churches, and both national and transnational organizations that engage in politics and cultural production.

The element of communal infrastructure that has had the most direct effect on the emergence of Armenian-American literature has been the Armenian press. Political and social features of Armenian life before the immigration had already necessitated the investment of financial and social capital, not only in churches and communal schools but also in an extraordinary profusion of ephemeral newspapers and periodicals, which played a central role in the emergence of Armenian nationalism in the diaspora.[4] The immigrants brought the habit of print with them. In 1888, when there were not more than 1,500 Armenians in the United States, a (short-lived) newspaper was published. The oldest Armenian-language paper still publishing today is *Hairenik,* established in 1899 as the political organ of the socialist and nationalist Armenian Revolutionary Federation (the ARF or Tashnag Party), which welcomed the involvement of factory workers as well as intellectuals in cultural production. In a pre-Gramscian recognition of the importance of hegemonic cultural production, the ARF also published *Hairenik Amsakir,* a literary and intellectual monthly in which a significant portion of the best Armenian-language writing of North America and, in fact, the global diaspora was published between 1922 and 1965. Today, the more than 200,000 Armenian Americans who retain reading competence in Armenian support one daily newspaper (*Asbarez,* 1908–), six weeklies, and many periodicals.

The Anglophone Armenian community is served by five weeklies and many periodicals as well, and the readership of these overlaps, to some degree, with the one previously mentioned. The most significant publication for writers and critics is *Ararat* (1960–, New York), a literary quarterly published by the Armenian General Benevolent Union (AGBU). Any scholar searching for the patterns of development in Anglophone Armenian-American writing since the early 1960s must begin here. In addition, the quarterly *Armenian Review* has published essays on literature and history since 1948, and *Raft* (1987–) publishes a mixture of poems, criticism, and English translations of work from all over the diaspora. The Canadian Armenian-language weekly *Horizon* (1979–, Montreal) continues to publish North American Armenophone literature in monthly special inserts, as do "middlebrow" periodicals such as *Navasart* (1981–), whose contents are sociologically telling, if not aesthetically compelling. While mainstream American publishers have issued only a handful of literary works by Armenian-American authors, community cultural organizations have maintained a large and steady flow of publications in both languages. With such periodicals publishing short fiction and poetry and with academic publications that host the works of a small but growing scholarly community,[5] the "tripod" of popular, highbrow literary and academic publishing that supports all American nonelectronic cultural production is in place. Nevertheless, today the actual role of literature is as precarious in this community as in the larger sphere of all American literature, haunted as it is by the electronic media.

As a result of the widespread availability of outlets for publishing and because of the prestige Armenian intellectuals enjoy in a diaspora where they have been an important component of the leadership elite (along with wealthy philanthropists and clergymen), a vast amount of *writing* has been produced by Armenian Americans since the 1890s, only a small portion of which a critic trained in modernist esthetics would consider "literature." Much of this writing is of uncertain generic status and appeared first in the press: essays, columns, polemical articles of great passion and rhetorical eloquence, patriotic verse, sentimental poetry, short stories (a few of them very good), autobiographies and memoirs that make no pretense of narrative sophistication. It is true—and, in the wake of recent theory, it is easy to argue—that this work shares images, themes, and concerns with the far less numerous works of literary merit. But such an affirmation does not forestall the necessity of exclusion in our context.

The language proper to that precarious category, "Armenian-American literature," is equally problematic. The pre-World War I immigrants were surprisingly literate in Armenian. Of those who arrived between 1899 and 1910, 76 percent were literate (compared to a high of 99 percent for Finns and a low of 46 percent for southern Italian immigrants in the same period; Mirak, *Torn* 74). They wrote abundantly in Armenian, whereas Armenian-American literature in English dates from the 1920s and began to achieve prominence only after the watershed of the 1960s. Is one to exclude the texts written in Armenian and therefore inaccessible to the majority of scholars of ethnicity and to many Anglophone Armenian-American ethnics, even if the concerns of these texts spring from the shared experiences of immigrants, exiles, refugees, and survivors? They depict diasporan dislocation, the contradictory yearning for a home in the homeland and at-homeness in the host land, the fear and fascination of the encounter with the *odar* (the Other, the Alien). Is literature written by Americans of Armenian descent "ethnic" only when certain concerns about identity and hybridity, the master figures of contemporary ethnic criticism, are central to the text and articulated in ways familiar to the contemporary critic? What particular constellations of origin, language, experience, figure, and theme qualify a work as "ethnic" and as "literature" in this or any other context?

Neither the question of identity nor any other issue or experience that at any one moment seems pivotal to a group necessarily enjoys long-term prominence in literature. For example, slavery is indisputably a central historical experience for African Americans and has mattered greatly to pre-abolition and contemporary writing by African Americans. But from the 1890s to the 1960s, its representation was not a dominant enterprise; African-American writers most often addressed contemporaneous oppressions and aspirations. Arguably, slavery again became a central topic of literary fiction only in the 1960s.[6] Analogously, among Armenian critics there is agreement approaching consensus that the genocide of the Armenians by the Turkish state is the central formative experience of diasporized Armenians and of Armenian ethnic literatures (not only in North America but also in France, Lebanon, and Syria).[7] It is a trauma that has been denied recognition and healing, to which other experiences of pain and loss are routinely, if symbolically, assimilated and even subordinated. The problem is that, as in all definitions, circularity is unavoidable: the experience that is considered central to a community helps to define the texts that are considered specific to that community, and the experience and the canonized texts, taken together, help to establish the identity of that community by the exclusion of other experiences and representations.

Yet the Armenian Americans have been, and are, composed of segments that have had different collective experiences. For example, most of those coming from the Iranian primary diaspora are not descendants of genocide survivors. At a minimum, they feel differently about this and other unequally shared experiences, or, alternatively, they contest the meanings assigned to shared experiences, for example, the relationship of diasporans with the host land's majority people. These contestations can be found in the articles and columns of the flourishing press but are also constructed in the literature. Both diachronically and at any one synchronous moment, including the present, the Armenian-American "community" has been made up of segments that must be enumerated.

There have been immigrants seeking economic opportunity; refugees from massacres; exiles fleeing political persecution; and survivors of genocide. There are those who came from the conquered homeland and others who came from long-established primary diasporas. Today, some Armenian-American "ethnics" are, in fact, fully *assimilated* Americans of Armenian descent, who are counted by the ethnic leadership in order to inflate the size of the community they claim to lead. The majority are true *ethnics,* who acknowledge their Armenian descent and display "ethnic pride" symbolically, retain voluntary associations with communal organizations (the church, compatriotic, youth, and sports organizations, cultural and lobbying groups) but are emphatically American at the same time. They have gone, in the words of one student of the community, from "being to feeling Armenian" (Bakalian). For those ethnics who routinely live as Americans, act only occasionally in specifically Armenian ways and contexts, but continue to feel Armenian in some way, identity and the genocide do remain major and linked issues, explored primarily in English. Yet another significant segment of the community is made up of *diasporic*[8] Armenians, recent arrivals who are vital to the struggles over communal self-definition. They give their various forms of allegiance to an Armenian nation that they see as having three components: a *nation-state* (the Republic of Armenia, which until the December 1991 demise of the Soviet Union was a constituent national republic of that state); a *region* of traditional Armenia called Nagorno-Karabagh, which was placed, by arbitrary partition, under the rule of the neighboring state of Azerbaijan; and a *transnational nation,* that is, a nation that exists not just in the homeland but also across the borders of other nation-states, "transnationally," and is made up of communities in thirty-four countries, from Egypt to Australia, linked by transnational institutions such as the Armenian Apostolic Church, political organizations like the ARF, and philanthropic groups like the AGBU, through which wealthy notables also exert political and cultural influence. In these communities, where diasporic, ethnic, and assimilated identities intersect and coexist, issues ranging from intermarriage to national liberation matter variously to artists, intellectuals, and writers.

Unlike traditional diasporas that aspired to return to the homeland, the contemporary North American ethnodiaspora "returns" repeatedly and transnationally toward the homeland and other diasporan communities by managing a circulation of people, cultural productions, financial aid, and political ideas. Within the Armenian-American community, the ethnics are often in muted conflict with the diasporans, who range from the involved, to the committed, to a few militants on issues of culture and politics. Since 1965, their ranks have produced writers who now live in the United States but have continued to write in Armenian, a language they share with both those left behind in their diasporan communities of origin and the inhabitants of the homeland.

Armenian-American literature written in English cannot, and does not, pay equal attention to all these points of origin or to all of their historically significant experiences and concerns. Is it the purpose of the scholar to validate the existing unevenness of this bilingual economy of representation? Are the shared concerns that inhabit both linguistic domains the ones that must claim priority? What ethical and political obligations might underpin our response to either question? The discussion that follows will be primarily devoted to constructing a taxonomic and interpretive narrative of both the "literature" of Anglophone Armenian-American ethnics and the community that produced it. Since, as Althusser has taught us, we must all acknowledge the reading we are guilty of,[9] this chapter has begun by acknowledging the exclusionary, canon-forming enterprise of writing an overview. I end this section by briefly discussing those who wrote and still write primarily in Armenian.

In his encyclopedically inclusive, anticanonical anthology and study of modern Armenian literature in the homeland and in ethnic diasporas, Minas Tololyan pays homage to the literary productivity of diasporan communities. For the period from 1890 (when there were 2,000 Armenian immigrants in America) to

1980 (when there were around 700,000), he names forty-six writers who produced in the Armenian language at least one work deserving mention. He cites
twenty-three who wrote in English, overlooking another dozen who might well
have been included. However approximate, the numbers (forty-six/thirty-five)
are telling: the volume of writing in Armenian at least matches that in English
and surpassed it until the 1960s. In the Armenian-language literature, the depiction of the often idealized homeland left behind by immigrants and memories
of the horrors from which the survivors of massacre and genocide fled are far
more frequent than immigrant interrogations of identity. However, since the
second and third generations of ethnics generally do not know Armenian well
enough to *read* it, they have no access to the mass of these writings, and oral
transmission from the grandparents, often in broken English, remains very important to them. Memories of the traumatic event of genocide and of immigrant
humiliation are transmitted to subsequent generations more by familial oral narrative—a category to which scholars have only highly mediated access—than
by writing. (Oral histories recorded in the past fifteen years are a new, inter-
mediary, primarily videotaped but occasionally transcribed genre and text).
Oddly, the work written in Armenian by the earlier generation of Armenian
Americans remains accessible for the mass of more recent immigrants who read
Armenian and who came after changes in the immigration law in 1965 from
both the (Soviet) homeland and the Middle Eastern diasporan communities of
Syria, Lebanon, Egypt, and Iran. We thus have the unusual phenomenon of
third-generation Armenian Americans ignorant of the literary production of their
own direct ancestors, while recent immigrants from the Middle Eastern diaspora
learn some of what they know about the pre-1914 homeland and early immigrant
experience through the commemorative narratives written in the United States
in Armenian (between the late 1920s and early 1970s) by authors like Hamas-
degh, Benjamin Noorigian, Aram Haigaz, Vahe Haig-Dinjian, and Hagop Asa-
doorian. As adolescents in the Middle Eastern diasporas, many of these same
readers were thrilled by the heroics of Armenian guerrilla fighters, narrated in
a series of six *Zartonk* (The Reawakening) novels penned in America in Armenian by Malkhas.

The point is that Armenian was the common language that linked, and to a
considerable extent still links, the intelligentsia and artists of the Armenian diaspora to each other and to the homeland; the emergence of the Republic of
Armenia in 1991 is likely to strengthen its status. The Armenophone Armenian-
American writers of pre-1968 both learned from these literary circuits and contributed to them, and this remains true, to a reduced degree, even today.
Furthermore, ethnic Armenian Americans who have written in English can be
divided into two groups: those, like William Saroyan and Michael Arlen, who
became famous enough to be translated into Armenian and to be read everywhere in the diaspora and in Armenia; and those who remain the authors of a
particular American ethnodiasporic community, writing for, and read by, that
community in English. While the rest of this chapter focuses on the latter, this

prolonged gesture of recognition of those who wrote in Armenian remains essential. A similar gesture, toward translation, is also necessary. Armenian reverence for the literature produced before the genocide and indeed since A.D. 428 in classical, medieval, and modern traditions has led to a significant effort of translation since the 1960s: scholars, as well as the poets Diana Der Hovanessian (who writes her own poetry in English), Garik Basmajian, and Ralph Setian, translators such as Ara Baliozian, Marzbed Margossian, and Tatul Sonentz-Papazian (who are also columnists in Armenian), Arra Avakian, and Aris Sevag have contributed. The result is—again—that the Anglophone ethnics ironically know more of the older literature originally written overseas and in Armenian than of the work written in Armenian in America by their own grandparents.

This Armenian-American writing/literature has changed and kept pace with post-1960s phenomena that are also manifest in the literature of other ethnic communities. Once produced mostly by men and often concerned with coming-of-age stories or with fathers and sons, writing and literature are now more ''feminized'' (or made familial, or domestic): more of the writers and readers of fiction and poetry are women than ever before. (Drama is not a major genre.) More fictional, lyrical, and memoiristic representations of women's lives are available than before (Avakian, Der Hovanessian, Edgarian). Journalistic essays and polemics—in both Armenian and English—remain vigorous and strident and rehearse themes that reappear in the fiction, if not in the poetry. I now turn to a chronological and highly selective survey of the concerns, themes, discourses, and figures that have dominated the Anglophone portion of these writings.

DOMINANT CONCERNS AND MAJOR AUTHORS

The immigrants who arrived in the period between 1880 and 1925 experienced widespread prejudice as ''Asians'' whose legal status as ''Caucasian'' was called into question until the end of this period. They encountered judgments that will be familiar to scholars of many immigrations:

I have found [the Armenians] ungrateful, deceitful and unreliable without exception. . . . If you treat them civilly, they are ungracious. If you are brutal and rough with them, they respect you. Very few of them ever smile—they have a sour countenance, as though every thought was mean, not sad, just mean. If their conduct in Turkey is as it is here, no wonder the Turks kill them.[10]

The encounter with such attitudes predictably led many to the desire to find solace in the family and the ethnic enclave. Yet three-quarters of the immigrants of 1880–1914 were single men; family life was not available to most. Engendered by this lack, as well as the language barrier and discrimination, loneliness and feelings of isolation and alienation became formative experiences; literary responses to that experience made their way into memoir and autobiographical narrative, as well as, by greater indirection, into fiction and poetry.

However, literary representation does not simply reflect; it refracts, mediates, and displaces experience, recoding it. This activity of recoding would best be traced, with intertextual amplitude, across the work of many writers. The oeuvre of the most famous Anglophone Armenian-American writer, the Pulitzer Prize-winning author William Saroyan (1908–1981), will serve as an emblem in this study, for it captures one way of recoding alienation very effectively. Many of his characters do not manifest the aggressively inexpressive, "sour" faces that dominate prejudice assigned to Armenian immigrants. Rather, his older immigrant characters, the ones born in Armenia, are often portrayed as joyous, eccentric, even lovable "madmen" who contain, but cannot always fully control, a secret, lonely, darkly melancholy self. This "mad" male self is apologized for by grandmothers who understand the special suffering of their men: Manuk "was mad, of course, but all great men are," says Lula, the Armenian grandmother who is his wife (*Rock* 74). This "mad" self is formed not only in response to the insults and impotence experienced in America, against which it has adopted the protective camouflage of eccentricity, but also by the pre-migration experience of helplessness in the homeland, which was dominated by Turkey and devastated by massacres, then genocide. Surviving the double misery of homeland and migrancy leads to oscillations between disabling grief and "mad" energy in the fictional Armenian-American characters, who are regarded with confusion and ambivalence by their children.

In Saroyan's work, as in his life, the drama of ethnic ambivalence is never resolved. It is stated, depicted, and then evaded. One of his authorial personae ends a meditation with: "I am both and neither. I love Armenia and I love America and belong to both, but I am only this: an inhabitant of the earth" ("Antranik," *SS* 82).[11] His fictions frequently begin by celebrating the enduring Armenianness of his characters; next, they note the duality of their identities; then they insist on the *integration* (incomplete, hence rarely amounting to *assimilation*) of these characters into American life. Saroyan's authorial personae insistently assert the uneasy compatibility of these two identities, even as his stories fail to demonstrate plausibly such a reconcilability in narrative terms. Saroyan finally insists, in humanistic terms that were convincing to American audiences during the ascendancy of left-populism in the 1930s but sound merely hollow now, that all people are the same, in that they experience, at bottom, dualities that can be mapped upon, and assimilated to, the original duality of the mad/sad Armenian.

It has been argued that the Armenian is the powerful archetype who, stripped of his ethnic name and manner, reappears as the all-American figure, indeed as Everyman, in Saroyan's work (Shirinian, *Literature* 163). This tactic recurs in an analogous maneuver elsewhere in that work, leading to what we might call the parallel positing of "Everyplace." Saroyan—who in later life lived on a circuit consisting of Fresno, California, Paris, and Armenia—insistently turns to the "identity of place": he points, correctly, to the geographical similarity between the Central Valley of California, where he grew up, and Armenia (a similarity that drew immigrants): "The grapes of the Armenian vineyards were not yet ripe, but there were fresh green leaves, and the vines were exactly like the vines of California. . . . The sun was warm and kindly, no less than in California" ("Antranik," *SS* 83). But, elsewhere, this assertion of similarity is replaced by a claim that recalls the phrase "an inhabitant of the earth": "There is a small land in Asia Minor that is called Armenia, but it is not so. It is not Armenia. It is a place. . . . There is no Armenia, gentlemen, there is no America and there is no England, and no France, and no Italy, there is only the earth" ("The Armenian," *SS* 127). Sentences like these are, as Derrida would put it, performatives disguised as constatives:[12] in describing what does not exist, they seek to evoke and perform into textual existence a humanist utopia beyond ethnicity and nation, homeland, and host land. Curiously, they do so as a result of, and in flight from, their representations of ethnicity and geographical specificity in the longings of the emigrants.

Saroyan's work is instructive because it oscillates between this kind of humanism, toward which he moves through a depiction of specifically ethnic Armenian dilemmas, and the opposing insistence that all identity is like ethnic Armenian identity, in that it is always and everywhere irrecoverably multiple and never fully integrated. Long before post-modern theory, he noted the irresolvable multiplicity of all identity; but in declaring this the general, human predicament, he usually avoided the task of concretely representing the struggle to hold together a self and a community in a diasporan setting, where power is unevenly distributed, and the porousness of social boundaries is both an exciting temptation and a threat to the immigrant. His evasions make Saroyan's fiction less than satisfactory today, for many diasporic Armenians; but it remains required reading for aspiring writers, in part because the Pulitzer he received marks the greatest recognition by the mainstream that any Armenian-American writer has attained and in part because Saroyan's career trajectory is, in some ways, exemplary. He began with short stories published in Armenian publications; he abandoned Armenian-American topics and became famous; he returned intermittently to specifically Armenian issues (chiefly in the novel *Rock Wagram;* then, in the last decade of his life, he fully embraced Armenian issues again, with an intensity that is manifest in his 1970s plays, edited after his death by Dickran Kouymjian as *An Armenian Trilogy.* This trajectory of the prodigal ethnic son's departure from, and return to, the ethnic fold reveals the conflicting pressures under which he and other Armenian-American writers worked before the acceptance and even celebration of ethnicity in the past two decades.

Overall, Saroyan's hortatory ambivalence repeatedly enacts an avoidance of the social sphere. His plays are often monologues, his fictions a series of events punctuated by the editorializing outbursts of his authorial persona; they usually fail to represent directly Armenian-American social life and conflict (as opposed to Sourian, discussed later). His favorite sites are the psychic landscape and a

landscape of places devoid of social markers. Even when he addresses the relationships of fathers and sons within families and returns fully to Armenian
themes, his work remains as evasive as it is suggestive.

The family is a crucial theme not just in all of Saroyan's ethnically oriented
fictions but also in Armenian-American literature at large. From the 1930s to
the 1970s, this concern manifests itself in two ways. First, the *narrative* thrust
takes the form of a search for the Father: a young man's coming-of-age also
becomes a search for a connection with, an understanding of, a father who is
dead, silent, or absent in some way. Second, the *descriptive* work of the text
evokes the ambience of the often extended family, in which mothers and especially grandmothers are central figures, catalysts of the search for, and pro-
viders of, information. Saroyan's *Rock Wagram* (1951), Peter Sourian's *The
Gate* (1965), and Peter Najarian's *Voyages* (1971)—the three most important
novels of this tradition—demonstrate that the search of the male protagonists
for a way to recover paternal, indeed patriarchal, authority and continuity is
central. The disruption of continuity is initiated by massacres and genocide. The
historical destruction of the male line and its power to protect the family is
sometimes literal, but just as frequently it can be recoded in representations of
fathers who have committed suicide (Saroyan's novel) or are paralyzed by stroke
(Najarian's).

Saroyan's novel traces the transformation of a Fresno Armenian named Arak
Vagramian into that most "American" of figures, a Hollywood star renamed
Rock Wagram, at the Christological age of thirty-three. Wagram is a potential
Gatsby figure: he has the quintessential opportunity of the American newcomer
to remake himself, which is also sporadically refigured as the Christian's opportunity to be "reborn." His subsequent experiences—failure at marriage and
unproductive, picaresque journey—are a virtual catalog of the themes of male-
authored Armenian-American fiction. In a crucial scene, Rock finds a poem his
late father had written in Armenian on the day of his suicide; significantly, this
discovery takes place in the office of *Asbarez,* an actual Armenian newspaper
(see p. 22) whose editor interprets the poem to him. Through the experience,
Wagram must learn to forgive his father (for suicide) and perhaps to feel for-
given by him for having grown into the kind of "Armenian" he believes his
father would not have wanted him to be. In fact, his father wanted him to know
the Armenian language, "whose majesty we all know" (*Rock* 101), and to
become his ideal of an Armenian American: neither a doctor nor a businessman,
neither a nationalist nor an assimilated American bourgeois, but rather "a man
who reads, who writes, who lives in a proud, lonely world" (*Rock* 106). Saroyan's familiar Armenian eccentric of the 1930s is reenvisioned in the Mc-
Carthyite 1950s as the ethnic artist and intellectual. In this text, the writer is
sketched as a man of the Word, emphatically capitalized and understood in two
senses. First is the sense of the Christian Word: "[A] man travels through a
mournful dream seeking many things, but in the end they are all only one thing:
the Word, and nothing in the lonely world is lonelier, for the name of the word

is Love" (*Rock* 103). The proper vehicle for ethnic, Armenian-American love is Family: "A man is a family thing. His meaning is a family meaning" (*Rock* 282). Again, Saroyan slips into paradox, contradiction, even incoherence: his writer is lonely, yet seeks love and constructs Family, the altar of ethnic religion and not customarily a site of loneliness; he is more an organic than an oppositional intellectual. Second, the Word is the Armenian language itself, in which so many Anglophone Armenian-American authors, like Saroyan himself, lack fluency and toward which they enact a profound ambivalence in their writing.

In a 1979 play published posthumously, Saroyan—this time as himself—returns to the scene of the *Armenian Sign,* the office of yet another Armenian newspaper. *Haratch* (Forward) is the name of both the play and the diaspora's leading newspaper, founded in Paris in 1925 by Shavarsh Missakian and now published by his daughter Arpik. She is a character in the play, as is the author of this overview, "Khachig."[13] Saroyan creates a meditation on the diaspora, which he insistently calls the "Dispersion." The play, which has been described as a Platonic symposium whose dialogue is concerned not with Love but with "being Armenian" (Kouymjian 34), offers various definitions of that issue, the sort of issue that rarely, if ever, arises in homelands but is discussed insistently by ethnodiasporans. One meaning of being Armenian is the maintenance of the Word itself, which in the diaspora has survived in the Armenophone press. *Haratch* and its editor are celebrated as the ministering angels of the language: "She is herself Armenia—in the Dispersion. She has kept Armenia alive in our hearts and minds through the pages of *Haratch*" (126). The language of the fathers and grandmothers, maintained in a medium that serves a shrinking and increasingly allophonic diasporan readership, comes to haunt the author as the embodiment of the not quite translatable Armenian Other. The Anglophone ethnodiasporan subject—here, Saroyan—repeatedly awakes to his double alienation from both Americanness and Armenianness and must articulate both in English.

Near the end of *Haratch,* the character Zohrab Mouradian turns to the discourse of Family and speaks synechdochically of the group gathered in the newspaper's office: "We are the family that we are, and all of our talk here is out of that condition of being a family" (176).

The trope of the Armenian nation, the diaspora, of Armenian-American ethnicity as the Family is—not surprisingly—to be found everywhere in this literature, mostly celebrated, sometimes interrogated. Peter Sourian's *The Gate* narrates the story of three generations of the men of the Stepanyan family. Paul, the compiler of the text, is an aspiring writer and the son of Sarkis, Massachusetts Institute of Technology-graduated engineer who thinks he has successfully distanced himself and his children from the pettiness and insularity of ethnic Armenian life. Paul aspires to write about his grandfather Vahan, who survived a Turkish massacre and left behind some notebooks in which he had begun to write an account of the homeland and family; some of the notebooks were burned in a fire that symbolizes the conflagration and disruption of the genocide.

Like Rock, confronted with his father's poem, Paul is unable to read the grandfather's text and asks his father to translate the Armenian for him. Sarkis begins,
is overcome by memory and emotion, and refuses to continue. The silenced
father cannot even transmit the grandfather's voice. Yet the past will not be
forgotten, nor can the Armenian community of the text's present be avoided.
Despite the pleas of his wife, Sarkis is drawn into designing a major Armenian
church, a "cathedral"; given the centrality of Apostolic Christianity to Armenian identity, his willingness to do the work signifies his willingness to construct
the ethnic community in diaspora. Sarkis is eventually shot dead by another
Armenian, a mad chauvinist. The intricate plot wholly (and with some animus)
devalorizes political nationalism and sees limitations in the sort of engagement
that chooses church and religion as the pillars of ethnodiasporan continuity. The
alternative Sourian prefers is the son's persistent attempt to recover a past despite the silent resistance of the father and imposed silence of the grandfather
and, if this fails, to *imagine* one. As in *Rock Wagram,* the Word, memory,
imagination, and the writer who employs them become the "rock" on which is
founded not so much the church Sarkis means to design as the ethnic community
itself. The limitation of Sourian's emphatically ethnic position is that the Armenian portion of his characters' identity lies in the past; he rejects the diasporic
insistence that the "Armenian" in Armenian-American must not be projected
and mapped upon a hyphenated "past-present" dichotomy that equates "Armenian" with "past."

Sourian's narrative acknowledges that ethnic life is something of a family
affair but insists that the family is shattered not only by Turkish massacres but
also by intra-Armenian violence. Until recently, most Armenian (and other)
ethnic fictions idealized the ethnic enclave, hiding the signs of all but peaceful
generational conflict, suppressing the memory of other intracommunal conflicts,
and engaging in celebrations of a nonexistent ethnic unity. Sourian's novel melodramatically acknowledges violence: it links Sarkis's death to the genocide
inflicted by the Turks, since the killer uses an ancient pistol confided to his care
by the victim's mother the year the genocide began. Thus, since Sarkis is the
architect of a cathedral, his death evokes what is historically the most significant
act of Armenian-American conflict, the murder of an Armenian bishop in church
in 1933 (see p. 21).

Even more important, the events of Sourian's novel become possible because
a writer seeks to reach the otherwise unreachable past of his family and people
to bridge discontinuity, through a text. The scene of reading one's way into the
past is as American as it is Armenian: Ike McCaslin of Faulkner's *The Bear,*
reading in the old commissary the ledgers that reveal his family's tale of rape,
incest, miscegenation, and suicide, is perhaps the canonical example. Memory,
so essential to the ethnic narratives of America, is not easily come by in these
texts: it is found in the inscriptions left by the Fathers, and, in the Armenian-
American case, the language is Armenian. It is also gendered: the fathers write,
and the mothers and grandmothers narrate orally. The mothers' tales have the

power of immediacy, of her body, and are recalled like the familiar smells of cooking in childhood. But the elusive dream of a common language haunts the Armenian-American "family" and ethnic group, or at least the Armenian-American literary tradition: the written, standard Armenian of the fathers is not identical to, or as accessible as, the Armenian dialect and broken English of the mothers; and the sons are ultimately native users of neither.

Unlike its predecessors, Peter Najarian's *Voyages* (1971) is stylistically our contemporary but shares a sensibility with the earlier texts. His protagonist is called Aram, named after the central figure of Saroyan's Fresno-idealizing collection of short prose pieces, *My Name Is Aram* (1940). Najarian's protagonist repeatedly evokes the "mad" Armenians of Saroyan. But there is nothing idyllic or Californian about Najarian's story. His life in a New Jersey tenement and lower Manhattan apartment alternates with voyages that lead him to remembrance and imaginative reconstruction of his family's past before, during, and after the repeatedly evoked genocide. They also take him on picaresque wanderings as he alludes to, or explicitly invokes, Saroyan, Kerouac, and Whitman, singers of a multiethnic "America." Once again, the father is not active in the text—he is paralyzed (literally, by a stroke) and then dies. A detailed journey into his past is not possible because there are no memoirs to decipher. Aram compensates: "Imagination is yet more than memory. My father is a broken voice" (50). To assist his imagination, Aram has the chorus of his mother and her circle of friends, many of whom are survivors of rape or massacre, and he also has old Vahan (named after the grandfather in Sourian's novel; the name means Shield, hence guardian, the safekeeper of memory). Vahan wishes to keep his memoirs safe and to transmit them as a keepsake to his grandchildren as a means of keeping them safely Armenian, just as Sourian's Vahan left behind half-burned notebooks for his grandchildren. Even if they can't be published, Najarian's Vahan reasons, "that's all right, as long as my grandchildren can read [them] some day" (37). Aram, who prefigures those grandchildren in that he can't read Armenian but understands it, is translating the notebooks into English with the old man's help and asks why the old man cares. He answers: "You ask why? They are my children's children, no? They're Armenian, no? . . . They should know what it means, no?" (37). This identification of the meaning of young lives with the suffering undergone by the old is both a central trope of ethnic writing and, in the Armenian case, a cause as well as a symptom of the frustration of the third generation of immigrant writers. They feel the necessity to retell the tale and to bring closure to it and can do so only at considerable cost.

In the act of translation—itself pregnant with meaning—that Aram carries out for the old man, he wishes to be an "amanuensis" (50), a pen through which the voice of the fathers will narrate and give meaning to the past that meant mostly suffering, impotence, and shame. But after delving into that past, he cannot come to terms with settling down as a conforming ethnic, like his half-brother Yero. The latter is one of the best-delineated portraits that Armenian-American literature has to offer of the uneasy reconciliations effected in, and as, "ethnicity." His American ranch house is, in many ways, an Armenian home, full of memorabilia. In his pursuit of money as the mark of success, he is double, simultaneously intensely American and yet an immigrant who focuses his energies on that aspect of the American dream that makes most sense to him. He is most fully American, in the text's terms, when he argues that to be American is to forget the past ("Let the dead bury their dead" [108]). He chides Aram for not becoming a professional, failing to take advantage of the opportunities America offers. But America as Aram sees it cannot yet be a true home for the son of Armenian refugees: it is his "foster home" and "orphanage" (21–22), where the Statue of Liberty is equated to "the Old Bitch gone in the teeth" (76). He sees America as a racist and classist place that deceives and abandons its children (31). Being an Armenian, Aram claims, makes one an orphan in America (58), because true parenthood requires a patriarchal continuity, a transmission of authority, at the very least the authority to make or remake a self. Armenian rupture and American indifference combine to make that impossible.

Significantly, the Armenians of the first generation are doubly stripped of authority, first as genocide survivors and then as impotent immigrants who are patronized. In such a situation, to be told, as he is, by his *mother* that he is like his father is terrifying to Aram. He sees his alternative, potential selves as either the paralyzed artist-father, fully Armenian, or as his brother, the ethnicized Armenian American reconciled to suburban subsistence. Responding to what he perceives as a lack of choices he can aspire to and in a pattern that is characteristic of mainstream American modernism, he becomes an expatriate (Hemingway is mentioned, 149), goes to London, variously thinking of himself as an "exile" and a "pilgrim" in reverse, and there comes to terms—unconvincingly—with his Armenian and American identities. As James Joyce's Stephen Dedalus in *Portrait of the Artist as a Young Man* aspires to do, Aram "forges" in exile an identity with which he can be comfortable. The mark of his having accomplished this is that he can imagine the conversation he never had with his father, as a result of which he is reconciled with himself: " 'I'm not going to be crippled, Papa!' 'My son,' he said, 'I never wanted you to be. Why did you think I did?' " (150).

The dilemma the novel enacts has to do with the costs of continuity: how to "accept" the extraordinary pain of the first generation, how to remember or sympathetically imagine it, without becoming crippled by it as they were or without being driven to elude it, as Yero seeks to do ("Let the dead bury the dead" [108]). While often melodramatic and lacking the formal discipline that would make it a truly successful novel, *Voyages* remains an exceptional Armenian-American and indeed ethnic-American fiction, in its refusal to glorify the "pastel colors" and saccharine emotions common to so many representations of immigrant life and in its insistence on the very high costs of *either* retaining or surrendering ethnic subjectivity. Aram does not compartmentalize his ethnic and American selves: he is at war; indeed, his identity *is* the conflict between two cultural traditions, and the truce he attains by the end of the novel is as precarious as it is satisfying.

In 1986, Najarian explored another path for attaining that truce. His *Daughters of Memory,* which he also illustrated, is a quasi narrative. It is pivotal in that it moves beyond the patriarchal text and seeks to balance the search of an Armenian-American man, Zeke, for some sort of closure to post-genocide trauma, with the story and portrait of his aging mother. The "Greek chorus" (Bedrosian 123) of the old Armenian women in the mother's circle is success-fully used; their staccato conversations (on matters major or mundane) illuminate the relatively banal narrative of Zeke's journey to the old Armenian lands now incorporated into Turkey and his encounters with old Armenian men who were taken into Turkish homes as orphans. Taking a leaf out of Saroyan's work, Najarian announces that, in the end, all men are so much the same he can't really differentiate between the old Turkish and Armenian-born men. Elsewhere in the text, it becomes difficult to differentiate the old mother from Mother Earth: "her feet like the ground itself, the bunions and calluses like a transition into the world of rocks and trees" (117).

As the genocide survivors approach their deaths, and Zeke moves toward a new life in which he will no longer carry the grandparents' pain, the book falters. The painful inadequacy of the closure Najarian grants his protagonist is not simply the result of esthetic misjudgment. He can achieve closure only by de-nying difference and declaring no longer relevant the history that "the daughters of memory" embody and recover elsewhere in his text. He seals the deliberate pact with amnesia in a scene in which Zeke has intercourse with a Turkish prostitute. Not surprisingly, she proves no different from other prostitutes in other countries: it seems that Turks, Armenians, and others are all people, not so distinguishable when really old or naked; in such pseudoinsights, the text finds a separate peace. Like Saroyan, Najarian wants both to portray the damage that the genocide inflicts across three generations and to move beyond it: he can do so only by neglecting difference—of culture, power, and pain inflicted on the Armenians—and by balancing it with and against our common humanity. Such a "balance," in the context of an otherwise astute portrayal of the effects of past inhumanity, creates contradiction, not truce, let alone resolution.

This resolution is additionally problematic because it disavows what really makes such a "resolution" possible for white, middle-class Armenian Ameri-cans: the option of moving on into the mainstream of American culture. Their ethnicity, in the third and fourth generations, is a matter of elective affinity, not a burden imposed by the majority. Emancipation requires only shrugging off the burden of memory imposed *from within* the ethnic group. After the 1960s, this burden of memory and difference, not the Turk or the genocide or the humiliation inflicted by WASPs (themselves virtually invisible in an immigrant-filled America, as Edgarian's novel points out) becomes the chief source of pain.

But some truces with the ethnic past work only for one generation. Michael

J. Arlen's two autobiographical narratives, *Exiles* (1970) and *Passage to Ararat* (1975), reflect on the apparent success and eventual failure of the peace his father, Michael Arlen (born Dikran Kouyumdjian), sought to make with his Armenian past. He changed his name, refused to speak of the past, married an equally displaced Greek woman, attained success as the author of romantic best-sellers in the Anglophone world, and sent his son to British private schools, then Exeter and Harvard. After the death of the father, the younger Arlen—by then a successful essayist and television critic for the *New Yorker*—sought to understand both the roots of his father's pained silence about his past and his own vague anxiety about his "Englishness": "I realized that there was at least one genuine certifiable 100 percent *English* thing I could do reasonably well, which was to catch a cricket ball" (*Exiles* 143) and about his own identity as Armenian, Greek, and American. The investigation he conducted is chronicled in *Exiles* (the finer book) and *Passage,* which won the National Book Award for contemporary affairs in 1976 and speaks more extensively of the Armenians.

Passage to Ararat is an atypical Armenian-American text, since Arlen's exploration begins not from within ethnicity but rather in the midst of a life more assimilated than those of the authors hitherto discussed. Also, his concern with the father—the ghostly legacy that will not let him rest—dominates the text to an extraordinary degree: there are no mothers and grandmothers here, only history, a journey to Armenia, a visit to the genocide memorial there, then to Turkey, and an extended internal dialogue with the father, an emblem of all the silently raging, humiliated fathers whom, he thinks, the Armenian "young will begin to set . . . free" (292). The son's engagement with the past is over as soon as he truly lays his father to rest. That engagement is an indispensable but parenthetical rite of passage rather than an initiation into ethnicity or hybridity as a way of life.

Carol Edgarian's *Rise the Euphrates* (1994) has enjoyed considerable commercial success and enacts a matrilineal turn. While some of the assumptions and categories that govern this well-wrought novel are not very different from those that shape Najarian's, its texture is. It concerns three generations of women, living in the aptly named Connecticut town of Memorial: the grandmother, Casard, her daughter Araxie, who marries an *odar,* a non-Armenian named George Loon, and their daughter, Seta Loon, who narrates the tale of her own coming-of-age, the imaginative labor of recovering the grandmother's past and—after the latter is killed in an accident—of dealing with it. There are no documents to be read. Fragments of memory and a synthetic imagination "reconstruct" and "recover" the past. This tale is interspersed with a full account of Araxie's marriage and its partial failure, stories of other teenagers, and evocations of two other generations of women: Casard's murdered mother, Seta, after whom the narrator is named, and the unborn, as yet unnamed child who is in the unmarried, thirty-three-year-old Seta's womb at the end of the novel. The Christological age (cf. *Rock Wagram*) is ironically dealt with: "Seta . . . has reached an age of no significance. In the store there are no special, funny cards

for her. She is on the other side of potential now, where everything counts"
(355). As in Najarian's *Daughters of Memory* and Arlen's *Passage to Ararat,*
what counts is to make peace with the past, and that, in turn, means not to pass
on either the pained silence or the painful stories to another generation: "You
passed your fears on to us as kids" (362), Seta says to her American-born
mother, who, in turn, received them from Seta's grandmother; Seta does not
wish to pass them on to her unborn child, to give yet another hostage to history.[14]
Translation, transmission, and transfer again emerge as issues, but Edgarian's
way of dealing with them is more nuanced than what has come before.

Like the older Chinese women of *The Joy Luck Club,* to which this text bears
several similarities (Amy Tan praises the novel in a blurb), Casard's friends
know her story, yet guard it for a long time as they continue to watch over her
family: "[T]he ladies I carry with me like chromosomes," Seta writes (355).
The full story is not revealed in any one epiphanic moment but in dreams and
historical recollections that punctuate the strong narrative of the younger generations, whose lives are not painless: an Armenian-American woman is raped;
Vietnam is invoked as offering a kind of parallel to the genocide; Araxie, of
the middle generation, does not behave as an Armenian daughter and mother
should. Having married an *odar* she loves against her mother's wishes, fifteen
years later she cuckolds him with an Armenian man, only to return to her husband. Desire is a force in this novel. In the Armenian-American tradition of
narrative, where even male desire has not been generously acknowledged (there
are prostitutes and masturbation in *Voyages,* but only as symptoms), the sudden
emergence of female desire as a repeatedly empowering force is evidence that
this tradition has managed to narrate its way through and past rape, shame, and
silence.

CONCLUSION

This overview has concentrated on long narratives at the expense of short
stories and poems, because doing so provided the axis of an indispensable generational analysis. The regrettable, if in this context necessary, neglect of the
poetic tradition must be partially redeemed. Like other West Asian cultures, the
Armenian is richest in poetry, and that tradition is invoked by the poets who
came of age in the 1960s and after. Michael Akillian, Harold Bond, Peter Balakian, Diana Der Hovanessian, and David Kherdian are among those who have
written many fine poems. It must be emphasized that a majority of their works,
especially Balakian's (technically the most accomplished), have no discernibly
Armenian or ethnic concerns. Those that do can be crudely categorized as belonging to either the vatic or the personal lyric tradition.

Der Hovanessian is the prominent oracular poet, who apostrophizes the murdered generations and the land: "O Kovkas/I too have seen your ice glory,"
she writes (*Selected Poems* 35). She has also "seen," that is, has read and
translated (often with Marzbed Margossian), the work of the major poets killed

in the genocide. In "How to Become an Armenian," each stanza consists of lines she attributes to the last century's poets, whose relay of statement and response reconstitutes the broken chain of the tradition. In "Diaspora," she speaks of herself as a "tourist" and "stranger" visiting the homeland. Though a poet, she is also a "stranger" to her two languages: "I spoke English with a slight accent / even after three generations. / Someone was calling / in a forgotten language" ("Diaspora," *Selected Poems* 10).

Of course, the forgotten do not stay forgotten here. Balakian invokes the genocide repeatedly in images both gory and quiet: "Men and women who bore my name / have gone from face to bone," and the blood-red poppies are "all my aunt remembered of Armenia" ("Poppies," *Reply* 42). Other flowers in his poems evoke the Euphrates he has never seen, the river of Edgarian's title, in which tens of thousands died ("Jack-in-the-Pulpit," *Reply* 49). In a poem dedicated to the Armenian-American painter Arshile Gorky, a genocide survivor who eventually hanged himself in a Connecticut barn, Balakian tenderly, fiercely evokes Armenia, Gorky's paintings of his mother, of nature and still lifes, and his suicide:

> Somewhere between your lake in Armenia
> and this place there is a trail
> of ash—almost chalk—to bring
> the limbs back to fullness.
> Your mother's stomach is a dried fig
> on your palette. Though swallows
> glide and turn through the rope
> still hanging in your barn,
> in this ghostly light you are a shadow:
> off-white, then gray, then a wisp
> of flame rising in the dust. ("To Arshile Gorky," *Reply* 29)

The condensation of references and their reworking into a poem that stands by itself yet is richly intertwined with Armenian history are masterful and characteristic of the best of Balakian's work.

Michael Akillian has described the life of even a third-generation ethnic as "a step forward, a glance back" ("The Song," *Eating* 21). His sensibility is closest to Edgarian's, and his images of nightmarish visions of the genocide, of relatives speaking Armenian, of a dead grandmother's kitchen could easily be interpolated as descriptions in her novel. In a powerful poem, "The Eating of Names," he evokes the helpless rage engendered by the immigrant's experience of having his name transmogrified at Ellis Island. The immigration officials "eat" his true name, and he silently "eats" his rage and pain in order to be allowed in. Akillian's insight is to see that the sons and grandsons of the humiliated immigrant will be his family, his "home" in a sense, but not "from" home, the homeland—and they will therefore be, in some measure, foreigners and strangers to him, immensely multiplying the distance that exists between any parent and child, any past (which is "a foreign country") and the beckoning present.

With Najarian's second novel and Edgarian's book, Akillian's poems stand firmly in the Armenian-American present, which is a moment of settling accounts with the past, of putting down a burden. Whether those who do so will turn, in the twenty-first century, to a redefinition and diasporization of Armenian Americanness in some interaction with the homeland Republic of Armenia is unclear. It is a plausible hypothesis. But it is also possible that the power and glamour of white ethnicity have already peaked and that white ethnics will henceforth affect and display only whatever items of their culture are deemed fashionable for middle-class consumers of lifestyles. Perhaps the title "Consuming Ethnicity" should be copyrighted for the next edition of a reference text like this volume: by then, it may be clear whether ethnicity will flourish as it consumes the signs and texts of its past or whether it will prove itself to be a self-consuming entity as ethnics make their peace with the past and fail to produce a diasporan future.

NOTES

1. "Primary" because the diasporan population came to the site directly from the homeland; "secondary" diasporas are formed when such a population migrates again, as the Jewish diaspora of Spain was forced to migrate in 1492 to the Ottoman Empire, or as the Indians of Uganda were forced by Idi Amin to depart for the U.K. and the United States. "Intrastate" because, having left a homeland ruled by an alien empire, the diasporans settled elsewhere in the territories of that empire. For details and implications, see Tololyan, "Exile Governments."

2. "Ethnodiasporan" is an awkward but necessary term, because the Armenian-American community contains both ethnics and diasporans. Italian Americans offer an excellent model of ethnicity: they take pride in their names, food, music, culture, and symbolic affiliations with the homeland; they rally against defamation; they maintain strong kinship groups and compatriotic associations. But unlike the Armenian diaspora, for example, they are not organized transnationally, to maintain, as a collectivity, active political, cultural, or economic interaction with the homeland or with other Italian communities in, say, Canada or Australia. Nor do they seek to lobby the U.S. government with a specifically Italian/American agenda.

3. Despite its promising title, Lorne Shirinian's *The Republic of Armenia and the Rethinking of the North-American Diaspora in Literature* does not adequately address this issue.

4. The importance of print culture to the emergence of homeland nationalisms is well known; cf. Anderson, Benedict. *Imagined Communities: Reflections on the Origin and Spread of Nationalism* (London: Verso, 1983). But their role in the creation of diasporan national movements such as the Armenian and the Jewish (Zionist) is not equally well understood.

5. The scholarly *Journal of the Society for Armenian Studies* has been published intermittently since 1984, and *The Journal of Armenian Studies* since 1975.

6. Ashraf Rushdy, *NeoSlave Narratives,* MS.

7. The thesis of the centrality of genocide to North American-Armenian ethnic texts is argued powerfully by Marc Nichanian in Armenian and by Shirinian in English. Rubina Peroomian's *Literary Responses to Catastrophe: A Comparison of the Armenian and the Jewish Experience* (Atlanta: Scholars Press, 1993) is a useful text that draws all its examples from Armenophone classics.

8. The adjectives "diasporic" and "diasporan" are used interchangeably here, as in much writing on the topic. "Diasporic" has been constructed on the model of, and in rhyme with, "ethnic"; "diasporan," with "American" or "Armenian." Not a lexical investigation but the consensus of those who use the term professionally will eventually determine the "victor."

9. Louis Althusser and Etienne Balibar, *Reading Capital,* trans. Ben Brewster (London: Verso, 1979 or 1968), 14.

10. Comments by two Americans in Fresno, documented in Richard T. La Piere, "The Armenian Colony in Fresno County, California," Ph.D. thesis, 1930, 339, 341.

11. *SS* stands for *Saroyan Special,* a collection of his stories. See Bibliography.

12. Jacques Derrida, "The Time Is Out of Joint," *Deconstruction Is/In America,* ed. Ansel Haverkamp (New York: NYU Press, 1995), 30.

13. All the characters are based on real people. Some retain their first names; others are renamed but are transparent to those who know the milieu. However, the words and thoughts assigned to these characters entirely serve Saroyan's purposes: a few of the things they say are nearly verbatim reproductions of what they actually said during Saroyan's frequent after-hours visits to *Haratch*'s office, when alcohol and conversation created a small salon of diasporic thinkers. But most of their speeches are ventriloquized: Saroyan gives these characters the words and positions he needs to create a dramatic debate concerning ethnic identity caught between homeland and host land.

14. In one of those coincidences that indicate how often art represents not what is, but will soon become, life, less than a year after Edgarian's work was published, the government of the Republic of Armenia asked (in March 1995) whether the teaching of genocide to those aged under twelve might transmit trauma too effectively. In homeland and diaspora both, the form in which the genocide must be remembered is now in dispute.

SELECTED PRIMARY BIBLIOGRAPHY

Akillian, Michael. *The Eating of Names: Poems.* New York: Ashod Press, 1983.

Antreassian, Jack. *The Cup of Bitterness and Other Stories.* New York: Ashod Press, 1979.

Arlen, Michael. *Exiles.* New York: Farrar, Straus, and Giroux, 1970.

———. *Passage to Ararat.* New York: Farrar, Straus, and Giroux, 1975.

Arzoomanian, Ralph. *Four Plays.* New York: Ararat Press, 1980.

Avakian, Arlene Voski. *Lion Woman's Legacy: An Armenian-American Memoir.* New York: CUNY-The Feminist Press, 1992.

Balakian, Peter. *Reply from Wilderness Island.* Riverdale-on-Hudson, New York: Sheep Meadow Press, 1988.

———. *Sad Days of Light.* New York: Sheep Meadow Press, 1983.

Baliozian, Ara. *In the New World.* New York: Voskedar Press, 1982.

———. *In the New World: Essays.* New York: Voskedar Press, 1982.

Basmajian, Garik. *Armenian-American Poets: A Bilingual Anthology.* Detroit: Manoogian Cultural Fund of the Armenian General Benevolent Union, 1976.

Bedoukian, Kerop. *The Urchin: An Armenian's Escape.* London: John Murray, 1978.

Bedrosian, Margaret, and Leo Hamalian, eds. *Crossroads: Short Fiction by Armenian-American Writers.* New York: Ashod Press, 1992.

Bond, Harold. *The Way It Happens to You.* New York: Ararat Press, 1979.

Der Hovanessian, Diana. *How to Choose Your Past.* New York: Ararat Press, 1978.

———. *Selected Poems.* Riverdale-on-Hudson, New York: Sheep Meadow Press, 1994.

Der Hovanessian, Diana, and Marzbed Margossian, trans. and eds. *Anthology of Armenian Poetry.* New York: Columbia University Press, 1978.

Edgarian, Carol. *Rise the Euphrates.* New York: Random House, 1994.

Hagopian, Richard. *The Dove That Brings Peace.* New York: Farrar and Rinehart, 1944.

———. *Faraway the Spring.* New York: Scribner, 1952.

Hamalian, Leo, ed. *Ararat: 25th Anniversary Issue* [An anthology from the leading Armenian-American literary quarterly]. New York: Armenian General Benevolent Union, 1985.

Hashian, Jack. *Mamigon.* New York: Coward, McCan, and Geoghegan, 1982.

Herald, Leon Serabian. *This Waking Hour.* New York: Thomas Seltzer, 1925.

Housepian, Marjorie. *A Houseful of Love.* New York: Random House, 1957.

Kalpakian, Laura. *Dark Continent.* New York: Viking, 1989.

Khachadoorian, Haig. *Shadows of Time.* New York: Ashod Press, 1983.

Kherdian, David. *Homage to Adana.* Fresno, CA: Giligia Press, 1971.

———. *The Nonny Poems.* New York: Macmillan, 1974.

Mardikian, George. *Song of America.* New York: McGraw-Hill, 1956.

Melikian, Lucik. *From Hunger to Caviar.* La Verne, CA: University of La Verne Press, 1985.

Najarian, Peter. *Daughters of Memory.* N.p. [San Francisco]: City Miner Books, 1986.

———. *Voyages.* New York: Pantheon, 1971.

Saroyan, William. *Haratch,* [a play in] *William Saroyan: An Armenian Trilogy.* Ed. Dikran Kouymjian. Fresno, CA: CSU-Fresno Press, 1986.

———. *The Man with His Heart in the Highlands and Other Stories.* New York: Dell, 1968.

———. *My Name Is Aram.* New York: Harcourt Brace, 1940.

———. *Rock Wagram.* New York: Doubleday, 1951.

———. *The Saroyan Special: Selected Short Stories.* Freeport, New York: Books for Libraries Press, 1970.

Setian, Ralph. *Cahier Noir.* Pasadena, CA: Corybantic Press, 1975.

Shirinian, Lorne. *Armenian-North American Poets: An Anthology.* St. Jean, Quebec: Manna, 1974.

Sourian, Peter. *The Gate.* New York: Harcourt, Brace, and World, 1965.

Surmelian, Leon Z. *I Ask You Ladies and Gentlemen.* New York: E. P. Dutton, 1945.

Varandyan, Emmanuel. *The Well of Ararat.* New York: Doubleday, Doran, 1938.

SELECTED SECONDARY BIBLIOGRAPHY

Bakalian, Anny. *Armenian-Americans: From Being to Feeling Armenian.* New Brunswick, NJ: Transaction Press, 1993.

Bedrosian, Margaret. *The Magical Pine Ring: Culture and the Imagination in Armenian-American Literature.* Detroit: Wayne State University Press, 1991.

Calonne, William. *William Saroyan.* Chapel Hill: University of North Carolina Press, 1983.

Kouymjian, Dikran. "Introduction." *William Saroyan: An Armenian Trilogy.* Fresno, CA: CSU-Fresno Press, 1986. 1–38.

Mirak, Robert. "Armenians." *Harvard Encyclopedia of American Ethnic Groups.* Ed. Stephan Thernstrom. Cambridge: Harvard University Press, 1980. 136–149.

———. *Torn between Two Lands: Armenians in America, 1890 to World War I.* Cambridge: Harvard University Press, 1983.

Oshagan, Vahe. [Editor, Special Issue 13, on Armenian Literature, of] *Review of National Literatures.* New York: Council on National Literatures, 1984.

———. "The Theme of the Armenian Genocide in Diaspora Prose." *Armenian Review* 38.1 (1990): 50–60.

Shirinian, Lorne. *Armenian-North American Literature: A Critical Introduction to Genocide, Diaspora and Symbols.* Studies in Comparative Literature 11. Lewiston, New York: Edwin Mellen Press, 1990.

———. *The Republic of Armenia and the Rethinking of the North-American Diaspora in Literature.* Lewiston, New York: Edwin Mellen Press, 1992.

Tololyan, Khachig. "Exile Governments in the Armenian Polity." *Governments-in-Exile in Contemporary World Politics.* Ed. Yossi Shain. London: Routledge, 1991. 166–187.

Tololyan, Minas. *Tar Meh Kraganootyun* [A Century of Literature, in Armenian.] 2d ed. 2 vols. New York: Voskedar Press, 1977.

Waldstreicher, David. *The Armenian Americans.* New York: Chelsea House, 1985.

3
Chinese-American Literature
Shan Qiang He

INTRODUCTION

Chinese-American immigrant literature can be defined as literature by or about Chinese immigrants in America. The word "immigrant" may cause some controversy, for most of the literary works in this field are written by native-born Americans of Chinese descent, while "Chinese immigrant literature" usually refers to the works written by Chinese immigrants in Chinese. However, since the theme of immigration and cultural difference is prominent in many works written in English by native-born Americans of Chinese descent, a thematic term, "Chinese-American immigrant literature," is possible for focusing on the immigrant heritage in literature.

The history of Chinese immigration into the United States has been overshadowed by official policies of racist exclusion and vigilante violence. "Chinese-American immigrant literature" covers not only the immigrant experience across different historical periods but also the aftermath of the history of racism in Asian America, which Asian Americans have been trying to claim and define as a unique space of political and cultural contestation.

The word "immigrant" has a verbal felicity. Its literal meaning, "moving into," has the connotation of "settling down" and "reaching the destination of assimilation," whereby the word itself will be put under erasure. This seems to be the manifest destiny of European immigrants in America. However, that destination of assimilation always moves a little beyond the reach of Chinese immigrants, "strangers from a different shore."[1] Reading Chinese-American immigrant literature involves a perpetual process of questioning and negotiating among different Chinese cultural traditions, different versions of historiography, different immigrant experiences, and, last but not least, readers' own cultural assumptions and political persuasions. The reading process is also a process of crossing borders of race, culture, language, and gender, through an intricate relationship of power, dominance, and subaltern resistance.

This chapter begins with the Chinese cultural backgrounds and the early immigrant experiences across the Pacific Ocean, and Asian America as an interstitial space between different cultures under an asymmetrical relationship of power and dominance. Then it traces the development of Chinese-American immigrant literature as a minority discourse of resistance, shaped by various forces of political movements, transculturation, and institutionalization in the United States. The focus is to highlight thorny issues and raise problems within the limited space available for a survey of this kind. Translations of immigrant literature written in Chinese are discussed, as a subject rarely included in "Asian-American literature." Finally, general trends and developments are outlined with both a historical view of the development in this field and recent revisions and explorations.

LITERARY-CULTURAL HISTORY

Reading Chinese-American immigrant literature requires a basic background knowledge of Chinese culture, American racist stereotyping of the Chinese, and the history of Chinese immigration to the United States. These three intersecting categories form a unique interstitial space for Chinese-American immigrant literature as a minority discourse.

In reading Chinese-American literature, we invariably come across "Chinese culture" in one way or another. The most familiar in the field is the warrior traditions, male and female, advanced by Frank Chin and Maxine Hong Kingston, respectively. In Chin's version, the warrior tradition in Chinese popular culture is best represented by Chinese classic novels like *Water Margin* and *The Romance of the Three Kingdoms.*[2] It is a tradition of universal brotherhood, of taking justice into one's own hands when the country is ruled by a tyrant, of opposing the rich and powerful on behalf of the poor and downtrodden. Frank Chin resurrected this tradition in the late 1960s in order to recover Chinese masculinity against the white emasculation of Asian America. Here the Chinese heroism serves to shatter the white myth of the effeminate Chinamen. Yet this tradition is in itself problematic: popular uprisings are contained within the ideal of finding a good emperor; universal brotherhood excludes women.

In contrast, the Chinese-American woman writer Maxine Hong Kingston's work *The Woman Warrior* invents the tradition of the woman warrior (from a famous classical narrative poem). Feminist critics have uncovered a list of heroic women in Chinese history who have made great achievements, ranging from the battlefields to music and poetry, in spite of the patriarchal cultural oppression. Indeed, many of the woman warriors are conscious fighters against the feudal patriarchal oppression.[3] The common emphasis on warrior in both types of cultural invention underlines the urgency of Chinese-American writers waging a war of pens for minority rights. Yet even Kingston's woman warrior Fa Mulan has taken on details borrowed from a male warrior, Yue Fei, in Chinese history, a nationalist hero loyal to the emperor, fighting the Huns who have now become assimilated into the Chinese Han nationality. Cultural translation and repetition blur the line between "authenticity" and "fakeness," thereby opening up the space for a genealogy of "origins" both as a source of patriarchy and as a history of subaltern insurgency.

Chinese culture is marked by geographical and historical diversity. Confucianism as a dominant ideology of Chinese culture is not a religion but a humanist philosophy, a secular ethics of *reason and fairness* (*qing li*) governing human relations. In its various manifestations both as doctrine and in practice, reason and fairness have often exceeded their limits and turned into rigid hierarchies of patriarchal oppression. Complementary to this dominant worldly ethics are Taoism and Buddhism, with their Oriental mysticism, yin/yang dialectics and supplementarity, and transcendentalism. There are also various folk traditions such as Chin's Cantonese opera and Kingston's "talk story," as unofficial, alternative cultures deeply embedded in the immigrants' daily life and traceable to their roots/routes across the Pacific. Most of the early immigrants such as represented by Chin and Kingston came from the Cantonese-speaking rural southern China, while the immigrants in the works of Gish Jen and Amy Tan spoke Mandarin and Shanghai dialect and came from an urban background. Since China in this century has witnessed a history of Westernization, colonialism, and modernity, cultural hybridity often makes it difficult to tell the East from the West, a convenient division that has often led to racial stereotypes whether in their nineteenth-century format of biologism or in their twentieth-century format of culturalism.

The American stereotypes of the Chinese originated from Western Orientalism, which, inventing the Orient as its Other in order to consolidate the Self, was part of the European global conquest and colonization in the age of colonialism and imperialism. As America joined other European powers after the Opium War (1840) to force numerous concessions and open ports of trade from China, it also sent missionaries there to convert the "heathens." The missionary literature continued the Christian tradition in Orientalism, whose moral imperative was the final racialized barrier against the assimilation of the Chinese.

When Chinese immigrants came to America in the mid-nineteenth century as gold miners, railway builders, factory workers, and agricultural laborers, racial stereotypes began as a cultural deployment of rational practicality for whites to define and contain the "yellow" other. In the American racist discourse, Chinese identity was constituted through different uses and functions for the whites: while, morally and physically, they were the same as the animalistic and barbaric blacks and deserve the same fate as the American Indians, they were a source of more efficient labor than the blacks and cheaper than the white workers. This unique position translated into many threats in the racial fantasies of whites: sexual perverts after white women, cheap competitors against white workers, greedy hoarders of wealth siphoned off back to China, harbingers of yet more numerous brute hordes to swamp America, armed with sly cunning, and low-wage competition. These ambiguous racial feelings built up quickly during economic downturns and led to the popular reception of Bret Harte's "The Heathen Chinee" (1870), which portrayed a Chinese Ah Sin beating two white opponents at card-game cheating, thus demonstrating that for "ways" "dark" and "tricks" "vain," the "heathen Chinee is peculiar."[4]

The Chinese and the Asians in general represented the "yellow peril" for white America, a phrase Jack London adopted for the title of his book (*The Yellow Peril*, 1904). His and white America's nightmare was that the fecund Chinese, awakened to Western mechanization by Japan, would invade and overwhelm the Caucasian race. This "yellow peril" was epitomized in the stereotypical image of Fu Manchu, created in 1913 by British author Sax Rohmer. Fu Manchu had mastered Western knowledge and science and turned them to satanic abuse. He embodied the primordial Chinese evil, without moral, without compassion, totally dedicated to pure intellect and impersonal projects of human sacrifice.

Racial stereotypes were intertwined with sexual fantasies. In the racist economy of the American imaginary, while the black phallus remains the white fetish, the Chinese race was feminized, with the Chinaman as a sexual joke to highlight white male virility. At best, he could be a Charlie Chan (created by Earl Derr Biggers from 1925 to 1932), an asexual clever Chinese detective solving murders for his white masters, while remaining bowing, unobtrusive, and amiable. In contrast, Chinese women were cast in the roles of either the dragon lady or the Shy Lotus Blossom and China Doll. The 1870s white racist focus on Chinese prostitution created the stereotype of Chinese (and Asian) women as depraved sex slaves of white men, which persisted in the 1960 film *The World of Suzie Wong,* as well as in the more recent musical *Miss Saigon,* an update of Puccini's *Madame Butterfly.* Such sexual fantasies usually ended in the death of the Oriental women as the end of the white male desire and obsession.

The geographical location of all the Chinese evil was imagined in the Chinatowns in the big American cities. Stereotypes in popular culture portrayed Chinatowns as sites of opium dens, brothels, gambling houses, *tong* wars, and other criminal underground vices behind the quaint facade of lions and dragons and amid the strange smells of exotic drugs. The inscription of Chinatown in the American imaginary as a panoptic object of anthropological gaze was first initiated by the turn-of-the-century photographer Arnold Genthe (1869–1942), who made over 200 photographs of the Chinese there between 1895 and 1906, all meticulously cropped and framed to produce a Chinatown of darkness, evil, and exoticism.[5] The image has persisted today in guidebooks as well as in movies such as Polanski's *Chinatown* (1974) and Michael Cimino's *The Year of the Dragon* (1985).

Racist discourses are constantly reconfigured for new deployment of power amid changing realities in new versions like the model minority and the Asian gangs. If Chinese Americans are made, not born (according to Frank Chin in his play *Chickencoop Chinaman*), then their making, unmaking, and remaking constitute a field of cultural contestation where racist discourse works through division, differentiation, recodification, and strategic deployment of stereotypes across gender, class, and race.

As to their entry to the United States, the Chinese came in large numbers (20,026 by 1852) as forty-niner gold rush prospectors in the mid-nineteenth century, driven by the political and economic disturbances in rural southern China after the Opium War. They joined gold mining in the Sierra Nevada and established numerous small Chinatowns there. Competition and the declining profits in gold mines led to widespread white hostility and racist violence, in which the Chinese were driven out, tortured, and lynched, their living quarters burned down, while the Californian legislature passed laws imposing taxes on the Chinese and discouraging Chinese immigration. From the mid-1860s, the Chinese turned to work on the construction of the Central Pacific Railway. After the completion of the first transcontinental railway in 1869 and with the economic crisis in America, the Chinese found themselves competing in a racist job market. They were not only exploited as cheap labor but also more and more singled out as scapegoats in politicians' racist propagandas and white mobs' riots, which finally led to the 1882 Chinese Exclusion Act, banning all Chinese labor immigration to the United States and prohibiting Chinese immigrants from becoming naturalized citizens.

The American exclusionary immigration laws led to the creation of a bachelor society for Chinese-American men, who could not bring their wives and sons over nor marry the whites here due to antimiscegenation laws. Not until the 1906 San Francisco earthquake, which destroyed government documents, did many Chinese have a chance to falsely claim native-born citizenship status and manage to send for their family members. Some Chinese had to come as "paper sons" by purchasing birth certificates of American citizens born in China. The immigrants were detained for screening on Angel Island off the coast of San Francisco, underwent racist humiliations, and suffered from loneliness and anxiety for months or even years.

The Chinese in America remained mainly an urban population. They were forced by white racism to work in menial jobs and concentrated mainly in Chinese restaurants, corner stores, and laundries, where the family members and Chinese employees worked long hours at substandard wages. During the long years of racist exclusion, the Chinese formed various organizations within Chinatowns to take care of each other and develop their own community. They also adopted various strategies for negotiation and petitioning for fair treatment. During the Second World War, the Chinese actively participated in military service and war efforts, and their contributions helped to induce the U.S. Congress to repeal the Chinese exclusion acts in 1943.

Since the Second World War, the U.S. immigration policies for the Chinese have been subjected to changes in political and economic climates. After 1943, the quota for the Chinese immigration was only 105 a year. The communist takeover of mainland China in 1949 led to the Refugee Acts, allowing Chinese political refugees to immigrate to America. The Immigration and Naturalization Act of 1965 replaced the national-origin quota system (much biased against Asians) with hemispheric quotas at 170,000 for the Eastern Hemisphere and 20,000 annual maximum per country. "Brain drain" sent to America thousands of students and scholars from Taiwan in the 1960s and 1970s, and from China in the 1980s and 1990s due to the 1989 Tianamen Square massacre. Vietnamese "boat people" of Chinese descent were accepted as refugees in the late 1970s. Taiwan and Hong Kong business entrepreneurs have also moved to America for a "First World" passport and a Western education for their children. Besides, there are also illegal immigrants smuggled into America and working underground in the strict control of gangs and criminals.

Chinese immigrants are a diverse community with a long history in America. Writers have been trying to uncover and explore various facets of the Chinese immigrant experience, which has not been properly recognized in official American history. Diverse historiographies, indeed, have created points of difference according to which the writers' works and literary criticisms articulate themselves, whether through an appeal to the interest of the whole community or through asserting difference in class, gender, dialects, regions of origin, education, and ideologies or through a "post-modern" play of diversity and difference. The battle between cultural dominance and subaltern resistance over texts is also a battle over contexts constructed or erased by different historiographies.

DOMINANT CONCERNS AND MAJOR AUTHORS

When we trace Chinese-American immigrant literature to its early days, we find not a single origin but diverse concerns and structures of sensibilities. Because there was not much critical self-awareness of Chinese-American identity and literary tradition in the pre-1960s, these concerns and sensibilities did not form any conscious trends; instead, they emerged into different formations in the contention, negotiation, and collaboration among Chinese culture(s), American racial discourse and institutional apparatuses, and the different personal and communal experiences of Chinese immigrants. From the songs of the Gold Mountain to Sui Sin Far, from Lin Yutang through Jade Snow Wong to Louis Chu, we see different and discrete combinations of cultural production and ethnic inventions, which, in some ways, foreshadow many of the concerns and dilemmas faced by Chinese-American writers today.

Songs of Gold Mountain, one of the earliest publications of Chinese-American immigrant literature, appeared in two volumes in 1911 and 1915. Written in

Chinese and anonymous in authorship, the two volumes contain poems expressing the feelings and experiences of Chinese immigrant laborers stranded in an alien land of hostility and racism. They were written for fellow Chinese immigrants, in folk rhymes of the common people, in the long-standing Chinese tradition of poetry and folk songs as self-expression, as protest against injustices, as signals for popular rebellions. These folk rhymes use vernacular Cantonese to express the immigrants' dilemma between a poverty-stricken homeland and the white men's racist oppression, see their present victimization in the larger context of a weak nation and a weak race bullied by Western powers, vow revenge, and expose the white mythology of liberty and democracy when race is dealt with otherwise in America. The Chinese eloquence contrasts sharply, as one folk rhyme describes, with the stuttering in English and silencing under the coercive power of the white language. As the precursor of the Chinese-American immigrant literature in Chinese, *Songs of Gold Mountain* maintains an alterity closely connected to the Chinese-speaking immigrant community and insists on dialogue in their own linguistic and cultural terms as basic paradigms of reference.

One of the earliest spokeswomen in English for the Chinese immigrant community is Sui Sin Far (Edith Maud Eaton). Born of a Chinese mother and an English father, Sui Sin Far (1867–1914) grew up amid poverty and as a stranger between cultures and races during the years of mounting white racism against the Chinese. She wrote in newspapers fighting for the rights of the Chinese and published many stories about Chinese immigrant experiences. Most of her stories are autobiographical, depicting her personal experiences as a Eurasian who looks white but chooses to fight for her Chinese mother's people, who possess a high civilization and a humanity more kind and reasonable than the white stereotypes and the whites themselves. She has many feminist ideas. In ''The Story of One White Woman Who Married a Chinese,'' she has one white woman breaking away from her white husband's sexist marriage and falling in love with a caring Chinese businessman, a scenario surprisingly different from the more usual representation of patriarchy in images of the Chinese. Her story ''In the Land of the Free'' tells the poignant experience of a Chinese merchant's wife forced to be separated from her baby by the immigration officers at the California immigration detention center and waiting in a Kafkaesque limbo for months for a special order from Washington, before she gets reunited with a by now estranged and renamed toddler. To say that her story reflects the harsh reality in the land of the free would be an understatement, for later historians have uncovered many cases of poor Chinese immigrants simply being forgotten at the detention center for years and driven to madness and suicide, as well as widespread cases of U.S. officials' rampant corruption and venality. On a deeper psychic level, the final twist when the toddler son tells his mother to go away marks a cultural break in which a Kafkaesque law (not even represented by the biological Chinese father and his naming) effects a fatal split in the child and the mother. More than mere realism or protest, Sui Sin Far's voice explores deeply the split psyche of double consciousness in immigrant life. Her highly personal autobiographical writings and fiction are always informed with an antiracist political position while acknowledging her own distance as a Eurasian from the immigrant community, endowed with a noble vision of transcending racial barriers for a common humanity while carefully noting cultural differences in concrete details of daily life.

There were many Chinese scholar-travelers writing their experiences and impressions of America and carrying on a high-level cultural dialogue between Chinese and Western traditions. The most prominent among them was Lin Yutang (1895–1976). A professor of philosophy educated first in missionary schools and universities in China and then in graduate schools in the West, he was well read both in Western and Chinese cultures and well known for his humorous essays. Before he came to live in America in 1930, his "apolitical" writings were already criticized in the political context of class conflicts and foreign invasion. In America, he wrote and published many books introducing Chinese culture and people to the American readers, including *My Country and My People* (1935), *The Importance of Living* (1937), and *Chinatown Family: On the Wisdom of America* (1948). The image he created for himself was a cultural gentleman of passivity and compromise, which was then projected onto Chinese culture as a whole. His writings on Chinese culture and Western culture are superficial, typical of an amateur man of letters and a widely read humorous essayist. They express both an enlightenment critique of Chinese culture and Chinese character and a Chinese literary gentleman's pride about his own cultural tradition as distilled in its best essence.

Lin Yutang's popularity with the American audience marked the first major institutional deployment of a Chinese man of letters' voice as the mainstream cultural production of Orientalist discourse. His writings have to be read as a cultural event across the neutrality of knowledge and personal integrity. It was the same political climate of mainstream ethnic cultural production that brought about Chinese-American autobiographical novels by Pardee Lowe and Jade Snow Wong. Pardee Lowe's *Father and Glorious Descendant* (1943) and Jade Snow Wong's *Fifth Chinese Daughter* (1950) contain autobiographies of second-generation Chinese Americans who grew up torn between their immigrant parents' cultural insistence and the American mainstream cultural coercion. Typically, it is a liberationist version of a young self going through the stage of rebellion against parental authority, fitting at the same time into the ready-made racialized discourse of critiquing the old Oriental culture and embracing the Western enlightenment. On one hand, there is much self-hatred and self-contempt. On the other hand, there is also much complaint about the self's not being accepted and assimilated by the mainstream culture, for at that time the Chinese were just beginning to be distinguished as American allies and were still confined to Chinatown. The personal experiences of racism in their texts betray a gap between the racialized self and the assimilationist ideology that informs their autobiographies.

The second-generation autobiographies follow the convention of confessions of the self in the language of personal truth. In contrast, China-born elites such as Lin Yutang and Chin Yang Lee (*Flower Drum Song* [1957]) resort more to asserting cultural wisdom of passivity and forbearance, as well as an inner pride in the ancient Chinese culture that has guided the survival of its people in their unbroken history. One may well abstract a cultural essence, if there is such a thing, in both kinds of writings about survival of the Chinese in adverse circumstances, among which white racism is just a special instance for diasporic Chinese. A more political criticism may opt to see the limits of the discourse allowed for Chinese, especially as best-sellers, in the American cultural market before the 1960s and question what kinds of truths were selected and produced about the Chinese. Often, racial stereotypes and insiders' cultural and personal information are not so different as materially repeatable discourses and images.

There are, of course, exceptions, such as Louis Chu's *Eat a Bowl of Tea* (1961), which portrays a bachelor society in Chinatown on the verge of change. The bachelor society, a product of racist Chinese exclusion laws, is thrown off balance when a Chinese girl is brought over to America by an impotent bachelor. The young couple have to work through the husband's father's anxiety about continuation of the family, through adultery brought on by a villain and symbolically through the guilt of the whole bachelor society that have left their wives in China, before they can start as a new and normal family to carry on the Chinese diaspora in America. The realistic narrative is belied by comic, absurd situations that subtly engage with, and deconstruct, racial stereotypes as half-truths between fantasy and fiction. Ostensibly, the journey is manhood lost and regained in the new world of the Gold Mountain; the process of telling undermines and subverts patriarchal authority, against the larger background of racist exclusion and emasculation as virtual killing of the Chinese race in America. The fascination of the novel lies in the gaps and silences in the comically real tale of an absurd entrapment.

From Sui Sin Far and the Gold Mountain songs to Louis Chu, pre-1960s Chinese-American literature is marked by a series of firsts—first collection, first novel, first woman writer, first second-generation writer—and though one tends to use the phrase ''break the silence'' today to mark new anthologies, the silence was broken long ago, often in a way that may intersect, but is not totally compatible, with our more contemporary political position of antiracism, cultural difference, and feminisms. Diverse and heterogeneous, overdetermined by Chinese culture, American racist discourse, and the Chinese-American experience of survival, the pre-1960s literature remains a cultural legacy for later writers and critics concerned with the identity politics informed by contemporary radical ideologies. Territories can be drawn and redrawn, with different maps of cultural and political contestations. The pre-1960s literature, especially the more popular books in the mainstream market, helped invent and solidify a Chinese identity between black and white, a composite of images defined through certain positivities of passivity and endurance and a series of differences in the American context. This sliding of identities provides the background for new uncertainties and attempts at new beginnings in the post-1960s creative and critical awareness of ethnic identity and political alliance.

The era of the Vietnam War and the civil rights movement in America was marked by increased awareness of racial and cultural identity. It was the era in which minority students seized buildings on campuses and established black studies programs, while, on the larger scene of cultural production, antiracist movements and assertion of ethnic pride posed a threat to the cultural dominance of white Anglo-Saxon America. Amid this politicized atmosphere of intense cultural and racial sensitivity grew various organizations and movements seeking to claim Asian America as a new ethnic identity, whose very name bears the traces of racist history that had thrown all Asians under one racial category.

In 1969, four young Asian-American writers, Jeffery Chan, Lawson Inada, Frank Chin, and Shawn Wong, formed an organization called the Combined Asian-American Resources Project, aimed at producing oral histories of Asian Americans, carrying out in-service training for teachers of Asian-American studies, and arranging for the publication of Asian-American writing such as Louis Chu's *Eat a Bowl of Tea.* The same group produced in 1974 the first influential anthology of Asian-American literature, *Aiiieeeee!,* which not only asserted the Asian-American voices on the cultural scene but also laid down in the introduction the general tone of anger and militancy as part of the aftermath of the rebellious 1960s and the civil rights movement. In the realm of theater, as early as 1965, a group of Asian-American actors in Los Angeles formed the first Asian-American theater group, East West Players, which dramatized the work of Asian novelists and staged Asian actors. In 1973, Frank Chin, Janis Chan, Jeffrey Chin, and others founded the Asian American Theater Workshop in San Francisco, which later produced the first major play by an Asian-American author: Frank Chin's *The Chickencoop Chinaman.*

The preceding may suggest a general concerted effort of minority writers, who inevitably chose to write about their own ethnic history and culture. Chinese-American writers Frank Chin and, later, Maxine Hong Kingston (*Woman Warrior,* 1976) prove to be the most influential in shaping the sensibilities of Chinese-American culture, gender, and ethnicity in this period.

Frank Chin has been called the ''godfather'' or the conscience of Asian-American writing. He is a controversial and influential figure, whether through his scathing criticism or through being a sexist, authoritarian target in the eyes of many Asian-American critics and writers. His works up to this moment include poems, short stories, plays, and one novel. Frank Chin writes as a conscientious oppositional voice, topical, chip-on-shoulder, and with a witty tangent. Many of his early works bear a clear influence of Afro-American literature, and the 1960s rebellious back talk may sound a clear product of the period.

Frank Chin's works show a wide-ranging view of cultural and racial problems. He thinks that racism emasculates Asian men; therefore, in his works, there are fantasies of sex with white women, in which ecstasy is mingled with loathing, conquest with hatred.[6] In his story "Railroad Standard Time," the protagonist realizes his manhood through sex with a woman almost as part of the natural scene, the sea, described in lyrical passages reminiscent of such writers as Henry Miller and D. H. Lawrence, who likewise find some mystical power in sex and nature. In *The Chickencoop Chinaman,* the protagonist would openly flaunt his manhood in his conversation with the Hong Kong dream girl so as to erase any stereotypically Chinese traits of effeminacy.

Frank Chin is concerned with what he perceives as the decline of Chinatown in America. Most of the protagonists in his stories are alienated young men dissatisfied with the stultifying quaint costumes and old-age decay of Chinatown and yet unable to gain acceptance in racist mainstream society. They find their mothers and fathers dying slowly, amid quaint festivals and funerals. In one story, "The Chinatown Kid," for example, the narrator says:

The Chinese in America seemed to live that long, live beyond endurance, beyond the limits of interest and curiosity and die slowly like cities blacking out a light bulb at a time, and even then not dead; a few more years of being not quite dead, a living corpse painfully sensing what he wanted to say what she wanted to say but not caring to speak or to have to hear.[7]

Such self-loathing is not uncommon among racial minority writers, though Chin might argue that his derives from anger and frustration at the mainstream culture, rather than as a part of the wholehearted embracing of white dominance. The very decay of Chinatown is precisely the result of the longtime racist immigration policy of exclusion. The story "The Only Real Day" describes an old Chinese man spending his last days in Oakland reminiscing about his life and passing on the heroic tradition stories to a young kid, Dirigible. As a symbol of the burden of history, the old man's story weighs heavily on the young kid, who later will retell the scene of bathtub death in *The Chickencoop Chinaman.*

Frank Chin is at his best with his witty, racy dialogues of barbed satire and back talk, targeting everything from model minority myth to racist stereotypes, from Chinese culture of the past to sexual/racial fantasies, from political speechifying to self-directed ironies and abasement. Tam Lum in *The Chickencoop Chinaman* quite sums up Chin's language and its problems: "I am the natural born ragmouth speaking the motherless bloody tongue. No real language of my own to make sense with, so out comes everybody else's trash and don't conceive" (*Aiiieeeee!* 119). Chinese-American identity is neither Afro-American nor Euro-American. What is it? What is its distinct language? Frank Chin cannot offer an answer; perhaps there is no answer, for there is no identity, only identification of various kinds.

Chin has explored various traditions of the Chinese-American subject, producing a strange company: on one hand, Chin embraces the heroic tradition in Chinese culture; on the other hand, he would call himself a cowboy; yet on a more historical level, he would declare the tradition of Chinese forefathers who came to America to build railways as pioneers. Only the first and the third stay on in his most recent novel, *Donald Duk,* in which one white child and one Chinese child learn to appreciate Chinese culture and the history of Chinese Americans. This work shows a more mellow Chin, exploring the daily community life of Chinatown and bridging gaps between whites and Chinese, between different generations. Much of the usual criticism against him no longer applies in this novel; nor is there the characteristic sharpness of tongue and wit. Frank Chin has written himself into a certain language and posture, a trademark that he cannot break out of easily.

Maxine Hong Kingston made a major literary event in Chinese-American literature with the publication of her work *The Woman Warrior* in 1976. Her second book is *China Men* (1980). If the first traces a Chinese woman's tradition with a modern feminist stance and carries the bewilderment of a Chinese-American girl lost between two cultures, the second book explores the history of Chinese male immigrants as they worked on the railways and farms amid racist oppression. Kingston's works bear influences from both the civil rights movements and feminism and experiment with (post-)modernist techniques to reflect on a racial and gendered self as a writer and a daughter of the Chinese immigrants. In both works, the hard line between fiction and nonfiction is blurred. Her latest book, *Tripmaster Monkey,* came out in 1989, this time as a post-modern novel that breaks in style from her earlier works and blends ethnicity amid myriads of intertextual references and images of a multiracial America.

The Woman Warrior has become such a literary masterpiece with numerous criticisms that it would be difficult to summarize what it is about. Generally, it depicts a Chinese-American girl growing up in an immigrant family and puzzled by stories about China, where there were woman warriors as well as woman victims of feudal patriarchy. The book inherits the tradition of autobiographies by Chinese-American writers trying to define their self-identity in a society of racist discrimination where immigrant minorities are remade in various racist images. The protagonist feels anger at Chinese patriarchal oppression of women, but she also feels powerless as she is inevitably lost amid competing images about China and about her self as a gendered and racialized subject. The tradition she will inherit or criticize is bound to be lost amid revisionist ethnic making and remaking so that her autobiography cannot escape fictionalization. As a major literary event, the book has been canonized as *the* Chinese-American writing and has become the most talked-about book in Asian-American literature. It has spawned many themes and shaped many sensibilities for later works dealing with Chinese immigrants and their offspring in America. Numerous sophisticated readings of the work have displaced an early impression of cultural authenticity created by hasty reviews and the work's initial classification as an autobiography. Many critics have pointed out that what the nameless first-person, naive narrator sees and says is itself symptomatic of a troubled racial and gendered self caught between two cultures in an asymmetrical relation of power.

In *China Men,* Kingston portrays images of Chinese male immigrants as pioneers claiming America despite racist oppression and immigration policies restricting women from joining their husbands. The Chinese men are not silent but very talkative, venting their anger and frustration through words and curses in Chinese. They claim America by persisting in their hard work with a strong will to stay and fight back racism, even though they are merely talking among themselves in a language unknown to the white employers and missionaries. *China Men* is the history of Chinese immigrants, the history of Chinese maleness in America, denigrated but persistent, with the will to endure and assert their claim of the land and the New World. The female narrator recedes most of the time, though sometimes she wonders if her scholar father toiling in the laundry really means to hurt women when he makes sexist curses in Chinese. In the narrator's voice, one may still see the history as made up, inevitably tinged by the writer's subject position as a feminist of a minority race.

While the early two nonfiction/fiction works raise questions about the precarious authenticity of a minority writer's voice in a predominantly white culture, Kingston's recent novel, *The Tripmaster Monkey,* is a pastiche of various quotes and images that foreground race and ethnicity in a post-modern mélange. The protagonist, Wittman Ah Sing, is an idealistic hippie of fifth-generation Chinese in America, a graduate in English Literature from Berkeley. Through him we see a combination of an irreverent attitude toward authority, a sharp tongue ironizing about race politics in America, self-contempt mingled with anger at racism—in sum, a hippie of the 1960s with a particular grudge as a minority in white America. Kingston distinguishes between this male protagonist and the female narrator, who is sometimes sympathetic and sometimes ironic toward Wittman.[8] If Wittman represents such literary figures as Frank Chin, then obviously a certain type of literary/political language is made the object of representation. There is an inevitable split between the narrator and the protagonist, who speaks the 1960s language as the only language of commitment, while the narrator also shows the limitations thereof. Is the author showing a reconciliation, a synthesis? Or is she trying to show a parody of a certain language to which we are still pulled back from time to time? Whatever the answer, the novel becomes a summation of Chinese-American literary criticism.

Jeffery Paul Chan's stories show a similar concern with identity that we can find in Frank Chin. Within his Chinatown, there is no hope for the Chinese immigrants caught in their pathetic conditions of forced bachelorhood and the racist image they see in the white culture and their treatment by white men. Self-loathing and despair suffuse his stories such as "Jackrabbit" (1974) and "Auntie Tsia Lays Dying" (1972). In "The Chinese in Haifa" (1974), the protagonist, Bill Wong, a Chinese-American teacher, is alienated from his divorced wife and all the Chinese culture that she seems to represent. Instead, he finds love and consolation in his adulterous relationship with his neighbor's blond Jewish wife. Identity is problematized in the confusion of the narrators and characters in Chan's stories, as their dreams and desires border on fear, fantasy, and loathing.

Shawn Wong's novel *Homebase* (1979) shows the fourth-generation protagonist, Rainsford Chan's, coming to terms with his Chinese-American identity through searching the history of his forefathers in a land that Rainsford claims as his America. The first-person narrator Rainsford is named after a town in California. Through his lyrical prose, Shawn Wong moves back and forth in the narrator's memory as it recalls, remembers, and searches for his personal experiences, which also expand and merge into those of his parents, grandparents, and great-grandparents' 125 years of toil and struggle across the American West. Memory re-creates history, re-creates his ancestors' spirits and voices. The lyricism of his prose records both his painful experience of alienation from the American white culture and his affirmation of the Chinese roots in the land of America as his home base. For Shawn Wong, Chinese-American identity is formed in their history of labor, humiliation, and perseverance on the new land, in their contribution to the land that they have claimed as home for more than 100 years.

Most of the Chinese-American writers writing in English are the offspring of immigrants, looking back and retracing the immigrant experience as American-born minority members, writing and negotiating their place in a predominantly white market. A different perspective on the Chinese immigrant experience can be obtained through reading Chinese immigrant literature written in Chinese, which reached its zenith in the 1970s due to large numbers of Taiwan students staying in the United States and finding themselves placeless and homeless between the two worlds. Writers like Nieh Hua-ling, Yu Li-hua, and Pai Hsien-yung had been writing in Chinese before they came to the United States. It is difficult to place them on the spectrum of Westernization and Chineseness, for they not only are well versed in Chinese culture and tradition but also have pursued Western literature, and the modernist influence and even Western syntax are unmistakable in their works.

The most famous of Nieh Hua-ling's works, *Two Women of China: Mulberry and Peach* (1976; English translation 1981), is narrated by a Chinese woman whose subjectivity is split between Mulberry in China and Peach in America, two names denoting a state of already dead and not yet born. She flees civil war in China, and wanders to Taiwan and finally to the United States, but wherever she goes, she is haunted by memories of violence in China, and since she is illegal in the United States, she is an object of easy prey in this land of the free. The style is post-modern pastiche with an ironic reflection on grand events of history in modern China and on Chinese tradition, as well as on the American dream, which attracted many Chinese from Taiwan in the 1960s and 1970s. The immigrant officer keeps on asking her who she is, but she cannot tell, since her tradition, the modern history, and her personal experience of exile render rememoration almost impossible. Although the novel is mainly about the victimization of Mulberry/Peach (much like Anna Morgan in Jean Rhys's *Voyage in the Dark*) as a strong indictment of patriarchy and racism in China and the United States, toward the end of the novel, the protagonist does develop an emerging sense of new responsibility toward her own life and another life inside her, a feminist consciousness of the female body. It is difficult to gauge whether her fiction is a China-oriented sojourner's mentality or an American root-taking commitment, directed as it is really toward the linguistic homelessness of a literary consciousness and an alternative sense of women's time/space.

The son of a Taiwanese general, Pai Hsien-yung came to the United States and pursued his studies in modernist poetry. His fiction, often nostalgic in tone, is often described as "the dirge of a lost paradise." His protagonists are often the socially and economically privileged who come to America with a deep sense of loss and homelessness. With their minds set in the past, the rich cultural tradition, and the life of leisure, America for them is alien, banal, and humiliating. His typical characters include a former general eking out an existence in Chinatown, a Ph.D. holder who sees no future either in America or in Taiwan and finally commits suicide, a general's daughter who had to adjust to the life of a housewife performing mundane household chores. Pai's works have a sense of modernist alienation particularized in the division of China and the life of exiles in a foreign land they can never claim as their own.

Most of Yu Li-hua's fiction about Chinese immigrants focuses on Taiwanese students as they change their status and manage to make America their home, yet not strictly their home, as their life seems uncertain and bittersweet. Her most famous novel about Taiwanese students in America is *See the Palm-trees Again* (1966).[9] The protagonist finishes his Ph.D. in journalism and settles with a Chinese-teaching job at a college. Although he feels empty in his life and would like to return to Taiwan to engage in more meaningful cultural work, he also finds himself alienated from the life there. America offers more freedom in personal lifestyle. Underlying the apparent cultural conflict are his cynicism and pessimism, his loss of youth and vitality when the American dream fails to materialize.

The certainty about one's Chinese cultural identity may be more illusory than real in the preceding novels and stories, since they are all set in a modern America, where the culture and the race still suffer from discrimination and neglect. Yet paradoxically, the immigrant characters all cling to that culture as the only real spiritual support, even in a critical sense. While this sentiment may not be politically effective, it should not be used in any way as a justification for white racist charges of Chinese unassimilability. On the contrary, the failure of assimilation for certain ethnic minorities points to the racist shadow right at the heart of the mainstream culture. In an age of multiculturalism and cultural difference, a sense of exile should not be denied as part of the immigrant experience and sensibilities.

MULTIPLICITY OF LITERARY EXPLORATIONS SINCE THE 1980s

Chinese-American literature has undergone a booming period since the beginning of the 1980s, not only in scholarly research and university curriculum but also in the variety of literary creations and experiments. While certain concerns and themes persist, more spaces are opened for various kinds of literary explorations of identity, politics, and cultural expressions.

Chinese immigrant history continues to be a fascinating subject. Laurence Yep's play *Pay the Chinaman* (1987) is based on the playwright's research into the history of early Chinese immigrants' gold mining and pioneering in the West and the eventual wiping out of many small Chinatowns during the ensuing racist waves. The play explores the trickster figure as an immigrant survivor who has to lie and change himself and his lifestyle in order to make a living in a hostile and volatile environment. Genny Lim's play *Paper Angels* (1991) is directly inspired by the discovery of the poems in the Angel Island detention center and focuses on the story of poor immigrants who had to fake "paper-son" identity (with purchased birth certificates of American citizens born in China) after the 1882 Exclusion Act and often spent months waiting in limbo on the island. In his play *FOB* (1979), David Henry Hwang telescopes Kwan Kung, the early immigrant protector god, with the contemporary context of new immigrants from Hong Kong, thereby seeking a way to solve the contradictions between the second-generation, American-born Chinese with troubled racial feelings and the new arrivals who find themselves targets of a new kind of racism. In an aside to the worship of Kwan Kung by Frank Chin and the *Aiiieeeee* group, Hwang introduces a woman character impersonating the woman warrior Fa Mulan to interpose as a gendered subject in the male heroic tradition. Thus, in the interstices of generations, histories, cultures, and genders, identities are scattered and shattered in a multiplicity of disguises. Histories and traditions are both explored for inspiration and inheritance and subjected to invention and modification.

Feminism continues to be a strong voice in the recovery of history. In *Thousand Pieces of Gold* (1981), Ruthanne Lum McCunn resurrects Lalu Nathoy, a woman kidnapped from China, shipped to America, and sold at auction to be a slave. Yet through all these vicissitudes of life, her resourcefulness and inner strength keep her alive from one hardship to another, until she finally marries the man who has bought her, and starts to own land in the western frontier. The book is interlaced with historical photos of Lalu, so that historical facts, fiction, and feminist revision fuse into one work of literary creation. Genny Lim's *Bitter Cane* (1991) goes back to the sugarcane fields of Hawaii in the early days of Chinese immigrant labor. A son comes to the sugarcane plantation with dreams of paradise similar to the dreams of his diseased father, who has died from hard labor and opium, and the son seems to have the same obsessions and dreams as his dead father. The play deals not only with the men as slave laborers on the plantation but also with the victimization of a Chinese prostitute, a former

concubine, who offers another feminist view of both the American racial oppression and the Chinese patriarchal tradition.

The same strong women can also be found in Amy Tan's novel *The Joy Luck
Club* (1989), which explores the tensions, jealousies, and love-hate relationship
between immigrant mothers and their American-born daughters. All the four
mothers have gone through many hardships in China, such as wars, abandon-
ment, and abuse by men they have married or been sold to as child brides. They
survive and become pioneers in coming to America and making a new life. The
novel opens up a space for the daughters to recognize and embrace a female
tradition in their ethnic culture that they need to treasure in their own life.

The depiction of Chinese students/immigrants apparently secure in their cultural identity is a theme usually found in immigrant literature in Chinese. Two
recent novels in English seem to have made a new attempt in that direction.
Steven Lo's *The Incorporation of Eric Chung* (1989) and Gish Jen's *Typical
American* (1991) portray the loss of idealism in Chinese students/immigrants as
their American dream fails. In Lo's novel, the protagonist, Eric Chung, tells his
experience as a student who stays on in America to make a living. Yet the better
break that he and his fellow Taiwanese students hope to achieve through getting
a well-paying job is always undercut by the uncertainty and ruthlessness of the
American corporate culture during times of recession. In Gish Jen's novel, the
protagonist is lured into a short-lived dream of getting rich quick through a take-
out restaurant business, only to be driven to the brink of suicide by the ruthless
competition and tricks of a villain in a melodrama of sex and intrigue. His very
survival in America is finally brought about by resorting to an inner strength of
his Chinese cultural tradition of forbearance and hope and by renouncing the
American dream of materialism.

The contemporary scene of Chinese immigrant literature is marked by diversity in subjects and volatility in political and aesthetic concerns, overdetermined
by American race politics, minority discourses, feminisms, and post-modern
sensibilities. Realistic representations and retrieval of past and present immigrant
experiences sit side by side with sophisticated experimentations of subjectivity
and form; the persistent task of restoring a human subject in opposition to racist
stereotypes sits side by side with formalistic anxieties in a market already glutted
with various old and new images of the Chinese. Challenges to racism and
dismantling of patriarchy become a double task in which alternatives have to
be negotiated by developing new languages and adopting new perspectives.

CRITICAL PERSPECTIVES

Serious criticism of Chinese-American literature started in the early 1970s
with the work of Frank Chin, Jeffrey Chan, and their *Aiiieeeee* anthology group.
Riding on the wave of the American civil rights movement and having their
anthology published by a black publishing house, their critical language is characterized by rage against nearly 100 years of racism in American mainstream

culture. Since they see white racism mainly working through castrating the masculinity of Asian Americans and co-opting Asian women who enter interracial
marriages at an alarming rate, they set themselves the task of restoring Asian-
American manhood, as well as critically examining all the past Asian-American
literature in the context of racist stereotyping, mainstream co-optation, and active
antiracist resistance. They have also resurrected the Chinese heroic warrior tradition as proof of manhood in Chinese culture. The issue of gender is subsumed
under a masculinist ideology.

Chinese-American literature is divided into that actively protesting racism and
that complicit with the white culture's denigration and feminization of Chinese
culture. In addition, there are finer distinctions between Chinese immigrants
secure in their identity of an elitist Chinese culture and those second-generation
Americans of Chinese descent who bear the brunt of white racism; between sell-
out literature and protest literature; between proponents of a Confucian Chinese
culture of a museum type and proponents of popular Chinese culture of the
heroic type. Cultural nationalist critics have also set up a binary opposition
between fake and authentic Chinese-American writers, the fake ones inventing
and distorting Chinese cultural traditions while the authentic ones truly inherit
them and keep their integrity.

The most controversial claim by Frank Chin is his criticism of what he calls
Christian Chinese-American writers, such as Maxine Hong Kingston, Amy Tan,
and David Henry Hwang, citing these authors' popularity with the white publishing industry as evidence of their complicity in racist stereotyping and denigration of Chinese culture. Although this evaluation remains an ongoing
polemic, Chin's persistent critique of racial stereotypes does ring a warning bell
in this media age when racism works through an active production of ethnic
images. In the movie version of *Thousand Pieces of Gold* (1990), Lalu is ob-
jectified in an interracial erotics played out in the politics of racism and sexism.
Her liberation from her villainous Chinese master/husband follows closely the
familiar Spivakian rhetoric of "white men saving brown women from brown
men," while her final decision to claim the American West "home" contrasts
sharply with the exodus of her fellow immigrants driven out of their homes by
racist mobs. A similar liberationist ideology also works in the movie *The Joy
Luck Club* (1993) through contrasting the tragic misery of old China (rendered
authentically other in the Chinese dialogues with English subtitles) with the
comedic American middle-class episodes in the family saga of the Chinese immigrants. The Hollywood treatment of Tan's novel may have developed from
Orientalist traces in the text itself.

Much of the critical debate around Maxine Hong Kingston's *The Woman
Warrior* bears on the controversial issues of tradition, feminism(s), cultural authenticity and revision, and stereotyping. With that novel now occupying a central position in the Asian-American literary canon, there is a general consensus
that in Chinese-American literature there are different kinds of traditions and
that patriarchy needs to be continually challenged by feminist positions. Writers

have every right to experiment with, and invent, Chinese cultural traditions, which need to be critically examined in the new experience of Chinese diaspora. The politics of racial identity is exploded by the fragmentation of subjectivity, as the ''I'' is subject to different kinds of identifications—minority, women, American, Chinese, immigrants, and so on. New critical vocabularies borrowed from feminism, post-modernism, Afro-American literary criticism, and various literary theories have superseded image criticism originally meant to correct racial stereotypes, thus making the field of Chinese-American immigrant literature complex and diverse, with competing interests, conflicting discourses, and complicated political positions. There is neither privileged genre nor privileged critical space outside the power play of cultural dominance and minority resistance/subversion.

The climatic changes and varieties of criticism in the field can be sampled through a brief look at some of the most prominent critics and their works: Frank Chin's numerous essays; Elaine Kim's *Asian American Literature: An Introduction to the Writings and Their Social Context* (1982); Amy Ling's *Between Worlds: Women Writers of Chinese Ancestry* (1990); King-Kok Cheung's *Articulate Silences* (1993); Sau-ling Cynthia Wong's *Reading Asian American Literature: From Necessity to Extravagance* (1993); and James S. Moy's *Marginal Sights: Staging the Chinese in America* (1993). Chin's and Kim's criticisms mainly focus on the history of racism and the various images of Asians constructed in the space between white culture and subaltern minority resistance. Amy Ling's position represents a feminist effort at recovering a women's literary history. Cheung's and Wong's works, while still carrying on the antiracist and feminist political positions, shift the focus to recurring themes and forms in Asian-American literature in an intertextual dialogue with European, Anglo-American, and other minority literary traditions and critical theories, tracing their influences as well as delineating peculiar Asian-American characteristics. James Moy's book, however, returns to a sociohistorical narrative of racist stereotyping up to the contemporary scene, ranging from flawed self-representations to popular media images.

The shifts between sociohistorical criticism and thematic/formal analysis suggest the wide-ranging possibilities open to critics with different political and critical agendas. It is also symptomatic of the explosion into multiplicity of critical reading positions through the 1980s with the proliferation of literary and cultural theories, feminisms, and the politics of cultural difference and multiculturalism. In this context of competing theories and conflicting readings, it may no longer be possible to write a literary history or a general introduction to the field, since evaluation is continually subject to revisions of various kinds. The crisis is also a moment of opportunities for various reading positions reflecting different critical responsibilities. In this sense, reading Chinese-American immigrant literature is a negotiation with an other that is already part of ourselves, a process of critical (self-)reflection on the world of massive migrations, on the country founded by different kinds of immigrants, and on the self that is not whole.

NOTES

1. Ronald Takaki, *Strangers from a Different Shore: A History of Asian Americans* (New York: Penguin Books, 1989).

2. Frank Chin et al., *"Aiiieeeee!* Revisited: Preface to the Mentor Edition" (1991), in *Aiiieeeee!: An Anthology of Asian American Writers* (New York: Mentor, 1991); and Frank Chin, "Come All Ye Asian American Writers of the Real and the Fake," in *The Big Aiiieeeee! An Anthology of Chinese American and Japanese American Literature.*

3. See Amy Ling, *Between Worlds: Women Writers of Chinese Ancestry* (New York: Pergamon Press, 1990), 1–9.

4. Bret Harte, "Plain Language from Truthfull James," *Overland Monthly* 5 (September 1870): 287–288. Quoted in Takaki, *Strangers from a Different Shore,* 105.

5. See Moy, 64–81.

6. See his poem "Song of the Monogram Warner Bros. Chine," in Ishmael Reed, ed., *Yardbird Reader,* vol. 1 (Berkeley, CA: Yardbird, 1971).

7. Frank Chin, "The Chinatown Kid" (first published in 1973), in Frank Chin, *The Chinaman Pacific & Frisco R.R. Co.,* 35–36.

8. See Marilyn Chin's "A *MELUS* Interview: Maxine Hong Kingston," *MELUS* 16.4 (Winter 1989–1990): 57–74.

9. *See the Palm-trees Again* [You Jian Zhong Lu, You Jian Zhong Lu]. (Chinese still untranslated) (Taiwan: Crown, 1966).

SELECTED PRIMARY BIBLIOGRAPHY

Berson, Misha, ed. *Between Worlds: Contemporary Asian-American Plays.* New York: Theater Communications Group, 1990. (The collection includes Ping Chong's *Nuit Blanche,* David Henry Hwang's *The Sound of a Voice* and *As the Crow Flies,* and Laurence Yep's *Pay the Chinaman.*)

Chan, Jeffrey Paul. "Auntie Tsia Lays Dying." *Aion* 1.2 (1971): 82–87. Rpt. in Hsu and Palubinskas, *Asian-American Authors.* 77–85.

———. "The Chinese in Haifa." Chin et al., *AIIIEEEEE!.* 12–29.

———. "Jackrabbit." *Yardbird Reader* 3 (1974): 217–238.

Chao, Evelina G. *Gates of Grace.* New York: Warner, 1985.

Chiang, Fay. *In the City of Contradictions.* New York: Sunbury Press, 1979.

Chin, Frank. *The Chickencoop Chinaman and The Year of the Dragon: Two Plays.* Washington: University of Washington Press, 1981.

———. *The Chinaman Pacific & Frisco R.R. Co.* Minneapolis: Coffee House Press, 1988.

———. *Donald Duk.* Minneapolis: Coffee House Press, 1991.

Chin, Frank, et al., eds. *AIIIEEEEE! An Anthology of Asian-American Writers.* Washington, DC: Howard University Press, 1974.

———. *The Big AIIIEEEEE! An Anthology of Chinese American and Japanese American Literature.* New York: Meridian Book, 1991.

Chin, Marilyn. *Dwarf Bamboo.* New York: Greenfield Review Press, 1987.

Chu, Louis. *Eat a Bowl of Tea.* Introd. Jeffery Paul Chan. 1961. Seattle: University of Washington Press, 1979.

Chuang, Hua. *Crossings.* New York: Dial, 1968. Foreword Amy Ling. Boston: Northeastern University Press, 1986.

Hagedorn, Jessica, ed. *Charlie Chan Is Dead: An Anthology of Contemporary Asian American Fiction.* New York: Penguin, 1993.

Hom, Marlon K. *Songs of Gold Mountain: Cantonese Rhymes from San Francisco Chinatown.* Berkeley: University of California Press, 1987.

Hsu, Kai-yu, and Helen Palubinskas, eds. *Asian-American Authors.* 1972. Boston: Houghton, 1976.

Hwang, David Henry. *Broken Promises: Four Plays.* New York: Avon, 1983.

Jen, Gish. *Typical American.* Boston: Houghton Mifflin/Seymour Lawrence, 1991.

Kingston, Maxine Hong. *China Men.* New York: Knopf, 1980.

———. *Tripmaster Monkey: His Fake Book.* New York: Knopf, 1989.

———. *The Woman Warrior: Memoirs of a Girlhood among Ghosts.* New York: Knopf, 1976.

Lai, Him Mark, Genny Lim, and Judy Yung, eds. and trans. *Island: Poetry and History of Chinese Immigrants on Angel Island, 1910–1940.* San Francisco: Hoc Doi, 1980.

Lee, C. Y. *The Flower Drum Song.* New York: Farrar, 1957.

Lee, Gus. *China Boy.* New York: Dutton, 1991.

Lim, Genny. *Paper Angels and Bitter Cane: Two Plays.* Honolulu: Kalamaku Press, 1991.

Lin, Yutang. *Chinatown Family.* New York: John Day, 1948.

Lo, Steven C. *The Incorporation of Eric Chung.* Chapel Hill, NC: Algonquin Books, 1989.

Lowe, Pardee. *Father and Glorious Descendant.* Boston: Little, 1943.

McCunn, Ruthanne Lum. *Thousand Pieces of Gold.* San Francisco: Design Enterprises, 1981.

Nieh, Hua-ling. *Two Women of China: Mulberry and Peach.* Trans. Jane Parish Yang and Linda Lappin. New: Sino, 1981; Boston: Beacon, 1988.

Pai, Hsien-yung [Kenneth]. "A Day in Pleasantville." *Born of the Same Roots: Stories of Modern Chinese Women.* Ed. Vivian Ling Hsu. Bloomington: Indiana University Press, 1981. 184–192.

———. "Li Tung: A Chinese Girl in New York." Trans. author and C. T. Hsia. *Twentieth Century Chinese Stories.* Ed. C. T. Hsia, with Joseph S. M. Lau. New York: Columbia University Press, 1971. 220–239.

Sui, Sin Far [Edith Eaton]. *Mrs. Spring Fragrance.* Chicago: A. C. McClurg, 1912.

Tan, Amy. *The Joy Luck Club.* New York: Putnam, 1989.

———. *The Kitchen God's Wife.* New York: Putnam, 1991.

Tsiang, Hsi Tseng. *And China Has Hands.* New York: Robert Speller, 1937.

Wong, Jade Snow. *Fifth Chinese Daughter.* New York: Harper, 1950.

Wong, Shawn H. *Homebase.* New York: I. Reed Books, 1979.

SELECTED SECONDARY BIBLIOGRAPHY

Chan, Jeffery Paul, et al. "An Introduction to Chinese-American and Japanese-American Literatures." In Houston A. Baker, Jr., ed., *Three American Literatures.* New York: MLA, 1982.

Chan, Jeffery Paul, Frank Chin, Lawson Inada, and Shawn Wong. "Resources for Chinese and Japanese American Literary Traditions." *Amerasia* Journal 8. 1(1981): 19–31.

Chen, Jack. *The Chinese of America.* San Francisco: Harper and Row, 1981.

Cheung, King-Kok. *Articulate Silences: Hisaye Yamamoto, Maxine Hong Kingston, Joy Kogawa.* Ithaca, NY, and London: Cornell University Press, 1993.

Cheung, King-Kok, and Stan Yogi. *Asian American Literature: An Annotated Bibliography.* New York: MLA, 1988.

Chua, C. Lok. "Golden Mountain: Chinese Versions of the American Dream in Lin Yutang, Louis Chu, and Maxine Hong Kingston." *Ethnic Groups* 4.1–2 (1982): 33–59.

Gong, Ted. "Approaching Cultural Change through Literature: From Chinese to Chinese American." *Amerasia Journal* 7.1 (1980): 73–86.

Hom, Marlon. "A Case of Mutual Exclusion: Portrayals by Immigrant and American Born Chinese of Each Other in Literature." *Amerasia Journal* 11.2 (1984): 29–45.

———. "Some Cantonese Folksongs on the American Experience." *Western Folklore* 42.2 (1983): 126–39.

Juan, Karin Aguilar-San, ed. *The State of Asian America: Activism and Resistance in the 1990s.* Boston: South End Press, 1994.

Kim, Elaine H. *Asian American Literature: An Introduction to the Writings and Their Social Context.* Philadelphia: Temple University Press, 1982.

Kim, Hyung-chan. *Dictionary of Asian American History.* New York: Greenwood Press, 1986.

Kingston, Maxine Hong. "Cultural Misreadings by American Reviewers." In Guy Amirthanayagam, ed., *Asian and Western Writers in Dialogue: New Cultural Identities.* London: Macmillan, 1982. 55–65.

Lai, Him Mark, et al., eds. *Chinese America: History and Perspectives.* San Francisco: Chinese Historical Society of America, 1987.

Lim, Shirley Geok-lin. "Twelve Asian-American Writers in Search of Self-Definition." In A. LaVonne Brown Ruoff and Jerry W. Ward, Jr., eds., *Redefining American Literary History.* New York: MLA 1990. 237–250.

Lim, Shirley Geok-lin, ed. *Approaches to Teaching Kingston's "The Woman Warrior."* New York: MLA, 1991.

Lim, Shirley Geok-lin, and Amy Ling, eds. *Reading the Literatures of Asian America.* Philadelphia: Temple University Press, 1992.

Ling, Amy. *Between Worlds: Women Writers of Chinese Ancestry.* New York: Pergamon Press, 1990.

Miller, Margaret. "Threads of Identity in Maxine Hong Kingston's *The Woman Warrior.*" *Biography* 6.1 (1983): 13–32.

Moy, James S. *Marginal Sights: Staging the Chinese in America.* Iowa City: University of Iowa Press, 1993.

Nomura, Gail M., et al., eds. *Frontiers of Asian American Studies: Writing, Research, and Commentary.* Pull: Washington State University Press, 1989.

Rabine, Leslie W. "No Lost Paradise: Social Gender and Symbolic Gender in the Writings of Maxine Hong Kingston." *Signs* 12.3 (1987): 471–492.

Rabinowitz, Paula. "Eccentric Memories: A Conversation with Maxine Hong Kingston." *Michigan Quarterly Review* 26.1 (Winter 1987): 177–187.

Rubenstein, Roberta. "Bridging Two Cultures: Maxine Hong Kingston." Roberta Rubenstein, ed., *Boundaries of the Self: Gender, Culture, Fiction.* Urbana: University of Illinois Press, 1987. 164–189.

Takaki, Ronald. *Strangers from a Different Shore: A History of Asian Americans.* New York: Penguin Books, 1989.

Thompson, Phyllis Hoge. "This Is the Story I Heard: A Conversation with Maxine Hong Kingston and Earll Kingston." *Biography* 6.1 (1983): 1–12.

Tsai, Shih-shan Henry. *The Chinese Experience in America.* Bloomington: Indiana University Press, 1986.

Wang, Alfred S. "Maxine Hong Kingston's Reclaiming of America: The Birthright of the Chinese American Male." *South Dakota Review* 26.1 (Spring 1988): 18–29.

Wong, Sau-ling Cynthia. *Reading Asian American Literature: From Necessity to Extravagance.* Princeton: Princeton University Press, 1993.

Wu, William F. *The Yellow Peril: Chinese Americans in American Fiction 1850–1940.* Hamden, CT: Archon, 1982.

4

Filipino American Literature

Nerissa Balce-Cortes and Jean Vengua Gier

INTRODUCTION

In 1974, Oscar Peñaranda, Serafin Syquia, and Sam Tagatac wrote the first historical overview of Filipino American literature in *Aiiieeeee! An Anthology of Asian-American Writers.* At the time they stressed the desperate "urgency and necessity" for a critical overview because of the apparent ignorance that publishers have displayed toward Filipino American writers (Chan il). Since the publication of *Aiiieeeee!,* we have been able to mark the beginnings of a more concerted critical attention toward this group, especially by Asian-American critics and anthologists. However, this does not, by any means, give pause for celebration since Filipinos in the United States continue to earn among the lowest wages of any Asian-American group (Chan 170), and even our inclusion in the groundswell of Asian-American literary publications may have resulted in yet another marginality within the rubric of "Asian America." Therefore, the exhortation of "urgency and necessity" still applies.

This "overview" of Filipino American literature is a demarcating, rather than a definitive, introduction of a continuing literary tradition. We hope—and indeed see the necessity—to do more than acknowledge and catalog the existence of Filipino American literature. We recognize the importance of continuing historicization, even as we delineate concerns of form and content in the literature and discuss new directions.

Our concern is specifically with those Filipino American writers who emerged after World War II. As such, a critical overview must include second- and third- and even fourth-generation writers. The concerns that surface in the writings of the Filipino American writers we surveyed are varied: the insistence on "history" (as personal or family narrative and as sociopolitical theme), on collective memory, and a regard for the "pioneering work"— for example, both physical labor and the work of art—of the first-generation immigrants. This concern for the pioneering writers is partly an attempt to heal the wounds of obscurity suffered by them.

To begin any discussion on "Filipino American literature," one must deconstruct the various meanings and issues inscribed in the term "Filipino American." E. San Juan explains the problematic relationship between the terms "Filipino" and "American": "the addition of the hyphen which spells a relation of subordination and domination" ("Mapping the Boundaries" 125). This hyphen signals a power dynamic with the term "American" even as Filipinos in the United States have always been constructed as racial subjects. A hyphenated identity, however, poses political possibilities for other peoples of color in the United States. Ketu H. Katrak writes that a hyphenated "condition" illustrates the predicament of a writer who "straddles" continents and whose writings attempt to reconcile issues of "home" or what one might have to consider home for certain economic, personal, or political reasons (652).

The issue of "home" is especially central to Filipino American writing. While Filipino American writing is inscribed with the particular historical experiences of Filipinos in the United States, some of the writings are inscribed with an "ancestral" focus, history that borrows from "official" or documented sources on the homeland. In the poems and short stories of Filipino American writers, various and multilayered meanings of "home," "place," or "history" resist easy definitions or categorizations.

Although one may meet many self-identified Filipino Americans, the term "Pilipino American" is also a preferred term. Sucheng Chan notes that "1960's and 1970's community activists and leftist academics in Hawaii and the Pacific Coast chose to spell the word with a *p* as a way to honor the old immigrants, many of whom were laborers without much education" (xvi). Since the letter *f* did not exist in most Filipino dialects, words beginning with *f* were pronounced with a *p* (xvi), such as "Pilipino" instead of the Hispanized "Filipino."

One may view the unease regarding the term "Filipino American" as a generational and political issue. Older generations, who remember the discrimination and violence they experienced as migrant farmworkers toiling in the fields of California or Hawai'i, during the 1920s, cling to the terms "Filipino" or "Pilipino." While they may have become American citizens decades ago, they still prefer to identify themselves as "Filipino" because of nationalistic or personal sentiments. Many first-generation immigrants continue to maintain ties with their relatives in the Philippines, dreaming and planning for the time when they will return home to retire and be taken care of by family members. Their children or grandchildren, however, born and raised in the United States, may have no problems identifying themselves as Filipino Americans or "Asian Americans."

For the purpose of this chapter, we designate the term "Filipino American literature" to mean writings, particularly fiction and poetry, by United States-born Americans of Filipino ancestry and Filipinos who claim the United States as their home, be it a temporary or permanent one. Certainly, the term has its limitations, as do all terms that refer to the sociopolitical and historical experiences of a heterogeneous group of peoples. But, as Campomanes has pointed out, the term "Filipino American" can be tactically deployed as a "conditional but meaningful category" (51).

Our task at hand is to map the issues, contexts, and texts that constitute "Filipino American literature" by presenting the writers and their milieu. We begin with a brief history of Philippine-American relations, the establishment of Filipino communities in the United States, and a survey of the major writers and their political-aesthetic concerns. Ultimately, we seek to define what constitutes "Filipino American literature" and how it is different and similar to other U.S. immigrant literary traditions.

LITERARY-CULTURAL HISTORY

While the history of most U.S. immigrant literary traditions starts with a discussion of immigration history, our discussion of Filipino American literature begins with the notion not of immigration but of imperialism. The impact of American imperialism on the history and culture of Filipinos in the Philippines and in the United States is a significant tool in understanding and reading Filipino American writing. After all, before Filipinos came to the United States and wrote about their experiences, their homeland was a colony of the United States at the turn of the century. Here lies a significant historical distinction between Filipino Americans and other Asian Americans. While other Asian groups experienced racial discrimination upon their arrival, Filipinos experienced their "victimization" as colonial subjects even before emigration (San Juan, *On Becoming Filipino* 4). For Filipinos, colonial subjugation was at once "coercive and consensual" (4), signaled by the establishment of an American military government and a public educational system in the islands in the early 1900s. The institutionalization of English through colonial education "forged the chains of acquiescence to the superior racial power" (San Juan, "Philippine Writing" 73). Thus, American colonization, by military force and by colonial acculturation, marked the beginnings of the neocolonial relationship between the United States and the Philippines.

The annexation of the Philippines, along with Cuba and Puerto Rico in 1898, marked the beginnings of American empire building, a historic moment that launched the United States as a colonial power. This moment of empire building did not come without a cost. The Philippines today, like other former U.S. colonies, continues to experience the socioeconomic effects of American colonization decades after its independence from the United States (Liu and Cheng 74–99; Appadurai 326). A recent book on Filipino American oral histories instructively begins with a discussion on the "impact of U.S. colonization of the Philippines" (Espiritu). Citing the work of Oscar V. Campomanes, the author writes that "the institutional invisibility of the Philippines and Filipino Americans is connected to the historical amnesia and self-erasure regarding the U.S. colonization of the Philippines in particular and U.S. imperialism in general" (1). Symptomatic of this invisibility are the questions raised by cultural workers in the Filipino American community. The "(non)existence" (Campomanes 50) of Filipino Americans and their literature surfaces in various cultural expressions: the first collection of poetry by the Bay Area Filipino American Writers, *Without Names* (1985), and Fred Cordova's picture book and oral history project, *Filipinos, Forgotten Asian Americans* (1983), suggest the anxieties of (non)presence. As such, the anxieties of invisibility, despite the reality of the Filipino American population as the second largest Asian-American group in the United States (Espiritu 1), are connected to the colonial or, to be more specific, the neocolonial relationship of Philippine-American relations.

The beginnings of Filipino emigration to the United States date from the early 1900s, when a select group of Filipino students was offered scholarships by the American colonial government. The *pensionado,* or the government-scholar program, was instituted in 1903 as a move to win the favor of the Filipino elite (Constantino 310; Lawcock 61). As members of the Filipino elite were offered positions in the new colonial government, they were also wooed to send their sons and daughters to America, since an American degree promised important positions once they returned to serve in the colonial government. By the early 1920s, while many of the early *pensionados* had returned to the Philippines to pursue various professional careers, some stayed on and became "unintentional immigrants" (Posadas and Guyotte 27). Circumstances such as the Great Depression and failed ambitions (27) were some of the factors that forced them to settle in the United States.

Large-scale emigration to the United States began in Hawai'i when the islands' sugar companies enticed Filipinos to work in the sugarcane fields. During the second half of the 1920s, a total of 44,000 Filipinos arrived in Hawai'i, mostly young men (Espiritu 5). By 1930, however, the number of Filipino women had increased to over 10,000 (6). Filipino men and women were "willing" emigrants, since economic policies by the American colonial government, particularly "the shift to an agricultural export economy led by sugar" (5), paralyzed the native economy in the homeland. With a colonial culture, poverty in the countryside, and grand illusions of wealth waiting for them in America, thousands of young Filipinos started to migrate to the United States (7). What awaited them were years of back-breaking labor, oppressive working and living conditions, racial discrimination, and loneliness. By 1932, Filipinos constituted 70 percent of Hawai'i's labor force (7). Filipinos received the worst treatment, since they were U.S. nationals with no representation in either the homeland or in Hawai'i to protect them from exploitation (8). Assigned the least desirable jobs and the lowest wages, it was no wonder that Filipino laborers, led by the likes of Pablo Manlapit and, later, Philip Vera Cruz, led the protest against these working conditions.

The 1920s also witnessed the rise of Filipino communities on the Pacific Coast. Thousands of Filipinos emigrated to California, lured by the prospects of work. With the great variety of crops grown along the coast, Filipino farm laborers "moved with the crops" according to periods of harvest (9). Between 1910 and 1930, the Filipino population in California grew to 30,470 (9). The majority of these immigrants were single young men with little formal education, most of whom "were between sixteen and thirty years of age" (9). Filipinos also found their way to the canneries of the Pacific Northwest and Alaska (11).

The Great Depression of 1930 brought "severe unemployment, intense labor exploitation, and rampant vigilante violence" against Filipinos (San Juan, *On Becoming Filipino* 5). As "U.S. nationals" with indeterminate status, Filipinos all over the United States were subjected to various racist and exclusionary acts and antimiscegenation laws and were prohibited from owning land or seeking employment in government (4).

From the 1930s to the 1950s, Philippine-born writers living in the United States—such as Jose Garcia Villa, Marcelo de Gracia Concepcion, Carlos Bulosan, Bienvenido Santos, and N.V.M. Gonzalez—emerged as pioneers of Filipino American writing. In the 1950s, several significant events in the publishing of Filipino American literature occurred: Jose Garcia Villa was nominated for the Bollingen and Shelley Awards, and his *Selected Poems and New* was published with much fanfare in 1959. Carlos Bulosan's papers, including his letters and poems, were collected in the late 1950s (he had died of exposure on the Seattle streets in 1956), to be published in 1960 as *Sound of Falling Light,* a collection of his letters. It seemed that the fortunes of these two writers rose with the escalation of World War II (which switched public perception of Filipinos from being vicious "monkeys" to being friendly allies) and, conversely, fell with the advent of the cold war and the rise of the communist "Huks" against the new, "independent" Philippine Republic. Villa was caught in the net of highly politicized literary conflicts in the Philippines and was branded a bourgeois "smart aleck" by some of his own countrymen (Gonzales 113). Thus, declaring himself apolitical, he was received into the arms of the formalists in the United States and in Europe. Bulosan, with his communist and labor affiliations, suffered the most; after a period of prolific publication during World War II (Kim 45), the publishing world turned its back on him during the 1950s, precipitating his decline in health and fortune.

In the 1960s, Bulosan was rediscovered by a generation of Filipino American writers politicized by the antiwar and civil rights struggles (San Juan, "Introduction" 1). As such, the reissuance of Bulosan's autobiography *America Is in the Heart* in 1973 is considered a landmark of Filipino American writing.

The 1970s saw the emergence of United States-born Filipino writers whose works would be published in this country. This cohort of writers consisted almost entirely of the members of BAYPAW or the San Francisco-based Bay

Area Pilipino American Writers, who called themselves the "Flips," their appropriation of what was once a pejorative term for Filipinos. Members of BAY-PAW were poets, fiction writers, and artists who were predominantly from the West Coast (Los Angeles), with some colleagues from the North (Seattle), the East Coast (New York), and Hawai'i. The group grew out of the Kearny Street Workshop, a collective of Asian-American artists and writers formed during the Third World Strikes in the 1960s and the 1970s.

The fiction and poetry produced by the Flip writers grew out of the labor and human rights struggles in which the writers were involved, such as the Delano grape harvesters strike, the student strike at San Francisco State University (Aguilar-San Juan 25–26), and the antieviction strike for the elderly Filipino residents of the I-Hotel in San Francisco. These struggles were influenced, in part, by the "worldwide resurgence of 'Third World' national liberation movements" (San Juan, "Introduction" 1). Many of the Flip writers involved in these demonstrations continued their community work long after the initial furor subsided. For these writers, community-oriented grassroots organizing, with its emphasis on the sociopolitical issues of labor and cultural production, confirmed the lessons of Bulosan's insistently proletarian or political writing. As Bulosan connected the labor struggles in California to the peasant struggles in the Philippines, the Flip writers saw the need to align their literary and political concerns with various "Third World" issues that would later mark the beginnings of the Asian-American movement (Aguilar-San Juan 32).

Virginia Cerenio's poem "at city planning" is an example of Flip poetry grounded in the experience of the tenants' rights struggles in San Francisco and also explores interconnections with the Third World. Its language moves from a reference to the unfulfilling touch of the impersonal grids laid out on a map, to her local experience of the concrete textures of San Francisco's south Market Street area. This, in turn, evokes a memory of visiting the Philippines, walking the streets, and the call for revolution bridging the gap between the shores of the two countries. "Revolution" as a force of irrepressible change surfaces in the last stanza, where, in a local context, developers "are planning the relocation of you and me" (27).

Indeed, Flip poetry took its cues from Bulosan's proletarian writing, the many oral history projects in conjunction with the "Third World strikes," local labor strikes, and movements to revamp curricula in American educational institutions. Poetry, whether written or performed, was explored in its relationship to oral "talk-story" and even to music and dance. This was a way of honoring oral recitative forms normally ignored by a mostly white readership that had fetishized written texts and their production. It also explored a more direct communication of poetry, invoking popular culture and cutting across class lines in order to build political coalitions. The universal experience was eschewed for local, community, and ethnic cultural experience. Thus, one finds frequent references to food and to rhythms of dance and music in the works of Cyn. Zarco and Jessica Hagedorn, while Al Robles's poetry embodies in text the speech rhythms and folkloric and historical content of talk-story. Drawing upon traditional oral forms and popular culture constituted a critique against "progressive," modernist, and individualist paradigms of the previous decade, those literary forms that emphasized the "New"—from New Criticism to the many anthologies that announced "new" American poets or poetics but that tended to exclude the poetry of ethnic writers.

In the 1970s and 1980s, small press and college publication of books, chapbooks, and anthologies became, and continue to be, crucial to the dissemination of works by Filipino American writers. The groundbreaking anthology *Aiiieeeee!*, published in 1974, was the first anthology to introduce Flip writers to the literary scene.

This was followed by a "grassroots" San Francisco Bay Area anthology, *Time to Greez! Incantations from the Third World,* published in 1975 by Third World Communications. The book included ten Flip poets who were placed in the "Asian" section. Distinct cultural differences in this anthology were subsumed under general ethnic categories for the sake of presenting a united Third World front. As the editors observed, the featured writers all shared "the common problems of racism, lack of capital and tools; but [also] the common beauty of understanding and expressing the rhythm and color of our lives" (v). Thus, the anthology declared itself at once united, revisionary, and oppositional to dominant narratives about the Third World and its peoples. In the poem "Islands on Fire," Luis Syquia, Jr., evokes the bloodshed and violence of the Vietnam War while addressing the need "to speak out against U.S. aid" to Marcos (22–23). While Oscar Peñaranda and Al Robles write of the *manongs,* or the old-timers who worked in the fields of Hawaii and California, the poetry of Cyn. Zarco, Emily Cachapero, and Jessica Hagedorn addresses the problems of Filipino women trying to adapt to life in the United States. In Cachapero's "Did You Bring . . . ," the persona of the poem is a second-generation immigrant, a child hoping that her mother's gambling has been able to reap the promise of the American dream (68). In Zarco's "Pacific Lover," the persona finds herself still divided between the Philippines and the United States and dreams of being planted symbolically beneath the nourishing mango tree (63).

In 1975, two anthologies appeared that expressed how complex and shifting the terms of national and ethnic affiliation can be when applied to Filipinos. In *Speaking for Ourselves: American Ethnic Writing* (1975), Philippine-born writers writing in English (such as Bulosan, Santos, and Villa) who were published in the United States and the Philippines were placed in the "Asian-American" section. Both American-born and Philippine-born writers were designated "Filipinos in America" in another anthology, *Liwanag: Literary and Graphic Expression by Filipinos in America* (1975).

In the late 1970s and during the 1980s, many of the students involved in political organizing became professionals. Ethnic studies programs were instituted in a number of undergraduate and graduate programs, while the market for Asian-American literature slowly began to increase. Anthologies devoted more space to featuring works of single poets, while continuing to introduce new writers.

Acknowledging the special influence of Carlos Bulosan upon Filipino American writing, *Amerasia Journal* published a special issue of Carlos Bulosan's prose and poetry in May 1979. While Bienvenido Santos was an accomplished poet and fiction writer in the Philippines, his collection of stories, entitled *Scent of Apples,* was published in the United States for the first time only in 1979. Santos's short stories chronicle the lives of old-timers, the lonely *manongs* he met in his U.S. travels and his years of exile in the United States.

Poet and performance artist Jessica Hagedorn published her first book in 1975, entitled *Dangerous Music: The Poetry and Prose of Jessica Hagedorn.* The work in this volume reflects the influence of the beat poets in its streetwise and experimental tone while expressing deep ironies that American culture holds for new immigrants. This was followed by a work of fiction, *Pet Food and Tropical Apparitions,* in 1981. Her work has continued to be featured in numerous anthologies and has remained influential well into the 1990s.

In the later 1980s, several anthologies and short story and poetry collections saw print. In *October Light* (1987), poet Jeff Tagami, a third-generation Flip writer, expresses a close familiarity with the land, complicated by the author's personal and historical knowledge of the oppression of Filipino laborers in the United States. Often dark and elegiac, the poems' images can be disturbing, although there are occasional moments of transcendence and even contentment (Gier 9).

Virginia Cerenio's *Trespassing Innocence,* a collection of poems, was published in 1989. Cerenio's poems, such as "lunch with manong benny" (36–37) and "family photos: black and white: 1960" (53), reflect upon the lives of both young and elderly Filipinos in the San Francisco urban area as well as in the Philippines. Many of the poems are decidedly feminist in tone, expressing a special concern for the lives of oppressed women and children in the Philippines.

The 1980s saw the rise of emerging Filipino American women writers. Linda Ty-Casper, an accomplished fiction writer who publishes both in the Philippines and in the United States, published several works of fiction with historical themes ranging from the Philippine-American war at the turn of the century to the Marcos regime. Some of her works include *Dread Empire* (1980), *Fortress in the Plaza* (1985), *Awaiting Trespass* (1985), *Wings of Stone* (1986), and *Ten Thousand Seeds* (1987).

Another fiction writer, Michelle Cruz Skinner, constructs life under dictatorial rule juxtaposed by "American neocolonial support for Marcos" (Campomanes 71) in her short stories in *Balikbayan, A Filipino Homecoming* (1988).

In 1988, journalist Ninotchka Rosca published her first novel, *State of War.* The novel examines the neocolonial history of an imagined "Philippines," traveling through various historical periods. Rosca continued her explorations and appropriations of Philippine "history" with her second novel, *Twice Blessed,* published in 1992.

Pioneering writers and new voices published their works in anthologies and books. Jessica Hagedorn published her first novel, *Dogeaters*, in 1990. The novel, with its historical allusions to the Marcos regime, employs a post-modern idiom that questions the notions of "history," authenticity, linear narration, and the narrative form. In 1993, the anthology *Charlie Chan Is Dead, An Anthology of Contemporary Asian American Fiction*, edited by Hagedorn, includes the work of new and established Filipino American fiction writers.

Another anthology, *Fiction by Filipinos in America*, was published in 1993, edited by fiction writer Cecilia Manguerra Brainard. In 1994, Brainard published a novel entitled *When the Rainbow Goddess Wept*, set in the Philippines during World War II. The novel had been previously published in the Philippines as *Song of Yvonne* (1991).

Peter Bacho's *Cebu*, published in 1991, is another novel with an ancestral and historical focus. *Cebu* follows the journey of a Filipino American priest, Ben, to the Philippines to bury his late mother. The novel is darkly comic, interspersing humor with political commentary, history, and various subplots that construct the novel as a cyclical rather than a linear narrative. Throughout the novel, Ben is constructed as an ambivalent figure. As a second-generation immigrant reared and raised with a Catholic upbringing, Ben vacillates between love and hate for his Filipino roots and his family's immigrant experience. As such, Bacho's novel constructs contemporary Filipino American life with the tensions, contradictions, and dilemmas experienced by an immigrant in the land of his ancestors and in his own adopted homeland.

The 1990s saw the rise of books by Filipino American writers who "straddle continents" by publishing their works in the United States while sending their writings to the Philippines as well. Marianne Villanueva's *Ginseng and Other Tales from Manila*, a short story collection, was published in 1991. In 1993, N.V.M. Gonzalez's short stories were published for the first time by a major university press in the United States and were entitled *The Bread of Salt and Other Stories*. Gonzalez, a contemporary of Santos, had been publishing his short stories in the Philippines and the United States for decades while living in this country. In 1994, an anthology edited by journalist and poet Luis Francia featured the writings of Filipinos and Filipino Americans, entitled *An Anthology of Twentieth-Century Philippine Literature in English*.

The year 1995 witnessed a revival of Bulosan as a major figure in Filipino American literature. E. San Juan, Jr., edited two books devoted to Bulosan's writings: *On Becoming Filipino, Selected Writings of Carlos Bulosan* (1995) and *The Cry and the Dedication* (1995). The latter, posthumously published decades after Bulosan's death, is a historical novel set in the Philippines that spans the years from 1915 to 1950. The novel was previously published in the Philippines as *The Power of the People* (1986).

In 1993, Garrett Hongo's anthology, *The Open Boat: Poems from Asian America*, was published by Anchor/Doubleday. Besides the work of Jessica Hagedorn and Jeff Tagami, it contained works of several "new" Filipino American poets, Vince Gotera, Eugene Gloria, and Alfred Encarnacion. These three poets recapitulate many of the concerns that were expressed by the Flip poets during the 1970s, although—approaching, as they are, the millennium—the tone of these poems seems much more reflective, moving back in time from the 1920s, through the more vocal struggles of the 1960s and 1970s, to the present transnational moment.

Both Alfred Encarnacion and Vince Gotera's meditations on Carlos Bulosan and the old-timers reflect a concern for the disappearance of these men (most of whom have died or will soon die), whose stories have so enriched the lives of the Flip poets. Encarnacion's image of Bulosan walking down a road and disappearing "through the eye of a needle" evokes in its title the "miles" the old-timers have clocked and the threads they have woven into the fabric of Filipino American life. Vince Gotera's "Dance of the Letters" and "Gambling" mourn the promise of America unfulfilled for the elderly *manongs*. Eugene Gloria's poetry seems to circulate constantly between the United States and the Philippines, drawing cultural connections to the ancestral homeland, invoking the names of things—"blood soup with chili peppers"—as if the words themselves conjure home, draw friends and relatives closer, and revive the dead.

Recent writings by Filipino American fiction writers explore the interconnections between gender and ethnicity. In the anthology *Charlie Chan Is Dead,* the emerging voices of a new generation of Filipino American short story writers employ "history" and the narrative in creative, transgressive forms. In Lawrence Chua's "No Sayang Lost," the reader encounters four "voices" who narrate disparate moments of their lives as gay Asian-American men. Chua's work tackles the complexities of homosexuality and ethnicity with experimental narrations that are erotic, humorous, and political. Similarly, the vignettes by R. Zamora Linmark explore the connections between gender and ethnicity. Zamora Linmark's vignettes are anchored by the voice of an unnamed narrator, a young boy who is initiated into the realities of racial discrimination, sex, and sexuality. In the poignant and powerfully written vignette "The Pen Is a Mirror, Lonely," the narrator and his friend Florante endure jokes about their accents from the schoolchildren, discover the writings of Filipino writers, and learn how to write poems and short stories of their own. The vignette ends with cultural affirmation—the young immigrant protagonist discovers his ethnic roots and the power of the written word.

Aside from Jessica Hagedorn's work, we find few examples of experimental poetry by Filipino Americans; for these, one must often turn to anthologies that are not generally oriented to Asian American literature. In 1995, the anthology *Chain* published a long "documentary" poem, "His Civil Rights," by Catalina Cariaga. Her poetry generally addresses tensions and contradictions that arise from the ideological use of language and text. "His Civil Rights" could be described as a "post-modern" poem in its intertextuality and genre-crossing, yet Cariaga remains suspicious of overarching categories such as "post-modern." Her "Working Notes" to the poem summarize many of the issues that Filipino American writers are addressing in the last decade of the twentieth century: "I deal with issues of race and gender. I document a reclaiming, retrieval and remixing of cultural metaphors, symbols, nuance, queues—not merely to freeze them in an anthropological or archival depository of "art"— but to enliven and set them in motion in a world and time that is most intent on forgetting or denying them" (Osman and Spahr 61).

DOMINANT CONCERNS

In discussing dominant concerns of Filipino American writers, it is necessary to place them within the context of two strands of thought—or poetics, if you will—that have been both influential and problematic. These two strands are represented by the proletarian prose and poetry of Carlos Bulosan and the formalist poetry of Jose Garcia Villa. It is important to note that the two are by no means the only Filipino writers working in these traditions who are influential or controversial; however, they have received the most scrutiny and—despite the unwillingness of at least one of them—have become representative of Filipino and Filipino American writing in general.

Carlos Bulosan's *America Is in the Heart* has provided a backdrop for much of Filipino American writing after World War II. The novel focuses on the oppression of Filipino field laborers in the western United States during the depression. Its politics is collectivist and proletarian; often mistaken as the autobiographical account of one Filipino "national," the narrator's voice is, in fact, multiple, relating the experiences of many. The book begins in the Philippines, recounting Bulosan's childhood in a rural locale and narrating the changes effected by capitalist economic forces upon the peasant population. Bulosan's novel was perhaps the first to detail the Filipino national's experience of migration in "steerage" to the United States and his subsequent alienation and mobilization into the desperate, depression-era workforce. "*America Is in the Heart*—perhaps more than any other literary influence—has helped to articulate to Filipino Americans the continuum of colonial/neo-colonial experience, especially in its relationship to labor and social rights movements in the U.S." (Gier 16). Just as Bulosan's prose articulates the disjunctures of the Filipino national, so do his poems speak of exiled men living with failure who are "betrayed . . . under the fabulous city," of factory towns and factories that "vomit black-faced . . . toil-worn" and "voiceless" men (*On Becoming Filipino* 163). Within the context of classical Marxism, he calls for the classless society with its necessary counterparts of revolution and unity among the proletariat. It is important to remember that Bulosan's mature literary influences stemmed first from his work with labor activists and second from his autodidactic readings in Marxist literature and from writers who focused on social life in America: Steinbeck, Hemingway, Whitman, and Richard Wright. Bulosan did not finish high school. Partly because of his social and educational limitations, his poetry has a "populist" feel; yet it must be understood that he also consciously styled his work to appeal to the "masses."

Bulosan might be considered, for the most part, a social realist. However, he made forays into the fantastic and romantic with enough frequency to warrant some attention. His concern for the people, or the proletariat, did not always remain on a pragmatic level, a habit that has proved problematic to some critics, but at times extended into the realm of the ideal or the metaphysical. Also, unlike most strict social realists, Bulosan evinced a concern for the place of art and beauty in the lives of the people; indeed, he seemed to view art as an ennobling tool, a means of emotional and spiritual transcendance, that is also able to articulate the material situation. For this reason, the artist—or the pro-toartist—has remained a recurring and enigmatic figure in Bulosan's fictive and prose works, especially in those works that focus on Filipino peasants, *The Philippines Is in the Heart* (1978) and *The Laughter of My Father* (1944). Nevertheless, while Bulosan at times expressed a rather romantic and idealistic hope for a democratic America, he remained committed to the problems of the worker, and he retained his concern for the oppression of the Filipino people by U.S. imperialism and capitalism.

It has been a tragedy for Filipino writers—as for most writers of colonized countries—that whatever form they choose is subject to the overarching definitions of culture issuing from an increasingly mobile and transnational center. These definitions then divide the subject communities into polarizing cultural hierarchies. What little attention the American publishing industry gave to Bulosan and Villa has only helped to fuel the oppositions between proletarian and formalist writing among Filipinos and Filipino Americans. This conflict may have contributed to the self-imposed obscurity of Garcia Villa, who continues to teach in New York but who refused to publish his work (except under the pseudonym of Doveglion in the Philippines) until the advent of the recent anthology, *Charlie Chan Is Dead,* edited by Jessica Hagedorn. This recent publication of his works constitutes a reunion, of sorts, for Garcia Villa and Filipino American readers and writers.

Garcia Villa's work is unabashedly formalist, and for this reason, he has been labled a petty bourgeoisie. A few lines from one of Garcia Villa's earliest published short stories, "She Asked Him to Come" (1933), illustrate the level of difficulty readers might experience in reading his work: "Did she. Ask him. To come. Did she. Or. Did she. Not. Ask him. To. Come. Did she. Ask him. To. Come. She asked. Him. To Come" (Alegre and Fernandez 287). For those who require a straightforward narrative, that is, a mimesis of linear or historical activity, the writing is problematic. Yet, when viewed against the backdrop of American experimental writing, the work does not present any more difficulty than a reading of, say, Gertrude Stein, whose writing influenced Hemingway and whose oeuvre is mined, increasingly, by feminists and post-modernists alike.

But Garcia Villa has not been a conventional formalist. He has consistently subverted the "progressive" complacencies of formalism by injecting metaphysical and romantic content into his work. Although formalism seems to claim an avant-garde status, it can, in fact, be viewed as traditional. Luc Ferry observes, "The search for novelty and innovation (in modernist formalism) has degenerated into its opposite: simple repetition of the formal gestures of innovation for its own sake . . . the break with tradition [thus] itself becomes tradition" (quoted in Docherty 16). This "weaving in" of romantic and metaphysical motifs into an otherwise strictly formalist mode accounts for some of the more startling effects in Villa's poetry—effects that seem almost post-modern in their juxtaposition of generic modes. In "The Angel," Villa divides his content into lexical units, each word separated by a comma. In this way, he poses ideas and images of spiritual "paradox" and transcendence; certainly, few poets in the formalist genre can, in one poem, speak of intellect, bridges to God, the voices of angels, and spiritual "truth" so successfully, without seeming trite or hopelessly archaic (*Selected Poems* 147)

As a new generation of Filipino American writers returns to the homeland through memory and imagination, the works by the pioneering generation of Filipino writers reveal how their "exilic" (Campomanes, "Filipinos in the United States" 57) voices articulate neocolonial history.

Bienvenido Santos's short story "The Day the Dancers Came" (1979) explores loneliness and displacement in the lives of two elderly immigrants, Fil and Tony. The two old-timers are trapped in their dead-end jobs and their dead-end lives, symbolized by their decrepit apartment, which reeks of age and decay. Analogous to the motif of entombment in African-American texts such as Ellison's *Invisible Man* and Morrison's *Jazz,* the characters of Santos's story are entombed by the poverty and the alienation they must live with as two old men who have no family or community to support them. Throughout the story, the whiteness of the snow covering the cityscape contrasts Fil's obsession with the brown, young Filipino dancers who come to Chicago for a brief performance. In effect, the dancers are metonymic representations of his idealized homeland, which he has left for good but frequently returns to through memory. The young Filipino dancers "in memory or in the flesh, are deified to represent a prelapsarian (pre-immigration) perfection" (Wong 117)

Filemon's own nickname, "Fil," invites the reader to view the character as more than the focalizer of the narrative and, rather, as the representation of the countless "Fils" or Filipinos who migrated to America in their youth only to find menial jobs, shabby apartments, and loneliness waiting for them in their old age. Santos writes:

To a new citizen, work meant many places and many ways: factories and hotels, waiter and cook. A timeless drifting; once he tended a rose garden. . . . As a menial in a hospital in Cook County, all day he handled filth and gore. He came home smelling of surgical soap and disinfectant. . . . He took charge of a row of bottles on a shelf, each bottle containing a stage of the human embryo in preservatives. . . . Now he had a more pleasant job as special policeman in the post office. (114)

The detail of the bottled embryos in different stages of development, which gave Fil nightmares years after he worked in the hospital, suggests the disconnected and arrested lives of old-timers (Campomanes 61). More important, the embryos metonymize "the utter disconnection of the oldtimer from the flow of time and from the Philippines whose birthing as a nation itself has been aborted by American colonialism" (61). Fil and Tony are thus "nationless" individuals with no connection or emotional ties to the homeland or their adopted land. They are bereft of any motherland. In many ways, their "timeless drifting" is likened to the embryos perennially afloat and preserved, aborted lives that parallel their own. The repeated image of Tony bundled up in his bed like "an oversized fetus in the last bottle" (Santos 125) depicts their preserved, unnatural existence. As old, lonely, and poor immigrant bachelors, Fil and Tony negate the immigrant mythology of happiness and success. The traumas experienced in their immigrant life surface in the different kinds of suffering the characters experience. Tony ultimately pays the price of wanting to be like a white man. His physical transformation is a freakish and painful fate. Fil, on the other hand, is haunted by his loneliness and sense of displacement. He has no "homeland" to return to. The metaphor of drifting and floating echoes in the dialogue of both characters, reflecting their castaway-like state. They wish they could come ashore, find a "home," and establish roots. But this is denied to the immigrant/ colonized subject by the colonial/First World culture.

N.V.M. Gonzalez's short story "A Warm Hand," published in the anthology *Fiction by Filipinos in America,* edited by Cecilia Manguerra Brainard (1993), is one of his early works when he was a student on a fellowship at Stanford University during the 1940s. His story was so well received by Katherine Anne Porter, then a professor at Stanford, that she prodded him to submit the story to the *Sewanee Review,* where it saw print for the first time.

Similar to Carlos Bulosan's construction of the homeland populated with hardworking, kind peasants, the stories of N.V.M. Gonzalez focus on the lives of peasants, farmers, fishermen, and other barrio folk. Inevitably, his lyrical valorization of peasant life "has been critiqued for creating a literary brand of nativism and ethnography about a 'bygone rural Philippines' " (Campomanes 66). But, like the stories of Santos, Gonzalez "mirrors his exilic condition in the patterns of migration, dispersal, and self-hood" through his reconstruction of his past (66). Central to his stories are the metaphors of the sea and voyage suggesting "exilic distances, departures and arrivals" (66).

In Gonzalez's story "A Warm Hand," the protagonist is a maid named Elay, a woman utterly obedient to her vain, citified mistress. The text explores a subaltern subject embodied in Elay, the servant who is the focalizer of the narrative. Her relationship with Ana, her young and vain employer, is defined by her "acceptance" of her class position. Elay's "feudal" relationship with Ana has defined her identity and the ways she interacts with others.

The narrative brings to the surface the concepts of taboo and transgression as they relate to the social classes of a hierarchized society. The characters in the short story represent a composite portrait of Filipinos from different classes. The sense of apathy, irritation, and impatience of the other passengers toward Elay, a servant girl "violated" by the unknown "warm hand," can be read as the dominant culture's attitude toward members of the lower class. Elay embodies both asexuality and sexuality. In effect, as a "servant girl," she is an automaton existing only for the needs of her mistress, with no "needs" of her own. Yet she is also a female body capable of arousing sexual desire. Gonzalez's story thus focuses on the dynamics between class and gender oppression in a colonized culture.

The latter part of the 1980s and the beginning of the 1990s saw the publication of two novels by two Filipino American women writers. Both novels are set in an imagined "Philippines" reconstructing the country's neocolonial history. Ninotchka Rosca's *State of War* (1988) and Jessica Hagedorn's *Dogeaters* (1990) have an "ancestral" and historical focus. In both texts, an imagined Manila is the topos of colonization, totalitarian power, corruption, decadence, and beauty (Balce-Cortes 97). The "Manila" of these novels is also the metonymic representation of the Philippines. The novels claim a rewriting of Philippine history by reexamining or constructing "Manila." Symptomatic of this rewriting of Philippine history are the synecdochic moves of *State of War,* where the interconnecting tales of three families become not only the history of three bloodlines but the history of the nation as well (97). Toward the end of Rosca's novel, for example, we encounter the ruminations of the central character, Anna, widow of an antigovernment activist. The sight of drunk carnival revelers who chant a song about Magellan, the Portuguese explorer credited with "discovering" the Philippines, propels Anna into an interior monologue of her country's "mangled history" (336) caught in the warbled lyrics of a "four hundred year old song." In Anna's narrative strand, her search for the body of her missing activist husband, the novel unravels a chapter of martial law history.

In Hagedorn's novel, the history of the Philippines is represented in the fragmented tales of the city "Manila," as told through the lives of its famous, infamous, and neglected citizens: prostitutes, generals, politicians, socialites, starlets, gossip mongers, slum dwellers, and criminals. The novel ends with a chapter ironically titled "*Kundiman*" (250), a Tagalog word for "love song." The song of the final chapter is a bittersweet, even nostalgic coda patterned after the prayer "Our Father" (250). The sacred *mater* imaged in the prayer becomes the suffering and insufferable homeland or motherland that the central character Rio leaves and returns to via memory.

In these two first-novels, landmarks of Filipino American women's writing, we see two trajectories in the narration of the homeland—in Hagedorn's text, the narrative suspects and presents "history" as "fabulation" or as a fantastic *cuento* (or, in this case, *kwento,* the Tagalog-Hispanized word for "story") reminiscent of the magic realist accounts of Latin American colonial history (Saldivar 534); Rosca's text, on the other hand, articulates a desire for a unifying narrative. In the novels by Hagedorn and Rosca, we thus read the desire and suspicion for "history."

In Jessica Hagedorn's *Dogeaters,* the novel's episodic structure, shifting narrators, disparate images, and texts present a "cinematext of a Third World scenario" (San Juan, *Mapping the Boundaries* 118) caught in a contemporary "neocolonial milieu." As cinematext, the novel is a montage, a text borrowing from the idiom of filmic representation. Such a strategy is significant in the light of the medium of film and its complicity with the colonial project for close to a century. A text that appropriates the filmic medium short-circuits the notions of a static image or a passive "native" narrated or documented by the Western eye/camera (Balce-Cortes 105). Hagedorn's novel moves in this interventionist manner with the abundance of pseudoevents and "real" events or documents in the narrative. As such, the novel *Dogeaters* evokes the post-modern strategy of questioning the authority of "history" (Hutcheon 71), a field of knowledge written by and through Western hegemonic discourse surrounding the native body, the Other. The novel's self-reflexivity generates theoretical and textual self-consciousness about "the act of narrating in the present the events of the past" (71). The metafictional convention of paratextuality—or the inclusion of "subtitles, prefaces, epilogues and epigraphs, etc."—signals both the "narrativity" (and thus the "fictionality") of the text while asserting its historicity (82, 85). Thus, *Dogeaters* presents "the text as stereography," a "spatial polyphony of textual forms," "linguistic registers," "fonts," and "fictions" (Hau 119–120) in historicizing the truth of neocolonialism (Balce-Cortes 106).

The chapter "Paradise" best exemplifies the deromanticized and demystified re-presentation of the imagined homeland. Manila or the Philippines is far from paradise as the chapter re-presents its dark and seamy images: the accident at the state-owned film center where several workers are buried alive and the nightclub life as told through Joey's story. In this scene from the novel, Joey, the Amerasian "rent-boy," takes his new john, a German film director in town for the government-sponsored film festival, to see the infamous "shower dancers" of Manila:

I chuckle softly, tell Rainer about Boy-Boy and his job at Studio 54, how the club is located at 54 Alibangbang Street, how the owner is a cop who's never been to New York. It's a gold mine, a kinky haven. . . . Hungry young boys crowd the stage, lathering their bodies with soap while an audience watches. Some of the boys soap each other, all part of their routine. . . . "Are they hungry or greedy?" Rainer asks. I look at him, perplexed by his question. "There's a difference, you know," he adds, gently.

What a pain in the ass. "Hey, man. How should I know? Boys are hungry, so they perform. . . ." . . . The German stares at me in the darkness. I recognize myself in the absence of light in his eyes, the junkie in him. And something else, something that bothers me. I remember the same doggish look about Neil, how it always made me angry, how my anger always fueled the American's desire. (141–142)

Rainer as a film director is significant because of the "historical" ties between film, or the camera, and the colonizer's construction of the Filipino as savage or primitive. Joey's previous client was also a white man, an American serviceman named Neil. In this scene, "white love" is evoked, how Filipinos are given "an opportunity to perform before the solicitous gaze" of the West (Rafael 189). The word "perform" becomes suggestive in this example, mirroring the sexual nature of Joey's relationship with his white clients. The character of Rainer becomes the metonymic representation of the totalizing white/racist gaze that eroticizes and dehumanizes the Other, represented here by Joey.

The novel's Manila is a garish and occasionally nightmarish theme park created by and for the West (Balce-Cortes 107). "Manila" is the nightmarish metropolis of the post-modern imagination as violence, both the psychic and the physical, looms large in every street corner. Inevitably, Hagedorn's *Dogeaters* is not just about Manila but is about the United States and its legacies for its former colony. Both visible and invisible are the effects of American imperialism on Philippine contemporary life cataloged in the novel—the Amerasian male prostitute embodying "special Filipino-American relations" (San Juan, "Mapping the Boundaries" 125), the "K Mart/ mass cultural realism" (Saldivar 535) seen in details of American pop culture transported to the Third World, and the mestizo characters symbolizing the worst of "colonial mentality." An American reader is given a "tour" of the empire, how America and the rest of the Western world continue to maintain hegemonic control over a Third World country without having to engage in war or colonial occupation.

After Hagedorn and Rosca's nightmarish neocolonial Manila, Jeff Tagami's book of poetry, *October Light* (1989), illustrates just how widely Filipino American writing can differ in both tone and setting. Tagami is a third-generation Filipino American who was brought up working in the agricultural fields of the Pajaro Valley. His is a pragmatic poetry grounded in a place known intimately and tempered by moments of lyric intensity that seem to spring from this knowledge of the land and its history. The setting is in rural central California, and Tagami's focus is on the lives of agricultural farm laborers and their families. The Pajaro Valley is itself an area full of contradiction for Filipinos. It is rich in terms of its agricultural yield for the United States, yet it has provided little sustenance for those who work its fields. Filipinos have worked the crops in the valley since the 1920s; for the writer, then, it is an area rich with history. But, ironically, that history is one of violence and resistance, since the Pajaro and the surrounding areas were a locus of Filipino race riots and labor strikes during the 1930s and again in the 1960s, when the momentum of the Delano grape harvester strikes reached the area. It is not surprising, then, that Tagami's poems thread back and forth between the experiences of the old-timers and those of his family and friends. The people he portrays live, for the most part, at near-poverty level, and their lives are drained by the daily grind of hard, physical work.

Despite the rootedness of Tagami's poetry in a particular locale, one of its singular ironies is its reflection upon the exilic experiences of the *manongs* who worked as migrant laborers. Tagami is keenly aware of the relationship between Filipino laborers in the United States and their peasant counterparts in the Philippines. Memory is at issue here—the importance of remembering a history that can actually be traced on the land itself, on the riverbanks, the roads, the remnants of farmworkers' bunkhouses, and in the apple orchards gone to seed. Thus, the working *manongs* are haunted by the memory of their families at home in the islands, to whom they cannot return. Decades later, the offspring of those farmworkers are, in turn, haunted by the ghost of Fermin Tobera, a Filipino laborer who was murdered in his bed during the race riots of the 1930s. But Tobera's haunting is not only that of a wasted life and lost potential; it is also a haunting of rage that lies beneath the surface history of Filipino Americans.

Although many of Tagami's poems are elegiac and even bitter in tone, a few express an almost unexpected happiness: remembering a moment when, leaning against a car and drinking a beer, Tagami felt happy "just to have come from someplace" (33–34) or when, standing high up in a tree picking apples with his mother, he felt the impulse to sing. Family, as portrayed in Tagami's poems, is both a source of grief and happiness, a way of articulating the abuses that a history of oppressive working conditions (linked to the history of colonialism in the Philippines) has wrought upon family members and a way of voicing hope and love. In *October Light,* Tagami insistently invokes the passage of time, the revision of history, and the influence of place. Through the memories of the people who work the land and remember its stories, the poet questions the dehistoricization and displacement imposed by the monolithic narratives of settlement and incorporation in the United States.

CONCLUSION

Filipino American literature is a literary tradition imbued with "histories." By "histories," we refer to the literary-historical ties between Filipino American writing and Filipino literatures, as well as the insistence of revisionary histories of both "local" resistance in the United States and neocolonial resistance in the Philippines. Villa, Santos, and Gonzalez began their literary careers in the Philippines and emigrated to the United States as students. They continued to publish their writings in the Philippines while they lived in the United States, since very few publishers would accept writings by ethnic writers at the time. As such, the pioneering generation of Filipino American writers finds itself included in the canon of another "world literature": Filipino literature. Bulosan came to America to work as a "national." During his years as a political activist, he returned to his native land through memory and imagination. In his writings, Bulosan examines neocolonial history by constructing the homeland and legacies left by American colonization and linking them with the experiences of Filipino farm laborers.

Having come through an era in which historical and political contexts have become crucial to an understanding of the experiences of Filipinos in the United States, emerging Filipino American writers are synthesizing what they have learned from these contexts in ways that address the ironies of the post-modern cultural and political complex. As these writers continue to articulate their experience in the United States in relation to its continuum with neocolonial experience in the Philippines, it is important to acknowledge the full scope of textual, as well as oral, tradition in Filipino writing. The positioning of Filipino Americans in the United States easily lends itself to capitalist specularity and fetishization of Third World cultural productions. Due to its geographic positioning, Filipino literature has, for centuries, been itself a crossroads of cultural production, although the meeting and mixing of cultures on its terrain have, at times, been violent and confrontative. Despite this violent meeting—and perhaps even *because* of it—Filipino *literatures,* by Filipinos and Filipino Americans, hold great potential for presenting new paradigms and disrupting universalizing, dominant narratives.

Keeping this in mind, Filipino American writers should encourage the "incursion" of Filipino texts into the dense network of American culture and literary production. Consider, then, the publication of Filipino texts in the United States exhibiting a range of works in different dialects; translations of these works giving both the original dialect as well as English; critical reviews of translated works, including a critique of methodologies used in translating Filipino texts. This is all, of course, easier said than done: past experience has taught us that funding for such projects must often encompass a range of political and economic strategies. Nevertheless, the case must be made, first, that translation projects such as these would not only reinforce the idea of an ongoing, boundary-crossing tradition of Filipino textual production but also revise and complicate the simplistic notions commonly held in American literary enclaves about Filipino and Filipino American writing (much of which seems derived from the detritus of American imperialist sentiment about the Philippines); second, as Filipino Americans continue to engage in both a dialectical and coalitional politics with the Philippines, such projects also help to put into perspective their own cultural, geographical, and political positioning in the United States in relation to that of Filipino writers and artists within their own political and cultural contexts. For, while there is a continuum and colonial and neocolonial experience and resistance between both countries, each also has its local forms.

We also need to take a fresh look at textual traditions in Filipino literature— especially those traditions that have proved problematic in juxtaposition to dominant (Western) poetics and canonical norms; if romantic and metaphysical poetics has continued to be expressed in Filipino poetry and fiction, let us explore the relevance of those concerns and forms to a Filipino American poetics. If Filipinos in the United States have found social realism relevant to their experiences here, as well as in the Philippines, let them also explore and continue to articulate that relevance to their lives.

For Filipino American writers, the creation of prose or poetry has often been a matter of balancing local issues with global issues and political concerns with the ongoing questions and problems of artistic form. This "balance" no doubt, at times, takes on the contour of a razor's edge. Some Filipino writers in the United States will choose to see their work as independent of national, canonical, and generic boundaries. Some will focus on local coalitions and community issues, while others will choose to range more widely, drawing lines of cultural and political connection between both shores of the Philippines and the United States. All of these threads of literary work come together to form a complex and variegated tapestry of Filipino American literature.

SELECTED PRIMARY BIBLIOGRAPHY

Alegre, Edilberto N., and Doreen G. Fernandez, eds. *The Writer and His Milieu.* Manila: De La Salle University, 1984.

Ancheta, Shirley, Jaime Jacinto, and Jeff Tagami, eds. *Without Names: A Collection of Poems [by] Bay Area Pilipino American Writers.* San Francisco: Kearny Street Workshop Press, 1985.

Asian Women United of California. *Making Waves: An Anthology of Writings by and about Asian American Women.* Boston: Beacon Press, 1989.

Bacho, Peter. *Cebu.* Seattle: University of Washington Press, 1991.

Brainard, Cecilia Manguerra. *Song of Yvonne.* Quezon City: New Day, 1991.

———. *When the Rainbow Goddess Wept.* New York: Dutton, 1994.

———, ed. *Fiction by Filipinos in America.* Quezon City: New Day, 1993.

Bruchac, Joseph, ed. *Breaking Silence: An Anthology of Contemporary Asian American Poets.* Greenfield Center, NY: Greenfield Review Press, 1983.

Bulosan, Carlos. *Sound of Falling Light: Letters in Exile.* Ed. Dolores S. Feria. Quezon City: Dilliman Review, University of the Philippines, 1960.

———. *America Is in the Heart.* 1946. Seattle: University of Washington Press, 1973.

———. *The Philippines Is in the Heart.* Quezon City, Philippines: New Day, 1978.

———. *If You Want to Know What We Are: A Carlos Bulosan Reader.* Ed. E. San Juan, Jr. Minneapolis: West End Press, 1983.

———. *The Power of the People.* Afterword, E. San Juan. 1977. Manila: National Book Store, 1986.

———. *The Cry and the Dedication.* Ed. E. San Juan, Jr. Philadelphia: Temple University Press, 1995.

———. *On Becoming Filipino: Selected Writings by Carlos Bulosan.* Ed. E. San Juan, Jr. Philadelphia: Temple University Press, 1995.

Cerenio, Virginia. *Trespassing Innocence: Poems by Virginia Cerenio.* San Francisco: Kearny Street Workshop Press, 1989.

Chin, Frank, et al., eds. *Aiiieeeee! An Anthology of Asian-American Writers.* 1974. Washington, DC: Howard University Press, 1983.

Chin, Marilyn, ed. *Dissident Song: A Contemporary Asian American Anthology.* Santa Cruz: University of California Press, 1991.

Concepcion, Marcelo de Gracia. *Azucena.* New York: Putnam's, 1925.

Francia, Luis, ed. *Brown River, White Ocean: An Anthology of Twentieth-Century Philippine Literature in English.* New Brunswick, NJ: Rutgers University Press, 1993.

Gonzalez, N.V.M. "A Warm Hand." *Sewanee Review* 58.1 (1950): 118–129.

———. *The Bread of Salt and Other Stories.* Seattle: University of Washington Press, 1993.

Hagedorn, Jessica. *Dangerous Music: The Poetry and Prose of Jessica Hagedorn.* San Francisco: Momo's Press, 1975.

———. *Pet Food and Tropical Apparitions.* San Francisco: Momo's Press, 1981.

———. *Dogeaters.* 1990. New York: Penguin Books, 1991.

———, ed. *Charlie Chan Is Dead, An Anthology of Contemporary Asian American Fiction.* New York: Penguin Books, 1993.

Hongo, Garrett, ed. *The Open Boat: Poems from Asian America.* New York: Anchor Books/Doubleday, 1993.

Osman, Jena, and Juliana Spahr, eds. *Chain* 2 (Spring 1995).

Rexroth, Kenneth, ed. *Four Young Women: Poems by Jessica Tarahata Hagedorn, Alice Karle, Barbara Szerlip, and Carol Tinker.* New York: McGraw-Hill, 1973.

Rosca, Ninotchka. *State of War.* New York: Norton, 1988.

———. *Twice Blessed.* New York: Norton, 1992.

Santos, Bienvenido. *Scent of Apples.* Seattle: University of Washington Press, 1979.

Skinner, Michelle Cruz. *Balikbayan, A Filipino Homecoming.* Honolulu: Bess Press, 1988.

Tagami, Jeff. *October Light.* San Francisco: Kearny Street Workshop Press, 1987.

Third World Communications. *Time to Greez! Incantations from the Third World.* San Francisco: Glide/Third World Communications, 1975.

Ty-Casper, Linda. *Dread Empire.* Hong Kong: Heinemann, 1980.

———. *Awaiting Trespass.* New York: Readers International, 1985.

———. *Fortress in the Plaza.* Quezon City, Philippines: New Day, 1985.

———. *Wings of Stone.* London: Readers International, 1986.

———. *Ten Thousand Seeds.* Quezon City, Philippines: New Day, 1987.

Villa, Jose Garcia. *Have Come, Am Here.* New York: Viking Press, 1941.

———. *Selected Poems and New.* New York: McDowell, Oblensky, 1942.

Villanueva, Marianne. *Ginseng and Other Tales from Manila.* Corvallis, OR: Calyx, 1991.

SELECTED SECONDARY BIBLIOGRAPHY

Aguilar-San Juan, Karin. *The State of Asian America: Activism and Resistance in the 1990s.* Boston: South End Press, 1994.

Appadurai, Arjun. "Disjuncture and Difference in the Global Cultural Economy." *Colonial Discourse and Post-Colonial Theory, A Reader.* Ed. Patrick Williams and Laura Chrisman. New York: Columbia University Press, 1994. 324–339.

Balce-Cortes, Nerissa. "Imagining the Neocolony." *Critical Mass* 2.2 (forthcoming).

Campomanes, Oscar V. "Filipinos in the United States and Their Literature of Exile." *Reading the Literatures of Asian America.* Ed. Shirley Lim and Amy Ling. Philadelphia: Temple University Press, 1992. 49–78.

Chan, Sucheng. *Asian America: An Interpretative History.* Boston: Twayne, 1991.

Cheung, King-Kok. *Articulate Silences: Hisaye Yamamoto, Maxine Hong Kingston and Joy Kogawa.* New York: Cornell University Press, 1993.

Constantino, Renato. *The Philippines: A Past Revisited.* Manila: Tala, 1975.

Cordova, Fred. *Filipinos: Forgotten Asian Americans, A Pictorial Essay, 1763–1963.* Iowa: Kendall/Hunt, 1983.

Docherty, Thomas, ed. *Postmodernism: A Reader.* New York: Columbia University Press, 1993.

Espiritu, Yen Le. *Filipino American Lives.* Philadelphia: Temple University Press, 1995.

Faderman, Lilian, and Barbara Broadshaw, eds. *Speaking for Ourselves: American Ethnic Writing.* Glenview, IL: Scott, 1975.

Gier, Jean Vengua. " '. . . to have come from someplace': *October Light, America Is in the Heart,* and 'Flip' Writing after the Third World Strikes." *Critical Mass* 2.2 (forth coming).

Gonzales, Joseph Ignatius B. *Philippine Poetry in English 1928–1950.* Manila: Dispatch, 1986.

Hau, Caroline S. "Dogeaters, Postmodernism and the 'Worlding' of the Philippines." *Philippine Post-Colonial Studies: Essays on Language and Literature.* Ed. Cristina Pantoja-Hidalgo and Priscelina Patajo-Legasto. Quezon City: Department of English Studies and Comparative Literature and the University of the Philippines, 1993. 113–127.

Hutcheon, Linda. *The Politics of Postmodernism.* London: Routledge, 1989.

Katrak, Ketu H. "Colonialism, Imperialism, and Imagined Homes." *The Columbia History of the American Novel.* Ed. Emory Elliot. New York: Columbia University Press, 1991. 649–678.

Kim, Elaine H. *Asian American Literature: An Introduction to the Writings and Their Social Contexts.* Philadelphia: Temple University Press, 1982.

Lawcock, Larry Arden. "Filipino Students in the United States and the Philippine Independence Movement: 1900–1935." Diss., University of California, Berkeley, 1975.

Lim, Shirley Geok-lin, ed. *Asian America: Journal of Culture and the Arts* 2 (Winter 1993).

Liu, John M., and Lucie Cheng. "Pacific Rim Development and the Duality of Post-1965 Asian Immigration to the United States." *The New Asian Immigration in Los Angeles and Global Restructuring.* Ed. Paul Ong, Edna Bonacich, and Lucie Cheng. Philadelphia: Temple University Press, 1994. 74–99.

Posadas, Barbara M., and Rolando L. Guyotte. "Unintentional Immigrants: Chicago's Filipino Foreign Students Become Settlers, 1900–1941." *Journal of American Ethnic Studies* 19.2 (1990): 26–48.

Rafael, Vicente L. "White Love, Surveillance and Nationalist Resistance in the U.S. Colonization of the Philippines." *Cultures of United States Imperialism.* Ed. Amy Kaplan and Donald E. Pease. Durham, NC, and London: Duke University Press, 1993. 185–218.

Saldivar, Jose. "Postmodern Realism." *The Columbia History of the American Novel.* Ed. Emory Elliot. New York: Columbia University Press, 1991. 521–540.

San Juan, Epifanio, Jr. "Mapping the Boundaries: The Filipino Writer in the U.S.A." *Journal of Ethnic Studies* 19.1 (Spring 1991): 117–131.

———. "Philippine Writing in English: Postcolonial Syncretism versus a Textual Practice of National Liberation." *ARIEL: A Review of International English Literature* 22.4 (1991): 69–88.

————. ed. "Introduction." *On Becoming Filipino: Selected Writings of Carlos Bulosan.* Philadelphia: Temple University, Press 1995. 1–44.

Wong, Sau-ling Cynthia. *Reading Asian American Literature, From Necessity to Extravagance.* Princeton: Princeton University Press, 1993.

5

Indian-American Literature
Gurleen Grewal

INTRODUCTION

Indian-American literature is among the very "young" literatures in the United States, barely forty years old. Indians came in significant numbers to the United States only after the changes in the U.S. immigration policy of 1965. This chapter attempts to situate the emergent literature in several contexts. I begin by framing the question of identity that concerns Indians in the United States, explaining the significance of terms such as "South Asian" and "post-colonial" that often identify this literature. I then sketch the basic sociocultural formations relevant to a discussion of a post-1947 "Indian" identity. This is followed by a brief history of Indian emigration, from the turn of the century to the present, followed by an examination of the literature and its dominant concerns.

Until very recently, most scholarship encompassing the term "Asian" in America tended to exclude Indian presence and identity. The *Columbia Literary History of the United States* (1988) has a chapter on Asian-American literature, defined as "published creative writings in English by Americans of Chinese, Filipino, Japanese, Korean, and Southeast Asian (for now, Burmese and Vietnamese) descent about their American experiences" (811). Anthologies of Asian-American literature have tended to assume this definition. "Asian Indian" as a separate category came into existence with the 1986 U.S. census, and only in the 1990s have Indians, whether as South Asians or as diasporic Indians, acquired a distinct literary identity. The volume *Writers of the Indian Diaspora* (Nelson 1993) brought together writers of Indian origin dispersed through-out the globe, featuring among them some expatriates-permanent residents-immigrants-citizens of the United States. Its appendix carries an instructive roll call of Anglophone nations: U.K., Canada, Trinidad, Guyana, Mauritius, Fiji, Singapore, Kenya, New Zealand, Tanzania, Uganda, South Africa. The volume thus showcases the remarkable heterogeneity in cultures, identities, and histories in the diaspora labeled Indian; also evident in this scattering to Anglophone regions is the role of British colonialism in India.

The term "South Asian" has acquired a resonance and currency as those scattered from the region regroup in North America. From 1989 to the present, six significant anthologies have been published under this rubric: *Desh-Videsh: South Asian Expatriate Writing and Art* (1988); *Our Feet Walk the Sky: Women of the South Asian Diaspora* (1993); *A Lotus of Another Color: An Unfolding of the South Asian Gay and Lesbian Experience* (1993); *Her Mother's Ashes and Other Stories by South Asian Women in Canada and the United States* (1994); *Blood into Ink: South Asian and Middle Eastern Women Write War* (1994); and *Living in America: Poetry and Fiction by South Asian American Writers* (1995). Of course, neither nomenclature—diasporic Indian or South Asian—is entirely satisfactory, for South Asia includes Pakistan, India, and Bangladesh, Bhutan, Nepal, Afghanistan, Sri Lanka, and the Maldives. The introduction of one of the anthologies acknowledges this medley of differences, clarifying that the term does not posit any "essence," yet its author, Arun Prabha Mukherjee, concludes: "[W]e need that term because despite our ethnic, religious, linguistic and national diversities, we *are* bound together by all kinds of subtle bonds. As long as the term South Asian does not get used to compress our specificities into a homogenized blob, it does serve the legitimate purpose of denoting the fact that South Asians do have what Wittgenstein might have called family resemblances" (*Her Mother's Ashes* x). The article brings to the fore the potentially disconcerting realization that once having been uprooted by political boundaries emerging out of colonialism, the diasporic South Asian community in North America "cuts across border lines" of nation states "with ties of kinship, custom, ritual and religion" (ix). These ties enable collaboration and coalitional work, especially among women of South Asian descent who face similar barriers rooted in a common patriarchal, sociocultural milieu; it answers the genuine need for women to share feminist insights across cultural and national borders. Arjun Appadurai and others have commented upon the ways in which global diasporas operate to undermine the exclusive narratives and politics of nation and national identity: "America may yet construct another narrative of enduring significance, a narrative about the uses of loyalty after the end of the nation-state. In this narrative, bounded territories could give way to diasporic networks, nations to trans-nations, and patriotism itself could become plural, serial, contextual and mobile" (Appadurai 806). The previously mentioned anthologies certainly seem to confirm the latter. However, the nation-state is not so easily overcome. Both the necessity and limitation—indeed, the dilemma— of using the term "South Asian diaspora" are summed up by Emmanuel Nelson: "If I were to limit my definition of the diaspora to people who are linked only to India—the post-1947 political entity—I would be, justifiably, accused of historical inaccuracy and nationalist chauvinism. Yet, if I were to broaden my definition to include all the nation-states of the subcontinent . . . [it] could be viewed . . . [as] a sign of imperialist appropriation and absorption of India's smaller neighbors'' (Reworlding x). Because Indian-Americans are the largest immigrant group from the region, ''South Asian'' often risks becoming synonymous with ''India.''

Since we are dealing with the new immigrant literatures after World War II, there is something to be said in favor of retaining the consciousness of national origins. As Frantz Fanon tells us, ''The consciousness of self is not the closing of a door to communication. Philosophic thought teaches us, on the contrary, that it is its guarantee. National consciousness, which is *not* nationalism, is the only thing that will give us an international dimension'' (247; emphasis mine). In the literature of a people, especially of new immigrants, the ''national consciousness'' is prevalent. In such a context, it becomes necessary to emphasize the specificity of Indian-American identity, while recognizing the importance of coalitional terms such as ''South Asian'' and ''Asian-American.''

In the academy, South Asian and Indian-American writing is often subsumed by the term ''post-colonial''—a term that seems to have been given currency by first-generation immigrant academicians. It is a theoretical term that signals an orientation toward a constellation of concerns, including anticolonial/imperialist discourses. The term grew out of the concern of Third World post-colonial intellectuals in Anglophone Western academies with the enduring effects of the hegemony of empire—a collective critique also broadly understood as the empire writing back. It is also a contested term that covers too many groups of various histories, geographies, and national origins—more than half the globe—to be of much help in understanding *specific* literatures. As many have said, it is a term now being emptied of political significance, merely serving consumption in the global publishing circuits of the international market. Conceding that the analyses generated under the rubric of ''post-colonial'' have been illuminating and necessary, let us say it is not a category that can distinguish between literatures or even attend to the diversity of concerns within a specific body of literature. It is a theoretical discourse that engages with history, Western imperialism, power and its claims upon truth and truth-making apparatuses, and, only broadly speaking, an identity.

LITERARY-CULTURAL HISTORY

Language

The most noteworthy feature of India is, of course, its heterogeneity. Prior to British rule, consolidated by 1765, India was under the Mughal Empire for five hundred years, and Urdu, an amalgam of Persian, Arabic, and Hindi, was a dominant language. With the power and promotion of English, Urdu declined in prestige and currency, coexisting with at least fourteen other scripted languages. A fundamental reality of most first-generation Indian Americans is that they have grown up bilingual, if not multilingual. Those who have had the privilege of being educated in English-medium schools have grown up with English as another "native" language. Upon independence from the British in 1947, India declared English a national language alongside Hindi. Given the hegemonic status of the English language, the privileged in India covet the education offered by "convent" schools built by Christian missionaries and "public" schools originally built for the children of the English bureaucracy. In the southern regions of India, English is preferred to Hindi, which is perceived as an imposition from the central government based in New Delhi in the north. Thus, national consciousness includes a strong and highly differentiated regional consciousness, having to do with language, food, religious affiliation, dress, and degree of historical interaction with, or isolation from, the British rulers. There are regions and communities known for their close connections (whether in antipathy or collaboration) with the English. The Parsee community (Zoroastrians from Persia who migrated to India in the thirteenth century to flee persecution in their own country) benefited from the patronage of the British. Certain port cities, such as Calcutta, Bombay, and Madras, became centers of maritime trade for the British East India Co. and are among the oldest urban centers of English education in India. For most educated Indians—themselves a minority who constitute the ruling bureaucratic and professional class—English either is their first language alongside their mother tongue or ranks second after their mother tongue. Novelist Bharati Mukherjee may well speak for the predicament of many upper-class, convent-educated Indians:

"How does the foreignness of the spirit begin?" Tara wondered. "Does it begin right in the center of Calcutta with forty ruddy Belgian women, fat foreheads swelling under starched white headdresses, long black habits intensifying the hostility of the Indian sun?" The nuns had taught her to inject the right degree of venom into words like "common" and "vulgar." (*The Tiger's Daughter* 37)

However, the hegemony of English aside, the various regional languages of India have their own literatures, a rich tradition of several hundred centuries. In their introduction, "The Twentieth Century: Women Writing the Nation," Susie Tharu and K. Lalita, editors of the groundbreaking double anthology *Women Writing in India, 600 B.C. to the Present* (1991, 1993), offer a complex socio-cultural history of the nation as refracted through women's literature in the regional languages. In contrast to English, literatures written in the regional languages are markedly heterogeneous in terms of class. In the United States, too, some Indians are writing in the regional languages. One such work is Susham Bedi's Hindi novel, *Fire Sacrifice,* translated into English in 1993. Hopefully, we can expect more such translations in the future.

Religion

Secular India is home to many religions. Hinduism is dominant, its texts going back to at least 1500 B.C.; others include Buddhism and Jainism, both founded in India in the sixth century B.C.; Islam; Zoroastrianism; Sikhism, founded in the fifteenth century A.D., a reformist movement incorporating unorthodox elements of Hinduism and Islam (Sufism); and Christianity, with one particular sect, the Syrian Christian community in Kerala, predating the Christianity accompanying colonialism. Over the centuries there have been significant cross-influences and conversions. Here, it is important to note the multiethnic, multilingual, multireligious constitution of the region. With the ousting of the British in 1947 came the bloody partition of India and the carving of the Indian territories of Kashmir, Punjab, and Bengal into India and Pakistan. This splitting along communal lines is the trauma that haunts the national bodies of Pakistan, India, and Bangladesh. East Bengal, severed from the Indian state of West Bengal, became East Pakistan in 1947 and eventually the nation of Bangladesh in 1971 after a war with (West) Pakistan, involving India as Bangladesh's chief ally. Contemporary Indian novelist Amitav Ghosh's *Shadow Lines* (1989) revisits the bitterness of this colonial legacy as it affects his own identity as a Bengali Indian. Recently, in the 1980s and 1990s, the politics of communalism and regional separatism has erupted violently, pitting against each other the Sikhs and the Hindus, and the Hindus and the Muslims. In the northern state of Kashmir, whose border with Pakistan has long been a tense zone, communal conflict has intensified in recent years.

Gender and Class

Today, the hierarchies of class are more salient than historical caste divisions—or, caste divisions have reconfigured along class lines—and, together with gender, create the dramatic differences in Indian subjectivities and life expectations. The contemporary Indian women's movement, one of the most vibrant in the Third World, has its roots in the social reform movements of the nineteenth century and the anticolonial nationalist movement of the twentieth century. Women gained both the right to vote and the right to abortion, both controversial events in U.S. history, in independent India's progressive democratic constitution. The Indian constitution guarantees sex, caste, and religious equality; laws for women included divorce, inheritance, the right to a husband's income and pension for widows. Nevertheless, misogynous double standards for men and women are pervasive in society, and while education affords middle- and upper-class women some control over their lives, poverty and illiteracy keep many women trapped in oppressive circumstances. In the United States, Indian women have gathered in Asian/South Asian feminist organizations to attend to the needs of immigrant women. *COSAW* [Committee on South Asian Women]

Bulletin, a journal that grew out of these concerns, also keeps abreast of women's issues in South Asia.

"India Abroad"

For a large segment of the Indian immigrant community, the ties to India endure. Given the present-day technology of communications and the increasingly transnational flow of capital, geographical distances are not what they were for earlier American immigrants. For most first-generation immigrants, political conflict in the nation of origin is felt swiftly and in many ways. Such was the case with every major upheaval in India of recent memory, whether the earthquake in Maharashtra, the sacrilegious entry of Indira Gandhi's troops into the Sikhs' sacred temple in Amritsar, Punjab, and her consequent assasination, the 1992 razing of the mosque in Ayodhya by Hindu fundamentalists, and the consequent Hindu-Muslim rioting in Bombay, or the current violence in Kashmir. These catastrophes have reverberated in the lives of many Indian immigrants. Then there are those in the immigrant population who are emotionally and financially invested in the emerging economic and political structure of India. There is economic power in the various immigrant communities in America, and they (whether Hindus or Sikhs), wooed by politicians in India, exercise their remote control. First-generation poet Meena Alexander expresses her concern over the financial support being garnered in New York for the anti-Muslim campaign: "How long did one have to live somewhere to make it one's home? Was there no protection for minorities anywhere? . . . Why could they [some Hindus in America] not feel the predicament of minorities in their own homeland? Why this terrible need to claim one's cultural identity, singular and immovable, for India?" ("Foreword" xiii). Insecurity in the adopted country, nostalgia for the country of the past, and a desire for influence in its future enable in certain immigrants a curious slippage, a frightening erasure of the violence unleashed in the present.

A BRIEF HISTORY OF INDIAN EMIGRATION

Although mercantile connections between the United States and India go back to the late 1700s, and a few hundred Indian emigrants arrived through the nineteenth century, significant emigration from India to the United States has occurred in two distinct phases, from 1904 to 1924 and after 1965. The first phase is part of a larger Indian diaspora created by British colonial oppression in India; the emigrants were mostly Sikh farmers, laborers, and veterans of the British army from the Punjab province, along with political refugees and activists, middle-/upper-class students from various groups, who came to gain political support against British rule. The immigrant farmers and laborers on the West Coast, from Canada to California, met with the same kind of resistance Euro-Americans and Canadians reserved for the Chinese and Japanese immigrants before them. Anti-Asian sentiment grew steadily after the turn of the century, leading to acts of virulent racism against a visibly foreign labor force threatening white jobs in lumber factories, sawmills, railroads, and farms. Riots, evictions, and expulsions were accompanied by discriminating laws ensuring the subordinate status of these hard workers. Between 1920 and 1940, nearly 3,000 Indians returned to India. Among the anti-Asian legislation directly affecting these early Indian immigrants up until 1946 were laws preventing them from owning land beyond three years, called the California Alien Land Law Act, 1913; the Barred Zone Act, 1917, whereby laborers from certain zones, practically all Asians except Japanese, were barred from emigrating; the *United States v. Thind* ruling, which made aliens from India ineligible for American citizenship; and the Asian Exclusion Act, 1924. In addition, those living in the United States were prevented from marrying white women or from sponsoring wives and kin in India, with the result that, for years, families remained divided across continents, and many Sikh men turned to Mexican women for a family life in California. Over time, these beleaguered immigrants managed to acquire some economic and political foothold, but their struggle has been hard. Although some recent anthologies include brief glimpses into this world—for example, poet Chitra Divakaruni has attempted brief sketches—literature of the lived experience of this community has yet to emerge. However, we do have contemporary documentaries, notably, independent filmmaker Beheroze Shroff's *Sweet Jail* (1985) and Ritu Sarin and Tenzing Sonam's *The New Puritans: The Sikhs of Yuba City* (1986).

Since there was little migration from India to the United States between 1917 and 1965, those who came after 1965 do not have much connection to the early history of Indian immigration. Also, the experience of the post-1965 second wave has been radically different. Enabled by the 1965 Immigrant Act providing quotas for professionals, that is, those with occupational skills desirable in the United States, the second wave comprised mostly students and professionals from the educated middle and upper classes in search of a better standard of living. After independence, India underwent rapid industrialization, developing technologically and becoming among the world's largest "exporters" of Anglophone scientists, who emigrated to countries like the United States, where their expertise was readily absorbed. It is this group of highly educated, post-1965 Asians (from Taiwan, India, and so on) whose visible success in America earns the Asian population the title of "model minority."

However, those who came in the late 1980s are a different lot and have quite another story to tell. Economic recession in the early 1970s "forced the federal government to revise the 1965 Immigrant Act in 1976, severely curtailing the entry of occupational immigrants" (Min 12). The majority who came after the subsequent Immigration and Reform Control Act (IRCA) of 1986 were "family reunification immigrants" and those less proficient in English and unqualified for white-collar jobs. Journalist Nita Shah notes that "their arrival has reawakened nativist fears": "Underpaid and exploited, the recent immigrants are forced to live in ethnic ghettos, lacking the confidence to make it to the Big League mainstream. An unassimilable segment of society, they are impeded by poor communication skills, . . . the women even more so than the men'' (72–74). Indian businesses in cities with a large Indian population have not been spared racist attacks, the most blatant instance being the New Jersey Dotbusters of the late 1980s, a group of white youth targeting Hindu women wearing ''dots'' on their foreheads.

Many who came after 1965 agree that while they have made strides in their professional careers, they have not always received their due, and this is perhaps because of their perceived cultural difference. While racism functions more subtly in the case of Indian professionals, the glass ceiling does manifest itself. The tag of ''model minority'' implies that Indians (and other Asians) have made it in America because of their Asian cultural traits, good work habits, and so on and that they should be regarded as models by the rest of the ethnic/racial minorities, such as Chicanos and African Americans (Woo 186). Among the insidious effects of this pronouncement are the stereotyping of an ''Asian character,'' the creation of hostility among minority groups toward Indian/Asian Americans, and the rendering invisible of racism meted out to Asians, even as it *dehistoricizes* the inequality experienced by other racialized minorities in the United States.

DOMINANT CONCERNS

So far, the literature by Indian Americans primarily reflects the conflicts and aspirations of its middle- and upper-class writers, mostly first-generation, although the various anthologies are beginning to reveal a number of exciting new voices from the American-born generations as well, predominantly women's. Absent in the following discussion are the several Indian writers whose work has been influenced by, often composed and published during, their sojourn in the United States but who are now permanent residents in India or elsewhere. Some of these United States-related writers are poets Sudeep Sen and Sujata Bhatt, a recipient of several international poetry awards; accomplished Indian novelists Amitav Ghosh and Anita Desai; and the poet and novelist Vikram Seth, celebrated for his rhymed metrical verse novel set in the San Francisco Bay Area, *Golden Gate*. Here, I focus on those writers living in the United States who have produced a sizable body of work and on the themes that pertain to the literature as a whole. For detailed appraisals of some works and writers I have been unable to discuss in this brief exposition, the reader should find in Nelson's sourcebook *Writers of the Indian Diaspora* a useful beginning.

One of the abiding concerns for most first-generation immigrants, poised between living ''back home'' and in the present, is how to balance their dual affiliations in a country with the myth of the melting pot. On one end of the spectrum is that ''need to claim one cultural identity, singular and immovable,'' a position critiqued by Meena Alexander (''Foreword'' xiii); on the other end is the shedding of Indianness, as in Bharati Mukherjee's positioning of her characters in the introduction to *Darkness* (1985): "Indianness is now a metaphor, a particular way of partially comprehending the world. Though the characters in these stories are, or were, 'Indian,' I see most of these as stories of broken identities and discarded languages, and the will to bond oneself to a new community against the ever-present fear of failure and betrayal" (3). Between these two positions, Indianness as "singular and immovable" and Indianness as "metaphor," lies a range of identities and affiliations, worked out in the genres of memoir, short story, novel, and poetry.

It is instructive to compare the work of first-generation writers Bharati Mukherjee and Meena Alexander, both of elite backgrounds. A prolific writer who has written in all genres except poetry, Bharati Mukherjee's oeuvre highlights some of the transitions made on the journey from expatriate/exile to immigrant/citizen. Having immigrated to the United States as a student in the early 1960s, she lived in Canada before making the United States her permanent home. Mukherjee's works follow a visibly autobiographical trajectory from *The Tiger's Daughter* (1972), a novel about a young woman's unsettling return home to Calcutta after years abroad; alienated from both her elite circle of family and friends and the revolutionary cause of the underclass, she is left with a lonely awareness of the hypocrisies of a patriarchal, class-conscious post-colonial society. This society is the subject of a memoir, *Days and Nights in Calcutta,* coauthored with her husband. It is a work in which Mukherjee, with her intimate outsider's eye, sheds her nostalgia for her home city. The next novel, *Wife* (1975), is about the despair of an immigrant woman of middle-class Bengali origin shorn of her support structure in an alien country. Depicting psychic violence in the lives of transplanted women is a specialty of Bharati Mukherjee, her hand gloved in a distancing irony. The violence unleashed in the novel seems excessive but underscores the upheaval and trauma of displacement. *Darkness* (1985), perhaps an allusion to the racism in Canada, is a collection of short stories that register the despair produced by the encounter with Canadian racism. Mukherjee's bitter experience of the latter makes her a particularly grateful American immigrant; her declaration "I'm one of you [Americans] now" ("Immigrant Writing" 1) carries a note of defiance but also relief. *Middleman and Other Stories,* drawing upon immigrant experience in Canada and the United States, reveals Mukherjee's confidence in being the detached and ironic purveyor of the immigrant experience, not just of Indians but of the various newcomers from the developing world.

The novel *Jasmine* (1989) expresses Mukherjee's position on the immigrant condition: "There are no harmless, compassionate ways to remake oneself. We murder who we were so we can rebirth ourselves in the images of dreams" (*Jasmine* 29). This novel best reveals the pressure felt by an immigrant in American society—the pressure to assimilate—and describes without apology the necessity of doing so. "To bunker oneself inside nostalgia, to sheathe the heart in a bulletproof vest, was to be a coward" (165). Elsewhere, Mukherjee declares,

"I am an American writer, in the American mainstream, trying to extend it. . . . I am not an Indian writer, not an exile, not an expatriate. . . . I look on ghetto-ization—whether as a Bengali in India or as a hyphenated Indo-American in North America—as a temptation to be surmounted" ("Four-Hundred-Year-Old Woman" 34). However, *Jasmine,* a narrative about the "mainstreaming" of an illegal alien, her becoming Jyoti-Jasmine-Jase-Jane, is silent about the conditions of successful assimilation. As Ketu Katrak has observed, "In general, Mukherjee stays within a safe 'political' space with regard to the politics of race in the United States" (678). Jasmine is a young woman, not well versed in English, belonging to the group of immigrants who came after 1980; as discussed before, this group is markedly different from the white-collar group that directly pre-ceded it. Mukherjee's facile conflation of the two in Jasmine's case, perhaps invisible to "mainstream" American readers, is troubling to discerning Indian ones. So far, for sensitive representations of class issues in the lives of the less privileged immigrants, we must look to other media, such as Mira Nair's short film *So Far from India* (1982), about a newspaper vendor in New York City, and *Taxi-Vala* (1994), Vivek Renjen Bald's look at South Asian taxi drivers in New York City, which has a greater concentration of Indians than any other U.S. city.

Meena Alexander's work in the genres of poetry, novel, and memoir provides an alternative understanding to Mukherjee's. Her immigrant credo is somewhat different: "The present for me is the present of 'multiple anchorages.' . . . How-ever, it is a fiction, a very dangerous one, to think that we can play endlessly in the post-modernist fashion, because our ethnicity is located in our bodies and comes in as a pressure to resist this sort of fracturing" ("Is There an Asian American Aesthetics?" 27). Her memoir *Fault Lines* (1993) seems to engage a dialogue with Mukherjee: "Can I become just what I want? So is this the land of opportunity, the America of dreams?" (202). It is tempting to read the fol-lowing as a gloss upon *Jasmine:* "I can make myself up and this is the entice-ment, the exhilaration, the compulsive energy of America. But up to a point. . . . I may try the voice-over bit, the words-over bit, the textual pyrotechnic bit, but my body is here, now, and cannot be shed. No more than any other human being can shed her or his body and still live" (202). Having grown up in two countries/continents, in India and Sudan, and having then moved to two more, Britain and the United States, the poet needs to link herself to a history, a lineage. In *House of a Thousand Doors* (1988), the poet constructs a literary foremother in the figure of her educated, revolutionary maternal grandmother, bypassing her domestic mother with her inimical advice to be seemly and silent. *Fault Lines* is a candid and poignant examination of all her losses, the vertigo of displacement, the liminality of exile, the shock of being "a woman without history in this new world" (160). The memoir explicates her earlier poetry, especially the volume *House of a Thousand Doors:* "It's as if in all these years as a poet I had carried a simple shining geography around with me: a house with a courtyard where I grew up in Tiruvella. My mother's ancestral house with its garden, . . . a well with clear water'' (197).

Fault Lines recounts her life as a student of English studies in Britain, immersed in "tortuous academic knowledge" that made her own identity irrelevant: "no color there, no female flesh, no postcolonial burden" (141). She voices the pain of a belated awareness also registered by other post-colonial intellectuals and writers: "Colonialism seemed intrinsic to the burden of English in India, and I felt robbed of literacy in my own mother tongue" (128).

Importantly, *Fault Lines* marks the narrator's evolution from a consciousness of exile and its carefully assembled picture of the past, to the immigrant awareness of the claims of the present: " 'That picture I spoke of? It's all shattered. Into tiny little bits. It doesn't work anymore. . . . What is, is all around. Here. Now. . . . It's all exploded now . . . house, courtyard, well, guava tree, bowl, pitcher'' (201). She asks what is surely the most recurring and poignant question in all immigrant literatures: "[A]m I American now I have lost my shining picture? Now I have no home in the old way? Is America this terrible multiplicity at the heart?'' (201). Mukherjee, we recall, has already answered an unremorseful yes. Noting the inevitable process of change, Alexander acknowledges the hyphenated ethnic American identity: "But as my shining past fractures, never to be reassembled, ethnicity enters. And with it a different sort of priority'' (201). Here, Alexander differs from Mukherjee. She speaks of "an ethnicity that breeds in the perpetual present, that will never be wholly spelt out," a past that will never be wholly cast out. For Alexander, the somatic body, history *incarnate,* carries the "hunk of what needs to be told," demands accountability, and pulls us into the "overt acknowledgement of the nature of injustice" (203). Thus, the body "transcends individualism" (203):

Like ethnicity, like the labor of poetry, it is larger than any single person, or any single voice. . . . It is shaped by forces that well up out of us, chaotic, immensely powerful forces that disorder the brittle boundary lines we create, turn us toward a light, a truth, whose immensity . . . casts all our actions into relief, etches our lines into art. (203)

The preceding lines of Meena Alexander may well anticipate the credo of poet Agha Shahid Ali, also a faithful chronicler of loss. *The Half-Inch Himalayas* (1987) is an exquisite collection of poems mapping in four sections the various spaces opened up in exile. The spectacular shrinkage of the Himalayas in "Postcard from Kashmir" is emblematic of the migrant's loss of home, reduced now to "a neat four by six inches" (1). The poems in this collection are remarkable for their lyric beauty and unposturing integrity; here, aesthetic verbal forms present emotions in their raw vulnerability, affirming gently and powerfully the experience of displacement shared by countless nomads of the Indian subcontinent. The poems achieve this universality by their fidelity to the poet's particular world. The first group of poems re-creates elegant "heirlooms" (8) of the poet's native Kashmiri Muslim lineage of ancestral "Snowmen,"

"Cracked Portraits," "Prayer Rug," and "Dacca Gauzes." The second section has poems that return us to a lost or distanced geography and heritage, paradoxically ensuring that what is lost also survives, proclaiming that what is far is also near. Notable for their lyric eloquence are two elegies commemorating the late *ghazal* (lyric) queen Begum Akhtar and the influential Urdu poet Faiz Ahmed Faiz. The third group of poems, describing the shifting occupancy of American apartments and American cities in the present, gives way to the concluding section, in which the poet's psychic life remains bound to India. However, in these final moving poems, such as "Survivor" and "In the Mountains," a part of the self remains estranged and "never found" (51); in "I Dream It Is Afternoon When I Return to Delhi," the poet becomes the very figure of loss so that even the destitute offer sympathy to him whose "hands are empty" (53). But, as in the poem "The Tiger at 4:00 A.M.," the poet-survivor continues at his table "to print on this blankness" (55), bearing witness to that which stirs and stalks through the night spaces of the Himalayan heart and dawns onto the page.

Ali's six collections of poetry include *The Rebel's Silhouette,* sensitive and necessary translations of renowned Urdu poet Faiz Ahmed Faiz. The influence of this older poet—and indeed the whole tradition of Urdu poetry—is evident in Ali's later work, *A Nostalgist's Map of America* (1991), also notable for its stunning improvisations of Greek myths and Emily Dickinson. This is a volume announcing a poet whose voice continues to occupy the alien spaces of a hyphenated identity. In this collection the poet turns toward the American landscape, appropriating it with his own imagination. Significantly, it is prefaced by "Eurydice," a unique rendering that highlights loss and farewells in a political setting—the guard at the gates of hell barring Orpheus from taking Eurydice on a train "along the upper Rhine" (18) is a Belsen camp officer with papers. The poet of this volume is a nomadic figure pursuing the glimpsed face of "evanescence," driven by a keen sense of injustice, recording on his journey from Pennsylvania through Arizona "ghost towns" (39), vanished tribes, other nomads of the desert that was once an ocean, a friend dying from AIDS. There are disturbing conjunctions and welcome echoes, when the past resonates in the present, as "[w]hen on Route 80 in Ohio" (41), the poet passes an exit to Calcutta or when a European legend merges with a Persian one, as the Arizona desert recalls "another desert," that of Arabia and its lover Majnoon, whose longing for Laila is rivaled only by Orpheus's for Eurydice. Like his Orpheus, Ali's Majnoon is especially sensible to the "plaint" of "feet in chains" (79). The collection ends with "Snow on the Desert," a poem that *sings* itself to the muse of loss, transporting us in a smooth exit from Tucson airport, befogged site of farewells, to a concert in New Delhi, where maestro Begum Akhtar's voice carries us to the very pinnacle of loss. What Ali has said of Faiz's poetry in his preface to *The Rebel's Silhouette* may also be said of his own later work with its "mingling of the political and the romantic": "Though deeply personal, it is almost never isolated from a sense of history and injustice" (n.p.). To date,

Ali's literary contribution, with its particular qualities of heart and craftsmanship, already assures him an eminent place on the map of American poetry.

Abraham Verghese's *My Own Country* is a moving memoir of how human involvement and engagement with a community make any place a home, how for the author "this parcel of land that I stand on" (347) becomes "my own country." This autobiography of a doctor specializing in infectious disease, battling with AIDS patients in a small town in Tennessee, speaks of the satisfaction that many professional Indian Americans feel about their specialized work here. After five years of living "in a culture of disease, a small island in the sea of fear," where "life speeds up and heightens in climates of extreme pain and emotion," the narrator is exhausted but feels "connected: legs to earth, shoulders to sky" (346–347).

In *their* own country, the second and third generation of Indian Americans, those born here, are coming of age and attending colleges and preparing to assume positions of visibility. Their ties to India are mediated by those of their parents. Understandably, their loyalties to the country of their birth and to the company and ways of their American peers are more pronounced. It is important to note here that the term "model minority" frequently conflates first-generation immigrants with second and third generations, who, as Kamla Visweswaran points out, are "born on American soil, born as well to different experiences of racism and discrimination":

[I]f second-generation Indian voices are coming to terms with citizenship, Americanness and cultural belonging, they must also face questions of race, and in ways that immigrant parents have not been forced to confront. Indeed, I would argue that race is perhaps the most crucial juncture distinguishing South Asian post-colonial from second-generation subjectivities. (Women of South Asian Descent Collective 306)

According to Visweswaran, second-generation writers, "because they have been interpolated from early childhood into the racialized structure of U.S. identity politics, are compelled to confront race in their narratives" (308). This claim is certainly backed by the anthologies *Living in America* and *Our Feet Walk the Sky.* The second generation is more aware of the struggles of people of color in the United States and attempt to critique the inequities of race and class as well as politicize concerns of gender within their own communities.

What effectively links the work of first- and second-generation women writers is the experience of gender. Second-generation women often find that they are subject to more parental pressures and restrictions than their male counterparts. Dating often becomes an uneasy issue in the lives of teenage daughters as women are expected to bear the burden of maintaining tradition. Discussing Indu Krisnan's *Knowing Her Place,* a documentary about the pain and conflict felt by a second-generation Indian woman, Lata Mani points out the "gendered nature of cultural conflict": "Given that there is no rupture in patriarchal power with migration, merely its reconfiguration, the consequences

of diaspora are specifiably different for women and men'' (Women of South
Asian Descent Collective 33–34). Conflicts faced within the home by the second generation of Indian-American women are the subject of Susham Bedi's
novel, *The Fire Sacrifice,* and a recurring theme of the fiction and poetry in
the recent anthologies.

Hema Nair, Lalita Gandbhir (anthologized in *Her Mother's Ashes*), Neila
Seshachari (in *Living in America*), Padma Hejmadi (''Weather Report'' in *Birthday, Deathday and Other Stories*), and Vijay Lakshmi (see *Writers of the Indian
Diaspora*) are writers of short stories that deal with the immigrant woman's
isolation and peculiar limbo, especially those who, after following their husbands
to the United States without careers of their own, find themselves at the mercy
of husbands who either cheat, desert, or abuse them. Their turbulent inner worlds
of despair and courage form the stuff of much of the fiction in the anthologies.
In a lighter vein, Kirin Narayan's hilarious, yet moving, first novel *Love, Stars,
and All That* (1994) explores with humor a young Indian female graduate student's confusion about issues of gender, sexuality, and cultural identity as she
attempts to fulfill her ''destiny''—finding her *jori* (mate), whose presence in
her life has been predicted by an astrologer. As we follow her on her way from
naïveté to maturity, we get satiric glimpses into the absurdities of both the
''East'' and the ''West.''

In *The Journey* (1990), first novel of Indira Ganesan, who immigrated to the
United States at the age of six, we find some of the themes shared by first- and
second-generation Indian women writers. Death of a beloved cousin, a twinlike
alter ego, inaugurates this narrative of a young Indian woman's return from the
States to her homeland, an imaginary island of Pi (named ''Prospero's Island''
by a Dutch explorer) in the Bay of Bengal. The narrator, Renu, journeying
through conflicting cultural identities and through loss, is an ''unattached female'' for whom plans of an arranged marriage are being considered by her
mother and aunts. Sunk in melancholia, Renu seeks escape. She meets Marya
the Seer, who warns her of the falseness of a ''holy'' renunciation that is really
a repudiation of the heart and its complex demands for connection. The seer,
urging her to make ''a choice of life,'' voices Renu's dilemma: ''You see, in
this life, women are constantly asked to become brides. You can be the bride
of a man, of another woman, of your parent, of a teacher, or a god. Whose bride
are you, Renu?'' To the young woman void of direction she assures that ''reconstruction is possible'' but cautions that ''it requires enormous discipline and
imagination'' (126).

This particular work of reconstruction is specific to, and evident in, the writings of Indian-American women. The ''fault lines'' of migration are perhaps
more jagged for women than men and demand this reconstruction of the ruptured
self. As Meena Alexander observes from her own experience of displacements,
it is ''as if the condition of being fractured had freed the selves jammed into
[the] skin'' (*Fault Lines* 2). Ganesan ends her novel by inviting the reader to

speculate about Renu's trajectory of self-reclamation:

> Imagine Renu like this, cut off from the inside of herself and aware of the world—a teeming, passionate world—around her. Imagine that with each step, she was walking away from her superstitions and fears, away from her self-wrought sickness, her desire to live in the past. Imagine her stepping away from her inherited weights, demanding flight.
>
> This is our secret dream, our need to break free from the ground on which we half the time drag our feet resentfully, because we have been told that it is important and correct to feel the earth beneath, even while flight is in our hearts. Weightless travel, metaphorical soul-soaring, a shedding of swallowed stones, a mobility that can hold the keys of the universe.
>
> Our heroes are those who defy gravity, the gods who live in the clouds, beings who walk on water, those with magic boots and capes. There are some of us forever at our windows, waiting for rescue from the world outside. But even the sages walked on the earth; they gathered staffs and bowls, placed foot after foot further into life, eyes open, palms open.
>
> Renu Krisnan stood on the beach on the island of Pi, ready for her journey. (173–174)

That this feminist flight/journey is not read negatively as an escape from life is ensured by the reference to the gravity, vision, and receptivity of sages, ''placing foot after foot further into life, eyes open, palms open.''

It is befitting to end the present survey of Indian-American writers on this shared note of constructive endings and beginnings. It is, after all, this ''shedding of swallowed stones'' that we find in Meena Alexander's *Fault Lines,* this ''stepping away from her inherited weights'' in Bharati Mukherjee's *Jasmine,* this reclamation of a ''teeming, passionate world'' in the poetry of Chitra Divakaruni and Sujata Bhatt and Shahid Ali, this desire to ''break free from the ground'' that unites the ''women of the South Asian Diaspora'' whose feet tread the sky. We can look forward to significant work by American-born generations, and, as the distinct identity of this literature becomes apparent, hopefully many more voices will be encouraged. Here, let us also be aware that the writing of this chapter, indeed the publication of this volume, is a small instantiation of the fact that ethnic and national literary traditions are also *constructed* and fostered—and that we have begun that important task.

SELECTED PRIMARY BIBLIOGRAPHY

Alexander, Meena. *House of a Thousand Doors.* Washington, DC: Three Continents Press, 1988.

———. *The Storm, A Poem in Five Parts.* New York: Red Dust Press, 1989.

———. *Nampally Road.* San Francisco: Mercury House, 1991.

———. *Night Scene, The Garden.* New York: Red Dust Press, 1991.

———. ''Is There an Asian American Aesthetics?'' *Samar* (South Asian Magazine for Action and Reflection) (Winter 1992): 26–27.

————. *Fault Lines.* New York: Feminist Press, 1993.

————. "Foreword: Translating Violence: Reflections after Ayodhya." *Blood into Ink: South Asian and Middle Eastern Women Write War.* Ed. Miriam Cooke and Roshni Rustomji-Kerns. Boulder, CO: Westview Press, 1994. xi–xviii.

Ali, Agha Shahid. *The Half-Inch Himalayas.* Middletown, CT: Wesleyan University Press, 1987.

————. *A Walk through the Yellow Pages.* Tucson: Sun/Gemini Press, 1987.

————. *A Nostalgist's Map of America.* New York: Norton, 1991.

————. *The Rebel's Silhouette/Faiz Ahmad Faiz.* Trans. Salt Lake City: Peregrine Smith Books, 1991.

Bedi, Susham. *The Fire Sacrifice.* Trans. from Hindi by David Rubin. Portsmouth, NH: Heinemann, 1993.

Bhatt, Sujata. *Brunizem.* New York: Carcanet, 1988.

————. *Monkey Shadows.* Toronto: Carcanet, 1991.

Divakaruni, Chitra Banerjee. *The Reason for Nasturtiums.* Berkeley, CA: Berkeley Poets Press, 1990.

————. *Black Candle.* Corvallis, OR: Calyx Books, 1991.

————. *Arranged Marriage: Stories.* New York: Anchor, 1995.

Ganesan, Indira. *The Journey.* New York: Knopf, 1990.

Hejmadi, Padma. *Birthday, Deathday and Other Stories.* London: Women's Press, 1985.

Mehta, Ved. *Daddyji.* New York: Farrar, Straus, and Giroux, 1972.

————. *The Ledge between the Streams.* New York: Norton, 1984.

————. *Sound-Shadows of the New World.* New York: Norton, 1986.

————. *The Stolen Light.* New York: Norton, 1989.

Mukherjee, Bharati. *The Tiger's Daughter.* Boston: Houghton Mifflin, 1972.

————. *Wife.* Boston: Houghton Mifflin, 1975.

————, with Clark Blaise. *Days and Nights in Calcutta.* Garden City, NY: Doubleday, 1977.

————. *Darkness.* New York: Penguin, 1985.

————, with Clark Blaise. *The Sorrow and the Terror: The Haunting Legacy of the Air India Tragedy.* Markham, Ontario: Viking, 1987.

————. "Immigrant Writing: Give Us Your Maximalists!" *New York Times Book Review,* August 28, 1988: 1, 28–29.

————. *The Middleman and Other Stories.* New York: Grove Press, 1988.

————. *Jasmine.* New York: Grove Weidenfeld, 1989.

————. *The Holder of the World.* New York: Knopf, 1993.

————. "A Four-Hundred-Year-Old Woman." *The Writer on Her Work,* vol. 2. Ed. Janet Sternburg. New York: Norton, 1992. 33–38.

Narayan, Kirin. *Love, Stars, and All That.* New York: Pocket Books, 1994.

Rao, Raja. *Kanthapura.* 1938. New York: New Directions, 1963.

————. *The Chessmaster and His Moves.* New Delhi: Vision Books, 1988.

Sen, Sudeep. *Dali's Twisted Hands.* New York: White Swan Books, 1994.

————. *Mount Vesuvius in Eight Frames.* New York: White Swan Books, 1994.

Seth, Vikram. *The Golden Gate.* London: Faber and Faber, 1986.

Sharat Chandra, G.S. *Heirloom.* Delhi: Oxford University Press, 1982.

————. *Family of Mirrors: Poems.* Kansas City: Bookmark Press, 1993.

————. *Immigrants of Loss.* Frome, Somerset: Hippopotamus Press, 1993.

Verghese, Abraham. *My Own Country.* New York: Simon and Schuster, 1994.

Anthologies and Collections of South Asian/Indian-American Literature

Azia, Nurjehan, ed. *Her Mother's Ashes and Other Stories by South Asian Women in Canada and the United States.* Toronto: Toronto South Asia Review, 1994.

Bahri, Deepika, ed. *Between the Lines: South Asian Theorists and Writers in the United States and Canada.* Temple University Press, forthcoming.

Cooke, Miriam and Roshni Rustomji-Kerns, eds. *Blood into Ink: South Asian and Middle Eastern Women Write War.* Boulder, CO: Westview Press, 1994.

Katrak, Ketu H., and R. Radhakrishnan, eds. *Desh-Videsh: South Asian Expatriate Writing and Art.* Special issue of *Massachusetts Review* 29.4 (Winter 1988).

Ratti, Rakesh, ed. *A Lotus of Another Color: An Unfolding of the South Asian Gay and Lesbian Experience.* Boston: Alyson, 1993.

Rustomji-Kerns, Roshni, ed. *South Asian Women Writers: The Immigrant Experience.* Special issue of *Journal of South Asian Literature* 21.1 (Winter–Spring 1986).

———. *Living in America: Poetry and Fiction by South Asian American Writers.* Boulder, CO: Westview Press, 1995.

"Telling Tales." *Committee on South Asian Women Bulletin.* 9 (1995): 1–4.

The Women of South Asian Descent Collective, ed. *Our Feet Walk the Sky: Women of the South Asian Diaspora.* San Francisco: Aunt Lute Books, 1993.

Selected Titles in Indian-American Film and Video

Features

In Custody. Ismail Merchant, 1993, 124 min., 35mm.
Mississippi Masala. Mira Nair, 1992, 118 min., 35mm.
West Is West. David Rathod, 1988, 80 min., 35 mm.

Documentaries

A Crack in the Mannequin: South Asian Working Women in America. Keshini Kashyap, Dharini Rasiah, 1993, 15 min., video.
Home. Michell Taghioff, 1992, 38 min., 16mm.
Knowing Her Place. Indu Krisnan, 1992, 40 min., video.
The New Puritans: The Sikhs of Yuba City. Tenzing Sonam, Ritu Sarin, 1986, 27 min., video.
None of the Above. Erica Surat Andersen, 1993, 30 min., 16mm.
So Far from India. Mira Nair, 1982, 28 min., 16mm.
Straight for the Money: Interviews with Queer Sex Workers. Hima B., 1994, 58 min., video.
Taxi-Vala. Vivek Renjen Bald, 1994, 45 min., video.

SELECTED SECONDARY BIBLIOGRAPHY

Aguilar-San Juan, Karin, ed. *The State of Asian America: Activism and Resistance in the 1990s.* Boston: South End Press, 1993.

Appadurai, Arjun. "The Heart of Whiteness." *Callaloo* 16.4 (1993): 796–807.

Breckenridge, Carol A., and Peter Van Deer, eds. *Orientalism and the Postcolonial Predicament: Perspectives on South Asia.* Philadelphia: University of Pennsylvania Press, 1993.

Dasgupta, Sathi S. *On the Trail of an Uncertain Dream: Indian Immigrant Experience in America.* New York: AMS Press, 1989.

Dharwadkar, Vinay. "Indian Writing Today: A View from 1994." Special issue of *World Literature Today* (Spring 1994): 237–241.

Elliot, Emory, ed. *Columbia Literary History of the United States.* New York: Columbia University Press, 1988.

Fanon, Frantz. *The Wretched of the Earth.* New York: Grove Press, 1963.

Helweg, Arthur W., and Usha M. Helweg. *An Immigrant Success Story: East Indians in America.* Philadelphia: University of Pennsylvania Press, 1990.

Jensen, Joan. *Passage from India.* New Haven, CT: Yale University Press, 1988.

Katrak, Ketu H. "Colonialism, Imperialism, and Imagined Homes." *The Columbia History of the American Novel.* Ed. Emory Elliot. New York: Columbia University Press, 1991. 649–678.

Min, Pyong Gap, ed. *Asian Americans: Contemporary Trends and Issues.* Thousand Oaks, CA: Sage, 1995.

Nelson, Emmanuel S., ed. *Reworlding: The Literature of the Indian Diaspora.* Westport, CT: Greenwood Press, 1992.

————. *Bharati Mukherjee: Critical Perspectives.* New York: Garland, 1993.

————. *Writers of the Indian Diaspora: A Bio-Bibliographical Critical Sourcebook.* Westport, CT: Greenwood Press, 1993.

Roy, L. Somi. "From India to America: New Directions in Indian-American Film and Video." Film festival pamphlet, the Whitney Museum of American Art, September 21–October 16, 1994.

Shah, Nita. *The Ethnic Strife: A Study of Asian Indian Women in the United States.* New York: Pinkerton and Thomas, 1993.

Tharu, Susie, and K. Lalita. "The Twentieth Century: Women Writing the Nation." *Women Writing in India, 600 B.C. to the Present.* Vol. 2. Ed. Susie Tharu and K. Lalita. New York: Feminist Press, 1993. 43–116.

Vaid, Jyotsna. "Seeking a Voice: South Asian Women's Groups in North America." *Making Waves: An Anthology of Writings by and about Asian American Women.* Ed. Asian Women United of California. Boston: Beacon Press, 1989. 395–405.

Welch, John. "South Asian Voices." *Poetry Review* 78. 1 (Spring 1988): 18.

Woo, Deborah. "The Gap between Striving and Achieving: The Case of Asian American Women." *Making Waves: An Anthology of Writings by and about Asian American Women.* Ed. Asian Women United of California. Boston: Beacon Press, 1989. 185–194.

6

Iranian-American Literature
Nasrin Rahimieh

INTRODUCTION

If the history of modern Persian literature has been dominated by Western influence, Iranian immigrant writing in the United States has found itself in a
paradoxical proximity with some of the very literary and cultural sources that
initiated the modern phase of literary development in Iran. While the earlier
stages of transformation in modern Persian literature, further elaborated later,
took the form of importations from foreign sources into the native literary scene,
the literature of immigration is confronted with what would at first seem to be
a reversal of this movement: the "other," regarded as a model for a new Iranian
national literary institution, is now deeply implicated in a "self," one, at best,
divided. The homogeneous and tangible identity, whose construction in the early
modern period depended on maintaining a clear demarcation between native and
other, is destabilized in the process of immigration and exile. The position of
immigrant writers on the borders of two languages, cultures, and nationalities
has led to attempts at critical reexamination of the notion of a unitary identity.
This has enabled some Iranian immigrant writers to challenge the Iranian nationalist erasure of minority languages and discourses. By and large, however,
Iranian-American writers retain a sense of nostalgia and a fear of being irrev-
ocably cut off from life in Iran. At its most extreme, this anxiety of loss finds
expression in re-creations of pre-revolutionary Iranian social setting or of events
immediately preceding the revolution of 1979. As Bahman Sholevar indicates,
transplanted Iranians have brought to America what they were (*Dead Reckoning*
22). The return to the historical moment that severed their ties with their home-

land betrays a desire to contain the effects of immigration and to preserve that part of their past that a crisis has eternally frozen in time. But even this apparent immobility is constantly challenged through interferences from the literary scene in Iran and their adopted cultural milieu.

For the exile and the immigrant, the dislocation from ''home'' sometimes translates into an idealized and frozen vision of Iran. This imaginative and imaginary stasis, however, in no way corresponds to the flourishing literary production in post-revolutionary Iran. In the domain of cinema, there has been a parallel movement in the aftermath of the revolution. The immigrant Iranian community in the United States is not unaware of these developments, but it does not have the palpability of the immigrants' own remembered experiences of the past. Nevertheless, these developments compel expatriate Iranians to make a difficult adjustment in their vision of their culture. What expatriates used to identify as the inner core of their self is now curiously transferred to the borders of their consciousness. Given that the opposition between the external (*zaher,* or *birun*) and the internal (*baten,* or *aendaerun*), as described by William Beeman (72), dominates and determines the nature of Iranian social and cultural interaction, it is not surprising that the reversal of these two poles of identification has disrupted the familiar patterns of self-recognition for immigrant writers. The inner life with which writers used to identify is now transformed into a reality seemingly external to their existence.

In their adopted home, the immigrant writers are subjected to a double displacement of the two psychocultural poles of inner and outer. The Western literary movements and figures that provided the impetus for change in modern Persian writing are now part of the cultural fabric of the world into which these writers have been transplanted. The Western literary figures and paradigms may retain their flavor of alterity, but they have become an uncannily close other. This sense of alienation is reinforced in the stereotypes and clichés of Iran, generated during the hostage crisis and revisited in the Rushdie affair, with which the immigrant writers have to contend. The dilemma caused by such essentializations is evoked by Taghi Modarressi, an immigrant writer living in Baltimore, in his essay ''Salman Rushdie and the Immigrant's Dilemma'':

The whole experience leaves me with a sense of betrayal. To hear your native country and its culture being publicly discussed is like eavesdropping on a conversation about myself. I experience the loss of that sense of authority that any immigrant possesses about his own background. (*Pilgrim's Rules* 7)

This double alienation further complicates and shifts the poles of inside and outside, self and other, the alien and the familiar.

In this survey of Iranian immigrant writing in the United States, I focus on the ways in which these shifts in paradigm filter through their works and, strangely, replicate the patterns of cross-culturalism already present in the history of Persian literature. Yet, because the modern prototypes of influence and borrowing have intensified into what Hamid Naficy has called a "process of perpetual becoming" (*Making of Exile* 8), what was characteristic of certain moments of transition in the history of Persian literature (i.e., shuttling between different literary systems) has now become the mainstay of literature of exile and immigration:

[E]xile is a process of perpetual becoming, involving separation from home, a period of liminality and in-betweenness that can be temporary or permanent, and incorporation into dominant host society that can be partial or complete. It must be emphasized that the three phases of exile are not just consecutive but also simultaneous—so that a unified or stable culture seldom results. (Naficy, *Making of Exile* 8–9)

As the next section illustrates more fully, it is ironic that a literary system that sought out the alien and the distant to remake itself, particularly in the modern era, should have spawned a literary corpus fixated on alterity.

LITERARY-CULTURAL HISTORY

The literary production of immigrant Iranian writers in the United States can best be appreciated against the background of the history of Persian literature, since the processes of linguistic change and cultural adaptation that so mark the experience of the contemporary immigrant writers have been integral to the history of this literature from its earliest days to the present. In the following historical sketch, I first provide an overview of those patterns and dynamics.

Of the pre-Islamic Iranian (up to A.D. 652) literary culture, very little has been preserved. In spite of the scarcity of Old and Middle Persian sources, to be distinguished from Persian, the language now spoken in Iran, scholars have been able to trace the development of the "new" Persian epic (i.e., of the Islamic era) to its ancient Iranian roots. Some inscriptions, tracts, and epistles in Middle Persian provide us with a glimpse of what was committed to writing in the pre-Islamic era. However, as Ehsan Yarshater points out in his survey of the development of Iranian literatures, the attempt to reconstruct a history of Old and Middle Persian literatures is impeded by the fact that "the secular literature of Iran prior to Islam was essentially oral" (10).

After the introduction of Islam in the seventh century, the Arabic alphabet replaced Middle Persian script, and Arabic words were adopted, while the language itself evolved along the patterns of its Indo-European roots. Arabic, as the lingua franca of the Islamic world, also exerted literary influences: "It was now fashionable to write poetry, like the Arabs, in qualitative meters . . . and the adaptable Persians proceeded to apply the rules of Arabic prosody to their favorite meters, making them even more strictly quantitative than Arabic ones" (Yarshater 13). This particular adaptability is crucial to an understanding of the course of evolution of Persian literature. Itself subjected to the hegemony of Arabic, Persian soon reached out to neighboring states (what is now part of

Afghanistan, the Central Asian Republics, and, eventually, India) and established a new Persian literary hegemony that was to last, at least in Moghul India, well into the nineteenth century.

Poetry is the most prominent genre of this period of Persian literary history. While epic poetry provided the initial motivating force for the revival of Persian letters, particularly in Ferdowsi's eleventh-century *Shah Nameh* (Book of the Kings), various forms of lyric poetry gradually gained dominance.

The predominance of poetic forms was to hold sway until the end of the classical period and the beginning of the modern period, the two phases into which Persian literature of the Islamic era is divided. The poets most often associated with the golden days of classical Persian poetry are Nezami (d. 1209), Attar (d. 1220), Rumi (d. 1273), Sa'di (d. 1292), and Hafez (d. 1390). Although the poetic genres inaugurated and embellished by these poets continued to be in circulation, by the fifteenth century they had entered a period of decline. In Yarshater's words, "The culmination of Persian lyric poetry was reached about a hundred years after Sa'di with Hafez" (27).

Given that the modern period in Persian literature does not begin until the twentieth century, it is imperative to account for the apparent halt to which Persian poetry seems to have come at such an early phase. This is far from saying that Persian poetry ceased to dominate Iranian literary tastes. On the contrary, conventionality and adherence to past models gave later poetry the reputation of being derivative. Classical Persian poetry was, by and large, associated with the court and the patronage of the ruling princes. This close alliance between the poet and the court served a distinct social purpose: "In keeping with the ethical dimension of the court poet's function, panegyric preoccupations were never far removed from didactic ones" (Meisami 11). This may, at least partially, explain the apparent stagnation in the development of Persian poetry; the social and ethical function of the poet inevitably changed with the times so that the poet's position in the life of the court was diminished.

Prose forms, except in satirical writings (see Javadi), never gained the same prominence as poetry. Yet prose was not exempt from ornamentation. As Hamid Dabashi demonstrates, not until translations of European languages began to appear in Persian in the nineteenth century did the highly ornate "Indian style" (*Sabk-e Hendi*) both in poetry and prose lose its appeal: "The translation movement was crucial in the gradual formation of a simple and deliberately democratic language" (165). Equally significant were the introduction of journalism, which employed prose as a means of reaching out to a wider public, and the establishment of new schools modeled on European institutions (for instance, Dar ol-Fonun, established in Tehran in 1851). In these schools "under the supervision of European teachers, a great number of celebrated political leaders of the forthcoming years were trained, and many technical and scientific books were either adapted or directly translated from European sources" (Kamshad 12).

Literary translation exerted the greatest influence on Persian prose. This is reflected in the immense popularity of the Persian translation of the Englishman James Morier's *The Adventures of Hajji Baba of Ispahan*—cited as one of the earliest examples of accessible Persian prose. Not only were Western literary texts translated into Persian, but they also provided models upon which Iranians could draw for their own creations. As we have seen in the example of the translation of Morier's novel, the genre of the travelogue proved most suitable to the sensibilities of Iranian readers. *Siyahat Nameh-e Ibrahim Beg* (The Travel Diary of Ibrahim Beg), which appeared in three volumes in the first decade of the twentieth century, is the most instrumental example of travel writing in Persian. It, too, marks a "break away from the old traditional style of ornate composition" (Kamshad 20).

If linguistic innovation was to become the hallmark of modern Persian prose fiction, equally significant was the fact that much of early modern literary production first appeared outside Iran or was written by Iranians living abroad. The three volumes of the *Siyahat Nameh* appeared in Cairo, Calcutta, and Istanbul and were imported into Iran. Mohammad Ali Jamalzadeh's *Yeki Bud Yeki Nabud* (Once upon a Time), yet another foundational text of modern Persian literature published in 1921, was composed outside Iran. In fact, after the age of twelve, Jamalzadeh left Iran for Egypt, Lebanon, France, and Switzerland. This absence from Iran made Jamalzadeh particularly conscious of the need to overcome his linguistic handicap. He set out to relearn Persian in a painstaking process he describes in his 1954 autobiography:

My knowledge of the written language was slight and I used to write Persian with utmost difficulty. When, still very young, I left Iran, Persian was not properly taught in Iranian schools and my Persian was extremely weak. But as I was passionately fond of it, I used to read and practice a great deal. Gradually writing became easier for me and I was deeply imbued with a zest for writing things which has never flagged in me. In other words, without any preliminary, without any teacher or lesson, I learnt Persian entirely on my own by whatever means came to hand. Still, day and night, I continue to be engrossed in this process: from every book or article I read in Persian, pencil in hand, I extract notes. I note idioms, expressions and even words and phrases, which I generally con afterwards. (quoted in Kamshad 93–94)

What needs to be stressed in this candid personal account is the defamiliarizing process that returned Jamalzadeh to his mother tongue. Because of his distance from Persian, he was less restricted by the dominant norms of prose composition. That is to say, he re-created for himself and his avid readers in Iran a new literary idiom derived from spoken Persian. In "New Lamps for Old," Donné Raffat argues that the renaissance in Persian letters was largely due to this type of displacement, or, to borrow Gilles Deleuze and Félix Guattari's term, deterritorialization. Far from suggesting that all modern Iranian writers found it necessary to leave Iran to find a new medium of expression, Raffat draws upon figures like Jamalzadeh and Bozorg Alavi, who has, since 1953, lived in what used to be East Berlin, to underline the extent to which literary Persian thrived in settings of exile. Furthermore, by stressing the fact that many modern Iranian writers were also literary translators, Raffat seizes on another crucial factor in the evolution of modern Persian prose fiction: "[T]he secondary task of the Iranian writer has been to translate. In some cases . . . , he [sic] is as much a translator as an author. Iranian letters in the twentieth century, in this respect, is singularly fortunate in having as its translators its major authors" (14). In other words, translation, metaphorical and physical, has been the conduit to linguistic and literary transformation in the modern era—the very elements that we will revisit in the context of Iranian immigrant literature.

Although translation facilitated the reshaping of the Persian literary system, once a popular medium of expression had been forged, its prominence and influence were gradually replaced by political and ideological concerns.

Reacting against what they believed to have been an excessive preoccupation with aesthetics in classical Persian poetry, a significant group of twentieth-century Iranian poets and writers declared themselves committed to issues of social and political relevance. As underlined by Hamid Dabashi, this engagé literature took on the ambitious project of revolutionizing not only literature but also society: "This literature, like the ideology behind it, was committed to reconstituting the culture, restructuring the society, and reforming the psyche. The guiding factor in this grand effort was the revolutionary ideal to which the ideologues and the literati subscribed" (Dabashi 173).

Although another group of writers, referred to by their rivals as *kohneh parastan* (worshipers of the old), refused to partake of this notion of commitment, the sociopolitical fervor of the *nevisandegan-e ejtema'i* (socially committed writers) was to hold sway until after the 1979 revolution. Their political commitment compelled these writers to seek their characters and settings from amid the very social groups whose cause they believed themselves to be promoting. The drastic transformations that had already opened up the possibility of using spoken and colloquial Persian in literature created an even more conducive environment for the literary expression of the 1960s and 1970s. In the domain of poetry, there was a parallel break with tradition whose effects Thomas Ricks describes: "By the 1950s and 1960s, the classicists turned with vengeance upon engagé writers, such as Nima Yushij and the 'New Poetry' movement" (xxi). The confrontation between the old and the new poetic traditions served to reinforce the new wave poets' commitment to their vision.

The decades following the revolution have seen radical revisions of this type of political commitment. In "Poetry against Piety," Ahmad Karimi-Hakkak demonstrates that the "oppositional categories of a simple discourse of antagonism" (525) have lost their force in the post-revolutionary sociocultural context. The transformation necessitated by the perceived failure of the artists to communicate their social objectives has occasioned a drastic reexamination of the very foundations of the literary discourse of the past:

In the case of the post-revolutionary literature of Iran, instances of efforts aimed at changing the bases of literary signification disguised as literary and social criticism, "true" historical accounts and rereadings of past cultural artifacts—particularly perennial myths perceived as possessing continued social significance—bespeak a wide variety of purposes and reveal an impressive diversity. (Karimi-Hakkak, "Poetry against Piety" 525)

These revisions might well be responsible for the flourishing of literary genres such as the magical realist novel and post-modernist prose, which lend themselves to multiple interpretations or, at least, do not espouse a singular view of "social reality." In another departure from the past, an ever-increasing number of women are joining the Iranian literary establishment (Milani 177–227). As a result, issues of gender and sexuality are becoming part of the post-revolutionary literary fabric. In women's writing, too, there is evidence of experiments with new modes of literary expression. Notwithstanding the censorship laws and the strictures imposed on the appearance of women actors and their mode of acting, this same trend can be observed in post-revolutionary Iranian cinema (Naficy, "Women and Semiotics of Veiling" 64).

Most noteworthy among the changes in post-revolutionary Iranian discourse is a new preoccupation with the linguistic, ethnic, and cultural diversities of Iran. While in pre-revolutionary times, few writers experimented with the use of regional dialects in their fiction, literary and artistic production in Iran today reveals a marked interest in ethnic identities. This development is part and parcel of the move away from the prevailing nationalist and unifying agenda of the engagé writers of the two decades preceding the revolution. It may be said that post-revolutionary Iranian is no longer suffering from Westitis, a term coined by the writer and social activist Jalal Al-e Ahmad in the early 1960s to encompass Iran's intellectual dependence on the West. Seen within the larger framework of the history of Iranian literatures, the new direction in Persian letters would seem to be in keeping with the spirit of innovation and adaptation that has always fostered literary creativity in Iran. Yet, in this most recent phase, there are indications that the clearly demarcated binaries of self/other and native/foreign have given way to a fascination with inner diversity.

DOMINANT CONCERNS

As the preceding overview has demonstrated, displacement and exile are not recent phenomena in Persian literary history. In fact, Persian literati living outside the borders of their country have often been the most prominent agents of renewal and change in Persian letters. It must be borne in mind, however, that such figures also saw themselves as inextricably bound to their native language and its literary manifestations. Immigration and exile, particularly in the last two decades, have redefined the nature of this relationship: not all Iranian writers abroad cling to notions of linguistic and cultural authenticity. Some have opted to write in English rather than Persian. This trend has problematized the classification of the works of Iranian writers. As I have argued elsewhere, those who continue to write in Persian and seek to publish their works primarily in Iran are subject to the psychological mechanisms of exile (Rahimieh, "Quince-Orange Tree" 39). As Bozorg Alavi indicates in a 1989 interview, for these writers the frame of reference has never shifted from the Iranian scene:

As I have gathered, there are currently a few hundred Iranian poets and writers in North America and Europe. They write poems and short stories, some of them excellent. I would not dare claim that the work of a given writer living in Iran, which I have also enjoyed, is better than that produced in exile. But I am certain that if some of these exiles lived in Iran, they would have markedly better productions. (quoted in Rahimieh, "Quince-Orange Tree" 39)

The model against which Alavi assesses the work of Iranian writers does not allow any space for the immigrant Iranian writers precisely because, like many literati of his generation, Alavi understands identity in terms of language and national borders. Yet, by choosing to write in English or translating their works from Persian into English, the new generation of immigrant writers appears to be calling for a more complex and intercultural view of identity. Donné Raffat, who grew up in the United States and published his first novel, *The Caspian Circle,* in English, offers this rebuttal to critics who begrudge him his self-proclaimed status as an Iranian writer:

[A]t the moment of the writing, I was Iranian to my core and marrow; for what I had, in lieu of language, was the vision: more than that, the experience of the vision. From nowhere else could that vision have come: this was the country's gift to me. Not the language—which I was fated to lose—but the vision. ("Nom de Plume" 59)

It is worth noting that Raffat himself is the English translator of Alavi's *Prison Papers.* For Raffat, the process of learning about Alavi, meeting him in person in East Berlin, interviewing him, and commenting on his works becomes a means of accessing his own childhood in Iran:

Alavi was the Iranian writer I was most anxious to meet: the one person alive whose works I could actually see myself sitting down and translating. And identity was a part of the attraction. I, too, was Iranian, by birth and parentage, although I had come to America at the age of five and was a citizen. What Alavi wrote about took me back to a period of time which, to me, was almost primordial: that period around my birth and just prior to my coming to America. . . . The rather rosy world of my recollection overlapped in large part with the rather grim one of his experience. Somehow the two merged, and more than any other writer he had told me about what those missing years had been about. (Raffat, *Prison Papers* 2–3)

What Raffat wants to translate, to bring across, of Alavi's writing is that which sharpens the vision that shapes for him an identity as a writer on the border of two cultures. The way in which the experiences of these two writers converge, in their attempt to come to terms with what it means to live as an Iranian abroad, and eventually diverge on this very point of self-positioning encapsulates the modalities of exile and immigration. While Alavi's generation, inside and outside Iran, avidly read, translated, and borrowed from the work of European and American writers to launch a new phase of Persian writing, Raffat's generation of immigrant writers carries from Persian into English experiences and visions whose focus is no longer exclusively trained on the construction of a cohesive national identity.

For Taghi Modarressi, who has lived in the United States since the late 1950s, the problems of identity continue to revolve around questions of language and culture. He still writes in Persian but translates his works into English. The two novels he has published in the United States, after years of silence, *The Book of Absent People* and *The Pilgrim's Rules of Etiquette,* have appeared simultaneously in Persian and English. But, unlike Alavi, Modarressi welcomes the new voice he has acquired as an immigrant writer:

The new language of any immigrant writer is obviously accented and, at least initially, inarticulate. I consider this "artifact" language expressive in its own right. Writing with an accented voice is organic to the mind of the immigrant writer. It is not something one can invent. It is frequently buried beneath personal inhibitions and doubts. The accented voice is loaded with hidden messages from our cultural heritage, messages that often reach beyond the capacity of the ordinary words of any language. ("Writing with an Accent" 9)

Modarressi's notion of the inner voice of the immigrant writer transcends the binaries of the kind Karimi-Hakkak outlined in his analysis of pre- and post-revolutionary Persian literature, as well as the simple duality of inside and outside, native and foreign; this new voice and vision draw for inspiration upon those very unresolved paradoxes of cross-cultural encounters:

On the plane from Iran to the U.S., a strange idea kept occurring to me. I thought that most immigrants, regardless of the familial, social, or political circumstances causing their exile, have been cultural refugees all their lives. They leave because they feel like outsiders. Perhaps it is their personal language that can build a bridge between what is familiar and what is strange. They may then find it possible to generate new and revealing paradoxes. Here we have our juxtapositions and our transformation—the graceful and the awkward, the beautiful and the ugly, sitting side by side in perpetual metamorphosis of one into the other. It is like the Hunchback of Notre Dame trying to be Prince Charming for strangers. ("Writing with an Accent" 9)

The way in which Modarressi conveys this "perpetual metamorphosis," or the constant linguistic and cultural juxtaposition, in his fiction is to leave traces of the untranslatable in his English. Through literal translations of Persian idioms, Modarressi demands that his readers partake of his voice and vision. For instance, in *The Book of Absent People,* we read: ''Even now, after some thirty-odd years, they still talked about it as though it had happened yesterday. They had never given any thought to the children of Homayundokht, God forgive her soul, and used to melodramatically *describe the onion and garlic of that story* in front of my Khan Brother Zia and my sister Iran as though those two were deaf and couldn't hear them'' (15; emphasis mine). The context clarifies that ''describing the onion and garlic of the story'' means to describe in great detail, as does this exclamation: ''He threw his hands up, but began to cough. 'Ohoo, ohoo, what can I do? I don't have radar to figure out who's running things, who's alive and who's dead. I'm not the top of the onion, nor am I the roots. I'm only an old agent of the Security Organization, Agha-jun' '' (*Absent People* 55).

This type of cross-linguistic experimentation is the expression of a particular cross-cultural graft whose paradoxical status is echoed in the words of the protagonist of *The Pilgrim's Rules of Etiquette,* who offers this response to an American colleague's attempts at persuading him to stay in the United States:

''To be sure there are common features between the Easterner and the Westerner, and in certain respects each can benefit the other. But in the end their encounters remain barren. It's like the quince-orange tree, which is a graft between a quince and an orange, or the mule, which is the result of horse-and-donkey copulation. Of course each has some use. But they themselves are barren and fruitless.'' (8)

Modarressi's linguistic counterpart to the quince-orange tree has its own limitations. Because his language is so dependent on context, its function does not extend beyond prose forms. Although poetry is not the most common medium employed by Iranian-American literati, in its limited manifestation, it is not cast into a new hybrid language.

Bahman Sholevar is the only Iranian immigrant writer who has turned to poetry. True to his literary heritage, Sholevar began his career in Iran as a translator. Among his translations from English into Persian are William Faulkner's *The Sound and the Fury* and T. S. Eliot's *The Waste Land.* Perhaps his craft as a translator has made him conscious of the need for smooth transitions from one language into another. Both in his prose fiction and in his poetry, Sholevar adheres to idiomatic American English. The clarity of his language and style is nevertheless pitted against expressions of displacement. In ''Night Traveler,'' a poem from his collection *Rooted in Volcanic Ashes,* we read that his ''rest'' will occur only once he has ''shot past [his] beginning'' (30). A similar preoccupation is betrayed in *Making Connection: Poems of Exile.* The elusive connection to which Sholevar's literary works allude is reinforced in the range of professional activities he has undertaken since his immigration to the United States in 1967; in addition to being a translator and literary critic, he has worked as a physician, psychiatrist, political activist, television commentator, and professor of literature. His poetry and prose bear witness to his intellectual and cultural wanderlust. Writing from the position of someone who has already experienced a cultural uprooting, Sholevar goes beyond his own specific context. He draws as much on his own literary heritage as on that of his adopted homeland. This is a rather uncommon phenomenon in Iranian immigrants' writing.

For writers like Manoucher Parvin, Majid Amini, Hooman Majd, Javad Mohsenian, and Barry Chubin, the frame of reference has never shifted from Iran, or at least its imaginative geography, which, in Hamid Naficy's words, they have made into a fetish object (*Making of Exile* 125–165). Intertwining elements of Iranian history, confrontation between Iranian and American cultures, and perceptions and stereotypes of Iran, they write, whether in works of adventure or political intrigue (*Cry for My Revolution, Iran,* and *The Feet of a Snake*), romance (*Persian Moonlight*), or psychological portraits (*Dreams of a Native Son*), with an immediacy that sometimes borders on the autobiography. I do not wish to imply that these writers' fiction is to be equated with autobiography, but rather that the voice and the tone they employ are imbued with the type of claims to authority and authenticity we would otherwise find in an autobiographical account or a political tract.

In the writing of two Iranian-American women, Nahid Rachlin and Gina Barkhordar Nahai, a similar personal investment takes on broader fictional dimensions. This provides Rachlin and Barkhordar Nahai with a larger canvas on which to experiment with the problems of voice, authenticity, and identity.

Although Rachlin's protagonists, especially in her two novels, *Foreigner* and *Married to a Stranger,* are plagued by the illusion and reality of cultural borders, they demonstrate a desire to transgress and to problematize those real and imaginary frontiers delimiting their existence. In *Foreigner,* for instance, when the protagonist's sense of alienation compels her to return to Iran, after years of living in the United States, she realizes that she has always played the image of Iran against that of the United States only to now be confronted with her own duplicity:

I tried, futilely, to recall the sense of urgency I had about the trip. The plan had begun to form in my mind one late afternoon as I stood behind the picture window of our living room. . . . How different this was from that other world, I had thought. (37)

The position the protagonist, Feri, takes up behind the window is emblematic of her cross-cultural existence. She sees herself through narrow fields of vision of her own making. When her experiences in the two "worlds" do not coincide with her construct, she flees one for the other. Her return to Iran raises more questions than it answers; there is not now, and there never was, a secure and centered world in which she can take refuge. By the end of the novel, Feri has discovered a certain temporary peace: "I turned over and looked at my mother.

Her face was serene in her sleep. I knew soon I would have to make decisions, think beyond the day, but for the moment I lay there. Tranquil'' (192). But the precariousness of this state of calm no longer forces her into flight. The foreigner she has made herself in the two worlds of her imagination is now conscious of what Julia Kristeva has called "radical strangeness": "A paradoxical community is emerging, made up of foreigners who are reconciled with themselves to the extent that they recognize themselves as foreigners" (195). In other words, Feri's anxieties about her status as a foreigner are now transformed into a source of strength. Recognizing the stranger within frees her from the illusory constructs of identity that had dominated her past. Her sense of minority ultimately becomes the source of her liberation. In an interesting turn away from the rhetoric of national identity and commitment to the cause of a nation, Rachlin, like her post-revolutionary Iranian counterparts, breaks with the restraints of a fixed national identity.

In Gina Barkhordar Nahai's novel, *Cry of the Peacock,* the experience of marginality and its potential for empowerment are even more concretely underlined. The novel chronicles the life of Iranian Jews from 1796 to 1982 and, as pointed out by the author in the Acknowledgments, mingles the personal, the historical, and the fictional:

I began with my own memories, and then asked questions. I spoke to hundreds of Iranians, Jews and Muslims, old and young. Through years of interviews and volumes of books, I became familiar with a history—albeit recent—that had been buried by the last of the "ghetto generation" as if to wipe away three thousand years of suffering. (341)

The Prologue of *Cry of the Peacock* begins with the character of Peacock, who has been imprisoned by the Iranian revolutionaries, and the narrator returns to her in the Epilogue. The novel itself begins with the life history of Peacock's great-grandmother, Esther the Soothsayer, and traces that of the next generations of the family.

This family history allows Barkhordar Nahai to manipulate historical discourse and to present female characters who are not imprisoned in time. At the opening of the novel, for instance, we encounter Esther the Soothsayer, who has the unique gift of reading into the past as well as the future: "She knew how to read people's eyes, walk into their dreams when they were asleep, and probe their minds" (10). If at first this knowledge does not rescue Esther from her subordination and loneliness, eventually she takes control of her own destiny and, disguised as a Muslim, goes to another city. Even here, a rabbi's refusal to allow her into the Jewish ghetto does not discourage her. She follows through with her convictions and, using her secret talents, finds an appropriate mate.

Esther is not allowed to enjoy her newfound independence, as she is finally humiliated and driven away from the ghetto. Yet her rejection at the hands of her community only strengthens her powers. Not only does she continue to keep an astute eye on her offspring through vast expanses of time and space, but she also gains a reputation as a reliable soothsayer among the ruling family. Generation after generation of her children are guided by her spirit. In this sense, her presence and role defy the limitations of history.

Following Esther's footsteps, her great-granddaughter Peacock also refuses to give in to the dictates of time. The Prologue, the scene in which she is being questioned by the Iranian revolutionary guards, gives us a glimpse of the same resilient spirit she has inherited from her great-grandmother:

"So how old were you?" . . .

"I am a hundred and sixteen years old," she said, "and still, I intend to live." (5)

Only in the Epilogue do we see the outcome of this encounter. Like Esther the Soothsayer, Peacock cannot be subjected to a permanent imprisonment. This is not to say that Esther, Peacock, or the other women characters have complete control of their destinies, but rather that they enter into battle with the currents of history. This determination and passion for life are epitomized in the defiant cries Mad Marushka utters as Ezraeel the Avenger shoots her in the ankles: " 'The hell with you!' Marushka screamed as she fell in pain. 'I lived' " (141). The women's stubborn will to survive enables them to claim their rightful place in their family's chronicles. At every turn, they make sure that they have not become the forgotten subjects of a history that would perhaps want to capitalize upon their double marginality as women and Jews.

Barkhordar Nahai's own family history has fed her imagination. When she recalls her childhood, she is drawn to a grandfather whose single passion in his later years was to have male grandchildren. Barkhordar Nahai's retelling of her grandfather's fate is imbued with a terrible historical irony: "My parents had three girls. Agha would have no heirs" (339). Interestingly, the same utterance that appears to cut her off from the patriarchal figure of authority underlines the significant position she ended up occupying in spite of her gender. It is she, the unacknowledged heir, who reanimates her family's history and, thus, reestablishes the ambiguous coexistence of the patriarchal and the matriarchal.

On another level, Barkhordar Nahai uses the historical framework as a means of entering into a dialogue with her past as well as her present. This is not an escape into the distant and idealized past but rather a recognition that physical displacement does not equal a loss of cultural location.

In Gina Barkhordar Nahai, as in Taghi Modarressi, Nahid Rachlin, Donné Raffat, and Bahman Sholevar, we find a movement away from territoriality toward a radical and liberating dislocation and, to once again borrow from Deleuze and Guattari, ultimate reterritorialization. No longer exclusively beholden to the poetics of nostalgia, they revel in their position as outsider and use it as a first step toward critiquing the discourse and politics of home and belonging. They disrupt the binaries of "home" and "exile" in an attempt to translate themselves metaphorically. For these immigrant writers, the reversal and interplay of those dichotomies that contributed to a redefinition of modern Persian letters have become a vehicle to a transformation with interesting echoes of the changes taking place inside Iranian borders: "The two settings, Iran and Iranian habitations abroad, mirror each other at acute or oblique angles, mutually affecting each other's representations, setting off mutating variations" (Fischer and Abedi 255). The conditions that have created this synchronicity are not exactly the same in the two settings. Writers living in Iran respond to linguistic, social, political, and cultural challenges that the immigrant writers, who are themselves subject to other forces of contestation, experience only secondhand. Even for those immigrant writers who cling to memories of the past and relive them in their obsessive repetitions, simple oppositions of the past can remain unchallenged only at the risk of producing works that reach neither the immigrant nor the "home" communities. The similarities between patterns of transformation in the Iranian literary scene and the immigrant setting could stem from the fact that writers inside and outside Iran have inherited the same mechanisms for coming to terms with moments of transition and rupture. Or, returning once again to Sholevar's *Dead Reckoning*, Iranian immigrant writers may have brought to America only what they were, both literary innovators and preservers of established tradition.

SELECTED PRIMARY BIBLIOGRAPHY

Amini, Majid. *Dreams of a Native Son*. Los Angeles: Afsaneh, 1986.

———. *The Howling Leopard*. Los Angeles: Afsaneh, 1986.

———. *The Sunset Drifters*. Los Angeles: Afsaneh, 1989.

Barkhordar Nahai, Gina. *Cry of the Peacock*. New York: Crown, 1991.

Chubin, Barry. *The Feet of a Snake*. New York: Tom Doherty, 1984.

Majd, Hooman. "Nobody Leaves a Winning Table." *Border Lines: Stories of Exile and Home*. Ed. Kate Pullinger. London: Serpent's Tail, 1993.

Modarressi, Taghi. *The Book of Absent People*. New York: Doubleday, 1986.

———. *The Pilgrim's Rules of Etiquette*. New York: Doubleday, 1989.

Mohsenian, Javad. *Persian Moonlight*. Durham, NC: Moore, 1981.

Parvin, Manoucher. *Cry for My Revolution, Iran*. Costa Mesa, CA: Mazda, 1987.

Rachlin, Nahid. *Foreigner*. New York: Norton, 1978.

———. *Married to a Stranger*. New York: E. P. Dutton, 1983.

———. *Veils: Short Stories*. New York: City Lights, 1992.

Raffat, Donné. *The Caspian Circle*. Boston: Houghton Mifflin, 1978.

Sholevar, Bahman. *The Angel with Bush-Baby Eyes and the Love Song of Achilles*. Philadelphia: Concourse, 1982.

———. *Dead Reckoning*. Philadelphia: Concourse, 1992.

———. "Dead Reckoning: Excerpt from Part Two." *North Atlantic Review* 4 (1992): 20–32.

———. *Making Connection: Poems of Exile*. Philadelphia: Concourse, 1979.

———. *The Night's Journey and the Coming of the Messiah*. Bibliotheca Persica: Modern Persian Literature Series, 7. Philadelphia: Concourse, 1984.

————. *Odysseus' Homecoming and the New Adam: Poems of Renewal.* Philadelphia: Concourse, 1982.

————. *Rooted in Volcanic Ashes: Collection of Poems.* Philadelphia: Concourse, 1987.

SELECTED SECONDARY BIBLIOGRAPHY

Al-e Ahmad, Jalal. *Plagued by the West.* Trans. Paul Sprachman. Bibliotheca Persica: Modern Literature Series, 4. Delmar, NY: Caravan, 1982.

Beard, Michael, and Hasan Javadi. "Iranian Writers Abroad: Survey and Elegy." *World Literature Today* 60.2 (1986): 257–261.

Beeman, William O. *Language, Status, and Power in Iran.* Bloomington: Indiana University Press, 1986.

Dabashi, Hamid. "The Poetics of Politics: Commitment in Modern Persian Literature." *Iranian Studies: Journal of the Society for Iranian Cultural and Social Studies* 18.2–4: (1985): 147–188.

Deleuze, Gilles, and Félix Guattari. *Kafka: Toward a Minor Literature.* Trans. Dana Polan. Theory and History of Literature, 30. Minneapolis: Minnesota University Press, 1986.

Fischer, Michael M. J., and Mehdi Abedi. *Debating Muslims: Cultural Dialogues in Postmodernity and Tradition.* Madison: University of Wisconsin Press, 1990.

Javadi, Hasan. *Satire in Persian Literature.* Cranbury, NJ: Associated University Presses, 1988.

Kamshad. Hassan. *Modern Persian Prose Literature.* Cambridge: Cambridge University Press, 1966.

Karimi-Hakkak, Ahmad. "Poetry against Piety: The Literary Response to the Iranian Revolution." *World Literature Today* 60.2 (1986): 251–256.

————. "Revolutionary Posturing: Iranian Writers and the Iranian Revolution of 1979." *International Journal of Middle East Studies* 23.4 (1991): 507–531.

Kristeva, Julia. *Strangers to Ourselves.* Trans. Leon S. Roudiez. New York: Columbia University Press, 1991.

Meisami, Julie Scott. *Medieval Persian Court Poetry.* Princeton: Princeton University Press, 1987.

Milani, Farzaneh. *Veils and Words: The Emerging Voices of Iranian Women Writers.* Syracuse: Syracuse University Press, 1992.

Modarressi, Taghi. "Salman Rushdie and the Immigrant's Dilemma." *Washington Post Book World,* March 12, 1989: 7.

————. "Writing with An Accent." *Chanteh* 1 (Fall 1992): 7–9.

Naficy, Hamid. *The Making of Exile Cultures: Iranian Television in Los Angeles.* Minneapolis: University of Minnesota Press, 1993.

————. "The Poetics and Practice of Iranian Nostalgia in Exile." *Diaspora* 1.3 (1991): 285–302.

————. "Women and the Semiotics of Veiling and Vision in Iranian Cinema." *American Journal of Semiotics* 8.1–2 (1991): 47–64.

Raffat, Donné. "Iran: A Culture in Exile." *Confrontation* 27–28 (1984): 28–31.

————. "New Lamps for Old: Or the Western Influence on Iranian Fiction during the Pahlavi Period (1925–1979)." *North Atlantic Review* 2 (1992): 12–19.

————. *The Prison Papers of Bozorg Alavi: A Literary Odyssey.* Syracuse: Syracuse University Press, 1985.

————. "When a Nom de Plume is Not a Pseudonym: Or, Writing in English What Oft Was Thought But Ne'er So Well Expressed in Persian." *Contention* 1 (1991): 51–59.

Rahimieh, Nasrin. "The Enigma of Persian Modernism." *New Comparison* 13 (1992): 39–45.

————. "The Quince-Orange Tree, Or Iranian Writers in Exile." *World Literature Today* 66.1 (1992): 39–42.

————. "Scheherazade in Exile: Iranian Women Writers Abroad." *North Atlantic Review* 4 (1992): 36–47.

Ricks, Thomas M., ed. *Critical Perspectives on Modern Persian Literature.* Washington, DC: Three Continents Press, 1984.

Yarshater, Ehsan, ed. *Persian Literature.* New York: Bibliotheca Persica, Persian Heritage Foundation, 1988.

7

Japanese-American Literature

Benzi Zhang

INTRODUCTION

"Immigrant," a term used frequently in the past to refer to a person who, passing a geopolitical border, leaves one society for another, has much more complex meanings today. In a sense, the crossing of a geopolitical border is the least important aspect of immigrant experience in terms of the long process of adjusting to the new society; immigration, as an important part of "American experience," is a sociocultural practice that thrives on a process of constant resignification of the established assumptions and meanings of ethnic/national identity. Today, the phrase "immigrant literature" refers not only to the writing by the actual immigrants who moved from one country to another but also to the texts of the descendants of the early immigrants. Immigrant literature—literature both by and about immigrants—concerns not only the movement across the borders of a country but also the experience of traversing the boundaries and barriers of space, time, race, culture, language, history, and politics and the complexities and ambivalences associated with defining an (im)migrant identity between and beyond boundaries.

Japanese-American immigrant literature, with its strong ethnic characteristics, chronicles a perpetual process of interaction and negotiation between different cultural traditions. Despite their shared immigrant heritage, Japanese-American writers exhibit differing attitudes toward their immigrant experience: some favor mutual assimilation and acculturation, while others advocate cultural distinctness and separateness. The "assimilation-separation dilemma" and the problem of immigrant identity in relation to their old and new "homes" are important issues to Japanese-American writers. In previous years, Japanese immigrant writers expressed either an intense desire to keep their distinct culture in North America or a strong nostalgia of their "homeland." Today's writers of Japanese descent are concerned more with recovering or constructing an identity in North American society; their increased awareness of the value of their immigrant heritage and ethnic background has given rise to diverse expressions of a wide range of experiences and concerns. Recent Japanese-American authors, in addition to asserting ethnic community distinctness, also emphasize their individuality both within the community and at the boundary that separates their community from the society at large.

The effort to adjust to two cultural backgrounds is related to the need to redefine the identity of the younger generations of Japanese immigrants, who are actually American-born but inherit an immigrant culture. To reflect the different responses by the four generations to the collision and interaction of two unlike cultures, the Japanese-American community designates the generational distinction by separate nomenclatures—issei, nisei, sansei, and yonsei—to mean the first, second, third, and fourth generation of Japanese Americans. Like other native-born Asians, Japanese-American writers of the younger generations are not very familiar with the old, distant land from which their parents or grandparents came. But this distant land is related to every aspect of their heritage and identity. The need to understand and appreciate their cultural heritage has prompted the younger writers to rediscover the immigrant elderly, whom they portray with passion and relate to their own experience of crossing the boundary separating their ethnic community from the dominant society. Movement across social and ethnic boundaries compels the writers to determine where they stand in relation to their immigrant tradition. Caught between cultures, Japanese-American writers, in general, try to represent the survival and growth of individuals who, depending on effective self-definition, gain strength from their (im)migrant experience.

As Elaine H. Kim observes, "Japanese Americans have written more prolifically in English than any other Asian American group" (73). Most Japanese-American writers are English-speaking, native-born nisei, sansei, and yonsei. It is something of a misnomer to call their writings "immigrant literature," for the nisei, sansei, and yonsei writers are actually America-born. In their daily lives, however, these writers frequently migrate between the dominant European-American culture of the United States and the culture brought here by their parents and grandparents from across the Pacific Ocean. In their attempt to express the richness and complexity of their own (im)migrant experience, the writers of the younger generations dive deep into their elders' and forebearers' immigrant experience. Although their writing shows a variety of attitudes toward their cultural roots—some assert their distinct cultural tradition; some attempt to minimize ethnic difference for acculturation; and some try to create a new cultural identity that takes elements from both traditions but belongs to neither—these writers, taken together, represent an increasing desire among Japanese

Americans to understand and to express themselves authentically in a new immigrant discourse. This chapter examines the authorial and critical production of Japanese-American (im)migrant literature as the nature and method of its representation unfold in increasing complexity.

LITERARY-CULTURAL HISTORY

The first flow of Japanese immigrants to Hawai'i and the West Coast of the United States increased in the four decades from 1885 to 1924. During this period, the vast majority of Japanese immigrants to Hawai'i were contract laborers recruited by the plantations to fill unskilled jobs. The early immigration of Japanese to California began in the 1900s, about ten to twenty years after the initial immigration wave to Hawai'i. At that time, as Chinese labor was banned from immigration by the Chinese Exclusion Act of 1882, and white workers changed to nonfarming jobs, the rapidly developed agriculture in California demanded a large number of immigrant farmhands. The shortage of farm labor in California concurred with the difficult economic situation in Japan, which drove many Japanese farmworkers into the search for a better life in America. While most of the Japanese immigrants were farm laborers, a small portion of the immigrants from Japan to mainland America were students and merchants. The Immigration Exclusion Act of 1924, however, obstructed almost any immigration from Japan until after World War II. During the early years after the war, the main Japanese immigrants were the wives of American soldiers who had served in the occupation force. From 1952 to 1965, a very small quota for Japanese immigration was granted under the McCarran-Walter Immigration Bill. Only after the immigration reform of 1965, which allocated comparable quotas to both Eastern and Western Hemisphere countries, did the Japanese start to immigrate to the United States in notable numbers again.

In history, Japanese immigrants, like immigrants from other Asian countries, have tremendous difficulty in obtaining U.S. citizenship. The Naturalization Act of 1790 explicitly discriminated against Asian immigrants by establishing racial criteria restricting citizenship only to "free white persons." Japanese immigrants in particular, with their salient cultural tradition and small community, often found themselves in a vulnerable position vis-à-vis racial discrimination. For a long time, racial prejudice and unjust law in America treated Japanese immigrants as "unassimilable aliens" and proscribed them from becoming American citizens. Even though many Japanese immigrants had lived most of their lives in the United States, their applications for naturalization were more likely to be rejected than those of the immigrants from other countries. Moreover, Japanese immigrants and their children were often suspected of retaining their national allegiance without any justifiable reason. Even being born in the United States did not guarantee them to be accepted as "completely American." During World War II, about 110,000 Japanese Americans, including native-born nisei and sansei, were interned by the U.S. government in concentration camps. Born and raised in the United States, the nisei and sansei were fully American citizens, but the government chose to ignore their citizenship when it locked them up in the camps. The anti-Japanese prejudice remained rampant until the mid-1950s.

Like Chinese groups in the United States, the first generation of Japanese immigrants attempted to keep their own language, culture, and customs. However, unlike a Chinese community, where "Chinatown" is an obvious banner, Japanese Americans were scattered in cities and suburbs, where "Li'l Tokyo" or "Li'l Yokohama" is seldom used as a symbol for the Japanese community. In the geographic sense, the Japanese-American community was more diffused and dispersed than many other Asian groups; however, the Japanese had a long tradition of being a "culturally homogeneous people." Problems such as regional sectarian differences, which often impeded other Asian immigrant groups from developing an ethnic unity, hardly ever occur in the Japanese community. In the late 1960s, the Japanese-American community underwent significant change. Demographically, the immigration reform of 1965 brought new Japanese immigrants to the United States; socially, anti-Vietnam War activism and the black power struggle encouraged Japanese Americans to question the racial roles that were imposed upon them by the dominant society; psychologically, they began to explore the deep impact that the camp experience had made on their sense of identity; culturally, Japanese Americans and other Asian groups began to challenge and change the old myths and stereotypes of "yellow peril." As a result, Japanese-American writers became ever more eager to express their deep feelings and social concerns through literature. The themes that underscore Japanese-American literature are the search for identity and self-fulfillment, the soul-searching journey in history, the struggle for justice, the need for community and communication, and the healing power and therapeutic use of literature.

DOMINANT CONCERNS AND MAJOR AUTHORS

In the 1910s and 1920s, most Japanese-American writing, which was published in Japanese-American community newspapers and journals, had a very limited readership; however, some literary works, such as the early poems by Yone Noguchi and Sadakichi Hartman, received wide popularity. The Oriental flavor and "quaint" style of Noguchi's *From the Eastern Sea* (1910) and Hartman's *My Rubaiyat* (1913) and *Tanka and Haikai: Fourteen Japanese Rhythms* (1915) brought in a breath of fresh air, which had some influence on American modern poetry. Although these poets wrote from an Oriental perspective and in a typical Japanese style, they did not express the concerns of Japanese Americans, and, therefore, they are normally called "Americanized Japanese" rather than "Japanese Americans." The early writers did not have a clear definition of their own identity, and some of them expressed a confused attitude toward themselves. In 1925, Etsu Sugimoto published her first book, entitled *A Daughter of the Samurai* (1925). As a Western-educated daughter of Japanese aristocratic class, Sugimoto depicted a feeling of dislocation that was caused not by immigration to the United States but by the modernization in both Japan and America. While painting the old Japan with a rosy touch, she admitted that the passé glory of samurai and old Japan must be replaced by the new era of modernization represented by aggressive America. This book was well received by white readers, who "found favor with it as an apologia for Japan and a hymn of praise to America by an endearing Japanese who has 'no superiority complex, pleads no cause, asks no vexing questions' but instead 'tells a tale with delicacy and taste' " (Kim 27).

During the 1930s and 1940s, Japanese-American literary magazines were flourishing. Even in the most painful period of internment during World War II, Japanese-American literary journals persisted in the concentration camps. These years witnessed a significant literary and journalistic production and also the beginning of the process of identity search. The identity of Japanese Americans is explored in relation to the wartime treatment, to the immigrant heritage, and to the difference and affiliation between issei and nisei. The result of the camp experience helped Japanese-American writers crystallize their immigrant experience and develop a sense of confidence in writing. During this period, Japanese-American journalists such as Bill Hosokawa and Larry Tajiri received quick recognition, but most Japanese-American writers of fiction and poetry remained obscure. However, in the magazines and newspapers of their community, Japanese-American literary writers started their formative years, developing their own distinctive language, honing their writing skills, and searching for appropriate forms to express their unique experience. At this time, well-known writers such as Toshio Mori and Hisaye Yamamoto embarked on their writing career in the 1940s and helped the tradition of Japanese-American literature come into form.

Toshio Mori, generally regarded as "the first real Japanese-American writer" (quoted in Inada 1982, 255) was born into a Japanese immigrant family in California. Toshio Mori's collection of stories, *Yokohama, California,* after being delayed for several years, appeared in 1949. From the very beginning, Mori was conscious of the language problem as related to the confusing identity of Japanese immigrants and their children. Mori was described by some critics as a "natural-born writer," because he was one of the most original, innovative "stylists" of Japanese descent who tried to find or invent an immigrant language to express his experience. The influence of Sherwood Anderson and John Steinbeck on Mori's writing was obvious, but the influence was balanced by Mori's rebellious individuality. Mori's stories are Japanese Americans' vernacular tales of immigrant community. As he indicates years later in a self-reflexive piece, "Confessions of an Unknown Writer" in *The Chauvinist and Other Stories* (1979), his early stories were told from the perspective of a Japanese-American folk artist who, limited in terms of social possibilities, is obsessed with language practice.

In Mori's *Yokohama, California,* the social and linguistic dialogue, which arises from the language problem, has profound implications. As suggested by the story "Akira Yano," writing and living or linguistic and social discourses are interrelated. Rather than a straightforward presentation of his experience in California, Mori's stories demonstrate a self-reflexive use of language in which the meanings of the linguistic signs become metaphorical. In the story "The Woman Who Makes Swell Doughnuts," Mori tells a local tale about a Japanese immigrant woman who sells plain doughnuts. Mori's language is plain and simple, but at the same time, his language is poetic and suggestive, which reaches something beneath the surface where the essence of things will be touched. In his stories, a sense of community bond is evoked, and the Japanese immigrant's common experience is transformed into significant growth.

Mori's narrative varies in tone, from the shrewdly down-to-earth to the piercingly sardonic. Some readers of *Yokohama, California* may be surprised by Mori's special way of using language, which does not have "correct" or "legitimate" rules. Critics, who even otherwise praise Mori's work highly, find Mori's English "too bad" and too offensive about the dominant, canonized language rules. While critics notice the transgressive use of language in Mori's work, what they miss, unfortunately, is the social/racial implication of Mori's transgressive discourse and his intention to break the canonizing power of "elegant" and "correct" English and to voice the Japanese immigrant's experience in the United States in a transgressive and decanonizing discourse. As Jeffery Chan et al. observe:

The minority experience does not yield itself to accurate or complete expression in the white man's language. Yet minority writers, specifically Asian-American writers, are made to feel morally obligated to write in a language produced by an alien and hostile sensibility. (Chan 1982, 217)

In his stories and later work *Woman from Hiroshima* (1978), Mori tries to find an immigrant language that reflects a critical self-consciousness of ethnic elements—linguistic and social—that may be directed to oppose the force of a canonizing cultural hegemony.

The 1950s were important years for the development of Japanese-American literature. After the war, Japanese Americans were released from the internment camps, and their community was more dispersed across the country than it had been before the war. Motivated by the will to reflect the changing community, Japanese-American writers tried to accommodate diverse perspectives and to make their writing accessible to a broad audience; at the same time, they attempted to challenge old myths and stereotypes about Japanese immigrants. The tension between assimilation and separation attitudes was also intensified, as writers asserted their own individual understanding and interpretation of immigrant identity and experience. While diversity of literary expressions of immigrant experience marked the development and maturation of Japanese-American literature, the most important writers during this period were Monica Sone and

John Okada, who represent the two extremes of the Japanese-American literary tradition in their search for identity.

Monica Sone's *Nisei Daughter* (1953) is a book that attempted to express the confusing experience of nisei, the second generation of Japanese immigrants. Under the pressure of racism, some Japanese Americans have difficulty in acknowledging their immigrant heritage. Kazuko, the protagonist in the book, is troubled by the question of identity. On one hand, born in America, she seems confident in assimilation by disengaging herself from her Japanese cultural heritage; on the other hand, she cannot deny the "Japanese blood" inside her. The dilemma in which Kazuko finds herself is the loss of an authentic sense of self. In order to succeed in a racist society, she tries to minimize her ethnic difference to assimilate to the white cultural standard. Kazuko's assimilation for success is an oblation of identity and a sacrifice of cultural difference. The ironic situation of the book is that when she is compelled by American racism to give up her Japanese identity, Kazuko is not able to obtain an American one—she is not treated equitably as a white American. In spite of the author's painstaking efforts to create a hopeful tone, the book does not really offer a hopeful picture for an assimilationist.

The difference between issei and nisei is depicted clearly in *Nisei Daughter* by their attitudes toward Japanese cultural heritage. Issei, the first generation of Japanese immigrants, suffered the most in American racist society; however, the prejudice and discrimination only make them cherish their heritage even more. They set up their own schools to teach Japanese language and culture in the hope that their nisei children will not forget their tradition. However, many nisei children find Japanese school boring and their parents' tradition outdated. To Kazuko, following issei tradition means to separate herself from practical values of the dominant society. Kazuko regards self-negation as a necessary sacrifice for assimilation, which, in her opinion, is the only way to dreamed success. But what we find in her sacrifice is victimization by American racism. Even if she rejects her Japanese self, Kazuko is not able to get what she wants—to be treated as a "complete American" by the white society.

John Okada's *No-No Boy,* a book ahead of its time, was published in 1957, only four years after Sone's *Nisei Daughter;* however, in contrast to Sone's immediate "success," *No-No Boy* was neglected not only by the white literary establishment but also by the Japanese-American community. But today, the value of this novel has been rediscovered, and it is widely regarded as "the first Japanese-American novel in the history of American letters" (Chan 1982, 215). Okada's novel started a unique tradition of Japanese-American fiction and developed a new sensibility. For Okada, neither Japanese nor American seems to be an authentic identity for a Japanese American, and therefore he refuses to make a choice. Instead, Okada tries to imagine Japanese-American identity as a mobile body of interrelationships, where the enunciatory interaction among the differential cultural presences trans(re)lates various historical, political, and psychological discourses into an accumulative proxy, which contests a single cultural hegemony by rejecting both Japanese and American—to say "No" and "No," as the novel's protagonist asserts, to any domination. As a gesture of independence, *No-No Boy* demands and activates a decentered transnational experience that is neither Japanese nor American—nisei identity is not simply a mixture of two incompatible elements. *No-No Boy* is a cry for independence from injustice, discrimination, and stereotyping; Okada attempts to define Japanese Americans' identity in terms of immigrant heritage, while refusing to accept the discourse of convenient assimilation.

To express his original perception of Japanese-American experience, Okada develops a unique, carnivalized style. This style suggests some basic features of the discourse by which Okada translates experience into words. The "ungrammatic" or "unconventional" style Okada employs is not merely an incidental trick or technique of writing but is, rather, a literary configuration that reacts to the larger issues challenging Japanese-American writers. *No-No Boy* is in a form of textual democratization or absence of hierarchy, which encompasses multiple focuses and voices in a carnivalistic, simultaneous achievement. Okada seems to write an oral tale, changing voices freely and defying character consistency. The style itself is part of an immigrant discourse that asserts an ethnic distinctness. Okada's *No-No Boy* manifests a rebellion against a "tyranny of language" that marginalizes and ostracizes ethnic discourse from entering the mainstream. Okada attempts to carnivalize the dominant language/discourse in which he never felt comfortable. He tries to codify the (im)migrant experience that has never been expressed in white cliché. His consciousness of the linguistic problem operates at a point where a language carnivalization borders on social critique, as the question of "language domination" is always related to racial discrimination.

A large number of Japanese-American writers are female—Monica Sone, Hisaye Yamamoto, Shelley Ota, Yoshiko Uchida, Patsy Saiki, Joy Kogawa, Jeanne Wakatsuki Houston, Wakako Yamauchi, Clara Jelsma, Doris Kawano, Cynthia Kadohata, and Gail Tsukiyama, to name only a few. These women writers normally experience double pressure in the context of a male dominant and patriarchal heritage. Unlike their male counterparts, they are the most disadvantaged members of their ethnic community in the United States, where they have to write against the dominant and immigrant cultures, both of which contain depressive values for women. To write within the context of a male dominant and patriarchal tradition is a challenging task faced by all Japanese-American women writers. With their traditionally subordinate position in society, they must fight against both racist and sexist stereotypes. Challenging traditional patriarchy and sexual prejudice, they try to break constraints inherent in Japanese women's sex roles in a racist society and to redefine their identity in terms of both race and gender. Their special concern with gender issues makes the relationship between race and gender an important theme in their writing. Thus, race should always be considered with gender when analyzing the writing by Japanese-American women authors, who attempt to subvert oppression by relocating the site of their ethnic identity outside the existing male discourse.

Hisaye Yamamoto is one of "Asian America's most accomplished short story writers" (Chan 1982, 215). Her *Seventeen Syllables and Other Stories* (1988) contains a selection of her best stories since 1949. Within the framework of immigrant experience, Yamamoto subtly describes Japanese-American women's difficult situation and articulates their frustrated feelings about sexuality, patriarchy, and racism. Yamamoto's short story "Seventeen Syllables" (1949) is about an issei woman of literary talent who is married to Mr. Hayashi, a Japanese immigrant farmer in California. In this subtle tale of unhappy marriage, the central conflict is between patriarchal domination and woman's self-assertion in terms of artistic creativity, erotic desire, and longing for freedom. Mrs. Hayashi's absorption in the narcissism of artistic creation, in a sense, reflects her longing for self-fulfillment and freedom in an oppressive marriage and society. Yamamoto's story, by examining an immigrant woman's prescribed social roles, suggests a limited freedom, or rather transgression, for immigrant women under the double tyranny of racial and male dominance. Mrs. Hayashi's poetic avocation is regarded as transgressive by her husband and society, because artistic creation is one of women's self-empowering devices, a sociocultural practice, and a way of achieving freedom and independence.

Immigrant women, with a feeling of alienation and isolation, try to establish a self-reflexive dialogue with themselves, when their attempt to communicate with others is frustrated. Moreover, the longing for a meaningful self-fulfillment beyond a stifling life of oppression is often related to a shadowy erotic passion. Yamamoto's "Yoneko's Earthquake" (1951) presents the tragic life of Mrs. Hosoume through the innocent eyes of a ten-year-old girl. Mrs. Hosoume, much younger than Mr. Hosoume, an abstemious Japanese issei farmer whose nerves were injured in the Long Beach earthquake of 1933, is attracted to a kind and energetic Filipino farmworker. Unfortunately, however, Mrs. Hosoume's affair results in an illegal abortion, which, like the earthquake, destroys the dream and hope she cherished. Social convention and the hardship of immigrant life that quenched Mrs. Hosoume's emotions eventually destroy her mentality and sanity. Yamamoto's story is not merely about an immigrant woman's domestic tragedy, but also about women's awakening into sexuality and happiness as well as the consequent suffering and pain in an oppressive society. As Yamamoto expresses later in "Life among the Oil Fields: A Memoir" (1979), her stories present the limited life that immigrant women have in a white- and male-dominant society and their painful efforts to transcend the dominance. Yamamoto has strong influence on other women writers such as Wakako Yamauchi, whose stories "And the Soul Shall Dance" (1966) and "Songs My Mother Taught Me" (1976) express a similar theme and sensibility.

Yoshiko Uchida, a prolific nisei woman author, depicts a vivid portrait of Japanese immigrant women in her best-known novel, *Picture Bride* (1987). In this book, Uchida explores the experience of a Japanese woman, Hana, who first comes to the United States as a "picture bride"—a woman who accepts an arranged marriage through viewing a man's picture. From the early years of Japanese immigration to the 1940s, arranged marriage, an old custom in Japan, was one of the affordable and convenient ways a Japanese immigrant male could marry in the United States. The man usually had to toil and moil for a number of years before he could save enough money to cover his bride's transportation and living expenses in the United States. Hana, a young girl from a small village in Japan, comes to California to marry Taro, a Japanese immigrant who is much older than she. When they actually meet each other at Taro's home in California, Hana realizes that she does not love this man. Disappointed at the marriage and at the condition of Japanese immigrants' hard life, her dream of the golden-mountain-like America is shattered. Later on, she comes to know and falls in love with a younger man. This only causes much inner contradiction and emotional stress for Hana.

Through describing the inner stress and pain of Hana in a patriarchally and racially dominant society, Uchida highlights the cultural retention that has survived since the early Japanese immigrant generation. *Picture Bride* reflects and articulates the value of Japanese heritage as well as the limitation of this legacy. The novel chronicles Hana's life as a young girl, bride, and mother, expressing vividly the feelings of loneliness, isolation, and unfulfillment that are crucial to Hana's immigrant experience. Similar to Yamamoto's short stories about immigrant women's dilemma, Uchida's *Picture Bride,* a book dedicated to "those brave women from Japan who travelled far, who endured, and who prevailed," combines gender issues with an unsparing criticism of racism. It reveals a Japanese immigrant woman's journey from self-sacrifice to self-independence, asserting both gender and ethnic identity in opposition to the institutions of male/racial domination. This theme is resonated in a different context in Uchida's other novels about internment experience, such as *Journey to Topaz* (1971) and *Journey Home* (1978).

WIND FROM THE PACIFIC: JAPANESE-AMERICAN LITERATURE IN HAWAI'I

Japanese-American literature in/about Hawai'i requires and deserves a special discussion. Japanese immigrated to Hawai'i earlier than they came to mainland America. By the 1900s, the residents of Japanese ancestry made up more than 39 percent of the total population of Hawai'i; and the descendants of these early Japanese immigrants now constitute Hawai'i's largest ethnic community. The lives of these immigrants and their children are depicted vividly and powerfully in numerous literary works such as Shelley Ota's *Upon Their Shoulders* (1951), Margaret N. Harada's *The Sun Shines on the Immigrant* (1960), Kazuo Miyamoto's *Hawaii: End of the Rainbow* (1964), Jon Shirota's *Lucky Come Hawaii* (1965) and *Pineapple White* (1972), Milton Murayama's *All I Asking for Is My Body* (1975), Patsy Saiki's *Sachie: A Daughter of Hawaii* (1977), Clara Jelsma's

Teapot Tales and Other Stories (1981), and Doris Kawano's *Harue, Child of Hawaii* (1984). These works are characterized by a combination of distinctive features of Japanese heritage and Hawai'ian local color. When Hawai'i was officially accepted as America's fiftieth state, the question of what Americanism means to Japanese Americans in Hawai'i also arose. These Japanese-American writers plunge deeply into the sea of their experience to explore from various perspectives the suffering, struggle, and heroism involved in their lives.

Kazuo Miyamoto's epiclike novel *Hawaii: End of the Rainbow* is regarded as one of the highest achievements in Hawai'i's Japanese-American literary circle. It chronicles the life and death of a pioneering Japanese immigrant, Sei-kichi Arata. When Arata immigrated from Japan to Hawai'i in 1891, he was a young man full of dreams. Although he had lived most of his life and raised his family in Hawai'i, he was never accepted by the dominant society because of his racial difference. During World War II, he was interned in a concentration camp by the U.S. government. The structure of the novel is unique: it is divided into five sections, and each section has a "prologue" that provides a current framework for the following account of Arata's early life. The five prologues mainly tell of the dying Arata, who suffered from a heart attack; as Arata lay dying, his physician, Dr. Murayama, a nisei son of Arata's old friend, reminisces and reflects on Arata's life. The thoughts and memories of Dr. Murayama are intertwined with historical descriptions; thus, the novel presents a multidimensional picture of two generations of Japanese immigrants. Dr. Murayama, a representative member of the nisei generation, felt the need and urgency to understand the older generation—how the war and imprisonment smashed their dream of a peaceful and idyllic life in Hawai'i. For many Japanese immigrants in Hawai'i, at the end of the rainbow are tears. As a whole, the novel affirms a hope for the future—a future based on our ability to remember history.

Milton Murayama's novel *All I Asking for Is My Body* is about a Japanese-American family in Hawai'i before World War II. The novel consists of three parts of odd lengths. The first two parts are fairly short in comparison with the lengthy third part, which carries the novel's title. These three parts are connected around the growth of the narrator, Kiyo, who recalls his childhood and youth in a sugar plantation in Hawai'i. This small plantation town represents the hierarchical structure of a racist society, with the white overseer's luxury residence at the top and the Japanese and Filipino laborers' shabby huts at the bottom. As a bildungsroman, the novel reveals Kiyo's increasing awareness of the oppression, hypocrisy, and deception in society and his slow understanding of the rebellion of his elder brother Tosh. "All I asking for is my body" is Tosh's defiant cry for independence from injustices, abuses, and a miserable life. This novel combines a penetrating examination of racism with an unflinching satire of the "American ideal." While Kiyo hears the praises of the great "American ideal" in school, the most immediate example of "American ideal" he can find in reality is the oppressive, exploitative plantation. In this miserable plantation town, Kiyo and his brother grow up, determined to struggle for freedom and dignity. This novel is characterized by Murayama's realistic and candid style.

Patsy Saiki, one of the Hawai'ian women writers who came of age in the post-World War II era, published her book *Sachie: A Daughter of Hawaii* in 1977. This book presents a vivid picture of the life of a young nisei woman, Sachie, in a Japanese community in Hawai'i. Sachie's issei parents, settled in Hawai'i for many years, still keep their native customs, etiquette, and tradition. Recognizing that she is by birth American, yet comes from a family that is not "American" by appearance, Sachie has a feeling of being caught in the middle, not knowing whether to adhere to traditional values or to assert her difference from her parents. Aware of the boundary between the "Japanese" values of her parents and the "American" values she learns from the society at large, Sachie attempts to blend the two to develop a Japanese-American individuality. As she crosses the boundary separating the life sphere of her parents from that of the white Americans, she resolves to transform the boundary into a connection rather than a barrier. *Sachie* contains abundant narrative sketches that illustrate the difficult experiences of Japanese immigrants and their contribution to Hawai'i's economic development.

PREVAILING GENRES

Apart from the genre of fiction just discussed, autobiography and poetry constitute significant literary forms for Japanese-American writers. From the late 1960s to the 1980s, a substantial amount of Japanese-American writing employed the form of (auto)biographical reminiscences. Varying in degrees from nonfictional autobiography to autobiographic fiction, Japanese-American autobiographical writings are well known beyond the Japanese-American community. Daniel Inouye and Lawrence Elliot's *Journey to Washington* (1967), Daniel Okimoto's *American in Disguise* (1971), Jim Yoshida and Bill Hosokawa's *The Two Worlds of Jim Yoshida* (1972), Jeane Wakatsuki Houston and James D. Houston's *Farewell to Manzanar* (1973), Sono Osata's *Distance Dances* (1980), Yoko Kawashima Watkins's *So Far from the Bamboo Grove* (1985), and Mike Masaoka's *They Called Me Moses Masaoka* (1987) are all notable works, although they differ from one another in terms of their content and sociopolitical position. The works mentioned earlier, such as Sone's *Nisei Daughter* and Saiki's *Sachie,* also have autobiographical elements. Some of the autobiographies are "success stories" that reflect a strong assimilationist attitude, while others attempt to present their experience of hardship, including the camp experiences. Some of the autobiographical works obviously move beyond the representation of self in an attempt to react to the larger issues challenging Japanese Americans. They are no longer personal histories, since (auto)biographical reminiscences provide opportunity for the writers to mediate on larger issues of history, race, and politics. For some Japanese-American writers, the more self-absolved they become, the more urgently they want to express the richness and complexity of the common experience of the Japanese community, which has not been properly recorded in canonized, white historical discourse. Works like Joy Kogawa's *Obasan* (1981) and Yoshiko Uchida's *Desert Exile: The Uprooting of a Japanese-American Family* (1982) resemble an (auto)biography; but the scope of their presentation moves beyond the narrowly circumscribed ethnic individuality. Broad and far-reaching in their historical vision of Japanese-American experience, these works should be regarded as historiographies.

Joy Kogawa is a Japanese-Canadian writer whose masterpiece *Obasan* has a strong impact on the Japanese community in North America. At first glance, the book seems to be an "autobiographical" story of the life of a Japanese-Canadian girl, Naomi. However, the author adeptly combines the history of Canada's mistreatment of Japanese Canadians during World War II with the girl's narrative of her nightmarish memories of the loss of parents, sexual abuse, and displacement. The "silent" history of the Japanese Canadians' suffering during World War II is not presented in a straightforward way but in a symbolic, self-reflexive discourse. In *Obasan* we find a combination of self-reflexivity and a sense of sociohistorical inclusiveness—the narrator's personal life is transposed to a larger canvas of history. It seems that the "silent" history is so deep in the heart of Japanese immigrants that it must be translated through a personal experience. *Obasan* has an effect of interrupting the canonized history and of laying bare the process of history making. Thus, through making Naomi's personal story "historical," this book uncovers a new historiographical dimension that challenges various historical misrepresentations of the Japanese community and unfolds a "silent" history that is never recounted in white discourses.

Obasan, with a structure of concentric narrative circles, embeds different issei, nisei, and sansei experiences of history in one book. The issei, as represented by the title character Obasan, are strongly attached to the Oriental values of "silence" and "forgetting"—afraid of discrimination and persecution, they try to avoid social involvement in their adopted society; the nisei individuals such as the Western-educated Aunt Emily are much more vocal and aggressive in fighting for justice and for redress of their wartime treatment through political protest. The two discourses—"silence" and "voice"—however, are not adequate in representing the "unspeakable" reality of their deep suffering, the lived history. The sansei narrator, Naomi, unwilling to follow either way of her two aunts, attempts to explore deeper implications behind the cruel treatment from a new perspective. Within the context of three interwoven perspectives, *Obasan* offers itself as a multidimensional work that accommodates a profound historical insight.

Poetry is another important literary form for Japanese-American writers. With diverse styles and concerns varying from traditional *senryu* and *tanka* to modern imagism, Japanese-American poets demonstrate prominent craftsmanship and achievement. Although a poetic tradition has long existed in the Japanese-American community, the works of early poets were largely confined to the world of community newspapers and magazines. However, in recent decades, quite a few poets of Japanese origin have achieved wide critical recognition, for instance, Lawson Fusao Inada's *Before the War* (1971), James Mitsui's *Crossing Phantom River* (1978), Ai's *Killing Floor* (1979), Geraldine Kudaka's *Numerous Avalanches at the Point of Intersection* (1979), Ronald Tanaka's *The Shino Suite* (1981), Garrett Hongo's *Yellow Light* (1982) and *The River of Heaven* (1988), Mitsuye Yamada's *Desert Run* (1988), and David Mura's *After We Lost Our Way* (1989), a winner of the National Poetry Prize. These volumes, fashioned in unique and ingenious poetic forms, express a variety of feelings, experiences, and sensibilities. For Japanese Americans, poetry is not only the expressive medium of people's feeling but also the way of strengthening the bond of their community.

Lawson Fusao Inada's *Before the War* started a new tradition of Japanese-American poetry. When it was first published, Inada's rugged, robust, and vigorous volume shocked critics, who were used to the "quaintness" and "smoothness" of Oriental art. Inada's volume, although not entirely about the wartime treatment, is titled *Before the War,* because for Japanese Americans the most critical period of their immigrant history is identified with the relocation experience during World War II. Inada wrote of love/life as well as hatred/death in a tough language that does not paint, but exposes, the truth that many dare not see. Refusing to subordinate himself to conventional "rhythm" and refusing to betray his soul for success, Inada bolts himself "into the open," declaring his independence and maturity. In his poems, Inada expresses his true feelings and experience in a unique voice, a voice never heard before. *Before the War* explores personal identity and communal heritage in a defiant, provocative, carnivalistic discourse, rather than in a delicate, submissive, and assimilationist one. The prevalent power of such a carnivalistic discourse subverts conventions that adhere to various modes of stereotyping from a white, canonizing perspective.

Ayumi, edited by Janice Mirikitani and one of the most important anthologies ever published by Japanese Americans, contains both poetry and prose; however, the poetry section is particularly impressive. As the title *Ayumi* (Ongoing Journey) suggests, the works collected in this anthology chronicle the "progress" of the Japanese-American experience, with the distinct sections of issei, nisei, sansei, and yonsei. In poems by the issei, the *senryu* and *tanka* are popular forms in creating a compact and intensive expression of their pains and sufferings, including the experience in relocation camps. Poems by nisei and sansei writers, which are normally preoccupied with the complexities, contradictions, and ambivalences associated with balancing and adjusting two cultural backgrounds, demonstrate diversity of styles and forms. Poems such as Janice Mirikitani's "For My Father," Lawson Fusao Inada's "My Father and Myself Facing the Sun," and Jonny Kyoko Sullivan's "Obasan" attempt to redefine their identity in relation to their immigrant heritage and to challenge discourses of convenient stereotyping. Some women poets also express their concern with gender issues. The poems by Kyoko Sullivan and Lonny Kaneko, for instance, suggest the constraints inherent in traditional gender-defined roles. This anthology, in terms of both its content and form, must be viewed as one of the most valuable treasure books of Japanese-American literature.

RECENT JAPANESE-AMERICAN FICTION

The experience of the internment during World War II, which deeply influenced Japanese America's perception of place and sense of displacement, constitutes a recurrent theme in literature, from John Okada's *No-No Boy* to Yoshiko Uchida's *Desert Exile*. Generations of authors, haunted by the memory of the horrible "uprooting," try to define themselves in terms of "place and displacement" (Inada 1982, 254). Writers of different generations present their experiences of dislocation within various contexts. Recent Japanese-American fictions—Edward Miyakawa's *Tule Lake* (1979), Lonny Kaneko's *Coming Home from Camp* (1986), Holly Uyemoto's *Rebel without a Clue* (1989), Cynthia Kadohata's *The Floating World* (1989) and *In the Heart of the Valley of Love* (1992), and Gail Tsukiyama's *Women of the Silk* (1991)—continue to map the topography of their identity and to explore the liminality of their place in American society. From the confinement in a concentration camp to the dissemination in a post-modern city, the experience of "uprooting" and "floating" is repeatedly explored in recent Japanese-American literature. Imbued with a new awareness of their (dis)placement in America, these writers regard their own experience of dislocation as part of a larger immigrant tradition of "reworlding" that contributes to the distinctive feature of their identity.

The strain of confinement versus movement has been an important theme in Cynthia Kadohata's *The Floating World* and *In the Heart of the Valley of Love*. From the confinement experience of her parents and grandparents to her own experience of displacement and dislocation in American society, Kadohata desperately searches for a place of her own in a new immigrant discourse. *The Floating World,* which has strong autobiographical elements, is about the on-the-road experience of a Japanese-American girl, Olivia, and her family, who move around the Pacific Northwest looking for a stable life. Kadohata examines the experience of "floating" in relation to the identity of a Japanese American. Lacking the sense of "rootedness" and "at-homeness," Kadohata expresses a deep yearning for a place of home—both in the outside world and in the heart. In addition to the immigrant heritage, she delineates a migrant dimension for her own identity. Her perception of spatial possibilities is closely related to her understanding of ethnic heritage and expression of a Japanese American's place in the overall social structure of America. For American-born nisei, sansei, and yonsei, floating across the borders of time, race, gender, culture, and history becomes part of their daily experience. Kadohata's fiction is preoccupied with the complexities associated with the younger generation's attempt to rediscover and redefine their identity in relation to their (im)migrant experience—to grasp their place in a "floating world."

SELECTED PRIMARY BIBLIOGRAPHY

Ai. *Killing Floor.* 1979. New York: Thunder's Mouth, P, 1987.

Chan, Jeffery Paul, Frank Chin, Lawson Inada, and Shawn Wong, eds. *The Big Aiiieeeee!: Chinese-American and Japanese-American History in Literature.* New York: Meridian, 1991.

Chin, Frank, Jeffery Paul Chan, Lawson Fusao Inada, and Shawn Wong, eds. *Aiiieeeee!: An Anthology of Asian-American Writers.* Washington, DC: Howard UP, 1974.

Harada, Margaret N. *The Sun Shines on the Immigrant.* New York: Vantage, 1960.

Hongo, Garrett. *The River of Heaven.* New York: Knopf, 1988.

Houston, Jeanne Wakatsuki, and James D. Houston. *Farewell to Manzanar.* San Francisco: San Francisco Book/Houghton Mifflin, 1973.

Inada, Lawson Fusao. *Before the War.* New York: William Morrow, 1971.

Jelsma, Clara Mitsuko Kubojiri. *Teapot Tales and Other Stories.* Honolulu: Bamboo Ridge, 1981.

Kadohata, Cynthia. *The Floating World.* New York: Viking, 1989.

———. *In the Heart of the Valley of Love.* New York: Viking, 1992.

Kaneko, Lonny. *Coming Home from Camp.* Waldron Island, WA: Brooding Heron, 1986.

Kawano, Doris Kimie. *Harue, Child of Hawaii.* Honolulu: Topgallant, 1984.

Kogawa, Joy. *Obasan.* Toronto: Lester and Orpen Dennys, 1981.

Mirikitani, Janice, ed. *Ayumi: A Japanese American Anthology.* San Francisco: Japanese American Anthology Committee, 1980.

Miyamoto, Kazuo. *Hawaii: End of the Rainbow.* Rutland, VT: Charles E. Tuttle, 1964.

Mori, Toshio. *Woman from Hiroshima.* San Francisco: Isthmus, 1978.

———. *The Chauvinist and Other Stories.* Los Angeles: UCLA Asian American Studies Center, 1979.

———. *Yokohama, California.* 1949. Seattle: U of Washington P, 1985.

Mura, David. *After We Lost Our Way.* New York: E. P. Dutton, 1989.

Murayama, Milton. 1959. *All I Asking for Is My Body.* San Francisco: Supa P, 1975.

Okada, John. 1957. *No-No Boy.* Seattle: U of Washington P, 1976.

Okimoto, Daniel. *American in Disguise.* New York: Walker-Weatherhill, 1971.

Ota, Shelley Ayame Nishimura. *Upon Their Shoulders.* New York: Exposition P, 1951.

Saiki, Patsy. *Sachie: A Daughter of Hawaii.* Honolulu: Kisaku, 1977.

Shirota, Jon. *Lucky Come Hawaii.* New York: Bantam Books, 1965.

———. *Pineapple White.* Los Angeles: Ohara, 1972.

Sone, Monica. *Nisei Daughter.* 1953. Seattle: U of Washington P, 1979.

Tsukiyama, Gail. *Women of the Silk.* New York: St. Martin's, 1991.

Uchida, Yoshiko. *Journey to Topaz.* New York: Scribner, 1971.

———. *Journey Home.* New York: Atheneum, 1978.

———. *Desert Exile: The Uprooting of a Japanese-American Family.* Seattle: U of Washington P, 1982.

———. *Picture Bride.* Flagstaff, AZ: Northland, 1987.

Uyemoto, Holly. *Rebel without a Clue.* New York: Crown, 1989.

Yamada, Mitsuye. *Desert Run: Poems and Stories.* Latham, NY: Kitchen Table: Women of Color P, 1988.

Yamamoto, Hisaye. *Seventeen Syllables and Other Stories.* Latham, NY: Kitchen Table: Women of Color P, 1988.

Yamauchi, Wakako. "And the Soul Shall Dance." 1966. *Aiiieeeee!: An Anthology of Asian-American Writers*. Ed. Frank Chin et al. Washington, DC: Howard UP, 1974. 193–200.

———. "Songs My Mother Taught Me." *Amerasia Journal* 3 (1976): 63–73.

Yoshida, Jim, and Bill Hosokawa. *The Two Worlds of Jim Yoshida*. New York: William Morrow, 1972.

SELECTED SECONDARY BIBLIOGRAPHY

Chan, Jeffery Paul, Frank Chin, Lawson Fusao Inada, and Shawn H. Wong. "An Introduction to Chinese-American and Japanese-American Literatures." *Three American Literatures*. Ed. Houston A. Baker, Jr. New York: MLA, 1982. 197–228.

Cheung, King-Kok. *Articulate Silences: Hisaye Yamamoto, Maxine Hong Kingston, Joy Kogawa*. Ithaca, NY, and London: Cornell UP, 1993.

Cheung, King-Kok, and Stan Yogi. *Asian American Literature: An Annotated Bibliography*. New York: MLA, 1988.

Crow, Charles L. "Home and Transcendence in Los Angeles Fiction." *Los Angeles in Fiction*. Ed. David Fine. Albuquerque: U of New Mexico P, 1984. 189–205.

Fugita, Stephen S., and David J. O'Brien. *Japanese American Ethnicity: The Persistence of Community*. Seattle and London: U of Washington P, 1991.

Ghymn, Esther Mikyung. *The Shapes and Styles of Asian American Prose Fiction*. New York: Peter Lang, 1992.

Inada, Lawson Fusao. "Of Place and Displacement: The Range of Japanese-American Literature." *Three American Literatures*. Ed. Houston A. Baker, Jr. New York: MLA, 1982. 254–265.

Kim, Elaine H. *Asian American Literature: An Introduction to the Writings and Their Social Context*. Philadelphia: Temple UP, 1982.

O'Brien, David J. *The Japanese American Experience*. Bloomington and Indianapolis: Indiana UP, 1991.

Ong, Walter J. "Introduction: On Saying We and Us to Literature." *Three American Literatures*. Ed. Houston A. Baker, Jr. New York: MLA, 1982. 3–7.

Oyama, Richard. "Ayumi: 'To Sing Our Connections.' " *A Gift of Tongues*. Ed. Marie Harris and Kathleen Aguero. Athens and London: U of Georgia P, 1987. 249–256.

Peck, David R. *American Ethnic Literature*. Pasadena, CA: Salem P, 1992.

Sumida, Stephen H. *And the View from the Shore: Literary Traditions of Hawai'i*. Seattle: U of Washington P, 1991.

Takaki, Ronald. *Strangers from a Different Shore: A History of Asian Americans*. New York: Penguin Books, 1989.

Wong, Sau-ling Cynthia. *Reading Asian American Literature: From Necessity to Extravagance*. Princeton: Princeton UP, 1994.

8

Korean-American Literature
Jae-Nam Han

INTRODUCTION

The last four decades have seen a significant increase in the number of Koreans immigrating to the United States. In that time, the Korean community has grown from around 10,000 to at least 800,000 today and is expected to grow to 1.3 million by the year 2000 (Patterson and Kim 48; Mayberry 38, 60). Not surprisingly, this growing community has given rise to a significant Korean-American literary movement, but its existence has remained largely undiscovered by both academe and the general public.

LITERARY-CULTURAL HISTORY

During the thirty-six years of Japanese domination, from 1910 to 1945, Koreans were subject to political repression and economic hardship. Many Koreans went overseas to the United States in order to escape poverty and/or to fight for national liberation. (Others migrated to China or to Russia.) The first Korean immigrants to this country were farm laborers on Hawai'ian plantations, ''picture brides'' (who came to their prospective husbands on the plantations matched through photos), political refugees, and students. Because of restrictive immigration laws, only a few hundred Koreans were permitted to immigrate to America from 1907 until 1952 (Mayberry 18). Although the pre-World War II immigrants ultimately intended to return to Korea, most of them remained in the United States because of the continued troubles in their home country. The post-war Korean-American writers who came to, or were born in, the United

States before 1945 include Morris Pang, Mary Paik Lee, Margaret Pai, the older Peter Hyun, and Induk Pahk. Cathy Song is the granddaughter of the first-generation immigrants to Hawai'i.

A new wave of Koreans began immigrating to the United States following the aftermath of World War II and the Korean War (1950–1953). Most of these were from South Korea. Between 1946 and 1964, most of the Korean immigrants came as students, "war brides," and adoptees. More than 10,000 Korean students came to study at higher institutions when the Korean War ended, 7,542 of whom later changed their legal status to permanent resident (Hyung-chan Kim, "Koreans" 18). A large number of Korean "war brides," who married American servicemen during the Korean conflict, arrived with their husbands. Thousands of Korean children also came to America as adoptees after the end of the Korean War.

Kim Yong Ik, a fiction writer, and the younger Peter Hyun, a journalist and fiction writer (author of *Darkness at Dawn: A North Korean Diary* [1981]), came to the United States in 1948, and Richard E. Kim, a fiction writer, like many others, arrived in America immediately after the end of the Korean conflict. These writers were well educated and were later formally trained in writing and literature. They were a part of the first group of Korean Americans who regarded writing as their profession and who worked hard for recognition from the American reading public.

The Immigration Act of 1965 allowed large numbers of Koreans to come to the United States for the first time. The continued post-1965 Korean immigration reached its peak during the 1970s. South Korea was stifled by its dense population, economic and political instabilities, and widespread fear of a second Korean War, all of which drove many intellectuals and professionals from their homeland to seek economic prosperity, political freedom, and better educational opportunities for their children in the United States. "War brides" brought their Korean relatives to the United States for permanent residency, and Korean orphans continued to find adoptive homes in America.

The yearly number of Koreans entering America as immigrants reached its peak in 1987 with 35,849 and has since declined. According to a recent report from a Korean-American newspaper, a total of 17,949 Koreans immigrated to America during the fiscal year 1993. This number was the lowest in twenty years ("Korean" 1). During the 1980s and early 1990s, some Korean Americans returned permanently to Korea. South Korea's improved living conditions and the difficulty of assimilating to American culture seem to have contributed to their decision to return. Nevertheless, many Koreans still want to adopt the United States as their home.

Most of the younger Korean-American writers, including Ty Pak, Chungmi Kim, Myung Mi Kim, Min Paek, and John J. Song, either immigrated since 1965 or were American-born of post-1965 Korean immigrants.

DOMINANT CONCERNS

As with any other immigrant literature, the pleasures and/or pain of living on adopted soil is probably the most popular theme of Korean-American writing. Morris Pang's "A Korean Immigrant" (1949) may be the earliest post-war Korean-American work that records a first-generation immigrant's recollection of his past life. The narrator's father tells of his experiences in Korea, China, Russia, and Japan and on a Hawai'ian sugarcane plantation. Now too old to remember his own parents in Korea, the old man wants to live his remaining years in Hawai'i.

Alice Chai's memoir, "A Picture Bride from Korea: The Life History of a Korean American Woman in Hawaii" (1978), records the oral history of a Korean-American woman who was born in Korea in 1904 and came to Hawai'i as one of the "picture brides." The interviewee recalls the bitter farewell to her parents in Korea, her first meeting with her husband-to-be, her struggle for mere survival in Hawai'i, and her consolation in having lived in a land offering creature comforts and in having contributed her resources to the Korean independence movement. She recalls how hard she worked as an army soldiers' laundrywoman: "I was working 16 hours every day. No Sundays off, even no Christmas, no New Year's Day. I missed church. It was too far and they don't give me a day off. That time they make us work like animals" (38). After living in the United States for ten years, she longed to return to Korea; when she finally visits her homeland, however, she is disappointed. Even as a blue-collar worker in the United States, her standard of living was higher.

Kumi Kilburn's "No Dogs and Chinese Allowed" (1978) is a story of a Korean-American woman who struggled with a mixed ethnic identity and resolved this conflict by reclaiming her original Korean identity. She drops her American name, Grace, and reclaims her Korean name, Kumi, symbolizing her refusal to be like an "American" and affirming her "Oriental" identity. She closes her essay with the thought: "What's in a name? A Cliche [*sic*]? No! The origins of awareness, the reality of language and culture" (74).

Kim Ronyoung's *Clay Walls* (1986), set in Los Angeles of the 1920s through the 1940s, explores the ordeal of a Korean immigrant family. Originating from the nobility class (*yangban*) in Korea, Haesu, the heroine, resents having to clean toilet bowls for a living. Her husband, Chun, stoically endures disgrace, which angers her. They suffer not only from racial discrimination but also from other people's ignorance of their ethnicity. The Las Vegas death certificate lists father Chun as Chinese, and, during World War II, Koreans are misidentified as Japanese. When the heroine returns to her Japanese-occupied home country, she soon discovers, as Alice Chai's interviewee did, that neither the United States nor Korea is wholly satisfactory.

Mary Paik Lee's *Quiet Odyssey: A Pioneer Korean Woman in America* (1990) is an excellent sociohistorical source for the study of the first-generation Korean immigrant experience. Born in North Korea in 1900, the author came with her family to the United States at the age of five and grew up in abject poverty. She worked at various odd jobs but eventually attained financial security—and peace of mind. In *Quiet Odyssey,* the author records countless cases of racial prejudice she has undergone. Once, as a high school student, Lee was invited to an American church by her white friend. At the entrance, however, Lee and her brothers were stopped by the church minister, who said, "I don't want dirty Japs in my church." Lee protested, "Would it make any difference if I told you we are not Japanese but Korean?" He replied, "What the hell's the difference? You all look alike to me" (54). Despite such an excruciating experience, Lee did not lose her faith in America, "where [now] everything is possible if they work hard enough" (129). At the close of the book, the author says: "Now I am free of cares and worry and am just trying to relax and enjoy what little time is left. I attend a church regularly where most of the members are black, because it is there I feel most comfortable" (130).

Lee Ki Chuck's "From Korea to Heaven Country" (1989), an autobiographical account based on an oral interview in 1975, poignantly describes the discrepancy between popular stereotypes about America and its reality. Before he came to the United States, he thought it "was really heaven country" (30), but that is not his experience. He suffers from loneliness and from the lost purpose of living. He despairs, but he also admits that America offers a luxurious life for immigrants. He adds, however, that heaven is not given but made.

Richard E. Kim represents another group of post-war Korean-American writers who frequently find their literary sources in major historical events of twentieth-century Korea. He once said, "Korea is the foundation of my literature, my eternal pursuit of my literary way and all of my literary resources" (quoted in Choy 284). Kim's *The Martyred* (1964), a final nominee for the National Book Award and one of the most representative books dealing with Korean history, revolves around the execution of twelve Christian ministers by North Korean communists and the survival of two others during the Korean War. The story's physical setting is Korea, the characters are all Koreans, and the actions loosely follow the Korean War.

The Innocent (1968) and *Lost Names: Scenes from a Korean Boyhood* (1970) complete Richard E. Kim's trilogy of modern Korean history. *The Innocent* draws on the South Korean military coup d'état of 1961 in order to explore the question, Does the end justify the means? In his *Lost Names,* Kim covers the 1930s and 1940s, when he was a child in the Japan-occupied Korea. The title of the book refers to the Koreans' forced assumption of Japanese names by their Japanese rulers.

Although Sook Nyul Choi's *Year of Impossible Goodbyes* (1991) is targeted toward young readers, it still attracts adult readers interested in mid-twentieth-century Korean history. Based on her own experiences, the author presents, through the eyes of a Korean girl named Sookan, the stories of the North Koreans' harrowing experiences under the Japanese and later under the communists and her dangerous flight to the then American-occupied South.

Korean immigrant writers have also created an impressive body of fiction recording the lives of Koreans living in Korea. Although these works do not directly reflect the authors' American experiences, they still constitute a body of immigrant literature in the sense that each story reflects the author's longing for the Old World. While he does not totally turn a blind eye to the immigrant experience, Kim Yong Ik has set most of his stories in Korea. For instance, *The Diving Gourd* (1962), one of his earliest works, is set in a Korean seaside, with a hardworking and independently minded fisherwoman named Bosun as its heroine. *Blue in the Seed* (1964), another of Kim's books, focuses on a blue-eyed student in a school of uniformly dark-eyed children in Korea. Chun Bok, the protagonist, has a hard time being called "Bird Eye" or "Fish Eye." Kim's *Love in Winter* (1969) is a collection of short stories, with only one set outside Korea. The title story deals with a harelipped boy's love for a beautiful tearoom girl who dies; another story, "Mother's Birthday," concerns a boy who cooks a fish he salvaged from a trash can for his ill mother on her birthday, only to cause her death.

In Korea's male-dominated society, the woman's voice was suppressed for centuries. Submission was regarded as a woman's indispensable virtue. However, some Korean-American women authors have stood up for their freedom. Induk Pahk's *September Monkey* and Chungmi Kim's poems both treat the theme of women's voice within family and society, but female sensibility finds its most explosive expression in Willyce Kim's poems and novels. Willyce Kim is the atypical Korean-American writer in that her works all but totally disregard racial issues. A lesbian and women's rights activist, she instead devotes her creative energy to depicting the lesbian experience and fighting for the feminist cause. In Kim's first collection of poems, *Eating Artichokes* (1972), the poet/ speaker rejects the submissive roles of an Asian woman. In one poem, she declares that she and her sisters seek emancipation from the role that has enslaved their Oriental mother. In another poem, she likens herself to a woman who swims "against the current."

Kim's second collection of poems, *Under the Rolling Sky* (1976), again takes up the themes of lesbianism and women's liberation. The poem "Sunday Afternoon Jam" graphically details homosexual lovemaking between two women. In the poem "A Fistful of Flowers for Vivian's Kid," women actively seek their freedom. The poem "Adventure #7 for French Jeanne the Scourge of Paris" narrates two women's successful bank robbery. Willyce Kim has also written two lesbian novels, *Dancer Dawkins and the California Kid* (1985) and *Dead Heat* (1988).

Philosophical speculations and Christian confessions also constitute a part of post-war Korean immigrant writing. Despite their Korean settings, Richard E. Kim's *The Martyred* and *The Innocent* wrestle with metaphysical questions. *The Martyred* advocates religious pragmatism, which is similar to Jamesian philosophy. The author dedicates it to the memory of the French writer Albert Camus, and his work unmistakably involves existential concerns. Meanwhile, *The Innocent* shows the author's uneasiness with idealistic pacifism.

Induk Pahk's deep Christian spirituality finds its voice in her three autobiographical works: *September Monkey* (1954), *The Hour of the Tiger* (1965), and *The Cock Still Crows* (1977). *September Monkey,* for which Pahk is best known, recollects her life from her birth in Korea to her eventual success as an educator and "cultural" ambassador to America. The author's two aims in writing the book are "to witness what can happen in a life when the power of God grips a heart, mind and soul" and "to express my gratitude to my friends who have contributed so much that is endearing and broadening and inspirational to my life on two continents" (Pahk 1954, 9). *The Hour of the Tiger,* Pahk's second testimonial book, concerns her opening Induk Vocational High School, "Berea in Korea" (Pahk, *Hour* 7), on March 20, 1964, in Seoul, Korea. The establishment of a training school for Korean boys was the author's thirty-year dream come true. *The Cock Still Crows,* a sequel to the previous book, is dedicated to her "friends in North America with gratitude and love." It testifies how God has helped her found a junior college in Korea.

PREVAILING GENRES

Autobiography and fictional prose are the two most popular genres of postwar Korean-American literature. Induk Pahk is a pioneer Korean woman writer who started the autobiographical tradition. Pahk is not an "immigrant" writer, for she eventually went back to Korea; however, her three autobiographies (*September Monkey, The Hour of the Tiger,* and *The Cock Still Crows*) describe much of her life in America.

Following Induk Pahk, a group of autobiographical writers began to publish in the 1980s and the early 1990s. They recorded their own stories or transcribed those of their immigrant forefathers. The younger Peter Hyun, who authored *Darkness at Dawn: A North Korean Diary* (1981) and is occasionally confused with the older Peter Hyun, was born and reared in Hamhung in North Korea. After attending American University in Washington, D.C., and Columbia University, he studied Spanish literature at the University of Madrid and French literature at the Sorbonne in Paris. During his stay in Europe, he introduced Korean literature and music to European audiences. Back in the United States, he worked as senior editor of children's books at Doubleday. His articles have seen publication in various newspapers and magazines, including the *New York Times, Wall Street Journal, San Francisco Chronicle, London Times, Sunday Observer,* and *L'Express.* Peter Hyun's book *Darkness at Dawn* recounts the author's trip to North Korea, his home country, as an American citizen. Written in diary form, it records the events and impressions of his visit to such places as Pyongyang, Chongsan-Ri, Panmunjom, and Hamhung.

The older Peter Hyun authored a memoir entitled *Man Sei!: The Making of a Korean American* (1986). According to his account, he was the first Korean baby boy born on the Hawai'ian island of Kauai. His father was the Reverend Soon Hyun, a revolutionary and pastor of the historic Jung Dong First Methodist Church in Seoul during the early part of the century. Hyun's story of his childhood, spent in Hawai'i, Korea, and Shanghai, provides insight into the Korean independence movement.

Margaret K. Pai, another autobiographical writer, was born to first-generation labor immigrant parents in 1914. Her *The Dream of Two Yi-min* (1989) is a personal memoir of her early life with her parents. The book is a revised and extended version of her essay entitled "Growing Up in a Factory," published in 1978 in the *Honolulu Magazine*. Although the book primarily focuses on her family history, it also offers a glimpse of the Korean independence movement, as does Peter Hyun's *Man Sei!*.

Mary Paik Lee's *Quiet Odyssey: A Pioneer Korean Woman in America* (1990), which has been discussed in the previous section, is an autobiography of a first-generation immigrant woman in her almost century-long life in the United States. Brilliantly edited with an introduction by Sucheng Chan, this work is based on a sixty-five-page copyrighted typescript (1984) by the then eighty-six-year-old Korean immigrant woman.

Along with autobiography, fictional prose is another prevailing genre among Korean-American writers. Richard E. Kim, Kim Yong Ik, and Ty Pak are three representative fiction writers. Richard E. Kim was born in Hamhung, North Korea, in 1932 and fled to the South during the communist persecution of the landowners. He met the Korean War as a freshman at Seoul National University and served in the South Korean army as an aide-de-camp to General Arthur Trudeau, then commander of the U.S. 7th Army. Thanks to General Trudeau and Charlotte D. Meinecke of New York University, Kim came to Middlebury College in Vermont to finish his college studies. He subsequently earned three master's degrees, from Johns Hopkins, the University of Iowa, and Harvard. Kim is the author of two major novels and one autobiography, *The Martyred, The Innocent,* and *Lost Names: Scenes from a Korean Boyhood,* which have been introduced earlier. He taught English at various institutions, such as Long Beach State College, University of Massachusetts at Amherst, Syracuse University, and San Diego State University. He is currently president of the Trans-Literary Agency in Shutesbury, Massachusetts.

Kim Yong Ik is one of the most active and prolific Korean-American writers ever. He was born in South Korea's Kyongsangnam-do Province in 1920. After attending high school and college in Korea and Japan, respectively, Kim came to the United States in 1948 and went to Florida Southern College, the University of Kentucky, and the Writers Workshop at the University of Iowa. He began his writing career at the age of forty-two and has written a few novels, including *The Happy Days* (1960), *The Diving Gourd* (1962), *Blue in the Seed* (1964), and *The Shoes from Yang San Valley* (1970). Among these, *The Happy Days* was honored by the American Library Association as a notable children's book of 1960 and West Germany's best youth book for 1965; *Blue in the Seed* was on the honor list in the 1967 Austrian State Prize. Kim Yong Ik also has written a significant number of short stories. The story "From below the Bridge," which originally appeared in *Mademoiselle* in 1957 and was later included in the author's *Love in Winter,* was cited as an outstanding story by a foreign author in Martha Foley's *The Best American Short Stories of 1958.* Kim has taught writing at many universities on both sides of the Pacific Ocean, including the University of California at Berkeley, Duquesne University, and Korea and Ewha Woman's Universities.

Ty Pak is a short story writer living in Hawai'i. Born in Korea in 1938, he earned his law degree from Seoul National University and then worked as a reporter for English daily newspapers in Seoul. He came to the United States in 1965, earned his Ph.D. in English from Bowling Green State University, and has since been on the faculty of the English Department at the University of Hawai'i. All his stories are set against the backdrop of the Korean and Vietnam Wars. The memory of the Korean War hangs over the stories "Guilt Payment," "The St. Peter of Seoul," "Identity," "The Boar," "Nostalgia," "A Second Chance," "A Regeneration," and "Exile" (all 1983). "Steady Hands" (1983) and "The Foe" (1984) are stories related to the Vietnam War.

Kim Ronyoung, the author of *Clay Walls* (1986), was born in Los Angeles. In writing the novel, the author had a sense of mission as a Korean-American writer. The dust jacket of the novel quotes her as saying: "A whole generation of Korean immigrants and their American-born children could have lived and died in the United States without anyone knowing they had been here. I could not let that happen." Unfortunately, shortly after the publication of *Clay Walls,* she was killed in a car accident.

Korean Americans did not begin publishing poetry until the 1970s. Willyce Kim's *Eating Artichokes* (1972) and *Under the Rolling Sky* (1976) were two of the earliest collections of poems ever published by a Korean-American writer. She is a unique Korean-American poet in that her poems rarely reflect on the immigrant experience.

Ko Won, whose real name is Sung-Won Ko, was born in Korea, attended Dongguk University in Seoul, and studied English at the University of London. He earned an M.F.A. in English from the University of Iowa and a Ph.D. in comparative literature from New York University. The winner of the *Kansas City Star* Award in poetry contests for 1966, he authored two collections of poetry, *The Turn of Zero* (1974) and *With Birds of Paradise* (1984), and translated works from Korean, Chinese, and Japanese.

Chungmi Kim, born in South Korea, graduated from Ewha Woman's University in Seoul with a B.A. in English. After working as a dramatist and producer/director for a broadcasting company in Seoul, she came to the United States. In 1973 she began writing poetry in Seattle, taking part in Nelson Bentley's Poetry Workshop at the University of Washington. In her *Chungmi: Se-*

lected Poems (1982), she ponders such issues as women's suffering, immigrant life, and Christian faith.

Cathy Song, a Korean Chinese-American born in Hawai'i in 1955, is perhaps the best-known of the second- and third-generation Korean-American poets. As Song says in the title poem of her first collection of poetry, *Picture Bride,* her grandmother came from Korea as a "picture bride" to marry a stranger who was "thirteen years older than she" (Song, *Picture* 3). Song earned a B.A. from Wellesley College in 1977 and an M.A. in creative writing from Boston University in 1981. She has published two collections of poems whose main focus is on her ancestral roots: *Picture Bride* (1983), the 1982 winner of the prestigious Yale Series of Younger Poets Competition, and *Frameless Windows, Squares of Light* (1988).

Theresa Hak Kyung Cha's *Dictee* (1982) combines multiple genres. Unlike other Korean-American works, her writing is in multiple languages (English, French, and Chinese) and combines prose and poetry with often shocking photos representing modern Korean history. One of the few 1.5 generation Korean-American writers (those writers who were born in Korea but grew up in America), Cha was born in Pusan, Korea, in 1951, and soon after the publication of *Dictee,* she was tragically murdered.

CONCLUSION

Despite its widening scope and increasing depth, Korean-American literature has not received much critical attention. When Korean-American writing is reviewed, critics sometimes regard it as being of little literary merit and of poor stylistic quality. While the language of the first generation of post-war Korean immigrant literature is often choppy or awkward, those critics have oftentimes ignored its sociohistorical value and the depth of its emotional power. These writers have left an important legacy to the newest Korean-American writers in their presentation of the stories of the earliest Korean immigrants to the United States.

Newer writers, building upon the foundations laid by the first Korean-American writers, have expanded their literary scope and vision. The newer writers, like Willyce Kim, Theresa Hak Kyung Cha, Chungmi Kim, Myung Mi Kim, Walter Lew, and John J. Song (whose short story "Faith" deals with incest), are embracing new forms and/or subject matters. Unlike the earlier-generation writers, especially Induk Pahk, who regarded the United States as Korea's generous big brother, they generally do not consider America as heaven on earth. Many of the newer writers have experienced an identity crisis as Korean Americans, and their agony over who they are in the United States has found its way to their literary imagination. As such, younger writers, with their greater command of the language, infuse their writing with a more aggressive tone and vision. Unlike the earlier generation, who primarily sought to record, this generation seeks to galvanize yet another generation of Korean-American writers. Perhaps the aggressive tone and vision of newer Korean-American writers parallel those of other ethnic writers who have begun to assert their own voices.

SELECTED PRIMARY BIBLIOGRAPHY

Binari [Korean-American Cultural Troupe]. *When the Green Mountain Stirs Our Hearts Again: A Madang-Gut (An Epic Drama)*. New York: privately printed, 1985.

Cha, Theresa Hak Kyung. *Dictee*. New York: Tanam P, 1982.

Chai, Alice. "A Picture Bride from Korea: The Life History of a Korean American Woman in Hawaii." *Bridge* 6.4 (1978): 37–42.

Choi, Sook Nyul. *Echoes of the White Giraffe*. Boston: Houghton, 1993.

———. *Halmoni and the Picnic*. Boston: Houghton, 1993.

———. *Year of Impossible Goodbyes*. Boston: Houghton, 1991.

Hyun, Peter. *Man Sei!: The Making of a Korean American*. Honolulu: U of Hawaii P, 1986.

Hyun, Peter. *Darkness at Dawn: A North Korean Diary*. Seoul, Korea: Hanjin, 1981.

———. "A Korean-American Saga." *Korea–U.S.A. Centennial, 1882–1982*. Ed. Yonhap Tongsin. Seoul, Korea: Yonhap News Agency, 1982. 88–91.

———. "The Tale of Chuyong's Lament as Told by Peter Hyun." *Korean Culture* 1.2 (1980): 40–41.

———. "Zen, American Style." *Yardbird Reader* 5 (1976): 73–75.

Kennel, Nancy Lee. "Mirrors." *Gathering Ground: New Writing and Art by Northwest Women of Color*. Ed. Jo Cochran, J. T. Stewart, and Mayumi Tsutakawa. Seattle: Seal P, 1984. 43–44.

Kilburn, Kumi. "No Dogs and Chinese Allowed." *The Ethnic American Woman: Problems, Protests, Lifestyle*. Ed. Edith Blicksilver. Dubuque, IA: Kendall/Hunt, 1978. 171–174.

Kim, Ahn [Andrew]. "A Homeward Journey." *75th Anniversary of Korean Immigration to Hawaii, 1903–1978*. Ed. Samuel S. O. Lee. Honolulu: 75th Anniversary of Korean Immigration to Hawaii Comm., 1978. 22–27.

Kim, Alison. "Sewing Woman." *The Forbidden Stitch: An Asian American Women's Anthology*. Ed. Shirley Geok-lin Lim and Mayumi Tsutakawa. Corvallis, OR: Calyx Books, 1989. 203.

Kim, Andrea. "Born and Raised in Hawaii, but Not Hawaiian." *Asian Americans: Oral Histories of First to Fourth Generation Americans from China, the Philippines, Japan, India, the Pacific Islands, Vietnam and Cambodia*. Ed. Joann Faung Jean Lee. New York: New P, 1992. 24–31.

Kim, Chungmi. "Brother." *Amerasia Journal* 10.2 (1983): 109–111.

———. *Chungmi: Selected Poems*. Anaheim, CA: Korean Pioneer P, 1982.

———. "A Girl on the Swing." *Making Waves: An Anthology of Writings by and about Asian American Women*. Ed. Asian Women United of California. Boston: Beacon, 1989. 80–92.

Kim, Elaine H. "War Story." *Making Waves: An Anthology of Writings by and about Asian American Women*. Ed. Asian Women United of California. Boston: Beacon, 1989. 80–92.

Kim, Elizabeth M. "Detours down Highway 99." *Quilt* 2 (1981): 103–110.

———. "Experience Preferred." *Express* [Berkeley, CA] November 21, 1980: 1+.

Kim, Jonathan. "Girls. Are They Worth It?" *Bamboo Ridge* 3 (1979): 44–49.

Kim, Kichung. "America, America!" *San Jose Studies* (Spring 1988): 113–124.

———. "A Homecoming." *Bridge* 2.6 (1973): 27–31.

———. "What's in a Name." *Career: A Teacher's Guide.* Ed. Adele Meyer. New York: Asian Society of New York, 1986. 44–46.

Kim, Leigh. "Da Kine." *Echoes from Gold Mountain.* Long Beach, CA: California State University, 1982. 95–106.

Kim, Myung Mi. "A Rose of Sharon." *The Forbidden Stitch: An Asian American Women's Anthology.* Ed. Shirley Geok-lin Lim, and Mayumi Tsutakawa. Corvallis, OR: Calyx Books, 1989. 20.

———. *Under Flag.* Berkeley: Kelsey St. P, 1991.

Kim, Richard. "Picture Love." *75th Anniversary of Korean Immigration to Hawaii, 1903–1978.* Ed. Samuel S. O. Lee. Honolulu: 75th Anniversary of Korean Immigration to Hawaii Committee, 1978. 47.

Kim, Richard E. *The Innocent.* Boston: Houghton, 1968.

———. *Lost Names: Scenes from a Korean Boyhood.* New York: Praeger, 1970.

———. *The Martyred.* New York: Braziller, 1964.

———. "Notes from the Underground." *Koreana Quarterly* 12.3 (1970): 24–27.

Kim, Ronyoung [Gloria Hahn]. *Clay Walls.* New York: Permanent P, 1986.

Kim, Ruth. *The Family of Chung Song.* New York: Vantage, 1968.

Kim, Willyce. *Dancer Dawkins and the California Kid.* Boston: Alyson, 1985.

———. *Dead Heat.* Boston: Alyson, 1988.

———. *Eating Artichokes.* Oakland, CA: Women's Press Collective, 1972.

———. *Under the Rolling Sky.* N.p.: Maud Gonne P, 1976.

Kim, Yong Ik. "Andy Crown." *Korea Journal* 27.11 (1987): 41–46.

———. *Blue in the Seed.* Boston: Little, Brown, 1964.

———. "A Book-Writing Venture." *Writer,* October 1965: 28–30.

———. *The Diving Gourd.* New York: Knopf, 1962.

———. "The Gold Watch." *Stories* 5 (May–June 1983): 19–33.

———. "Gourd Dance Song." *Confrontation* 27–28 (1984): 44–51.

———. *The Happy Days.* Boston: Little, Brown, 1960.

———. *Love in Winter.* Garden City, NY: Doubleday, 1969.

———. *The Shoes from Yang San Valley.* Garden City, NY: Doubleday, 1970.

———. "The Snake Man." *TriQuarterly* 58 (Fall 1983): 133–151.

———. "Spring Day, Great Fortune." *Sewanee Review* 86 (1978): 495–512.

———. "Translation President." *Hudson Review* 33 (1980): 233–244.

———. "Village Moon: A Comedy in One Act." *Korea Journal* 23.12 (1983): 56–66.

———. "Village Wine." *Atlantic* (May 1976): 70–73.

———. "Village Wine: A Play in One Act." *Korea Journal* 23.12 (1983): 46–55.

Ko, Won [Sung-Won Ko]. *The Turn of Zero.* Merrick, NY: Cross-Cultural Communications, 1974.

———. *With Birds of Paradise.* Los Angeles: Azalea P, 1984.

Koh, Taiwon. *The Bitter Fruit of Kom-Pawi.* New York: Holt, 1959.

Lee, Ki Chuck. "From Korea to Heaven Country." *New Worlds of Literature.* Ed. Jerome Beaty and J. Paul Hunter. New York: Norton, 1989. 28–30.

Lee, Marie G. *Finding My Voice.* Boston: Houghton, 1992.

———. *If It Hadn't Been for Yoon Jun.* Boston: Houghton, 1993.

Lee, Mary Paik. *Quiet Odyssey: A Pioneer Korean Woman in America.* Ed. Sucheng Chan. Seattle: U of Washington P, 1990.

Lee, Saebang. "To the Stars." *Amerasia Journal* 10.2 (1983): 103–104.

Lee, Tony. "Nowadays Not like Before." *Bamboo Ridge* 1 (December 1978): 3–11.

Lew, Walter. "Black Korea." *Charlie Chan Is Dead: An Anthology of Contemporary Asian American Fiction.* Ed. Jessica Hagedorn. New York: Penguin, 1993. 230–235.

———. "Fan." *Breaking Silence, An Anthology of Contemporary Asian American Poets.* Ed. Joseph Bruchac. Greenfield Center, NY: Greenfield Review P, 1983. 155–156.

———. "Leaving Seoul: 1953." *Breaking Silence, An Anthology of Contemporary Asian American Poets.* Ed. Joseph Bruchac. Greenfield Center, NY: Greenfield Review P, 1983. 152.

———. "Two Handfuls of *Waka* for Thelonious Sphere Monk (d. Feb. 1982)." *Breaking Silence, An Anthology of Contemporary Asian American Poets.* Ed. Joseph Bruchac. Greenfield Center, NY: Greenfield Review P, 1983. 157–58.

Paek, Min. *Aekyung's Dream.* San Francisco: Children's Book P, 1988.

Pahk, Induk. *The Cock Still Crows.* New York: Vantage, 1977.

———. *The Hour of the Tiger.* New York: Harper, 1965.

———. *September Monkey.* New York: Harper, 1954.

Pai, Margaret K. *The Dreams of Two Yi-min.* Honolulu: U of Hawaii P, 1989.

Pak, Ty. "The Foe." *Hawaii Review* 15 (Spring 1984): 25–28.

———. "The Gardner." *Bamboo Ridge* 21 (1983): 49–64.

———. *Guilt Payment.* Honolulu: Bamboo Ridge, 1983.

Pang, Morris. "A Korean Immigrant." *Social Process in Hawaii* 13 (1949): 19–24.

Ryu, Charles. "Koreans and Church." *Asian Americans: Oral Histories of First to Fourth Generation Americans from China, the Philippines, Japan, India, the Pacific Islands, Vietnam and Cambodia.* Ed. Joann Faung Jean Lee. New York: New P, 1992. 162–164.

———. "1.5 Generation." *Asian Americans: Oral Histories of First to Fourth Generation Americans from China, the Philippines, Japan, India, the Pacific Islands, Vietnam and Cambodia.* Ed. Joann Faung Jean Lee. New York: New P, 1992. 50–54.

Song, Cathy. "Beginnings (for Bok Pil)." *Hawaii Review* 6 (Spring 1976): 55–65.

———. *Frameless Windows, Squares of Light.* New York: Norton, 1988.

———. *Picture Bride.* Foreword, Richard Hugo. New York: Yale UP, 1983.

Song, John J. "Faith." *Charlie Chan Is Dead: An Anthology of Contemporary Asian American Fiction.* Ed. Jessica Hagedorn. New York: Penguin, 1993. 440–449.

Yim, Louise. *My Forty Year Fight for Korea: The Thrilling Personal Story of Korea's Joan of Arc.* New York: A. A. Wyn, 1951.

Yoon, Esther. "Vanishing Point." *Hawaii Review* 16 (Fall 1984): 61–63.

SELECTED SECONDARY BIBLIOGRAPHY

"Best-Selling Korean." *Life,* March 20, 1964: 125–126.

Bowers, Faubion. "Rich Bull, Poor Bull." Rev. of *The Diving Gourd,* by Kim Yong Ik. *New York Times Book Review,* November 4, 1962: 55.

Chan, Sucheng. Introduction. *Quiet Odyssey: A Pioneer Korean Woman in America.* By Mary Paik Lee. Ed. Sucheng Chan. Seattle: U of Washington P, 1990. xxi–lx.

Chang, Yunshik. Rev. of *The Martyred,* by Richard E. Kim. *Pacific Affairs* 40 (1967–1968): 387–390.

Choy, Bong-youn. *Koreans in America.* Chicago: Nelson, 1979.

Clifford, William. "Cupid and the Cow." Rev. of *The Diving Gourd,* by Kim Yong Ik. *Saturday Review,* November 24, 1962: 32–33.

"The Courage to Be." Rev. of *The Martyred,* by Richard E. Kim. *Time,* February 28, 1964: 108.

Elman, Richard M. Rev. of *The Innocent,* by Richard E. Kim. *New York Times Book Review,* November 10, 1968: 4.

Engeler, Amy. Rev. of *Clay Walls,* by Kim Ronyoung. *New York Times Book Review,* January 11, 1987: 18.

Engle, Paul. "The Story of Kim." Rev. of *The Martyred,* by Richard E. Kim. *New York Times Book Review,* February 16, 1964: 35.

Fisher, Dexter, ed. *The Third Woman: Minority Women Writers of the United States.* Boston: Houghton, 1980.

Fujita-Sato, Gayle K. " 'Third World' as Place and Paradigm in Cathy Song's *Picture Bride.*" *MELUS* 15.1 (1988): 49–72.

Galloway, David D. "The Love Stance: Richard E. Kim's *The Martyred.*" *Critique* 7 (1964–1965): 163–171.

Greenbaum, Jessica. "Family Albums." Rev. of *Picture Bride,* by Cathy Song. *Women's Review of Books,* October 1988: 19.

Hata, Nadine Ishitani. Rev. of *Quiet Odyssey: A Pioneer Korean Woman in America,* by Mary Paik Lee. *Journal of American History* 79 (1992): 700.

Hill, William B. Rev. of *The Martyred,* by Richard E. Kim. *America,* February 22, 1964: 264–265.

Hugo, Richard. Foreword. *Picture Bride.* By Cathy Song. New Haven, CT: Yale UP, 1983. ix–xiv.

Kim, Elaine H. *Asian American Literature: An Introduction to the Writings and Their Social Context.* Philadelphia: Temple UP, 1982.

———. "Asian American Writers: A Bibliographical Review." *American Studies International* 22.2 (1984): 41–78.

———. Rev. of *Quiet Odyssey: A Pioneer Korean Woman in America,* by Mary Paik Lee. *Pacific Affairs* 64 (1991): 290–292.

———. "A Survey of Asian-American Literature: Social Perspectives." Diss., U of California, Berkeley, 1976.

Kim, Hyung-chan, ed. *The Korean Diaspora: Historical and Sociological Studies of Korean Immigration and Assimilation in North America.* Santa Barbara, CA: ABC-Clio, 1977.

———. "Koreans in the United States." *Dictionary of Asian American History.* Ed. Hyung-chan Kim. New York: Greenwood, 1986. 13–22.

Kim, Hyung-chan, and Wayne Patterson. *The Koreans in America, 1882–1974: A Chronology and Fact Book.* Ethnic Chronology Series 16. Dobbs Ferry, NY: Oceana, 1974.

Klausler, Alfred P. "Unbeliever as Saint." Rev. of *The Martyred,* by Richard E. Kim. *Christian Century,* May 6, 1964: 639.

"Korean Immigration the Lowest in 20 Years." *Korean Central Daily Chicago,* April 30, 1994: 1. (In Korean.)

Lash, Richard G. " 'The Martyred' in Theological View." Rev. of *The Martyred,* by Richard E. Kim. *Korea Journal* 5.3 (1965): 55+.

Lee, John Kyhan. "The Notion of 'Self' in Korean American Literature: A Socio-Historical Perspective." Diss., U of Connecticut, 1990.

Lim, Shirley. Rev. of *Picture Bride,* by Cathy Song. *MELUS* 10.3 (1983): 95–99.

Mayberry, Jodine. *Koreans.* Recent American Immigrants Series. New York: Franklin Watts, 1991.

McCune, Evelyn. Rev. of *Lost Names,* by Richard E. Kim. *Journal of Asian Studies* 30 (1971): 472–473.

Min, Yong Soon. "Promised Land, Broken Promises." Rev. of *Quiet Odyssey: A Pioneer Korean Woman in America,* by Mary Paik Lee. *Women's Review of Books,* February 1991: 11.

Nahm, Andrew C. Rev. of *Man Sei!: The Making of a Korean American,* by Peter Hyun. *Journal of Asian Studies* 47 (1988): 385–386.

Nichols, Christopher. "The Tough and the Tender." Rev. of *The Innocent,* by Richard E. Kim. *National Review,* February 25, 1969: 183–184.

Nomaguchi, Debbie Murakami. "Cathy Song: 'I'm a Poet Who Happens to Be Asian American.' " *International Examiner,* May 2, 1984: 9.

O., S. K. "Korean Memories." Rev. of *Lost Names,* by Richard E. Kim. *Newsweek,* July 13, 1970: 100.

Oka, Takashi. "Land of the Morning Calm." Rev. of *September Monkey,* by Induk Pahk. *Christian Science Monitor,* October 28, 1954: 11.

Patterson, Wayne, and Hyung-chan Kim. *The Koreans in America.* In America Series. Minneapolis: Lerner, 1977.

Sakurai, Patricia A. Rev. of *Under Flag,* by Myung Mi Kim. *Minnesota Review* n.s. 38 (Spring–Summer 1992): 97–101.

Simpson, Hassell A. "A Bitter Lesson of Brutal Passion." Rev. of *The Innocent,* by Richard E. Kim. *Saturday Review,* November 23, 1968: 66–67.

Smith, Robert Aura. "Story from Korea." Rev. of *September Monkey,* by Induk Pahk. *New York Times Book Review,* November 7, 1954: 34.

Stephens, Michael. "Korea: Theresa Hak Kyung Cha." *The Dramaturgy of Style: Voice in Short Fiction.* Crosscurrents Modern Critiques Third Series. Carbondale: Southern Illinois UP, 1986. 184–210.

Wade, James. "Author Richard Kim Looks Homeward." *Korean Journal* 5.3 (1965): 53–54.

Walsh, Chad. "Another War Raged Within." Rev. of *The Martyred,* by Richard E. Kim. *New York Times Book Review,* February 16, 1964: 1+.

Wilson, Rob. Rev. of *Man Sei!: The Making of a Korean American,* by Peter Hyun. *MELUS* 14.1 (1987): 99–103.

Wolf, Susan. "Theresa Cha: Recalling Telling ReTelling." *AfterImage* (Summer 1986): 10–13.

Yang, Eun Sik. Rev. of *Clay Walls,* by Kim Ronyoung. *Los Angeles Times Book Review* April 26, 1987: 1+.

Yonhap Tongsin. *Korea–U.S.A. Centennial, 1882–1982.* Seoul, Korea: Yonhap News Agency, 1982.

Yu, Pyong-ch'on. "Korean Writers in America." *Korea Journal* 7.12 (1967): 17–19.

Yun, Chung-Hei. "Beyond 'Clay Walls': Korean American Literature." *Reading the Literatures of Asian America.* Ed. Shirley Geok-lin Lim and Amy Ling. Philadelphia: Temple UP, 1992. 79–95.

9
Pakistani-American Literature
Sunil Sharma

INTRODUCTION

Although immigration from South Asia to the United States began in the early decades of this century, when Punjabis arrived and settled down as farmers in California, Pakistani nationals as such did not, of course, come here until the creation of Pakistan in 1947 after the partition of British India. However, only after the 1965 Immigration Act did Pakistanis settle here in substantial numbers. In keeping with the general trend of immigrants from South Asia, while the more recent arrivals have been from diverse socioeconomic backgrounds, the early post-1947 immigrants were largely professionals and academics. Their writing is mainly in English and is part of the larger post-colonial writing scene in South Asia. Due to the cultural and historical links between the different countries of South Asia, the category of Pakistani-American immigrant literature cannot be entirely separated from the larger one of South Asian. Specific categories like Pakistani-American literature and general ones like literature by South Asian Muslims or South Asian women overlap to a great extent and ideally would be contained under the general rubric of South Asian-American literature, as is seen in many of the anthologies mentioned later. However, this survey is limited to writers of Pakistani origin who reside in the United States. Canada has an equally significant and perhaps even more active expatriate Pakistani literary community, and while Canadian writers of Pakistani origin are not included here, it should be noted that the Canadian journal *Toronto Review of Contemporary Writing Abroad* (*Toronto South Asian Review* until recently) is the chief publication of South Asian writers in North America. Those who chose to write in English are mostly part of the American academic world and, more often than not, were educated in the United States. In addition to English, Pakistani Americans also write in Urdu and Punjabi, but this literature has a different audience and has received less critical attention. As far as I know, there is no writing published in the United States in other regional languages such as Punjabi and Sindhi, although several writers residing here have their works published in Pakistan or India, among other places, in these languages.

The experiences of these immigrants are relatively recent, and despite the diversity of voices from the community, as yet there are no significant second-generation voices to tell their stories. In general, Pakistani Americans have written about the problems of deracination and alienation, themes common to all immigrant groups and peoples. What they share in common with other writers of the South Asian diaspora worldwide is the memory of colonialism, partition, and the problems of nationalism. Apart from these recurrent themes, transnationalism, with its problems of cultural and geographical separation between people, is the most human and touching aspect of this literature. However, most Pakistani-American writers who write in English, especially Zulfikar Ghose and Bapsi Sidhwa, have received very little critical attention in Pakistan despite the efforts of critics like Tariq Rahman and Alamgir Hashmi, who regularly review their works. In addition to providing multifarious topics, the immigrant experience has enabled writers to express themselves freely in ways not possible otherwise.

WRITING IN ENGLISH

Zulfikar Ghose is a writer who transcends categories and exemplifies the complex nature of the Pakistani-American experience. He is not a spokesperson for one particular nation, culture, or community. Born in Sialkot (now in Pakistan) before partition, he lived in Bombay for a few years, where he witnessed the communal wars between Muslims and Hindus, until he moved to England. He now resides in the United States. Given the story of his life, writing about alienation and exile has been a major preoccupation of his. But at the same time, although he started off by writing about being uprooted from India and Pakistan, his work is situated on a global plane, as is reflected in the settings of his novels, sometimes all in one work: Pakistan, India, England, Texas, and South America. His breadth of work is prodigious: he has authored novels, poetry, literary criticism, and essays. *The Review of Contemporary Fiction* devoted the summer 1989 issue to him (along with Milan Kundera); it has a selected bibliography of his works by C. Kanaganayakam, who is also preparing a study on him. Ghose's first collection of poetry, entitled *The Loss of India,* was shortly followed by his autobiography, *Confessions of a Native-Alien.* His early novels are concerned directly with recent Indian and Pakistani history, while the later, experimental ones, although not set there, explore issues such as the politics of nationalism, post-colonialism, and the relationship between language and reality, in the words of Kanaganayakam, "in a manner that avoids both the snares of essentialism and the temptations of obscurity" ("Zulfikar Ghose" 133). Going back home and journeys of all kinds are treated in various genres; his novel *The Triple Mirror of the Self* is described as the "imaginative transformations of what is documented in his autobiography" (Kanaganayakam, "Re-Tracing the Past" 82). The title of his latest short story, published in *Toronto Review of Contemporary Writing Abroad,* "Arrival in India," suggests an autobiographical piece. The story is a superb irony about imaginary utopias, narrated by a Spanish Muslim scholar from Granada who sets sail with Columbus, and on reaching America thinks he has found the India of his dreams. Set in a different time and age, it seems to capture Ghose's life, which has seen many homes, but going back is the ultimate delusion. In 1986, he said in an interview, "I have not been back to India or Pakistan for twenty-three years. Neither country has given me the slightest recognition. But this has nothing to do with writing" (Kanaganayakam, "Zulfikar Ghose" 180).

Bapsi Sidhwa is from the minority Parsi community in Pakistan, a background that provides much rich material in her novels. Of her four novels, the first three are set in the subcontinent, and the fourth in the United States. Her first novel, *The Crow Eaters,* is an insider's ironic look at the life of the Parsis. *The Bride* and *Cracking India* (published as *Ice-Candy Man* in Britain) both have partition as a historical backdrop, an event that has informed the work of almost every post-colonial South Asian writer. *The Bride* explores the effect of the clash of values between the modern urban and traditional tribal segments of Pakistani society on women. *Cracking India,* narrated from a child's perspective, is monumental in scale and directly concerned with partition, in the tradition of Rushdie's *Midnight's Children.* Her latest novel, *An American Brat,* is a delightful social comedy of the way America is seen by a sixteen-year-old Parsi girl from Pakistan, as she simultaneously deals with the problems of cultural differences and adolescence. This is a subject that has been more often explored in film than in the novel by South Asians. In an interview, Sidhwa emphasizes her Pakistani identity as a writer but also comments on her loneliness while growing up as a Parsi in predominantly Muslim Pakistan.

Apart from Sidhwa's fictional account of experiencing life in America, the Pakistani poet Waqas Ahmad Khwaja, who writes in English, attended the Iowa Writing Program in 1988 and has published a memoir of his time in the United States, entitled *Writers and Landscapes.* This includes poetry, a travelogue, stories about the people he met, and impressions of American life.

Whereas the novel has been mainly utilized to explore the larger themes of partition and post-colonial realities, the short story has been a more popular and successful genre in narrating the day-to-day experiences of Pakistani immigrants. Tahira Naqvi, who was born in Iran and grew up in Pakistan, has written short stories that sensitively deal with the special problems of transnational Pakistani families. Her touching short story "Journeys" is about an old Pakistani woman who reluctantly visits her son in the United States. She only wants to be buried in Pakistan on her death and fears dying in America and the problems that would cause her son. In "Hiatus," the protagonist is a Pakistani-American woman who, on a visit home, becomes emotionally caught up in a plot of land that she and her husband own there. The land symbolizes her last tie to her homeland, and it is not easy letting go of it. Naqvi has also done fine translations of short stories of the Urdu writers Sadat Hasan Manto, published as *Another Lonely Voice,* and Ismat Chugtai, published as *The Quilt and Other Stories.* Javaid Qazi is another short story writer whose work has appeared in various journals. Excerpts from his novel *Alien Harvest,* published in the *Toronto South Asian Review,* are episodes from the life of a Pakistani foreign student in the United States, depicting the different sexual mores of the two cultures. "Beast of Bengal," a satirical sketch of a foreign student whose sense of reality becomes embroiled with the past as he studies an Indian historical text, comments on the nature of South Asian studies in American academe. "President Sahib's Blue Period," a satire on the regime of General Zia ul-Haq in the 1980s in Pakistan, allows Qazi as a nonresident to scathingly criticize the political situation there. Syed Afzal Haider, who was born in India and grew up in Pakistan, writes short stories chiefly with non-South Asian characters. His "Brooklyn to Karachi via Amsterdam" deals with a Pakistani American's coming to terms with his alienation from his family in Pakistan as well as his American wife and kids.

The travel essay by expatriates who go back home for a visit is a newly cultivated genre. Javaid Qazi's essay "A Passage to Pakistan: A Personal Memoir," on going back to Pakistan after living in the United States for several years, highlights the emotional and cultural detachment that develops after being away from one's homeland for an extended period of time. Zulfikar Ghose also has such an essay, "Going Home," which allows him to reestablish connections and heal old wounds caused by leaving his place of birth. Expatriates are critical and insightful observers about people, places, and things in their homeland that were once familiar but have now become alien to them.

Sara Suleri's kaleidoscopic autobiographical work *Meatless Days* is a memoir of growing up in Pakistan as the daughter of a Pakistani father and Welsh mother and then moving to the United States. In a complex metaphorical style, Suleri weaves her rich narrative back and forth from the present to the past and, touchingly but without sentimentality, recounts the story of her large family, especially the women who have experienced displacement. She attempts to make sense of the past in terms of the different realities of the present, in both temporal and cultural terms. Ties to one's homeland eventually must be broken, but at the same time one's "new" identity must be forged. Another problem that members of transnational families face, as in the case of Suleri and her siblings, is living in different parts of the world and becoming separated from each other not just by distance but by disparate experiences; thus, the only connection left is the past.

(Aurangzeb) Alamgir Hashmi, like other post-colonial South Asian writers, has lived in various places in the world. A resident of the United States in the

1970s, he also lived in Switzerland before deciding to return home to Pakistan. His poems appear in a wide variety of publications, and he has published several collections of poems, *The Oath and Amen, America Is a Punjabi Word,* and *My Second in Kentucky.* His poetry is impressionistic and highlights psychological and geographical differences in the poet's experiences. Western critics have commented on the influence of the Urdu tradition in his poetry, which is really a reflection of his cross-cultural consciousness and cosmopolitan perspective.

Two Pakistanis are included in the impressive anthology of writing by American women of South Asian origin, *Our Feet Walk the Sky: Women of the South Asian Diaspora.* Huma Dar's poems are a deeply felt emotional expression of her experience as a battered wife and a single mother. Ruxana Meer's poem and short prose piece deal with issues of female sexuality. A representative of the second generation of Pakistani Americans is Umair Haque, whose poems have been published in Pakistan.

WRITING IN URDU

The audience for Urdu literature by Pakistani-American writers is mainly based in Pakistan and India, although the works published there make their way west and are read by Pakistanis there. Given the fact that they belong to a different literary sphere, some of their work is enriched by drawing on the immigrant experience. A recent anthology of Urdu short stories, *Fasânah kaheñ jise,* is representative of the variety of writing in Urdu outside South Asia and includes short stories by authors in Europe and North America. Three Pakistani-American writers, Rifat Murtaza (previously Mirza), Shaista Aiman, and Anwar Khwaja, are included in this work. All three stories deal with the encounter of Pakistanis with Americans and depict Pakistanis in culturally alien situations: in Murtaza's ''Qâtil,'' a woman becomes emotionally entangled in the life of her housekeeper, whose son has been involved in a holdup and shooting; Aiman's ''Be Únvân Rishta'' deals with the recurrent theme of a woman's discovering that her lover, Pakistani in this case, is involved with her merely to get a green card; Khwaja's ''Roz'' is about the common feeling of selfishness that lies beneath the desires of young people, in spite of cultural differences between a young Pakistani-American man and an American woman.

Iftikhar Nasim is a poet whose Urdu and Punjabi work is published in journals in Pakistan and India. Nasim has written frankly on gay themes and has introduced this topic into modern Urdu poetry. Some English translations of his poems have appeared in the United States, including a poem in the anthology *A Lotus of Another Color: An Unfolding of the South Asian Gay and Lesbian Experience.* Muhammad Umar Memon has translated and edited many works from Urdu; he has written short stories in Urdu that he has himself translated into English. Humera Rahman writes poetry in Urdu. Razia Fasih Ahmad, a novelist, who was a well-established writer in Pakistan, has continued to write in Urdu after moving to the United States and is published in Pakistan.

JOURNALISM AND SCHOLARLY PUBLICATIONS

Numerous weekly and monthly newspapers are published in English and Urdu, both for a national and a local audience. In English there are the *Pakistan Link* (Los Angeles), *Pakistan Herald* (New York), and *Minaret* (New York); and in Urdu, *Urdû Tâimz* (New York). The journal *Annual of Urdu Studies,* previously published in Chicago and now in Madison, Wisconsin, has been the primary source for scholarly writing about Urdu literature. *The Journal of South Asian Literature* (previously, *Mehfil*) also includes relevant material, including original writing by Pakistanis. Each issue provides information about new publications with respect to Urdu studies. *Urdû Intarneshnal* (Karachi) is a journal that includes work by writers living outside Pakistan.

SELECTED PRIMARY BIBLIOGRAPHY

English

Abbasi, Talat. "Going to Baltistan." *Massachusetts Review* 29.4 (Winter 1988–1989): 633–636.

Dar, Huma. "The Battle Cry of an Ex-Battered Ex-Wife!" *Our Feet Walk the Sky: Women of the South Asian Diaspora.* Ed. Women of South Asian Descent Collective. San Francisco: Aunt Lute Books, 1993. 252.

———. "The Little Yellow Jacket: The One I Made Before You Were Taken Away." *Our Feet Walk the Sky.* Ed. Women of South Asian Descent Collective. San Francisco: Aunt Lute Books, 1993. 71.

———. [Untitled poem.] *Our Feet Walk the Sky.* Ed. Women of South Asian Descent Collective. San Francisco: Aunt Lute Books, 1993. 31.

———. "Kamala Das." *Massachusetts Review* 29.4 (Winter 1988–1989): 682.

Ghose, Zulfikar. "Arrival in India." *Toronto Review of Contemporary Writing Abroad* 12.1 (1993): 1–11.

———. *Confessions of a Native-Alien.* London: Routledge and Kegan Paul, 1965.

———. *The Contradictions.* London: Macmillan, 1966.

———. *Crump's Terms.* London: Macmillan, 1975.

———. "Daniel Zwernemann's Flight." *Transatlantic Review* 41 (Winter–Spring 1972): 79–81.

———. *Don Bueno.* New York: Holt, Rinehart, and Winston, 1984.

———. *Figures of Enchantment.* London: Hutchinson, 1986; New York: Harper and Row, 1986.

———. "Going Home." *Toronto South Asian Review* 9.2 (1991): 15–22.

———. *Hulme's Investigations into the Bogart Script.* Austin: Curbstone, 1981.

———. *The Incredible Brazilian: A Different World.* London: Macmillan, 1978; New York: Overlook, 1984.

———. *The Incredible Brazilian: The Beautiful Empire.* London: Macmillan, 1975; New York: Overlook, 1983.

———. *The Incredible Brazilian: The Native.* London: Macmillan, 1972: New York: Holt, Rinehart, and Winston, 1972; New York: Overlook, 1983.

———. *Jets from Orange.* London: Macmillan, 1967.

———. "The Last Watermelon in Texas"; "Surprising Flowers"; "Bells in Goliad." *Chelsea* 46 (1987): 214–216.

———. "Lila of the Butterflies and Her Chronicler." *Latin American Literary Review* 13.25 (1985): 151–157.

———. *The Loss of India.* London: Routledge and Kegan Paul, 1964.

———. "Maggie's Orchard." *Journal of Indian Writing in English* 16.2 (1988): 191–209.

———. *A Memory of Reality.* Austin: Curbstone, 1984.

———. *The Murder of Aziz Khan.* London: Macmillan, 1967; New York: John Day, 1969.

———. *A New History of Torments.* New York: Holt, Rinehart, and Winston, 1982.

———. "Redbrick Ritual." *Twentieth Century* (October 1959): 275–279.

———. "The Rough Ride." *Ambit* 16 (1963): 24–30.

———. "The Savage Mother of Desire." *Chelsea* 46 (1987): 279–290.

———. "Schooldays: In Bombay." *Twentieth Century* (October 1960): 312–320.

———. "The Sealed Light of Being." *Exile* 12.2 (1987): 89–93.

———. "The Sounds of Cricket." *Allsorts 2.* Ed. Ann Thwaite. London: Macmillan, 1969. 18–24.

———. "Three Poems." *Toronto South Asian Review* 6.1 (1987): 14–16.

———. *The Triple Mirror of the Self.* London: Bloomsbury, 1992.

———. "Two Poems." *Toronto South Asian Review* 4.3 (1986): 11–13.

———. *The Violent West.* London: Macmillan, 1972.

———. "The Waxahachie Coincidence." *Transatlantic Review* 45 (Spring 1973): 86–94.

———. "With Music by Dmitri Tiomkin." *New Quarterly* 3.1 (1978): 25–33.

Haider, Syed Afzal. "Brooklyn to Karachi via Amsterdam." *No Worst, There Is None.* Ed. E. Beverly and A. Dawid. (forthcoming)

Haque, Umair. *Blighted Within.* Lahore: Maktaba, 1992.

Hashmi, Alamgir. *America Is a Punjabi Word.* Lahore: Karakoram Range, 1979.

———. "Bahawalpurlog." *Toronto South Asian Review* 2.2 (1983): 75–79.

———. "Eight Poems." *Journal of South Asian Literature* 13.1–4 (1977–1978): 295–305.

———. "Five Poems." *Toronto South Asian Review* 6.1 (1987): 63–66.

———. *Inland and Other Poems.* Islamabad: Gulmohar Press, 1988.

———. *My Second in Kentucky.* Lahore: Vision Press, 1981.

———. *Neither This Time/Nor That Place.* Lahore: Vision Press, 1984.

———. *The Oath and Amen.* Philadelphia: Dorrance, 1976.

———. *This Time in Lahore.* Lahore: Vision Press, 1983.

———. "Six Poems." *Toronto South Asian Review* 4.2 (1985): 44–51.

———. *Sun and Moon and Other Poems.* Islamabad: Indus Books, 1992.

Ibrahim, Huma. *See* Dar, Huma.

Khwaja, Waqas Ahmad. *Writers and Landscapes.* Lahore: Sang-e-Meel, 1991.

Meer, Ruxana. "love supreme/you can name your daughter." *Our Feet Walk the Sky.* Ed. Women of South Asian Descent Collective. San Francisco: Aunt Lute Books, 1993. 205.

———. "we're not mean, we're just hardheaded." *Our Feet Walk the Sky.* Ed. Women of South Asian Descent Collective. San Francisco: Aunt Lute Books, 1993. 264–266.

Memon, Muhammad Umar. "The Apocalypse." *Versions of Truth: Urdu Short Stories from Pakistan.* Ed. Khalid Hasan and Faruq Hassan. New Delhi: Vikas Publishing House, 1983. 188–199. (Urdu version "Bijli basant" in *Târîk galî,* 141–152, see next section.)

———. "The Dark Alley." *The Tale of the Old Fisherman: Contemporary Urdu Short Stories.* Ed. Muhammad Umar Memon. Washington, DC: Three Continents Press, 1991. 139–156. (Urdu version is title story in *Târîk galî,* 103–122, see next section.)

———. "The Worm and the Sunflower." *Toronto South Asian Review* 1.2 (1983): 17–30. (Urdu version "Kenchua aur surajmakhkhi" in *Târîk galî,* 123–139, see next section.)

Naqvi, Tahira. "Hiatus." *Massachusetts Review* 29.4 (Winter 1988–1989): 744–761.

———. "Journeys." *Journal of South Asian Literature* 21.1 (1986): 71–79.

Nasim, Ifti. "Narman." *A Lotus of Another Color: An Unfolding of the South Asian Gay and Lesbian Experience.* Ed. Rakesh Ratti. Boston: Alyson, 1993. 71–72.

Qazi, Javaid. "Alien Harvest." *Toronto South Asian Review* 6.1 (1987): 66–76.

———. "The Beast of Bengal." *Toronto South Asian Review* 4.2 (1985): 34–42. (Also in *Chelsea* 46 [1987]: 266–273.)

———. "From Alien Harvest—The Ski Trip." *Toronto South Asian Review* 7.3 (1989): 56–67.

———. "Gloria Mundy and Other Depravities." *Kansas Quarterly* 12.1 (Winter 1980): 153–157.

———. "A Passage to Pakistan: A Personal Memoir." *Chelsea* 46 (1987): 157–180.

———. "President Sahib's Blue Period." *Massachusetts Review* (Winter 1988–1989): 683–700.

———. "Slouching towards San Hozay." *Sequoia* 25.1 (Winter 1982): 6–10.

Sidhwa, Bapsi. *An American Brat.* Minneapolis: Milkweed Editions, 1993.

———. *The Bride.* London: Cape, 1983.

———. *Cracking India.* Minneapolis: Milkweed Editions, 1991. (Published as *The Ice-Candy Man,* London: Michael Joseph, 1985.)

———. *The Crow Eaters.* Lahore: Privately published, 1978.

Suleri, Sara. *Meatless Days.* Chicago: University of Chicago Press, 1989.

Urdu

Aiman, Shaista. "Be Unvân Rishta." *Fasânah kaheñ jise: maghrib meñ mukhtasar afsânah aur bayâlis Urdû afsâneh.* Ed. Sayyid Ashur Kazimi. Dihlî: Ejukeshnal Pablishing Haus, 1993. 321–324.

Khwaja, Anwar. "Roz." *Fasânah kaheñ jise: maghrib meñ mukhtasar afsânah aur bayâlis Urdû afsâneh.* Ed. Sayyid Ashur Kazimi. Dihlî: Ejukeshnal Pablishing Haus, 1993. 325–338.

Memon, Muhammad Umar. *Tarîk galî.* Lâhaur: Sang-e mîl pablîkeshanz, 1989.

Murtaza, Rifat. *Âdam kî paslî.* Lâhaur: Sang-e mîl pablîkeshanz, 1991.

———. "Qâtil." *Fasânah kaheñ jise: maghrib mēn mukhtasar afsânah aur bayâlis urdû afsâneh.* Ed. Sayyid Ashur Kazimi. Dihlî: Ejukeshnal Pablishing Haus, 1993. 314–320.

Nasim, Iftikhar. *Ghazaal.* Chicago: South Asian Performing Arts Council of America, 1992.

———. [Poems.] *She'r va hikmat: dawr-i duvvum.* Hyderâbâd: Maktaba-e Sher va Hikmat, 1990. 216–227.

SELECTED SECONDARY BIBLIOGRAPHY

Ali, Hina Babar. "Alamgir Hashmi's Wandering Soul." *Journal of South Asian Literature* 23.1 (1988): 146–150.

Campbell, Ewing. "Encountering the Other in *The Fiction of Reality.*" *Review of Contemporary Fiction* 9.2 (1989): 220–224.

Harris, Wilson. "A Note on Zulfikar Ghose's 'Nature Strategies.' " *Review of Contemporary Fiction* 9.2 (1989): 172–178.

Kanaganayakam, Chelva. "Interview with Bapsi Sidhwa." *Toronto South Asian Review* 11.1 (Summer 1992): 43–53.

———. "The Luminous Comprehension: From Realism to Counter-Realism in the Writings of Zulfikar Ghose." *Review of Contemporary Fiction* 9.2 (1989): 225–235.

———. "Re-Tracing the Past." *Toronto South Asian Review* 11.1 (Summer 1992): 81–85.

———. "Zulfikar Ghose." *Writers of the Indian Diaspora: A Bio-Bibliographical Critical Sourcebook.* Ed. Emmanuel S. Nelson. Westport, CT: Greenwood Press, 1993. 129–136.

———. "Zulfikar Ghose: An Interview." *Twentieth Century Literature* 32.2 (1986): 169–186.

Lim, Shirley Geok-lin. "A Poetics of Location: Reading Zulfikar Ghose." *Review of Contemporary Fiction* 9.2 (1989): 188–191.

Naim, C. M. "Narmân kâ shâ'ir." *She'r va hikmat: dawr-i duvvum.* Hyderâbâd: Maktaba-e Sher va Hikmat, 1990. 212–215. (On Iftikhar Nasim.)

Rahman, Tariq. *A History of Pakistani Literature in English.* Lahore: Vanguard Books, 1991.

Sadana, Rashmi. "Making a Space for Women in the Third World: Displacement and Identity in Suleri's *Meatless Days.*" *Our Feet Walk the Sky.* Ed. Women of South Asian Descent Collective. San Francisco: Aunt Lute Books, 1993. 320–324.

Scheick, William J. "Fictional Self and Mythical Art: *A New History of Torments and Don Bueno.*" *Review of Contemporary Fiction* 9.2 (1989): 209–219.

Vassenji, M. G. "A Conversation with Zulfikar Ghose." *Toronto South Asian Review* 4.3 (1986): 14–21.

II
CARIBBEAN-
AMERICAN
LITERATURES

10

Anglophone Caribbean-American Literature

Aparajita Sagar

INTRODUCTION

Immigration, not just to the United States but also to other First World nations such as Canada and England, has had a more profound effect on Caribbean cultural production than perhaps anywhere else in the post-colonial world. As the contemporary Jamaican-American writer Michelle Cliff says, "The Caribbean doesn't exist as an entity; it exists all over the world. It started in diaspora and it continues in diaspora" (Cliff, Interview). Caribbean cultural production within or outside the borders has always engaged the legacy of a brutal 500-year colonial past that saw the decimation of entire groups of indigenous people followed by the forced importation of others—of Africans through slavery and of Asians through indenture processes designed to replace slaves with what was, in effect, bonded labor. Left to negotiate new identities, often vis-à-vis groups of other brutally displaced Third World communities, and often while their African and Asian languages and cultural practices were being eroded through colonial education and forced "acculturation," Caribbean people have, from the start of their history, been violently inserted into a diaspora premised on absence. Post-independence migrations to Europe and North America in the twentieth century have reconfigured this already diasporic culture, scattering it across an even wider terrain. Caribbean literature, immigrant and nonimmigrant, is born of these experiences of erasure, enforced transculturation, and diaspora. The imaginative resilience and power with which it counters these experiences unite an array of Caribbean cultural practices.

This chapter is a broad overview of these practices as developed in the literature of U.S. immigrants from the English-speaking Caribbean. In the section titled "Migration and Diaspora," I examine the historical context of Caribbean migration to the United States in this century. A subsequent section, "Literary-Cultural History," focuses on the specific ways in which the past of historical erasure, colonial violence, and resistance has informed Anglophone Caribbean literature. In "Dominant Concerns," I examine similar concerns in the narrower context of U.S. immigrant Caribbean literature.

MIGRATION AND DIASPORA

Despite vast cultural, linguistic, economic, and political differences among the Anglophone independent nations and dependencies in the Caribbean Sea, these nations share structural similarities resulting from their common past of colonization by England and from their proximity and enforced economic dependency on the United States. Critical to any historical understanding of Caribbean immigration is an awareness of the ways in which Caribbean economies and cultures have been underdeveloped through European colonization and present-day U.S. domination. This theme unites all the varied stages of Caribbean history: the days of the Middle Passage, of slavery and white plantocracy; of the importation of indentured Asian labor after the emancipation of slaves in 1838; of U.S. control through the Monroe Doctrine; of many stages of Caribbean anti-imperial resistance, including the widespread riots of the 1930s and 1940s and the independence movements of the 1950s and 1960s; of the nominal decolonizations of the 1960s; of the short-lived attempts to forge a West Indian federation of nations in the 1950s; of the present structures of U.S. hegemony through the New World order. Through all of these phases, as Carmen Diana Deere et al. note, the Caribbean has never been seen as anything but a generator of surplus value, "a source for cheap labor and a market for U.S. goods," an economy intended to "produce what it does not consume" (3). Among the resources that it produces without using are a highly skilled workforce, a significant percentage of which has been migrating to the First World throughout this century. Taking the case of Jamaica as paradigmatic, Robert A. Pastor notes that between 1950 and 1980, as many as one in five Jamaicans emigrated to the United States; in the 1970s, "the equivalent of more than half" of Jamaican university and vocational school graduates left for North America (13). Pastor concludes that emigration has turned the Anglophone Caribbean as a whole into "a moveable object" (4). The cost of migration on such a scale is crippling, as is widely recognized. Yet, given the pressures to which the small economies of the Caribbean have been subjected through the centuries—"chronic overpopulation, scarce resources, seclusion, and limited opportunities of small island nations"—emigration has come to be seen as "a survival strategy . . . a normal and expected part of the adult life cycle, a virtual rite of passage" (Kasinitz 19–20).

There have been three waves of migration to the United States from the Caribbean. The first, which lasted from 1900 to 1930, began slowly, with around 200 to 300 immigrants every year. But this number grew steadily, doubling every few years, until by 1930, roughly 178,000 immigrants from the Caribbean had arrived in the United States (Maingot 63). The second wave, between the 1930s and 1960s, was the weakest, with the majority of emigrants from the Caribbean in this period going to England. The last wave, from 1965 to the present, has been the strongest of the three, with non-Hispanic Caribbean immigrants to the United States numbering about 50,000 a year in the 1980s. In the 1990s, the Caribbean presence in major U.S. cities, particularly in New York, is highly visible, with the establishment of specifically Caribbean neighborhoods, educational and social institutions, and cultural events such as Carnival (Kasinitz 27).

The First Wave

The first wave of migration covers the first three decades of the twentieth century. Most immigrants to the United States came from the working and landless classes at home but rose quickly to prominence in the limited avenues open to blacks in the United States, becoming landlords, professionals, and businesspeople. When the first wave of immigration ended, Afro-Caribbeans already formed "a disproportionately high percentage of . . . the professional, economic, and political leadership of New York's black community," the city where most had settled (Kasinitz 25). By 1930, Caribbean immigrants constituted between 1 and 1.5 percent of the entire black American population and a quarter of the population of Harlem (Maingot 63).

Although very few among this group pursued literature as a profession, their presence in the tradition of U.S. Caribbean writing is vivid and indelible. The reason is their unforgettable depiction in literature by their U.S.-born offspring, including major contemporary American writers such as Paule Marshall and Audre Lorde. The struggles of this first immigrant group to survive, their complex and sometimes troubled relationships with the African-American community, and their rich cultural traditions have been commemorated in U.S. Caribbean classics such as Marshall's *Brown Girl Brownstones* (1959) and Lorde's *Zami, A New Spelling of My Name, A Biomythography* (1982). Both Marshall and Lorde have written of the tremendously formative influence on their writing and their feminism of oral Caribbean culture, to which each was introduced by her mother.

A second reason for the importance of the first immigrant generation is the work of a small subset of literary and political activists who came in the first wave. The most influential figure here is Claude McKay (1890–1948), the Jamaican-born poet, novelist, and political activist who was to play a pivotal role in the Harlem renaissance. Before his arrival in the United States, McKay had already published some "dialect poetry" celebrating rural and underclass

Jamaican culture. In the United States he was a central presence in the Harlem renaissance and a founding member of the Black Writers Guild, which included renowned African-American writers, including Jean Toomer, Zora Neale Hurston, Countee Cullen, and Arna Borntemps. McKay's stay in the United States partly overlapped with the stays of two other famous Caribbean political activists: C.L.R. James, the Marxist novelist, playwright, and cultural critic from Trinidad, and Marcus Garvey from Jamaica, the founder of the United Negro Improvement Association (UNIA), which stands for the first widespread political resistance in the African diaspora. Vociferously critical of both European colonialism in the Caribbean and the United States' systemic exploitation of its African-American minority, this group has been credited with creating "the first major alliance between the Communist party and the black community" (Maingot 68). Their views subjected them to continual harrassment by U.S. authorities, who classified them as "agitators" and "subversives" and eventually, by denying them immigration and visas, forced them to leave for England or the Caribbean. McKay, however, returned to the United States on a British passport and lived here, often in conditions of poverty, until his death in Chicago in 1948.

McKay's poetry and novels have been critical in inviting later writers to engage questions of class and ethnicity and to inflect the language of the printed text with the oral culture and poetry of the underclass. His dialect poetry in Jamaica had celebrated the strength and resilience of oppressed peasant culture. His fiction, most of which was written either in the United States or Europe and which included works such as *Home to Harlem* (1928), *Banjo: A Story without a Plot* (1929), and *Banana Bottom* (1933), criticized black middle-class values as the sterile and oppressive legacies of Western imperialism. McKay's political views shifted radically over the course of his career, taking him from a conviction that black resistance needed to organize around the axis of class rather than race, to a near reversal of this position. His relationship with African-American culture, meanwhile, was always close but rarely untroubled. While he is often criticized on this and related grounds—for instance, for his depiction of women and his romanticization and even exoticization of poverty—McKay is also appreciated for evolving a tradition that could bring the language and culture of the people to the forefront of African-American and Caribbean literature. His influence on later Caribbean thinkers and writers, including Aime Cesaire and Rene Depestre, has been considerable.

The Second Wave

In the 1920s and 1930s, a series of U.S. policies and historical developments, such as immigration restrictions in 1924, the Immigration Act of 1932, and the depression, caused Caribbean immigration figures to drop sharply, a trend that continued until the 1960s. Between the 1930s and 1960s, a small number, comprising mainly students or relatives of earlier immigrants, came to the United

States; other emigrating Caribbeans went to England, which had loosened immigration restrictions in order to meet "postwar labor shortages" (Kasinitz 26). Literary figures within this English immigrant group exercised a crucial influence on later traditions of U.S. immigrant Caribbean writing. Prominent figures here include Wilson Harris from Guyana, Edward Kamau Brathwaite and George Lamming from Barbados, V. S. Naipaul and Sam Selvon from Trinidad, and Derek Walcott from St. Lucia. In both their education at home and their sojourns abroad, this generation contended with empire and Englishness, and their writing typically negotiates post-coloniality vis-à-vis colonial/imperial England rather than the United States. Later in their careers, however, and especially from the 1970s onward, the writers of this generation traveled extensively to the United States, often for extended stays as invited professors and writers-in-residence in U.S. universities. This fact, as well as the overpowering cultural and political presence of the United States in the Caribbean, has caused some writers within this generation to engage more closely with U.S. culture in their later works. The outcome of this engagement is works such as Walcott's *The Arkansas Testament* (1987), a collection of poems that weave the narrator's experience in the United States with his returns to the Caribbean, or Naipaul's *Turn in the South* (1988), a narrative of his travels in the southern United States. Since the base of these writers continues to be the Caribbean and/or England, they do not belong to a U.S. immigrant literary tradition. However, as a highly prominent generation, whose works are sometimes seen as inaugurating the first flowering of Caribbean print literature, their influence on Caribbean-U.S. writers has been significant, though not always direct or uncritically embraced.

The Third Wave

In the 1950s and 1960s the pattern of Caribbean emigration shifted again as England severely curtailed immigration from Caribbean nations that were now beginning to gain independence. Meanwhile, the U.S. Hart-Cellar Immigration Act of 1965 made it easier for Caribbean citizens to gain entry. The third wave of immigration to the United States, which dates from the 1960s to the present, has made it possible for Caribbean-born men and women across the classes to come to the United States. The artists, writers, musicians, academics, cultural critics, and political thinkers among this generation, in conjunction with the United States-born offspring of earlier immigrants, have put the immigrant experience of the United States in the forefront of Caribbean cultural production. Prominent writers among this group include Jan Carew (Guyana), Michelle Cliff (Jamaica), Rosa Guy (Trinidad), Ismith Khan (Trinidad), Audre Lorde (Grenada, United States-born), Garth St. Omer (St. Lucia), Jamaica Kincaid (Antigua), Paule Marshall (Barbados United States-born), Orlando Patterson (Jamaica), Michael Thelwell (Jamaica), and Sylvia Wynter (Jamaica). Writers of African descent dominate in this group, although Khan, who emigrated to the United States in the 1950s, and Selvon, who emigrated to Canada after his stay in Britain, are indications of the East Indian-Caribbean presence in North America.

In contrast to the first two phases of Anglophone Caribbean literature, the role of women in the present generation is strongly visible. One reason for this is the significant number of Caribbean women who, having emigrated to the United States on their own in search of higher education and work, have later turned to writing. Second, women born in the United States of immigrant Caribbean parents, such as Lorde and Marshall, are being published and read in greater numbers, frequently as part of an African-American feminist tradition. Such writers have sometimes sought other affiliations in addition to the Caribbean immigrant tradition. Lesbian and political activist writers such as Lorde and Cliff have allied themselves with a global community of women of color, or, as Cliff has described it, a tradition of "political novelists" united by "political enthusiasms" rather than "origins" (Cliff, Interview 598). The counterparts of this generation of U.S.-Caribbean women are Dionne Brande and Marlene Noubrese Philip in Canada, Beryl Gilroy and Zee Edgell in England, and Merle Hodge and Merle Collins in Grenada.

The twentieth-century history of the Caribbean diaspora indicates that migration is more readily accepted in the Caribbean than perhaps other Third World nations and is less frequently construed as a sign of the emigrant's disaffection or lack of national feeling. Even so, Caribbean immigrant writers, like other Third World immigrants, are sometimes taken to task over their "authenticity" and their ability to represent the world they have left behind. In response, writers of the second wave tended to cite the difficulty of publishing in the Caribbean and the general lack of resources to support literary activity. Later immigrant writers, particularly in the United States, have focused on a second, primarily political reason for their departure. Thus, when informed of a controversy over whether or not Caribbean writers abroad could be included in a Caribbean studies program being developed at University of Hartford, Cliff replied with the words quoted in the beginning of this chapter (Cliff, Interview 597). She added that only in emigrating could she find a political community. In Jamaica, her light skin and economically privileged background became a wedge, distancing her from activist groups. For such writers, the contemporary First World is alluring not because, as is conventionally supposed, it is the site of absolute freedom and egalitarianism but, rather, because the removal to it allows the writers paradoxically to overcome the distance between themselves and the masses at home: political activism becomes a reason to leave rather than to stay. Cliff suggests that the grip of neocolonialism in Jamaica has made it impossible for her to "see extreme political change . . . as a possibility" (Cliff, Interview 600). If the fact of being a majority rather than minority culture at home frees Afro-Caribbeans from the widespread political and institutional racism with which African Americans and black British populations have to contend in the First World, it is also true that race hierarchies in the Caribbean, displaced onto those of color-class, gender, and ethnicity, have produced a comparably stratified culture. With this in mind, the Guyanese-American writer Jan Carew has said:

[T]he colonizing zeal of the European made indigenous people exiles in their own countries—Prospero made Caliban an exile in his. The West Indian writer by going abroad is, in fact, searching for an end to exile. (quoted in Gikandi 39)

The argument that emigration is an act of conscience for Caribbean writers is unfortunately sometimes extended to mean that all significant cultural and political activity in the Caribbean takes place outside its borders. Still, some Caribbean immigrant and United States-born writers have been careful not to eclipse the vital literary and cultural traditions of those who do not have the resources to migrate and those who have chosen to return and work within the Caribbean. Caribbean immigrant writing in the United States or elsewhere must be read with some awareness of those who have stayed behind, for instance, writers such as Merle Hodge or grassroots organizations such as Sistren, the Jamaican working-class womens' collective based in Kingston slums, which formed under the socialist government of Michael Manley in the late 1970s and continues to be engaged in a remarkable theater, testimonial writing, and political activism.

LITERARY-CULTURAL HISTORY

The rest of this chapter focuses more closely on specifically literary responses to the Caribbean history of colonialism and diaspora. This section concerns such responses as they have evolved in Caribbean literature as a whole; the next section examines the ways in which this literary and cultural history has been reshaped by Caribbean immigrant writers in the United States.

The history of large-scale colonial violence and erasure has compelled Caribbean writers to figure, in their writing, the complex processes through which landscapes and received colonial texts—historical, cultural, and literary—can be read as palimpsest structures marked by gaps and absences and carrying traces of historical violences, of the effaced and the erased. It has simultaneously urged writers to reclaim the past through transgressive acts of naming, mythmaking, and rehistoricizing. A compelling account of this process comes from the Barbadian poet and historian Edward Kamau Brathwaite:

You have to begin with me in the small island of Barbados, this little island, this coral island of Barbados in the Atlantic where we have this tremendous landscape which has no word attached to it, no word, no sound, no touch, no history. And, like all of us growing up in the Caribbean, my responsibility was to try to find words for this amazing landscape which is awesome not only in its magnificence and the range of its architectural beauty, but because it is so absent of words. This is a landscape where the original population was destroyed within thirty years of Columbus' crunch upon the sand.

Therefore there was in fact no native tradition, no tongue spoken, no whisper, no memory coming out of these islands. And we who inherited these islands had the responsibility of finding a way of speaking, finding a way of remembering and finding a way of projecting that memory into a future. (25)

The refrains of "small island" and "absence of words" structure much of Caribbean cultural texts and historiography. Thus, Jamaica Kincaid, the Antiguan immigrant writer, titles her revisionist history of Antigua *A Small Place* and asks in what way the "unreal" beauty of her island, its "heightened, intense surroundings," could be written into history, given that Antiguans "have nothing to compare this incredible constant with, no big historical moment to compare the way they are now to the way they used to be. No Industrial Revolution, no revolution of any kind, no Age of Anything, no world wars, no decades of turbulence balanced by decades of calm" (79). What is clear from Brathwaite's and Kincaid's accounts is that the highly eventful past of these "small islands"—involving great movements of people, the uprooting and decimations of vast numbers, oppression and resistance on an unprecedented scale—has still not been seen as worthy of the monumental history that the first and even nondiasporic Third World has been able to claim.

The act of recovering and imaging a Caribbean past in the absence of record and ready-made "words" has called for a great act of collective imagination and produced a rich repertoire of strategies of cultural resistance, of subversive tactics of reading and naming. Some of the most innovative of such strategies have been drawn from the history of the genocide of Amerindians, African slavery, and Asian indenture. The Guyanese poet, philosopher, and novelist Wilson Harris, for instance, proposes the term "limbo" as a metaphor for the creativity and resilience of a people under conditions of extreme oppression, such as the Middle Passage. In "limbo dance," which was born on the slave ships and drew on African roots, the dancer executed a series of complex movements under an iron bar that was gradually lowered on the dancer's body. Nathaniel Mackey points out that in this "outspread, spiderlike sprawl," the dancer's body invoked the African figure of Anancy, "a cunning trickster-god in the form of a spider" (168). The word "limbo," at the same time, figures the Middle Passage as a purgatorial space between Africa and the New World, while the presence of "limb" in the word suggests "the idea of the phantom limb related to amputation, or, in this context, geographical and cultural . . . dislocation" (Mackey 169). Harris's image of resistance thus points to the ways in which the creative energies of the Caribbean people survived in the brutally constricted spaces of the slave ship and the Middle Passage.

A second metaphor, that of "maroonage," commemorates an equally complex and ambiguous resistance born of the experience of slavery. Maroons were slaves who successfully escaped the plantations in places such as Jamaica and Dominica and managed to live in small communities outside, but in proximity to, the white colonial world. Significantly, they survived not only by waging a guerrilla warfare on the plantocracy but also, in some cases, by agreeing perforce to the plantocracy's demands to turn in later fugitives. As Simon Gikandi notes, immigrant Caribbean writers have "adopted maroonage as a metaphor for cultural production in foreign lands, and specifically, for writing in a colonial situation" (20). Cliff's novel *Abeng* offers a feminist perspective on maroonage by invoking the figure of Nanny, leader of the Windward Maroons of Jamaica, a group that waged war on white slave owners from 1655 to 1740. Nanny was the "sorceress," "obeahwoman," "the magician of this revolution," known for her ability "to catch a bullet between her buttocks and render the bullet harmless" (*Abeng* 14). The difficulty of writing Nanny and other elided histories of the Caribbean into texts becomes apparent when Cliff insists that "there is absolutely no doubt that [Nanny] actually existed" but adds immediately that "the ruins of her Nanny Town remain difficult to reach" (14). The title of Cliff's novel, *Abeng,* is itself a tribute to creative and subversive strategies of survival. As she glosses it in an author's note, *abeng* is an African word meaning "conch shell"; used to summon slaves to the cane fields, *abeng* was also, however, used by Maroon armies to communicate with each other. Limbo dance and maroonage are but a small sample of the ways in which Caribbean literature has sought to refashion a cultural resistance out of historical violence and erasure.

Like erasure and renaming, a powerful imprint on Caribbean literature is the experience of diaspora. The history of the Caribbean begins with violent and large-scale dislocations of people for whom the possibility of sealing off ethnic and cultural identity is always already forestalled, in a way it might not be for other First *or* Third World cultures that have, for extended periods, been free of enforced contact with others. In contrast, Caribbean writers, who have always lived in the experience of diaspora, have also used this experience to offer radical reformulations of culture and subjectivity. Wilson Harris observes that in the Caribbean,

despite the mixed blood section of the population, that had its cross-racial roots (if I may so put it) in generations of colonialism and in immigration policies in which women were at a premium whatever their race or culture, cross-cultural rapport was discouraged. The deficiencies of such a hierarchical system accentuated a sense of malaise within the society as a whole, a sense of lost opportunities. (20)

To recover such opportunities, Harris argues, one must eschew a "withdrawal into cells of ideological or racial or cultural purity" (10). The experience of diaspora has urged Caribbean cultural theorists and writers from early on to question closed, unitary, and essentialized notions of culture and identity inherited from Western humanism and to offer alternative accounts of cultures and identities that are "creolized" and "on the borders," existing in constant contact and negotiation with others. This process is evocatively staged by Frantz Fanon, the Martinican psychiatrist, philosopher, and revolutionary, in his important es-

say of the late 1950s, "The Fact of Blackness" in *Black Skin/White Masks.*
Later Caribbean thinkers have continued to develop theories of subjectivity,
language, and culture that are premised on the possibility of boundary
crossing—processes variously described as "transculturation," "creolization,"
or *"metissage."* Such tropes differ from present-day Caribbean state policies of
"creolization": as Gikandi observes, they "counter the orthodoxy of state doctrines of creolization which sometimes create the illusion that the relationship
of all the parts that make the whole is egalitarian" (18). Creolization and *metissage* also work against a "will to cultural synthesis which sometimes obscures
the racial, ethnic, and caste tensions" within creolized cultures (Gikandi 18).
Instead, they image identities, cultures, and languages as fluctuating, as constantly crossing their own boundaries and being inflected and displaced through
each other.

Such transculturation has invited Caribbean writers to counter the "absence
of words," of which Brathwaite and Kincaid spoke earlier, with dialogism and
a Creole language inflected by the voices of the different classes, genders, and
ethnicities—African, Amerindian, European, and Asian—within the diaspora.
The use of the "Creole" or "patois" languages of the people, frequently in
counterpoint to colonial-derived "standard" English, is responsible for the remarkable vibrancy and suppleness of not only Caribbean oral culture but also
print literatures borrowing from oral traditions.

If "creolization," which contests originary and foundational notions of identity and culture, is one consequence of the experience of diaspora, so also is the
narrative of return that informs some traditions of Caribbean writing. The Rastafari movement, a revisionist form of Christianity that evolved in Jamaica,
images Ethiopia as Eden and the Caribbean (and First World metropoles in
general) as Babylon and thus projects paradise as the return to Africa. Rastafarian philosophy, which was central to the works of earlier writers such as
Roger Mais, is also invoked in some immigrant Caribbean literature, for instance, Michael Thelwell's *The Harder They Come* (1980), the novel based on
Perry Henzell's film of the same title. The narrative of return both to Africa and
to the Caribbean is evident also in the writings of immigrant Caribbean women,
for instance, in Lorde's *Zami* and poetry and in all of Marshall's fiction. This
narrative, which is examined briefly in the next section, does not replace creolization by promising an uncomplicated return to origins but instead typically
works with the latter metaphor to point to the contingency of absolutist concepts.

While these strategies of resistance affirm the imaginative reach and resilience
so characteristic of Caribbean writing, they are also especially resistant to romanticization. However creatively subversive the potential might be of various
acts of cultural resistance—of reading history as palimpsest, naming in "the
absence of words," and creolizing—this potential can be lost when the resistance is itself read as being founded on absolutes and fixity. Belinda Edmondson's criticism of Brathwaite, in which she charges him with using creolization
in restricted and closed ways, is important in this connection.

DOMINANT CONCERNS

The repertoire of cultural resistance is continually being expanded and re-shaped by writers of different generations, races, classes, sexual orientation, and gender within the Caribbean disapora. Caribbean immigrant writing in the United States, which itself comprises a vast and varied literary output, is no exception. This section provides a brief glimpse of some of the ways in which some Caribbean immigrant writers have envisioned acts of "renaming" and writing over erasure, creolization, and the narrative of return.

Acts of Rewriting/Writing over Erasure

A recurring pattern in Caribbean literature, particularly in the works of the Caribbean-English generation of Walcott, Lamming, and Brathwaite, is the re-or overwriting of Western colonial texts, histories, and paradigms. Thus, Naipaul's novel *A Bend in the River* is a rewriting of Conrad's *Heart of Darkness*. Similarly, the paradigm of Prospero and Caliban and, to a lesser extent, of Crusoe and Man Friday is frequently engaged, reversed, and subverted by writers such as Lamming and Walcott. In a woman's tradition, the white Dominican writer Jean Rhys chooses in her novel *Wide Sargasso Sea* (1966) to write over a different Western text, Charlotte Brontë's *Jane Eyre*. Rhys's novel is written from the viewpoint of Brontë's madwoman in the attic, Bertha Rochester, the "Creole Heiress" who eventually provides the financial wherewithal for the happy ending of Jane's bildungsroman, after first having served the plot function of being a temporary obstacle to Jane and Rochester's love. Brontë's portrayal of Bertha as a subhuman, bestial, and insane alter image of Jane, the prototypically questing figure of Western feminism, is invoked elsewhere in Caribbean women's literature, for instance, by Cliff in *Abeng* and in Sistren's collective testimony, *Lionheart Gal* (1987).

Among U.S. Caribbean writers, the act of writing back to the center has changed contours, in accordance with the shift in the center from colonial England to the imperial United States. Entire works structured as creative (mis)readings of canonical literary texts are rare (although Cliff, who has recently speculated that Emily Brontë's Heathcliffe might be black, might be contemplating another such rewriting). U.S.-Caribbean writers do, however, continue to be engaged in innovative acts of overwriting received colonial texts and paradigms.

One of the most powerful examples of this comes from Kincaid's novel *Annie John* (1985), itself, in part, her rewriting of her earlier poetic-prose fragment text *At the Bottom of the River* (1983). The overwriting takes the form of the adolescent protagonist Annie's scribble across a picture depicting Columbus on his third voyage, in chains, being transported to Spain. The picture is in Annie's schoolbook, titled *A History of the West Indies,* and she defaces it while she is sitting in a class focused on Columbus's "discovery" of Dominica. Annie, who has instinctively detested Columbus (and such events as the celebrations of Queen Victoria's birthday), makes an immediate connection between the picture of a temporarily vanquished Columbus and some family gossip she has recently overheard concerning a mysterious ailment that has descended on her patriarchal grandfather, affecting his legs in particular. On getting the news, her mother had laughed and said, "So the great man can no longer just get up and go" (78). Remembering this, Annie John now carefully traces over the caption to Columbus's picture ("Columbus in Chains"), in her best Old English lettering, the sentence "The Great Man Can No Longer Just Get Up and Go." Columbus appears again, somewhat more obliquely, in Kincaid's *At the Bottom of the River,* where the narrator first muses over sexuality and the cohering of her own identity, envisioned as a transparent embryo "swimming upside down"—in limbo—and then worries over the "great discovery" she has made and whether it will mean her being sent home in chains. Annie John's instinctive connection between the patriarchal domination of her grandfather and the colonial brutality of Columbus and all that he represents, her creative substitution of official schoolbook history with a lesson learned from her mother, and *At the Bottom*'s narrator's ability to connect colonial violence with the traumatic onset of a closed narrative of self-identity are glimpses of the kind of innovative over-writing of colonial history that characterizes all of Kincaid's work and much of Caribbean writing in general.

The history of erasure has also led immigrant Caribbean writers to a form of historical-literary fiction in which the gaps and fissures of received history become occasions for rehistoricizing. Michelle Cliff's early novel *Abeng* (1984) and her most recent novel, *Free Enterprise* (1993), are examples of such fictional rewritings of history. *Abeng* is Cliff's account of Clare Savage, an adolescent born to privilege in Jamaica. The narration of Clare's bildungsroman is continually overlaid with the history of maroonage and Nanny (discussed briefly in the previous section), with Columbus, and with later historical figures such as Claude McKay and Marcus Garvey. In *Free Enterprise,* set in the mid-nineteenth century, Cliff writes the lives of two women, African-American and Jamaican, into history, specifically into the historical raid on Harper's Ferry.

Creolization

In U.S. Caribbean immigrant literature, one form of creolization is the incorporation of street and popular culture in print literature and the creation of a heteroglossic Creole or patois inflected with the experience of various ethnic groups and classes. This technique is especially evident in the genre of what C.L.R. James has called "barrackyard" literature, focusing on the lives of urban underclasses in the Caribbean, and of the genre of the peasant novel inaugurated by McKay. U.S. immigrant writing continues to draw on this tradition, with writers such as Orlando Patterson, Ismith Khan, Garth St. Omer, and Michael Thelwell, many of whom set their works in the Caribbean rather than in the new immigrant spaces of the First World.

If creolization means the negotiation of ethnic identities and languages, then it is an appropriate rubric also for works not set in the Caribbean but born more directly of the experience of immigration and focusing on the relationship of the immigrants with other U.S. cultures, particularly the African-American. This theme is a constant even in the children and young adult fiction of Caribbean immigrants, for instance, the Trindad-born Rosa Guy. One of her early novels, *The Friends* (1973), recounts the slow and difficult process through which the protagonist, Phyllisia, with the help of her African-American friend Edith, gradually overcomes the split induced in her by growing up surrounded by a vibrant Harlem culture but in an ambitious immigrant Caribbean family that sees its relationship to African Americans as one of antipathy, of competition for the limited resources doled out by a white world. As a child of this experience, Phyllisia must also confront the fact that those outside either community, such as the mainstream white world, cannot recognize this division, since it is not manifested in any visible or physical way: as Wilfred Cartey has noted, "[T]he outer reality, Harlem, though disconsolate, does not select [Phyllisia] out because of race, does not regard her with surprise or amazement because of color; rather in Black Harlem she is most often indistinct, faceless, customary," and terrified by her frequent immersion into "the violent anonymity of the streets" (Cartey 289). Guy's novel urges that Caribbean immigrants recognize their common destiny and shared history with African Americans, a theme that continues to inform all of her fiction for adolescents. The complex differences and wished-for convergence of the two communities are central to much adult Caribbean immigrant literature as well. In *Abeng,* set in Jamaica, Cliff develops the theme through a character who has lived in Harlem and then returned to Jamaica and who observes that both groups, though of common African descent, "had been colonized differently. The differences between them ranged from food to music to style to their way of being in the world" (86). As Guy suggested, these differences are complicated by the fact that the two groups can pass for each other in the white mainstream imagination. Lorde overcame these differences by affiliating herself with the tradition of black feminist and lesbian literature, a group commemorated in the title of her work, *Zami, A New Spelling of My Name.* Lorde indicates that *Zami* is a "Carriacou name for women who work together as friends and lovers" (*Zami* 255). Marshall's equally complex resolution to this question, posed in all of her writing, does not involve lesbian identity but similarly urges an imaginative return to Africa and the history of a shared oppression. Both writers also celebrate the coming together of the two communities, an impulse that structures Cliff's *Free Enterprise* as well.

The Narrative of Return

This narrative structures a wide range of U.S. immigrant literature, from novels invoking the experience of the Rastafari, such as Thelwell's *The Harder They Come* (1980), to, as suggested before, Lorde, Cliff, and Marshall. In Thelwell's novel, the philosophy of Rastafarianism promises a space outside the widespread violence of a neocolonial culture in which every billboard proclaims the U.S. presence and its commodification of Jamaican culture and in which all institutions of the state and civil society, including the official church and music industries, are riddled with neocolonial corruption. In such a world, however, Rastafarian culture can only be a small and always besieged enclave. In Kincaid's *Lucy,* the first novel she sets outside Antigua and in the new immigrant world of New York, the protagonist conflates her relationship with the Caribbean with her immensely intimate and immensely troubled relationship with her mother. In an ambiguous and bitter gesture, Lucy decides never to read or even open the many letters sent to her by her mother but instead always carries all of them, sealed, inside her brassiere. Intended to be grimly triumphant, a proof of her power over her past, the gesture, of course, doubles on itself: the letters scratching Lucy's skin are unrelenting reminders of the presence of the past.

A similar complexity and lack of closure inform the narrative of return in Paule Marshall. Whether it is literal and physical or symbolic, the metaphor of return structures all of Marshall's fiction. One of the most powerful of these narratives comes in an early story, ''To Da-Duh, in Memoriam,'' published in 1983 in the collection titled *Reena.* The protagonist is a nine-year-old girl, taken by her Caribbean immigrant mother to meet her grandmother in Barbados, Da-Duh, an old woman, strong, fearless, and imperious, who has never left her island. A strange competition begins between Da-Duh and her grandchild, in which Da-Duh confronts the latter with some miracle or wonder of her life in Barbados—for instance, a towering and ancient tree—and the grandaughter counters this with tales of First World marvels, such as Shirley Temple, the machinery of the modern world, and the Empire State Building. Da-Duh is gradually silenced in this exchange, to be finally defeated when her granddaughter reveals that in New York she has taken on the white world and has actually beaten up a white girl. Yet the victory, if that is what it is, of immigrant possibilities over Old World ways is of little eventual solace to the nine-year-old. She leaves the island, never to return, for Da-Duh dies the following year. But on growing up, the narrator finds that the Old World had won, after all, for it could neither be blotted in her imagination nor controlled through representation:

For a brief period after I was grown I went to live alone, like one doing penance, in a loft above a noisy factory in downtown New York and there painted seas of sugar-cane and huge swirling Van Gogh suns and palm trees striding like brightly-plumed Tutsi warriors across a tropical landscape, while the thunderous tread of the machines downstairs jarred the floor beneath my easel, mocking my efforts. (106)

Perhaps this passage can be made to serve as a final word in this survey of Caribbean immigrant literature. The elegaic tone in this passage, the mediations of Van Gogh, on one hand, and the thunderous presence of First World machines of modernity, on the other, the need to invoke Africa in some way, if only through the exoticized figure of the Tutsi warrior, together constitute a powerful statement on the (im)possibility of return. While the tones and modalities of the return narrative may vary sharply among Caribbean immigrant writers, in almost all, this narrative continues to collide with that of the present. The filtering of the Caribbean past not only through the First World present but also through earlier systems of representation (in Marshall's example, the European as well as African) itself testifies to the many worlds that move and become brilliantly reconfigured in Caribbean immigrant writing.

SELECTED PRIMARY BIBLIOGRAPHY

Carew, Jan. *Green Winter.* New York: Stein and Day, 1965.

———. *Third Gift.* Boston: Little, Brown, 1974.

Cliff, Michelle. *Abeng.* New York: Dutton, 1984.

———. *The Land of Look Behind: Prose and Poetry by Michelle Cliff.* Ithaca, NY: Firebrand Books, 1985.

———. *No Telephone to Heaven.* New York: Dutton, 1987.

———. *Bodies of Water: Stories.* New York: Dutton, 1990.

———. *Free Enterprise.* New York: Dutton, 1993.

Guy, Rosa. *The Friends.* New York: Holt, Rinehart, and Winston, 1973.

———. *The Music of Summer.* New York: Bantam-Doubleday, 1992.

Khan, Ismith. *The Crucifixion.* Leeds, U.K.: Peepal Tree P, 1986.

———. *A Day in the Country and Other Stories.* Leeds, U.K.: Peepal Tree P, 1990.

Kincaid, Jamaica. *At the Bottom of the River.* New York: Farrar, Straus, Giroux, 1983.

———. *Annie John.* New York: New American Library, 1985.

———. *A Small Place.* New York: Farrar, Straus, Giroux, 1988.

———. *Lucy.* New York: Penguin, 1990.

Lorde, Audre. *The Black Unicorn.* New York: Norton, 1978.

———. *Chosen Poems, Old and New.* New York: Norton, 1982.

———. *Zami, A New Spelling of My Name: A Biomythography.* Freedom, CA: Crossing P, 1982.

Marshall, Paule. *Reena and Other Stories.* New York: Feminist P, 1993.

———. *Brown Girl Brownstones.* 1959. New York: Feminist P, 1984.

———. *The Chosen Place, The Timeless People.* 1969. New York: Vintage, 1984.

———. *Daughters.* New York: Atheneum, 1991.

McKay, Claude. *Home to Harlem.* New York: Harper, 1928.

———. *Banjo: A Story without a Plot.* 1929. New York: Harcourt Brace, 1957.

———. *Banana Bottom.* 1933. Chatham, NJ: Chatham Bookseller, 1970.

———. *The Dialect Poetry of Claude McKay.* 2 vols. Vol. 1, *Songs of Jamaica.* Vol. 2, *Constab Ballads.* Freeport, NY: Books for Libraries, 1972.

Patterson, Orlando. *The Children of Sisyphus.* London: New Authors, 1964.

———. *Die the Long Day.* New York: Morrow, 1972.

St. Omer, Garth. *The Lights on the Hill.* London: Heinemann, 1968.

Thelwell, Michael. *The Harder They Come.* New York: Grove Weidenfeld, 1980.

Wynter, Sylvia. *The Hills of Hebron, A Jamaican Novel.* New York: Simon and Schuster, 1962.

SELECTED SECONDARY BIBLIOGRAPHY

Brathwaite, Edward Kamau. "History, the Caribbean Writer and *X/Self.*" *Crisis and Creativity in the New Literatures in English.* Ed. Geoffrey Davis and Hena Maes-Jelink. Amsterdam and Atlanta, GA: Rodopi P, 1990: 23–47.

Cartey, Wilfred. *Whispers from the Caribbean: I Going Away, I Going Home.* Los Angeles: Center for Afro-American Studies, UCLA, 1991.

Cliff, Michelle. Interview by Meryl F. Schwartz. *Contemporary Literature* 34.4 (Winter 1993): 594–619.

Cudjoe, Selwyn R. *Resistance and Caribbean Literature.* Athens, OH: Ohio UP, 1980.

———, ed. *Caribbean Women Writers: Essays from the First International Conference.* Wellesley, MA: Calaoux P, 1990.

Dance, Daryl Cumber. *Fifty Caribbean Writers: A Bio-Bibliographical Critical Sourcebook.* New York: Greenwood P, 1986.

Deere, Carmen Diana, et al. *In the Shadows of the Sun: Caribbean Development Alternatives and U.S. Policy.* Boulder, CO: Westview P, 1990.

Edmondson, Belinda. "Race, Tradition, and the Construction of the Caribbean Aesthetic." *New Literary History* 25.1 (Winter 1994): 109–120.

Fanon, Frantz. *The Wretched of the Earth.* Trans. Constance Farrington. New York: Grove P, 1961.

———. *Black Skin/White Masks.* Trans. Lars Markmann. New York: Grove P, 1967.

Gikandi, Simon. *Writing in Limbo: Modernism and Caribbean Literature.* Ithaca, NY: Cornell UP, 1992.

Harris, Wilson. "Oedipus and the Middle Passage." *Crisis and Creativity in the New Literatures in English.* Ed. Geoffrey Davis and Hena Maes-Jelink. Amsterdam and Atlanta, GA: Rodopi P, 1990. 9–22.

Kasinitz, Philip. *Caribbean New York: Black Immigrants and the Politics of Race.* Ithaca, NY: Cornell UP, 1992.

Lionnet, Françoise. *Autobiographical Voices: Race, Gender, Self-Portraiture.* Ithaca, NY: Cornell UP, 1989.

Mackey, Nathaniel. *Discrepant Engagement: Dissonance, Cross-Culturality, and Experimental Writing.* New York: Cambridge UP, 1993.

Maingot, Anthony P. "Political Implications of Migration in a Socio-Cultural Area." *Migration and Development in the Caribbean: The Unexplored Connection.* Ed. Robert A. Pastor. Westview Special Studies on Latin America and the Caribbean. Boulder, CO: Westview P, 1985. 63–90.

Marshall, Paule. "From the Poets in the Kitchen." *Reena and Other Stories.* New York: Feminist P, 1983. 3–12.

Pastor, Robert A., ed. *Migration and Development in the Caribbean: The Unexplored Connection.* Westview Special Studies on Latin America and the Caribbean. Boulder, CO: Westview P, 1985.

11
Cuban-American Literature
Ricardo L. Ortíz

INTRODUCTION

The exiled Cuban novelist Guillermo Cabrera Infante opens his *Tres Tristes Tigres* with an *advertencia* or "warning" to readers that *"[e]l libro está en cubano,"* literally, that his novel *is* "in Cuban." Cabrera Infante's pronouncement works simultaneously as both a warning and an invitation, however; *Tres Tristes Tigres,* written in a recognizably Cuban dialectal deviation from normative Spanish, also *enacts something Cuban* in its play of vocalizations. Cabrera Infante goes on in the passage to describe this enactment as an attempt to "capture the human voice in flight," particularly the nocturnal jargon of those *habaneros* who, in the 1950s, haunted Havana's decadent underground. But to insist, as Cabrera Infante does here, that one "writes in Cuban" or, better put, that one's text "is in Cuban" is not, I think, to insist that one's Spanish merely deviates from some normative concept of Spanish. It seems less, even, about the attempt to include all the possible Spanish dialects spoken in Havana at the time of which Cabrera Infante writes, so much as about the attempt to have one's written language capture something constitutively "deviant" about the human voice, that is, of the *spoken* voice, at once "underground, secretive," *and* "in flight." What Cabrera Infante seems to propose here is the possibility of writing "in Cuban" even if one does not literally write in Spanish. Because Cabrera Infante settled in Europe rather than North America, his work does not figure prominently in the following survey, but the survey owes a profound debt to his ingenious formulation: that a text "is Cuban" to the extent to which it manages to inscribe its own fleeting quality, its own capacity for emergence *and* disappearance, its underground, secretive (non)being, its radical sense of exile from itself.

Nowhere is this proposition more significantly tested than in the writing of a number of young Cuban-American poets, novelists, and critics who, as the children of the great wave of Cuban immigration to the United States that followed Castro's revolution, write technically in English, but with an ear for the polyvalent richness of language as such, a richness, however, uniquely problematized for them by the complex positionings available to them in *their* language. In his introduction to *The Cuban Condition: Translation and Identity in Modern Cuban Literature,* Gustavo Pérez-Firmat sizes up the linguistic and cultural situation of our generation of Cuban-American writers thus: "As a 'native' Cuban who has spent all of his adult life away from the island, the notion of a 'Cuban' voice is for me as alluring as it is problematic. A Cuban voice is what I wish I had, and what I may never have" (14). Other current writers, as disparate as Cristina García, Elías Miguel Muñoz, and Ricardo Pau-Llosa, have posed much the same question for themselves, in similar, if not identical, terms. The question of Cubanity, of Cubanness (*"lo cubano"*), as posed for and by these writers in their (English) language, calls up the primal quasi-oedipal struggle between mother and father tongues, between a nostalgic longing for our lost *patria,* our feminine-gendered fatherland and the language in which we (only) remember *her,* and our grudgingly grateful capitulations to our adoptive patron-nation and *his* generous but dispassionate language.

The experience of Cuban immigration to North America has been both internally and externally divisive. Externally, Cubanos in the United States find themselves often the exception rather than the rule in discussions of the larger Latino immigrant experience here. Internally, Cubanos find themselves divided politically, culturally, and linguistically according to their generation and the relative degrees of direct experience they have had or are having with island culture, the unassimilated "ghetto" culture in Miami and the Northeast, and the larger mainstream culture of the United States. It is largely on the borders between these divided spaces of experience that the emerging generation of Cuban-exile writers write, taking such paradoxical positions in their work that they often seem to build bridges between generations and ideologies and with the same gesture mark their divisions so powerfully as to suggest their irreconcilability. Writing in Cuban is "impossible" to the extent that it may never coalesce into one voice, one language, but for the writers I treat here it is precisely this condition of impossibility that challenges, indeed *obligates,* them to write. As Cabrera Infante attempted to characterize a "Cuban" language that was simultaneously subterranean and airborne, I hope in the following pages to explore an alternative paradox, that writing "in Cuban" may indeed be simultaneously necessary and impossible.

LITERARY-CULTURAL HISTORY AND
DOMINANT CONCERNS

Any attempt to narrate the "history" of Cuban-American writing must begin with an examination of the phases of exile. This attempt immediately raises the question of the relation between historical continuity and discontinuity. Cuban writing since the revolution, both within and beyond the island, undergoes a tortuous and oftentimes bewildering set of historical and geographical displacements and superimpositions that defies easy thematic and formal classification. Profound differences in both aesthetic and political orientations can be observed among writers and other artists, as some effect of their histories in and out of exile. Those who stayed and were either disaffected with Castro or not cannot be easily classified together; a José Lezama Lima and a Nicolás Guillén, for example, ultimately formed such divergent relationships with the regime, leading to the departure of the former from the island, that it makes little sense to combine two such prominent poetic voices to find some coherent project in their work. Those who left before the revolution, like Alejo Carpentier, cannot easily be classed with those who left, as adults, as an immediate effect of the revolution. These, in turn, cannot be classed with those who, like Pérez-Firmat and the poet Pablo Medina, left, as children with their families, in the same historical moment. These last, finally, also cannot be classed with those born or raised primarily in the United States (Hijuelos, García, Muñoz), who bear additional differences, depending on whether they grew up in, say, Miami or New York or on the West Coast. Finally, there are those who were raised in and by the revolution but who came to leave much later, say, in the Mariel boat lift of 1980, like Reinaldo Arenas, or, even more recently, after the dissolution of the Eastern bloc. Three very useful recent reference texts already cover much of the ground I have briefly charted here; they are the volumes, cited in the bibliography, edited by Maratos and Hill, Kanellos, and Zimmerman. I hope in this chapter to augment much of what they say about the early efforts of exile writers like José Sánchez-Boudy, Lydia Cabrera, Celedonio González, Dolores Prida, and Iván Acosta, by focusing primarily on work by the most recent Cuban writers to rise to prominence in the United States.

Some recent books have tried in various ways to make sense of the Cuban exile experience. Interestingly, the manner in which these largely cultural and sociological studies approach their analyses hinges on the turn of some potent metaphors; what is clear from the work of young Cuban writers emerging from the culture that these analysts study is that their writing attempts to literalize these metaphors, to give voice to fictions that shape, and make real, their history. In his sweeping study *Latinos,* Earl Shorris observes that the Cuban experience of exile borrows from tradition the identification of exile and death. "The Greeks," Shorris argues, "understood exile as a form of capital punishment: not travel, relocation or emigration, but death. Nothing else radicalizes a person

quite so thoroughly, nothing makes one quite so daring, as to be already dead"
(68). While Shorris focuses as much on the generation of older Cubans who
are, in fact, dying without realizing their wish to return to the homeland, he also
suggests in his discussions of literary figures from succeeding generations, like
Jorge Valls (346–350) and Roberto Fernández (386), something of a posthumous
quality in their writing. Much Cuban-exile writing, Shorris suggests, explores
an almost de facto nostalgia that takes as its premise the absolute irretrievability
of the past it still stubbornly desires. David Rieff in his more recent book, *The
Exile: Cuba in the Heart of Miami,* makes frequent reference to what we term
el tema, the theme, which Rieff tells us "describes for Cuban Miami everything
from relating to the exile, to the possibility of change on the island, and to the
role Cuban-Americans might play in it" (28). Between the uncompromising
symbolic equation of exile and death and the exhaustive operation of the "catch-
all" *tema* that some argue dominates Cuban cultural life outside Cuba, there
would seem to be little space left for viable literary expression. This is part of
what I term the condition of impossibility for Cuban-exile writing.

Yet, in this impossible space, Cuban exile writing happens. In that space
created, for example, by the mutual exclusion of ideas of exile and assimilation,
which, as Rieff observes, "were ideas that did not mix" because "to assimilate
was to accept that the exile was over, and, on a political level, that Fidel Castro
had won" (30), and by the simultaneously obsessive nostalgia for a past inscribed in Spanish and the lure of a successful present promised and delivered
in and by American English, Cuban exile writers *necessarily* write. Rieff, in a
study bolstered by his own fine writing, comments at length on "the unquench-
able fantasy of return" and its power to keep Cuban exiles from ever settling
for, or accepting, one status or another, one side of this cultural and political
endgame or the other:

[W]hatever distinctions it might have been rational to expect the Miami Cubans to draw
among the wound, the wish and the reality, or for that matter, between what it was to
be an exile and what it is to be an immigrant, drawing them came to seem the unlikeliest
act of all for *el exilio* to perform. For to do so would have been, imaginatively at least,
the grossest act of self-mutilation. The contradictions were infinitely preferable. (29–30)

These then, are the stakes in current Cuban-exile writing. While it may seem
that a good deal of current work on the Cuban-exile political and cultural scene
has been written by non-Cubans, like Shorris and Rieff, and by other prominent
North American writers, like Joan Didion and John Sayles, the specifically literary exploration and articulation of the "contradictions" intrinsic to writing *in
Cuban* or *from exile* have been taken up by a heterogeneous but uniformly
excellent and courageous group of young Cuban Americans and Cuban exiles.
These writers cover a varied landscape of thematic concerns, a landscape, however, in no way islandized or isolated by the overwhelming *tema* of exile and
return; I pay as much attention in the following section to explorations of race,

class, gender, and sexuality, which give more full-bodied, practical occasion to the larger exile-related thematics of nostalgia and the often simultaneous desire for, and skepticism about, return.

PREVAILING GENRES AND MAJOR AUTHORS

Cuban history is literary to its core. From the poetry of the founder of Cuban democracy, José Martí, to the present obsession with a theme, exile and return and their attendant symbolism, Cuban culture and its diasporic extensions have always embraced an understanding of themselves mediated by metaphor and music. Canonical Cuban literature can be characterized more as an amalgam of fiction and poetry, though its dramatic output speaks in its own unique voice to the Cuban character as well. Cuban and Cuban-American literary output, because of this privileged marriage of story and symbolism, often manifests itself in intensely poetic, lyrical fiction. Cuban drama, on the other hand, is more popularly based. It can be characterized by the broad comedy of the *teatro bufo* form and the more elusive camp quality of the *picúo,* a specifically Cuban brand of kitsch theatrics. These theatrical tendencies persist today in the camp aesthetics of Cuban-American performance artist Carmelita Tropicana, whose work has been brought to critical attention by Lillian Manzor-Coats. For an informative introduction to the variety and experimental nature of recent Cuban exile dramaturgy, I recommend the collection of pieces edited by Rodolfo J. Cortina entitled *Cuban American Theatre.* The collection features a number of lesser-known playwrights as well as a useful introductory essay and brief but comprehensive biographies of all the contributors. While I do not treat Cuban drama here, it bears saying that Cuban theater reflects the larger theatricality in Cuban life. Without appealing to sterile prejudices, there is no denying that, from the music to the food, the Cuban cultural temperament is passionate, its characteristic sensibility given to spectacle, to intensities of rhythm, to much that can be termed complex, though perhaps little that can be called subtle.

As I hope to demonstrate in this section, it is perhaps not so coincidental that today it is possible to speak of current Cuban-American literary and cultural output as occupying as ''special'' a period of evolution as that which Castro has ascribed to the island, in political and economic terms, as it struggles through the post-Soviet phase of its history. It seems that no sooner have we achieved a place for ourselves in elite, serious culture than we find ourselves sprinting just as quickly into inclusion in the American popular-cultural mainstream. It seems that for the ''serious'' successes of every Cristina García and Oscar Hijuelos, there is the parallel success of a Gloria Estefan or of talk-show host Cristina or even of a screenwriter like Cynthia Cidre, who has written both ''from the Cuban,'' in her adaptation of Oscar Hijuelos's *Mambo Kings* into a screenplay and in her own original work in *Little Havana,* as well as her successful adaptation of Bobbie Ann Mason's *In Country.* I mention these formidable pop-cultural figures not in counterpoint to the higher-brow accomplishments of their literary counterparts but to acknowledge that, despite its own best efforts to the contrary, Cuban-exile culture has never fully shaken its profound identification with the image of itself produced by a commercial culture driven by the North American media, especially as it developed in the fifteen years between the end of the Second World War and the fall of Batista. It seems to me that, despite the current revival of interest in alternative Cuban mythologies originating in the exotic practices of Santería and Afro-culturalism in general, there is still a great power left in the mythology Hollywood produced for Havana, and chiefly with the latter's full-hearted cooperation.

This struggle between the traditional past and the untethered present of modern democracy takes some acute turns when filtered through the issue of gender. While certain prominent women writers like Dolores Prida and Lydia Cabrera have certainly made significant contributions to the emergence of a Cuban literary voice in exile, only with the publication of Cristina García's *Dreaming in Cuban* in 1992 has a Cubana finally risen to mainstream national attention as a writer. This is due, I believe, in part to García's ability to position herself in a more general tradition of writing in the United States by immigrant women and women of color. While in content, *Dreaming in Cuban* is profoundly "Cuban," in general form and in more local aesthetic strategies, it owes a great deal to a set of non-Cuban literary foremothers, from Toni Morrison to Amy Tan.

Dreaming in Cuban traces the history of three generations of women in the del Pino family: Celia, the matriarch, grew up in pre-Castro Cuba and stayed after the revolution, a loyal supporter of Castro until the 1980s; of her two daughters, Felicia, the locus of much of the *santera* magic in the text, also stays and raises three children, twin girls named Luz and Milagro and a son named Ivanito; the other, Lourdes, leaves with her husband, Hugo, and their daughter, Pilar, for the United States, where they open a successful bakery in Brooklyn. The novel's "action" (it is intricately plotted, but emphasis is often given to eloquent lyrical observations that suspend the momentum of the plot) alternates largely between Cuba and New York, between the past, which is traced to Celia's girlhood and an affair with a Spaniard that haunts the rest of her life, and the present, which revolves largely around Pilar's restless disaffection with much that she finds lurid in the (North American) materialism her parents have embraced and her desire to see her grandmother again, if only to reaccess something more authentic from her past. The connections and disconnections among the women characters drive, indeed, all the desire in García's text; they do more than personalize history; they emphatically feminize it.

That a mainstream North American audience embraced García's novel upon its publication attests to the author's remarkable ability to translate a foreign experience into a language at once accessible and not entirely familiar. The intense lyricism of her prose, like Amy Tan's, invites, rather than alienates, her reader, at the same time that it often articulates harrowingly painful experiences, which are as close to the real as writing about the body can get. It would be wrong, though, to lump García exclusively with Tan or Morrison or with the

Latin American magical realists whose work her writing might also recall. She balances, in different ways, her lyricism with a journalistic directness that both reveals her own professional background and suggests something of her appreciation for the historical and political urgency of her themes. For every scene in which we find García exploring the obscurer aspects of the Cuban cultural past, as in her depiction of Felicia's experiences with Santería, we find one in which she speaks in balanced but unambiguous terms about the political and material divisions between the del Pino women and the nation(s) they represent symbolically. García can thus bring us into the mystery of *santera* ritual: "On the morning of her initiation, sixteen santeras tore Felicia's clothes to shreds until she stood naked, then they bathed her in river water. . . . After many more rituals and a final bath in the omiero, the santeras led Felicia to Obatalá's throne. . . . They painted circles and dots on her forehead and cheeks—white for Obatalá, reds and yellows and blues for the other gods—and crowned her with sacred stones. It was then Felicia lost consciousness, falling into an emptiness without history or future" (187). In equally effortless writing, she confronts us with the unambiguous emotion separating Cubans from each other in the political present; she places Lourdes in Havana the week in 1980 that mobs stormed the Peruvian embassy, an event that led directly to the Mariel boat lift with which her novel culminates, and allows Lourdes to confront Castro himself: "Lourdes realizes she is close enough to kill him. She imagines seizing El Líder's pistol, pressing it to his temple, squeezing the trigger. . . . She wants him to see her face, to remember her eyes and the hatred in them. . . . She takes a deep breath and concentrates on extracting a phrase from the reeling in her brain. . . . *'Asesino!'* she shouts abruptly, startling everyone in the courtyard" (236–237). While instructive to a non-Cuban audience, scenes like this speak to the heart of everything in Cuban-exile experience that David Rieff argues might be denoted by *el tema*. There is something at once vindicating and terrifying about Lourdes's and García's gestures; while the author's is more cautionary than her character's, each speaks to precisely the complications with which divisions in the Cuban past will rifle any Cuban future.

While I do not mean to give short shrift to a writer as important as Oscar Hijuelos, it is important to consider that he, like Cristina García, has achieved a level of prominence in the United States that few of the other writers I analyze have. For this reason, I focus on some limited aspects of Hijuelos's fiction, particularly his own ambivalent romance with the glamorization of the Cuban in the popular culture of the United States. In defense of Hijuelos, I argue that his last two novels reflect a legitimate acknowledgment of the power of moving pictures to record and make sense of specifically twentieth-century historical events and movements like the Cuban diaspora; in this sense his novels reflect Walter Benjamin's assertion that twentieth-century historical consciousness is structurally filmic, and by extension, televisual. In both *The Mambo Kings Play Songs of Love* and *The Fourteen Sisters of Emilio Montez O'Brien,* Hijuelos places his main characters in Hollywood, in both cases involving them in scenes crucial to their negotiations with their own evolving self-images.

In *Mambo Kings*, for example, the Castillo brothers' meeting with Desi Arnaz and their consequent appearance on "I Love Lucy" provide Hijuelos with the opportunity to explore more fully the range of cultural (mis)identifications available not only to the Castillos, but to all Cubans. He has Arnaz, of all people, ponder especially about the somber quality of Nestor Castillo's composition "Beautiful María," and, "as he did so," Hijuelos tells us, "he wondered about the terrible somberness that seemed to plague Nestor. He thought, 'Of course, he's a *gallego,** and gallegos are melancholic at heart' " (132). Hijuelos adds a curious historical footnote (hence the asterisk) about the term *gallego,* especially what it signifies in Cuban: "Who were the *gallegos?* . . . gallego referred to those Cubans whose ancestors had come from Galicia . . . in the northwest corner of Spain . . . El Cid was a *gallego,* . . . Another *gallego?* Franco. Others? Ángel Castro, a Spanish soldier who settled in Oriente Province, became a land baron, and whose son, Fidel, ambitious, arrogant, cocky, would become absolute ruler of the island" (132). Giving his readers Castro's Galician genealogy in a footnote prompted by a passing thought in the head of a fictionalized Desi Arnaz speaks directly to the capacity of Hijuelos's imagination to slip the historical into his fiction in various guises. The gesture also suggests something of the way that fictions can, dangerously, swallow up history; Arnaz presents a more comforting picture of a Cuban past, a picture Hijuelos can use to lure a precisely televisually oriented generation of readers into a confrontation with a history that television especially seduces us into forgetting.

A similar moment occurs in the heart of the narrative of *Emilio Montez O'Brien.* The United States-born protagonist and title character, who has a go at a film career in 1950s Hollywood under the stage name of "Monty" O'Brien, has an opportunity to visit Cuba in 1958, practically on the eve of the revolution, after filming *Cuban Rebel Girls* with Errol Flynn in the Florida Keys. In ironic counterpoint to Flynn's brainstorm of filming a story that knowingly and positively anticipates Castro's revolution, Hijuelos has his "Americanized" character ponder his fate had he been raised in Cuba. Visiting his sister at his mother's ancestral house in Santiago de Cuba, Emilio thinks, "No doubt he would have looked very much the same, but his head would have been filled with Spanish perhaps and his demeanor and his heart might have been different, for he noticed an open emotionality to the people" (349). This insight is underscored by Emilio's lack of familiarity with Cuban culture, elite and popular; as his brother-in-law, "intent on impressing on Emilio that Cuba was thick with culture and art" (350) fails in this project, Emilio's thoughts turn instead to the romanticism his own past can lend to the scene around him:

Emilio would go wandering through the streets of Santiago, . . . and on the way he would wander through the working of his own heart, hearing the voices around him and imagining how, perhaps years before, his father, an Irishman, once also heard foreign voices around him and at a certain moment, with tripod and camera in his arms during a hike up the steep hills of the city, he'd been enticed to stay and had pursued his destiny of meeting a Cuban woman named Mariela Montez. And years later his movie-actor son would have the privilege of standing by a stone wall looking out, pensive and filled with wonder, over the splendid harbor of the city. (350–351)

The story Emilio tells himself is, of course, more than just romantic: it is cinematic. At the heart of the memory and at the heart of twentieth-century history as we construe it, as we see it, there is camera. Rather than just glamorizing the tragedy of exile by rendering it cinematic or belittling a Cuban cultural past in the United States by appealing in some manner to the universally recognized image of Ricky Ricardo, Hijuelos suggests in each gesture that we cannot ignore the power of the moving image in our reconstruction of our past; it is, for Hijuelos, a technique for placing the events of Cuban history surrounding the revolution in a specific historical environment, one shaped for better or worse by a technology and its attendant culture industry whose aims and values did not emanate from Cuba, even though many Cubans do from time to time fall back in love with the images of themselves it continues to generate.

One writer whose work bridges and breaches the more continuous tradition in Cuban writing among those who stayed on the island after the revolution and the current state of Cuban writing in exile is Reinaldo Arenas. Arenas, who spent a decade of exile in the United States between his expulsion from Cuba in the Mariel boat lift and his suicide during the last stages of his bout with AIDS, was both a student and protégé of José Lezama Lima and Virgilio Piñera from the time of his arrival on the literary scene in Havana in the 1960s and a political and cultural martyr like Heberto Padilla, Armando Valladares, and Jorge Valls, once his work was identified as counterrevolutionary and subversive in the following decade. These four writers (Arenas, Padilla, Valladares, and Valls) comprise in their work in exile a significant movement in the writing of prison memoirs. In his brilliant autobiography, *Antes que Anochezca,* Arenas's writing grapples not only with the simultaneous transition from one cultural or political environment to another but also with the redoubled exile into which his open and defiant homosexuality cast him. Arenas's experiences with varying levels of imprisonment distinguish him significantly from his heterosexual counterparts. Arenas's writing orients him sexually and politically in one and the same gesture; it tests prevailing conceptions of freedom and criminality, of pleasure and power, in more problematically aestheticized ways than we find in the more classically oriented testimonies of imprisonment, torture, and humiliation of Padilla, Valladares, or Valls.

While Cuban sections of his autobiography, dealing with his various experiences of flight and imprisonment and with the confiscation and destruction of various of his manuscripts, provide a compelling indictment of Castro regime's repressive practices, Arenas's equally painful memories of his rejection by some elements of the Cuban-exile community in the United States speak more directly to his immigrant experience. Arenas's descriptions of his alienation from Miami's bourgeois Cuban culture often draw from the vocabulary of fantasmatization fashioned by literary analyses of immigrant writing in recent times. "In exile," he writes, "one is nothing but a ghost, the shadow of someone who never achieves full reality" (293). This sense of being forced into a partialized, incomplete existence is specifically tied to more than the general political state of exile; in Miami, Arenas contends, artists and, in particular, writers were considered with an odd kind of suspicion: "The sad fact is," he observes, "that Cuban exiles were not much interested in literature; a writer was looked upon as a strange, abnormal creature" (290). It is impossible not to hear in the term "abnormal" its conventional concomitant, *"maricón"* (fairy or pansy in Spanish). What strikes the conventional *machista* Cuban sensibility as culturally suspect immediately also strikes it as sexually suspect. Miami culture seemed to Arenas a distillation of some of the worst features of the Cuban character, especially in terms of its sexual politics: "The typical Cuban machismo has attained alarming proportions in Miami. I did not want to stay long in that place, which was like a caricature of Cuba, the worst of Cuba" (293). It is not surprising, therefore, that Arenas's investments in his writing and in his sexuality so strongly paralleled each other. Cuba, both at home and in exile, treated its writers as badly as it treated its homosexuals; indeed, it seemed not to distinguish the one from the other.

In the last chapters of the autobiography, Arenas inscribes the dissolution of his last years in the dissolution of reason and sense, a surrender to the forces beyond order that had always governed his life. These include madness, witchcraft, and dreams, terms that serve as titles to some of the later chapters. The embodiment of madness is his lifelong friend Lázaro Gómez, who also served as the inspiration for the title character of Arenas's novel of exile, *The Doorman.* Juan, "a young man who was dying of grief" (3), suffers from the doubled disenchantment of having been forced to leave his own childhood behind in immigrating to the United States and in having to confront a culture profoundly alienated from its own innocence, its own authentic past or history. The "million" narrators of *The Doorman,* the Cuban-exile community speaking typically with one voice, sum up Juan's predicament thus:

Ten years ago Juan had fled his native Cuba in a boat, and settled in the United States. He was seventeen then, and his entire past life had been left behind: humiliations and warm beaches, fierce enemies and loving friends whom the very persecutions had made even more special. Left behind was slavery, but the complicity of night as well, and cities made to the measure of his restlessness; unbounded horror, but also a human quality, a state of mind, a sense of brotherhood in the face of terror—all things that, just like his own way of being, were alien here. (3)

While the choice of an (ironically) univocal communal voice raises its own aesthetic and philosophical questions of subjectivity and the force of ideological group think, in Arenas's hands these questions are always directed back toward the individual and the limits of the collective to "make something" of him. This is clear, for example, in the limited sympathy with which the narrative bloc treats its subject:

But we, too (and there are a million of us), left all that behind; and yet we are not dying of grief . . . so hopelessly as this young man. . . . He arrived in the United States an unskilled laborer, like most of us, just one more person escaping from Cuba. He needed to learn, just as we did, the value of things, the high price one must pay for a stable life: a well-paying job, an apartment, a car, vacations, and finally one's own house, preferably near the ocean. (3–4)

More than an exemplary narrative of immigrant success through hard work and the acquisition of real property, Arenas's impersonation of this community and his ironic take on its values undermines the distinction it would place on "value," "price," and "cost." He leaves open the question of whether the inventory of acquisitions signifies either the signs of "a stable life" or the "high price" one must pay for that life.

Another writer who seems to appreciate the fatal cost to a displaced but materially successful culture of mistaking value and price is the poet Ricardo Pau-Llosa. The success of Pau-Llosa and some other poets of his generation, especially in fashioning a poetic Cuban voice in English, should not completely overshadow the achievements of a number of older poets who write primarily in Spanish. The collection edited by Felipe Lázaro in 1986, *Poetas Cubanos en Nueva York,* establishes the achievement of this earlier wave of Cuban-exile poetry. The collection includes a fine introductory analysis by José Olivo Jiménez, as well as selections from a rich variety of poets, from Reinaldo Arenas to Arminda Valdés Ginebra to Luisa M. Perdiga to Jorge Valls. The collection is also valuable in that it represents the voices of Cuban women poets as equal in value and number to their male counterparts.

In an evolving body of poetic work covering three volumes of sometimes stunning lyrics, Pau-Llosa has been able to devise in his own manner a voice with which to articulate the impossible but necessary contradictions that I have been arguing characterize Cuban-exile writing. In his last two collections, *Bread of the Imagined* (1992) and *Cuba* (1993), Pau-Llosa has confronted particularly the difficulty of finding a poetic idiom in English for the articulation of Cuban-exile experience that can retain the Cubanness of that experience. Pau-Llosa has characterized himself in a recent interview for *Poet's Market '93* in almost unflinchingly serious tones, stating, "Among other subjects, I am concerned with the desperate history of my native country, Cuba, but I am not at all interested in catchy, simplistic and marketable ethnic themes. I don't mambo" (78). While the refusal to "mambo," as Pau-Llosa puts it, can be taken merely to mean a refusal to succumb to marketable stereotypes of the Cuban, there is nevertheless a sense that he is willing to sacrifice some of his Cubanness for the sake of the seriousness of his project. For better or worse, Cubans mambo. There are a laughter, a playfulness characteristic of the Cuban character that, Arenas observed in his memoir, current political divisions seem to have stolen from Cubans. Arenas is especially good at articulating the profound philosophical and political dimensions of that laughter, in a manner that would please a theorist of the comic like M. M. Bakhtin. In Pau-Llosa's work, laughter is not altogether absent, but it is always cautious, always a controlled irony cast in the service of serious ends.

In *Bread of the Imagined,* Pau-Llosa's interests appear to be primarily philosophical; poems like "The Island of Mirrors," with its epigraph from Descartes and its optical play, and "Freedom as Etymology," with the curious interchangeability of the terms of its title, ropewalk meticulously between image and concept, between sensation and linguistic abstraction with undeniable mastery. But in the more relaxed "abundance" that philosophical pose is surrendered somewhat to the force of desire, as a father negotiates with both his adolescent son and their lusty pet shepherd for the best way to act on the burgeoning appetites of each. Below the immediate scene is a meditation on Cuban affluence and Cuban materialism (the family owns a pool; the boy's professional ambitions are lofty), but the poetic voice is that of a detached, bemused father; it merely patronizes those in the heat of desire. In *Cuba* Pau-Llosa turns an even more acute eye on the political issues haunting his earlier work; in poems like "President for Life" and "Conscience," Pau-Llosa manages even more complicated arrangements of philosophical, political, and poetic themes and effects. The former, a monologue of a sexual encounter from the perspective of the arrogant male partner speaking over the sleeping body of the woman, ironically parallels marital betrayal with political tyranny, figuring thus the political infidelity of Fidel's lifelong "commitment" to husband the Cuban nation. The latter narrates the rape by Cuban prison guards of a young male detainee, as an outraged poetic comment on the epigraph, a quote from Nelson Mandela, who, speaking in Angola in 1990, praised Castro's Cuba for "its love for human rights and liberties" (86). Ironically, his elegy "Reinaldo Arenas" may typify both the strengths and limitations of Pau-Llosa's refusal to mambo best. Here, in a masterfully controlled villanelle that balances the contradictions of our exile, of what he terms a "voyage" whose destination we envision as "a Cuba free from itself," free of the paradoxical condition of "the bondage of freedom in exile" (11.5–7), Pau-Llosa's formal grip chokes much of the laughter that exploded from Arenas to the end. While other poets have shown that the villanelle, for all its restrictions, can afford some room for play, in Pau-Llosa's hands it serves to reconstitute a "spirit" broken "like glass in a clenched hand," (1.19) but in effect, I would argue, only "clenches" it anew, reviving it via a tension it always, laughingly, resisted.

As we have already seen with Reinaldo Arenas, autobiography has also figured as a prominent genre in the literary output of Cuban-exile writers. One of the useful aspects of a life story like the one that poet Pablo Medina recounts in his autobiography, *Exiled Memories: A Cuban Childhood,* is that it bears testimony to a compelling historical fact often ignored or suppressed in the discourse of immigration in the United States. Long before most immigrants come to the United States, the United States has come to their home countries in many forms, but significantly via the powerful images generated by the American popular media and the values of the commercialist/capitalist machine it seductively globalizes. Especially in his chapter entitled, aptly enough, "English," Medina recalls his middle-class childhood in the Havana of the 1950s, where, "[g]iven the proximity of the United States and Cuba's virtual economic dependence on it, it was natural for English to become the second, and ever more important, language of Havana" (54). This linguistic invasion articulates what in more material terms is an economic invasion: "the everyday speech of the city," Medina remembers, reverberated largely with the idiom of consumer culture, especially "consumer goods, movies and sports" (54).

Medina concludes this chapter by describing the manner in which Cuban and American cultural values vied for his heart and soul long before his family fled the revolution in 1960. On one hand, Medina says, "[m]ore than anything I wanted to be American and live in a suburb . . . and have a pretty blonde wife who waited on me as Doris Day waited on Rock Hudson . . . I yearned for the reality of celluloid, the truth of fiction" (59), while, on the other, he experienced as facts of life qualities he later realized were exclusively Cuban: "On the other hand . . . , there was José Martí, whose poetry I memorized and whose life I accepted as a model . . . there were carnivals and Nochebuenas and trips to La Luisa and Sunday outings through El Malecón, . . . [t]here was family, too: raucous, anarchic, unpredictable, joyful, accepting, loving, secure" (59). It is the loss, with exile, of this last experience that Medina most poignantly describes in conclusion; the tumultuous train of adjectives arrives finally, eloquently, at the quality of security that familiality and a construction of nationality based on familial notions seem to guarantee most and that seem to leave exiles from such nations, like Medina, Arenas, and others, in such a profoundly orphaned state in this America.

The nostalgia that drives Medina's childhood memories and Cabrera Infante's more adult depictions (in *Tres Tristes Tigres*) of the glamorous, decadent Havana of the 1950s persists as a ghost that haunts a good deal of the writing produced by contemporary Cuban-American writers. This may be chiefly due to the embarrassingly banal fact that the one universally accessible image of Cubans with which my generation grew up was that of Ricky Ricardo, as portrayed by Desi Arnaz in "I Love Lucy" through the 1950s and in interminable reruns through the present day. It appears that, for the generation of Cuban-American writers I am treating here, there has been no other way to exorcise this legacy than to confront it, in more or less direct ways, a confrontation I have tried to explore in various ways in the course of this discussion. Less banal, but no less compelling, may be the phenomenon to which Cuban exiles may lay no exclusive claim, of having had to reconstruct their own pasts and those of their parents and grandparents, through a fragmented collection of chiefly photographic images that suggest an impossibly elegant, glamorous time, during which even the poorest of the poor seemed to muster some real *style* as subjects sitting for photographic portraits. Medina's text is exemplary in this respect; the photographs oftentimes appear to rise to the status of text around which the writing hovers like gloss. This may, of course, be due to little more than some constitutive glamour of which black-and-white photography is said to be possessed, but that does not justify dismissing the power these particular vestigial images have over the imaginations of current writers who are out to mine the past for the most potent symbolic language with which to shape the present.

RECENT SHORT FICTION

While the tendency for nostalgia I describe in concluding the preceding section may be most apparent in the work of Hijuelos and Medina, it is not exclusive to them. Of the Cuban writers represented in *Iguana Dreams,* a recent anthology of short fiction by Latino/a writers, half make at least passing mention to this crucial cultural and ideological mediation. In "Nellie," by novelist Roberto G. Fernández, the main character, who significantly stores her family's clothes "in suitcases" in order to "keep her faith . . . that all that had happened was not lasting, not permanent," spends a good deal of her day-to-day existence rapt in a delusive identification with Donna Reed, from whose television show she learns English, as well as "reconstructing her old life with the pictures" that an old family servant still in Cuba "was sending in exchange for Gillette razor blades and flints she could sell in the black market" (Poey and Suarez 63–65). In the course of rummaging through photos, Nellie comes across one of her group of friends, from "the time of American actors, of smoking Lucky Strike and dreaming yourself blonde, pale, and freckle-faced. From left to right, forming a bouquet . . . : Pituca, Maria, Rosa, Loly, Cuqin, Helen, Ignacia and Nellie, though, among themselves, they went by Joan, Ginger, Hedy, Betty, Debbie, Lana, and Irene" (66). The subsequent scene, a mixture of reminiscence and fantasy inspired by the photo, opts for the iconic power of each woman's pseudonym.

A similar displacement of one set of cultural symbols by another occurs in Gustavo Pérez-Firmat's story in the same collection, "My Life as a Redneck" (221–234). Pérez-Firmat's fiction exhibits the same appreciation for the oedipal cast of the Cuban psyche, individually and collectively. His protagonist in "My Life" finds himself split between an allegiance to his Cubanity and its fundamental ties to the "Mami"/"Miami" matrix (and the uncompromising moral rectitude associated with them) and an adulterous passion for an Anglo-American woman named Catherine. Acquiring some independent identity means "unmooring" himself from both "Mami" and "Miami," a tall order, given the protagonist's "theory . . . that if you're born male and born in the Caribbean, you have a complicated relationship to water . . . [because] Geography has a gender [and in it] Cuba is a feeble phallic epiphenomenon awash in an endless mothering ocean'' (224). Once he does, separating from his Cuban wife and taking up with Catherine, Pérez-Firmat's self-deprecating and genuinely funny hero suffers the worst kind of guilt, in a form only the most insidious operations of the superego we call pop-cultural ideology could make possible:

In my eyes Catherine and I became the protagonists of the great Cuban-American love story, a Lucy and Ricky for the nineties. Sleeping with her was like making cross-over dreams come true. I was bewitched, bewildered, and bicultural. . . . [but] It was around this time . . . that I had my first Gary Morton dream. Gary Morton . . . was Lucille Ball's second husband—the guy on whom Lucille, no longer Lucy, took revenge for all that Desi, no longer Ricky, made her go through. (228)

Displacements in the narrator's dream space proliferate, even after this passage, but the significance here is the manner in which ''real'' actors displace their fictive characters, in which history disturbs fantasy and teaches the narrator a lesson in realism and possibility. He returns at story's end, having had his great erotic flirtation with the dream of assimilation, to Marta, who ''received me with open arms, like the sea retrieving a piece of driftwood'' (234). Pérez-Firmat's critical sensibility is as playful as the one he displays in his fiction; in a recent article on Hijuelos's *Mambo Kings* entitled ''I Came, I Saw, I Conga'd,'' Pérez-Firmat exhibits a fine appreciation of the Cuban tendency to inflect all artistic genres with an insistent musicality and lightness. He analyzes the function of musical and dance forms in *Mambo Kings* through the various symbols in the novel, among them the name ''Ricky Ricardo'' and the significance of the dancing figure(s) behind it.

In ''The Movie-Maker,'' also from *Iguana Dreams,* Elías Miguel Muñoz gives us a young female narrator, Gina Domingo, who, having grown up in Los Angeles in the 1980s, is given to mimicking ''the apathetic empty-headed teenager in the hit sitcom *Growing Up Is a Pain,*'' even when joking about the difficult life of her grandmother, who is due to visit from Cuba. Gina's only resource for making sense of this event in her family's life, what she calls ''my abuela's saga and the Cuban 'thing' '' (190) is to cast it in the same terms as other events she's had to actively analyze, and that is as something to report to her high school paper. Searching ''for a fresh and original form'' in which to cast ''her'' story, Gina decides she'll ''film [her] grandmother's arrival and describe the video clip in [her] article'' (191). Muñoz, himself a playwright as well as a fiction writer, suggests here his own sincere concern for the fine line between dramatization for an inescapably fetishistic cinematographic recording and the always possible exploitation of people's ''real'' suffering for the purposes of art, even of ''responsible'' art.

Gina is later shown to be remembering the events surrounding her grandmother's visit in guilty flashback. Working in the futuristic present of the story as an adult filmmaker for a diabolically hegemonic cultural industry, Gina reflects back on the events connecting her own past with her present. She remembers having "had the seed in her, the potential for 'making things happen,' " which she turns into commercial success until this crucial "instance of remembrance" in her adult life. And it is precisely "remembrance" which becomes Gina's ultimate act of defiance; forbidden by a culture industry which no longer even officially tolerates cultural difference, the act of memory allows Gina to counter the "fabricated and desired whole" proposed by that industry as "our last hope for union." "Remembering my grandmother Estela," Gina tells us, she is "prepared to start somewhere (yes: somewhere in time)" to "remake us" (193). Gina's remarkable interior monologue brings me back to precisely the issues with which this brief survey of Cuban-American narratives began: each in its own way contributes to the larger project of confronting and negotiating their own position between a "fabrication" and a "desire," between the seductively false image of themselves presented to them by the prevailing and nowadays pervasive culture industry and their own self-destructive pleasure in (mis)recognizing themselves, however illusively, in that image.

Another fine story in *Iguana Dreams,* "Abuela Marielita" by Cecilia Rodríguez-Milanés, explores the alienation of an aging woman who, having escaped Cuba in the Mariel boat lift, now lives in relative comfort but profound alienation with her Americanized daughter's family in the suburbs of Miami. The most remarkable thing about "Abuela Marielita" is the manner in which the United States-born Rodríguez-Milanés captures the Cubanness of her characters' language. In an English shrewdly punctuated, invaded, by Spanish Cubanisms, the author's protagonist and narrator articulates her own personal and cultural reasons for holding her daughter's family's materialist values with suspicion. In her daughter's house, Soledad tells us, "It seems that the television is on almost as much as the air conditioner sometimes and of course, *la niña* has her own little color t.v. in her room" (292–293).

Soledad's distaste for the manner in which her family takes their prosperity for granted resembles that of another Marielito, Reinaldo Arenas, who seemed to realize the difficulties this would portend for anything like an economic and cultural reunification of the two Cubas. This apprehension, I suggested earlier, also haunts García's *Dreaming in Cuban.* For Rodríguez-Milanés, the profound apprehension of these difficulties is already figured in the first-wave exiles' treatment of Marielitos; Soledad's daughter rents out a back room to another Marielita, a single mother named Yamile, for whom Soledad feels a deep sympathy. On a particularly hot day, as her family celebrates their son's birthday with a party to which they do not invite their embarrassing tenant, Soledad secretly takes her food from the party: "Angel of God, to remember that poor girl with that whimpering baby, ay, it just breaks my heart" (295). Through the bond between Soledad and Yamile and through the hope that emanates from Yamile's baby's name, "Luz," Rodríguez-Milanés indicates both one of the more troubling divisions within the Cuban exile community and a way of overcoming it through the recognition and embrace of some common Cubanity.

Earl Shorris observes in his brief discussion of Roberto Fernández in *Latinos* that, "[l]ike all emerging literatures, the work of the Latinos is a neighborhood conversation, people talking to each other of a shared experience" (386), but while this may well characterize Fernández or Rodríguez-Milanés or even Arenas, it seems less true of either García or Hijuelos. While the choice of audience may, in this case, help us to determine whose writing might ultimately be "more Cuban," what might be more important is the implicit acknowledgment among all these writers that fashioning a Cuban voice necessarily entails some negotiation of the voice and the attention of the overwhelming Other into whose immediate environs Cubans have ventured out of political and economic necessity.

CONCLUSION

Ironically, this struggle with, and against, symbols and images imposed on Cubans from elsewhere is being waged not only in the fiction, poetry, and drama emerging from this generation of Cuban-American writers but even in the cultural work of artists who, like Estefan and Cidre, seem more directly invested in the mythmaking operations of the culture industry of which they are a part. In a recent review for *The Nation* of an exhibit of visual artwork by Cuban-American women entitled "Arte Cubana," María de los Angeles Torres observes that "Miami today is home to a new wave of exiles: the children of the Cuban revolution, . . . the revolution's own cultural elite, who critique it because it has betrayed its own nationalist and socialist principles." These recent exiles, especially in their coexistence and communication with "the children of the original exiles," who have similarly "rejected the dominant political culture of their community, . . . are bringing down the aquatic wall that has separated the island/nation for thirty-five years" (95). In an equally recent analysis of the current state of the arts in Cuba, Coco Fusco also comments on the exodus in the 1980s of some of Cuba's major artistic figures. Fusco observes in her article for the *Los Angeles Times* that while these "young Cuban artists raised within the revolution had revised their country's understanding of popular culture and used satire to question the staid political order," that same order's response to its own economic instability in the post-Soviet world was a repressive political and cultural retrenchment that "prompted many of Cuba's best and brightest creators to leave for good" (F1–F27). The confrontation of young Cuban artists raised here and there will ultimately contribute to the opening of the necessary dialogue among the many disparate elements that make up the complex patchwork that Cuban culture has become; and, with Coco Fusco, I suspect that it may be in the sphere of popular culture and its most accessible idioms that this opening initially takes place.

Already in an immensely successful recording like Gloria Estefan's *Mi Tierra*, we hear the optimistic anticipation not only of Cuban-to-Cuban reconciliation and reintegration but of an even larger Pan-Hispanist movement that crosses and dissolves borders with the same exhilarating force of liberation that we find in the poeticized theoretical work of Gloria Anzaldúa, in her *Borderlands/La Frontera*. In addition to this, we find in a film like *Mambo Kings* a utopian rather than nostalgic vision of a Cuba that, because of its unique historical and geographic positions, holds in itself both the memory and the promise of a pan-racial culture; historically, we know that Cubans were not exclusively of African and Hispanic descent but were also, and as significantly, Chinese, Arab, Jewish. While I have not addressed matters of racial and ethnic differences among Cubans directly in this chapter, it bears mentioning that the mostly white Cuban writers I have discussed in the preceding pages all embrace a view of Cuban cultural traditions as intrinsically multicultural, and that, despite the work of Afro-Cuban writers like Nicolás Guillén and Lydia Cabrera to bring to light the African foundations of much of Cuba's culture, there remains a great deal of work to be done on the part of non-European Cubans living in exile to sustain this endeavor. History leaves no doubt that there never really was "one" Cuba; Cuba, as a singular term, paradoxically denotes a complex of profoundly differential qualities, tastes, rhythms, passions, and pleasures. To write, therefore, "in Cuban" is not one thing, one act, one performance; it is, as Cabrera Infante observed, flight, dance, and song, impossible and necessary at once, a pleasuring that simultaneously loves and resists itself. It may be in this contradictory, paradoxical combination of the pleasure and pain in being Cuban that Cuban writers inscribe themselves.

SELECTED PRIMARY BIBLIOGRAPHY

Arenas, Reinaldo. *Antes que Anochezca.* Barcelona: Tusquets Editores, S.A., 1992.
———. *Before Night Falls.* Trans. Dolores M. Koch. New York: Viking, 1993.
———. *The Doorman.* Trans. Dolores M. Koch. New York: Grove Weidenfeld, 1991.
———. *Farewell to the Sea.* Trans. Andrew Hurley. New York: Penguin Books, 1986.
Cabrera Infante, Guillermo. *Tres Tristes Tigres.* Barcelona: Editoria Seix Barral, S.A., 1983.
Estefan, Gloria, and Emilio Estefan. *Mi Tierra.* Epic Records, 1993.
Fernandez, Roberto G. *Raining Backwards.* Houston: Arte Público P, 1988.
García, Cristina. *Dreaming in Cuban.* New York: Knopf, 1992.
Hijuelos, Oscar. *The Fourteen Sisters of Emilio Montez O'Brien.* New York: Farrar, Straus, and Giroux, 1993.
———. *The Mambo Kings Play Songs of Love.* New York: Farrar, Straus, and Giroux, 1989.
Lázaro, Felipe, ed. *Poetas Cubanos en Nueva York.* Madrid: Editorial Betania, 1986.
Medina, Pablo. *Exiled Memories: A Cuban Childhood.* Austin: U of Texas P, 1990.
Muñoz, Elías Miguel. *Crazy Love.* Houston: Arte Público P, 1988.
———. *The Greatest Performance.* Houston: Arte Público P, 1991.
Padilla, Heberto. *Self-Portrait of the Other: A Memoir.* Trans. Alexander Coleman. New York: Farrar, Straus, and Giroux, 1990.
Pau-Llosa, Ricardo. *Bread of the Imagined.* Tempe: Bilingual P, 1992.

————. *Cuba.* Pittsburgh: Carnegie Mellon UP, 1993.

Poey, Delia, and Virgil Suarez, eds. *Iguana Dreams: New Latino Fiction.* New York: Harper Perennial, 1992.

Sayles, John. *Los Gusanos: A Novel.* New York: HarperCollins, 1991.

Valladares, Armando. *Against All Hope: The Prison Memoirs of Armando Valladares.* New York: Knopf, 1987.

Valls, Jorge. *Twenty Years and Forty Days/Life in a Cuban Prison.* New York: Americas Watch, 1986.

SELECTED SECONDARY BIBLIOGRAPHY

Anzaldúa, Gloria. *Borderlands/La Frontera.* San Francisco: Spinster/Aunt Lute, 1987.

Benítez-Rojo, Antonio. *The Repeating Island: The Caribbean and the Postmodern Perspective.* Trans. James Maraniss. Durham, NC, and London: Duke UP, 1992.

Bhabha, Homi. "Anxious Nations, Nervous States." Keynote lecture delivered, March 4, 1994, at the Annual Meeting of the American Comparative Literature Association, Claremont, CA.

Cinnamon, Deborah. "Close-Up: Ricardo Pau-Llosa." In *Poet's Market '93,* ed. Michael J. Bugeja and Christina Martin. Cincinnati, OH: Writer's Digest Books, 1993. 77–78.

Cortina, Rodolfo J., ed. *Cuban American Theatre.* Houston: Arte Público P, 1991.

Didion, Joan. *Miami.* New York: Simon and Schuster, 1987.

Echevarría, Roberto González. "Outcast of the Island." *New York Times Book Review,* October 24, 1993: 1–8.

Foster, David William. *Gay and Lesbian Themes in Latin American Writing.* Austin: U. of Texas P, 1991.

Fusco, Coco. "Cuba's Art World Comes Undone." *Los Angeles Times,* December 24, 1993: F1, F27.

Kanellos, Nicolás, ed. *Bibliographical Dictionary of Hispanic Literature in the United States.* New York: Greenwood P, 1989.

Kipnis, Laura. "Aesthetics and Foreign Policy." *Ecstasy Unlimited: On Sex, Capital, Gender, and Aesthetics.* Minneapolis and London: U of Minnesota P, 1993. 207–218.

Kutzinski, Vera M. *Sugar's Secrets: Race and the Erotics of Cuban Nationalism.* Charlottesville and London: UP of Virginia, 1993.

Levine, Robert M. *Tropical Diaspora: The Jewish Experience in Cuba.* Gainesville: U of Florida P, 1993.

Manzor-Coats, Lillian. "Stagings between Two Cubas: Toward an Ethic of Resistance." Lecture presented at the Annual Meeting of the American Comparative Literature Association, Claremont, CA, March 5, 1994.

Maratos, Daniel C., and Marnesba D. Hill. *Cuban Exile Writers: A Bibliographic Handbook.* Metuchen, NJ., and London: Scarecrow P, 1986.

Martínez, Julio A., ed. *A Dictionary of Twentieth-Century Cuban Literature.* New York: Greenwood P, 1990.

Menton, Seymour. *Prose Fiction of the Cuban Revolution.* Austin: U of Texas P, 1980.

Oppenheimer, Andrés. *Castro's Final Hour.* New York: Simon and Schuster, 1992.

Pérez-Firmat, Gustavo. *The Cuban Condition: Translation and Identity in Modern Cuban Literature.* Cambridge: Cambridge UP, 1990.

————. "I Came, I Saw, I Conga'd: Contexts for a Cuban American Culture." Unpublished manuscript.

Retamar, Roberto Fernandez. *Caliban and Other Essays*. Minneapolis: U of Minnesota P, 1991.

Rieff, David. *The Exile: Cuba in the Heart of Miami*. New York: Simon and Schuster, 1993.

Rozencvaig, Perla. "Reinaldo Arenas's Last Interview." Trans. Alfred MacAdam, Jr. *Review* 44 (January–June 1991): 78–83.

Shorris, Earl. *Latinos: A Biography of the People*. New York: Norton, 1992.

Sontag, Susan. "Some Thoughts on the Right Way (for Us) to Love the Cuban Revolution." *Ramparts* (April 1969): 6–19.

Soto, Francisco. "*El Portero:* una alucinante fábula moderna." *Revista de Literatura Hispánica* 32–33 (Fall 1990–Spring 1991): 106–117.

Torres, María de los Angeles. "Dreaming in Cuban." *Nation,* (January 24, 1994): 95–97.

Young, Allen. *Los Gays Bajo La Revolución Cubana*. Trans. Máximo Ellis. Madrid: Editorial Playor, 1984.

Zimmerman, Marc. *U.S. Latino Literature: An Essay and Annotated Bibliography*. Chicago: MARCH/Abrazo P, 1992.

12

Dominican-American Literature
Carrie Tirado Bramen

INTRODUCTION

Although Dominicans are currently one of the largest immigrant groups from Latin America and now constitute the most numerous immigrant population in New York City, their literary presence has been largely overlooked. Not only has the work of such writers as Franklin Gutiérrez, Sherezada Vicioso, and Héctor Rivera been excluded from multicultural revisions of the American literary canon, but they have also been frequently omitted from anthologies, bibliographies, and biographical guides to U.S. Latino literature. This double marginalization of Dominican immigrant literature, which falls between the cracks of Latino studies' triadic structure (Chicano, Puerto Rican, and Cuban), presents certain challenges and creates specific priorities for critics of this literature.

One such challenge is inaccessibility. Published mainly in Santo Domingo and written primarily in Spanish, Dominican literature about emigration is beginning to be translated and/or distributed through bilingual journals and small presses in North America. In 1988, Daisy Cocco de Filippis from York College, City University of New York, and Emma Jane Robinett from the Polytechnic University in Brooklyn edited the first collection of Dominican immigrant poetry in the United States, entitled *Poemas del exilio y otras inquietudes/Poems of Exile and Other Concerns*. In her introduction to this collection, Daisy Cocco de Filippis admits that the first hurdle of researching U.S. Dominican literature is ''the scarcity of material'' (9). This is partly due to the fact that several journals have experienced economic hardships and have had to cease publication after only a few issues. For example, *Letras e imágenes,* edited by Juan and Esteban Torres from 1981 to 1982, ceased circulation after eight issues; *Inquietudes,* edited by José Carvajal between 1981 and 1982, ended after only six issues; *Alcance,* edited by Franklin Gutiérrez and started in 1983, has also ended (Cocco and Robinett 9–10). Only *Punto 7 Review: A Journal of Marginal Discourse,* edited by Silvio Torres-Saillant and Ramona Hernández and published annually by the Council of Dominican Educators, still continues publication.

Making Dominican emigrant literature more accessible to U.S. readers is, according to the critic Silvio Torres-Saillant, only part of the story. For Torres-Saillant, who is a professor of literature and composition at Hostos Community College in New York, as well as the director of the Dominican Studies Institute at City College of New York, academics must go beyond libraries and bookstores and redefine literary research to include fieldwork. He refers to local workshops such as "El Taller Juan Sánchez Lamouth" and "Colectivo de Escritores Dominicanos en Nueva York," which constitute the literary center of the community. Both Torres-Saillant and Cocco de Filippis emphasize their active roles as critics in defining, consolidating and distributing a nascent literary emigrant tradition. In establishing such a tradition, they stress the need for the Dominican immigrant community to produce "organs of dispersion" and institutional resources "[que] impulsen sus textos hasta las puertas de la academia" (that will push their texts to the doors of the academy) (Torres-Saillant "La literatura dominicana" 24).

As an emergent tradition, Dominican immigrant literature is distinct from the already well established canons of Nuyoricans and Chicanos. This is largely due to the fact that the Dominican presence in the United States is relatively recent, beginning with the assassination of Generalissimo Trujillo in 1961 and accelerating after the April revolution of 1965, when the U.S. Marines invaded. These events encouraged migration not only to the United States but also to Puerto Rico, where Dominicans still constitute the largest immigrant group. Therefore, to distinguish the literary tradition of U.S. Puerto Ricans from that of Dominicans is sometimes difficult, since intra-Caribbean migrations have created numerous cultural and literary convergences. I want to reflect such convergences by including in my definition of Dominican immigrant literature such seemingly unlikely authors as Enrique Laguerre, Sandra María Esteves, and José Luis González Coiscou. Laguerre, who is a central figure in Puerto Rican letters, spent a number of years studying and working in New York City, where he wrote *El laberinto* (The Labyrinth, 1959), a scathing attack on the Trujillo regime. I also discuss the work of Sandra María Esteves, a well-known Nuyorican poet, whose mother came from the Dominican Republic and lived in St. Thomas and Puerto Rico. Her mother then moved to New York in 1935 at the age of nineteen. Finally, I include in the bibliography José Luis González Coiscou, the well-known Puerto Rican author associated with the famous "Generation of 1940," since he was born in Santo Domingo, the son of a Puerto Rican father and a Dominican mother, and moved to Puerto Rico at the age of four. His mother,

Mignon Coiscou Henríquez, came from one of the most prestigious families in Dominican letters. I mention these writers to demonstrate that Dominican emigrant literature is both familiar and unfamiliar. It includes a young generation of poets whom Cocco de Filippis calls "pioneers" as well as a few long-established writers who have been traditionally associated with the Puerto Rican or Nuyorican canons.

LITERARY-CULTURAL HISTORY

The Dominican Republic has been not only a sending nation in the context of global migratory flows but a receiving nation, especially earlier in the twentieth century. The establishment of U.S. sugar refineries in the 1900s attracted immigrants from Puerto Rico and Cuba. According to Dulce Cruz in *High Literacy, Ethnicity, Gender and Class: The Case of Dominican Americans,* the various ethnic groups were drawn to specific commercial activities: "Cubans and Puerto Ricans contributed to education, Germans traded tobacco; Italians established commerce; Sephardic Jews were involved in financial and commercial activities; and Arabs (Syrians, Lebanese and Palestinians) contributed to the retail trade. Chinese immigrants began to set up laundries, restaurants and cafes in the early 1900s" (66). Haitian migration to the Dominican Republic represents the oldest migratory flow of Haitians to any foreign country, a migration that got under way after 1915 with the fall of Haiti's president Vilbrum Guillaume Sam (Latortue 18). Since then, they have worked as sugarcane cutters, a job that Dominicans regard as beneath their dignity (Schoenhals 17). During the depression of the 1930s, at the height of anti-Haitian sentiment among Dominican elites, Trujillo ordered their massacre in 1937, which resulted in the death of 30,000 Haitians.

Two years later Trujillo supported the founding of DORSA (the Dominican Republic Settlement Association), which encouraged the settlement of Austrian and German Jews. The general told DORSA's president that he would sell the prospective settlers 25,000 acres of his own land at Sosua (a town in the northern part of the island) for a reasonable price. According to the historian Kai Schoenhals, this was an attempt to whiten the population, since Trujillo, who was of mixed race, firmly believed in the supremacy of whites (17).

During his thirty-one-year reign, General Trujillo maintained strict control of his nation's borders; however, after his assassination in 1961, people began to emigrate to the United States and Puerto Rico. The number accelerated after 1965, in the aftermath of the April revolution and the passage of the Immigration Law of 1965, which dramatically relaxed the borders of the United States. From 1966 to 1978, most immigrants did not intend on settling permanently in the United States; however, when the Dominican Republic's economy collapsed in the early 1980s, emigration grew more popular (Dwyer 105). According to the 1980 U.S. census, there were 169,000 Dominicans living in the continental United States, with 75 percent living in New York City. This does not include the illegal count, which some estimate as high as 400,000 in New York City (Pessar, "The Dominicans" 104). The largest concentrations of Dominicans are in Washington Heights and in northern Queens (Corona, Jackson Heights, and Woodside).

Dominican literary and cultural critics prefer to describe Dominicans living in the United States as economic exiles rather than emigrants, a point underscored in the title of Daisy Cocco de Filippis and Emma Jane Robinett's collection of U.S. Dominican poetry *Poems of Exile*. Silvio Torres-Saillant makes a similar claim: "Pues salir de la tierra natal para huirle a la persecución política no es más inminente que salir para no morirse de hambre. En este sentido, nuestros escritores viven la condición del exilio" (Leaving one's native land in order to flee political persecution is not necessarily more imminent than leaving to escape starvation. In this sense, our writers live in a state of exile) ("La literatura dominicana" 18). High unemployment, poverty and illiteracy make the future of the nation bleak. According to the poet Sherezada (Chiqui) Vicioso, 40 percent of the population are entirely illiterate, and another 40 percent are functionally so (Horno-Delgado 232). In the early 1990s, there was 25 percent unemployment, a 60 percent average inflation rate, and a \$4 billion foreign debt. What tends to unite the writers and critics of the Dominican diaspora is a strong historical and political knowledge of their "home" country's material reality. Critics, such as Torres-Saillant, insist that a critical and aesthetic language about the Dominican literature of emigration/exile must foreground this context, that is, demonstrate a serious engagement with the sociocultural space and the historically specific imperatives of this emigrant experience (Torres-Saillant, "La literatura" 23).

DOMINANT CONCERNS

Literary Relations between New York and the Island

Similar to the Nuyoricans' call in the 1970s for a distinct literary tradition that synthesized Puerto Rican and North American literary traditions, critics of Dominican immigrant literature have insisted on their distinctiveness vis-à-vis the island. To illustrate the tensions between island writers and New York-based writers, Silvio Torres-Saillant refers to the first International and Multidisciplinary Conference about the Dominican Republic, held in April 1986 at Rutgers University ("La literatura" 8). A well-known poet from the island was deeply offended when he arrived at the conference and realized that he would have to comment on a panel of Dominican writers from New York. Accusing the organizers of being inconsiderate (*desconsideración*), this poet exemplifies the contempt and inferiority with which a certain class of island writers perceives Dominican literature of the United States.

This anecdote, however, tells only half the story, since U.S. Dominican writers seem to be on far better terms with the island than Nuyoricans and Puerto

Ricans a generation earlier. Take, for example, the recent best-seller in the Dominican Republic, *Los que falsificaron la firma de Dios* (Those Who Forged the Signature of God), which was written by Viriato Sención in New York City, where he has resided for the past fourteen years. Others include the Dominican poet Alexis Gómez Rosa, who now lives in New York and works with the Northern Manhattan Coalition for Immigrant Rights, though most of his poetry has been published in the Dominican Republic. Similarly, Chiqui Vicioso has published her three books of poetry in Santo Domingo, where she has returned to teach at the University of Santo Domingo after having lived in New York City for eighteen years. That these writers publish predominantly in Spanish and work through publishing houses in the Dominican Republic ensures an ongoing connection between emigrant writers and Dominican audiences. The relationship between the island and its diasporic artists is illustrated in Daisy Cocco de Filippis's introduction to *Poems of Exile and Other Concerns,* when she describes the book as a ''gift of a generation of emigrant poets to those who have remained in the homeland'' (18).

Redressing History

A number of novels depict Dominican politics and culture under the Trujillo regime, and they are committed to disclosing the fears, paranoia, and clandestine murders that occurred on the eve of Trujillo's assassination in 1961. Enrique Laguerre's *The Labyrinth* (1959) was inspired by the murders of the journalist Andrés Requena in 1952 and the 1956 ''disappearance'' of Columbia University professor Jesús de Galíndez as he entered a New York subway station. Both men published articles from New York City exposing the Trujillo regime's violence and corruption, and Galíndez was not only an exile of the Trujillo regime but a Spaniard who arrived in the Dominican Republic years earlier as a political exile from Franco. Laguerre demonstrates the proximity of island and metropolis in Trujillo's efforts to control criticism and subversive acts beyond the borders of the Dominican Republic. Given Trujillo's success in having his enemies in foreign capitals killed, *The Labyrinth* was a courageous and even dangerous undertaking. So strong was this sense of fear that many reviewers of the novel refrained from overtly identifying the ''Santiagan Republic'' of the novel as the Dominican Republic. In the novel, an Antillean unity of Puerto Ricans and Santiagans in New York band together and gradually infiltrate the inner circles of the ''General'' (Trujillo is never explicitly named). As a way of surviving in such a suspicious environment, ''passing'' is an important theme, exemplified by the architects of the General's assassination, Sebastián Brache and Juan Lorenzi, whom the General considers to be his closest advisers and allies.

Passing is also a central trope in Viriato Sención's 1992 novel, *Los que falsificaron la firma de Dios,* which captures the climate of terror and fear in the Trujillo and post-Trujillo years. The novel begins in the final years of the ''Tirano'' regime, when a seminary student, Antonio Bell, is imprisoned within the school for his protests against the dictatorship. Since it is suspected that he will soon die from a mysterious "suicide" as his father did in Tirano's jails, Antonio masquerades as an old man to flee his cell in the seminary. He is rescued by two students, Arturo Gonzalo and Frank Bolaño, who arrange for Bolaño's sister to hide him in her home in Santo Domingo. The second half of the novel begins roughly ten years later, when Arturo and Frank have become associates of Dr. Ramos (fictional version of Dr. Joaquin Balaguer, the current president of the Dominican Republic, whom many consider to be another dictator), while Antonio has joined a leftist guerrilla group and is killed in 1968. At the end of the novel, the reader discovers that there has been another form of passing: the character Arturo Gonzalo is actually the author, who was an assistant to the president from 1971 to 1978 and witnessed the corruption among key members of the Balaguer residence. The character Gonzalo has written a novel entitled *Los que falsificaron la firma de Dios,* published in 1992 (the actual publication date of Sención's novel), which exposes the corruption of the Balaguer regime. We are told that Gonzalo, who predicts that this novel will cost him his life, dies in 1993, a victim of "el único crimen ordenado, clara y directamente, por boca del doctor Mario Ramos" (the only crime that was ordered, clearly and directly, from the mouth of Dr. Mario Ramos) (316).

In confronting the terror and fear of living under various dictatorships, these authors reproduce in their narratives the survival strategies of passing, of disguising oneself as a friend of the despot, an aged man in the case of Antonio Bell, or as one of the actual characters in the novel. But for Viriato Sención, the strategy of passing as Gonzalo must ultimately be disclosed to the reader, as Sención courageously takes on a direct attack of the Balaguer regime from the position of someone, like Gonzalo, who has worked within its most intimate circles. Fortunately, Sención's fate has been luckier than that of his fictional counterpart.

Creating a "Home" through Language

One of the more notable aspects of recent Dominican emigrant literature is the absence of a nationalist poetics of homeland that is equivalent to the Nuyorican notion of "Boricua" or the Chicano myth of "Aztlán." Instead, poets such as Tomás Rivera Martínez prefer a more intimate process of "retracing a homeland in [his] heart" (Cocco and Robinett 17). According to Daisy Cocco de Filippis, "taking '*la carreta*' [the oxcart] back home is impossible for most writers, [therefore] language has become the true homeland and the sword to be wielded when dislodging old misconceptions" (*Poemas del exilio* 16). Cocco de Filippis refers to the epigraph of Julia Alvarez's *Homecoming,* which begins with Czeslaw Milosz's adage, "Language is the only homeland." For Dominican poets living in the United States, the word is the means of constructing and imagining a community outside the *isla.*

Also through language, one witnesses the sense of losing a home, as in Franklin Gutiérrez's *Helen*. Written in an epistolary tone, the poem's authorial voice chastises "Helena" for dropping the "a" of her name to sound North American. He blames this on her American boyfriend, whom he accuses of exoticizing "a dark-skinned Mama like you" and secretly sleeping with a blonde American woman. According to the narrative voice, Helen tears letters from "the beloved homeland" so as to rupture an emotional and sentimental connection with the island. The word, in other words, stands for the place, a place that Helen must ultimately forget. This poem exhibits the frustrations and contradictions of the immigrant experience, but by projecting these frustrations onto a female figure, Gutiérrez problematically configures "Helen/a" as the Dominican "La Malinche," as the betrayer of her people.

Women and Emigration

As with the majority of the new immigrants, most Dominicans emigrating to the United States are women. In her study of Dominican women in the New York garment industry, Patricia Pessar argues that wage work has brought immigrant women several personal gains, which include higher self-esteem and greater authority in the household. "Women realize that if they returned to the Dominican Republic they might well end up cloistered in the home since the sexual division of labor in the Dominican economy militates against productive employment for women of their training and class background" (Pessar, "The Dominicans" 123). In his poem "Laborer," Guillermo Francisco Gutiérrez individualizes the anonymous female labor of the sweatshops through the sketches of Ana and Altagracia, the latter of whom carries in her bag a few remnants of the island, such as a crucifix and "mud from her village" (Cocco and Robinett 51).

Chiqui Vicioso describes in an "oral testimonio" how her experiences in New York gave her a greater sense of personal insight and feminist consciousness: "Being in New York was very essential to my development. I would not be the woman I am today had I not gone to New York. I would have been the classic *fracasada* (failure) in my country because I know that I would not have found happiness in marriage and having children" ("Oral History" 231). While in New York, Vicioso was also exposed to the writings of Frantz Fanon and Angela Davis, who played formative roles in Vicioso's decision to identify as a "*caribeña*" and "caribbean *mulata*." Furthermore, in New York Vicioso rethinks the deeply ingrained racism of Dominicans toward Haitians. In a poem entitled "Haiti," she represents, rather than resolves, the ambivalence toward her island neighbors: "I found out that love and hate/share your name" (Cocco and Robinett 40).

For Julia Alvarez, the best-known Dominican writer in the United States, New York represents a similar place of exploration and, more specifically, a site of female pleasure and adventure. In *How the García Girls Lost Their Accent*, which won the 1991 PEN Oakland/Josephine Miles Book Award for works that present a multicultural viewpoint, Alvarez portrays the experiences of four sisters growing up in the United States and the new freedoms that they associate with their new home: "We could kiss and not get pregnant. We could smoke and no great aunt would smell us and croak. We began to develop a taste for the American teenage good life, and soon, Island was old hat, man. Island was the hair-and-nails crowd, chaperones, and icky boys" (108–109).

Although Julia Alvarez's poem "Homecoming" is included in Cocco de Filippis and Robinett's collection, Alvarez actually occupies a rather contentious position in the emergent canon of Dominican emigrant literature. Some critics accuse her of not being representative of the majority of immigrants from the island, who are mainly working-class; and although this is true, her poetry, stories, and essays offer a valuable representation and critique of the highly stratified society of Santo Domingo and the experiences of women within that culture and in the United States. For the Puerto Rican feminist critic Luz María Umpierre, Alvarez courageously brings a Latina sexuality to literature, recovering writing as "una fuente de poder para la mujer y debe utilizarla con ese propósito" (a source of power for women, which should be used with that purpose in mind) (112).

The Core and the Periphery

First arriving in the United States in April 1967, Chiqui Vicioso views New York as "the second most important city for Dominicans," and she has never felt far from Santo Domingo while living in what Guillermo Gutiérrez calls "the rotten apple." The intimate ties between the two regions are not only cultural but also economic. In 1987 the Dominican consulate reported that Dominican immigrants annually send $800 million home to their families, while U.S. foreign aid to the nation during the same year amounted to $62 million (Dwyer 16). The Dominican Republic's most valuable resource is its economic exiles. In his study of a small village in the northern part of the island, Glenn Hendricks comments on the daily contact between the village and New York City, where typically a car departs for the airport in Santo Domingo, carrying passengers destined for, and returning from, New York (23). Local villagers commonly refer to the northern metropolis not as "Nueva York" and say not "los Estados Unidos," but simply "por allá" (up there). This signals the degree of familiarity and intimacy between these two widely separated spaces.

Traveling Music and Immigrant Identities

Music plays an important role in the Dominican diasporic experience, linking geographically disparate places through the familiar themes of migration from, and nostalgia for, the homeland. One of the most popular musical forms is merengue, a type of folk ballad and dance, which the Argentinean theater director Hugo Medrano describes as "the most authentic expression of the Dominican spirit'' (Dwyer 71). Initially played with a *tambora* (bass drum) and a *güiro* (a dried gourd scraped with a stick), the merengue ensemble now includes an accordion. The origin of this popular musical form coincides with the island's independence from Haiti in 1844, and its modern form developed around 1915 in the Cibao region of the island, where it incorporated the polka in the late nineteenth century. Following the migratory flows of Dominicans, the merengue now dominates the contemporary musical scene in Puerto Rico, where it has replaced the traditional salsa (Dwyer 71). As a traveling cultural form, merengue often addresses the theme of migration and refers nostalgically to the island. Another ballad, ''A Cibaoen in New York,'' describes how the high-sounding claims of returning immigrants entice inhabitants of the island to pack and move north. Hence, merengue represents the immigrant experience in ambivalent terms, as both desirable and regrettable.

Popular musical forms also provide a strong sense of feminist identification for the Antillean immigrant, while also suggesting Pan-African alliances. In the short story ''Colita,'' Aida Cartagena Portalatín describes the immigrant experience of Colita, who finds employment as a housekeeper for Mrs. Sarah in New York. For Colita, who is renamed Dawn by her employer, Donna Summer's music provides continuity for the disjunctural experience of migration. Once associated with the memories of her shack and neighborhood on the *isla,* Donna Summer's voice now fills the emptiness of Mrs. Sarah's posh eleventh-floor apartment. The story ends with Colita's silent words, while Mrs. Sarah grabs her hair and screams at her for playing Donna Summer on her record player: ''I can't even hear myself cry now. Donna Summer, my dear little black girl, fill with your voice and excite with your rhythm Mrs. Sarah's house'' (93).

In Sandra María Esteves's most recent collection of poetry, *Bluestown Mockingbird Mambo,* she remembers in ''Sistas'' the strong female singers with whom she grew: Nina Simone, Celia Cruz, Billy Holiday, Bessie Smith, Aretha Franklin. This eclectic combination of salsa, blues, and Motown gave a Caribbean immigrant girl a sense of place, that ''they were fruit from the same feelin' tree'' (19). Portalatín and Esteves find in the strong female vocalist a sense of ''place'' or ''home'' that unites multiple musical traditions, languages, and nationalities into a Pan-American feminist culture.

PREVAILING GENRES

Among Dominican emigrant writers, poetry rather than prose seems to predominate. Silvio Torres-Saillant explains this phenomenon according to the limits of many immigrants' material reality: ''La prosa de ficcíon exige más requisitos sociales: más horas para escribir y reescribir, mayor continuidad mental, y hasta más tinta y papel'' (Fictional prose requires more social requisites: more hours to write and rewrite, greater mental continuity, and even more ink and paper) (''La literatura'' 16). Perhaps with Asa Zatz's forthcoming translation of Sención's *Los que falsificaron la firma de Dios* (Willimantic, CT: Curbstone Press), Dominican novels will reach a wider audience in the United States.

One genre that appears to be flourishing at the present time is that of migratory narratives written from the perspective of children and intended for young readers. Such books as Ginger Gordon's *My Two Worlds* (featuring Kirsy Rodriguez) and Mildred Leinweber Dawson's *Over Here It's Different: Carolina's Story* (told by Carolina Loranzo) emerge from the specific needs of the New York public school system to address the bicultural and bilingual backgrounds of many of the students. Told from the perspective of two elementary school students, both narratives depict the two largest *colonias dominicanas* in New York City, upper Manhattan and Queens, as well as representing the experiences of eldest daughters adjusting to either single-parent or two-income households. The narratives legitimate the existence of nonnuclear or regionally separated families, as well as portraying the reality of overcrowded apartments, return trips to visit grandparents, and the challenges of learning English. What is significant is how these narratives address the issue of divided loyalties between two different worlds, where students may have close family members in both places. Neither Kirsy nor Carolina is made to choose between being American and Dominican; instead they encourage the young readers to accept their biculturality. *My Two Worlds*, for example, concludes with the following affirmation: "Sometimes I wonder if I'd rather live in the Dominican Republic instead of New York City. Well, I don't know. I'm glad I don't have to choose. I belong to both worlds and each is a part of me" (44).

This emphasis on continuity rather than disjuncture largely characterizes the emergent immigrant literature of Dominicans living in the United States. This body of literature, currently in the process of definition, consolidation, and distribution, is truly a traveling literature that circulates between New York and Santo Domingo. The migratory nature of this literature, published and read in both the metropolis and the island, not only represents a nascent tradition of a relatively recent immigrant group but also provides an important basis for a Pan-American literary tradition.

SELECTED PRIMARY BIBLIOGRAPHY

Alvarez, Julia. "An American Childhood in the Dominican Republic." *American Scholar* 56 (Winter 1987): 71–85.

———. *Homecoming*. New York: Grove Press, 1984.

———. *How the Garcia Girls Lost Their Accents*. Chapel Hill, NC: Algonquin Books of Chapel Hill, 1991.

———. "My English." *Punto 7 Review: A Journal of Marginal Discourse* 2.2 (Fall 1992): 24–29.

Dawson, Mildred Leinweber. *Over Here It's Different: Carolina's Story*. Photographs by George Ancona. New York: Macmillan, 1993.

Espaillat, Rhina. "Learning Bones." *Sarah's Daughters Sing: A Sampler of Poems by*

Jewish Women. Ed. Henny Wenkart. Hoboken, NJ: KTAV Publishing House, 1990. 62.

———. "You Call Me by Old Names." *Looking for Home: Women Writing about Exile.* Ed. Deborah Keenan and Roseann Lloyd. Minneapolis: Milkweed Editions, 1990. 39.

Esteves, Sandra María. *Bluestown Mockingbird Mambo.* Houston: Arte Público Press, 1990.

———. *Tropical Rains.* New York: African Caribbean Poetry Theater, 1984.

———. *Yerba buena.* Greenfield Center, NY: Greenfield Review Press, 1980.

Gómez Rosa, Alexis. *Cabeza de alquiler.* Santo Domingo: Luna Cabeza Caliente, 1990.

———. "High Quality, Ltd." Trans. Kim Gerould. *Anthology of Contemporary Latin American Literature, 1960–1984.* Ed. Barry Luby and Wayne Finke. Rutherford, NJ: Fairleigh Dickinson University Press, 1986. 170–171.

———. *High Q.* Santo Domingo: Colección Luna Cabeza Caliente, 1986.

———. "Mercado Negro." *Cuadernos de Poética* 3.9 (May–August 1986): 67–68.

———. *New York City en transito de pie quebrada.* Santo Domingo: Casa de Teatro, 1993.

———. "Octavio Paz." *Cuadernos de Poética* 3.9 (May–August 1986): 69–70.

———. *Pluróscopo.* Santo Domingo: Ediciones Ahora, 1976.

González Coiscou, José Luis. *En Nueva York y otras desgracias.* 1973. 3d ed. Rio Piedra, PR: Ediciones Huracan, 1981.

———. *Paisas, un relato de la emigración.* Mexico, D.F.: Fondo de Cultura Popular (Editorial Popular), 1950.

Gordon, Ginger. *My Two Worlds.* Photographs by Martha Cooper. New York: Clarion Books, 1993.

Gutiérrez, Franklin. *Helén.* Santo Domingo, DR: Editorial Santo Domingo, 1986.

———. *Hojas de octubre.* Santo Domingo: Impresora Olga Palo Hincado, 1982.

———. "Literatura dominicana en New York: apuntes para un embrión." *Cultura* 106 (Supplement of *El Nacional,* August 21, 1983).

———. "New York, otra frontera de la literatura dominicana." *Cultura* 159 (Supplemento of *El Nacional,* September 30, 1984).

———. *Niveles del imán.* New York: Ediciones Alcance, 1983.

———, ed. *Voces del exilio.* New York: Alcance, 1986.

Gutiérrez, Guillermo Francisco. "Laborer," "Ana Freedom on the Sand," "Unlicensed Doctor in New York." *Poemas del exilio y otras inquietudes/ Poems of Exile and Other Concerns.* Ed. Daisy Cocco de Filippis and Emma Jane Robinett. New York: Ediciones Alcance, 1988. 51–58.

Laguerre, Enrique. *The Labyrinth* (*El laberinto,* 1959). Trans. William Rose. New York: Las Americas Publishing Co., 1960.

Luby, Barry, and Wayne Finke, eds. *Anthology of Contemporary Latin American Literature, 1960–1984.* Rutherford, NJ: Fairleigh Dickinson University Press, 1986.

Martínez, Tomás Rivera. "I ask Myself" and "From Here." *Poemas del exilio y otras inquietudes/Poems of Exile and Other Concerns.* Ed. Daisy Cocco de Filippis and Emma Jane Robinett. New York: Ediciones Alcance, 1988. 43–48.

Portalatín, Aida Cartagena. "Colita." Trans. Catherine Rovira. *Anthology of Contemporary Latin American Literature, 1960–1984.* Ed. Barry Luby and Wayne Finke. Rutherford, NJ: Fairleigh Dickinson University Press, 1986: 91–93.

————. *Escalera para Electra.* (*Ladder for Electra,* 1970). 2d ed. Santo Domingo: Editora Taller, 1980.

Rivera, Héctor. *Biografía del silencio.* New York: Systematic Color Printing, 1985.

————. *Poemas no comunes para matar la muerte.* New York: Ediciones Alcance, 1984.

Sención, Viriato. *Los que falsificaron la firma de Dios* (Those Who Forged the Signature of God). Santo Domingo: Biblioteca Taller No. 288, 1992. (Forthcoming English translation by Asa Zatz will be published by Curbstone Press, Willimantic, CT.)

Vicioso, Sherezada (Chiqui). *Algo que decir.* Santo Domingo: Editora Buho, 1991.

————. *Un extraño ulular traía el viento.* Santo Domingo: Alfa y Omega, 1985.

————. "An Oral History" (Testimonio). *Breaking Boundaries: Latina Writings and Critical Readings.* Ed. Asunción Horno-Delgado et al. Amherst: University of Massachusetts Press, 1989. 229–234.

————. *Viaje desde el agua.* Santo Domingo: Fundacion del Libro Casa de Teatro, 1981.

————, ed. *Julia, la nuestra.* Santo Domingo: Editora Alfa Omega, 1987.

SELECTED SECONDARY BIBLIOGRAPHY

Bosch, Juan. "Cañas y letras en las Islas." *El mundo* (San Juan), June 2, 1940: 17.

Cocco de Filippis, Daisy. "Entre dominicanos: Una lectura de 'Las cuatro niñas.' " *Bulletin Centro de Estudios Puertorriqueños* (Winter 1989–1990): 91–95.

————. *Sin otro profeta que su canto: Antología de poesía escrita por dominicanas.* Santo Domingo: Biblioteca Taller no. 263, 1988.

Cocco de Filippis, Daisy, and Emma Jane Robinett, eds. *Poemas del exilio y otras inquietudes/Poems of Exile and Other Concerns.* New York: Ediciones Alcance, 1988.

Cruz, Dulce. "High Literacy, Ethnicity, Gender and Class: The Case of Dominican Americans." Diss., Indiana University, 1993. Ann Arbor: UMI, 1994. 94-06597.

del Castillo, Jose, and Martin F. Murphy. "Migration, National Identity and Cultural Policy in the Dominican Republic." *Journal of Ethnic Studies* 15 (Fall 1987): 49–69.

Dwyer, Christopher. *The Dominican Americans.* New York: Chelsea House, 1991.

Fernández, Carmen Lara. *Historia del Feminismo en la República Dominicana.* Ciudad Trujillo: Imp. Arte y Cine, 1946.

Friedenberg, Daniel. "Our Creature in Ciudad Trujillo." Rev. of *The Labyrinth,* by Enrique Laguerre. *New Republic,* January 16, 1961: 17–18.

Garrison, Vivian, and Carol Weiss. "Dominican Family Networks and United States Immigration Policy: A Case Study." *Caribbean Life in New York City: Sociocultural Dimensions.* Ed. Constance Sutton and Elsa Chaney. New York: Center for Migration Studies, 1987. 235–254.

Georges, Eugenia. *The Making of a Transnational Community: Migration, Development and Cultural Change in the Dominican Republic.* New York: Columbia University Press, 1990.

Grasmuck, Sherri, and Patricia Pessar. *Between Two Islands: Dominican International Migration.* Berkeley: University of California Press, 1991.

Hendricks, Glenn L. *The Dominican Diaspora: From the Dominican Republic to New York City.* New York: Teachers College Press, 1974.

Hernández, Ramona. "The Pitfalls of Comparing Marginal Groups." *Punto 7 Review: A Journal of Marginal Discourse* 2.2 (Fall 1992): 36–48.

Horno-Delgado, Asunción, ed. *Breaking Boundaries: Latina Writings and Critical Readings.* Amherst: University of Massachusetts Press, 1989.

Latortue, Paul. "Neoslavery in the Cane Fields: Haitians in the Dominican Republic." *Caribbean Review* 14.4 (1985): 18–20.

Leavitt, Roy, and Mary Lutz. *Three New Immigrant Groups in New York City: Dominicans, Haitians, and Cambodians.* New York: Community Council of Greater New York, 1988.

Mateo, Andrés, ed. *Manifiestos Literarios de la Republica Dominicana.* Santo Domingo: Taller, 1984.

Perrier, Joseph Louis. *Bibliografía dramática cubana, incluye a Puerto Rico y Santo Domingo.* New York: Phos Press, 1926.

Pessar, Patricia. "The Dominicans: Women in the Household and the Garment Industry." *New Immigrants in New York.* Ed. Nancy Foner. New York: Columbia University Press, 1987. 103–130.

———. "The Linkage between the Household and Workplace of Dominican Women in the U.S." *Caribbean Life in New York City: Sociocultural Dimensions.* Ed. Constance Sutton and Elsa Chaney. New York: Center for Migration Studies, 1987. 255–277.

Ríos, Palmira. "Acercamiento al Conflicto Dominico-Boricua." *Centro* 4.2 (1992): 244–249.

Schoenhals, Kai. "An Extraordinary Migration: Jews in the Dominican Republic." *Caribbean Review* 14.4 (1985): 17.

Sommer, Doris. "Good-Bye to Revolution and the Rest: Aspects of Dominican Narrative since 1965." *Latin American Literary Review* 8.16 (Spring–Summer 1980): 223–228.

———. "Populism as Rhetoric: The Case of the Dominican Republic." *Boundary 2* 11.2 (Fall–Winter 1982–1983): 253–270.

Spalding, Hobart. "Dominican Migration to New York City: Permanent Residents or Temporary Visitors." *Migration Review* (May 1989): 47–69.

Sutton, Constance. "The Caribbeanization of New York City and the Emergence of a Transnational Socio-Cultural System." *Caribbean Life in New York City: Sociocultural Dimensions.* Ed. Constance Sutton and Elsa Chaney. New York: Center for Migration Studies, 1987. 15–30.

Sutton, Constance, and Elsa Chaney, eds. *Caribbean Life in New York City: Sociocultural Dimensions.* New York: Center for Migration Studies, 1987.

Torres, Esteban. "Perspectiva de la literatura dominicana en EE.UU." *Punto 7: Revista de letras e imágenes* 7 (1990): 16–22.

Torres-Saillant, Silvio. "La experiencia neoyoriquina de la literatura dominicana: narrativa de Juan Torres." *El Diario—La Prensa,* February 26, 1989: 40–49.

———. "La literatura dominicana en los Estados Unidos y la periferia del margen." *Cuadernos de Poética* 7.21 (1993): 7–26.

———. "Overview of Three Immigrant Writers." *Punto 7 Review: A Journal for Marginal Discourse* 2.1 (1989): 147–152.

———. Rev. of *Los que falsificaron la firma de Dios,* by Viriato Sención. *Brújula/Compass* (New York) 16 (1993): 12.

———. "Western Discourse and the Curriculum." *Punto 7 Review* 2.2 (Fall 1992): 107–167.

Umpierre, Luz María. "Sexualidad y Metapoesía: Cuatro poemas de Julia Alvarez." *Americas Review* 17.1 (Spring 1989): 108–114.

13

Puerto Rican-American Literature
Carrie Tirado Bramen

INTRODUCTION

Unlike other immigrant groups, Puerto Ricans arrive in the United States as citizens. In contrast to Mexicans and Central Americans, whose immigrant experience is largely defined by questions of illegality and fears of deportation, Puerto Ricans have a different relation to the United States, one born out of a colonial history. Claimed as a U.S. possession in the Spanish-American War of 1898, Puerto Rico is neither a sovereign nation nor a state of the Union, but a "commonwealth" (estado libre asociado), its official status since 1952. A Supreme Court decision in 1904 declared Puerto Ricans free to circulate within U.S. territories, creating the longest-standing open border in U.S. history. Three years later, the Jones Act conferred citizenship on Puerto Ricans. Migration from the island to the metropolis has played a formative role in the history and culture not only of Puerto Rico but also of the United States. This is especially true of New York City, with long-established *colonias* (extended neighborhoods) in the South Bronx, Spanish Harlem, and the Lower East Side. Frequently described as a "revolving door" or "commuter" migration, movement between Puerto Rico and New York has followed a circular pattern of settlement, along the lines of what the playwright Luis Rafael Sánchez has called "to-go-out-again-and-come-back-again" (Rodríguez de Laguna 25).

Puerto Ricans' colonial status as "immigrant-citizens" does raise the question of whether they do indeed constitute an immigrant group. While scholars such as Michael Lapp argue that Puerto Ricans are internal migrants, since they do not emigrate across a national border but instead move from one part of the

United States to another, other scholars, such as the political scientist Manuel Maldonado-Denis, prefer the term "emigration" to "migration." The former term recognizes that Puerto Rico is a Latin American nation in its own right and not an indissoluble part of the United States.

Just as there is debate about how to classify Puerto Ricans moving to the mainland, so there is discussion about where to locate Puerto Rican literature written about the immigrant experience. Produced within two different localities, the island and the continent, Puerto Rican immigrant literature poses certain questions that complicate the boundaries of national literary traditions: How are the conditions of a national literature challenged by the demographic reality that nearly 40 percent of puertorriqueños live outside the geographical boundaries of the island? Is U.S. Puerto Rican literature written in English part of the literary heritage of the *isla?* Finally, when is U.S. Puerto Rican literature no longer an immigrant literature?

Although I discuss island writers from the generation of the 1950s, the primary focus of this chapter is the literary production of Nuyoricans or "neoricans," first- and second-generation Puerto Ricans who were either born or raised in the United States. Located in the margins of Puerto Rican and North American literary traditions, Nuyorican literature asserts a nationalist identity of collective self-affirmation, as in Pedro Pietri's declaration that "PUERTORRIQUEÑOS ARE A BEAUTIFUL RACE," as well as an internationalist identity that draws upon dialects, tropes, and tempos from numerous diasporic cultures (Pietri 1973, 10). What Nuyorican writing demonstrates, with its engagement of black English, Caribbean rhythms, and familiarity with Jewish culture, is an implicit challenge to the way that American literature has been traditionally conceived and recently reconceived as a microcosm of distinct cultures. Recent multicultural renditions of the American canon, though important and progressive, still formally tend to arrange "ethnic" writing in discrete and self-contained chapter headings and sections. Nuyorican literature, emerging out of the circular movement between island and mainland and growing out of the multicultural and multiracial context of the metropolis, represents an ongoing dialogue between nationalist and internationalist alliances, situated in that interstitial space that Jose Angel Figueroa describes in his poem "Boricua" as between "sanjuan/& kennedy airport" (Turner 221).

LITERARY-CULTURAL HISTORY AND MAJOR AUTHORS

Puerto Rican literature about emigration to the United States can be divided into four stages: (1) the early period (1900–1945), (2) the post-World War II "Great Migration" (1945–1965), (3) Nuyorican renaissance (1965–1970s), and (4) the post-Nuyorican period (1980–present). Since the sociological studies of the 1950s, there has been a tendency to configure Puerto Rican emigration as a post-World War II phenomenon. However, from the 1980s to the present, much of the scholarship has focused on the historical antecedents of post-war Puerto

Rican emigration. Works such as Virginia Sánchez Korrol's *From Colonia to Community: The History of Puerto Ricans in New York City, 1917–1948* (1983) and Juan Flores's *Divided Borders: Essays on Puerto Rican Identity* (1993) have been instrumental in adding historical depth to our understanding of the Puerto Rican presence in the United States. In establishing the origins of an emergent literary tradition, Flores suggests that U.S. Puerto Rican writing begins in the late nineteenth century with the writings of political exiles from the independence struggles against Spain. Puerto Rico's major revolutionary and intellectual leaders spent time in New York City, where they united with Cuban exiles to establish organizations such as the Cuba and Puerto Rican Revolutionary Party, led by the Cuban exile José Martí. Such promoters of "Antillean unity" include Eugenio María de Hostos, Ramón Betances, Lola Rodríguez de Tío, and Sotero Figueroa.

Rather than focus on these individuals, however, literary historians have tended to see the primary figures of the first generation of U.S. Puerto Rican writers as Jesús Colón (1901–1974), a stowaway on the USS *Carolina* in 1918, and Bernardo Vega (1885–1965), who arrived in New York in 1916 as a second-class passenger on the *Cuamo* when he was thirty years old. Both were from Cayey, where the Puerto Rican Socialist Party was founded in 1915; both were *tabaqueros* (cigar makers), socialists, and union organizers, politically committed to the ideals of working-class internationalism and supportive of Puerto Rican independence, as well as chroniclers of New York's nascent Puerto Rican community. In occupational and political terms, they largely typified first-wave immigrants: skilled workers, carpenters, bricklayers, and artisans, coming primarily from San Juan rather than rural regions. The core were *tabaqueros,* apprenticed cigar makers looking for jobs in East Coast cities, and they represented the most militant and educated sector of the Puerto Rican working class.

Both Colón and Vega write within autobiographical and testimonial genres, retrospectively documenting their experiences of the first decades of the twentieth century. Jesus Colón completed *A Puerto Rican in New York and Other Sketches* in 1959, and Bernardo Vega wrote *Memorias de Bernardo Vega* in the 1940s, though it was not published until 1984. Despite these similarities, Colón and Vega write about Puerto Ricans in New York from significantly different angles. In *A Puerto Rican in New York and Other Sketches* and his recently published collection of articles and editorials *The Way It Was . . . ,* Colón focuses on the different experiences of labor, whether working on the docks, peeling labels from bottles, or translating Longfellow's "Hiawatha" into Spanish. Even Colón's arrival narrative, "Stowaway," reflects this emphasis on labor. He resists the readerly expectations of anxious first glimpses of the Manhattan skyline and the silhouette of the Statue of Liberty and concentrates instead on his activities on the ship: dishwasher, busboy, brass polisher, and janitor.

Throughout his work, Colón emphasizes the need to create multicultural alliances within the metropolitan working class as well as international links with other countries, such as Puerto Rico. In "The Two United States," he asks:

".... [W]hat kind of unity and understanding exists between the exploited here in this country and over there in Puerto Rico? Among those who have to get up every day—Black and white, Protestant and Catholic, Puerto Rican or North American—to sweat in a factory?" (1993, 62). The place of racism in hindering such unity is the focus in many of Colón's anecdotal essays, particularly those published in the *Daily Worker*. A precursor to Piri Thomas, Colón describes how his experience as a black Latino differs from that of one who is light-skinned. In "Hiawatha in Spanish," he recounts how his successful freelance translating at home earns him a full-time position at a New York office; but when he arrives for his first day of work, the employer is stunned, expecting a mestizo rather than a black Latino, and exclaims: "That was to be your desk and typewriter. But I thought you were white" (1993, 51).

In contrast to Colón's emphasis on racial prejudice and the particular incidents that he experienced as a black man, Bernardo Vega begins his narrative by describing his racial position as white: "I was white, a peasant from the high-lands, and . . . I had a round face with high cheekbones, a wide, flat nose, and small blue eyes" (1987, 5). The racial difference between Colón and Vega underscores the heterogeneity of Puerto Ricans and their contrasting immigrant experiences in the United States. Another difference between the two early chroniclers is Colón's emphasis on the need for interracial working-class alliances and Bernardo Vega's concentration on changes within the Puerto Rican community, namely, the transformation of scattered and small Puerto Rican neighborhoods in the World War I era to their consolidation as El Barrio or Spanish Harlem in the 1920s. According to Vega, the Puerto Rican population in New York in 1918 was roughly 10,000, and it increased to 150,000 by 1927, when Harlem became "a socialist stronghold." Where Colón focuses on the experience of work and labor unions, Vega gives us a cultural history of the nascent barrio, such as early "ethnic" restaurants, poetry readings, debates, and the arrival of Spanish-language theater companies. Vega expresses an internationalist bent in his portrayal of New York City as a "modern Babylon, the meeting point for peoples from all over the world" (1987, 15). He also depicts the dynamic and cosmopolitan character of New York localities, such as Spanish Harlem and the Lower East Side, which were largely Jewish prior to, and immediately after, the First World War and whose residual presence remains, a theme taken up by later Nuyorican writers.

Both Vega and Colón acknowledge the writings of Arturo Alfonso Schomburg (1874–1938), a black Puerto Rican who emigrated in 1891 at the age of seventeen. Primarily known as a bibliophile for the African-American community, Schomburg frequently wrote on Caribbean and Latin American issues in such major newspapers as the *New York Globe*, defending the right of Puerto Ricans to self-rule. Antithetical though contemporaneous with these three writers is Pedro Juan Labarthe (1906–), who wrote *Son of Two Nations: The Private Life of a Columbia Student* (1931). Considered by many critics as the Puerto Rican Horatio Alger, Labarthe subscribes to the conventional model of the immigrant success story along the lines of *The Americanization of Edward Bok,* an autobiography that he greatly admired. Labarthe's inclusion within a Nuyorican canon is a controversial one. Eugene Mohr, author of *The Nuyorican Experience,* which is the first and still the only book on Puerto Rican literature in the United States, defends Labarthe on the grounds that both negative and positive renditions of life on the continent need to be represented.

Where the first-wave writers tended toward autobiographical sketches and newspaper editorials, the writers of the post-war generation depicted the emigration experience through more conventional "literary" genres, such as plays, short stories, poetry, and novels. Writers such as Pedro Juan Soto, Jaime Carrero, René Marqués, Enrique Laguerre, and Julia de Burgos exemplify transitional figures both in Puerto Rico and in the United States. As the first generation of Puerto Ricans who felt the full impact of the American occupation of the island and the second generation of children taught entirely in English in the public schools (Spanish did not resume its position as the national language until 1949), the generation of the 1950s grappled with the impact of imperialism, mass migration, and the bicultural, bilingual quality of puertorriqueñidad. Additionally, the industrialization scheme of the 1950s, called Operation Bootstrap, dramatically altered the economic and social structures of the island. The development of large mechanized, agribusiness plantations uprooted a rural population, creating an internal migration to San Juan and then to New York. In 1940, there were roughly 69,000 Puerto Ricans living in New York, a number that dramatically grew to 1,429,396 by 1950. This post-war exodus, frequently referred to as the "Great Migration," consisted of a population that was largely rural and less skilled, educated, and politically organized than the first wave of immigrants.

A majority of the writers portraying the reality of migration and the immigrant barrio were island authors, who visited and lived in New York for certain lengths of time but who ultimately identified with, and lived on, the island. Take Pedro Juan Soto, for example, who lived through the emigration firsthand but ultimately resettled in Puerto Rico by the late 1950s. The critic Juan Flores refers to the majority of puertorriqueño writing about the "Great Migration" as "views from an island"—portrayals of New York from Puerto Rico—which remain some of the most familiar Puerto Rican literature in the United States. Mostly written in standard literary Spanish, the island literature of midcentury refrained from representing Nuyorican speech acts, an emergent language that was already immersed in bilingual mixing and code switching in Spanish, English, and black English.

With the increasing accessibility of travel, it is not surprising that the airplane became a recurring trope in the writing of this period, such as in Jaime Carrero's bilingual collection of poetry called *Jet Neorriqueño: Neo-Rican Jetliner.* As both a literal entity and poetic metaphor, the "neo-rican jetliner" plays a contradictory role. It makes possible the conditions for cultural and regional dislocation as well as easing that painful sense of duality by making the two contrasting worlds an immediate part of the puertorriqueño experience, bringing about a sense of direct contact that would gradually grow more distant in subsequent generations.

In contrast to the excitement and anticipation in Bernardo Vega's New York arrival narrative, the narratives of this later period portray the journey north as rather ordinary and familiar. In *Trópico en Manhattan,* Cotto-Thorner, one of the few writers of the period raised in New York and considered by some to be the first novelist who writes about the Nuyorican community "from a view within," describes the arrival of Juan Marcos Villalobos, a well-educated, middle-class teacher. Where Vega recounts the thrill of his first glimpse of the Statue of Liberty and impulsively decides to throw his wristwatch into the ocean (after hearing that watches were considered effeminate in New York), Juan Marcos Villalobos is disappointed even prior to landing, "because the clouds prevented him from seeing New York from the air, as he had so often dreamed." He has a similar reaction when he catches his first glimpse of the New York skyscrapers: "When all was said and done, it wasn't as spectacular as he had imagined. There were no dazzling lights; his hopes were dulled by the ordinariness" (Flores 1987, 60, 62). For the post-war writers, the metropolis of the first generation had lost some of its aura as a more sober and cynical portrayal of New York emerged, a portrayal that would reach fruition with the next generation. Cotto-Thorner differed not only from this earlier generation but also from his contemporaries. He was unusually sensitive toward the language practices of the Nuyorican community, evident in the appended glossary of "Neoyorkismos," which are code-switching expressions emerging from the New York *colonias.*

In *La Carreta* (The Oxcart), a play that was produced in Puerto Rico, Spain, and the United States in the late 1950s and 1960s, René Marqués represents migration in terms of an allegory of moral declension. In contradistinction to the airplane, that icon of technological modernity, the oxcart (*la carreta*) represents a sentimental metaphor of peasant (*jíbaro*) innocence and rural nostalgia; it conveys a sense of rootedness with the land, strong kinship bonds with the extended family and community, and a purifying form of physical labor that is comparatively unalienated. When Doña Gabriela moves her family to the slums of San Juan ("La Perla") and eventually to the South Bronx, a common trajectory for immigrants of the period, her family gradually falls apart, plagued by urban poverty, drugs, promiscuity, and gambling. Marqués dramatizes the personal impact of Operation Bootstrap, the dispossession of rural lands from families that owned them for generations. By the end of the play, Doña Gabriela decides to return to "the red earth of my village," preferring the rural poverty of a tenant farmer to the degenerate lifestyle of an urban slum dweller.

Although New York signifies moral corruption for some writers of this period, others see it as a place to experiment with taboo topics, such as female sexual desire as well as domestic violence. Pedro Juan Soto's short stories in *Spiks* feature female protagonists held "captive," the title of one story, not only by their personal relations to boyfriends, husbands, children, and mothers but also by their bodies. In "Scribbles," which won the Ateneo Puertorriqueño Prize in 1953, Graciela, the mother of two children and the wife of a wistful artist, is pregnant again, a burden that is compounded by her family's impoverished home in the basement of a New York tenement: "Holy God all I do is have kid after kid like a bitch and that man doesn't bother to look for work" (34). The need to create imaginary lovers in a world that denies female pleasure is the subject of Soto's short story "Absence," where Altagracia re-creates Mario, the husband who abandoned her three years before. The story concludes with a drunken, masturbatory spectacle, where she makes love to her absent husband. The scene is both a sad commentary on the inability of women to gain satisfaction in heterosexual relationships as well as a daring portrayal of women's sexual self-expression.

The poet Julia de Burgos (1914–1953) further explores the limits of female pleasure, both in her writing as well as in her life. Finding it difficult to live in Puerto Rico due to her unconventional lifestyle, de Burgos arrived in New York in 1942. Unable to make the adjustment to life in the metropolis, she eventually succumbed to alcoholism, depression, and a mysterious death on the streets of the city. One of her final poems, "Poema para mi muerte," prophetically describes her corpse "on the rock slab of a deserted island" (1979, 129). Today, Julia de Burgos has become an important icon for a puertorriqueña lesbian aesthetic, an aesthetic that has its early voice in de Burgos's poetics of transvestitism in "Pentacromía" (Pentachromatic). In this poem, the female voice imagines herself to be a man, who climbs over the walls of a convent to seduce the nuns and ultimately to rape (*violar*) the author, Julia de Burgos.

Although a nascent literary tradition from Jesus Colón to Julia de Burgos was in the making, writers of the late 1960s promulgated a poetics of the present that would create a "new language" for a "new day." Calling themselves "nuyoricans" and "neo-ricans," they insisted not only on a temporal break with the past but also on a spatial break with the island, a rhetorical gesture that affirmed their place within the United States, more specifically, in New York. This sense of place was made literal at Miguel Algarín's Nuyorican Poets' Cafe, a sort of cultural headquarters for the Nuyorican renaissance on 505 East Sixth Street in the Lower East Side (and now an official landmark of the city). With the existence of such a place, the Nuyorican literature of this period had a strong sense of social, spatial, and temporal coherence, fundamentally concerned with defining a distinctive identity that differed from mainstream America as well as from island culture.

The task of the poet was to create this new identity, one that would reject a previous generation's nostalgic bond with the island and focus on the problems of urban America. In Miguel Algarín's introduction to *Nuyorican Poetry,* a piece that can be read as a manifesto for the movement, he defines the function of the poet: "The poet is responsible for inventing the newness. The newness needs words. . . . The poet has to invent a new language, a new tradition of communication'' (9). This new language would retain the "rawness" of street language and preserve the "dynamic and erratic" qualities of ghetto culture. Nuyorican poets not only demystify poetic language and situate it in the everyday world of the inner city but also define a public role for the poet, one where "he tells the tale of the streets to the streets" (11). More concerned with the masculinized exterior spaces of El Barrio and the Lower East Side than with the feminized interior spaces of mothers, sisters, and daughters, this poetry depends on a conflictual relation with authority at two levels: (1) within the Puerto Rican community and especially toward the parent culture and the figure of the father, and (2) with the dominant culture and its figures and institutions of social control (i.e., police, prison, the corporation, and so on). In this sense, Nuyorican literature of this period can be understood as the cultural production of a post-war working-class youth subculture, which struggles to assert a youth identity that is simultaneously opposed to a parent immigrant culture and yet ultimately continuous with it.

Where "proto-nuyoricans" like Colón and Vega understand struggle and resistance in concrete and collective terms, the Nuyoricans frequently configure struggle in individual terms: the rebel versus society or, in Algarín's words, the outlaw versus the institution. This tension between historical continuity and a radical break with the past structures the first anthology of U.S. Puerto Rican verse, entitled *Nuyorican Poetry,* edited by Miguel Algarín and Miguel Piñero. The first section is called "Outlaw Poetry," while the following one is "Evolutionary Poetry"; these juxtaposing sections ironically situate the lawless poet alongside the laws of evolutionary, linear development. The editors of this anthology are aware of the tensions between lawlessness and laws that permeate the very heart of the project: anthologizing and thereby formalizing Nuyorican street language. Algarín fears standardizing the street-born language of Nuyorican poetry and seeks to preserve its "rawness" without imposing "grammatical rules."

Two major works of the period, Pedro Pietri's collection of poems entitled *Puerto Rican Obituary* and Piri Thomas's *Down These Mean Streets,* explore this tension between historical continuity and radical "newness" in terms of the generational gap between parent immigrant culture and youth subculture. Pedro Pietri criticizes his parents' and their generation's faith in the American dream of consumer success and their passive obedience to the work ethic. In the title poem, Pietri insists that commercialism combined with "electric appliances" is killing the creative energy of an older generation that he both honors and reproaches.

A generational split also appears in Piri Thomas's autobiography, *Down These Mean Streets,* especially in the chapter aptly entitled "Funeral for a Prodigal Son," when Piri Thomas argues with Poppa over the issue of being black and Puerto Rican. Poppa identifies as white, while Piri insists that neither his father nor he could pass as such, and he accuses his father of living in a "dream" of passing: "You protect your lying dream with a heavy strain for a white status that's worthless to a black man. You protect your dream, Poppa, protect it. . . . You gonna have to wake up to the fact that you ain't white" (151). Piri Thomas asserts the Nuyorican alternative formulation of "puertorriqueñidad," as a hybrid and multiracial identity composed of Taíno, African, and Spanish.

The Nuyorican generation celebrates, rather than denies, the tripartite dimensions of their identity. The poet Victor Hernández Cruz, who is often considered the generation's existentialist, discloses the layers that constitute the palimpsestic history of island culture in "African Things" (Turner 1991, 30). To be Puerto Rican, according to Cruz, is to be "indio" and "african," two indelible genealogies of island identity that have been historically considered inferior to Spanish blood. This insistence on recognizing the diasporic quality of Puerto Rican identity, where the history of the island is understood as a history of migrations, is also an important theme in the poetry of Rosario Morales and Tato Laviera. In "Africa," Morales likens not only herself but the Puerto Rican people to a tree, with Africa signifying the lifeblood that nourishes its roots. In his more positive reformulation of René Marqués's play *La Carreta* entitled *La Carreta Made a U-Turn,* Tato Laviera sees New York, specifically, Central Park, that performative site of jam sessions, as an eclectic space where various cultures blend through language and music. Employing musical metaphors of syncretism and organic tropes of nourishment, these writers render Africa not as a tangential component of a Nuyorican identity but as a constitutive element that permeates all of its aspects.

Besides challenging the binary of being Puerto Rican and being black, Nuyorican writers also undermine the polarity of assimilation and separatism, a familiar dualism in discourse on immigrant literatures. When the Nuyoricans declare that they will create a "new language," they do not mean a pure language, with an authentic and unproblematic connection to Boricua, the pre-Columbian name of the island. Instead, this language is, according to the Puerto Rican-Dominican writer Sandra María Esteves, "essentially street-rooted and evolves from the natural mixing of multiethnic people" (Algarín and Piñero 1975, 164). Tato Laviera demonstrates such linguistic eclecticism in the poem "asimilao," which acknowledges in a humorous yet profound way the dialectical complexity of acculturation. Rather than deny "assimilation," that is, the experience of adapting and adjusting to the dominant culture and language of North America, the poetic "I" (or "yo soy") confesses that the process has already occurred ("yo soy asimilao"). But in admitting that the process has occurred in Spanish, in "black spanish" at that, Laviera asserts the creative agency of the immigrant in rewriting, reconfiguring, and translating the dominant culture. This is a major theme in Laviera's collection entitled *AmeRícan,* where the very title is an assertion of not only an alternative spelling but an alternative way of conceptualizing the nation, as a "humane america."

Contrast this position with the more cynical attitude of Pedro Pietri, who often renders the immigrant as a passive and complicitous victim of advertisements and consumerism in *Puerto Rican Obituary.* Both poets insist on the need for pride and dignity within working-class Puerto Rican communities, but Laviera believes that the process is already under way, alive in everyday Nuyorican culture, while Pietri is less hopeful. Laviera's optimism is shared by writer and graphic artist Nicholasa Mohr, who is one of the most widely published Puerto Rican writers in the United States. In an essay entitled "Puerto Ricans in New York: Cultural Evolution and Identity," she argues that the "marginal" has radically transformed, and continues to transform, the metropolis: "The European culture that has dominated these United States since its beginning is continually being imbued with the cultures of the people of color, and most recently by Hispanics. . . . New York is indeed a bilingual city" (Rodríguez de Laguna 158). The dramatic post-war influx of immigrants from the Americas has resulted in the Caribbeanization of New York.

A dialectical way of understanding how Puerto Ricans are both influencing, and are influenced by, the dominant culture can also be applied to Nuyoricans' relations with other immigrant groups. As early as the 1940s, Bernardo Vega felt that what distinguished Puerto Ricans from other immigrants was their "racial open-mindedness" (1984, xiii). This is partly due to the fact that Puerto Ricans are themselves racially heterogeneous; but they also settled in primarily urban centers, where the congested urban space compressed manifold cultures. The proximity of other cultures creates instances of intercultural harmony, as well as moments of aggression and tension. A number of the short stories in Nicholasa Mohr's *El Bronx Remembered* address the problems and pleasures among different immigrant groups in these largely autobiographical sketches about growing up in the Bronx between 1945 and 1956. At this time, the Bronx was a transitional space, where the residual presence of an earlier generation of Jewish immigrants lived alongside the emergent, post-war population of Puerto Ricans. In the short story entitled "Mr. Mendelsohn," an elderly Jewish man, who never married but raised his many sisters, now lives alone in an apartment building that has changed from being primarily Jewish to Puerto Rican. His next-door neighbors, the Suarez family, regularly welcome Mr. Mendelsohn into their apartment for dinner, so that, in time, he becomes a part of their extended family, befriending Mrs. Suarez's first grandson, Tato. During the course of the story, Mr. Mendelsohn's sense of family changes, feeling much closer to the Puerto Rican immigrant family than to his own. Mohr enlarges the category of "family" and shows the importance of locality and proximity, suggesting that families do not necessarily form along discrete and self-contained national lines.

Interacting with other immigrant groups is not always harmonious. In *Down These Mean Streets,* Piri Thomas describes a boyhood incident in Harlem, when his family moved onto an Italian block. Rocky, the neighborhood bully, starts harassing Piri for being a "spic" and "black enuff to be a nigger" (26–27). The public spaces of the streets are racially and ethnically encoded as distinct territories for the boys and adolescents who inhabit them. The streets, for Thomas, constitute the site of masculine war games, where one's manliness is constantly tested through threats of violence, the pressure of drugs, and the presence of gangs. However, Piri does establish an important bond with Brew, an African American living in Harlem, who originally came from the Deep South. When Piri's racial consciousness as a black man in the United States grows, he and Brew take jobs on a coastal ship that travels along the southern coast, where Piri experiences segregation for the first time. This experience draws an important link between the black Latino and the black American.

Piri Thomas's pilgrimage to the Deep South, a journey of exile and return in the name of self-discovery, has a corollary with Nuyorican poems that address return journeys or first-time visits to Puerto Rico. In "This Is Not the Place Where I Was Born," Miguel Piñero visits the island in 1974 only to realize his spiritual and cultural disjuncture with the place. Nuyoricans arrive in search of spiritual identity, only to be "greeted with profanity" (Turner 1991, 20). Miguel Algarín expresses this same experience of disillusionment in "San Juan/ an arrest/ Maguayo/ a vision of Malo dancing" (Algarín and Piñero 1975, 139). Expecting the "motherland" to embrace, console, and protect him, Algarín instead finds himself in jail for not possessing a valid driver's license. Even on the island, he is subject to the law, unable to find respite from its jurisdiction.

Others find the island a dumping ground for North American fast-food chains, commercial goods, and tourists, as they witness the aftermath of Operation Bootstrap. Jose Angel Figueroa comments on the irony of finding consumer products in the midst of an exotic island in " 'Puerto Rico' Made in Japan" (Turner 1991, 33), where Puerto Ricans are "natives" on display for North American tourists, dressed like Carmen Mirandas and eating Uncle Ben's Minute Rice. Similarly, Amina Muñoz, a first-generation Nuyorican writer of the early 1970s, employs the advertising language of tourism in "welcome to San Juan, oldest city in the u.s.," where she juxtaposes the United States' cultural presence with their military presence (109). The Nuyorican generation returns to Boricua only to find a place looking more like New York than the Edenic island of childhood stories. In contrast to the generation of the 1950s, who had a much more immediate connection to the island, the Nuyorican generation sees it from a distance, feeling both shunned from the island as its "bastard" children and disgusted with its loss of cultural independence.

For others, such as Sandra María Esteves, Boricua is less a literal place and more a metaphor for configuring a Nuyorican identity. Similar to the metaphor of "the borderlands" in Chicana feminism in describing subjectivity and mestizaje, Esteves presents a divided and bicultural subject in the poem "Here" (Turner 1991, 186–187). Torn between the dual identities of "boricua" and "spic," this poem combines the optimism of Tato Laviera with the cynicism of Pedro Pietri. It asserts that she is both "alive" as well as "oppressed," in possession of "cultural beauty" but "robbed of a cultural identity." This poem conveys the contradictory position of the immigrant subject, caught between two worlds and two temporalities. Rather than unify this split subject into a whole, Esteves instead decides to keep the two poles of her identity separated by the slash, rather than connected through the hyphen. The two sides remain close enough to provide an ongoing tension, but far enough apart to remain irreconcilable.

Nicholasa Mohr also reconfigures Nuyorican identity by directly challenging the prevalent images of the Nuyorican poet as primarily male, an ex-con, drug addict, and imbued in a culture of violence. In an anecdotal essay entitled "On Being Authentic," Mohr describes why a major publishing house rejected her short stories: "[T]he editor suggested that he was really looking for something 'more authentic,' something that describes what *really* goes on in *El Barrio.* Someone along the lines of a female Piri Thomas—drugs, rape, crime, prostitution, the whole chilling spectacle of ghetto existence. That's what most readers seem to want" (73). From her first collection of short stories, *Nilda,* to her most recent book, *Rituals of Survival,* Nicholasa Mohr is committed to representing the domestic interiors of Puerto Rican culture, the everyday, nonspectacular happenings of mothers, daughters, and grandmothers.

By referring to the "post-Nuyorican" period of Nuyorican Literature, I do not want to suggest that there is a clear break between the writing of the 1970s and that of the 1990s, but rather to underscore how contemporary writing extends, modifies, and takes the Nuyoricans' concerns with identity and migration in new directions. One area that has changed significantly has been the theorizing of feminism. In specifying the differences, it is useful to compare Sandra María Esteves's early poem "A La Mujer Borrinqueña" (*Yerba Buena* 63–65), with her recent revision, "So Your Name Isn't María Cristina" (*Bluestown Mockingbird Mambo* 32–33), two poems that are in direct dialogue with each other. The figure of María Cristina was one of the first articulations of the borrinqueña viewpoint at a time when there were few women's voices within the Nuyorican movement. She represents the feminist nationalist position, which both expresses pride in a Boricua identity and empowers women's traditional domestic roles in the family. Although Esteves dignifies motherhood, she still ultimately reconfigures femininity within the rather narrow perimeters of the home. At one level, she merely celebrates the role of the good and dutiful housewife, having her family's concerns as her first priority. However, in her most recent collection of poems, *Bluestown Mockingbird Mambo,* Esteves revises this earlier poem and dedicates it to the lesbian puertorriqueña poet and scholar Luz María Umpierre. In this later poem, "So Your Name Isn't María Cristina," Esteves admits that when writing the earlier version, she was "just a young woman," who desperately sought "to define self within worlds of contradictions" (*Bluestown* 32). Since then, she has undergone dramatic changes, even though her name has remained the same. Critical of her earlier, static rendition of the "universal" puertorriqueña, Esteves insists that identity is malleable, dynamic, and always growing. But she refuses to reject this earlier version and tacitly suggests that the two poems be read together as part of a historical and personal process of "metamorphosis."

In a sense, María Cristina's transformation depicts a kind of feminist migration. In recent U.S. Puerto Rican writing, the very term "migration" has become far more expansive and metaphoric, referring to a wide range of experiences and discoveries. Where earlier generations, including the Nuyorican period, use "migration" in a specific historical sense, literally referring to the influx of Puerto Ricans to the mainland, the term gradually becomes distanced from the actual history of migration and consequently becomes more flexible at a figurative level. In his most recent collection of poetry and essays, *Red Beans*, Victor Hernández Cruz uses migration as a metaphor for change. It signifies mobility and the subsequent process of syncretism, which constitutes plural identities that are integral to the Caribbean, "a place of great convergence." The distinctiveness of each national ingredient breaks down and blends into others, so that what remains are composites of scrambled and rearranged fragments. Where early Nuyorican poetry has a strong performative element, evident in Algarín's description of the poet as a "troubadour," more recent U.S. Puerto Rican literature is more reflective, observing and commenting on one's own personal performance in the spectacle of identity formation.

Judith Ortiz Cofer opens her essay "The Story of My Body," in her most recent collection of poetry, *Latin Deli*, with an epigraph from Hernández Cruz: "Migration is the story of my body." This autobiographical essay describes how the color of her skin circulates in different geographic contexts: "I was born a white girl in Puerto Rico but became a brown girl when I came to live in the United States" (135). Migration also plays an important role in her novel *The Line of the Sun*, which was nominated for a Pulitzer Prize in 1988. In this novel, the second-generation daughter, Marisol, grows up in Paterson, New Jersey, and knows about the island only through the narratives of her mother, Ramona, and her Tío Guzmán and later from the letters of her *abuela* from the island, which kept "coming like installments in a biography" (286). Migration, for Marisol, is in the telling, a narrative performance from one generation to another.

For others, such as Luz María Umpierre, migration describes the process of coming out as a lesbian. In contrast to the use of the woman's body in Esteves's "A La Mujer Borrinqueña," the body for Umpierre is less concerned with "la patria" and more interested in exploring the realm of the erotic. As the successor to Julia de Burgos, Umpierre experiments with the theme of sexuality and lesbianism as a form of crossing over in her poem entitled "Immanence" (1987, 16). "Deviant" women, such as "whores" and "dykes," cross the river "Mad" together, representing a consecratory act that rinses off the "sinful" connotations of female dissidence.

Migration, for Aurora Levins Morales, does not suggest cultural disjuncture, as it did for earlier generations, but signifies a common historical thread that weaves together her Puerto Rican and Jewish identities. In "Ending Poem," written by both Aurora and her mother Rosario Morales (in Morales and Morales), the poetic "I" is comprehensive, including multiple generations, places, and cultures. But rather than render a fractured and divided subject, as in Esteves's "Here," Rosario and Aurora Levins Morales transfigure the "I" of the poem into a collective "we" and conclude: *"And we are whole"* (213).

CONCLUSION

Dislodged from the immediate experience of immigration, the term "migration" gradually evolves into a metaphor that describes explorations into sexuality, feminism, and the dynamic nature of identity. Not only does the term "migration" become referentially more diverse, but so does the geographic location of later Nuyorican writers. No longer centrally located in New York and affiliated with the Nuyorican Poets' Cafe, recent writers like Judith Ortiz Cofer and Aurora Levins Morales write from Georgia and California, respectively. With this ongoing, diasporic quality to Nuyorican literature, Puerto Rican writers in the United States will continue to complicate, challenge, and revise notions of identity, family, and community. Beginning with depictions of New York's *colonias,* Nuyorican literature will still show the multicultural, palimpsestic quality of the Puerto Rican immigrant experience, an experience that cannot be isolated from other immigrant groups nor understood solely as a discrete and self-contained culture.

SELECTED PRIMARY BIBLIOGRAPHY

Agüeros, Jack. *Correspondence between the Stonehaulers.* Brooklyn, NY: Hanging Loose Press, 1991.
———. *Dominoes & Other Stories from the Puerto Rican.* Willimantic, CT: Curbstone Press, 1993.
Algarín, Miguel. *Body Bee Calling from the Twenty-first Century.* Houston: Arte Público Press, 1982.
———. *Mongo Affair.* New York: Nuyorican Poets' Café, 1978.
———. *On Call.* Houston, TX: Arte Público Press, 1980.
———. *Time's Now/Ya es tiempo.* Houston: Arte Público Press, 1985.
Algarín, Miguel, and Bob Holman, eds. *Aloud, Voices from the Nuyorican Poets Cafe.* New York: Henry Holt, 1994.
Algarín, Miguel, and Miguel Piñero, eds. *Nuyorican Poetry.* New York: William Morrow, 1975.
Antush, John, ed. *Nuestro New York: Puerto Rican Plays.* New York: Penguin Books, 1994.
Babín, María Teresa, and Stand Seiner, eds. *Borinquen: An Anthology of Puerto Rican Literature.* New York: Knopf, 1974.
Barradas, Efraín, and Rafael Rodríguez. *Herejes y mitificadores: Muestra de poesía puertorriqueña en los Estados Unidos.* Río Piedras: Huracán, 1981.
Barreto, Lefty. *Nobody's Hero.* New York: New American Library, 1976.
Burgos, Julia de. *Antología Poética.* San Juan: Editorial Coquí, 1979.
———. *Llamita quiere ser mariposa.* San Juan: Escuela del Aire, 1935.
———. *El mar y tú, otras poemas.* San Juan: Puerto Rico Printing and Publishing, 1954.
———. *Obra poética.* San Juan: Instituto de Cultural Puertorriqueña, 1954.

————. *Poemas en veinte surcos.* San Juan: Imprenta Venezuela, 1938.

Carrero, Jaime. "The FM Safe." *Revista Chicano-Riqueña* 7.1 (1979): 110–150.

————. *Jet Neorriqueño: Neo-Rican Jetliner.* San Germán, P.R.: Universidad Interamericana, 1964.

————. *Pipo Subway no sabe reir. Teatro.* Río Piedras, P.R.: Ediciones Puerto, 1973. 113–157.

————. *Raquelo tiene un mensaje.* San Juan: privately printed, 1970.

Cofer, Judith Ortiz. *The Latin Deli.* Atlanta: University of Georgia Press, 1993.

————. *The Line of the Sun.* Atlanta: University of Georgia Press, 1988.

————. "Searching for the Mainland." *Triple Crowns: Chicano, Puerto Rican, and Cuban Amerian Poetry.* Ed. Robert Duran, Judith Ortiz Cofer, and Gustavo Perez Firmat. Tempe, AZ: Bilingual Press, 1987.

————. *Terms of Survival.* Houston: Arte Público Press, 1987.

Colón, Jesus. *A Puerto Rican in New York and Other Sketches.* New York: International, 1982.

————. *The Way It Was and Other Writings.* Ed. Edna Acosta-Belén and Virginia Sánchez-Korrol. Houston: Arte Público Press, 1993.

Cotto-Thorner, Guillermo. *Gambeta.* San Juan: Editorial Cordillera, 1971.

————. *Manhattan Tropic.* [selections]. *Divided Arrival: Narratives of the Puerto Rican Migration, 1920–1950.* Ed. Juan Flores. New York: Centros de Estudios Puertorriqueños, Hunter College, City University of New York, 1987. 51–73.

————. *Trópico en Manhattan.* 1951. 3d ed. San Juan: Editorial Cordillera, 1969.

Cruz, Victor Hernández. *By Lingual Wholes.* San Francisco: Momo's Place, 1982.

————. *Mainland.* New York: Random, 1973.

————. *Red Beans.* Minneapolis: Coffee House Press, 1991.

————. *Rhythm, Content and Flavor: Poems, Selected and New.* Houston: Arte Público Press, 1988.

————. *Snaps.* New York: Random, 1968.

————. *Tropicalization.* New York: Canon, 1976.

Espada, Martín. *City of Coughing and Dead Radiators: Poems.* New York: Norton, 1993.

————. *The Immigrant Iceboy's Bolero.* 4th ed. Maplewood, NJ: Waterfront Press, 1986.

————. *Rebellion Is the Circle of a Lover's Hands.* Willimantic, CT: Curbstone Press, 1990.

————. *Trumpets from the Island of Their Eviction.* Tempe, AZ: Bilingual Press, 1988.

Esteves, Sandra María. *Bluestown Mockingbird Mambo.* Houston: Arte Público Press, 1990.

————. *Tropical Rains.* New York: African Caribbean Poetry Theater, 1984.

————. *Yerba Buena.* Greenfield Center, NY: Greenfield Review Press, 1980.

Fernández, Roberta, ed. *In Other Words: Literature by Latinas of the United States.* Houston: Arte Público Press, 1994.

Figueroa, Jose A. *East 100th Street.* Detroit: Broadside, 1973.

————. *Noo Jork.* Trans. Victor Fernandez Fragoso. San Juan: Inst. de Cultural Puertorriqueña, 1981.

————. *Unknown Poets in the Full-Time Jungle.* New York: Noo Jork, 1975.

Flores, Juan, ed. *Divided Arrival: Narratives of the Puerto Rican Migration, 1920–1950.* New York: Centros de Estudios Puertorriqueños, Hunter College, City University of New York, 1987.

Gonzalez, Ray, ed. *Currents from the Dancing River: Contemporary Latino Fiction, Nonfiction, and Poetry.* New York: Harcourt Brace, 1994.

Labarthe, Pedro Juan. *Son of Two Nations: The Private Life of a Columbia Student.* New York: Carranza, 1931.

Laguerre, Enrique. *The Labyrinth [El laberinto].* Trans. William Rose. New York: Las Américas, 1960.

Laviera, Tato. *AmeRícan.* Houston: Arte Público Press, 1985.

———. *La Carreta Made a U-Turn.* 1979. Houston: Arte Público Press, 1992.

———. *Enclave.* Houston: Arte Público Press, 1981.

———. *Mainstream Ethics.* Houston: Arte Público Press, 1988.

Marqués, René. *The Oxcart [La Carreta].* Trans. Charles Pilditch. New York: Charles Scribner's Sons, 1969.

Marzán, Julio, ed. *Inventing a Word: An Anthology of Twentieth-Century Puerto Rican Poetry.* New York: Columbia University Press, 1980.

Matilla, Alfredo, and Iván Silén, eds. *The Puerto Rican Poets.* New York: Bantam, 1972.

Mohr, Nicholasa. *El Bronx Remembered.* Houston: Arte Público Press, 1986.

———. *Felita.* New York: Dial Press, 1979.

———. *Going Home.* New York: Dial Books for Young Readers, 1986.

———. *Nilda.* 1973. New York: Bantam, 1974.

———. *In Nueva York.* New York: Dial Press, 1977.

———. "On Being Authentic." *Americas Review* 14.3–4 (Fall–Winter 1986): 106–109.

———. *Rituals of Survival.* Houston: Arte Público Press, 1985.

Morales, Aurora Levins, and Rosario Morales. *Getting Home Alive.* Ithaca, NY: Firebrand Books, 1986.

Muñoz, Amina. "welcome to san juan, oldest city in the u.s." *Nuyorican Poetry.* Ed. Miguel Algarín and Miguel Piñero. New York: William Morrow, 1975. 109.

Pietri, Pedro. *Lost in the Museum of Natural History [Perdido en el Museo de Historia Natural].* Río Piedras: Huracán, 1981.

———. *The Masses Are Asses.* Maplewood, NJ: Waterfront, 1984.

———. *Puerto Rican Obituary.* New York: Monthly Review Press, 1973.

———. *Traffic Violations.* Maplewood, NJ: Waterfront, 1983.

Piñero, Miguel. *La Bodega Sold Dreams.* Houston: Arte Público Press, 1980.

———. *Short Eyes.* New York: Hill and Wang, 1975.

———. "The Sun Always Shines for the Cool." *Revista Chicano-Riqueña* 7.1 (1979): 173–204.

Reyes Rivera, Louis. "Introduction: By Way of Sharing Perspective." *Yerba Buena,* by Sandra María Esteves. New York: Greenfield Review Press, 1980.

———. *Poets in Motion.* New York: Shamal Books, 1976.

———. *Who Pays the Cost.* New York: Shamal Books, 1977.

Reyes Rivera, Louis, ed. *This One for You.* New York: Shamal Books, 1983.

———. *Womanrise.* New York: Shamal Books, 1978.

Sánchez, Luis Rafael. "The Flying Bus." *Images and Identities: The Puerto Rican in Two World Contexts.* Ed. Asela Rodriguez de Laguna. New Brunswick, NJ: Transaction Books, 1987. 17–25.

———. *Macho Camacho's Beat. [La Guaracha del Macho Camacho].* New York: Pantheon, 1980.

Santiago, Esmeralda. *When I Was a Puerto Rican.* Reading, MA: Addison–Wesley, 1993.

Schomburg, Arturo Alfonso. *The Arthur A. Schomburg Papers.* Microform. Bethesda, MD: University Publications of America, 1991.

Silén, Iván. *Los paraguas amarillos: Los poetas latinos en Nueva York.* Binghamton, NY: Bilingual, 1984.

Soto, Pedro Juan. *Ardiente suelo, fria estacion.* Xalapa, Mexico: Universidad Veracruzana, 1961. (*Hot Land, Cold Season.* Trans. Helen Lane. New York: Dell, 1971.)

———. *Spiks.* Mexico: Los Presentes, 1956. (*Spiks.* Trans. Victoria Ortiz. New York: Monthly Review Press, 1973.)

———. *Un oscuro pueblo sonriente.* Havana: Casa de las Américas, 1982.

———. *UsMaíl.* Río Piedras: Editorial Cultural, 1958.

Thomas, Piri. *Down These Mean Streets.* 1967. New York: New American Library, 1968.

———. *Savior, Savior, Hold My Hand.* New York: Doubleday, 1972.

———. *Seven Long Times.* New York: Praeger, 1974.

———. *Stories from El Barrio.* New York: Knopf, 1978.

Turner, Faythe. *Puerto Rican Writers at Home in the USA.* Seattle: Open Hand, 1991.

Umpierre, Luz María. *En el pais de las maravillas.* Bloomington, IN: Third Woman Press, 1982.

———. *The Margarita Poems.* Bloomington, IN: Third Woman Press, 1987.

———. *Y otras desgracias—And Other Misfortunes.* Bloomington, IN: Third Woman Press, 1985.

Vando, Gloria. *Promesas: Geography of the Impossible.* Houston: Arte Público Press, 1993.

Vega, Bernardo. *Memoirs of Bernardo Vega: A Contribution to the History of the Puerto Rican Community in New York.* Ed. Cesar Andreu Iglesias. Trans. Juan Flores. New York: Monthly Review Press, 1984.

———. *Memoirs of Bernardo Vega* [selections]. *Divided Arrival: Narratives of the Puerto Rican Migration, 1920–1950.* Ed. Juan Flores. New York: Centros de Estudios Puertorriqueños, Hunter College, City University of New York, 1987. 1–17.

Vega, Ed. *The Comeback.* Houston: Arte Público Press, 1985.

———. *Mendoza's Dream.* Houston: Arte Público Press, 1987.

SELECTED SECONDARY BIBLIOGRAPHY

Acosta-Belén, Edna. "Beyond Island Boundaries: Ethnicity, Gender, and Cultural Revitalization in Nuyorican Literature." *Callaloo* 15.4 (1992): 979–998.

———. "The Building of a Community: Puerto Rican Writers and Activists in New York, 1890s–1960s." *Recovering the U.S. Hispanic Literary Heritage.* Ed. Ramón Gutiérrez and Genaro Padilla. Houston: Arte Público Press, 1993. 179–195.

———. "Conversations with Nicholasa Mohr." *Revista Chicano-Riqueña* 8 (1980): 35–41.

———. "The Literature of the Puerto Rican Migration in the United States: An Annotated Bibliography." *ADE Bulletin* 91 (Winter 1988): 56–62.

Acosta-Belén, Edna, and Barbara Sjostrom, eds. *The Hispanic Experience in the United States: Contemporary Issues and Perspectives.* New York: Praeger, 1988.

Alarcón, Norma. "An Interview with Miguel Piñero." *Revista Chicano-Riqueña* 2.4 (Fall 1974): 55–74.

Barradas, Efraín. "Puerto Rico acá, Puerto Rico allá." *Revista Chicano-Riqueña* 8.2 (Spring 1980): 43–49.

Benítez, Jaime. "El problema humana de la emigracion." *La Torre* 4.13 (1956): 13–31.

Benmayor, Rina. "*Getting Home Alive:* The Politics of Multiple Identity." *Americas Review* 17.3–4 (Fall–Winter 1989): 107–117.

Benmayor, Rina, et al. *Stories to Live By: Continuity and Change in Three Generations of Puerto Rican Women.* New York: Centro, 1987.

Bonilla, Frank. "Ethnic Orbits: The Circulation of Capitals and Peoples." *Contemporary Marxism* 10 (1985): 148–167.

Bruce-Novoa, Juan. "A Case of Identity: What's in a Name? Chicanos and Riqueños." *Retrospace: Collected Essays on Chicano Literature, Theory and History.* Houston: Arte Público Press, 1990. 33–40.

———. "Hispanic Literature in the United States." *Retrospace: Collected Essays on Chicano Literature, Theory and History.* Houston: Arte Público Press, 1990. 25–32.

Centro History Task Force. *Labor Migration under Capitalism: The Puerto Rican Experience.* New York: Monthly Review, 1979.

———. *Sources for the Study of Puerto Rican Migration, 1879–1930.* New York: Centro, 1992.

Cruz-Malavé, Arnaldo. "Teaching Puerto Rican Authors: Identity and Modernization in Nuyorican Texts." *ADE Bulletin* 91 (Winter 1988): 45–51.

Flores, Juan. "Back Down These Mean Streets: Introducing Nicholasa Mohr and Louis Reyes Rivera." *Revista Chicano-Riqueña* 8 (Spring 1980): 51–56.

———. *Divided Borders: Essays on Puerto Rican Identity.* Houston: Arte Público Press, 1993.

———. "Puerto Rican Literature in the United States: Stages and Perspectives." *Recovering the U.S. Hispanic Literary Heritage.* Ed. Ramón Gutiérrez and Genaro Padilla. Houston: Arte Público Press, 1993. 53–68.

Flores, Juan, John Attinasi, and Pedro Pedraza. "*La Carreta Made a U-Turn:* Puerto Rican Language and Culture in the United States." *Daedalus* 110.2 (1981): 193–217.

Gordils, Yanis. "Island and Continental Puerto Rican Literature: Cross-Cultural and Intertextual Considerations." *ADE Bulletin* 91 (Winter 1988): 52–55.

Horno-Delgado, Asunción, ed. *Breaking Boundaries: Latina Writings and Critical Readings.* Amherst: University of Massachusetts Press, 1989.

Jiménez de Báez, Yvette. *Julia de Burgos, Vida y Poesia.* Río Piedras: Editorial Coquí, 1966.

Kanellos, Nicolás. *Biographical Dictionary of Hispanic Literature in the United States.* New York: Greenwood Press, 1989.

———. "Canto y Declamación en la Poesía Nuyoriqueña." *La Confluencia* 1.1 (1986): 102–106.

———. "Nuyorican Writing and Beyond: American Academic and Latino Writers." *Contact I* 6.34–35 (Winter–Spring 1984–1985): 21–23.

———. "Puerto Rican Literature from the Diaspora to the Mainstream." *American Book Review* 7.1 (November–December 1984): 16–17.

Kanellos, Nicolás, and Jorge Juerta, eds. *Nuevos Pasos: Chicano and Puerto Rican Drama.* Houston: Arte Público Press, 1979.

Lapp, Michael. "The Migration Division of Puerto Rico and Puerto Ricans in New York

City, 1948–1969.'' *Immigration to New York.* Ed. William Pencak et al. Philadelphia: Balch Institute Press, 1991. 198–214.

López, Adalberto. ''Literature for the Puerto Rican Diaspora.'' *Caribbean Review* 5.2 (1973): 5–11.

———. ''Literature for the Puerto Rican Diaspora: Part II.'' *Caribbean Review* 6.4 (1974): 41–46.

Miller, John C. ''Nicholasa Mohr: Neorican Writing in Progress: 'A View of the Other Culture.' '' *Revista/Review Interamericana* 9.4 (1979–1980): 543–549.

Mohr, Eugene. ''Fifty Years of Puerto Rican Literature in English—1923–1973.: An Annotated Bibliography.'' *Revista/Review Interamericana* 3.3 (1973): 290–298.

———. *The Nuyorican Experience.* Westport, CT: Greenwood Press, 1982.

Oral History Task Force. *Extended Roots: From Hawaii to New York. Migraciones Puertorriqueñas a los Estados Unidos.* New York: Centro, 1986.

Ramos, Juanita, ed. *Compañeras: Latina Lesbians.* New York: Latina Lesbian History Project, 1987.

Rodríguez, Emilio Jorge. ''Apuntes sobre la visión del emigrante en la narrativa puertorriqueña.'' *Primer seminario sobre la situación de las comunidades negra, chicana, cubana india y puertorriqueña en Estados Unidos.* Havana: Política, 1984. 445–485.

Rodríguez de Laguna, Asela, ed. *Images and Identities: The Puerto Rican in Two World Contexts.* New Brunswick, NJ: Transaction Books, 1987.

Sánchez Korrol, Virginia. *From Colonia to Community: The History of Puerto Ricans in New York.* 1983. Westport, CT: Greenwood Press, 1993.

Velez, Diana, ed. *Reclaiming Medusa: Short Stories by Contemporary Puerto Rican Women.* New York: Kitchen Table, 1988.

Zimmerman, Marc, ed. *U.S. Latino Literature: An Annotated Bibliography.* Chicago: March Abrazo Press, 1992.

III
EUROPEAN-AMERICAN
LITERATURES

14

Finnish-American Literature
Anita Aukee Johnson

The Finnish Americans, far from the land they had called home, found the American landscape "claiming" them, incarnating them into an American identity, as they learned to call new lake shores and farmyards and fishing grounds home. The transfer of affection and sense of identity from the homeland of Finland to the United States was not easy; in fact, the Finns arriving in the last waves of European immigration were among the least likely immigrants to learn English or marry outside their ethnic circle—and the most likely, for a time, to return to the homeland.

The Finnish immigrants to America in the late nineteenth and early twentieth centuries left behind a nation in turmoil, struggling for identity and political direction, but they also left behind a landscape that had shaped their personal and philosophical view. Nature and the experience of living close to the land were a common factor in Finnish life. In climate and topography, Finland is a challenge to the human community, but in its beauty and wildness, the Finns have always located their strength and sense of meaning. Rockwell Gray, in his discussion of the role of landscape, believes that

pleasure or displeasure in a particular landscape or interior carries within it roots deep in the first years of life. So we do not see landscape and the natural world without instruction from art—without the perceptual frames and visual conventions regnant in our own culture—neither do we respond to any place without the informing presence of many remembered places and experiences—layered palimpsest like in consciousness. (55)

Finnish immigrants sought out the landscapes that echoed the lakes and forests of Finland in their new home. They clung to the northern states of Minnesota and Michigan, venturing tentatively into Washington and Wisconsin as well. Finnish sailors, one of the first and largest groups to settle in the United States, tended to gather around port cities—Astoria, New York, San Francisco, Los Angeles—but all noted their longing for lakes and forests and often found their way to such American landscapes.

DOMINANT CONCERNS

In their literature, as in their location choices, the Finnish Americans chronicle their longing for a life lived close to the land. Many of the early immigrants found their first work in the iron mines of the upper-midwest iron range, and the contrast of work below ground to their lives on the sea or in the forest was enough to send more than a few Finns home—or to the nearest tavern! To have a small farm, with a patch of woods and a lake or a pond big enough to sustain a sauna, was the common dream. When realized, the romance of the farm life was often maintained, at least in the literature of the early Finnish farm communities. Lakes and the evergreen trees familiar in both the old country and the new are the most oft-repeated images in the tales, biographies, and poetry of the first-generation Finnish-American writers. Other images of nature that recur record the response of the Finnish mind and imagination to landscapes seen for the first time: the seemingly endless prairie, the multicultural mix of the eastern seaboard cities, the Rocky Mountains. As Barry Lopez has pointed out, "[D]iffering landscapes of the earth are hard to know individually. They are as difficult to engage in conversation as wild animals. The complex feelings of affinity and self-assurance one feels with one's native place rarely develop in another landscape" (255). The desire to live in affinity with land and wilderness, however, was articulated from immigrant parent to child, and the American-born generation turned with eagerness to the landscapes of their childhood.

The relationship of the Finn to the environment is grounded in tradition, Finnish folk literature, and the reality of living in a dynamic, respectful balance with nature. As a culture dependent on forestry, fishing, fur, and limited farming, a carefully cultivated view of humanity as resourceful steward was essential. Replanting trees, reserving areas for wildlife, rotating crops, and keeping operations small-scale were necessary in Finland, and these practices served the immigrant farming/forestry communities planted in America well. The sense of dependence on nature is married to a sense of unrestrained joy in the presence of nature in the Finnish-American texts. Autobiographers, such as Annie Ruissalo and Helmi Mavis Hiltunen Biesanz, record the struggle for sustenance even while describing with great pleasure the blueberry picking, scent of the sauna, sunsets on the lake, simple fare, and sense of comfort in the encircling pines. This strong positive association with nature and the land is also present in the early fiction of the Finnish-American writers and continues today in powerful ways in the poetry of Jim Johnson, Karen Mattson, Diane Jarvenpa, and Marlene Ekola Gerberick. The role of nature continues to hold a central place in the fiction of Laurie Anderson, Shirley Schoonover, and many other Finnish-American writers.

Annie Ruissalo's *The Floating Caravan* is an autobiography of a Finnish immigrant, but the subtext is the biography of the land on which Annie lives—and the natural companions with which she shares her new home. The wild birds, berries, and flowers around her farm remind her that

she is not alone, after all, but among good friends. . . . A small wren appears on a nearby fence post. Outwardly it seems insignificant . . . but just listen to its artistry! Its song is so incredible that it melts the frost from my mind. Its singing silences the heavy heart. (Jarvenpaa and Karni 67)

The music inherent in nature reverberates throughout Finnish literature and echoes in Finnish-American works. The Finnish epic *The Kalevala* is based in a culture that derives meaning from music and nature—and the focus is on Vainomoinen, a hero who is, first and foremost, a "singer" and one who hears the music in nature. The song of a "small wren" would not be insignificant to a Finnish woman; the early literature of Finland is full of birds offering wisdom, comfort, or warning. Annie Ruissalo recognizes a friend in the familiar sound of birdsong—and it is a cultural recognition of where meaning lies as much as it may be a reminder of a forest full of friends left behind.

The American forests that became homes to the Finnish immigrants provided them with a tentative sense of belonging. Not only was the land providing life in terms of firewood and pastureland, but it provided value and identification. A familiar physical environment meant survival; the Finn knew how to live by forestry, small-scale farming or fishing, woodcraft, or trapping. Identity, inasmuch as it is shaped by "vocation" and "activity," could be maintained. The common threads of life between Finnish America and Finland allowed the Finnish community to transport their social gatherings, religion, drama, and family structures. All of these aspects of life would be reconstructed on American soil and in contact with other ethnic groups, but the maintenance of a similar life, in a familiar environment, was achieved by the first wave of Finnish Americans.

Helmi Mavis Hiltunen Biesanz described growing up in a Finnish-American community as "sweet and wonderful" (Jarvenpaa and Karni 118). Although the work was constant and tedious, not unlike life in Finland, the pleasures of the sauna and fresh rhubarb pie were palpable enough to allow fatigue and drudgery to disappear from her memory, at least as she records her memories in her autobiography. Her text moves from a finely detailed walk in the woods to an exploration of the workings of the farm and descriptions of her adopted region. Common to many immigrant literatures/pioneer tales is the picture of the multifunctional, nearly self-sufficient family farm. What is striking, although, of course, not unique to the Finnish American, are the deep attachment and devotion to the land.

The affection for the farm, however, is no match for the Finnish American's passion for the sauna. A truly Finnish import, similar in experience to the sweat lodge or sweat bath, the sauna as location and experience is a crucial aspect of Finnish life. While saunas are found on farms throughout Finland, in the United States the sauna is most often found at the lake cottage, which might be visited only on weekends and in the summertime. Both Ruth Pitkanen Johnson and Helmi Biesanz detail the family rituals around the sauna and the lake. Finding lakes and evergreens familiar to the Finnish eye and spirit encouraged reclamation of an identity as it is celebrated in the Finnish sauna. The sauna is not only a place of relaxation after a workout but a social and familial gathering place. It was the place for birthing and for preparation for burial at death. Traditions of the sauna encoded many of the customs and relations within Finnish culture. It was a place of reconciliation and presence. The sauna experience in America and its transcription into literature in America are very important. A shared sauna, especially an intergenerational sauna, becomes the opportunity for cultural transmission. Values, embodied in old tales or stories of the homeland, were communicated in an atmosphere of purification and cleansing, of immersion into the natural: lake, cedar smoke, fire, and steam. The impact of that experience is clearly shown in the almost unanimous inclusion of sauna stories and images in Finnish-American poetry and fiction, along with the reflections included in autobiography. Jane Piirto's "Sauna" poem is only one example among many, reflecting the delight in the visceral, natural experience and the consciousness of the cultural aspect. Carol Staats describes the sauna as sanctuary, a site for rituals of nature and the human community:

the burning birches lending the heat of the summer's sun to the coldest winter; the white granite rocks, stones of the earth heated by birch, and the steam bursting in great puffs off the stone, the clean spring water, cleansing, purifying. A mortification for the body, leaving the mind clear, the soul free. (Jarvenpaa and Karni 316)

The familiar practice of the rituals that valorized land and recognized wildness in both environment and the self was crucial to the Finnish American in maintaining a clear sense of self. Finnish-American authors transcribed that ritual and relationship into a literature that would affirm the experience, past and present.

Finding the landscape and the life lived in the landscape to be reminiscent of Finland also meant that the Finns honored the land as they had the Finnish geography. The eclectic and sympathetic approach to sustainable living in Finland was also effective in the northern United States. The land of Finland is exacting and sparing in its gifts. A careful balance must be maintained for the limited arable land, animal resources, climate, forest, and fish resources to provide for each family.

Care must be taken with every aspect of the life lived close to the land and vulnerable to not only the changing moods of nature but also to a volatile political climate. Because of the political instability in Finland's relationship with Sweden or Russia, Finns were often forcibly removed from their land by either relocation to an area that the state wanted developed or drafted into foreign military conflicts. To stay on the land and be able to call it home for more than a generation became a persistent and insistent dream. This desire was transported to the United States and the political activity of the late nineteenth and early twentieth centuries. Land and opportunities were not available to the Finnish immigrant as they may have been to an earlier immigrant generation, before the so-called closing of the frontier in the 1890s. The Finn was often willing to work long and hard, mining, fishing, farming, to be able to stay in the landscape that felt like home.

Love and identification with place were an inheritance that could be passed on that surpassed any amount of wealth. The shared scenes of wild lakes and forests in Finland and in the American Northwest became a touchstone for immigrants and succeeding generations. The reshaping of these natural scenes in literature, either upon the immigrant's arrival in the United States or in the return pilgrimage of the child/grandchild to Finland, marks the poetry of Finnish America. Jim Johnson sketches the initial sense of displacement in ''Getting Off the Train at Brimson'':

> When
> she got off the train
> at Brimson there was
> no one there. she wept
> beside the pulpwood
> piled at the crossing
> she wept.
>
> the train, the tracks
> went on through
> swamp and trees;
> behind her
> frosted cattails, dead firs
>
> placed along the tracks
> like poles.
> she understood. it was so.
> she had not arrived. here
> there was no Vainomoinen,
> fingertips worn through
> knitted mittens
> strumming the wind. (Jarvenpaa and Karni 49)

Jim Johnson's poem points to meaning in the woman listening for Vainomoinen, the singer/hero of the Finnish *Kalevala,* for the assurance of home in the landscape marked out by dead firs and tracks. In the return trip to the grand-mother's Finland home, Marlene Ekola Gerberick seeks meaning and places in her poem "Twigs, Feathers, Stones, Moss":

> That summer
> when I finally got to your
> side of the ocean
> when I finally
> found your forests . . .
> the wildly fragrant
> wildflowers were filled
> with the waiting spirit of you.
> . . .
> my hands
> became your hands. (Jarvenpaa and Karni 81)

Gerberick recaptures in her poem the sense that the identification with the land of her grandmother not only is valuable for memory's sake or for confirmation of self-knowledge but is, in fact, an opportunity for becoming, for realizing the woman in the land and her link with both woman and land.

Nancy Mattson focuses on the identification with nature and wilderness in her poetry, but she integrates the natural into the emotive, the creative, and the expressive. In "Kanadalainen," she writes:

> To have left behind the language
> that flowed like spring water
> the easy seepage
> of fresh words every hour
>
> To have come to a land
> of thorough drought
> with a dry tongue. (Jarvenpaa and Karni 105)

Images of nature and wilderness are evoked in all of her pieces, in a way that mirrors an identity that does not separate the natural and the wild from the human everyday. The most immediate connection and bridge to meaning is made through the acknowledgment of the relationship of the human to the natural and that human life can be understood in terms of the natural and the wild.

Diane Jarvenpa is another contemporary Finnish-American poet who weaves the language of nature into her work, taking as her project the need to understand the world as a participant in the natural world. Her poems are inhabited by women and men, moths and lilies-of-the-valley, and "syllables grow in our mouths/familiar movements of reed and water on the earth's floor/spin on the spoon . . . As we learn to speak our lines, the earth once more gives up/a little more of itself" (Jarvenpaa and Karni 276). Tactile and sensual, her poetry draws the reader into the natural world through pieces like "Tuula's Nettle Soup."

The night opens her body
to the May earth,
lays a long dark sash
across the screen porch.
Guests sit around a table,
small candles burn like
tiny flames of monarch wings.
Conversation hangs quietly
in the air, swaying with the
lilies-of-the-valley,
their bells holding a power
inside each creamy light like
some small death we all share.

As we eat, the language of grass and
of flat arctic woods becomes clearer
in the moonlight, its beam as bright
as the rims of our bowls.
Syllables grow in our mouths,
familiar movements of reed and water
on the earth's floor
spin on the spoon
that softness there.
Our friend weaves her mother's magic
turning nettle fire into glacial water,
its stinging leaves cooked into
silky pieces of broken emerald.
Our friend has given us new words
with which to feel a spring night.
As we learn to speak our lines,
the earth once more gives up
a little more of itself. (Jarvenpaa and Karni 274)

Jane Piirto's ''Blueberry Season'' introduces a character living between seasons and places, trying to draw her daughter into the sensitivity Jarvenpa's poetry evokes. In fiction, Piirto crafts the setting that is so familiar to the Finn— and then comments on the newness, on the succeeding generation's lack of understanding. Poised between the grandmothers in Finland who ritualized the blueberry and the bear, and the daughter and granddaughters insulted by suburb and asphalt, she continues her walks in the woods by necessity, for essence, for life.

Wondering why she insists on this immersion into long grass and thorns, she is confronted by wildness, by nature, in the form of a bear:

Worshipped by ancient primitive tribes as a life-giver, where did she know that from? A constellation in the sky. Taunted in the city square, caged and dancing. . . . When he turned and glided, in a smooth gallop, up the rock and away into the cedar stand, she almost wept. She had not meant to fright him out of his place. . . . Her daughter called her up the other month and told her to get a pet, she said this show on "Nova" said without touch you shrivel up, Mother; you need to touch and be touched, and she had replied—I touch the trees, I touch the grass, I touch the plants and the fruit, as if it were a joke, but now she longed for the bear and she was unable to find the path to home . . . but yes, she had been on target again; her instinct for home, her internal compass, right again, an old woman of the woods. (Jarvenpaa and Karni 214–215)

Nature and wilderness are more than place and condition: for the Finnish-American writer, in nature and wilderness, life is enacted, and the way back to society may be lost because of the draw into the "blueberry and bear" country.

Laurie Anderson is of the grandchild's generation, and in "Hunting Hemingway's Trout," he translates the complicated desire by succeeding generations to respond to the identifying experience of nature. Cousin Toivo, who stayed in the north woods, unlike the protagonist, a graduate student of literature, uses literature to create a connection between his life, enacted still on the edge of wildness, with the "civilized" urban life of his cousin. Literature meets life as the two cousins search for Hemingway's fictional "Big Two-Hearted River" as a real-life fishing destination. In their search they meet a store clerk, and the clerk's recollections of the man Hemingway force acknowledgment that the river was fiction, while the man was real. The graduate student reveals his distance of a generation from Piirto's character, saying, "I'd rather read Hemingway's books than go fishing with him . . . I didn't need reality. Reality always included mosquitoes, wet feet, sweat and dirt. I'd take the fictional fishing world of Hemingway every time over reality" (Jarvenpaa and Karni 230). The river may not be genuine, but Anderson knows that Cousin Toivo and his values are genuine. Toivo's desire for the "reality" disdained by his cousin is exemplified in his ability to react as the steward of the situation when a car accident results in a dead moose. Toivo does not turn away from the reality of nature but takes care of the passengers in the car and the animal carcass, planning to use the moose as food for his family. He places the value of literature in a "reality" context: "If Hemingway hadn't invented that damn Big-Hearted River I guess we wouldn't have gotten the moose!" (Jarvenpaa and Karni 234).

Fiction provided Finnish-American writers with avenues for exploring the "reality" and the "invention" of a land that, when treated with care and awareness, could provide both sustenance and a sense of place, engagement, and identity.

Shirley Waisanen Schoonover presents both the real and the symbolized, in various generations, in her *Season of Hard Desires*. Like Jarvenpa and Mattson in their poetry, Schoonover sees and writes with a palette of nature imagery:

Henriika walked the slanting floor of the sod house built in Minnesota, the uncut land she came to as a bride, her damask tablecloths brought to set a table on the grassland, the lakes moraine region that groaned and heaved in winter under her feet, that wrenched the timbers of the house she helped build, that house haunted by the earth beneath it; earth heaving in waves that moved and groaned and foamed up boulders. (292)

Schoonover's sense of the earth as alive, wild, in motion implies that a relationship with the land is possible and necessary. It will not be ignored or unknown. Earth is a unifier; Minnesota is not Finland, but it is of the same earth, requiring the respect and care she and her people have always shown and providing the same sustaining elements of sauna, food, water, and farm. The evocation of land and wilderness scenes and themes in Finnish-American literature reflects a value found in acknowledging and celebrating the relationship between the land and the human community.

This central place of nature in the literary mind is a reflection of an attitude toward the environment within the Finnish-American community at large. Work by Arnold Alanen, University of Wisconsin–Madison, documents the integration of environmental concerns and ethics with wise and prudent twentieth-century resource management by Finnish Americans. Valuation of land and wildness within the literature encourages Finnish Americans to value nature in their politics, economics, and cultural environment. "Reclaiming the land" is a commitment to both environmental ideology and ethnic heritage and identity. Finnish-American literature captures ways in which the relationship of nature and the human community is important and how that relationship contributes to a sense of identity with the land, important to the immigrant, and a corresponding identity with the national culture, the American culture.

SELECTED PRIMARY BIBLIOGRAPHY

Gray, Rockwell. "The Nature Essay." *Essays on the Essay: Redefining the Genre.* Ed. Alexander J. Butrym. Athens: University of Georgia Press, 1989.

Jarvenpaa, Aili, and Michael G. Karni, eds. *Sampo: The Magic Mill. A Collection of Finnish-American Writing.* Minneapolis: New Rivers Press, 1989.

Lopez, Barry. *Arctic Dreams: Desire and Imagination in a Northern Landscape.* New York: Scribners, 1986.

Schoonover, Shirley Waisanen. *A Season of Hard Desires.* Rpt. in *Finnish Americana: A Journal of Finnish American History and Culture* 3 (1980): 1–2.

INFORMATION SOURCES

Finlandia Foundation, P.O. Box 2590, Grand Central Station, New York, NY 10163.

FinnFest USA, c/o Ray Lescelius, President. 412 Huntington Lane, Elmhurst, IL 60126.

Finnish American Literary Heritage Foundation, P.O. Box 1838, Portland, OR 97207.

North Star Press of St. Cloud, Inc., P.O. Box 451, St. Cloud, MN, 56302, has published a number of Finnish-American texts, including poetry collections by Aili Jarvenpaa and Jim Johnson, autobiographical works, and fiction.

15
Greek-American Literature*
Yiorgos D. Kalogeras

INTRODUCTION

Historical accounts of the Greek presence in America often begin with such semihistorical figures as Pytheas of Marseilles; they lay claims on Christopher Columbus's ethnic identity, or they speculate on the origin of Greek-sounding names of early settlers and explorers. However, the first Greek immigrants were from Mani and settled in New Smyrna, Florida, in 1768. By the middle of the nineteenth century, New Orleans had a substantial number of Greek merchants, while several orphans of the Greek War of Independence (1821–1827) had already been transported to New England, and a number of them had distinguished themselves as educators, politicians, and administrators. By the 1880s the numbers of Greek immigrants were swelling, to reach their peak years in the early twentieth century. Poverty, absence of ready cash, and a currant crop failure were the most common reasons for immigration. Subsequent to the Reed-Johnson Act (1924), the numbers dwindled to a few hundred. At the end of World War II, immigration to the United States resumed. This time the immigrants were fleeing not only poverty but also a civil war. The numbers have declined substantially since the 1970s due to economic difficulties in the United States, as well as more attractive work opportunities in European Community (EC) countries.

The majority of Greek immigrant literature dates from the early days of the twentieth century. However, until World War II, apart from Demetra Vaka

*To Helen Papanikolas, who made things possible in Greek-American Studies

Brown's work, Greek immigrant literature had not been visible to a wider public. The language barrier delayed its recognition; after all, it was primarily since the war that immigrant writers decided to make the transition to English. Still another factor has been the preoccupation of post-World War II authors with more experimental modes of writing and more "universal" themes. It is noteworthy, nevertheless, that the immigration story has always had little appeal to the Greeks, and this fact has determined, to an extent, their exclusion from the company of canonized immigrant writers such as Abraham Cahan and Anzia Yezierska. What remains a predominant issue and theme in their work is the definition of "Greekness." Very early, they realized that in order to be considered human in the new country, they had to create for themselves a Western identity that would coincide with Western assumptions of what constitutes the "Hellenic." Equally important were their explorations of the confluences and divergences between ethnic and gender issues. These themes have become even more prominent in the work of post-World War II Greek immigrant writers.

DOMINANT CONCERNS

The personal narrative, written in English, appears first in early Greek immigrant literature: John Stephanini's *Personal Narrative* (1827), Christophorus Castanis's *The Greek Captive* (1845), Demetra Vaka Brown's *Haremlik* (1909), George Demetrios's *When I Was a Boy in Greece* (1913). These books do not focus on the immigrant experience; they describe instead the Greeks' sociocultural position within the Ottoman Empire and their situation during the War of Independence. The Greek narrators mediate between the "exoticism" of their pre-American motherland and the modernity of their new country. Furthermore, they seek cultural and social legitimation by establishing connections between themselves and the classical heritage that a post-Enlightenment West idolized. To gain legitimation, in other words, they place themselves within a Western discourse on Greece, which nevertheless categorized the modern descendants of ancient Hellas as deficient and decadent.

The most prolific writer of this early period was Demetra Vaka Brown (1877–1946). She published fourteen books in English, some of them in collaboration with her husband, Kenneth Brown. Taking advantage of the American interest in the Orient, she cast in personal narratives her own experiences as a journalist among the women of the Balkans but primarily among the women of the Turkish harems. As a narrator she played with Western fantasies of the harem and subverted these fantasies and stereotypes; ultimately, she predicated an autonomy for these women, who moved precariously between modernity and tradition, between Muslim restrictions and Western cultural and social encroachment.

Equally interesting are the stories of Konstantinos T. Kazantzes (1864–1927). In 1910 the author, a Louisville tobacco merchant and an accomplished literary critic, published what is presumably the first Greek-American collection of short stories. *Istories tis patridos mou* (Stories of My Motherland) questions the nationalistic assumptions of the Greek rural story of manners/*ethographia*. Kazantzes's Gothic tales begin as innocuous Greek folktales and conclude as self-destructive fantasies of homogenized national landscapes.

Kazantzes wrote in the manner of post-1880 Greek writers: in other words, he employed the short story to articulate a more contemporary, "realistic" narrative in reaction to the romantic, historical romances of the previous generation. However, he proposed that this realism was nothing but a last phase of romanticism with a rigorous nationalistic agenda. This applied as well to the work of the immigrant poets. The first collection of Greek language poetry to appear in the United States was Demetrios Valakos's (1890–1958) *Tragoudia tis Ksenitias* (1912). He as well as other immigrant poets lived under the heavy shadow of Kostis Palamas—the foremost Greek poet of the turn of the century. A belated romanticism characterizes most of these collections, which focus on the nostalgic recollection of their pre-American motherland. The classical place-name and the mythological event(s) associated with these places figure prominently in the poems. The poets primarily promote a vision of a peaceful folk who exist in harmony with nature and the classical past. In the 1930s, Yiorgis Koutoumanos (1876–1962) added to this theme poems of social awareness and protest. Aristidis Phoutridis (1886–1923) and Dimitrios Michalaros (1897–1967) were among the first to write in the medium of English. Phoutridis, a classical scholar and a professor at Harvard University, is well known for his translations of Palamas's poetry. Less well known is his own collection of poems, *Light at Dawn* (1917), in which he borrows Palamas's patriotic and romantic themes in order to write poetry that emphasizes the romantic sublime of the American landscape. Michalaros, on the other hand, conceived the grandiose project of creating a Greek-American mythology in the true sense of the word. He wrote long epic poems about the imaginary discovery of America by ancient Greek explorers.

Post-World War II immigrant literature reflects both continuities and departures. Theano Papazoglou Margaris (1908–1991) was the first Greek immigrant writer to utilize extensively the immigration story in her writing. Although she published her first volume of short stories before World War II in Chicago, not until the 1950s did her work focus almost exclusively on the immigrant. Her early stories follow, to an extent, the lead of other Greek immigrant writers who wrote about their motherland. Margaris's immigrant fiction appears straightforward and realistic; however, she demonstrates the ambiguous relation of her protagonists to the Old World and New World by creating narratives whose realities are founded primarily on the imagination of the protagonists or narrators. Her main characters cross certain boundaries when they cross the Atlantic; consequently, they cannot ground themselves in reality. Stories that explore gender relations are particularly poignant in this respect. The women undergo a drastic process of "othering"; ultimately, they cannot ground themselves in any reality, even in an imagined one. Margaris refused while alive to allow any translation of her stories, so only two are accessible to an English-language public. She is little known in Greece as well, although she became the first diasporic writer to receive one of the most prestigious Greek literary awards.

Nikolas Kalamaris (better known under his aliases, Calas, Randos, Spieris) (1907–1988) first published his work in Greece in the 1930s, then took up residence in France, followed by a move to Portugal, and finally settled in New York in 1940. He had become known as the father of Greek surrealism by the time he moved to Paris. In fact, he worked both with and against the generation of artists who introduced modernism to Greek letters. He criticized his contemporaries from a Marxist perspective, and he ardently promoted Cavafy over Palamas as the foremost Greek poet. On this point his work departs radically from the work of most early immigrant writers. Calas's aesthetic agenda was to revolutionize Greek poetics and also to introduce new ideas on aesthetic appreciation to the American public. His articles have appeared in *Artforum, Art News, Arts Magazine,* and *The Partisan Review.* His books include *Icons and Images in the Sixties* (1971), *Art in the Age of Risk* (1968) and others. His poetry published in Greek is satirical and subversive. In the end, he shared with his contemporaries an anxiety of influence regarding the Hellenic past. The Greek identity is in the center of his preoccupations, as it is also for Odysseas Elytis and Giorgos Seferis, yet he attempts to deconstruct their reverential stance toward it. Kalamaris remained the least-known Greek-American artist, although one of the most articulate and innovative.

Since the war, Greek immigrant writers have acquired greater visibility and a wider audience. The transition they have made to writing in the English language as well as the translation of their Greek language work have helped them gain recognition in the United States and abroad. Kimon Lolos (b. 1917), Andonis Decavalles (b. 1920), Nanos Valaoritis (b. 1921), Stratis Haviaras (b. 1935), Nicholas Gage (b. 1939), Irini Spanidou (b. 1946), Olga Broumas (b. 1949), and Euridice (b. 1965) are among the better-known Greek-American names today. A preoccupation with the pre-American motherland continues to characterize both their prose and poetry, especially prevalent among the prose writers. Indeed, Kimon Lolos's *Respite* (1961), Stratis Haviaras's *When the Tree Sings* (1979), Nicholas Gage's *Eleni* (1983), and Irini Spanidou's *God's Snake* (1986) make little reference to the United States.

Kimon Lolos's *Respite* is the story of a peaceful interval in the lives of the men of a military unit on its way to the Greek Albanian front in World War II. The book is a critique of broken promises in both personal and political domains. Futility is a prominent mood that emanates from a feeling of powerlessness in the face of devastating natural and political forces in a narrative of understatement and irony. The main character is a young lieutenant disenchanted with life and the melodrama that people make of it. He seeks to control himself and his emotions, finding in the army discipline a perfect vehicle for his intentions; yet his youthful posturing and self-importance are constantly undermined by the mundane realities of everyday life and by the emotions and impulses of youth.

Stratis Haviaras's *When the Tree Sings* presents the ambiguous maturation story of a young boy in World War II Greece, and the narrative moves between realism and fantasy. The "stories of the tribe" that the early immigrant writers worked into their fiction and poetry in an attempt to gain legitimation under Western eyes acquire a very disturbing role in Haviaras's book. They become vehicles of indictment of Western political interference, and they help foreground the West's dehumanizing ahistorical vision of Greece/Hellas. This critique is predicated upon the carnivalistic spirit of the stories, yet cultural and political alienation remains a strong force in the end. The book concludes with a poetic chapter on immigration, exile, *xenitia*—departing for foreign lands, a Greek's most enduring metaphor for alienation.

Nicholas Gage's *Eleni* begins with the immigrant's return to the motherland. The narrator attempts to redress the psychic rift between past and present and to legitimate his American identity. This rift can be bridged only by the recovery of his mother's life story and especially by the discovery of the truth about her execution by the communists during the Greek civil war (1945–1949). *Eleni* is a work of investigative journalism that turns into the biography of a woman, the autobiography of the narrator, and the history of Greece in the 1940s.

The book became the source of a bitter controversy in Greece, where it was translated shortly after its publication in the United States. It was endorsed both by the *New York Times Book Review* and the *New York Review of Books,* was made into a movie, and had the dubious honor of being quoted in Ronald Reagan's address to the nation in 1987. Its immediate success was due to the fact that it combined a human interest story that was emotionally told with a politically correct ideological position. It appeared at a time when Eastern Europe was part of the "evil empire" and when the Reagan administration claimed Central America to be the "backyard" of the United States. Therefore, political demonization for the immigrant narrator went hand in hand with his attempt to legitimate his identity as an American Hellene. The interest of the book lies exactly in the way this identity is constructed: in a very traditional immigrant ideological gesture, the narrator claims America to be the completion of Greece.

Irini Spanidou's *God's Snake* deals with the ambiguities of gender construction. A young girl grows up in post-World War II Greece, experiencing the oppression of conservative political and social forces of the time. Her role model and strongest influence in life is her father, an army captain who rules his family the same way he rules his men in the barracks. The book is structured as a series of independent stories that are arranged in a nonlinear time sequence. Defying traditional autobiographical narrative patterns while structuring the book as an autobiography, the author offers only tentative answers to the ambiguities of sexuality. It remains Spanidou's only novel so far, although, at the time of this writing, her second book has been announced by Knopf.

Olga Broumas's poetry was first published in English as part of the series of the Yale Younger Poets. *Beginning with O* (1977) still remains a very popular collection of poems, although Broumas has since published four more collections, as well as two volumes of Odysseas Elytis's poetry in translation. Her work constitutes a radical departure from what we consider early twentieth-century Greek immigrant poetry. She poetically reconstructs her immigration as the moment of her sexual rebirth; furthermore, she perceives it as an occasion of political empowerment. Broumas's cultural legitimation comes from her connection with the feminist movement, yet Greece and Greekness as ideological issues involve her in an ironic project of reworking what traditionally has been perceived as the cultural legacy of Greece. In a well-known and widely discussed poem, "Twelve Aspects of God," she begins from within the context of a Western knowledge of Greek mythology: she draws on Robert Graves's book on Greek myths. She then introduces a contemporary and feminist perspective; in this manner she creates a revisionary text that works its way toward a more encompassing and universal philosophy of womanhood. This is her aim in her more ethnic poems as well, to move away from the "exoticism" of her ethnic history and into a broader political and historicized feminist discourse.

Andonis Decavalles is an immigrant poet who writes exclusively in Greek. A well-known poet in Greece today, he is one of the most profound and lyrical voices writing in the United States. Language for Decavalles is a mode of "return" to the motherland. His spiritual journeys to Greece are accomplished through a private mythology in which the local language of his parents' island plays an important role. Language militates against rootlessness and becomes the ransoms the poet pays to time to reach a temporary haven. In the excellent translation of Kimon Friar, the poet approaches this haven with an ironic awareness that in the language of his parents he seeks to find "the alphabet of all caresses and entreaties" (*Ransoms to Time* 90).

Another eminent poet living in the United States today is Nanos Valaoritis. Like Decavalles and Calas, he is a poet who has lived and worked in different countries; he has associated himself primarily with English and Greek, publishing his poetry and his poetic autobiography in these two languages. His poetry undertakes to explore desire and history or, more precisely, desire in history. He approaches his ethnic identity not through the purely Western constructions of the Hellenic or through a deconstruction of these models. On the contrary, at the center of his work is a self-conscious and satirical relationship to Western civilization and also to Greek history. He experiments with both the Western fantasies of the Hellenic and also the modern Greek fantasies of these fantasies. His spiritual journeys into his pre-American homeland evoke from him corrosive jeremiads and not the usual romanticized analyses to which Greek-American artists are prone.

Like Nanos Valaoritis, Greek poets living in the United States today write in both English and Greek. Regina Pagoulatou, Eleni Floratou-Paidoussi, Yiorgos Chouliaras, Panos Vozikis, Makis Tzilianos, Christos Tsiamis, Nikos Spanias, Theodosis Athas, and Lili Bita have seen their work translated into English. Dino Siotis, Eleni Fourtouni, and Miranda Cambanis write directly in English.

Dino Siotis (b. 1944), who lived and worked in San Francisco, explores the potentialities of surrealistic poetry and also acknowledges the influence of the beatniks. He has published in both languages and is the editor of the *Aegean Review,* a periodical publication devoted to Greek and Greek-American issues. Chouliaras (b. 1951) writes a minimalist poetry drawing on a post-modern aesthetics. Nikos Spanias (1924–1991) perceived himself as a *poete maudit.* He explored the darker and seamier side of New York in poems that occasionally remind one of Lorca's collection *A Poet in New York.* Theodosis Athas (1936–1973) was one of the most promising poets writing in Greek. He began with traditional poetic forms and themes to move by the end of his short life to more experimental ones. Influenced originally by the Greek folk song, he made a transition to more startling forms under the influence of the blues.

CONCLUSION

What remains controversial among Greek scholars today is whether writers such as Nikolas Calas and Nanos Valaoritis or Andonis Decavalles can be called Greek-American, since they had already formed their aesthetic sensibilities by the time they arrived in the United States. Moreover, Calas and Decavalles wrote only in Greek and published their poems in Athens. Thus they remain inaccessible to an English-language public and instead seem to belong to the Greek literary canon. The questions facing the American critic are inaccessibility of language and also the radical alterity of the themes and stories, since most of the English-language authors write about Greece and make little or no references to the United States or to immigration. The task that lies ahead, then, is not only to define the canon of this literature but also to find ways to talk about it without compromising its difference or integrating it within the canon of either American or Greek literature. The task is also to move beyond the easy paradigms that American critics have extrapolated from a limited number of texts or literatures such as the Jewish or the Italian-American. One should not deny the interface among different ethnic/immigrant literatures, yet the study of "smaller" literatures might offer interesting insights that overturn the critics' long-standing assumptions. Indeed, the "deviant" literary production of a certain group might reveal, in the end, the critics' own deviant critical/theoretical angle. But more significantly, the study of how a certain group crosses the ethnic boundaries in literature might offer paradigms of less deviant sociopolitical behavior than the ones we encounter in "real" life today.

SELECTED PRIMARY BIBLIOGRAPHY

Athas, Theodosis. "Poems." *Resistance, Exile, Love: An Anthology of Post-War Greek Poetry.* Trans. and ed. Nikos Spanias. New York: Pella, 1977. 32–41.
———. "10 Poiemata." *Argonaut.* Ed. Elias Ziogas. New York, 1962. 187–193.
———. *Tragoudia ton Kairo tou Sigan.* New York: Ivikos, 1969.
Bita, Lili. *Blood Sketches.* Trans. Robert Zaller. Miami: Guevara Press, 1973.
———. *Erotes: Five Love Poems.* Trans. Robert Zaller. Miami: Guevara Press, 1969.

————. *Furies.* Trans. Robert Zaller. Torrance: Hors Commerce Press, 1969.

Broumas, Olga. *Beginning with O.* New Haven, CT: Yale University Press, 1977.

————. *Caritas.* Eugene: Jackrabbit Press, 1976.

————. *Pastoral Jazz.* Port Townsend, WA: Copper Canyon Press, 1983.

————. *Perpetua.* Port Townsend, WA: Copper Canyon Press, 1989.

————. *Soi Sauvage.* Port Townsend, WA: Copper Canyon Press, 1979.

Broumas, Olga, with Jane Millers. *Black Stockings, Black Holes.* Port Townsend, WA: Copper Canyon Press, 1985.

Cambanis, Miranda. *The Traffic of the Heart.* Chapel Hill, NC: Carolina Wren Press, 1986.

Capri-Karka, Carmen. *Ampotis ke Palirioia.* Athens: Difros, 1962.

————. *O Kaimos tis Romiosinis.* New York: Greek Voice, 1971.

Chouliaras, Yiorgos. *Fast Food Classics.* Athens: Ypsilon, 1992.

————. *I Alli Glossa.* Athens: Ypsilon, 1981.

————. *O Thisavros ton Valkanion.* Athens: Ypsilon, 1988.

Decavalles, Andonis. *An mas Pligosei o Helios.* Athens: Diatton, 1992.

————. *Armoi, Karavia, Lytra.* Athens: Ekdoseis Filon, 1976.

————. *Okeanides.* Athens: Ikaros, 1970.

————. *Ransoms to Time: Selected Poems.* Trans. Kimon Friar. London and Toronto: Associated University Presses, 1983.

Euridice. *E/32. The Second Coming.* London: Virago Press, 1993.

Floratou-Paidoussi, Eleni. *Eikosi Strofes kai Alla Poiemata.* Athens: Synchroni Epochi, 1976.

————. *Ta Pedia tou Kronou.* Athens: Synchroni Epochi, 1984.

————. *To Telefteo Chelidoni.* Athens: Synchroni Epochi, 1992.

Fourtouni, Eleni. *Monovassia 76.* New Haven, CT: Thelphini Press, 1979.

————. *Watch the Flame.* New Haven, CT: Thelphini Press, 1983.

Friar, Kimon. *The Nativity.* Athens: Pleias, 1974.

Gage, Nicholas. *Eleni.* New York: Random House, 1983.

————. *A Place for Us.* New York: Houghton Mifflin, 1989.

Haviaras, Stratis. *Crossing the River Twice.* Cleveland: Cleveland State University Press, 1976.

————. *The Heroic Age.* New York: Simon and Schuster, 1984.

————. *When the Tree Sings.* New York: Simon and Schuster, 1979.

Kalamaris, Nikolas. *Grafi ke Fos.* Athens: Ikaros, 1982.

————. *I Odos Nikita Rantou.* Athens: Ikaros, 1976.

Kotsovolou-Masry, Youlika. *Esoterikes Diarithmiseis.* Athens: Nefeli, 1988.

Lolos, Kimon. "Mule No. 095." *The Best American Short Stories.* Ed. Martha Foley and David Burnett. Boston: Houghton Mifflin, 1964. 191–201.

————. *Respite.* New York: Harper and Brothers, 1961.

————. *Under the Circumstances.* New York: Harper and Row, 1962.

Nord, Paul. *Salamander, a Spiritravelore.* New York: Private edition, 1946.

Pagoulatou, Regina. *Angels.* New York: Pella, 1988.

————. *Motherhood.* Trans. Kali Loverdos-Streichler. New York: Pella, 1985.

————. *Pyrrhichios.* Trans. Apostolos Athanasakis. New York: Pella, 1979.

————. *Transplants.* Trans. Apostolos Athanasakis. New York: Pella, 1982.

Papazoglou-Margaris, Theano. *E Eftichia ke Alla Diegemata.* Chicago: Synchroni Skepsi, 1939.

————. *Hena Dakre gia ton Mparmpa Tzime.* Athens: Difros, 1958.

————. *Oi Peripeteies tou Theiou Platona.* Athens: Astir, 1972.

————. *To Chroniko tou Halsted Street.* Athens: Fexis, 1962.

Polentas, Manolis. *Agios Misanthropos.* Athens: Eridanos, 1983.

Samaras, Nick. *Paramythia sti Nea Iorki.* New York: Sylogos Apophiton Ellinikon Panepistimion, 1970.

Siotis, Dino. *Emeis kai o Vrohopoios.* Thessaloniki: Tram, 1973.

————. *Part Time Paradise.* Oakville (Ontario) New York, London: Mosaic Press, 1988.

————. *So What.* San Francisco: Panjardum Press, 1972.

Spanias, Nikos. *Ameriki.* Athens: Odos Panos, 1988.

————. *Foros Timis ston Giorgio de Chirico.* New York: Gnosi, 1981.

————. *Poiemata.* Athens: Gnosi, 1982.

————. *To Mavro Gala tis Avgis.* Athens: Odos Panos, 1987.

Spanidou, Irini. *God's Snake.* New York: Norton, 1986.

Tsiamis, Christos. *Polytropo.* New York: Ostraka, 1979.

Tzilianos, Makis. *Anises Fones.* New York: Ippokambos, 1979.

Valaoritis, Nanos. *Diplomatic Relations Followed by Birds of Hazard and Prey.* San Francisco: Panjardum Press, 1972.

————. *Flash Bloom.* San Francisco: Wire Press, 1980.

————. *Gia mia theoria tis grafis.* Athens: Eksantas, 1990.

————. *Hired Hieroglyphics: Poems and Collages.* San Francisco: Kayak Press, 1971.

————. *I Zoi mou meta thanaton engiimeni.* Athens: Nefeli, 1993.

————. *Poiemata 1.* Athens: Ypsilon, 1983.

————. *Poiemata 2.* Athens: Ypsilon, 1987.

Vozikis, Panos. *Alla Rysai Emas.* New York: Anthe, 1979.

————. *Elliniki Gi.* New York: Anthe, 1983.

————. *Erastis.* New York: Anthe, 1988.

SELECTED SECONDARY BIBLIOGRAPHY

Books

Giannaris, Yiorgos. *Oi Ellines Metanastes ke to Ellinoamerikaniko Mythistorima.* Athens: Filippotis, 1985.

Kalogeras, Yiorgos. "Between Two Worlds: Ethnicity and the Greek American Writer." Diss., Arizona State University, 1984.

Karanikas, Alexander. *Hellenes and Hellions: Greek Characters in American Fiction.* Urbana: Illinois University Press, 1981.

Articles

Carruthers, Mary J. "The Revision of Muse: Adrienne Rich, Audre Lorde, Judy Grahn, Olga Broumas." *Hudson Review* 36 (1983): 292–322.

Crist, Robert. "Image, Feeling, and Idea in the Poetry of Olga Broumas." *Hellenism and the U.S.: Constructions and Deconstructions.* Ed. Savas Patsalidis. Thessaloniki: Art of Text, 1994. 169–174.

Friar, Kimon. Introduction. *Ransoms to Time: Selected Poems* by Andonis Decavalles. London and Toronto: Associated University Press, 1984. 13–43.

Kalogeras, Yiorgos. "Apagorevmena ke Epikindina Ethnika Topia: Ta Prosopika Afigimata tis Demetra Vaka Brown." *Porphyras* 67–68 (November 1993–March 1994): 16–22.

———. "A Child of the Orient as American Storyteller: Demetra Vaka-Brown." *Working Papers of the English Department, Aristotle University.* Ed. Ruth Parkin Gounelas and Thanasis Kakouriotis. Thessaloniki: Aristotle University, 1989. 187–193.

———. "*Eleni:* Hellenizing the Subject, Westernizing the Discourse." *MELUS* 18.2 (1993): 77–89.

———. "Ellinoamerikaniki Logotechnia." *Grammata ke Technes* 49 (January–February 1987): 29–32.

———. "Greek-American Literature: An Essay and a Bibliographic Supplement." *Ethnic Forum* 7.2 (1987): 102–115.

———. "Greek-American Literature: An Introduction and an Annotated Bibliography of Personal Narratives, Fiction and Poetry." *Ethnic Forum* 5 (1985): 106–128.

———. "Greek American Literature: Who Needs It? Some Canonical Issues concerning the Fate of an Ethnic Literature." *New Directions in Greek American Studies.* Ed. Dan Georgakas and Charles Moskos. New York: Pella, 1991. 129–141.

———. "Historical Representation and the Cultural Legitimation of the Subject in Ethnic Personal Narratives." *College Literature, Special Issue: Teaching Minority Literature* 18.3 (1991): 30–43.

———. "Suspended Souls, Ensnaring Discourses: Theano Papazoglou-Margaris' Immigration Stories." *Journal of Modern Greek Studies, Special Issue: Empowering the Minor* 8.2 (1990): 85–96.

———. "*When the Tree Sings:* Magic Realism and the Carnivalesque in a Greek-American Narrative." *International Fiction Review* 16.1 (1989): 32–38.

Ollier, Nicole. "*Eleni* de Nicholas Gage: Antigone ou Hecube? Orestie ou Odyssee?" *Annales de CRAA* 14 (1989): 95–108.

———. "Nanos Valaoritis: Metamorphose et Surrealisme." *CRAA* 13 (1988): 151–161.

———. "Nicholas Gage: *A Place for Us:* Nulle Part Ailleurs." *Annales du CRAA* 16 (1991): 11–29.

———. "Stratis Haviaras: Le Chant des Racines." *Annales du Centre de Recherches sur l'Amerique Anglophone* 12 (1987): 41–60.

Raizis, Marios Byron. "Suspended Souls: The Immigrant Experience in Greek-American Literature." *Greek Letters* 1 (1982): 292–323.

Vistonitis, Anastasios. "Tessareis Sygrafeis tis Diasporas." *Leksi* 110 (July–August 1992): 558–565.

Interviews

Christon, Jean. "An Interview with Stratis Haviaras." *Publishers Weekly,* April 13, 1984: 73–74.

Georgakas, Dan. "An Interview with Stratis Haviaras." *Journal of the Hellenic Diaspora* 8.4 (1981): 73–82.

Hammond, Carla. "An Interview with Olga Broumas." *Northwest Review* 23.3 (1980): 32–48.

Keyishian, Marjorie. "An Interview with Andonis Decavalles." *Literary Review* 21 (1978): 394–412.

Shugart, Diana Alicia. "Perpetually O: An Interview with Olga Broumas." *Greek American,* May 26, 1990: 12–13.

Siotis, Dino. "Olga Broumas: The Hidden Self." *Aegean Review* 7 (Fall–Winter 1989): 12–25.

16
Irish-American Literature
Daniel J. Casey and Robert E. Rhodes

INTRODUCTION

With more than 44 million Americans—nearly one in six in the population—tracing their ancestry to Ireland, it stands to reason that the Irish should be well represented in American letters. Irish Americans have, in fact, produced major writers in all of the literary genres over the last century, though, with a few exceptions, they have in the last generation melded into the great American amalgam. Irish-American literature has, since the 1970s, fused with mainstream American literature.

This chapter begins with a consideration of the Irish immigrant experience as a prototype for the experiences of other established immigrant populations and posits ''loss of Irishness'' as a trade-off in the assimilation process. The second part studies the nineteenth- and twentieth-century literary development through 1945, as background to the new immigrant literature. The final sections—the body of the chapter—concentrate on Irish-American contributions to post-World War II and contemporary literature.

As a bibliographical survey, this chapter identifies recurring themes in the literature and moves chronologically, generation by generation, highlighting only the major and representative writers and their works. For reasons of space and emphasis, it neglects scores of competent writers in all genres who have contributed, some of them significantly, to the Irish-American cultural legacy.

The bibliography is also selective—150 citations covering the primary and secondary sources. The authors have published a fuller 170-page bibliography as part of *Irish-American Fiction: Essays in Criticism* (1979) and refer the reader to that and to other sources, like Charles Fanning's *Irish Voice in America* (1990), for further reference.

LITERARY-CULTURAL HISTORY

History confirms that, over two centuries, the American Irish have been successful. According to National Opinion Research Center data, they have the highest income and educational level of any Gentile group in the United States, and they are at the same occupational prestige level as the more "established" British Americans. They have proven themselves in politics, literature, journalism, trade unionism, and religious life and more recently in finance, industry, and commerce. But the cost of admission to the inner sanctum has been too high—they have, in fact, paid with their souls.

In "Irishness in America" (1961), John Kelleher says, "There is no point in talking about this or that people's contribution to America. The only contribution any people consciously make is what they want for themselves . . . what other Americans of older vintage already possess" (40). Lawrence McCaffrey, in his *Irish Diaspora in America* (1984), traces the complex and diverse pattern of the Irish-American experience and the shaping of the personal and community identity, but McCaffrey calls the century-long generational shift from Ireland to America, from ghetto to suburb, "a journey from someplace to no place" (178). In effect, McCaffrey echoes Kelleher's notion that "they [the immigrants] threw away what they had to content themselves with before" (40).

The complex and diverse patterns of the experience are by now reasonably well documented. The pre-Famine immigrants were, in the main, Scots-Irish and Protestant who settled in with minimal bother. The earliest Catholic Irish arrivals were a distinct minority until the eve of the Famine, though they had already begun to increase in number in the 1815–1845 period.

The Famine refugees and those coming on the heels of the Famine, up to 1870—approximately 2.5 million of them—were a rabblement, mostly Irish and Catholic, who disembarked at immigration centers in the Northeast and at the other Atlantic and Gulf centers in droves. They were "the huddled masses" who created instant slums and drained urban resources and left, in their wake, a trail of crime, disease, and prostitution.

Characterized in the literature as violent, lazy, shiftless, dirty, dishonest, and alcoholic, these Irish crowded into port cities that were ill equipped to accommodate them. They were economically and culturally bankrupt, and they sought survival on any terms. Their contribution to America was that they provided an endless pool of "unskilled, cheap, almost infinitely exploitable labor" (Kelleher, "Irishness in America" 38)—they were the dray horses, the railway gangers, the diggers of sewers and canals.

The later immigrants, those of the 1870–1900 period, provided a stark contrast to those of the Famine generation. They were more ambitious and literate, determined to make a life for themselves and their children in their adopted country. There were improved opportunities for employment in the cities, and the Irish were well poised to take advantage of the situation. "By 1900," writes William V. Shannon (1966), "the Irish as a group had acquired a stake in society and begun to move forward" (140).

Through the twentieth century the Celtic tide waned, and immigration, after the 1920s, slowed to a trickle. There was, however, a perceptible "upward mobility" among the American Irish, and by the post-World War II period, with the help of the GI Bill and GI mortgages, they became successful and educated middle-class suburbanites. There was no turning back, no looking back. They were third- and fourth- and fifth-generation American; their ethnicity had been left behind with the faded curtains on the windows in the urban neighborhoods.

In "The Last of the American Irish Fade Away" (1971), Andrew Greeley reflects on the tragedy of that trade-off. He says: "The legitimization of ethnicity came too late for the American Irish. They are the only one of the European immigrant groups to have over-acculturated. They stopped being Irish the day before it became all right to be Irish" (33). The trade-off may, in fact, have come on a blustery January Inauguration Day in 1960, when John F. Kennedy took the oath of office, and the Fitzgerald-Kennedy dynasty realized the ultimate American dream. On that January day, paradise had been regained, Camelot restored, the day won for the Kennedys and for the Irish.

Even Yankee poet Robert Frost, playing to the inauguration gallery, rasped this admonition to the president: "You are Harvard and you are Irish, but I tell you to be more Irish than Harvard" (Address at the Inauguration of John F. Kennedy, Washington, D.C., January 20, 1960). Whether Frost was high on the Irish or down on the Brahmins or simply caught up in "the Celtic rays" (Van Morrison, "The Celtic Ray," Essential Music and Rightsong Music, 1988) is perhaps less important than his awareness that "the indomitable Irishry" (Yeats, "Under Ben Bulben," *Last Poems;* London: Macmillan, 1939) had finally *arrived* and arrived en masse, to celebrate the coronation of their first Irish and Catholic president. By the time the flags of Camelot were furled three years later, the President, the Speaker of the House, the Senate Majority Whip, and the Chairman of the National Committee were all Catholic Democrats of Irish descent.

But, looking back, one also has to wonder if being Harvard wasn't as important as being Irish and wonder whether Kennedy's ascendancy didn't at once signal the capitulation and the demise of an ethnic identity and a tradition. JFK was, after all, different from the long line of Tammany-type ward politicians— from Jimmy Walker in New York and James Michael Curley in Boston and Richard Daley in Chicago—and he was different from Al Smith, who ran a flawed campaign and who wasn't Harvard. JFK had played the green card, as he had played the green card in earlier campaigns; but at this election the time was right; the green card was trump.

When he visited the Irish Parliament in Dublin in 1963, Kennedy remarked: "If this nation had achieved its present political and economic stature a century or so ago, my great grandfather might never have left New Ross and I might, if fortunate, be sitting down there with you. Of course, if your own President had never left Brooklyn, he might be standing up here instead of me'' (Address to Dail Eireann, Dublin, Ireland, June 29, 1963). The Kennedy wit charmed the Irish, but the address also recognized that four generations stood between New Ross and Brookline. While political expediency, which would continue to deliver an Irish vote, was dictated, there was a conscious effort to turn Irishness on and off to meet the occasion. However, the Honorable Joseph P. Kennedy, former ambassador to the Court of Saint James, insisted that his Massachusetts brood was American to the core. He once snapped: ''My family has been in this country for four generations, and we're still called Irish. What the hell do we have to do to be called American?'' (in Ralph G. Martin's *A Hero for Our Time,* 22).

It wasn't only the Kennedys who jockeyed for the post position in mainstream America. The writers, too, put distance between themselves and their Irishness. James T. Farrell, F. Scott Fitzgerald, Eugene O'Neill, Mary McCarthy, and others spent much of their lives trying to come to terms with an Irish past. ''I am a second-generation Irish American. The effects and scars of immigration are upon my life. The past was dragging through my boyhood and adolescence,'' Farrell once confessed (Casey and Rhodes, ''Echoes from the Next Parish'' 3). The others, too, lost faith in the past, though without that past, no one of them could have contributed as he or she did to American letters.

Make no mistake: the American Irish survived and succeeded against incredible odds, and their survival and their successes, given the circumstances, were no mean feats. The point of the story is that they survived and succeeded as Americans, no longer Irish, and that an ethnic history—all ethnic histories—is, by its nature, evolutionary and has an inevitable resolution that is especially troubling to ''ethnics.''

DOMINANT CONCERNS: PRE-WORLD WAR II LITERATURE

Before the Famine, literary views of the American Irish—in the fiction of Hugh Henry Brackenridge, James Fenimore Cooper, and Sara Hale—offered broad caricatures lifted from earlier British models. They were Yankee translations of a stage-Irish stereotype—the Irishman entered American fiction as a burlesque. The images of the rascally rapscallion, superstitious simpleton, and cowering lock-puller traveled well.

Post-Famine writers went a step further and vilified the immigrants. They were no longer comic fools; they became, after 1850, an economic burden. But, because they were illiterate and dependent, they were unable to respond to prejudicial attacks and unwilling to offend the Establishment. At mid-century the Irish in America were concerned with survival, not national pride.

Unfortunately, the earliest Irish-American novelists, writers like Mary Anne Madden Sadlier, in *Bessy Conway; or, The Irish Girl in America* (1861), *Con*

O'Regan; or, Emigrant Life in the New World (1864), and *Willy Burke; or, The Irish Orphan in America* (1850), advanced the stereotype and churned out moralistic pap exhorting the immigrants to disavow the past and emulate the Yank work ethic. As industrious laborers and steadfast domestics serving their "betters," the Irish would, they were told, earn high marks in this world and the next. Even the first serious challenge to Paddyism, Thomas D'Arcy McGee's *History of the Irish Settlers in North America* (1855), which extolled Ireland's ancient glories, accepted the immigrant's failings as consequences of his origin.

Despite the length and strength of the Irish tradition, then, Irish-American writers in the nineteenth century produced a body of second-rate literature that served to underscore nativist charges of inferiority. It was, for the Irish, a century of acculturation and adjustment, not an age of leisure and high art.

There were, of course, Irish immigrants like Fitz-James O'Brien, remembered for his dramas and tales of the supernatural, and John Boyle O'Reilly, editor of the *Boston Pilot,* who wrote popular fiction like *Moondyne: A Story of the Underworld* (1879). But Irish-American literature properly begins with the Chicago journalist Finley Peter Dunne, who contributed hundreds of humorous dialect sketches to the national press between 1893 and 1919. Dunne's spokesman was Mr. Martin Dooley, a bartender-philosopher who provided a chronologue of Bridgeport, an Irish neighborhood on Chicago's South Side. The sketches offered political commentary and social history that added a new dimension to Irish character. Dunne was witty and well informed, and, for millions of newspaper readers, his Mr. Dooley was the quintessential Irishman.

There was Eugene O'Neill, influenced by the Celtic revival playwrights, particularly Synge and O'Casey, arguably the most talented and inspired dramatist in American theater. O'Neill's early one-acters—*The Long Voyage Home* (1917) and *The Moon of the Caribbees* (1918)—as well as *The Emperor Jones* (1920), *Anna Christie* (1921), and *The Hairy Ape* (1921) show that influence.

In O'Neill's *A Touch of the Poet,* set in Boston in 1828, Con Melody, a hard-drinking Irish immigrant, seeks to raise himself above the social level of the Irish he has left behind. One mark of his success is that he has managed to shed his brogue, though the ultimate sign of his failure to achieve acculturation is the return of the brogue at the end of the play when he shares a drunken revelry with local low-life Irish.

When O'Neill moved from Provincetown to the Village and Broadway, he outdistanced his Irish mentors with a rush of major experimental dramas that established his preeminence as a world-class playwright in *Desire under the Elms* (1924), *The Great God Brown* (1926), *Strange Interlude* (1928), *Mourning Becomes Electra* (1931), and *Ah, Wilderness!* (1933).

O'Neill broke a long stage silence with *The Iceman Cometh* (1946), but his tour de force, *A Long Day's Journey into Night* (1956), an autobiographical drama about disintegration of the Tyrone family, exposed a nerve the Irish sought to shield. The play, a damning indictment of family and culture, magnifies the failures, "warts and all."

James T. Farrell was a South Side Chicagoan who, in the 1930s, published an autobiographical trilogy that cataloged the short, sordid career of William "Studs" Lonigan. Farrell's fiction offered a comprehensive sociological study, albeit an uncomplimentary one, of the Chicago Irish from 1915 to the Depression. *Studs Lonigan* (1932–35) traces the tribulations of that boyhood and adolescence. Betty Smith's *A Tree Grows in Brooklyn* (1943), set in the Williamsburg section of Brooklyn in the same time period, captures the ambience of the cold-water flats with empty larders and the Tammany-sponsored children's excursions up the Hudson River. Her heroine, Francie Nolan, was not as scarred as Studs; still, there was, in Smith's novels, a sense of desperation to "fly by those nets" of her ghetto neighborhood.

F. Scott Fitzgerald, Mary McCarthy, and John O'Hara were not graduates of street academies; they came from favored circumstances. Fitzgerald attended the Newman School and Princeton; McCarthy graduated from Vassar; and O'Hara, a doctor's son, aspired to Yale, though his father's untimely death put Yale out of reach. Irish backgrounds are sublimated in the fiction of these three: "Irish" was, after all, a stigma among the nouveaux riches. Yet, their fiction is also autobiographical: In *This Side of Paradise* (1920), Fitzgerald not only creates the Jazz Age but sheds his Irish identity; in *Memories of a Catholic Girlhood* (1957), McCarthy spurns her lace-curtain origins; and in *The Doctor's Son and Other Stories* (1935), O'Hara sounds a final salvo on his birthright. Jimmy Molloy, the young narrator of "The Doctor's Son," experiences disillusionment. It is, coincidentally, the same Jimmy Molloy who, in *Butterfield 8* (1935), says: "I want to tell you something about myself that will help to explain a lot of things about me. You might as well hear it now. First of all, I am a Mick. I wear Brooks Brothers clothes and I don't eat salad with a spoon and I probably could play five-goal polo in two years, but I am a Mick. Still a Mick." Fitzgerald, McCarthy, and O'Hara spent their professional lives coming to terms with Molloy's dilemma.

Though Finley Peter Dunne imbues his Dooley with native intelligence and wit, and Betty Smith adds a dash of sentiment to the character, the second-generation writers generally aspire to American respectability at the price of Irish culture. What we find in the best fiction of the period—in the works of Farrell, Fitzgerald, O'Neill, McCarthy, and O'Hara—are a frustration and bitterness with a transported Irishness that has restricted social movement and shackled the imagination. The Irish come off as ignorant, materialistic, and corrupt.

DOMINANT CONCERNS: POST-WORLD WAR II LITERATURE

By the first half of the twentieth century, the Irish had proven themselves. There was no longer the preoccupation with covering their "scars of immigration." With the Germans, they had been this country's first white ethnics, and most of them were already third- and fourth-generation American.

The Celtic wave had crested at the eastern seaboard and washed across the northern half of continental America. About 60 percent of the immigrants had settled in New England and the Middle Atlantic states. Another 25 percent had pushed on with the westward migration into the north-central states. The rest had been scattered across the country with concentrations in the major rail centers and in the port cities of Louisiana, Texas, and California.

But after World War II, regional differences became more pronounced. The Bostonians, heirs to the Old-World values, established the genteel tradition of the Yankee Irish. A majority of New Yorkers, Philadelphians, and Chicagoans who had risen in the ranks of business and the civil service melded into the wasteland of suburbia. In the Midwest and the South, where the Irish were often an indistinct minority, they sought a wider sense of community by emphasizing their religion over their Irishness.

Women are generally underrepresented in ethnic literatures, and they are underrepresented in the Irish. Mary McCarthy and Flannery O'Connor stand out as the writers of genius, and Betty Smith is recognized for her social realism in *A Tree Grows in Brooklyn, Tomorrow Will Be Better* (1948), *Maggie-Now* (1958), and *Joy in the Morning* (1963). But other gifted women whose regional works have been published regionally in limited editions have been all but ignored by the critics.

Among the post-war regionalists, Ruth McKenny, Mary Doyle Curran, and Ellen Berlin have made their marks. McKenny, best known for the popular 1940s stage version of *My Sister Eileen* (1938), made an important contribution in *Industrial Valley* (1938), a little-known novel that exposed the grotesqueries of life among the impoverished rubber workers in Akron, Ohio, during the Depression. Mary Doyle Curran's only novel, *The Parish and the Hill* (1948), set in the red-brick tenements of a Yankee milltown, contrasts squalor of the tenements with the poshness of life on the hill. Ellen Berlin, in *Lace Curtain* (1948), traces the social climb of the Irish from the shanties of the flats to Boston's Beacon Hill. Taken together, the fiction of these three women takes regional realism to a new level.

Edwin O'Connor's *The Last Hurrah* (1956), set "in a New England city" in 1948, is more than a political novel about the changing of the guard; it is an analysis of the passing of a tradition. O'Connor's Frank Skeffington calls himself "a tribal chieftain." Between wakes and dances, he liberally dispenses favors to petitioners, but he recognizes that he is the end of the line. In *The Last Hurrah,* O'Connor has fictionalized the final campaign of Mayor James Michael Curley of Boston and glossed over the corruption of his political machine, but he has also provided a memorable slice of New England Irish Americana. O'Connor's other major novels—*All in the Family* (1966), *The Edge of Sadness* (1961), and *I Was Dancing* (1964)—overshadowed by *Hurrah,* complement O'Connor's notion that his is an Irish "state o' chassis."

Elizabeth Cullinan perfectly catches the atmosphere of New York City, where she grew up in the security of pre-Vatican II. Her fiction, particularly her prize-winning novel *House of Gold* (1970) and the stories in *Yellow Roses* (1977), provides a chronicle of lower-middle-class Irish-American urban life and of the young women caught in the conflicts of tradition and modernism.

Though Cullinan's world is circumscribed—New York and, in *A Change of Scene* (1982), Dublin—she is more than a mere regionalist; she is a conscious artist with an eye for detail and an infallible narrative sense. Her characters move in ordered worlds and confront moral dilemmas that matter. As often as not, they fail themselves because they espouse tribal virtues that no longer apply. They are typically intelligent women preyed upon by a world that conspires to control them. As a stylist and a storyteller, Cullinan ranks with the best of contemporary American writers.

The Irish that turn up in the Midwest fiction of J. F. Powers are often clerics. Powers has, in five short story collections and a novel, decimated scores of them. He takes on the collared golf pros, television personalities, trigger-happy exorcists and bingo emperors, as well as the new liberals, the hippy priests promoting strobe-light masses and drive-in confessionals. In his novels *Morte D'Urban* (1962) and *Wheat That Springeth Green* (1988), and in the story collections— *Prince of Darkness* (1947), *The Presence of Grace* (1956), *Lions, Harts, Leaping Does* (1963), and *Look How the Fish Live* (1975)—Powers is the comic-satirist who balances the sacred and the profane, who makes Irish Americans laugh at their own excesses. He is one of the most talented writers in the tradition, one of the most skillful writers of fiction today.

Finally, among the regionalists, there is Flannery O'Connor, an important Southern writer of Irish background who was reared a Georgia Catholic. The Irish-American quality of her work is sublimated—it is *felt* rather than stated, expressed as an intellectualized Catholicism rather than an Irish consciousness. Her God-haunted novels, *Wise Blood* (1952) and *The Violent Bear It Away* (1960), are fantastic in plot, grotesque in characterization, surreal in reverie, nightmarish in metaphor, and clotted in sentence structure; but the ultimate purpose, perhaps, is to confirm orthodox religious belief through unorthodox content and form. Though she produced four major works and died in 1964 at the age of thirty-nine, O'Connor's literary reputation continues to grow even since her death.

Among the New Journalists, Jimmy Breslin, the late Joe Flaherty, and Pete Hamill have produced hard-hitting news copy and realistic fiction. In three autobiographical novels—Breslin's *World without End, Amen* (1973), Flaherty's *Fogarty & Co.* (1973), and Hamill's *The Gift* (1973)—the New York writers explore the tragic father–son generation chasm in Irish-American families. Later novels—Breslin's *Table Money* (1986), about a Medal of Honor-winning Vietnam vet Owney Morrison, and Flaherty's *Tin Wife* (1983), about the New York police and the Brooklyn Irish, and Hamill's *Loving Women, A Novel of the Fifties* (1989)—delve deeper into Irish life in the diocese of Brooklyn. Hamill's memoir, *A Drinking Life* (1994), makes real life more real.

The farther that Irish-American literature moved from Ireland and from the Irish ghettos, the less continuity it had. Some authors, writing from the crumbling citadels of the culture, mourn its passing like the death of an old friend, while others regard it a nightmare from which they have never quite awakened. The echoes from the next parish are, however, becoming fainter; Irish character is, in the regional fiction, evolving and producing a new hyphenate hybrid. But the personality is rooted in the New World, and the idiom is now distinctly American.

DOMINANT CONCERNS: CONTEMPORARY LITERATURE

The preserve of more avant-garde writers has been a feature of Irish writing from the start—the macabre, the grotesque, the black humor. J. P. Donleavy and Tom McHale have given us two of the most outrageous comic novels in *The Ginger Man* (1955) and *Farragan's Retreat* (1971), respectively. Donleavy's dastardly antihero, Sebastian Dangerfield, romps through "dear, dirty Dublin," shattering the saints-and-scholars myths of the "oul' sod," while McHale's Farragan clan churns up the bigotry stewing in the hearts of the Irish-American superpatriots during the Vietnam travesty. Mark Costello has offered a wonderfully crafted collection, *The Murphy Stories* (1973), a case study of the artist gone amok in a psychic tug-of-war. Like a number of Irish-American writers, Costello shows an Irish penchant and talent for the nonrealistic thinking and language that, like much in Joyce and Beckett, border on, and sometimes cross over into, the surreal in both content and shifting stream of consciousness.

The last two decades have yielded a number of promising titles, like John Gregory Dunne's compelling character contrast cum murder mystery, *True Confessions* (1977), a savage—and comical—satire of Irish-American priests, where the action is located in the "cloudcuckooland of Los Angeles." Monsignor Timothy J. O'Fay, nutty as a fruitcake, owns a string of useless titles and has a penchant for breaking into "My Old Kentucky Home" at the wrong time. Monsignor Mickey Gagnon dies in bed in a whorehouse. Augustus O'Dea, vicar-general, has seen *The Song of Bernadette* eleven times, a fact readers are more apt to remember than that he was "a kind, holy man." Father Des Spellacy, an "Irish Medici," exploits his wartime role as "the Parachuting Padre," fixes a raffle, golfs—perhaps the most popular sport among priests in fiction—is something of a fop, and is afflicted with hubris.

James Carroll's *Mortal Friends* (1978) is a classic replay of the Irish-American saga, and *Supply of Heroes* (1986) uses the big canvas to deliver a historical thriller that resurrects Irish Republican Army (IRA) men on the run and plays on two continents. Tom Clancy, who writes edge-of-your-seat, high-tech espionage-adventure novels, like *Patriot Games* (1987) and *Without Remorse* (1993), invents his heroes Jack Ryan and John Kelly to move the action. Carroll and Clancy reach millions of readers and tell a good story.

Mary Gordon's escape to reality, *Final Payments* (1978), offers one of the most memorable of first novels. Her realistic portrayal of Isabel Moore, who sacrifices to nurse an invalid father at home, rings true as tragedy in the Irish scheme of things. A later novel, *The Other Side* (1989), damns the Irish on both sides of the Pond (both sides of the Atlantic). As four generations of Mac-Namaras gather in Queens for the matriarch's funeral, Dan MacNamara reflects: "[T]hey could never be happy, any of them, coming from people like the Irish. Unhappiness was bred into the bone, a message in the blood, a code of weakness. . . . You saw it everywhere in Irish history; they wouldn't allow themselves to prosper" (160). In spite of its psychic bleakness, Gordon's novel tells the hard truths and invites introspection.

Thomas Flanagan stands above and apart from the others. His historical novels—*The Year of the French* (1979), *The Tenants of Time* (1988), and *The End of the Hunt* (1994)—are brilliantly conceived and executed. Grounded in nineteenth-century Irish history, they portray the events that matter with an authenticity that leaves formula novels in the dust. Flanagan is a stylist of genius who introduces multiple narrators and creates a vivid and credible history in fiction. In effect, he has reinvented the genre, beautifully reinterpreting a century full of turmoil, betrayal, and deceit.

Yet another master writer in the tradition is William Kennedy, whose Albany trilogy—*Legs* (1975), *Billy Phelan's Greatest Game* (1978), and *Ironweed* (1983)—has won him international critical acclaim. In Kennedy's talent for re-creating the urban microcosm, where machine politics rule from rectory to poolroom, his vision goes far beyond the reportorial. Set in the New York State capital in the mid-1920s to mid-1930s, the trilogy teems with life—there are, in Kennedy's world, journalists, politicians, young toughs, gangsters, and decent working-class people. Kennedy not only captures the ambience of his city but also creates flesh-and-blood characters like Francis and Billy Phelan. Like Joyce, he celebrates, in his fiction, the common virtues of common men and women. *Quinn's Book* (1988), set in the mid-nineteenth century, rehearses the plight of the immigrants and *Very Old Bones* (1992) continues the saga.

In an interview in 1985, Kennedy said: "I believe that I can't be anything other than Irish American. I know there's a division here, and a good many Irish Americans believe they are really American. They've lost touch with anything that smacks of Irishness as we used to know it" (Peter Quinn, "William Kennedy: an Interview" 78). Kennedy came late to fiction, and his vision is historical. Though he emerges as its principal spokesman, he recognizes the loss of an Irish-American identity, "Irishness as we used to know it."

The emphasis in this chapter has been fiction because most Irish-American writers came from a journalistic background and because the Irish have always loved to tell a good story. Apart, then, from Eugene O'Neill, the early playwrights produced period pieces, melodrama, and light comedy. But, in the 1950s, William Gibson made Broadway with *The Miracle Worker* (1957); in the 1960s, William Alfred's *Hogan's Goat* (1966), far better than its title, won rave reviews; and in the 1970s, John Guare's *House of Blue Leaves* (1971) proved that the Irish had staying power. Guare's recent *Six Degrees of Separation* (1990) has made a convincing case for the strength of an Irish-American stage presence. It isn't a Celtic revival, but it is respectable drama from accomplished playwrights.

The poets are another matter. Though the best of them, like the best of the dramatists, have come to the fore since the mid-twentieth century, they show stronger and more direct Irish influences. Among first-line poets in the tradition are Frank O'Hara, John Logan, X. J. Kennedy, Galway Kinnell, Robert Greeley, and Tess Gallagher, who, in literally scores of collections, model themselves on Yeats and company. Phyllis McGinley, who won a Pulitzer, began as a serious poet but abandoned the quest in favor of the witty epigrams she contributed to *The New Yorker* over so many years. The younger poets of promise are women of the 1980s whose works are, in fact, true to the tradition—poets like Kathy Callaway, Ethna McKiernan, Renny Golden, and Mary Swander, to name but four.

While some established Irish-American writers emphasize the paralyzing grip of church and family and neighborhood on the psyche, others stress the need to break the soul-fetters of the past. They mock—sometimes savagely—the narrowness of traditional values and find little or no consolation in modernism. Like William Kennedy, they see that "their kind" has been assimilated, that they need no longer prove themselves statistically as soldiers fighting wars not theirs or as builders of sewers and canals. They have graduated into the corporate structure and been admitted to the country club with an unlimited credit line. What has happened in recent years is part of the grand evolutionary scheme; it is a kind of cultural trade-off that is written into the price of emigration. If Irish-American writers draw now from non-Irish and non-ghetto experiences, their fiction simply reflects those experiences.

The current literature explores new ground; the conflicts that are played out emanate from an American subculture that is divorced from Ireland by generations. Apart, then, from an incidental reference or a "walk-on," by the 1990s, Irish-American fiction has made the transition. As John Kelleher says in his essay, "Like it or not, we're on our own" ("Irishness in America" 40).

To what degree are the promising younger writers with Irish surnames Irish? Is there "something in a name," or has Irish-American literature simply run its course? What of western writers like Larry McMurtry, whose *Last Picture Show* (1966) and *Lonesome Dove* (1985) give us pause? What of Cormac McCarthy, whose *All the Pretty Horses* (1992) and *The Crossing* (1994), set in the badlands of Texas and Mexico, who has recently attracted so much critical excitement? What of the daring of a T. Coraghessan Boyle in *World's End* (1987), *Budding Prospects* (1985), *East Is East* (1990), and *Without a Hero* (1994), his splendid story collection? It is becoming ever harder to measure the Irish-American dimension in the literature.

The phenomenon in America is that the Irish Americans, like other ethnics, have gained access to the universities in unprecedented numbers and that the writers among them have been introduced to literary traditions that deny American and British stereotypes and infuse a new pride. The younger generation of

Irish Americans will continue to explore American themes and give voice to the American imagination.

SELECTED PRIMARY BIBLIOGRAPHY

Alfred, William. *Hogan's Goat.* New York: Farrar, Straus, and Giroux, 1966.

Berlin, Ellen. *Lace Curtain.* Garden City, NY: Doubleday, 1948.

Boyle, T. Coraghessan. *All the Pretty Horses.* New York: Vintage Books, 1992.

———. *Budding Prospects.* New York: Viking Penguin, 1985.

———. *East Is East.* New York: Viking Penguin, 1990.

———. *Without a Hero.* New York: Viking Penguin, 1994.

———. *World's End.* New York: Viking Penguin, 1987.

Breslin, Jimmy. *Table Money.* New York: Ticknor and Fields, 1986.

———. *World without End, Amen.* New York: Viking, 1973.

Callaway, Kathy. *Heart of the Garfish.* Pittsburgh: University of Pittsburgh Press, 1982.

Carroll, James. *Mortal Friends.* Boston: Little, Brown, 1978.

———. *Supply of Heroes.* New York: E. P. Dutton, 1986.

Costello, Mark. *The Murphy Stories.* Urbana: University of Illinois Press, 1973.

Creeley, Robert. *Selected Poems.* Los Angeles: University of California Press, 1991.

Cullinan, Elizabeth. *A Change of Scene.* New York: Norton, 1982.

———. *House of Gold.* Boston: Houghton Mifflin, 1970.

———. *The Time of Adam.* Boston: Houghton Mifflin, 1971.

———. *Yellow Roses.* New York: Viking, 1977.

Curran, Mary Doyle. *The Parish and the Hill.* Boston: Houghton Mifflin, 1948.

Donleavy, J. P. *The Ginger Man.* Paris: Olympia Press, 1955.

———. *A Singular Man.* Boston: Atlantic Monthly, 1989.

Dunne, Finley Peter. *Mr. Dooley in the Hearts of His Countrymen.* Boston: Small, Maynard, 1899.

———. *Mr. Dooley in Peace and in War.* Boston: Small, Maynard, 1898.

———. *Mr. Dooley's Philosophy.* New York: R. H. Russell, 1900.

Dunne, John Gregory. *Dutch Shea, Jr.* New York: Simon and Schuster, 1982.

———. *Harp.* New York: Simon and Schuster, 1989.

———. *True Confessions.* New York: E. P. Dutton, 1977.

Farrell, James T. *The Face of Time.* New York: Vanguard Press, 1953.

———. *Father and Son.* New York: Vanguard Press, 1940.

———. *The Short Stories of James T. Farrell.* New York: Vanguard Press, 1937.

———. *Studs Lonigan: A Trilogy (Young Lonigan, The Young Manhood of Studs Lonigan, Judgement Day).* 1935. New York: Vanguard Press, 1978.

———. *A World I Never Made.* New York: Vanguard Press, 1936.

Fitzgerald, F. Scott. *All the Sad Young Men.* New York: Charles Scribner's Sons, 1926.

———. *The Beautiful and Damned.* New York: Charles Scribner's Sons, 1922.

———. *The Great Gatsby.* New York: Charles Scribner's Sons, 1925.

———. *Tender Is the Night.* New York: Charles Scribner's Sons, 1934; with author's final revisions, ed. Malcolm Cowley, New York: Charles Scribner's Sons, 1951.

———. *This Side of Paradise.* New York: Charles Scribner's Sons, 1920.

Flaherty, Joe. *Fogarty & Co.* New York: Coward, McCann, and Geoghegan, 1973.

———. *Tin Wife.* New York: Simon and Schuster, 1983.

Flanagan, Thomas. *The End of the Hunt.* New York: E. P. Dutton, 1994.

———. *The Tenants of Time.* New York: E. P. Dutton, 1988.

———. *The Year of the French.* New York: Holt, Rinehart, and Winston, 1979.

Gallagher, Tess. *Instructions to the Double.* Port Townsend, WA: Graywood Press, 1976.

Gibson, William. *The Miracle Worker.* New York: Knopf, 1957.

———. *Two for the Seesaw.* New York: S. French, 1960.

Gill, Brendan. *The Trouble of One House.* Garden City, NY: Doubleday, 1950.

———. *Ways of Loving.* New York: Harcourt Brace Jovanovich, 1974.

Golden, Renny. "Renny Golden." *Unlacing: Ten Irish-American Women Poets.* Ed. Patricia Monaghan. Fairbanks, Alaska: Fireweed Press, 1987.

Gordon, Mary. *Final Payments.* New York: Random House, 1978.

———. *The Other Side.* New York: Viking Penguin, 1989.

Guare, John. *The House of Blue Leaves.* New York: E. P. Dutton, 1971.

———. *Six Degrees of Separation.* New York: Random House, 1990.

Hamill, Pete. *A Drinking Life.* Boston: Little, Brown, 1994.

———. *The Gift.* 1973. New York: Ballantine Books, 1974.

———. *Loving Women, A Novel of the Fifties.* New York: Random House, 1989.

Howard, Maureen. *Before My Time.* Boston: Little, Brown, 1974.

———. *Bridgeport Bus.* New York: Harcourt, Brace, and World, 1965.

———. *Expensive Habits.* New York: Summit Books, 1986.

———. *Facts of Life.* Boston: Little, Brown, 1978.

———. *Grace Abounding.* Boston: Little, Brown, 1982.

Kelly, Robert. *Cat Scratch Fever.* Kingston, NY: McPherson, 1991.

———. *Kill the Messenger Who Brings Bad News.* Santa Rosa, CA: Black Sparrow, 1979.

Kennedy, William. *Billy Phelan's Greatest Game.* 1978. New York: Penguin, 1983.

———. *Ironweed.* New York: Viking, 1983.

———. *Legs.* 1975. New York: Penguin, 1983.

———. *Quinn's Book.* New York: Viking, 1988.

———. *Very Old Bones.* New York: Viking, 1992.

Kennedy, X. J. *Cross Ties: Selected Poems.* Athens: University of Georgia Press, 1985.

Kinnell, Galway. *Selected Poems.* New York: Houghton Mifflin, 1983.

Logan, John. *John Logan: The Collected Poems.* Brockport, NY: BOA Editions, 1989.

McCarthy, Cormac. *All the Pretty Horses.* New York: Vintage Books, 1992.

———. *The Crossing.* New York: Knopf, 1994.

———. *Suttree.* New York: Random House, 1992.

McCarthy, Mary. *Memories of a Catholic Girlhood.* New York: Harcourt, Brace, and World, 1957.

McGinley, Phyllis. *Times Three.* New York: Viking, 1961.

McHale, Tom. *Alinsky's Diamond.* Philadelphia: Lippincott, 1974.

———. *Farragan's Retreat.* New York: Viking, 1971.

———. *The Lady from Boston.* Garden City, NY: Doubleday, 1978.

———. *Principato.* New York: Viking, 1970.

———. *School Spirit.* Garden City, NY: Doubleday, 1976.

McInerny, Jay. *Bright Lights, Big City.* New York: Random, 1984.

McKenny, Ruth. *Industrial Valley.* New York: Harcourt, Brace, 1938.

———. *My Sister Eileen.* New York: Harcourt, Brace, 1938.

McKiernan, Ethna. *Caravan.* Minneapolis: Midwest Villages and Voices, 1989.

McMurtry, Larry. *The Last Picture Show*. New York: Penguin Books, 1966.

———. *Lonesome Dove*. New York: Simon and Schuster, 1985.

O'Brien, Fitz-James. *A Gentleman from Ireland: A Comedy in Two Acts*. New York: S. French, 1858.

O'Connor, Edwin. *All in the Family*. Boston: Little, Brown, 1966.

———. *The Edge of Sadness*. Boston: Little, Brown, 1961.

———. *I Was Dancing*. Boston: Little, Brown, 1964.

———. *The Last Hurrah*. Boston: Little, Brown, 1956.

O'Connor, Flannery. *The Complete Stories*. New York: Farrar, Straus, and Giroux, 1971.

———. *The Violent Bear It Away*. New York: Farrar, Straus, and Cudahy, 1960.

———. *Wise Blood*. New York: Harcourt, Brace, 1952.

O'Hara, Frank. *Art Chronicles*. New York: Braziller, 1990.

———. *Selected Poems*. New York: Random House, 1974.

O'Hara, John. *Appointment in Samarra*. New York: Harcourt, Brace, 1934.

———. *Butterfield 8*. New York: Harcourt, Brace, 1935.

———. *The Doctor's Son and Other Stories*. New York: Harcourt, Brace, 1935.

O'Neill, Eugene. *Ah, Wilderness!* New York: Library of America, 1933.

———. *Anna Christie*. New York: Random House, 1921.

———. *Desire under the Elms*. New York: Random House, 1924.

———. *The Emperor Jones*. New York: Random House, 1920.

———. *The Great God Brown*. New York: Boni and Liveright, 1926.

———. *The Hairy Ape*. New York: Random House, 1921.

———. *The Iceman Cometh*. New York: Random House, 1946.

———. *A Long Day's Journey into Night*. New Haven, CT: Yale University Press, 1956.

———. *The Long Voyage Home*. Mattituck, NY: Random House, 1917.

———. *The Moon of the Caribees*. New York: Boni and Liveright, 1917.

———. *Mourning Becomes Electra*. New York: Random House, 1931.

———. *Strange Interlude*. New York: Random House, 1928.

———. *A Touch of the Poet*. New Haven, CT: Yale University Press, 1946.

O'Reilly, John Boyle. *Moondyne: A Story from the Underworld*. Boston: Pilot, 1879.

Powers, J. F. *Lions, Harts, Leaping Does and Other Stories*. New York: Time, 1963.

———. *Look How the Fish Live*. New York: Knopf, 1975.

———. *Morte D'Urban*. Garden City, NY: Doubleday, 1962.

———. *The Presence of Grace*. Garden City, NY: Doubleday, 1956.

———. *Prince of Darkness and Other Stories*. Garden City, NY: Doubleday, 1947.

———. *Wheat That Springeth Green*. New York: Knopf, 1988.

Sadlier, Mary Anne (Madden). *Bessy Conway; or, The Irish Girl in America*. New York: Sadlier, 1861.

———. *Con O'Regan; or, Emigrant Life in the New World*. New York: Sadlier, 1864.

———. *Willy Burke; or, The Irish Orphan in America*. Boston: Patrick Donahoe, 1850.

Smith, Betty. *Joy in the Morning*. New York: Harper, 1963.

———. *Maggie-Now*. New York: Harper, 1958.

———. *Tomorrow Will Be Better*. New York: Harper, 1948.

———. *A Tree Grows in Brooklyn*. New York: Harper, 1943.

Smith, Dennis. *Report from Engine Co. 82*. New York: Saturday Review Press, 1972.

———. *Steely Blue*. New York: Simon and Schuster, 1984.

Swander, Mary. *Succession*. Athens: University of Georgia Press, 1979.

Toole, John Kennedy. *A Confederacy of Dunces.* Baton Rouge: Louisiana State University Press, 1980.

SELECTED SECONDARY BIBLIOGRAPHY

Bolger, Stephen G. *The Irish Character in American Fiction, 1830–1860.* New York: Arno Press, 1976.

Browne, Joseph. "The Greening of America: Irish American Writers." *Journal of Ethnic Studies* 2 (1975): 71–76.

Casey, Daniel J. "Echoes from the Next Parish: An Introduction to Irish-American Fiction." *An Gael* 11.2 (Spring 1984): 2–6.

———. "The Last Irish American." *Bostonia* (Spring 1994): 48–51.

Casey, Daniel J. and Robert E. Rhodes, eds. *Irish-American Fiction: Essays in Criticism.* New York: AMS Press, 1979.

———. *Modern Irish-American Fiction: A Reader.* Syracuse: Syracuse University Press, 1989.

Fanning, Charles. *The Irish Voice in America.* Lexington: University Press of Kentucky, 1990.

Fanning, Charles, ed. *The Exiles of Erin: Nineteenth-Century Irish-American Fiction.* Notre Dame, IN: University of Notre Dame Press, 1987.

Greeley, Andrew M. *The Irish Americans: The Rise to Money and Power.* Chicago: Quandrangle Books, 1981.

———. "The Last of the American Irish Fade Away." *New York Times Magazine,* March 14, 1971: 33.

———. *That Most Distressful Nation: The Taming of the American Irish.* Chicago: Quadrangle Books, 1972.

Handlin, Oscar. *Boston's Immigrants, 1790–1880, A Study in Acculturation.* Revised and enlarged ed. New York: Atheneum, 1969.

Kelleher, John V. "Edwin O'Connor and the Irish-American Process." *Atlantic 222,* July 1968: 48–52.

———. "Irishness in America." *Atlantic 208,* July 1961: 38–40.

Martin, Ralph G. *A Hero for Our Time.* New York: Fawcett Crest, 1993.

McCaffrey, Lawrence J. *The Irish Diaspora in America.* 1976. Washington, DC: Catholic University of America Press, 1984.

———. *Textures of Irish America.* Syracuse: Syracuse University Press, 1992.

McGee, Thomas D'Arcy. *A History of the Irish Settlers in North America.* Boston: Office of the American Celt, 1855.

Quinn, Peter. "William Kennedy: An Interview," *The Recorder: Journal of The American Irish Historical Society,* New Series, 1.1 (Winter 1985): 65–81.

Rhodes, Robert E. "F. Scott Fitzgerald: 'All My Fathers.' " *Irish-American Fiction: Essays in Criticism.* Ed. Daniel J. Casey and Robert E. Rhodes. New York: AMS Press, 1979. 29–51.

Shannon, William V. *The American Irish: A Political and Social Portrait.* New York: Macmillan, 1966.

Wittke, Carl. "The Immigrant Theme on the American Stage." *Mississippi Valley Historical Review* 34 (1953): 211–232.

17

Italian/American Literature

Fred L. Gardaphe

INTRODUCTION

Bibliographic in nature, this chapter first provides a general cultural backdrop against which the "new immigrant" writing can be viewed in relation to the Italian/American culture established earlier. Against this backdrop comes a closer look at a few selected writers who, while they cannot accept the burden of representing the many cultures of the new Italian immigration, provide insights into the subjects and themes that concern many of the Italian/American writers who immigrated to American since 1945.

LITERARY-CULTURAL HISTORY

Between 1920 and 1950, the number of Italians immigrating to the United States diminished each year. No longer were Italians leaving their homeland by the hundreds of thousands. Two reasons are usually given for this: during this period, living conditions in Italy had improved, and the American government had placed limits on the numbers of people who could immigrate to America from any one country. However, the end of World War II brought a new wave of Italian immigration, and these immigrants changed the definition of Italian America. For the children and grandchildren of the first major wave of Italian immigration, these new arrivals came as the enemy the Americans had defeated, the people America had liberated. Upon their arrival the immigrants after World War II found themselves alienated not only from American culture but also from the Italian/American culture that had sprung up since the major immigration of Italians to America during the early 1900s. The majority of Italians coming to America between 1880 and 1920 came from a peasant culture based on oral, rather than literate, traditions. Books were not among the possessions carried along in the move to America. In Italy, during this period, literacy was a tool used by those in power to exercise and protect their power over others. The Italian institutions of church and state controlled access to this power by controlling access to literacy. Only in 1877, when the Coppino law was enacted, was formal education made mandatory for all children between the ages of six and nine. This law was vigorously resisted by inhabitants of the Mezzogiorno, the southern region of Italy from which more than 80 percent of America's Italians emigrated. Thus, it is no wonder that the majority of Italians who immigrated to America were illiterate people who had no power to control their lives in Italy. In essence they were considered subhuman by those who held power over them. There are many references to the plight of the Italian peasant being the same as that of the donkey, the typical beast of burden in southern Italy. A Sicilian poem by Ignazio Buttitta, from the early 1920s "Lu sceccu," or "The Ass," is a prime example: "The wretch drags the chain/ and the dumb donkey bears it,/ harnessed from dusk till dawn/ to the mill, back and forth—/ a thrashing is the rule/ as the boss strides the rump./ Bray, the bridle will slash,/ paw, the spurs will grind,/ tote wheat, but straw/ and chaff is what you eat" (72).[1]

This was the way of life that many of those who immigrated to the United States were hoping to change. While immigration became the first step in gaining greater control over one's life, the acquisition of literacy in America became a way of maintaining and increasing that control. For the immigrant, acquiring the ability to signify this experience became the key to shifting from the powerlessness of an oral culture ruled by destiny to a written culture in which one could exercise greater control over one's life. This transition, however, did not happen cleanly nor completely in the life of every immigrant. The earliest Italian/American writing, primarily autobiographies and autobiographical fiction, fluctuates between oral and literate styles just as they fluctuate between identification with Italian and American cultures. *Rosa,* an as-told-to autobiography of Rosa Cassettari, is consistently much more closely tied to oral traditions than Pascal D'Angelo's *Son of Italy,* and Constantine Panunzio's *The Soul of an Immigrant* is even less connected to these traditions than the others. Together, these three narratives represent a foundation upon which a distinct Italian/American literary tradition has been built.[2]

EARLY AND RECENT EFFORTS

During the 1930s and 1940s, a number of Italian intellectuals emigrated to the United States, often in flight from fascism. Three writers whose work is characteristic of this period and whose subjects and themes differ greatly from the writing of earlier American immigrants are Arturo Vivante, P. M. Pasinetti, and Niccolo Tucci. These writers, discussed in greater detail in Rose Basile Green's *The Italian/American Novel,* chose to focus more on aesthetics than on exploring aspects of their ethnicity; this emphasis helped them enter mainstream American culture more easily than their predecessors. Arturo Vivante, a physician born in Italy in 1923, immigrated to the United States and contributed frequently to such major publications as the *New Yorker.* He has published short fiction, a collection of short stories, *The French Girls of Killini* (1967), and three novels, *A Goodly Babe* (1966), *Doctor Giovanni* (1969), and *Run to the Waterfall* (1965). An active fiction writer, Vivante has also, like many of the new immigrant writers, been involved in translation of Italian literature into English.[3]

Pasinetti was born in 1913 and raised in Venice. He came to study in the United States in 1935 and first published fiction in *The Southern Review.* He earned a Ph.D. at Yale in 1949 and went on to teach at the University of California–Los Angeles (UCLA). In 1965 he received an award from the National Institute of Arts and Letters. Pasinetti published three novels, *Venetian Red* (1960), *The Smile on the Face of the Lion* (1965), and *From the Academy Bridge* (1970). Tucci, like Pasinetti, first came as a student. His two novels, primarily autobiographical, *Before My Time* (1962) and *Unfinished Funeral* (1964), use European settings to depict liberation from the history that the emigrant experiences upon leaving his ancestral homeland. For these writers, their sense of the literary, while heavily drawn from their Italian education, was significantly shaped by the prominence in 1930s Italy of Italian Americanisti such as Elio Vittorini and Cesare Pavese, both translators and influential editors of American literature who helped introduce American literature to Italian culture. Along with these three earlier immigrants was a protégé of Pavese who has had a tremendous impact on both the perception of Italian literature in America and the progression of Italian/American culture: Giose Rimanelli.

In 1935, Rimanelli, a ten-year-old native of Molise, Italy, entered a Catholic seminary in Puglia with the intention of becoming a missionary. There he learned classical Greek and Latin, studied Provencal and French, and encountered and translated the French symbolists Rimbaud, Verlaine, and Apollinaire. Five years later he left, realizing that he had lost his vocation. His first novel, *Tiro al piccione* (1953, 1991), the publication of which was fostered by Pavese, is a fictionalized autobiographical account of his early years in Molise and his experiences during the Second World War. This novel, translated into English by Ben Johnson as *The Day of the Lion* and published by Random House in 1954, received critical praise and became an American best-seller. Six years and a number of novels later, Rimanelli came to America to give a lecture at the Library of Congress, after which he was invited to teach and travel throughout North and South America. Then he decided to remain in the United States, where he continued to write poetry and fiction, publishing all his writing, except for some academic work, in Italian.

Even before moving to America, Rimanelli was beginning to examine the American influence on life in Italy. In his second novel, *Peccato originale* (Original Sin 1957), he gives us the story of a Molisani family and the father's (Nicola) obsession with the dream of coming to America, which becomes a topic of debate among the villagers. "As far as I'm concerned, America is an illusion, one big illusion" (92), says Scocchera in response to Nicola's suggestion that, once settled there, he will send for his friend, Scocchera. Scocchera then takes out a letter from one Vincenzo Rimanelli, "the one whose son's a writer, and who took it into his head to go to America with that busted leg he had" which tells of the trials of living in America. Scocchera reads: "And then, I won't even tell you about the Italo-Americans. They're all hopping madmen, and if things keep on the way they're going we'll be off our heads too. And now, just thinking it over real good, America is a big fat bluff, they treat us like pack asses" (92).

The Italian living in North America served as a regular subject for his writing. In *Una posizione sociale* (1959), he recounts the life of the Italian living in New Orleans in the early 1900s and examines the lynching of thirteen Italians. In 1966 he collected, edited, and introduced *Modern Canadian Stories*. *Tragica America* (1968) contains his reflections of his first years in the United States. Seven years later he gave us a greater insight into the literature of Italy through *Italian Literature: Roots and Branches.* Now a professor emeritus of the State University of New York–Albany (SUNY–Albany), Rimanelli continues writing his fiction in Italian and publishing it primarily in Italy. However, over the years that he has lived here, Rimanelli has been writing poetry and novels in English and has accumulated a number of unpublished manuscripts. Early in the 1970s he wrote his first novel in English, entitled *Benedetta in Guysterland,* which was published for the first time in 1993 by Guernica Editions of Toronto, Canada.

The first question that comes to the reader of *Benedetta* is why this novel was not published until 1993. After all, by 1970, the year it was written, Rimanelli was an internationally acclaimed writer who had published seven very successful books in Italy that had been translated into eight languages.[4] At the time, Rimanelli was a well-known journalist and cultural critic. Since 1961 he had been a tenured professor in American universities such as Yale, promoted on the merits of his writing and not by virtue of his academic credentials. So why didn't he publish this novel right after it was written? Though Rimanelli made no attempt to publish it, perhaps because he lacked the confidence in his experimental exercises, he did send the manuscript to an impressive list of readers. The readers' responses are cataloged in an appendix that Rimanelli attaches to the novel. One of the respondents was the noted literary critic Leslie Fiedler, who wrote: "I'm sending back your manuscript with this. It gave me much pleasure, and I think it would be a great loss to all of us if you did not become an American novelist at this point" (191). That was back in 1972, and Fiedler was responding to Rimanelli's sophisticated literary experimentation, an experimentation that few American immigrant authors were capable of producing in the English language. The novel, to Rimanelli, was simply an experiment in

English, his first response to the demands of starting over again, from scratch, as a writer with a new language, a man of the world with a new toy.

Yet while the language was new, his knowledge of world literature and of America was not. North America had entered his imagination long before his arrival in the 1950s. His grandfather was born in New Orleans, and his mother in Canada. We can see images of America forming in his earliest novels. *Benedetta,* the record of his divorce from his native culture, which he chose to leave, is the result of his first two decades of immersion into American culture. As writer Anthony Burgess noted in an introduction to "Alien," Rimanelli's unpublished book of poems in English written between 1964 and 1970, "Rimanelli is one of those remarkable writers who, like Joseph Conrad . . . have turned from their first language to English, and have set out to rejuvenate it in a way few writers could do who were blessed and burdened with English as their first language" (244).

Benedetta in Guysterland fills a deep void in Italian/American literary history; that void is the cavity caused by the decay of a literary realism characteristic of the standard fare produced by early Italian/American writers. For too long, those imaginations have been held prisoners by the psychosocial borders of the Italian/American ghetto. While the emphasis of most Italian/American fiction has been the Italian/American experience, most authors have been unable to gain a distance from the subject that would enable them to gain the new perspectives necessary to renew the story of Italian life in America. What Mario Puzo romanticized in *The Godfather* (1969) and what Gay Talese historicized in *Honor Thy Father* (1971), Giose Rimanelli has parodied in *Benedetta.* Through parody he has transcended the Italian/American subject by, above all, writing a book about language and literature through the same subject of the Mafia used by Puzo and Talese. Like James Joyce, Rimanelli unites high culture with popular culture in this labyrinth of a text that reads like a map of Western civilization. Rimanelli balances his life on the border of tradition and the avant garde by making literary forays into both worlds.[5] *Benedetta* demonstrates that one culture could not satisfy Rimanelli. While Rimanelli dove into American culture with a youthful abandon, one of his contemporaries did so more reluctantly.

Born in San Marco in Lamis, the province of Foggia, Joseph Tusiani immigrated to the United States shortly after World War II. Educated at the University of Naples in English language and literature, Tusiani had written much poetry before emigrating. Tusiani was a translator of Italian. While his first novel, *Envoy from Heaven,* appeared in 1965, he is perhaps best known for his translations of the poetry of Michelangelo and Tasso. He was the first Italian American to be named vice president of the Poetry Society of America, a position he held from 1956 to 1968.

The alienation themes that characterized the episodic writing of the early Italian/American novelists such as Pietro di Donato were perhaps best crystallized in poetry by Tusiani. In his "Song of the Bicentennial," written in celebration of America's 200th birthday, Tusiani raises the question of the meaning of Italianita or Italianness in America and its relation to the immigrant's identity: "Then, who will solve this riddle of my day?/ Two languages, two lands, perhaps two souls . . . /Am I a man or two strange halves of one?" ("Song of the Bicentennial," *Gente Mia* 7). In questioning his own experience as an immigrant, Tusiani also begins to wonder about the experience of those who immigrated earlier, those who did not have his abilities to write in either language. Perhaps more than any other Italian American who has ventured into the arts in America, Tusiani gives voice to those who preceded his arrival. In the final stanza of "Song of the Bicentennial," he writes: "I am the present for I am the past/ of those who for their future came to stay,/humble and innocent and yet outcast./ . . . For this my life their death made ample room" (8).

Through such poems Tusiani takes on the responsibility of speaking for the earlier immigrants. As critic Paolo Giordano points out: "Tusiani shows the reader that the American cultural milieu has absorbed the superficial and stereotypical aspects of Italian immigrant culture while never understanding the true character of this populace. . . . It is up to the poet, who draws his inspiration from the injustice suffered by his people, to assure that their sacrifice will not be forgotten" ("From Southern Italian" 325). Though he is of Italian extraction and writes from his experience as an Italian immigrant, Tusiani speaks for every immigrant this country has taken in. Tusiani uses *Italianita* to speak to the larger issue of what it means to be American.

As an artist and academic, Tusiani has translated Latin and Italian literature into English. He is currently retired, having taught in American colleges for more than thirty-five years, and has completed three volumes of an autobiographical narrative epic. The first one is a novelization of his landmark poem, "La parola difficile" (The Difficult Word). The next two were *La parola nuova* (The New Word) and *La parola antica* (The Ancient Word). All three were written in Italian and are currently being translated into English.

Much of Italian/American literature is connected directly or indirectly to the experiences of those who came during the mass migrations that occurred during the last turn of the century. Very little of this literature has made its way into either American or Italian mainstream culture. Thus, the new immigrant writers, whose experiences a half-century or more later are quite different, often avoid association with the Italian/American community. They become, in the words of critic and writer Paolo Valesio, writers "between two worlds" (259).

Two younger writers whose works depict the struggle of the writer between two worlds are Peter Carravetta and Anne Calcagno. Carravetta, a professor of Italian and director of the World Studies Program at Queens College, has become a prominent voice in Italian/American culture; he writes in both Italian and English and has published in Italy and America. Until recently, he has primarily been known as a cultural critic, but he has been writing poetry and fiction since his teenage years. He is the founding editor of *Differentia, Review of Italian Thought* and a frequent contributor to *Voices in Italian Americana,* where he has published fiction and poetry. His poetry is characterized by its frequent allusions to ancient Greek and Roman mythology, as well as to various traditions of Italian, British, and American lyric and epic poetry. The interaction between these cultures becomes a basis for the creation of new myths that concern life and love between two worlds. While Carravetta has privately published a number of poetry chapbooks, he has recently placed a collection of his poetry with Guernica Editions of Montreal. *The Sun and Other Things* marks a major shift in his writing career. Ranging over the past twenty years of his life, he deals with such subjects as life, literature, linguistics, sensual and platonic love, and adolescent angst. He anxiously reacts to the influence on him by such classic poets as Dante, Shakespeare, and the English romantics. The entire collection is a metamorphic journey in which the poet, at home in English and Italian traditions, travels from thought to word. The result is that, for Carravetta, writing becomes the sanctuary of a self besieged by forces competing for the author's attention. One of his stylistic trademarks is frequent code switching between English and Italian; his work also includes phrases and sentences from other Romance languages such as French and Spanish.

At first glance, there doesn't seem to be anything particularly Italian about the short stories in Anne Calcagno's first collection *Pray for Yourself.* While two of the nine are set in Italy, the rest are scattered about urban and rural America and are peopled with characters peculiar to America. What is Italian about these remarkably American short stories can be found under the surface of the polished prose and carefully constructed sentences. Calcagno brings the beauty of poetry into the complexity of prose fiction by capturing the rhythms and sounds of the Italian language through English. Calcagno weaves Italian sensibilities with English syntax to create stories that resonate in the mind long after the last page has been turned.

Born in San Diego, Calcagno was raised in Milan and Rome since the age of four, when her father's job transferred the family. At the age of seventeen she returned to the United States to attend Williams College, where the late John Gardner encouraged her writing by calling her synthesis of Italian and English "original." After graduation from Williams College, Calcagno lived in New York City, where she worked for the Italian newspaper *La repubblica.* She then moved to Montana to work on a master's of fine arts in poetry and fiction at the University of Montana. She had published stories in such periodicals as the *North American Review* and the *Denver Quarterly,* as well as in the anthologies *Fiction of the Eighties* and *American Fiction,* prior to placing her collection with TriQuarterly Books, Northwestern University's new venture. Calcagno is an assistant professor of English and teaches creative writing at DePaul University in Chicago. She is currently at work on a novel that deals with a family and Italian immigration during this century.

CONCLUSION

By way of concluding this chapter, I include some brief sketches of major writers who, while they have primarily produced literature in Italian, are creating new dimensions of Italian/American literature, as more and more their works are written in, or translated into, English. At the forefront of this group is Paolo Valesio, a professor of Italian at Yale University. Valesio is the author of a number of books of criticism of Italian literature and has produced two novels and four books of poetry. His essay "The Writer between Two Worlds" has become a manifesto of sorts for those Italian writers who live in the United States, not as immigrants but as expatriates. While some question this appellation—and suggest that they are really immigrants who do not wish to be identified with the mass waves of immigration from Italy—there can be no doubt that these writers are beginning to carve out a niche for themselves in both Italian and American literary histories. Unlike earlier immigrants, these writers—most of whom are professors in American universities—write in Italian and publish in both the United States and Italy. Their frequent travel to Italy enables them to maintain a strong contact with their homeland culture. Their profession keeps their use of the Italian language alive, and thus, until recently, most of them have published only in Italian.

Gradiva, the international journal of Italian literature, recently produced a bilingual anthology entitled *Italian Poets in America.* Edited by Luigi Fontanella, *Gradiva*'s founder and editor, and Paolo Valesio, this collection includes bibliographies and brief interviews of each poet. Both the Foreword by Fontanella and the Introduction by Valesio are important essays on the phenomenon of the contemporary Italian expatriate writer.

Until only recently, the number of Italian women writers has been few. But writers such as Laura Stortoni and Rina Ferrarelli have begun to publish and fill the gender gap. Stortoni, who immigrated to the United States at the age of twenty-three in the 1960s, has published poetry in *Voices in Italian Americana, The Midwest Quarterly, Italian Americana, Women's Quarterly, Blue Unicorn,* and the *City Lights Review.* Educated in Italy, England, and France, Stortoni did graduate work at the University of California in comparative literature and has worked as a translator and professor. Her experience with the literatures of the world finds its way into her poetry, which covers a wide range of styles and subject matters. In *The Moon and the Island,* her first book, yet unpublished, she attempts to re-create the world that was lost to her once she left Italy for America. Like her predecessors, one of her major concerns is the need to use a new language that does not convey everything she wants to say. In "A Borrowed Tongue," she echoes a lament heard in Tusiani's poetry: "Who is poorer than I am?" she asks, then tells of those who borrow houses, cars, condiments, books, and "company in loneliness." She concludes with, "But the poorest of them all/is she who must borrow a tongue" (125). Stortoni does quite well with her borrowed tongue, and her achievements are lauded by Diane di Prima in the Preface to Stortoni's collection: "The work is variously a poetics of loss and a song of celebration" (unpub.). Some of her poems speak of the distant, mythic, and historic past, and others of the present in which she is creating a new history for the immigrant. The effect, then, is that for the reader the Old World is renewed through remembering, and the New World becomes a place to build a future that might possibly transcend time. Like Carravetta, Stortoni mixes the myths of both Old World and New, and in her latest work she turns her attention to the myths of Native American and Mexican cultures. The volume, entitled *From the New World,* presents poems from the point of view of the pre-European inhabitants of the land she now calls home. In this way, by focusing attention on the hosts who have been removed from their homes, Stortoni creates a unique parallel to her own uprootedness. Thus, the image of immigrant as a heroic explorer—used by many earlier Italian immigrant poets— becomes displaced by that of the immigrant as potential destroyer or potential ally of the descendants of those natives. In any case, Stortoni's poetry creates a powerful female presence in a world that has been dominated by men.

Rina Ferrarelli was a teenager when her family immigrated to the United States. She has received two national honors for her translation work, a National Endowment of The Arts fellowship in 1984 and the Italo Calvino Prize in 1988. She has also been writing and publishing her poetry in anthologies such as *The Dream Book, American Sports Poems,* and *Looking for Home.* Her poems have appeared in journals such as *la bella figura, BSU Forum, Footwork: The Paterson Literary Review, The Hudson Review, Kansas Quarterly,* and many others. She recently published *Dreamsearch,* her first collection of poems.

Born in Francavilla, Sicily, Gaetano Cipolla immigrated to America with his parents in 1955. Since then he has devoted himself to teaching and writing and is professor of Italian at St. John's College in New York. Cipolla's career has two distinct stages. The first, as a critic and scholar, had nothing to do with Sicily. This stage was marked by *Labyrinth: Studies of an Archetype.* Published in 1987 by Legas, this first book of a series on literary criticism presents a study of the labyrinth in Western culture. His next books, however, marked a change not only in his career but in himself. While in graduate school, Cipolla's professor, Luigi Ballerini, had students choose readings of works in their own dialects. Cipolla chose the writing of the Sicilian writer Giovanni Meli. Cipolla's subsequent verse translations of Meli's *The Origin of the World, Don Chisciotti e Sanciu Panza,* and *Moral Fables* were the first of Meli's works to be published in this country. Cipolla soon began editing books with Legas, a press founded in 1988 by Leonardo Sbrocchi, professor of Italian at Ottawa University. At the time, Legas was primarily publishing Italian textbooks and book projects in other languages. Since Cipolla's collaboration, Legas has added a specialty of publishing Sicilian writing in two series. One, called "The Poets of Arba Sicula," features the works of individuals such as Vincenzo Ancona and includes Cipolla's translations of Nino Martoglio's poetry. The second series is more scholarly and covers Sicilian history, sociology, and economics. The first volume in this series is Giuseppe Quatraglio's *A Thousand Years in Sicily.* Cipolla has been active with Arba Sicula since the early 1980s. Started by Joseph Palisi and Gaetano Giacchi in 1978, this organization is dedicated to the study, preservation, and promotion of the language and culture of Sicily. Cipolla also edits the periodicals *Arba Sicula* and *Sicilia Parra.*

Like Cipolla, Ferdinando Alfonsi is an Italian scholar and poet who has devoted much of his recent energy to developing the important dialogue between Italian and Italian/American cultures. These efforts have resulted in the bilingual anthology *Italo-American Poets* (1985), his *Dictionary of Italian/American Poets* (1989), and *Italian/American Poetry* (1991), all three important references.

Born in Lodi, Italy, Alessandro Carrera started writing poetry when he was eight years old and never stopped. He entered a 1985 Ministry of Foreign Affairs competition for teaching Italian abroad and was awarded the assignment of teaching in America for seven years. While in America, he has published a chapbook of poetry, *The Perfect Bride,* which reflects cross-cultural influences of American beat poetry and blues music, on one side, while, on the Italian side, the work echoes Italian giants such as Leopardi, Montale, Pasolini, and Ungaretti. A portion of his second novel, *The Tower and the Lowlands,* appeared in a recent issue of the *Review of Contemporary Fiction* devoted to contemporary Italian writers. His third novel, *When I'm Sixty-Four,* is close to completion and tells the story of the American immigration to Houston of an elderly English character based on former Beatle Ringo Starr. Though written in Italian, Carerra hopes to have it translated into English. He is currently with the Italian Cultural Center of Toronto and teaches at McMaster College in Hamilton, Ontario.

Antonio D'Alfonso's Guernica Editions of Montreal, Canada, has become a major publishing resource for new immigrant writers. Guernica is spearheading an attempt to enable the various branches of the Italian diaspora to speak to each other from Australia to Argentina, from Italy to Italian/North America, and D'Alfonso's creative, critical, and publishing efforts have all contributed to provide vital forums for Italian/American literature.

NOTES

1. Mario Puzo consistently makes this connection—most recently in a scene from *The Godfather III,* in which Don Altobello requests that an assassin's retarded son "[d]o the donkey," an act in which the son contorts his face and brays, and earlier in his novel *The Sicilian* (1984):

The Sicilian peasant has an affinity with his mule and donkey. They are hard-working beasts, and like the peasant himself have flinty, dour natures. Like the peasant they can work steadily for very long hours without breaking down, unlike the higher nobility horse, who must be pampered. Also, they are surefooted and can pick their way along the mountain terraces without falling and breaking a leg, unlike the fiery stallions or the high-blooded, flighty mares. Also, peasant and donkey and mule subsist and thrive on food that kills other men and animals. But the greatest affinity was this: Peasant, donkey and mule had to be treated with affection and respect, otherwise they turned murderous and stubborn. (58–59)

"The Ass," or "Lu sceccu," was translated by Justin Vitiello, whom I thank for bringing it to my attention. The translation is as yet unpublished.

2. For more on this tradition, see my dissertation, "Italian Signs, American Streets: Cultural Representation in Italian/American Narrative Literature."

3. Vivante's most recent translation is *Giacomo Leopardi, Poems.* Wellfleet, MA: Delphinium Press, 1988.

4. Rimanelli's novels, such as *Tiro al piccione,* are now best-sellers as they are being rediscovered and republished as classics.

5. Rimanelli is as much concerned with preserving folk culture through his dialect poetry and songs as he is with creating new literature through his Italian- and English-language experiments; see his *Moliseide.*

SELECTED PRIMARY BIBLIOGRAPHY

Alfonsi, Ferdinando. *Verso il mare: Toward the Sea.* Catanzaro: A. Carello Editore, 1987.
———. ed. *Poeti Italo-Americani: Italo-American Poets, A Bilingual Anthology.* Catanzaro: A. Carello Editore, 1985.
Ancona, Vincenzo. *Malidittu la lingua* (Damned Language). Brooklyn: Legas, 1990.
Barolini, Helen. *The Dream Book: An Anthology of Writings by Italian/American Women.* New York: Schocken, 1985.
Buttitta, Ignazio. "Lu sceccu." *Prime e nuovissime di Ignazio Buttitta.* Ed. M. Puglisi. Turin: Gruppo Editoriale Forma, 1983. 72.
Calcagno, Anne. *Pray for Yourself.* Evanston, IL: Tri-Quarterly Books, 1993.
Carravetta, Peter. "Eros e Nomos." *VIA* 2.2 (1991): 133–136.
———. "From *Ulcer.*" *Voices in Italian Americana* 3.2 (1992): 75–80.
———. *Dialogi V. Tam Tam* 54 (1987).
———. *Metessi.* Salerno-Roma: Edizioni Ripostes, 1990.
———. *The Sun and Other Things.* Montreal: Guernica, forthcoming.
Carrera, Alessandro. *The Perfect Bride. La Sposa Perfetta.* Houston: Thorn Books, 1992.
———. "The Rose of Yesterday." *Review of Contemporary Fiction. New Italian Fiction* (Fall 1992): 139–149.
Cipolla, Gaetano, ed. and trans. *The Origins of the World* by Giovanni Meli. New York: Arba Sicula, 1985.
———. *The Poetry of Nino Martoglio.* Jamaica, NY: Legas Books, 1993.
Corsi, Pietro. *La giobba.* Milano: Edizione Enne, 1982. Trans. Guernica: Montreal, forthcoming.
D'Angelo, Pascal. *Son of Italy.* New York: Macmillan, 1924.
Ets, Marie Hall. *Rosa: The Life of an Italian Immigrant.* Minneapolis: University of Minnesota Press, 1970.
Ferrarelli, Rina. *Dreamsearch.* San Francisco: malafemmina press, 1992.
Fontanella, Luigi. "Un'altra volta e vivi." *VIA* 3.1 (1992): 97–102.
Fontanella, Luigi, and Paolo Valesio, eds. *Italian Poets in America.* Special issue of *Gradiva* 5.1 (1992–1993).
Giordano, Paolo A., ed. *Joseph Tusiani: Poet, Translator, Humanist.* Vol. 2 West Lafayette, IN: VIA Folios, 1994.
Minni, C. D., ed. *Ricordi: Things Remembered, An Anthology of Short Stories.* Montreal: Guernica, 1989.
Nicolai, A. P. *La doppia finzione.* Chicago: Insula, 1988.
Panunzio, Constantine. *The Soul of an Immigrant.* New York: Macmillan, 1921.
Pasinetti, Pier Maria. *From the Academy Bridge.* New York: Random House, 1970.
———. *The Smile on the Face of the Lion.* New York: Random House, 1965.

————. *Venetian Red.* New York: Random House, 1960.

Rimanelli, Giose. *Benedetta in Guysterland.* Toronto: Guernica, 1993.

————. *The Day of the Lion.* Trans. Ben Johnson, Jr. New York: Random House, 1954.

————. *Italian Literature: Roots and Branches.* New Haven, CT: Yale University Press, 1975.

————. "A Mesmeric Sculpture: Tusiani, the Humanist." *Italian Ethnics: Their Languages, Literature and Lives.* Proceedings of the 20th Annual Conference of the American Italian Historical Association. Ed. Dominic Candeloro et al. Staten Island, NY: AIHA, 1987. 9–11.

————. *Modern Canadian Stories.* Toronto: Ryerson Press, 1966.

————. *Moliseide.* Campobasso, Italy: Edizioni Enne, 1990.

————. *Original Sin.* Trans. Ben Johnson, Jr. New York: Random House, 1957.

————. *Peccato originale.* Milan: Mondadori, 1954.

————. *Tiro al piccione.* 1953. Turin: Einaudi, 1991.

————. *Tragica America.* Genoa: Immordino, 1968.

————. *Una posizione sociale.* Florence, Italy: Vallechi, 1959.

Romano, Rose, ed. *La bella figura: A choice.* San Francisco: malafemmina press, 1993.

Stortoni, Laura. "A Borrowed Tongue." *Voices in Italian Americana* 2.2 (1991): 125.

————. "Red Geraniums." *Voices in Italian Americana* 3.2 (1992): 113.

Tucci, Niccolo. *Before My Time.* New York: Simon and Schuster, 1962.

————. *The Unfinished Funeral.* New York: Simon and Schuster, 1964.

Tusiani, Joseph. *Envoy from Heaven.* New York: Obolensky, 1965.

————. *Gente Mia.* Stone Park, IL: Italian Cultural Center, 1978.

————. *La parola antica.* Fasano di Puglia: Schena Editore, 1992.

————. *La parola difficile.* Fasano di Puglia: Schena Editore, 1989.

————. *La parola nuova.* Fasano di Puglia: Schena Editore, 1992.

————. "Two Languages, Two Lands, Perhaps Two Souls." *Italian Ethnics: Their Languages, Literature and Lives.* Proceedings of the 20th Annual Conference of the American Italian Historical Association. Ed. Dominic Candeloro et al. Staten Island, NY: AIHA, 1987. 1–8.

Valesio, Paolo. "Il viso." "The Face in the Mirror." *VIA* 2.2 (1991): 137–154.

————. "The Writer between Two Worlds: Italian Writing in the United States Today." *Differentia* 3–4 (Spring–Autumn 1989): 259–276.

Vivante, Arturo. *Doctor Giovanni.* Boston: Little, 1969.

————. *The French Girls of Killini.* Boston: Little, 1967.

————. *A Goodly Babe.* Boston: Little, 1966.

SELECTED SECONDARY BIBLIOGRAPHY

Alfonsi, Ferdinando, ed. *Dictionary of Italian/American Poets.* New York: Peter Lang, 1989.

————. *Poesia Italo-Americana: Italian/American Poetry, Essays and Texts.* Catanzaro: Antonio Carello Editore, 1991.

Ballerini, Luigi, and Fredi Chiappelli. "Contributi espressive delle scritture e parlate Americo-Italianie." *Atti di convegni Lincei.* Rome: Accademia Nazionale dei Lincei, 1985. 195–218.

Boelhower, William. *Immigrant Autobiography in the United States.* Verona, Italy: Essedue Edizioni, 1982.

————. *Through a Glass Darkly: Ethnic Semiosis in American Literature.* New York: Oxford University Press, 1987.

Burgess, Anthony. "Alien. Poems. (1964–1970)." *Misure critiche. Su/Per Rimanelli: Studi e Testimonianze* 17–18. 65–67 (1987–1988): 244–245.

Caroli, Betty Boyd. "Italian Women in America: Sources for Study." *Italian/Americana* 2.2 (1976): 242–251.

Gardaphe, Fred L. "From Oral Tradition to Written Word: Toward an Ethnographically Based Literary Criticism." *From the Margin: Writings in Italian Americana.* Ed. Anthony Tamburri et al. West Lafayette, IN: Purdue University Press, 1991. 294–306.

————. "Giose Rimanelli: New Directions of a Literary Missionary." *Misure critiche. Su/Per Rimanelli: Studi e Testimonianze* 17–18.65–67 (1987–1988): 235–243.

————. "Italian Signs, American Streets: Cultural Representation in Italian/American Narrative Literature." Diss., University of Illinois at Chicago, 1993. Ann Arbor: UMI, 1994.

————. *Italian Signs, American Streets: The Evolution of Italian American Literature.* Durham, NC: Duke University Press, 1996.

————. "Parody at the Border." Preface to *Benedetta in Guysterland.* Montreal: Guernica Editions, 1993. 11–23.

————. "Pietro Corsi's Chronicle of Rebirth." *Italian Canadiana* 8 (1992): 30–39.

Giordano, Paolo A. "Da italiano del Sud ad Americano riluttante: *Gente Mia and Other Poems* di Joseph Tusiani." *Campi Immaginabili* 1–2 (1991): 91–109.

————. "From Southern Italian Emigrant to Reluctant American: Joseph Tusiani's *Gente Me and Other Poems.*" *From the Margin: Writings in Italian Americana.* Ed. Anthony Tamburri et al. West Lafayette, IN: Purdue University Press, 1991. 316–328.

————. "Images of American Columbus in Italian/American Literature." *Annali italianistica* 10 (1992): 280–296.

————. "Tusiani Explores Lives of Italian Immigrants." *Fra Noi* (November 1987): 25+.

————. "The Writer Suspended between Two Worlds: Joseph Tusiani's 'Autobiografia di un Italo-Americano.' " *Differentia* 6–7 (Spring–Autumn 1994): 297–310.

Green, Rose Basile. "Recent Italian Immigrant Writers." *The Italian/American Novel.* Cranbury, NJ: Associated UP, 1974. 211–223.

Hobbie, Margaret, comp. *Italian/American Material Culture.* Westport, CT: Greenwood Publishing Group, 1992.

Mangione, Jerre, and Ben Morreale. *La Storia.* New York: HarperCollins, 1992.

Minni, C. Dino, and Anna Foschi Ciampolini, eds. *Writers in Transition: The Proceedings of the First National Conference of Italian-Canadian Writers.* Montreal: Guernica, 1990.

Peragallo, Olga. *Italian/American Authors and Their Contribution to American Literature.* New York: S. F. Vanni, 1949.

Perin, Roberto, and Franc Sturino, eds. *Arrangiarsi: The Italian Immigration Experience in Canada.* Montreal: Guernica, 1992.

Pivato, Joseph, ed. *Contrasts: Comparative Essays on Italian-Canadian Writing.* Montreal: Guernica, 1991.

Tamburri, Anthony. "From *Simulazione di reato* to *Round Trip:* The Poetry of Luigi Fontanella." *Voices in Italian Americana* 3.2 (1992): 125–134.

Tamburri, Anthony Julian, Paolo A. Giordano, and Fred L. Gardaphe, eds. *From the Margin: Writings in Italian Americana.* West Lafayette, IN: Purdue University Press, 1991.

Valesio, Paolo. "The Writer between Two Worlds: Italian Writing in the United States Today." *Differentia* 3–4 (Spring–Autumn 1989): 259–276.

18

Jewish-American Literature
Mark Krupnick

INTRODUCTION

Jewish writing in America is hardly one of the newer immigrant literatures. It goes all the way back to the 1890s, when William Dean Howells, then the reigning dean of American letters, hailed the emergence of Jewish immigrant writing in the work of Abraham Cahan. Cahan, the founding editor of the Yiddish-language newspaper the *Jewish Daily Forward,* went on to publish *The Rise of David Levinsky* (1917), a novel that established some of the main themes of subsequent Jewish-American writing. *David Levinsky* is about a poor East European immigrant who becomes a wealthy garment manufacturer but worries that acculturation and material success have cost more than they are worth emotionally and spiritually. *The Price,* the title of a 1968 play by a later Jewish writer, Arthur Miller, sums up a major preoccupation of Jewish writing from the time of Cahan to our own. The question of Jewish-American identity, which is more broadly the question of the fate of Jewishness in America, has continued to be the grand theme of this body of work.

Since Cahan, that worry has often been expressed in Jewish writing that is confessedly or obliquely autobiographical. At first, Jewish writers were limited to autobiographical material because American anti-Semitism excluded them from the wider life of America. They had little access to the social institutions and milieux that provided the setting and subjects of older-stock American writers. For example, no Jewish writer of the 1920s could have written a mainstream novel about the price of success in America like Scott Fitzgerald's *The Great Gatsby* (1925).

The radical politics of the 1930s seemed to promise an exit from Jewish parochialism. Certainly the left-wing movement was more open to Jewish writers and intellectuals than had been the universities, banks, clubs, and other institutions of mainstream Gentile culture. But the subject matter of Jewish fiction continued to be closely attached to the personal life histories of its creators, as it is now. Take, for example, Henry Roth's first novel, *Call It Sleep* (1934). Here the writer, not yet thirty, closely followed his fictional alter ego, David Schearl, to the age of eight. But what might have been a claustrophobic account of a deeply neurotic immigrant family is redeemed by Roth's linguistic virtuosity, which involves a blending of New York street English and transliteration of the Yiddish spoken at home by the Schearls.

Call It Sleep is possibly the most accomplished work of fiction by a Jewish-American writer. Yet it remains a sport, for Roth published no new novel during the next sixty years. Before his demise in 1995, however, he released the first volume of a sequel, *Mercy of a Rude Stream,* a projected six-volume autobiographical novel that intended to take up Roth's life where he had left off so many decades before. Another autobiographically based first novel is *The Unpossessed* (1934), Tess Slesinger's satire on a group of would-be leftists in their twenties and thirties. Like Roth, Slesinger adapted the stream-of-consciousness technique made popular by James Joyce's *Ulysses,* this time to register a woman's disillusionment about men possessed neither by genuine political faith nor by unambivalent sexual passion. Because these men are not possessed, neither are Slesinger's two main women characters, each of whom is based on the author herself. One of the women, Missus Flinders, is pressured to have an abortion; the other, Elizabeth, is allowed to persist in emotional self-destructiveness by the one man who could save her. The Jewish immigrant angle is that the inability of Slesinger's characters to find themselves is owing to their in-between identities, alienated from their respectable immigrant parents, on one hand, and not accepted in mainstream American society, on the other. One other representative body of work of the 1930s that is founded on relatively narrow autobiographical experience is the dramatic writing of Clifford Odets, who, in plays like *Waiting for Lefty* (1935), brought together the familiar post-immigrant themes of radical activism and personal liberation.

LITERARY-CULTURAL HISTORY

All three of these representative figures of the 1930s wrote New York stories. Through the 1950s, Jewish writing in America was the work mainly of the children of immigrants who had settled in big cities, notably, New York and Chicago; who usually spoke Yiddish at home; and who lived according to roughly the same (lower-middle-class) social conventions and customs. For these reasons Irving Howe, the primary historian of the Jewish writing of his generation (City College of New York class of 1940), regarded Jewish writing as a regional literature, a literature of local color, comparable with the southern writing (William Faulkner and his progeny) that first flowered in the 1920s.

Southern writing, of course, grew out of an old-stock American, rather than an immigrant, culture. It is like an immigrant literature, however, in detailing the disintegration of traditional values and ways of life. The southern writers' detestation of the "New South" has elements in common with the Jewish writers' ambivalence toward Americanization. The fear in both cases is of losing one's identity in the amorphous, homogenizing melting-pot culture of an early twentieth-century mass society with little respect for the past.

It is true that Jewish-American writing first emerged under the auspices of the political Left—Roth, Slesinger, and Odets were all caught up in the communist movement in the 1930s. But Jewish writing did not come into its own until after 1945, and then as a tragic literature suffused with the experience of suffering and defeat, like southern writing after the Civil War. It should be added, however, that, tragic as were their themes, the major Jewish writers— like Faulkner before them—often did their best work in the comic mode.

The comic mode defends against despair in this writing, but it owes something, also, to the distance of the Jewish writers from what they were writing about. The irony in post-war Jewish-American writing emerges from the pained awareness of these authors that their rise and that of American Jews generally were occurring at the same time as the extermination of Europe's Jews. But ironic distance had other causes as well. Irving Howe stresses the belatedness of the Jewish-American cultural flowering. It came at the end of the immigrant experience, at the end of the radical experience, at the end of the literary-cultural movement known as modernism.

Hegel said that the owl of minerva flies by night. Breakup and disintegration liberated Jewish literary self-consciousness. The anti-immigration legislation of the early 1920s put an end to the flood of newcomers from East Europe. The ban on immigration, together with Hitler's murder of the Jews trapped in Poland and the Soviet Union, hastened another death, that of Yiddish as a living language. Saul Bellow's translation from the Yiddish of Isaac Bashevis Singer's "Gimpel the Fool" launched that great Yiddish writer as a major literary presence in America. But around the same time as Bellow was translating Singer, he was also writing the novel that first brought *him* to general attention, *The Adventures of Augie March* (1953). Augie is a larky Jewish-American Huck Finn out of Chicago, and he was not the only avatar of Mark Twain's archetypally American hero in Jewish novels of the 1950s.

J. D. Salinger is not usually considered a "Jewish" writer because neither his characters nor his themes insist on their Jewishness. But Salinger's Holden Caulfield, the vulnerable central consciousness of *The Catcher in the Rye* (1951), is another version of Huck. Salinger, who went on to tell the stories of the no less vulnerable members of the Glass family, was participating in the same post-immigrant generational trend as Bellow. Salinger was announcing, in his own way, with characters from New York's Central Park West rather than the downscale Chicago West Side of Bellow, his arrival as an American, a child of Mark Twain rather than Sholom Aleichem.

The comedy tended to be bittersweet. One of the best examples is Cynthia Ozick's "Envy; or, Yiddish in America" (1969), which is about an old, neglected Jewish poet committed, heartbreakingly, to Yiddish, the *mamaloshen* (mother tongue) fated for death. This remarkable story holds out against the gloomy end that it envisages for Yiddish by being told in an English inflected by the rhythms of the East European Jewish masters. Yiddish may be dying, but it also remains a ghostly presence in Bernard Malamud's short stories, in the curious amalgam of Yiddish and university-refined English in Bellow, and even in the work of a younger writer, Steve Stern. In *Lazar Malkin Enters Heaven* (1986), Stern brings Yiddish myth and fable to unlikely material, the magical life of "the Pinch," the Jewish section of Memphis, Tennessee. Allowances made, however, the culture of *Yiddishkeit* has in the main become, for most American Jewish writers, only the memory of a memory. The classic eulogy for this lost immigrant culture is Irving Howe's masterwork, *World of Our Fathers* (1976).

THE NEW YORK INTELLECTUALS

The collapse of the radical political movement after 1945 was no less crucial for Jewish writers than the decline of the culture of *Yiddishkeit*. Jewish intellectuals were among the first Americans to be inspired by the Bolshevik revolution in Russia. Writers like Mike Gold and Joseph Freeman were active in the communist movement from the 1920s on, but these communist polemicists and functionaries are not most important for the history of Jewish writing in America. If Gold and Freeman were early in signing on with communism, so were other, slightly younger Jewish intellectuals among the first to declare their disillusionment and become, in Gold's unforgiving view, "apostates."

These early ex-communists and other anticommunists who arrived on the scene somewhat later include figures who have come to be known as the New York Intellectuals, among them Lionel Trilling, Philip Rahv, Alfred Kazin, Meyer Schapiro, Leslie Fiedler, Clement Greenberg, Harold Rosenberg, Daniel Bell, Irving Kristol, and Howe. Many of these writers started out in the 1930s, but none gained a national reputation until after 1945. These intellectuals and many others whose works appeared in the first years of *Partisan Review* (1937–) and *Commentary* (1945–) were primarily essayists and critics, not poets and novelists. But they, too, are part of Jewish-American "literature," if we allow that word the larger signification it has come to have in recent years.

Indeed, I would argue that the critical essay, rather than the lyrical poem or novel, has been the most important genre of Jewish writing in America. The children of the immigrants were drawn to criticism for a variety of reasons, including, no doubt, a residual Jewish distrust of original artistic composition as inevitably idolatrous. A writer might no longer believe in the Jewish God without having freed himself from ancient Jewish prohibitions, and a certain residual Jewish awe in the face of the Book may account, in part, for the Jewish-American preference for collections of essays to writing full-length studies.

But the major factors in explaining the Jewish specialization in criticism are political and intellectual. First, the corruption of socialism in Stalin's Soviet Union led to the collapse of the secular political faith that had itself replaced Judaism during the seedtime of many of the intellectuals. The communist "god that failed" occasioned a massive rethinking. That rethinking might take the form of a major treatise, like Hannah Arendt's *Origins of Totalitarianism* (1951). More frequently, that rethinking informed essays that aimed only to refract facets of a situation, that disowned the totalizing (and totalitarian) explanations of ideology. Having been burned by a totalizing substitute faith, Jewish intellectuals turned to the essay as a form that encouraged tentative forays as against philosophic system building. This is true even of Sidney Hook, the major philosopher of the group. We see a similar resort to the fragment, the aphorism, the short dash instead of the marathon run, in German-Jewish contemporaries like Walter Benjamin (in his *Illuminations*) and Theodor Adorno (most notably in *Minima Moralia*).

Another comparison suggests itself. One thinks of the skeptical Montaigne and his search for self-knowledge in the *Essais*. There is a link between the essay form that Jewish-American intellectuals favored and the autobiographical mode of Montaigne. It is striking how many of the New York Intellectuals essayed the memoir form or even spiritual autobiography. The major instance of the latter is Alfred Kazin's trilogy *A Walker in the City* (1951), *Starting Out in the Thirties* (1965), and *New York Jew* (1978). It is likely that Kazin's frequently eloquent self-writing will long outlast his work in literary criticism.

The autobiographical self-reflectiveness of the New York Intellectuals is inseparable from their deep commitment to literature and the visual arts. They were political writers but not specialists in political theory. A later cohort, including Daniel Bell and Irving Kristol, were mainly interested in social issues and policy, but the earlier group (including Trilling, Rahv, Greenberg, and Schapiro) were literary critics or art historians. Their most characteristic work is influenced by the question of Marxism and anti-Marxism, but the love of literature, art, and culture makes their writing considerably more than ephemeral political journalism.

In view of the contemporary currency of pop-culture studies, which really get under way with the much-read essays in the 1960s by yet another Jewish intellectual, Susan Sontag, it's important to underline the intransigent high-culture elitism of the earlier cohorts. The skeptical, high-culture stance of the New York Intellectuals owes something to the deep respect of the immigrant generation for secular sages like Tolstoi and Dostoevsky. It was also influenced by what I have described as their in-between status, "alienated" (a favorite word of theirs) from middlebrow American culture both in its WASP forms and in the form of middlebrow Jewish literary culture. The latter is represented by writers like Leon Uris, Irwin Shaw, and Budd Schulberg, popular novelists who also wrote for the movies. This is not the place for an account of Jewish involvement in the movie industry and later television. Suffice it to say that Jewish dreams and notions (especially of America) in the mass media have had an incomparably greater influence on the general culture than the critical writing of Jewish high-culture intellectuals.

MAJOR AUTHORS

The most accomplished of the Jewish writers who deal with post-immigrant themes are Bernard Malamud, Saul Bellow, and Philip Roth. These three have been bracketed for nearly thirty years, causing Bellow to complain about being locked in what he disparages as a journalistic version of Hart Schaffner & Marx, the clothing manufacturers. As always, Bellow has been restive about being labeled. With some reason, he has felt, especially in earlier years, that he was being ghettoized. The fact, however, is that this troika, notwithstanding differences of style and sensibility, has shared some central themes and dispositions. These have to do with a certain social history that we describe in shorthand as "the immigrant experience."

Malamud was born in 1914 but came to attention as a Jewish writer only with *The Assistant* (1957), a drably realistic story of a poor Jewish grocer, his daughter, and his Italian assistant. Even here, however, Malamud's primary feeling for fairy tale and folk legend is as important as his realistic depiction of Jews without money. During the early 1950s, Malamud was also writing short stories, and in these stories, beginning with his collection *The Magic Barrel* (1957), he found his form. The reading public focused on Malamud's themes of Jewish suffering and conscience, but his fiction may ultimately be remembered most for the way, especially in the short stories, he fused Isaac Bashevis Singer and Nathaniel Hawthorne in a new, Yiddish-inflected version of the American romance. Malamud's continuing interest in the merger of Yiddish folktale and American fable is evident in his most directly autobiographical work, *A New Life* (1961), about the encounter of a broken-down Jewish writer from New York and his innocently philistine academic colleagues at a less than arcadian "cow college" in the Pacific Northwest. From the point of view of immigrant writing, Malamud represents the Jewish literary attempt to hold onto the older Yiddish consciousness even while claiming the legacy of Hawthorne, Henry James, and their American successors. His autobiographical effort to be true to both terms of his Jewish Americanness makes of Malamud's literary career a great cultural-spiritual drama.

A year younger than Malamud, Bellow got off to an earlier start with *Dangling Man* (1944) and *The Victim* (1947), the latter a claustrophobic drama of anti-Semite and Jew. But despite Bellow's early fame, not until *Herzog* (1964) did he really hit his stride. Here, in a novel made up of countless unsent letters, an out-of-work, recently cuckolded academic reflects on his own private disasters amid the disasters of modern history. This was the first novel in which Bellow created a hero as intelligent and learned as himself, a hero beset by problems not very different from those that had afflicted Bellow himself in the preceding decade.

Writing frankly about an intellectual, albeit an intellectual skeptical about the powers of thought, liberated Bellow's talent and established him in the public mind as a Jewish wisdom figure. But it hasn't always been clear, in critical commentary on Bellow, what his Jewishness is supposed to consist of. Isolated and disoriented, Moses Herzog longs for "a politics in the Aristotelian sense." What he misses is community, the community, to be specific, of the lost immigrant world. This central theme of loss may be related to the pervasive discomfort of once-radical Jewish writers in the post-radical, privatized 1950s. But Bellow was never primarily a political man or even a member of groups, and what his hero laments is not so much the breakup of the old-left intellectual community as something deeper, more encompassing. Herzog suffers from the attenuation of emotional bonds in modern-day America. Hence his melancholy nostalgia for his illustrious dead. Some of Bellow's best writing is contained in Herzog's recall of a better time, when he was a little boy in a struggling Jewish family living on Napoleon Street in Montreal. The immigrant world was sorely beset, but Bellow has more and more made clear his preference for the warmth and loyalties of what he calls "the old system" of the immigrants to the ambiguous rewards of what came later.

Philip Roth, who was born some twenty years later than Malamud and Bellow, is the last of the triumvirate. Like Bellow, Roth is an accomplished essayist, and, in a number of essays he published in the early 1960s, he sought to separate himself from his erstwhile father figures. I am not a Jewish sage, Roth announced; I am a Jewish freak. The idea was to identify with the Jewish stand-up comedian Lenny Bruce rather than with the Jewish wisdom tradition.

Freakishness or freakiness was a positive in the radical 1960s, which found its voice in a generational rebellion against the conservative cultural synthesis of the preceding decade. For a young Jewish novelist, rebellion took the form of *épater le rabbi,* there being many rabbis of culture (Bellow, Trilling, Rahv the Marxist rabbi, and others) to rebel against. Roth's breakthrough novel was *Portnoy's Complaint* (1969), a parody of Jewish family life, which had been a staple theme of Jewish-American fiction from the time of Anzia Yezierska and Henry Roth to that of Delmore Schwartz and Bellow. What especially outraged Philip Roth's respectable literary elders was the flamboyant hedonism of Alexander Portnoy. Older readers understood Portnoy's story as a call to desublimation or, as Roth more colorfully phrased it, "putting the Id back in Yid."

In actuality, Roth has been the most austere of supposed libertines. His chief literary influences have included Kafka, the hunger artist, and Henry James, the self-abnegating priest of the religion of art. Like Norman Mailer in an earlier Jewish cohort, Roth has not wanted to appear as a tame Jewish humanist, a version of "the nice Jewish boy." But in his recent writing, especially in directly autobiographical works (*The Facts* and *Patrimony*), Roth appears as nothing if not the good Jewish son.

Roth's complicated modulations in his nonfictional memoirs and his autobiographical fictions reveal the persistence in Jewish post-immigrant writing of the theme of personal identity. Whereas Bellow has seemed to identify Jewishness with the "old system" of family loyalties and a moral code that is explicitly Jewish, Roth has, in the past decade, defined his Jewishness minimally, as a sense of difference that remains after everything else—Jewish family ties, nationality, religion, and so on—has atrophied or been exorcised. A negative view of Roth argues that his self-bemusement (or, more precisely, his absorption in his fictional not-quite-self Nathan Zuckerman) demonstrates the exhaustion in his work of what had hitherto provided the interest of Jewish-American fiction: the immigrant experience, the radical tradition, literary modernism. A more positive view, my own, points to the energy with which Roth explores the literary possibilities of his existential impasse.

Roth has been the most honored Jewish novelist in the generation that followed Malamud and Bellow, but he has hardly been alone. A culture that celebrated its writers as much as its television anchorpersons would also honor, among those older than Roth, Joseph Heller, Herbert Gold, and Wallace Markfield; among his contemporaries, Stanley Elkin, Leonard Michaels, and Chaim Potok; and in a younger cohort, Mark Helprin, Max Apple, and Ethan Canin.

MODES OF RETURN

One major trend in Jewish-American writing of the past quarter century has been the retrieval of traditional Jewish forms and topics. If the writers of the 1930s and 1940s were bent on escape, the most recent generation has been committed to a return. One need only compare two representative autobiographies. First, consider Norman Podhoretz's *Making It* (1967), a final paean to the success ethic that had driven the parvenu heroes of so many middlebrow Jewish novels of the 1940s. An autobiography that reverses Podhoretz's priorities and speaks to the new mood is Paul Cowan's *An Orphan in History: Retrieving a Jewish Legacy* (1982). Whereas Podhoretz celebrates his arrival as an American, recounting his progress from Brooklyn provincialism to Manhattan and its fields of light, Cowan describes what in a previous memoir he had called "the making of an un-American." Cowan celebrates his escape from the fashionable Park Avenue world of his highly assimilated parents and his retrieval of Judaism, his family's repressed Jewish past, and a mode of existence founded, at least in part, on the communal ethos of the old East European shtetl. By the journey's end—he died of leukemia, at age forty-eight—Cowan the orphan had become spiritual father and adviser to a growing community of young Jews on the Upper West Side of New York who were similarly determined to recapture the Jewish past.

The other major trend of recent years complements this orientation to retrieval: the increasingly important phenomenon of the emergence of talented Jewish women writers, who have created a new Jewish writing founded not on sociological themes but on specifically Jewish ideas. The most important exemplar of this turn is Cynthia Ozick. In a groundbreaking collection of essays, *Art and Ardor* (1983), Ozick called for a Jewish writing less absorbed in the surfaces of daily life—she had in mind the lox and bagels school of Jewish suburban nostalgia—than in large questions that have occupied Jewish thinkers through the ages.

Ozick's own great theme has been idolatry, the dubious involvement of creative art in graven images of the divine and in representation generally. She has created an intellectually challenging body of fiction out of her own anxieties about the rightness, for her as a Jew, to be writing fiction at all. As an author of stories, Ozick has not been as prolific or consistently successful as Bellow and Roth, but her hard-hitting essays helped to bring about a sea change in Jewish-American writing at a time, the 1970s, when older Jewish critics were announcing the exhaustion of the movement that had made such an impact twenty years earlier.

Some writing by Jewish women of Ozick's generation, like the feminist poet Adrienne Rich and the post-modernist critic-theorist Susan Sontag, has not been centrally concerned with Jewish themes. More relevant for a discussion of post-immigrant literature are writers like Tillie Olsen, especially in the stories collected in *Tell Me a Riddle* (1961), and Grace Paley, in such story collections as *Enormous Changes at the Last Minute* (1974). Paley's highly autobiographical stories of her fictional surrogate, Faith Darwin, juxtapose aged parents, who live according to the "old system" of decency and decorum, and a daughter, Faith, who loves, and is loved by, them despite the comparative messiness of her life as a divorced mother involved in affairs romantic and political. Other gifted senior Jewish women writers include Norma Rosen, Lore Segal, and Ann Birstein.

But the fusion of women's themes and Judaism is largely the work of more recent writers. A useful sampler is *Writing Our Way Home* (1992), edited by Ted Solotaroff and Nessa Rapoport. The transformation of Jewish-American writing may be suggested by comparing this new anthology with the collection that had heretofore been the standard work in the field, Irving Howe's *Jewish-American Stories* (1977). Howe's collection, of fiction mainly from the 1950s and 1960s, contains twenty-six stories, of which only four are by women (Olsen, Paley, Ozick, and Johanna Kaplan). Although the stories include titles like "No Kaddish for Weinstein" (Woody Allen) and "King Solomon" (Isaac Rosenfeld), few of the contributors show much interest in, or knowledge of, Judaism. The post-immigrant sensibility as we see it in Howe's collection is overwhelmingly secular and liberal.

The Solotaroff-Rapoport collection, on the other hand, features thirteen women among its twenty-four contributors. Many of these stories are concerned with Judaism, not only Jewishness. Rabbis drift in and out of these stories; young American Jews clean the house, polish the silver, bake bread, and cook dinner before sunset to be ready for the Sabbath; and characters invoke non-household Jewish names like the poet Bialik and the sage Rav Soloveichik. Some authors have recourse to ancient models of Hebrew textuality, like midrash; that is, a story may consist in a rewriting or commentary on a familiar Bible story. An example of modern midrash is Ozick's novel *The Messiah of Stockholm* (1985), which is, among other things, a commentary on the fiction of the Polish-Jewish writer Bruno Schulz, author of a lost manuscript entitled *The Messiah.*

One notes also how many of these American stories are set in Israel or have Israeli characters. Like the American economy, Jewish-American writing has gone global. The most original story, by Allegra Goodman, features Cecil Birnbaum, an unemployed American professor of literature who lives in Oxford, England, with his British mathematician wife, Beatrix. Cecil is very up-to-date. He looks after the children and does the housework, wears an abortion rights button on his lapel, and loves the writing of Jacques Derrida. At the same time, he is also an Orthodox Jew who takes pleasure in the structure of Jewish law and jibs when, at his shul, an unworthy congregant is allowed to come up to the Torah. Other stories of Goodman are set in the Jewish community of Hawai'i, where the author grew up.

It does appear that Cynthia Ozick's program for Jewish writing has been in the process of being carried out. Is it possible that the immigrant literature that includes the Napoleon Street section of *Herzog* and a novella like Philip Roth's *Goodbye, Columbus* has now turned into a post-immigrant literature more concerned with religion than with ethnicity? The dilution of the immigrant element would not be surprising. American Jews are by now a well-established, integrated group, not as accepted, perhaps, as the Irish, who have seen one of their own elected president, but certainly no longer marginal.

Still, the consciousness of marginality persists, after its disappearance in actuality. It appears in the writing of previously silenced groups, like Jewish gays and lesbians, among them the poet Irena Klepfisz and the novelist David Leavitt. In general, however, the form that marginality has taken is a self-determined particularism, a rejection of the old idea of Jewish universalism in favor of Jewish specificity. The emergence of Jewish studies in the universities is one by-product. A more directly literary portent has been the feminist activist group that includes Gloria Steinem, Letty Cottin Pogrebin, and Esther (E. M.) Broner. This group has met annually for some years to celebrate a women's-only Passover Seder, for which they have developed a new feminist liturgy without the patriarchal features of the traditional Passover Haggadah.

Broner's curious novel, *A Weave of Women,* reflects this new feminist Judaism. Set in Israel, Broner's novel is about a woman's group that, in addition to providing its members mutual support, is engaged in the creation and enactment of new religious rituals. The members of this group are as varied as the crew of Melville's Pequod. They include European women as well as Americans and

Israelis, and even some women who are not Jewish. The novel is Jewish in its concern for the law and ritual; it is feminist in focusing on the group and having no individual who stands out; and it is archaic, and at the same time modernist, in being told in a language redolent of epic, myth, and folktale.

It would be misleading to emphasize the religious dimension of this new writing. Secular-mindedness remains the norm, among younger Jewish women writers as among the men. One thinks of Cathleen Schine's *Rameau's Niece,* an irreverent send-up of New York intellectual types, and of Rebecca Goldstein's *The Mind-Body Problem* and *The Late-Summer Passion of a Woman of Mind.* Even Allegra Goodman, who draws on substantial Jewish learning, remains more an ethnic than a religious writer. She is basically a satiric observer of manners, in the tradition of Jane Austen. That her fourth- and fifth-generation Jewish-American characters display so odd a mix of traditional Judaic and avant-garde attitudes demonstrates, among other things, a new phase of post-immigrant experience. No longer as stiffly correct as they were fifty years ago, middle-class Jews feel safer now in America. So it's all right to "act Jewish."

That phrase itself points to a problem. Is the new Jewish consciousness mainly a matter of "acting" or of "lifestyle," the now-threadbare term that serves us in place of older, better words like "vocation" or "profession"? A recent book, *Saving Remnants,* answers yes to that question. The authors, Sara Bershtel and Allen Graubard, telegraph their conclusions in the subtitle, *Feeling Jewish in America.* Their view is that selective religious observance, determined by mood rather than tradition, makes feel-good Jews pretty much like other hyphenated Americans, who are often being most conformist when they are being most ethnic. Jewish religious law, as Bershtel and Graubard point out, is not compatible with an off-again, on-again impulse to "feel" Jewish.

Saving Remnants is attuned to the weightlessness of some parts of contemporary Jewish-American experience. But it is too early to pronounce on the fate of Jewishness in America or on the profundity of the changes in Jewish consciousness. It will take many more decades before it becomes clear just what has been the effect on Jewish identity of the Holocaust. Then, too, there is the ongoing drama of Israel. These two epochal historical actualities have brought about changes in self-awareness that make the Jewish experience in America different from that of other immigrant groups. Whether the Jewish sense of "feeling different" will be enough to overcome countervailing trends—accelerating percentages of intermarriage and assimilation, decline of Jewish education, and so on—remains uncertain. But clearly, many gifted writers are engaging with the Jewish past and present in a way that distinguishes them from the merely fashionable and light-minded.

SELECTED PRIMARY BIBLIOGRAPHY

Apple, Max. *The Oranging of America.* New York: Grossman, 1976.

Arendt, Hannah. *The Origins of Totalitarianism.* 1951. New York: Harvest Books, 1973.

Bell, Daniel. *The End of Ideology.* 1960. Chicago: University of Chicago Press, 1982.

Bellow, Saul. *The Adventures of Augie March.* 1953. New York: Viking Penguin, 1984.

Benjamin, Walter. *Illuminations.* 1968. New York: Schocken, 1977.

Birstein, Ann. *Dickie's List.* New York: Coward, 1973.

Broner, E. M. *A Weave of Women.* 1978. Bloomington: University of Indiana Press, 1985.

Cahan, Abraham. *The Rise of David Levinsky.* 1917. New York: Viking Penguin, 1993.

Cowan, Paul. *An Orphan in History: Retrieving a Jewish Legacy.* 1982. New York: Doubleday, 1990.

Elkin, Stanley. *Criers and Kibitzers, Kibitzers and Criers.* New York: Random House, 1966.

Fiedler, Leslie. *Fiedler on the Roof.* Boston: Godine, 1992.

Gold, Herbert. *Fathers.* 1967. New York: D. I. Fine, 1991.

Gold, Michael. *Jews without Money.* 1930. New York: Carroll and Graf, 1984.

Goldstein, Rebecca. *The Mind-Body Problem.* 1983. New York: Dell, 1985.

Goodman, Allegra. *Total Immersion.* New York: Harper and Row, 1989.

Greenberg, Clement. *Collected Essays and Criticism.* Vols. 1–4. Chicago: University of Chicago Press, 1988–1993.

Heller, Joseph. *Catch-22.* 1961. New York: Dell, 1985.

Helprin, Mark. *Ellis Island and Other Stories.* 1981. Harcourt Brace Jovanovich, 1991.

Howe, Irving. *Jewish-American Stories.* New York: New American Library, 1977.

Kaye/Kantrowitz, Melanie, and Irena Klepfisz. *The Tribe of Dina: A Jewish Women's Anthology.* Boston: Beacon Press, 1989.

Kazin, Alfred. *A Walker in the City.* 1951. New York: Harbrace, 1969.

Klepfisz, Irena. *A Few Words in the Mother Tongue: Poems Selected and New.* Portland, OR: Eighth Mountain Press, 1990.

Kristol, Irving. *On the Democratic Idea in America.* New York: Harper and Row, 1972.

Leavitt, David. *Family Dancing.* 1984. New York: Warner Books, 1985.

Malamud, Bernard. *The Stories of Bernard Malamud.* New York: New American Library, 1989.

Markfield, Wallace. *To an Early Grave.* New York: Simon and Schuster, 1964.

Michaels, Leonard. *The Men's Club.* 1981. San Francisco: Mercury House, 1993.

Miller, Arthur. *The Price.* New York: Boulevard, 1968.

Odets, Clifford. *Waiting for Lefty.* 1935. New York: Grove-Atlantic, 1993.

Olsen, Tillie. *Tell Me a Riddle.* 1961. New York: Delta, 1989.

Ozick, Cynthia. *Bloodshed and Three Novellas.* New York: Alfred A. Knopf, 1976.

Paley, Grace. *Collected Stories.* New York: Farrar, Straus, and Giroux, 1994.

Podhoretz, Norman. *Making It.* New York: Random House, 1967.

Potok, Chaim. *The Chosen.* 1967. New York: Fawcett, 1987.

Rahv, Philip. *Essays on Literature and Society.* Boston: Houghton Mifflin, 1978.

Rosen, Norma. *Touching Evil.* 1969. Detroit: Wayne State University Press, 1990.

Rosenberg, Harold. *The Tradition of the New.* 1960. Chicago: University of Chicago Press, 1982.

Rosenfeld, Isaac. *Passage from Home.* 1946. New York: Markus Wiener, 1988.

Roth, Henry. *Call It Sleep.* 1934. New York: Avon Books, 1976.

Roth, Philip. *The Counterlife.* 1986. New York: Viking Penguin, 1989.

Salinger, J. D. *The Catcher in the Rye.* 1951. Boston: Little, Brown, 1991.

Schapiro, Meyer. *Theory and Philosophy of Art.* New York: Braziller, 1994.

Schulberg, Budd. *What Makes Sammy Run?* 1941. New York: Vintage Books, 1993.

Schwartz, Delmore. *In Dreams Begin Responsibilities.* 1938. New York: New Directions, 1978.

Segal, Lore. *Her First American.* New York: Knopf, 1985.

Shaw, Irwin. *The Young Lions.* 1948. New York: Dell, 1984.

Singer, Isaac Bashevis. "Gimpel the Fool." *Jewish American Stories.* Ed. Irving Howe. New York: New American Library, 1977.

Slesinger, Tess. *The Unpossessed.* 1934. New York: Feminist Press, 1984.

Solotaroff, Ted, and Nessa Rapoport, eds. *Writing Our Way Home.* New York: Schocken, 1992.

Sontag, Susan. *Against Interpretation.* 1966. New York: Doubleday, 1990.

Stern, Steve. *Lazar Malkin Enters Heaven.* New York: Viking Penguin, 1986.

Trilling, Lionel. *The Liberal Imagination.* 1950. New York: Harcourt Brace Jovanovich, 1979.

Uris, Leon. *Exodus.* 1958. New York: Bantam Books, 1983.

Yezierska, Anzia. *The Bread Givers.* 1925. New York: Persea, 1975.

SELECTED SECONDARY BIBLIOGRAPHY

Aaron, Daniel. *Writers on the Left: Episodes in American Literary Communism.* 1961. New York: Columbia University Press, 1992.

Alter, Robert. *After the Tradition: Essays on Modern Jewish Writing.* New York: Dutton, 1969.

Baumgarten, Murray. *City Scriptures: Modern Jewish Writing.* Cambridge: Harvard University Press, 1982.

Berger, Alan. *Crisis and Covenant: The Holocaust in American Jewish Fiction.* Albany: State University of New York Press, 1985.

Bershtel, Sara, and Allen Graubard. *Saving Remnants: Feeling Jewish in America.* 1992. Berkeley: University of California Press, 1993.

Finkelstein, Norman. *The Ritual of New Creation: Jewish Tradition and Contemporary Literature.* Albany: SUNY Press, 1992.

Fried, Lewis, ed. *Handbook of American-Jewish Literature.* Westport, CT: Greenwood, 1988.

Howe, Irving. *World of Our Fathers.* 1976. New York: Schocken, 1989.

Klingenstein, Susanne. *Jews in the American Academy: 1900–1940.* New Haven, CT: Yale University Press, 1991.

Kremer, S. Lillian. *Witness through the Imagination: Jewish American Holocaust Literature.* Detroit: Wayne State University Press, 1989.

Krupnick, Mark. *Lionel Trilling and the Fate of Cultural Criticism.* Evanston, IL: Northwestern University Press, 1986.

Nadel, Ira. *Jewish Writers of North America: A Guide to Information Sources.* Detroit: Gale Research, 1981.

Ozick, Cynthia. *Art and Ardor.* New York: Knopf, 1983.

Pinsker, Sanford. *Jewish American Fiction.* New York: Twayne, 1992.

Shapiro, Ann R., ed. *Jewish American Women Writers: A Bio-Bibliographical and Critical Sourcebook.* Westport, CT: Greenwood, 1994.

Shechner, Mark. *After the Revolution: Studies in the Contemporary Jewish-American Imagination.* Bloomington: Indiana University Press, 1987.

Wald, Alan M. *The New York Intellectuals.* Chapel Hill: University of North Carolina Press, 1987.

Walden, Daniel, ed. *Dictionary of Literary Biography, vol. 28: Twentieth-Century American-Jewish Writers.* Detroit: Gale Research, 1984.

Wirth-Nesher, Hana. *City Codes: Reading the Modern Urban Novel.* Cambridge, England: Cambridge University Press, 1995.

Wisse, Ruth. *The Schlemiel as Modern Hero.* Chicago: University of Chicago Press, 1971.

19

Sephardic Jewish-American Literature

Diane Matza

INTRODUCTION

Sephardic Jews have been in the United States for more than 350 years. In the early seventeenth century, the first arrivals were primarily Conversos, unwilling Spanish Jewish converts to Christianity, who practiced Judaic rituals secretly because they were hounded by the Inquisition in Spain and Portugal and who traveled widely, often settling in England, France, and Holland for periods of time and then moving on. The first such Jews came to America during the colonial period, as early as 1623. Primarily traders and entrepreneurs, commercial success characterized their early experiences in the colonies, often providing them entrée into mainstream American life; yet their very small community participated little in the shaping of American literary culture. The first Sephardic American writer, Penina Moise, was a poet known best in her own South Carolina community, and she was followed by the playwright Mordecai Manuel Noah, whose reputation as a statesman far outweighed his fame as a belletrist. By the late nineteenth century the Sephardic poet Emma Lazarus achieved true American stature when her poem ''The New Colossus'' appeared on the base of the Statue of Liberty. Her sister, Josephine Lazarus, also published belles lettres, and her other relations, Annie Nathan Meyer and Robert Nathan, became noted figures in the twentieth century, Meyer as a founder of Barnard College and a playwright and publicist and Nathan as one of the most prolific popular writers of his day. Yet another descendant of this family is Nancy Cardozo Cowles, a poet and biographer of Maud Gonne. Also possessing a long history on American soil is the contemporary writer Lawrence Perreira Spingarn, who traces his ancestry on his father's side to a family derived from Granada, a branch of which settled in the United States in the 1820s, and on his maternal side to Portuguese Jews who arrived in the United States via Holland in 1687.

At the opening of the twentieth century, the American Jewish community changed profoundly in its ethnic makeup, religiosity, and relationship to the adopted nation. The tiny Sephardic community at this time was prominent, largely well-to-do, and fully integrated into American society. While members still proudly discussed their lineage, most had intermarried with one another, with German Jews, or with the Gentile population. Shearith Israel, the largest and one of two oldest Sephardic congregations in the United States, continued to use the Sephardic liturgy, although most members were not Sephardim. Into this community immigrated nearly 50,000 Jews of Sephardic background between 1890 and 1924. They are the primary focus of this chapter.

LITERARY-CULTURAL HISTORY

Coming from numerous small towns and major cities in the Levant, many of these Jews, described as Oriental or Levantine or Turkish by the fully American Sephardim and German Jews, traced their ancestry to Spain and retained the original home language (Judeo-Spanish) as well as the keys to the houses their ancestors had left so reluctantly more than 400 years before. Others in this new immigrant group were Greek-speakers, primarily Romaniot Jews who had resided in Greece long before the sultan invited the expelled Spaniards to his empire in 1492. Also emigrating from the Levant were Syrian Jews, mostly from Aleppo and Damascus, some who did trace their ancestry to Spain but most who did not. For the sake of simplicity, and because this is currently accepted practice, I call all these Jews "Sephardim."

Upon arrival in the United States, the new Sephardim appeared completely foreign to the established Jewish communities in the United States, speaking odd tongues, dressing colorfully, displaying attachments to rituals and beliefs alien to the American Jews' largely assimilated way of life. The Shearith Israel membership did not identify with the newcomers. Finding their religious services undignified, their manners unrefined, their foods and languages strange, the established community shunned integration. Nonetheless, the synagogue sisterhood was active in staffing a Hebrew school for immigrant children on the Lower East Side of Manhattan and in encouraging all immigrants to study English. Also, the synagogue membership supported creation of the Federation of Oriental Jewry—an offshoot of the Hebrew Immigrant Aid Society—to help Americanize the immigrants. Still, the majority of the Sephardic population remained physically isolated (most settled on the Lower East Side and in Brooklyn) and socially distant from the uptown Sephardi community. Separated, too, from the immigrant Ashkenazi community because they spoke no Yiddish, Sephardim found themselves largely on their own, hence settling into the new land in much the same way the Italians and Poles and Lebanese did: establishing religious and social institutions similar to those they had known at home, trying to find work comparable to what they had performed before and with a boss of the same ethnic background, marrying among their own, saving money to send home or to pay steerage passage for family members, learning English on the job and in the street.

A small number of Sephardic immigrants possessed job skills and education, but most were unskilled and often illiterate. Given this and the small numbers of the group, it is remarkable that they published their own newspapers (*La America* and *La Vara,* the two best known in New York, and *The Progress* in Seattle) and meagerly supported local theater groups and playwrights. Wherever they settled, Sephardim continued to tell the *romanzas* and sing the ballads they'd learned as children, and much of this material has been collected by second-generation foreign-language scholars. Clearly, the Sephardim were interested in culture, although the immigrants' efforts to preserve it were rarely formal, and their self-perception did not include a sense of themselves as artists or writers. To write about themselves and their experiences and to see themselves as contributing in a new way to American literature were not possible for them.

EARLY AND RECENT EFFORTS

Among the first-generation Sephardim to emigrate between 1880 and 1924, only one wrote an autobiography, the largely nostalgic post-World War II memoir of a destroyed culture, *Farewell to Salonika* by Leon Sciaky. The immigrant coming-of-age in American memoir, made so distinct a form by such East European Jews as Mary Antin and Marcus Ravage, does not exist in the Sephardic literature. A woman who might have written such a book, an emigrant at age five from Yanina (Joannina), was Rae Dalven, whose brief memoir, ''The Gold Chain,'' beautifully evokes tension between love for the past and rejection of it and perhaps explains why she never wrote more of her own past. Rae spent most of her life as a teacher of classics, translator of modern Greek poetry, and recorder of Yanioti history.

Recent creative work by Sephardic writers is varied in form, content, theme, and relation to Jewishness. The best of this work is as rich, complex and compelling as any in American literature, but it generally has a small critical and popular audience. For the work that is strongly flavored with Sephardism, the fiction of Ruth Knafo Setton, Gloria L. Kirchheimer, and Stanley Sultan, a perception of it as exotic may explain size of readership. This work has rarely been anthologized in collections of ethnic literature, although the surge of interest in microliteratures in the last fifteen years has perhaps been the impetus behind their inclusion in a few American Jewish literature anthologies. That several Sephardic writers are poets also determines the size of their audience; as we know, this genre is the least read by the American public. In addition, the Sephardim's belles lettres have been self-published, by small presses and in little magazines. No work to date displays the imprimatur of a major publishing house, and limited circulation may account for the short publishing history of *Adelantre,* Stephen Levy's Sephardi journal of the 1970s. While a part of Levy's purpose, to promote interest and development of Judeo-Spanish, was similar to the Ashkenazi promotion of Yiddish, Levy was far less successful than Irving Howe, for example, who had a well-known name, a strong connection to academe and mainstream publishers, and a much larger audience. It is interesting to note, however, that several writers I discuss here have achieved wide readership through their critical scholarship. For example, Stanley Sultan is a highly respected writer on James Joyce; Ammiel Alcalay's recent *After Jews and Arabs* has received much critical attention; and Michael Castro's *Interpreting the Indian: Twentieth Century Poets and the Native American* is a seminal work in that field.

DOMINANT CONCERNS

I have argued elsewhere ("Tradition and History: American Writers of Sephardic Background") that themes of tradition and history are particularly important for writers of Sephardic background, but beyond this, their work reveals no shared moral perspective or religious code. Some of the work has no discernible ethnic or religious content at all, although it is more common that these writers' domain straddles two worlds—a Sephardic one as well as an American or internationalist one. Nonetheless, it is possible to define some of the significant issues for the Sephardi writer. First, the Sephardi writer often conveys a strong sense of the culture, delineating the intersection among color, rhythm, and ritual and behavior, belief, and attitude. We can see this operating in a documentary-style historical novel such as David Raphael's *The Alhambra Decree,* which chronicles in great detail the Spanish Inquisition while offering passages depicting the prayer style of the Sephardim, their foods, their music, and their holiday rituals. Stanley Sultan's story "Ba'lawa" opens with the protagonist's preparing the traditional Syrian sweet as she contemplates the traditional filial duty of her Americanized and unmarried son. Similarly, in Gloria L. Kirchheimer's "A Case of Dementia," a daughter performs an evil eye exorcism on her mother, dramatizing the tension between one's cultural past and a shifting present.

Tension between traditional and modern practices also characterizes a second concern, gender relations. Ruth Knafo Setton's "Street of the Whores" examines the protagonist's responses to stereotypes of her as a Moroccan Jew and as a woman. Stanley Sultan's *Rabbi* and several stories by Gloria L. Kirchheimer also explore women's roles in the Sephardic and American cultures, not merely by questioning traditional expectations of women but—especially in Sultan's case—by positioning women characters within a moral debate and allowing them a voice often denied them historically.

A third significant theme is identification with the suffering of others, a powerful force particularly in the work of Rosaly De Maios Roffman, David Altabe, and Ammiel Alcalay. These are well-traveled poets, scholars in numerous literatures—Spanish, Hebrew, Japanese, Serbo-Croatian, and so on—and Altabe and Alcalay are both translators. Their poems infrequently confront the American experience but often address or allude to issues of international scope. For example, Roffman's "Sometimes people think" shows the poet's recognizing that images of contemporary human horrors immediately remind her of the Holocaust. In addition, Alcalay is at the forefront of the artistic movement to widen world understanding of the tragedy in the former Yugoslavia. To this end, he has edited a special issue of the journal *Lusitania* and Zlatko Dizdarevic's *Sarajevo, A War Journal.*

Given the prominence of the Holocaust in the Jews' twentieth-century history, it is not surprising that memory, history, sense of place, loss, and exile are a fourth issue pervasive in many works by Sephardic writers, though in quite different ways. Sciaky's *Farewell to Salonika,* written at the close of World War II, captures and preserves a pre-World War I world swathed in tradition but on the brink of enormous and violent changes. In America in 1946 Sciaky no longer hears ancestral voices pulling him toward a traditional life; he hears primarily the desire for freedom and peace expressed by the warring and innocent nationalities of a disintegrating empire. Ruth Knafo Setton's "Pieds Noirs" effectively reveals how folklore and ethnicity haunt children who have been encouraged to hide their identity. Alcalay's spectacular poem "I Had Thought of Writing a Play Based on the Following Facts" presents the complexities of national identity as well as the contemporary world's destruction of the past. Further, how the immigrant's memories of the old country's people, values, and assumptions shape his or her experience of America is one subject of Stanley Sultan's *Rabbi,* Gloria L. Kirchheimer's "Two Stories," and several poems by Stephen Levy. One more example is Sarah Melhado White, who is half Sephardic and who suggests that Jewish history informs the fragmented world depicted in many of her tales.

A fifth theme for Sephardic writers is multiple identity, first sounded in *Farewell to Salonika* as Sciaky detailed the impact on him of Sephardic and Islamic culture. Herbert Hadad's memoir pieces, Jordan Elgrably's soon-to-be-finished novel, and Ammiel Alcalay's poetry all explore the pleasures and dilemmas faced by those with hearts and minds embedded in more than one culture.

CONCLUSION

Offering a glimpse into a rich Jewish culture different from the widely known Eastern European one, the literature of twentieth-century American Sephardim deserves further attention. Much work by Sephardim also resonates with figures, attitudes toward ritual and the past, social and ideological concerns that are part of the fabric of American life. The best of it combines an emphasis on concrete and intimate detail and a concern with universal human issues.

SELECTED PRIMARY BIBLIOGRAPHY

Alcalay, Ammiel. "For Paul Metcalf." *Review of Contemporary Fiction* (Summer 1981): 287.

———. "The Order." *Bad Henry Review* (1981): 26.

———. "The Quill's Embroidery" and "Crescent Tale." *Frank* 1.2 (1984): 76.

———. "Highway Song." *Midstream* 31 (April 1985): 5.

———. "Charles River," "Blues" and "Old Flame." *Sun and Moon* 4 Fall (1987): 90.

———. "I Had Thought of Writing a Play Based on the Following Facts." *Caliban* 4 (1988): 144–147.

———. "For the Old Gang." *Literary Review* 33.4 (1990): 460–462.

———. "Culture without a Country." *Afterimage* 17 (May 1990): 16–17.

———. "In True Colors." *Afterimage* 19 (October 1991): 15.

———. "Atonement." *Grand Street* 10.3 (1991): 39.

———. "Independence Day." *Poetry New York* 4 (1992): 30.

———. *After Jews and Arabs: Remaking Levantine Culture*. Minneapolis: University of Minnesota Press, 1993.

———. *The Cairo Notebooks*. Philadelphia: Singing Horse Press, 1994.

Altabe, David. *Symphony of Love: Las Rimas*. New York: Regina, 1974. (Translation into English verse of Las Rimas de Gustavo Adolf Becquer with an analysis of his poetry and biographical information.)

———. *Chapter and Verse*. New York: Fintzenberg, 1978.

———. "Four Poems of the Holocaust in Judeo-Spanish." *Sephardic Brother* 19 (Spring 1978): 3.

———. "La recherche." *Poesie-U.S.A.* (Summer–Fall 1980): 12.

———. "Coplas por la muerte de mi padre." *La Prensa Israelita* 16 (January 1981): 8.

———. "La orasion de un djudio." *Aki Yerushalayim* 13–14 (April–July 1982): 67.

———. "Kina de Tesha beAv: Lament for the 9th of Av 5742." *Sephardic Scholar* 4 (1982): 133–135.

———. "Noche de shabat." *Aki Yerushalayim: revista de la emission en djudeo-espanyol de Kol Israel-La Boz de Israel* 24–25 (January–April 1985): 40.

———. "Los fijones de Salonik." *Aki Yerushalayim* 40 (January–June 1989): 83.

———. "Los gameyos karos." *Aki Yerushalayim* 40 (January–June 1989): 85.

———. "La Kara es espejo de la alma." *Salom* (Istanbul, Turkey) (June 14, 1989): 5.

———. "La dolor de la parida." *Salom* (June 28, 1989): 5.

———. "Mazal en los kazamientos." *Salom* (July 21, 1989): 5.

———. "Otra Konseja ke me konto mi padre." *Salom* (August 16, 1989): 5.

———. "Homage to Our Turkish Brethren." *Vision Magazine* (March 1991): 15.

Ashear, Linda. *Toward the Light*. New York: Croton Review Press, 1989.

Castro, Michael. *The Kokopilau Cycle*. Marvin, S. D.: Blue Cloud Quarterly Press, 1975.

———. *Ghost Hiways and Other Homes*. Arnold, MS: Cornerstone Press, 1976.

———. "Grandfathers," "Percolating Highway." *Voices within the Ark: Modern Jewish Poetry*. Ed. A. Rudolph and H. Schwartz. New York: Avon, 1980. 436–438.

Dalven, Rae. "The Gold Chain." *Weekly Review Proini* (December 23, 1983): 12–13.

Del Bourgo, David. *Fairfax and Other Poems*. Brea, CA: Quest, 1985.

————. *Composite Things.* Los Angeles: Medina Press, 1991.

Fresco, Sarah. "Carny." *Red Brick Review* (1992): n.p.

Hadad, Herbert. "Both Jewish and Arabic." Editorial. *New York Times,* August 3, 1985.

————. "My Family Reunion." *Northeastern University Magazine* (January 1994): 31–32.

Kirchheimer, Gloria L. "Food of Love." *Follow My Footprints: Changing Images of Women in American Jewish Fiction.* Ed. Sylvia Barack Fishman. Hanover, NH: New England University Press, 411–417.

————. "A Case of Dementia." *North American Review* 269 (March 1984): 10–13.

————. "Two Stories." *Kansas Quarterly* 16. 1–2 (1984): 129–135.

————. "Nona—A Recollection." *Jewish Currents* 38 (November 1984): 33–34.

————. "Talking in Tongues." *Jewish Currents* (April 1991): 31–32.

Levy, Stephen. "Some Sephardic Poems." *Adelantre!* (1975). (In addition to poems this issue contains translations of Ladino proverbs and a poem about the Nazi destruction of the Monastirli Jews: "Snowflakes Falling from the Black Sky," based on Uri Oren's book *A Town Called Monastir.* Copies of *Adelantre!* can be found in the Jewish Division of the New York Public Library on 42nd Street.)

————. "Home Alone These Last Hours of the Afternoon, Dusk Now, the Sabbath Setting In, I Sit Back, and These Words Start Welling Up in Me," "Friday Night after Bathing," "Freely, from a Song Sung by Jewish Women of Yemen," "A Judezmo Writer in Turkey Angry." *Voices within the Ark: Modern Jewish Poetry.* Ed. A. Rudolph and H. Schwartz. New York: Avon, 1980. 522, 523.

Luria, Emile. *Tornado Weather.* Lewiston/Queenston/Lampeter: Mellen Poetry Press, 1993.

Marshall, Jack. *Arabian Nights.* San Francisco: Coffee House Press, 1986.

————. "Thirty-Seven," "Letter to My Father on the Other Side," "The United Way," "The Months of Love," and "Still." *Grape Leaves: A Century of Arab American Poetry.* Ed. Gregory Orfalea and Sharif Elmusa. Salt Lake City: University of Utah Press, 1988. 179–191.

Raphael, David. *The Alhambra Decree.* North Hollywood, CA: Carmi House Press, 1988.

Reyez, Ivanov Yehudi. "Vigil." *Nebula 7: Eros.* Ontario, Canada: Nebula Press, 1978. 60–67.

————. "Gemutlichkeit." *Aileron: A Literary Journal* (1989): 22–23.

————. "Trip." *Gypsy* 17 (1991): 65.

————. "Wet in the Rain." *New Texas 93* (1993): 39.

————. "Tracks." *New Texas 93* (1993): 40.

Roffman, Rosaly De Maios. "Elegy for your dinosaur," "Taps at an Indonesian Rice Table," "Teahouse from Child's Playhouse Building." *Athaena, A Collection of Poetry.* Ed. Paula Rubenstein. 1972.

————. "It's 1985 and Now I'm Reading George Orwell's Poems." *Journal of Popular Literature* (1989): 51–66.

————. "Personals." *Studies in the Humanities* 19 (December 1992): 195.

————. *Going to Bed Whole.* Indiana, PA: University IV Press, 1993.

————. "Notes from the World Congress of Poets." *Pittsburgh Quarterly* (Winter 1993): 11–16.

Roffman, Rosaly De Maios, and Sue Walker, eds. *Life on the Line.* Mobile: Negative Capability Press, 1992.

Sciaky, Leon. *Farewell to Salonika.* New York: Current Books, 1946.

Setton, Ruth Knafo. "Traveling." *Journal of Canadian Fiction* 30 (1980): 37–44.
———. "Pieds Noirs." *Response* (Spring 1989): 61–66.
———. "Street of the Whores." *Follow My Footprints: Changing Images of Women in American Jewish Fiction.* Ed. Sylvia Barack Fishman. Hanover, NH: New England University Press, 1992. 403–410.
———. "Songs from My Mother's House." *Bridges* (Spring 1993): 39–42.
Spingarn, Lawrence P. *Poets West: Poems from the Western States.* Van Nuys, CA: Perivale Press, 1975.
———. *Journey to the Interior and Other Stories.* Van Nuys, CA: Perivale Press, 1992.
Sultan, Stanley. "And Jacob Called." *Epoch* (Spring 1948): 55–60.
———. "Fugue of the Fig Tree." *Kenyon Review* 14.3 (1952): 418–431.
———. "An Early Autumn." *University of Kansas City Review* 21 (March 1955): 192–202.
———. "Feigenbaum and Mary Jane." *Pequod* (Spring 1976): 43–49.
———. "Ba'lawa." *West Branch* (Fall 1977): 28–34.
———. *Rabbi.* West Whately, MA: American Novelists Cooperative, 1977.
———. "The Hills of the Chankly Bore." *A Shout in the Street* (Spring 1979): 170–190.
———. "Free Fire Zone." Brown Review (Spring 1983): 19–23.
Sutton, Joseph. "A Fellow Tribesman." *Cavalcade of Arts* (March 1974): 6–7.
White, Sarah Melhado. "After Louise Labe." *Spirales* 5 (June 1981): 27.
———. "God Creates Eve on a Prayerbook Page." *Chelsea* 40 (1981): 80.
———. "Six Words and Several Flowers." *Village Voice,* August 9, 1983: 38.
———. "Threaded Itineraries." *West Branch* 21–22 (1988): 62.
———. "The Cure of Folly." *Alea* 3 (Fall 1993): 112–121.

SELECTED SECONDARY BIBLIOGRAPHY

Adatto, Albert. "Sephardim and the Seattle Sephardic Community." Master's thesis, University of Washington, 1939.
Angel, Marc. "The Sephardim of the United States: An Exploratory Study." *American Jewish Yearbook* (1973): 77–136.
———. "The Sephardic Theatre of Seattle." *American Jewish Archives* 25 (1973): 156–160.
———. *La America: The Sephardic Experience in the United States.* Philadelphia: Jewish Publication Society, 1982.
Armistead, S. G. and J. A. Silverman. "Hispanic Balladry among Sephardic Jews of the West Coast." *Western Folklore* 19 (1960): 229–244.
Baumgarten, Murray. "Urban Failures, Fictional Possibilities." *Jewish Book Annual* 41 (1983–1984): 6–24.
Benardete, Jose Mair. *Hispanic Culture and the Character of the Sephardic Jews.* New York: Hispanic Institute in the United States, 1953.
Benyunes, J. A. de. "The Sephardic Jews of New York." *American Hebrew* (September 1916): 718–719, 737.
Besso, Henry. "The Character of the Sephardic Jews." *Jewish Quarterly Review* 46 (1956): 299–301.
Bunis, David. *Sephardic Studies: A Research Bibliography.* New York: Garland, 1981.

Cohen, Martin, and Abraham D. Peck, eds. *Sephardim in the Americas.* Tuscaloosa: University of Alabama Press, 1993.

Hacker, Lewis. "The Communal Life of the Sephardic Jews of New York City." *Jewish Social Service Quarterly* (December 1926): 32–40.

Herzberg, Bruce. "Stanley Sultan." *A Critical Survey of Short Fiction.* 7 vols. Ed. Frank N. Magill. Englewood Cliffs, NJ: Salem Press, 1981. Vol 7; 2848.

Hexter, Maurice B. "The Dawn of a Problem." *Jewish Charities* (December 1913): 2.

Lavender, Abraham D., ed. *A Coat of Many Colors.* Westport, CT: Greenwood Press, 1977.

Liptzin, Sol. *The Jew in American Literature.* New York: Bloch, 1966. 25, 151–152.

Matarasso, Albert. "Historique du Sefardisme aux U.S.A." *Les Cahiers Sefardis* (June 1947): 240–244.

Matza, Diane. *"Farewell to Salonika:* The Anomoly of a Sephardic Experience." *MELUS* (Spring 1987): 33–41.

———. "A Bibliography of Materials on the National Background and Immigrant Experiences of the Sephardic Jews in the United States, 1880–1924." *Immigration History Newsletter* 19 (May 1987): 4–9.

———. "Sephardic Jews in America: Why They Don't Write More." *American Jewish Archives* 39 (November 1987): 115–126.

———. "Sephardic Jews Transmitting Culture across Three Generations." *American Jewish History* 79 (Spring 1990): 336–354.

———. "Tradition and History: American Writers of Sephardic Background." *American Jewish Archives* 44 (Spring–Summer 1992): 379–409. Also in *Sephardim in the Americas.* Tuscaloosa: University of Alabama Press, 1993.

Miraglia, Dina Dahbany. "An Analysis of Ethnic Identification among Yemenite Jews in the Greater New York Area." Diss., Columbia University, 1983.

Papo, Joseph. *Sephardim in Twentieth Century America: In Search of Unity.* San Jose, CA: Pele Yoetz Books, 1987.

Pool, David de Sola. "On Spanish Jews of Levantine Origin in the United States." *Jewish Charities* (March 1913): 12–27.

Romey, David. "A Study of Spanish Traditions in Isolation as Found in Romances, Refranes, and Folklore of the Seattle Sephardi Community." Master's thesis, University of Washington, 1950.

Sassoon, S. D. "The Spiritual Heritage of the Sephardim." *Sephardic Heritage.* Ed. R. D. Barnett. New York: KTAV, 1971. 1–28.

Schlesinger, Emma Adatto. "A Study of the Linguistic Character of the Seattle Sephardi Folklore." Master's thesis, University of Washington, 1938.

Stern, Stephen. *The Sephardic Jewish Community of Los Angeles.* New York: Arno Press, 1979.

Sutton, Joseph. *The Magic Carpet: From Aleppo to Flatbush.* New York: Thayer-Jacoby, 1975.

20

Polish-American Literature
Dawn B. Sova

INTRODUCTION

Polish émigré literature is rooted in the experiences of the fiercely independent and nationalistic Polish people who, in various periods of history, have experienced both a flourishing of culture and the complete obliteration of their nation. The literature of Poland has evolved throughout centuries of unrest and severe threats to national identity to become a literature of exiles, even among those writers who have physically remained in their homeland. Latin, the first literary language of Poland, was itself an alien language adopted when Christianity became the dominant religion in tenth-century Poland. As did other European nations of the eleventh century, Poland pushed aside its pre-Christian oral culture, which included lyric poetry in the form of folk ballads and epic poetry containing fables, animal epics, apologues, religious legends, and historical tales, and replaced it with chronicles of the lives of saints, as well as annals and a range of allegorical and historical chronicles, prose sermons, and biblical translations written in Latin.

Although a strong Polish-language literature developed and flourished by the mid-fifteenth century, history decreed that Poles would have to struggle long and hard to maintain the right to their own language, literature, and land. Throughout centuries, a strong national spirit sustained the people and the literature. However the subject and form of this literature might have changed to conform to government dictates, the character of Polish literature remained constant, revealing, even to the present, ''the Poles' passionate sense of nationality, their experience of exile and oppression, their prejudices as well as their love of freedom'' (Gillon and Krzyzanowski 30).

In the period since World War II, these same influences can be seen in émigré writers whose experience with the occupation and the establishment of the Peoples' Republic in 1945 decisively affected the character of their output and fueled their literary anger, as well as in the works of younger émigré writers whose writings reflect the political events of 1968 and the challenges to the government of the 1980s.

As Czeslaw Milosz observes in his essay ''Biblical Heirs and Modern Evils'' in *The History of Polish Literature,* the outlook of post-World War II émigrés is relatively uniform in its regard for freedom. ''No less amazing is the idea that the power of the state should have limits prescribed by law and that nobody should be thrown in prison on the whim of uniformed men. . . . Yet only the experience of living in systems where the individual is at the mercy of the rulers enables one truly to prize democracy, which submits to the control of the citizenry, albeit incompletely and with reluctance'' (192). Thus, for both Poland and its émigré writers, the literature represents the collective consciousness of centuries of Polish life.

LITERARY-CULTURAL HISTORY

Despite early literary reliance on Latin, by the early fifteenth century, vernacular translations of prose sermon fragments and of biblical passages appeared, and use of the Polish language in literary output became more widespread. Historical, didactic, and religious songs, proverbs, and riddles were written in both Latin and Polish. This movement toward greater use of the Polish language ushered in the golden age of Polish literature, the Polish Renaissance, which spanned the sixteenth century in Poland. Although Latin continued to be used in social and political treatises, and even the major poets of the period— Pawel of Krosno, Andrzej Kryzycki, Jan Dantyszek, Miklolaj Hussowski, and Klemens Janicjusz—continued to write in Latin, by 1550 Polish began to supplant Latin as the literary language of the country. From this point, Polish writings flourished in a variety of genres, most notably, poetry, satires, dramatic dialogues, and moralistic and didactic works. By the close of the sixteenth century, Polish literature had secured its place as a national literature, a reflection of the growing power of the country with its far-flung boundaries, the evolution of the ruling class, and the increase in national economic prosperity. The political and military upheaval of the seventeenth century influenced writers to create poetical and prose works in which historical themes dominated as they described military triumphs and defeats of the period. Writers also produced sharply critical social and political comedies and satires.

During its stormy history, Poland has frequently been threatened with a loss of national identity. In three specific periods, conquerors overtook Poland and divided up the spoils. In 1772, Austria, Russia, and Prussia acquired large portions of Polish territory and forced upon the Polish people a constitution that forbade a resurgence of Polish nationalism. Renamed the Polish Commonwealth, the nation was inundated with political restrictions. In 1792, the Polish army arose in a failed attempt to overthrow the conquerors, after which the Russian and the Prussian governments annexed two-thirds of the remaining Polish territory. In 1794, a hastily formed Polish army, under the command of Thaddeus Kosciusko, began a revolutionary war to recover the lost territories. Despite initial victories, large numbers of Polish revolutionaries were massacred, and Poland experienced a third partitioning, in which the Russian Empire took one-half of the territory, and Prussia and Austria each took one-quarter of Polish lands.

With the third partitioning, the Polish nation was physically subsumed, and for 125 years the Polish people, as exiles in their own land, continued to exist and to preserve their literary and cultural history against heavy opposition from their foreign rulers. The Russian conquerors worked hard to eliminate Polish national identity by requiring that Russian be the teaching language in school and by making the Polish language one subject of study, as well as by severely limiting the activities of the Roman Catholic Church. The conquerors' goal was to culturally, politically, and economically transform all parts of Poland under their rule into provinces of the Russian Empire. Less severe, yet still active, were the efforts of the Prussians and the Austrians to similarly eliminate the Polish national identity. Not until 1918 was the right to Polish self-determination once again recognized, and a provisional government formed.

''The political obliteration of the country was not, as might have been thought, tantamount with the nation's spiritual and cultural death. Paradoxically enough, the political enslavement coincided with the greatest flowering of Polish Romantic poetry'' (Gillon and Krzyzanowski 21), if clandestinely, as early nineteenth-century writers found in Romanticism a means of keeping Polish national spirit alive. Adam Mickiewicz, proclaimed the ''Poet of Poland,'' was a major figure in this period. The poet's narrative poem *Konrad Wallenrod* and his great epic *Pan Tadeusz* inspired his countrymen with nationalistic zeal. His influence continues to be felt in the twentieth century, for ''Poles find in Mickiewicz, with his flights of passionate patriotism, his bitter satire on the enemies of his country, and his mystical vision of Poland's glorious future, a great spiritual leader who has captured in bright, deathless verse the full image and ultimate aspirations of his people'' (Simmons vii).

The urban intelligentsia that emerged in the late nineteenth century focused its attention on critical realism and creating literary works concerned with political and social problems in a movement called ''positivism.'' Henryk Sienkiewicz, the author of *Quo Vadis* and other historical novels less known outside Poland, was the first Polish writer to receive the Nobel Prize (1905), and he remains the best-known writer of this positivist era. He and others wrote two types of literature—what was officially permitted and the other, ''true'' literature of positivism, which was circulated among the knowledgeable few.

In the thirty years preceding the 1918 restoration of Poland, the "Young Poland" literary movement dominated and called for a return to the imagination. These neoromantics opposed the positivists, and from their pens flowed symbolist and psychoanalytic works that were published side by side with works of their naturalist contemporaries. With the existence of no Polish state, no normal political and community life, poets and writers became the chief spiritual leaders of the nation.

The nation itself considered them as such and placed correspondingly high demands on them; expected moral help, teaching, counsel and warning of them, and the greatness of their works was measured by these standards. Poets and writers not only recognized the nation's claim on their work, but themselves considered this service their vocation. (Kridl 476)

Bold literary experimentation seemed to set the stage for a return to political nationhood. The restoration of Polish independence in 1918 after the collapse of the Central Powers opened the world to writers whose increased contact with other European literatures encouraged a richness and variety in form and subject. Intense imagery and inventiveness flowed through revolutionary works that dealt with contemporary social and ideological problems.

Between the world wars, from 1918 through 1939, the continuing economic and political instability and threat to Polish security were reflected in the literature, which gained the label of "catastrophism," a forerunner of the better-known Theatre of the Absurd in other parts of Europe. The movement was mobilized by experimental dramatist Stanislaw Witkiewicz, whose works such as *Insatiable* and *The Madman and the Nun and the Crazy Locomotive,* like those of other catastrophists, expressed with surreal elements a concern with the disintegration of Europe, the growing danger from totalitarian ideology, and the increasingly strong attempts to create a uniform mass society. Nonheroic heroes commanded the attention of the writer who asked perturbing questions about social justice "even at the risk of alienating a large section of his reading public" (Gillon and Krzyzanowski 28).

The invasion of Poland by Germany on September 1, 1939, marked, once more, a return to domination for Poland. First the Third Reich, then the Soviet Union imposed an alien culture on the Polish people, making of them exiles in their own nation once again. For over fifty years, Poles produced an underground literature that expressed their nationalist sentiments while they also maintained their right to religious worship despite communist domination. In 1968, students and artists began a revolt for greater freedom of expression, a move that resulted in even more severe government repression.

Literature of the post-war period in Poland consisted of the publication of either material written during the occupation or material written by writers who had been in the concentration camps or prisons and whose experiences informed their writing. Writers exploring the themes of human depravity and degradation and the moral controversies that accompanied the political and social changes of the post-war period stood in direct contrast to those who followed the government-proscribed literary dictates of socialist realism, which emphasized the depiction of people employed in productive work with social elements that supported a view of revolutionary progress. This fantasy of socialist realism was similarly foisted upon Czechoslovakian writers by the communist regime.

Censorship, major outbreaks of unrest, political and social tensions, and economic crises in the 1970s and 1980s encouraged writers to challenge the system, and when communist rule was finally overthrown in 1990, with the dissolution of the Communist Party in Poland, writers could claim a role in the victory alongside participants in workers' riots and strikers whose Solidarity efforts had dealt the death blow to totalitarianism.

DOMINANT CONCERNS

Polish émigré writers who entered the United States after World War II brought with them the centuries of nationalism and the struggle for independence that had long characterized their ancestral land. In many ways, despite their youth and modernity, they carried with them the legacy of all who had come before. As Milosz expressed this paradox in his Nobel Prize lecture,

Every poet depends upon generations who wrote in his native tongue; he inherits styles and forms elaborated by those who lived before him. At the same time, though, he feels that those old means of expression are not adequate to his own experience. When adapting himself, he hears an internal voice that warns him against mask and disguise. When rebelling, he falls in turn into dependence on his contemporaries, various movements of the avant-garde. (324)

The Polish émigré writers who came to the United States in the immediate postwar years differed significantly from those of previous generations. Born in Poland, many were brought up in countries other than their own, frequently in England, the English dominions, and France. In addition, they were well educated, poised, intelligent, and determined to succeed in their new home. They were followed by a significantly different group of émigrés, ''the young creative artists, brought up in Marxist Poland, who have been coming to the United States in a steady flow since the 1960s. . . . seeking that freedom of expression that is impossible in a more regimented society'' (Kuniczak 172).

Joseph Wittlin and Kasimierz Wierzynski, among the earliest Polish émigré writers, arrived in the United States at different times during 1941 by way of France. In 1935, Wittlin had published the highly successful *Salt of the Earth,* which examines the thoughts and feelings of a simple foot soldier in World War I, an Everyman whose experiences mirror the human condition. Although he was also a poet, Wittlin placed particular emphasis on the importance of the essay, which he characterized in a 1957 essay, ''Sorrow and Grandeur of Exile'' as being

a kind of outline of the physiology of émigré literature. Ours is not a voluntary emigration, not one of free choice, but one to which writers are forced by bitter necessity, by
a catastrophe, by the ruin of their nations. . . . In any event it is a condition of peril, of
danger, if not to the writer's physical person, then to his literary personality and to his
creative work, that was the cause of his staying away from his native country. (81–82)

The essay form was used by many other Polish émigré writers to express their post-war experiences.

First and foremost a lyrical poet, Wierzynski, one of the cofounders of the Skamander poetic group of avant-garde stylists, had published several acclaimed poetry collections before leaving Poland in 1939. His poetry, currently out of print in the United States, focused on moral and national problems before World War II. Works written during and immediately after the war became more personal, expressing the innermost feelings of the Polish people in the face of the nation's tragic fate. Several of the author's prose works, also currently out of print, focused on the Nazi domination of Poland, but his widely acclaimed biography *The Life and Death of Chopin* remains available.

Jan Lechon (a pseudonym for Leszek Serafinowicz) and Alexander Janta both fled Poland after the war in the late 1940s, taking with them their experiences of an occupied homeland. Lechon, another cofounder of the Skamander poetic group, produced numerous pre-war poetry collections that combined lyricism with national motives. Although all of his works are currently out of print in the United States, his poetry and essays retain importance in contemporary literature published in Poland.

Essayist Janta joined the Polish army in 1939 and was captured by the Germans and incarcerated in a prisoner of war camp, from which he escaped before the end of the war. Although he wrote poetry about his pre-war and war experiences, the bulk of Janta's work is in essay form in which he covers a wide range of topics from travel and autobiography through literary studies and criticism. All of his works except the *History of Nineteenth Century American-Polish Music* are out of print in the United States.

The seething intellectual and artistic discontent of Marxist Poland in the 1950s brought two of Poland's best-known émigré writers, Jerzy Kosinski and Czeslaw Milosz, to the United States, albeit via different routes. Kosinski created brilliant novels of terrifying impact that earned him the National Book Award in 1969 and the deserved reputation of a formidable literary artist, while Milosz, the most widely translated contemporary Polish poet and later author of the monumental *History of Polish Literature,* sought political asylum in the West in 1951, in protest against the unenlightened policies of Poland's rulers (Kuniczak 174).

As a commercially popular novelist, Kosinski stands apart from his fellow émigrés, whose main output has been nonfiction. Only twelve years old when World War II ended, the novelist grew up in Russia and came to the United States in 1957, bringing with him terrifying memories of the Polish Occupation. His novels reflect this merging of the old with the new. In 1965, Kosinski published *The Painted Bird,* which provided a vivid, if horrifying, description of a young boy's experiences alone in Poland during World War II. He conveys the experience of terror and physical cruelty through his young narrator in a world in which innocence and adolescence are juxtaposed with a nightmarish world of excess and injustice. However widely acclaimed, none of Kosinski's later works deal so directly with the war experience. Rather, in novels such as the 1968 National Book Award-winner *Steps,* as well as *Being There* (1971), *Cockpit* (1975), *Blind Date* (1977), and *Passion Play* (1979), he explored modern life and the difficult moral choices it offers.

Poet, literary critic, and essayist Czeslaw Milosz was awarded the Nobel Prize in literature in 1980 for his poetry. As a young poet in Poland in the early 1930s, he was one of the founders of "catastrophism" whose poetry, along with that of others in the group, prophesied disaster and mirrored the uneasiness of the times. He emigrated to the United States in 1960, and both his early verse and more recent publications continue to reflect the spiritual pain of exile as well as the remembrance of life under a totalitarian regime and his experiences as an active member of the Warsaw underground during World War II. In the autobiographical novel *The Issa Valley,* published first in 1955 then translated into English in 1978, Milosz recalls the tranquil pre-war life of his youth. *The Captive Mind,* published in 1953, contains essentially an extended meditation regarding the spiritual slavery of writers who live under a totalitarian regime. In addition to individual collections of poetry, Milosz published a bilingual edition in 1984, *The Separate Notebooks,* which contains poetry from the war years as well as recent writings in Polish and English. As he noted in his Nobel Prize acceptance speech, throughout his writing, he remains cognizant that he is an exile, "always Dante. But how the number of Florences have increased!" (327).

The few Polish émigrés of the 1960s and 1970s were primarily poets and essayists, as were those who had preceded them. Literary critic and essayist Jan Kott, who emigrated to the United States in 1966, received wide acclaim for *Shakespeare Our Contemporary,* published in Poland in 1961 and widely translated since. A former Resistance fighter against the Germans in World War II, Kott relates in his autobiography, *Still Alive,* which he subtitles *An Autobiographical Essay,* that he had a long post-war involvement with the Communist Party in Poland before being dismissed from his teaching position at the University of Warsaw for political reasons. Since settling in the United States, Kott has published several books of essays, including *The Theatre of Essence, The Memory of the Body,* and the *The Bottom Translation,* in which he explores the universal concern of how to make sense of one's existence. In the preface to *Four Decades of Polish Essays,* published in 1990, the author explains why, for him, the essay form has become an eloquent expression of his role as an émigré writer.

Emigration is a difficult and painful choice. . . . But in the Polish essay of the last half century, the memory of history makes itself felt perhaps more often and certainly more clearly than it does in the reflections of writers from happier countries. (3)

Thus, whether the topic is literary or social, essayists infuse their experiences into the text.

Stanislaw Baranczak is among the most recently arrived of the Polish émigré writers of the late 1970s, and he carries with him no firsthand memories of World War II nor of a pre-war Poland, because he was born in 1946. As both a poet and an essayist, he combines the two genres, which predominate among Polish émigré writers and which appear to hold equal importance in their creative work. The author of eight collections of poems, eight books of literary criticism, and numerous volumes of translations, among them a collection of East European essays entitled *Breathing under Water* and the poetry collection *Under My Own Roof,* Baranczak permeates his work with a recognition of the limitations imposed on the émigré writer by his exiled state. He observes in the 1990 essay "Tongue-Tied Eloquence" that "the exiled writer is someone who has left the cage of an oppressive political system; but if he is to remain a writer at all, he must never really leave another cage—that of his native language" (348). Thus, despite the need for any writer if he is to say anything relevant to "break a norm. . . . this is precisely what an outsider cannot afford" (348), if he is to maintain credibility in his adopted land.

With rare exception, the majority of Polish émigré writers have channeled their thoughts into two genres, poetry and the essay, which have permitted them the greatest range for developing their distinct voices. Among the reasons for this may well be, as Kott suggests in his preface to *Four Decades of Polish Essays,* that both genres use the first person, "even if this first person is hidden under many stylistic disguises" (1). Therefore, both the poet and the essayist are able to relate real-world experience as a personal story that is, at the same time, "the most universal image and reflection" (1).

SELECTED PRIMARY BIBLIOGRAPHY

Baranczak, Stanislaw L. *Breathing under Water and Other Eastern European Essays.* Cambridge: Harvard University Press, 1990.
———. "Tongue-Tied Eloquence: Notes on Language, Exile, and Writing." *Four Decades of Polish Essays.* Ed. Jan Kott. Evanston, IL: Northwestern University Press, 1990.
———. *Under My Own Roof.* Trans. Frank Kujawinski. Portland, OR: Mr. Cogito Press, 1980.
Kosinski, Jerzy. *Being There.* New York: Harcourt Brace Jovanovich, 1971.
———. *Blind Date.* Boston: Houghton Mifflin, 1977.

————. *Cockpit.* Boston: Houghton Mifflin, 1975.

————. *The Painted Bird.* 1965. New York: Modern Library, 1983.

————. *Passion Play.* New York: St. Martin's Press, 1979.

————. *Steps.* New York: Random House, 1968.

Kott, Jan. *The Bottom Translation.* Evanston, IL: Northwestern University Press, 1993.

————. *The Memory of the Body: Essays on Theatre and Death.* Trans. Jadwiga Kosicka. Evanston, IL: Northwestern University Press, 1992.

————. *Shakespeare Our Contemporary.* 1961. New York: Norton, 1974.

————. *Still Alive: An Autobiographical Essay.* Trans. Jadwiga Kosicka. New Haven, CT: Yale University Press, 1994.

————. *The Theatre of Essence.* Evanston, IL: Northwestern University Press, 1984.

————, ed. *Four Decades of Polish Essays.* Evanston, IL: Northwestern University Press, 1990.

Milosz, Czeslaw. "Biblical Heirs and Modern Evils." *The New Immigrant Experience: The Anguish of Becoming American.* Ed. Thomas C. Wheeler. New York: Penguin Books, 1980.

————. *The Captive Mind.* Ann Arbor: Michigan Slavic, 1953.

————. *The Issa Valley.* 1955. Ann Arbor: Michigan Slavic, 1978.

————. "Nobel Prize Lecture." *Four Decades of Polish Essays.* Ed. Jan Kott. Evanston, IL: Northwestern University Press, 1990.

————. *The Separate Notebooks.* Trans. Robert Hass and Robert Pinsky. New York: Ecco Press, 1984.

Sienkiewicz, Henryk. *Quo Vadis.* New York: Dodd, Mead, 1955.

Wierzynski, Kasimierz. *The Life and Death of Chopin.* Trans. Norbert Guterman. New York: Simon and Schuster, 1949.

Witkiewicz, Stanislaw. *Insatiable: A Novel in Two Parts.* Ann Arbor: Books on Demand, 1976.

————. *The Madman and the Nun and the Crazy Locomotive.* New York: Applause Theatre Book, 1988.

Wittlin, Joseph. *Comissar: The Life and Death of Larenty Pavlovich Beria.* New York: Macmillan, 1972.

————. *Salt of the Earth.* 1935. Harrisburg, PA: Stackpole Books, 1970.

————. "Sorrow and Grandeur of Exile." 1957. *Four Decades of Polish Essays.* Ed. Jan Kott. Evanston, IL: Northwestern University Press, 1990.

SELECTED SECONDARY BIBLIOGRAPHY

Gillon, Adam, and Ludwik Krzyzanowski, eds. *Introduction to Modern Polish Literature: An Anthology of Fiction and Poetry.* New York: Twayne, 1964.

Kridl, Manfred. *A Survey of Polish Literature and Culture.* Trans. Olga Scherer-Virski. New York: Columbia University Press, 1956.

Kuniczak, W. S. *My Name Is Million: An Illustrated History of the Poles in America.* Garden City, NY: Doubleday, 1978.

Milosz, Czeslaw. *The History of Polish Literature.* London: Macmillan, 1969.

Simmons, Ernest J. Foreword. *Adam Mickiewicz: Poet of Poland.* Ed. Manfred Kridl. New York: Greenwood Press, 1951. iii–vii.

21

Slovak-American and Czech-American Literature

Dawn B. Sova

INTRODUCTION

Slovak and Czech émigrés in the United States have produced little in the way of lasting literature, despite having long established a presence in this nation. In part, this lack is due to the multiplicity of ethnic identities encompassed by both groups whose members, due to shifting boundaries in the European region from which they emerge, have at times also been identified as German, Moravian, Austrian, Hungarian, and even Polish.

The recent political division of Czechoslovakia into the Czech Republic and Slovakia is the culmination of centuries of separate ethnic identities and separate languages within the same nation. Since 906, the Slovaks had been separate from the Czechs, and the two were not officially brought together until 1918, when Czechoslovakia was created. The Slovaks, who had been part of Hungary, were fragmented in their language and had used Latin, Hungarian, or Czech in writing their literature until a standard Slovak was developed in the nineteenth century. The Czechs, on the other hand, had been relatively in control of their own state under Austria, and, as a result, they were more linguistically homogeneous. Despite their close physical proximity, language, customs, and even literature have developed in distinct paths that call forth a charge of ethnic favoritism against the critic who might choose to discuss the writings of both people under one heading. The fault, of course, lies not in the historical ignorance of the critics but more in the greater visibility of Czech immigrant writers who have published since the end of World War II.

As recently as 1982, the Toronto-based Czechoslovak émigré publishing house the Sixty-Eight Publishers Corporation published the *Dictionary of Czech Writers of the Twentieth Century,* which contained over 500 novelists, playwrights, poets, essayists, and scholarly writers of Czech or Slovak background who were simply classed under the one heading of Czech. When examining the two groups, many writers and critics fail to distinguish between the divergent histories of the Slovaks and the Czechs. Even the essentially careful scholarship of Fermi exhibits this failure to distinguish between their different cultures.

The difficulties [of defining the national characteristics of Czech émigrés] are even greater in the case of the Czechs. After centuries of obliteration from the maps, Czechoslovakia emerged as a nation from the ruins of the Austro-Hungarian edifice at the end of World War I. By that time many future Czech emigres had already been born as the subjects of the Habsburg monarchy and had been shaped by the forces of the old order. (131–132)

In essence, however, Slovak and Czech writers have themselves been responsible for the increased modern blurring of differences between the two cultures since the early 1960s, as the number of translations between the two languages has grown, leading readers to view the two cultures as interchangeable.

LITERARY-CULTURAL HISTORY

Slovak Literature

Although the Slovak dialects are closely related to the Czech language, the Slovaks have maintained a separate identity since the Middle Ages. In like manner, while the outside world may have classed Czech and Slovak literary works under one heading, the fiercely independent members of both groups maintained their distinctions, and Slovaks never did accept Czech as their written language. In the early nineteenth century, writers codified a new form of literary Slovak that was based on the central Slovak dialects, and this was used in Slovak literary expression as the literary Czech continued to be used by Czech writers.

As national consciousness increased, the strong national feeling of the Catholic Slovak majority found expression in romantic ballads and lyrics, as well as in the national epic *Marina,* written in 1846 by Andrej Sladkovic. The ballads, epics, and lyrics of Janko Kral, a romantic literary figure who had fought in the revolution of 1848–1849, further popularized the use of literary Slovak and came to represent Slavonic romanticism. Although some, such as Slovak dramatist Jan Chalupka, wrote their works in Czech, more followed the lead of playwrights such as Jan Palarik, who used the new literary Slovak to produce his comedies in the 1850s and 1860s.

In the twentieth century, the Slovak literature has concentrated on the lyric, which chronicled in the personal expressions of novelists and poets the problems of World Wars I and II and the aftermath of communist domination. Martin

Kujucin, often referred to as the father of Slovak realism, humorously chronicled Czech life. His contemporary and one of the leading poets of the Slovak modern school, Janko Jesensky, wrote antifascist verses and novels that satirized the upper classes. Later writers walked the fine line between creating accurate word portraits of the peasants and life under communism and meeting the stringent government-imposed restrictions of "socialist realism" (Smith 58). For such writers as Peter Jilemnicky, Milo Urban, and Ladislav Mnacko, the novel became a work of art with hidden meanings that conveyed their true themes.

Slovak writers were active through the 1960s, but little Slovak writing of consequence has emerged from the 1970s to the present.

Czech Literature

Czech literature, one of the oldest of the vernacular literatures of Central and Eastern Europe, had its beginnings in the introduction of Christianity into Moravia in A.D. 863 by Slav apostles Cyril and Methodius. Latin prevailed as the literary language of choice during the first few centuries, until the fourteenth-century Czech translation of the Latin *Alexandreid,* a life of Alexander the Great written by the twelfth-century French poet Gautier de Lille, and the growth of nationalism resulted in the writing of great legends in Czech verse. Political ideas dominated the literature, which reverted once more to expression in Latin after the Czechs lost political independence in 1620, when the Hapsburgs defeated the Protestant Bohemian forces, and the Czech provinces became part of the Hapsburg Empire. A new Jesuit literature emerged that obliterated the use of the Czech vernacular for higher literary works, although its use continued in popular poetry and folk songs and dramas, which expressed the extent of dissatisfaction among the peasants.

The decree in 1774 by Maria Therese, queen of Hungary and Bohemia, that German was the new language of instruction and literature provoked a revival of nationalism among Czech writers, who made extensive efforts to create a public for Czech literature in the vernacular, an effort that was aided by the social and political developments late in the eighteenth century. While some writers followed the romantics in their work, more authors sought to balance romanticism with a realistic prose that, in the nineteenth century, extended to psychological analysis and moral and social problems. Czechoslovakian literature exhibited a strong note of social optimism after the establishment of an independent republic in 1918. Writers experimented with both form and content, as some explored the industrial scene and individual psychology while others used satire or surrealism to examine the relation of the average citizen to society. One of the best-known plays of this period is "R.U.R.," written by Karel Capek in 1920, which exposed the problems of a centralized, machine society and which introduced the word "robot" into English as a derivation of the Czechoslovakian word for forced labor, *robota.*

The German occupation of 1938–1945 limited literary achievement, which suffered even more under the Russian domination that resulted from the coup d'état of 1948. With the rise of the Communist Party in Czechoslovakia came attacks on the newly declared "decadent" writings as political controls forced writers to adopt a theme of "socialist realism," which advocated the building of a socialist regime and a socialist society. Some liberalization of these controls occurred when Joseph Stalin died in 1953, and writers as well as the nation experienced a loosening of controls until a culmination of this move toward liberalization and democratization resulted in the "Prague Spring" of 1968. The euphoric flowering of the arts was short-lived, for the Soviet Union invaded Czechoslovakia in August 1968, and the works of many writers who had examined the contradictions inherent in a socialist society were repressed.

Émigré writer Josef Skvorecky points out in a 1989 article:

The Czech writer, from the beginning of the renaissance of Czech literature in the early nineteenth century, had been constantly admonished to mix politics with poetics; indeed, occasionally he was even exhorted to describe Czech life not merely as it is but also—perhaps predominantly—as it should be: an ominous foreshadowing of the demands of the much later Socialist Realism. (44)

Writing and politics have long been interwoven in Czechoslovakian history, as writers not only wrote of, but lived, the political life. Early nineteenth-century writer Frantisek Palacky, often called the "Father of the Nation" for both his extensive written history of the Czech nation and his political activities, exemplifies this duality, as does the founder of independent Czechoslovakia and its first president, Tomas Garrigue Masaryk, who was a philosophy professor and literary critic as well as a politician. More recently, the final president of Czechoslovakia was Vaclav Havel, a much-published writer.

Soviet control of Czechoslovakia after the 1968 invasion bred a mandatory "socialist realism" among writers who strove to gain the political acceptance that meant financial rewards. Thus, writers were instructed by the government to describe life as it should be, not as it was, and to follow a course of obligatory optimism. Silent at first, a group of "liberals" emerged who began in the 1970s and 1980s to produce literary neonaturalism that attacked society's ills, such as prostitution, bribery, and the black market, without attacking the system. Fear of reprisal suppressed many writers, yet the works of others such as Vaclav Havel, author of *Largo Desolato, Long Distance Interrogation,* and *Power of the Powerless,* and Ludvik Vaculik, author of *The Axe, A Cup of Coffee with My Interrogator,* and *The Guinea Pigs,* found their way to émigré publishing houses. While the dissenters may have been silenced in their own country, they found a voice abroad.

DOMINANT CONCERNS

Slovak émigrés to the United States from the mid-nineteenth century focused their writing talents in journalism rather than in producing literature. Large numbers of Slovak-language newspapers flourished over the years, as did periodicals that expressed a range of political and religious views, but most published either all or at least in part in the Slovak language. As Stolarik rightly observes, "[A]lthough newspapers and almanacs have provided a medium for Slovak expression and have offered some insight into the Slovak experience in North America, they scarcely qualify as literature" (87). In the effort to correct what they viewed as the lack of recognition of the Slovak contribution to the arts, a group of Slovak intellectuals emigrated to the United States and to Canada after World War II with the goal of stimulating interest in Slovak literature and art.

A number of poets and short-story writers published in American and Canadian Slovak newspapers and almanacs, and a group of these writers founded the Slovak literary review *Most* (published since 1954). Because they wrote exclusively in Slovak, however, none of these writers managed to establish a reputation outside the Slovak community.

Even among the Slovak population, only a handful of people read these writers. For the most part, working-class Slovaks lacked the time, money, and inclination to patronize the arts. (Stolarik 88)

In contrast, Czech émigré writers have made their mark on American literature, but their work shows little unity of thought. Early émigré writers of the World War II period, such as Franz Werfel, Hans Natonek, and Franz Weiskopf, wrote novels that dramatized the plight of Czechoslovakia during, and in the period immediately following, World War II. Czechoslovakia also gave America one of the highest-ranking contemporary scholars of the history and the theory of literary criticism, Rene Wellek, whose impressive knowledge of European, English, and American literature appeared in a monumental history of modern literary criticism.

Franz Werfel, the Czech-born poet, dramatist, and novelist, who emigrated in 1941, was well known to the American public for his *The Forty Days of Musa Dagh,* the epic of the Armenians' desperate resistance against the Turks on that now famous Syrian mountain, but his later work remains in the public eye. While escaping the Nazis, the Jewish Werfel found himself in Lourdes, France, and vowed that he would write the story of Saint Bernadette, which became *The Song of Bernadette,* the first novel he wrote on American soil. Published in 1942, it revived the popularity that Werfel had enjoyed six years previously with his story of the Armenians. Werfel later delved into science fiction in a posthumously published utopian novel that describes a trip 100,000 years into the future and a meeting with technospiritual life.

Egon Hostovsky, who settled in New York and became an American citizen but did not write in English, has been considered "the most important contemporary [1971] Czech writer" to emigrate (Fermi 131). After resigning from diplomatic service in 1948, Hostovsky entered the United States, where he wrote novels that examine in depth the psychological world of refugees from tyranny.

For the most part, his works "deal with the experiences of alienated and displaced personalities" (Smith 57).

For many writers, the increased controls that followed the Prague Spring of 1968 led to subsequent emigration to Western nations, where they could explore national themes without fear of reprisal. The best-known Czech émigrés of this period are Milan Kundera, who went to France, and Josef Skvorecky, who emigrated to Canada, both of whom have attained popularity in the United States. They have been joined in the 1990s by a new literary voice, Iva Pekarkova, whose writings are making her presence felt in the literary world. In contrast to their predecessors, the more recent émigrés have turned their analyses inward, from describing life within a restrictive political context to an exploration of the personal and philosophical implications as they examine the meaning of freedom for the individual.

Kundera's first novel, *The Joke,* chronicles the hard price that Stalinist Czechoslovakia extracts from a student who plays an innocent joke, and it joins *The Farewell Party* as a witty and ironic treatment of modern life and love. In particular, despite the insistence of both critics and translators that *The Joke* is a political novel, a point that Kundera has frequently contested, the author explores a theme of thwarted love and revenge as he focuses upon the very personal actions and feelings of people.

His best-known work, *The Unbearable Lightness of Being,* is a blackly humorous novel about two lovers and is set in Prague in 1968. The politically charged atmosphere of the period after the Soviet invasion provides the setting in which Kundera explores the theme of desolation for those individuals who are living life under a totalitarian state. This novel focuses on two couples who are coming to terms with their changed world. The well-respected Prague surgeon Tomas is a philanderer who desires to settle down with the bartender Tereza, but he finds that he does not have the willpower to resist other women. One of his temptations is Sabina, one-half of the other couple in the novel, who is having an affair with the married university professor Franz. In examining the intertwined lives of these four people, Kundera explores the metaphysical conflict between body and soul as well as the consequences suffered by those who confront the essential meaningless of life.

In the highly intelligent and humorous *Immortality,* Kundera again uses four contemporary characters to examine the existential nature of modern life. Through Agnes, husband Paul, her sister Laura, and the hedonist Rubens, the author explores the theme of conflict between the individual and his image. Kundera takes a surreal side trip to heaven in this novel, where he portrays a meeting between writers Ernest Hemingway and Johann von Goethe. The two discuss the sorrows of immortality, and, more important, they bemoan man's powerlessness before an image of himself over which he has no control.

Josef Skvorecky uses a largely autobiographical framework in his works to focus on the emotional reality of life for modern individuals and to explore the impact of the past on life in the present. In *The Engineer of Human Souls,* he chronicles life in Czechoslovakia under the Nazis as well as his later life and that of other Czech émigrés in Canada. In this novel, Skvorecky mixes images of the present with images of World War II-era Czechoslovakia as he explores the theme of the role played by the artist in exile. Patterning the life of his protagonist Danny Smirecky much after his own, the author moves from relating the experiences of the young Danny working for the Resistance and plotting sabotage with his lover and co-conspirator Nadia, a factory girl, to Danny's present as an émigré writer in Canada. Because Skvorecky filters his view of the freedom, security, and decadence of his New World life through a vision created by the suffering and experiences of life in a totalitarian state, his char- acters serve as useful critics of their new lives. Later in the novel, as a college professor of American literature for over a decade, Danny has adopted many New World views, but his world is peopled by a differentiated group of Czech émigrés—the prosperous and the impoverished, the gloomy and the ecstatic, the paranoid and the complacent—whose comments and concerns widen the themes of this novel to examine the role of fate in the lives of individuals, the goals and dreams of the working class, and the even greater issues of the nature of love and the finality of death. In sum, Danny as a writer learns that he has enough fodder for his writer's hunger and that he can reject out of hand the dictate fed to writers in his native Czechoslovakia under the social realism of Stalin, which declared that writers should be the engineers of the soul of the masses.

Skvorecky continues this autobiographical tone in *The Miracle Game,* in which his protagonist is, once more, Danny Smirecky. A combination of polit- ical thriller and cautionary tale, the novel examines with humor the often mis- guided actions of well-meaning people. Set first in Bohemia in the post-war turmoil of 1948 and later during the heady times of the Prague Spring of 1968, the novel moves its highly libidinous protagonist along a time continuum in Czechoslovakian history, moving from a seemingly obscure religious prank that takes place in 1948, to a full discovery of its vast social, political, religious, and personal implications during a period of intense turmoil and unrest. As a teacher in an all-girls' Catholic school in Bohemia where the chief activity is compe- tition among the girls to seduce the young male teachers, Danny is present at mass in the little village church when a statue of St. Joseph suddenly seems to bow to the congregation. The townspeople proclaim this a miracle, but the fledg- ling Communist Party powers in the area move quickly to disprove the occur- rence. They torture and kill the priest, whom they claim has misled the people. The second part of the novel takes place during the frenetic days of 1968, with the Soviet invasion imminent, as Danny, now a writer, moves freely throughout Prague and its squabbling intellectuals. The miracle of the St. Joseph statue once more takes center stage as the case is reopened, and questions are asked as to who or what was really responsible—was it a hoax of the church or a sinister deed by the Communist Party? Or was it truly a miracle? As he leads readers toward an answer, Skvorecky dissects human nature and human motivation, laying bare the often ignoble reasons for human action.

The themes of individual human frailty and the juxtaposition of the Old World with the New World exist throughout Skvorecky's novels, beginning with *The Cowards,* in which the protagonist of both *The Engineer of Human Souls* and *The Miracle Game* is first seen, as well as in *Miss Silver's Past, Dvorak in Love,* and *The Swell Season.* This combination of humor and insightful examination of human behavior is also found in his four mystery novels, which feature his sad-eyed detective Lieutenant Boruvka—*The Mournful Demeanour of Lieutenant Boruvka, Sins for Father Knox, The End of Lieutenant Boruvka,* and *The Return of Lieutenant Boruvka.* In the first three novels, Lieutenant Boruvka operates within the sometimes funny but more often sad milieu of Czechoslovakia under totalitarian rule. In the final novel, *The Return of Lieutenant Boruvka,* Skvorecky moves his protagonist to Canada, where, after escaping from a Czechoslovakian prison, he turns his talents to solving a murder and avenging an old war crime. Throughout, however, the author maintains his focus on individual human problems and feelings.

The newest generation of Czech émigré writers has no direct experience with the pre-World War II Czechoslovakia, the horrors of the war, or the restrictions of the post-war period. In many cases, even the 1968 Soviet invasion may have been an event experienced with little understanding by a writer who was too young at the time to understand its significance. This new generation of émigré writer is exemplified in the work of young novelist Iva Pekarkova, whose novels *Truck Stop Rainbows* (1992) and *The World Is Round* (1994) chronicle her life both in a communist-dominated nation and as a Czech émigré. Born in 1963, Pekarkova left Prague in 1985 and now lives in New York City. The author uses her first-person narrator in *Truck Stop Rainbows* to present a serious view of the desires and confusions of the modern Czech generation. The novel relates the story of a free-spirited young woman who blithely trades sex for Marlboros and cosmetics until she acquires a cause that forces her to demand money for sex. When her boyfriend develops multiple sclerosis, and the two learn that he cannot acquire a wheelchair from the state for five years, the narrator decides to turn her "hobby" into a business and, thus, outsmart the state. Rather than promiscuous, her narrator is adventuresome and expresses her desire to use her college English in the United States, daydreaming of traveling from coast to coast like Kerouac and listening to the purring of the trucks sounding out her freedom. For the time, her immediate goal and that of others in her circle are to simply try to create some kind rainbow of colors in their lives, even above the gray and overheated truck stops where she plies her trade.

In *The World Is Round,* Pekarkova provides an unflinching look at Eastern and Central European immigration as well as a poignant account of life in a refugee camp for a young woman who desperately wishes to emigrate to the United States. Narrator Jitka has become bored with her life in Prague and bored with her lover, so she decides to sneak over the border into Austria. She soon lands in an Austrian camp whose inmates provide a varied and detailed look at the strength of human longing and human will. After a series of mishaps, including being brutally gang-raped, Jitka learns that the United States has accepted her application as a political dissident. The novel ends with an epilogue set ten years later, as Jitka reflects on her emigration and her new life in New York City.

With World War II long behind them and even the events of 1968 long over, recent Czech émigré writers may not have abandoned a concern with political topics, but they have made such concern secondary to their exploration of the individual. Individual freedom, goals for happiness, and motivations in life have taken center stage, and writers have turned the analysis inward, from examining established institutions and events to placing focus on their impact on the individual.

SELECTED PRIMARY BIBLIOGRAPHY

Capek, Karel. "R.U.R." *Toward the Radical Center: A Karel Capek Reader.* 1920. North Haven, CT: Catbird Press, 1990.

Havel, Vaclav. *Largo Desolato.* Adapted by Tom Stoppard. New York: Grove-Atlantic Press, 1987.

———. *Long Distance Interrogation.* New York: Knopf, 1990.

———. *Power of the Powerless.* Ed. John Keane. Armonk, NY: M. E. Sharpe, 1985.

Kundera, Milan. *The Farewell Party.* Ed. Philip Roth. New York: Viking Penguin, 1987.

———. *Immortality.* Trans. Peter Kussi. New York: Grove Weidenfeld, 1990.

———. *The Joke.* Trans. Michael Heim. New York: Harper and Row, 1969.

———. *The Unbearable Lightness of Being.* Trans. Michael Heim. New York: Harper and Row, 1984.

Pekarkova, Iva. *Truck Stop Rainbows: A Road Novel.* Trans. David Powelstock. New York: Farrar, Straus, and Giroux, 1992.

———. *The World Is Round.* Trans. David Powelstock. New York: Farrar, Straus, and Giroux, 1994.

Skvorecky, Josef. *The End of Lieutenant Boruvka.* Trans. Paul Wilson. New York: Norton, 1991.

———. *The Engineer of Human Souls.* Trans. Paul Wilson. New York: Knopf, 1984.

———. *Miss Silver's Past.* Trans. Paul Wilson. Hopewell, NJ: Ecco Press, 1985.

———. *The Mournful Demeanour of Lieutenant Boruvka.* Trans. Rosemary Kavan. New York: Norton, 1987.

———. *Sins for Father Knox.* Trans. Paul Wilson. New York: Norton, 1991.

———. *The Swell Season.* Trans. Paul Wilson. Hopewell, NJ: Ecco Press, 1986.

Vaculik, Ludvik. *The Axe.* Trans. Marian Sling. Evanston, IL: Northwestern University Press, in press.

———. *A Cup of Coffee with My Interrogator.* Trans. George Theiner. Boca Raton, FL: Readers International, 1987.

———. *The Guinea Pigs.* Evanston, IL: Northwestern University Press, 1986.

Werfel, Franz. 1936. *The Forty Days of Musa Dagh.* New York: Carroll and Graf, 1988.

———. *The Song of Bernadette.* New York: Amereon, 1942.

SELECTED SECONDARY BIBLIOGRAPHY

Capek, Thomas. *The Czechs in America.* New York: Arno Press and the New York Times, 1969.

Chudoba, Frantisek. *A Short History of Czech Literature.* 1924. New York: E. P. Dutton, 1969.

Fermi, Laura. *Illustrious Immigrants: The Intellectual Migration from Europe, 1930-41.* 2d ed. Chicago: University of Chicago Press, 1971.

Flier, Michael, ed. *Slavic Forum: Essays in Linguistics and Literature.* Paris: Mouton, 1974.

Skvorecky, Josef. "Czech Writers: Politicians in Spite of Themselves." *New York Times Book Review,* December 10, 1989: 1, 43–45.

Smith, Martin Seymour. *Guide to Modern World Literature.* Vol. 4. London: Hodder and Stoughton, 1975.

Stolarik, M. Mark. *The Slovak Americans.* New York: Chelsea House, 1988.

IV
MEXICAN-AMERICAN
LITERATURES

22

Mexican-American Literature
Ada Savin

INTRODUCTION

Presenting Mexican-American literature as *one* of the immigrant literatures produced in the United States calls for a prompt caveat. Unlike any other group of immigrants, Mexican Americans "have been here for 450 years and for 45 seconds''; hence, some of them do not consider themselves immigrants, claiming that not they, but rather the border, has migrated. As a community they locate themselves somewhere between the native and the colonial experience, recognizing a centuries-long process of (im)migration while simultaneously claiming a presence prior to Anglo-Americans. Indeed, whether directly or indirectly, today's Mexican-American community traces its physical and spiritual presence in the North American Southwest to pre-Anglo-American times. One can claim, for that matter, that a writer like Rudolfo Anaya, whose roots in New Mexico go very deep, may well be a remote descendant of the union between a Spanish conquistador heading toward the seven cities of Cibola and an Indian woman from the northern provinces of New Spain.

Given the historical precedence of Spaniards, Indians, and Mexicans in the American Southwest, the question that arises is, When did Mexican-American literature begin? For one thing, the *Relaciones* or *Narracion de los naufragios* (1542) by Cabeza de Vaca—arguably, the "father" of Mexican-American literature—preceded by almost a century John Smith's *Generall Historie of Virginia, New England, and the Summer Isles* (1624). One can argue that the sixteenth-century Spaniard's encounter with the American Indians prefigured the leitmotif of cultural ambivalence that has been the hallmark of Mexican-American literature to this day.

The Spanish exploration narratives can also be regarded as the beginnings of a distinct Mexican-American autobiographical discourse, much like their English counterparts—William Bradford's *Of Plymouth Plantation* (1630–1651) or John Winthrop's *Journal* (1630–1649). "Both Spanish and British narratives constitute the beginnings of American literature since they express a literary response to the New World and were shaped by the experience in the Americas" (Padilla, "Recovery" 47).

The annexation of northern Mexico, sealed by the Guadalupe Hidalgo Treaty (1848), brought the local population under the political domination and cultural influence of the United States, thereby signing the birth certificate of the first generation of Mexican Americans. In retrospect, the nineteenth-century confrontation between Mexico and the United States was the source of the first significant encounter between the two main cultural traditions facing each other in the New World—the Anglo-American and the Latin-American.

The origin of the deep fracture between North and South America is to be found in the particular circumstances of their colonization by the Old World. Europe projected two diverse images of itself onto the Americas, which, to this day, account for the underlying difference between the Anglo-American and the Latin-American post-colonial experience and their respective literary representations:

The eccentricity of the English is insular and is characterized by isolation: an eccentricity that excludes. Hispanic eccentricity is peninsular and consists of the co-existence of different civilizations and different pasts: an inclusive eccentricity. (Paz, *Nobel Lecture* 3)

The distinction highlighted by Paz is particularly relevant in the perspective of this chapter, which argues that Mexican-American literature functions as a bridge between these two traditions while, at the same time, it is in the process of significantly expanding—spatially, temporally, and formally—the cultural boundaries of U.S. literature.

As Octavio Paz aptly pointed out, though diverse in their origins, both Latin-American and Anglo-American literature began as projections of Europe; they are written in "transplanted languages." English and Spanish "were rooted out from their native soil and their own tradition, and then planted in an unknown and unnamed world: they took root in the new lands and, as they grew within the societies of America, they were transformed" (Paz, *Nobel Lecture* 2). Historically the first literary works to feature a "double cultural and linguistic transplant" (through the use of the two languages, Spanish and English), Mexican-American writings thus seem "manifestly destined" to play a unique, crucial role within the cultural landscape of the Americas.

The adverse circumstances of the conflictual encounter between the United

States and Mexico, followed by the political and ideological domination exercised by the former, did not manage to erase the artistic and literary heritage of the Mexican tradition. Issued from the *mestizaje*[1] of Indian and Spanish blood, the Mexican people are inheritors of a twofold tradition, one European, with a long-standing literate culture, the other indigenous, based on the orally transmitted wisdom of the Indian ancestors.

Actually, the intercultural contact following the 1848 annexation unwittingly created a new literary space within which cultural differences as well as potential compatibilities could be confronted and dialogized. Through its use of Hispanic and Indian motifs and traditions and, most strikingly, by bringing another language into play—Spanish—Mexican-American literature was to add new dimensions to the U.S. literary space. Over a century ago, in a letter to the city fathers of Santa Fe, Walt Whitman had foreseen the new vistas that could open if the Hispano-Indo-Anglo cultural contact were renewed:

We Americans have yet to really learn from our antecedents, and sort them, to unify them. They will be found ampler than has been supposed, and in widely different sources. To that composite American identity of the future, Spanish character will supply some of the most needed parts. (quoted in Moquin 224–225)

This chapter intends to highlight the potential contribution of Mexican-American literature to the creation of a Pan-American literary paradigm in which the multiple cultural layers making up the New World imagination would coexist. From this point of view, Chicano literary works (and, more generally, Hispanic writings in the United States) can be regarded as attempts at dialogizing the Indo-Afro-Ibero-Américan (Carlos Fuentes's term) and the Anglo-American traditions.[2] After a closer examination of the Mexican Americans' literary-cultural history, the chapter focuses on the dominant concerns and specific features of the literature produced after World War II.

LITERARY-CULTURAL HISTORY

I find three levels of time-space, within which anybody lives and functions. The historical time-space, which is the collective time-space, one that describes reality as accorded by a consensus of people. There is a personal time-space that is very individual, psychological. It belongs to the individual and not to the collective group. And a third level, the mythological time-space that unifies the personal and historical time-spaces.
—Alurista, Interview with Juan Bruce-Novoa,
Chicano Authors: Inquiry by Interview, 279

The Pre-Columbian Heritage

Rediscovered, sometimes reinvented during the Chicano movement years, Aztec religion, symbols, and mythology underlie much of present-day Mexican-

American literature. The nationalist movement's myth of origin, Aztlan—a symbolic place on the map of the American Southwest, a counterpart to Plymouth, as it were—provided the Chicano writers with a necessary rallying symbol, thereby also opening up the vast repertoire of their ancestors' mythology to modern literary use. As the Chicano poet Alurista observed, Aztlan subsequently became a "state of mind," the rekindling of the old myth resulting in a new faith, in a new, assertive self-concept for the Mexican Americans.

The Spanish Colonial Heritage

Stricto sensu, Mexican-American literature dates back to 1848, the year Mexico ceded the large territory known today as the Southwest of the United States. However, as Luis Leal and Juan Bruce-Novoa, among others, have pointed out, there is a strong case for considering the writings of the sixteenth–eighteenth-century *cronistas* (chroniclers) as the literary predecessors of Chicano literature and, more generally, as forming part of the rubric of American colonial literature.

The colonization of New Spain's northern provinces has left behind an impressive number of *cronicas, historias, relaciones,* and *diarios* that provide the first descriptions of the region's countryside and inhabitants. Cabeza de Vaca's *Relaciones* (1542) or Pérez de Villagra's *Historia de la Nueva Mexico* (1610) are among the first written accounts of the cultural encounter between Spaniards and Indians in the present territories of Texas and New Mexico—the very site of the mythical Aztlan, which the Mexican Indians had crossed during their migration north to south on their way to Tenochtitlan (today's Mexico City) in the twelfth century. Four centuries later the Spanish colonizers began to explore, settle, and name the remote northern provinces of New Spain, a process that lasted well into the eighteenth century.

The "I"/"eye" of the Spanish explorers thus recorded and attempted to describe the realities of a world unknown to the Europeans: Cabeza de Vaca delights in the buffalo's meat, Pérez de Villagra writes about the helpful Indian vaqueros (the future cowboys) or names the mighty river that today separates Mexico and the United States, Rio Bravo.

The explorers' and missionaries' narratives—of Coronado, Onate, De Anza, and Serra, among others—testify to the gradual emergence of an identity that is somewhat distinct from that of the rest of New Spain. This difference can be ascribed, on one hand, to geographical distance from the center (Mexico), leading to isolation, and, on the other hand, to the frequent contacts, conflicts, and clashes with other populations—native Indians, French, Anglo-Americans. As Juan Bruce-Novoa has argued, Cabeza de Vaca's intercultural experience was to change both his and the others' perception of his identity: if in Spain he felt more like an Indian, in Mexico he was considered a Spaniard.

Mutatis mutandis, the Mexican Americans are facing a similar existential quandary: not entirely American in the United States, they are not regarded as

Mexicans south of the Rio Grande, either. The very essence of Chicanismo, according to some critics, this ambiguity accounts for the obsessive search for identity in Mexican-American literature, often in the form of (fictionalized) autobiographies.

The Mexican-Indian Heritage

No sooner had the Spanish-speaking population in the Southwest been reduced to the status of a foreign minority than the Spanish component of Mexican culture became a cult, especially in California (cf. Pitt). On the other hand, the native Mexican-Indian oral tradition has long been regarded with contempt, if not utterly ignored. Américo Paredes's pioneer study *With His Pistol in His Hand* (1958) focused scholarly attention on the folk base of Chicano literature. Paredes considers the *border corrido* as a peculiar Mexican-American expression of the cultural conflict between Mexico and the United States. Thus, Gregorio Cortez, the hero of the most famous *border corrido,* has become a Pan-Hispanic symbol of Latino resistance, popularized more recently through a television video. The *corrido* has accompanied the Mexican Americans' trials and tribulations north of the Rio Grande to this day, whether to express protest against social injustice or participation in events affecting the entire nation, like the assassination of the Kennedys or of Martin Luther King.

Many Mexican-American legends, myths, and folk beliefs trace their ancestry to Aztec and Mayan sources or to events linked with the 1519 conquest of Mexico. Having long been denied expression of their Indian heritage, the Chicano militant writers of the 1960s revived and sometimes reinvented this mythological legacy in their quest for cultural self-definition. More recently, contemporary Chicano writers have been using the legendary figures of La Llorona, La Malinche, or La Virgen de Guadalupe in a more personal, at times subversive, way (e.g., Bernice Zamora, Sandra Cisneros, Ana Castillo).

Folk beliefs in the existence of witches (*brujas*), *curanderos/as* (folk healers), ghosts, and evil spirits—some of which are part of a common Indian heritage of the Americas—have also proved to be a rich source of inspiration for Mexican-American writers from Rudolfo Anaya to Ana Castillo.

"Strangers in Their Own Country"

One of the few Californios to maintain a seat in the state Senate after 1848, Pablo de la Guerra was painfully aware of the changing power relationship that would silence his countrymen's political and cultural voice. Under the new circumstances, the first-generation Mexican Americans, who, in his words, had become overnight "strangers in their own country," felt the need to express their concerns about, and general attitude toward, the political, socioeconomic, and cultural upheaval. They did it mainly through the Spanish-language newspapers, of which about 132 were published in the Southwest between 1848 and 1900.

Among these, *El Clamor Publico* stands out due to the outspoken articles of its editor, Francisco Ramirez, whom Luis Leal considers a forerunner of the Chicano movement. While arguing the necessity for Mexican Americans to learn English, Ramirez nevertheless insisted on the need for a bicultural education as well as the publication of California state laws in English and in Spanish; thus, he defended outlaws like Joaquin Murrieta on the ground that they were ignorant of the criminal code because it had not been translated into Spanish.

Another important mode of expression was undoubtedly the autobiographical narrative, which has only recently received due attention. According to Genaro Padilla, the shock waves set off by the 1848 annexation may have generated an autobiographic impulse in the Mexican-American community:

> Social rupture led to a decontextualization of individual and communal life that required a form of verbal restoration of that community with which the individual had identified his or her very locus of meaning. Before relocating life in the new regime, the life of the past had somehow to be accorded purpose, dignity, integrity. Autobiographic social history served this re-integrative, psycho-social process. ("Recovery" 47)

The "autobiographic impulse" in Mexican-American writings has clearly persisted to this day. However, it has undergone momentous shifts in perspective matching the writers' collective or individual quest for identity in their old/new land; the relative emphasis placed on one or the other of the two cultural poles— Mexico and the United States—functions as the litmus test of Mexican-American cultural identity. This does not preclude the attempt to forge a "borderlands" identity, which is manifest in certain recent writings, like Gloria Anzaldua's *Borderlands—La Frontera: The New Mestiza*.

The late nineteenth-century *memorias, historias, reminiscencias,* and *vidas* from archives in Texas, New Mexico, and California have brought to light the manifold contradictions of the Mexicano self shaped in the turmoil of both intra- and intercultural conflicts. The recent reexamination of these narratives has, by the same token, considerably altered the rigid, somewhat monolithic construction of the Chicano self proposed by the ideologues of the Chicano movement.

From Immigrant to Ethnic—Mexican-American Identity in the Making

The Mexican Revolution can be considered a "distant degree zero" of contemporary Chicano fiction insofar as, in most works written since the 1950s, it indirectly represents the starting point for the evolution of the Chicano literary hero in the United States. Actually, the only historical novel set during the 1910 revolution is José Antonio Villareal's *The Fifth Horseman* (1974), which can be read as an exploration of the Chicanos' Mexican past, while its mythic revolutionary hero stands as a counterexample to the negative image of Mexican refugees in American and Mexican literature.

In the first two decades of the twentieth century, the Mexican-American community and its culture got a new lease on life with the arrival of numerous political refugees and thousands of Mexican farmworkers and laborers. While the first generation of Mexican Americans had clung to their traditions against all odds, this second *entrada,* not of hidalgos in search of gold and silver but of peons in search of bread and a job, ensured the revival of Mexican culture north of the Rio Grande (cf. McWilliams).

The early twentieth century witnessed the gradual crystallization of a Mexican-American identity distinct from that of the Mexicans'. The latter actually started evincing negative opinions on the Mexican-American *pochos,* who, in José Vasconcelos's opinion, had become "mexicano-yankee hybrids" through the betrayal of their culture of origin and the adoption of what he called "North-American primitivism." The author of *La Raza Cosmica* could not conceive of, let alone foresee, the gradual emergence of an intercultural borderlands identity that would bring together the Anglo-American and the Hispano-American worlds. Yet in the barrios of California and Texas this process was taking place, eventually turning this "invisible and inaudible minority" into a highly visible and articulate ethnic group.

DOMINANT CONCERNS AND MAJOR AUTHORS

The decades leading up to the Chicano movement saw the Mexican-American community engaged in a daily struggle for survival, which hardly left it time or opportunity for literary pursuits. Yet some of the most significant contemporary Mexican-American writers drew their inspiration from those very years when, as children, they had accompanied their parents on their journey north in search for a place of their own in the land of the gringos. The two landmark novels preceding the Chicano literary renaissance of the 1960s and 1970s—José Antonio Villareal's *Pocho* (1959) and John Rechy's *City of Night* (1963)—both draw their material from those years.

In *Pocho,* Villareal introduces the fictionalized autobiographic hero—the writer's adolescent alter ego—in the process of "transition from the culture of the old world to that of the new" (135). By presenting, in bildungsroman fashion, the Rubio family's difficulty in maintaining the old traditions under the day-to-day pressure of American society, Villareal is the first Mexican-American contemporary writer to use the genre and to pose the cultural identity theme. With numerous variations, Chicano writers would explore, in their turn, the effects of assimilation on the collective identity of their community or on the private self.

John Rechy's first novel had an altogether different reception and legacy. Excluded for many years from the literary "canon" established by the nationalist standards of the Chicano movement, only recently have Chicano critics started reappraising his work, in which "ethnicity ceases to be an explicit subject, becoming one alluded to through the metonymy of the author's background'' (Bruce-Novoa *Retrospace,* 101). As gay and lesbian topics have become increasingly present in recent Chicano literature, Rechy's work no longer appears marginal and isolated. Moreover, ethnicity itself is being treated in less blatant terms than in the 1960s and 1970s.

The political and social effervescence of the mid-1960s signaled the first conscious attempts within the Mexican-American community to break with over a century of Anglo economic and cultural domination, which had turned it into an ''invisible minority.'' The Chicano movement's ideological agenda crystallized the claims springing from two fronts: the farmworkers led by Cesar Chavez and the students from the barrios, whose spokesman became Rodolfo ''Corky'' Gonzalez.

Some of the landmark literary works of the community were rooted in direct contact with the movement's commitment to affirmation of cultural pride, the struggle for civil and human rights and, most important, the ferment instilled by the Chicano student activists. In the early phase of what has been termed the ''Chicano cultural renaissance,'' this contact was quasi-symbiotic, as in the case of the *Teatro Campesino* (1965), brought forth out of the farmworkers' struggle. Luis Valdez's *Actos* (e.g., ''Las dos caras del patroncito'' (1965) or ''Los Vendidos'' (1967)), brief sketches initially performed by Chicano farmworkers, were designed to primarily educate and entertain Chicano audiences through a Manichean satirical portrayal of Anglo and Chicano stereotypes in a specific social reality and use of the interlingual idiom of the people. Forever restless, Valdez would jump outside the defined boundaries of Chicano literature.

The other landmark work of the first stage of Chicano nationalism, Rodolfo ''Corky'' Gonzalez's epic poem *I Am Joaquin* (1967), was, according to its author, ''a journey back through history, a painful self-evaluation, a wandering search for my peoples and, most of all, for my own identity'' (1). Written first and foremost for the Chicano movement, *I Am Joaquin* prefigures its nationalist ideology, its search for a past ethnocultural unity as a springboard for the awakening of a collective Mexican-American identity. The poem ''swept through the Chicano Movement like a popular manifesto, and it is still considered the best crystallization of the early Movement rhetoric in its stage of cultural nationalism'' (Bruce-Novoa, *Retrospace* 77).

While the Chicano movement's role in the boosting of original literary creation was undoubtedly instrumental, in retrospect, one must also acknowledge its excessive ideological impact on most of the works written at the time. The monologic nationalist stance of the militant 1970s was probably an inevitable stage in the community's long history of cultural obliteration. But literature and the arts tend to resist ideological imposition if they are to be authentic. The desire to rekindle the community's collective memory and the need to reinvent a Chicano ethnocultural past or to write about one's own life in the barrio in the language of the barrio were certainly legitimate; but when the programmatic intention took over, it often yielded a literature of self-imposed ethnic stereotypes couched in linguistic clichés. As Juan Bruce-Novoa put it, "[T]he standard formula for a successful Chicano piece calls for five or six *carnales,* a dozen *eses* and *batos,* a sprinkle of Spanish and a well-placed '*Chinga tu madre*' " (*Retrospace* 16). Much of the didactic, overtly political writing of the period has long been forgotten.

However, the 1970s were crucial years for the subsequent evolution of Mexican-American literature, and the credit for putting the Mexican Americans on the contemporary U.S. literary map goes to the Chicano movement. Undoubtedly a watershed year for Mexican-American literature, 1971 saw the publication of major literary works in the three genres: poetry, prose (the novel, the autobiographical narrative), and drama. *Actos,* a compilation of *actos* written by Luis Valdez between 1965 and 1971, was published that year, as was Alurista's *Floricanto en Aztlan,* which remains to this day the best expression of the Chicanos' quintessential search for a collective identity.

One of the authors of *El Plan Espiritual de Aztlan* (1969), Alurista was the spokesman of *la raza,* a term abundantly used in the 1970s to highlight the Mexican-Americans' Indo-Hispanic heritage and to raise the community's awareness of the past and present domination, as well as the necessary affirmation of its identity (cf. the poem "When Raza?"). In consonance with the Chicano movement's ideology, Alurista's poetic universe is dominated by a dichotomous vision that pits the traditional virtues of *la raza* against the inhumanity of Anglo-America. From this point of view, his poetry, which rules out any possible dialogue with the Other, has become outdated; the monologic, didactic, and prophetic vision has given way to a more open, dialogic poetic mode in the past decade. Alurista's literary reputation and lasting influence lie more in the pioneering role he played in innovating a modern interlingual *ars poetica.* Defying the laws of the market, he resorted to frequent code switching not only between English and Spanish but also including black English, Nahuatl, or Maya, "the full range of colors, the full rainbow," as he said himself. In a way, Alurista's multilingual code-switching contradicts the dichotomous ideology that underlies his poetry (cf. "El sarape de mi personalidad").

Twenty-five years after its publication, Tomas Rivera's . . . *Y no se lo trago la tierra* (1971, translated as . . . And the Earth Did Not Devour Him) remains one of the few masterpieces of Mexican-American literature. The author's untimely death has probably deprived the Mexican-American literary community of one of its most gifted writers. Written in the third person, the book is a series of fourteen short stories and thirteen vignettes in which the narrator encapsulates a year in his adolescent life as the son of Mexican migrant workers. Taking his distance from the dogmatic precepts of the Chicano movement, Rivera was the first writer to create the Chicano as a complete figure in contemporary Mexican-American literature, which he considered part of the "whole American scene." The narrator-protagonist, clearly the writer's young alter ego, writes a bildungsroman of sorts, drawing both on the American tradition of the autobiographical narrative of a would-be writer and on the writer's knowledge and experience of

Mexican migrant life in the United States. To this day, the novel strikes the reader by the astonishing skill with which Rivera used the stream-of-consciousness technique to give coherence to the apparently disjointed, embedded episodes that make up the book. An admirer of the quest for mental and intellectual liberation that has been so important for the Americas, Rivera was a searcher himself who succeeded in finding his particular idiom, which blends folkloric and (post)modernist techniques. Rivera's book received the first Quinto Sol National Award, sponsored by the publisher of the renowned journal *El Grito*. A whole generation of Chicano novelists, known as the Quinto Sol Generation, came to occupy central stage in the early 1970s, rendering substance and credence to the Chicanos' presence within Anglo-American culture.

Before turning to their works, brief mention has to be made of Ernesto Galarza's autobiography, *Barrio Boy* (1971), in which the author narrates the story of his assimilation to American life in Sacramento, California, during the 1920s. Although Galarza accurately renders the geographical segregation of the barrio, he draws a somewhat idyllic portrait of his smooth cultural and linguistic assimilation, which, however, did not prevent him from retaining the link to his Mexican roots. (Eleven years later, another autobiographical narrative that favored assimilation to the American society, Richard Rodriguez's *Hunger of Memory* [1982], was going to create a scandal in the Chicano literary community, which largely perceived the author as a *vendido* [a sell-out] to white Anglo-America.)

Galarza's book fits only marginally into the Chicano literary scene of the early 1970s. If Mexican-American cultural identity was a central issue with most writers, the emphasis was rather on re(capturing) a sense of the community's collective identity than on one specific, individual experience. Thus, authors like Rudolfo Anaya and Rolando Hinojosa, who have become the classics of Mexican-American literature, expanded the Chicano literary space beyond the here and now by turning to ancient myths and folk motifs (Anaya's *Bless Me, Ultima*, 1972; Second Quinto Sol Prize) and to regional traditions along a border area (Hinojosa's *Estampas del Valle*, 1973). Set, respectively, in New Mexico and Texas, the two novels dwell on the endurance and sense of determination of Mexican Americans who were not only recent immigrants to Anglo-America but also inhabitants whose roots date back many generations. While, in his subsequent works, Anaya remained very anchored in his native soil, somehow impervious to the influences of the outside world, Hinojosa's historical novels about south Texas are an example of *"mestizaje,* a cross-breeding of traditional and non-traditional North American and Latin American literary and cultural traditions" (Saldivar, *Dialectics* 63). In 1976, Hinojosa's second novel, *Klail City y sus alrededores,* was awarded the prestigious Casa de las Américas Prize in Cuba.

Oscar Zeta Acosta's two autobiographical novels, *The Autobiography of a Brown Buffalo* (1972) and its sequel, *The Revolt of the Cockroach People* (1973), are both frenzied existential musings of an adrift Chicano lawyer in quest of his identity. Alienated from everyone, Acosta is caught up in the political movement of the late 1960s, when he becomes the lawyer of militant Chicanos in East Los Angeles. Although the *Autobiography* ends up with the protagonist's being crushed by those he had set out to help, Acosta has nevertheless come to an awareness of his ethnic identity:

Ladies and gentlemen . . . my name is Oscar Acosta. My father is an Indian from Durango. Although I cannot speak his language . . . you see, Spanish is the language of our conquerors. English is the language of our conquerors. . . . No one ever asked me or my brother if we wanted to be American citizens. We are citizens by default. They stole our land and made us half-slaves. . . . Now what we need is, first to give ourselves a new name. We need a new identity. A name and a language all our own. (198)

Through its ties and orientation, Miguel Méndez's *Peregrinos de Aztlan* (1974) represents the transition from the Quinto Sol Generation to the post-1975 Isolated Generation of novelists. At the same time, *Peregrinos* signaled the Chicano writers' affiliation with the experimental Latin American New Novel. Within the United States–Mexico border problematics central to migrant Chicanos and would-be Chicanos, Méndez fuses myth and history with linguistic variants to create an alternative interlingual aesthetics.

The early and mid-1970s witnessed an unprecedented flourishing of Chicano poetry whose content generally gravitated around life in the barrio or in the prison (the so-called *pinto* poetry). As Francisco Lomeli has pointed out, "[P]erhaps the most refined poetic encapsulation of a marginalized Chicano character is José Montoya's 'El Louie' (1970), an eloquent eulogy to a dead *pachuco*" (*Handbook* 94).[3] The poem brings back to life the image of the dead *pachuco:*

> Kind of slim and drawn,
> there toward the end,
> aging fast from too much
> booze y la vida dura. But
> class to the end.

Montoya symbolically restores to the Mexican-American community an essential cultural signifier. Starting with the famous line "Hoy enterraron al Louie" ("Today they buried Louie"), the poem remains to this day the epitome of a Chicano poetics whose salient feature is interlingualism, the blending of languages, mainly Spanish and English, into what Tino Villanueva has called a "bisensitive poetry," which goes beyond the binary phenomenon of bilingualism. According to Juan Bruce-Novoa, "Chicano speech (and poetry) expands both the connotative and the denotative range of words in both languages, creating not a binary phenomenon, but a new phenomenon unfamiliar to the bilingual" (*Chicano Authors* 29). This type of interlingual poetry was characteristic of the early 1970s, when poets like Abelardo Delgado with *Chicano: 25 Pieces of a Chicano Mind,* Raul Salinas with *The Trip through the Mind Jail,* or Ricardo Sanchez with *Canto y grito mi liberacion* tried to capture in a narrative mode the quintessential features of the Chicano—humane, in harmony with nature, a victim of the Anglo—the callous conqueror living in a dehumanized, sterile society. This essentially dichotomous stance, often accompanied by a didactic tone, actually went against the interlingual mode, which attempted to achieve a synthesis of the two languages, English and Spanish, into a third.

The publication of Tino Villanueva's *Hay Otra Voz: Poems* (1974) signaled the emergence of a distinct, powerful poetic voice; he considerably widened the range of Chicano poetry by composing intimate poems in which the poet drew his inspiration from writers like Dylan Thomas, Anne Sexton, Octavio Paz, or D. H. Lawrence, to whom he refers in "Love Taste." Villanueva also wrote interlingual poems about Chicano farmworkers, *pachucos* or *la raza.* Most remarkable was, and still remains, his "ability to slide along the spectrum of interlingual mixture from standard English to standard Spanish" (Martinez and Lomeli 169).

While, by the mid-1970s, poets like Alurista, Abelardo Delgado, and Ricardo Sanchez were still active, issuing, respectively, *Timespace Huracan, It's Cold: 52 Cold-Thought Poems of Abelando,* and *HechizoSpells,* two new poetic voices came to the fore with the publication of *Restless Serpents* (1976) by a Chicana poet, Bernice Zamora, and *The Elements of San Joaquin* (1977) by Gary Soto. The latter's vision of a sterile society from which God has disappeared, his windswept images suggesting a barren landscape, prompted Juan Bruce-Novoa to compare Soto's collection of poems to T. S. Eliot's *The Waste Land;* however, the persona's grandmother's migration from Mexico and the hovering, mistrusted figure of La Malinche turn *The Elements of San Joaquin* into a Chicanized wasteland.

Before Bernice Zamora, only one Chicana writer, Estela Portillo Trambley, had achieved public attention, with her play *The Day of the Swallows* (1971), followed in 1975 by a volume of short stories, *Rain of Scorpions.* However, Bernice Zamora's *Restless Serpents* poems prefigured the powerful emergence on the literary scene of the Chicana writers, whose voice had practically remained silent during the male-dominated Chicano movement. Deeply anchored in the traditions of her New Mexico ancestors, such as the religious rites of the Penitentes, Zamora's poetry is concerned with the spiritual condition of modern society and, to a large extent, with the condition of women in a culture of male-chauvinist traditions. Zamora's originality lies in her expanding the Chicano poetic discourse through poems of intertextual reference (to Shakespeare, Robinson Jeffers, or Hesse). In one of her most quoted poems, "So Not to Be Mottled," she masterfully conveys the complexity of Chicana identity, whose "divisions are infinite"—a definition to which many of her followers would subscribe, like Ana Castillo, Sandra Cisneros, and others.

In 1975 occurred another turning point in the evolution of contemporary Chicano fiction. While the Quinto Sol Generation writers continued to publish works conveying a macrocosmic, existential view of Mexicans/Chicanos meant to underscore their full humanity in somehow ahistorical terms, the writers of the Isolated Generation—Alejandro Morales, Ron Arias, and Isabella Rios— emerged independently onto the Chicano literary scene with novels that obviously modified the previously established paradigms. As Francisco Lomeli aptly put it:

If the Quinto Sol Generation presents a horizontal view of experience, the Isolated Generation of 1975 advances a vertical conceptualization of marginalized social sectors. The former sought to legitimize what Chicano meant and the latter proceeds to probe into the meaning of Chicanismo with a magnifying glass. ("State of Siege" 186)

Thus, Alejandro Morales's *Old Faces and New Wine* (originally published in Spanish as *Caras viejas y vino nuevo*) signals a radical departure from other Chicano novels in its crude, microscopic focus on life in a hard-core, nameless barrio during the civil rights decade of the 1960s. Morales's characters are caught in a vicious circle of rampant violence and self-victimization that belie any moralistic, academic categorization, since dichotomies like oppressed-oppressor paradoxically coexist within a deconstructed world of perverted alienation.

Ron Arias's *The Road to Tamazunchale* (1975) displays a different kind of narrative experimentation; an admirer of García Márquez and Borges, Arias artfully mixes reality and fantasy in the protagonist's (the old bookseller Fausto) imaginary construct of his last days as if it were a novel. With Morales and Arias, just as with Zamora or Soto, Chicano literature showed the first signs of a shift away from the community-oriented sociopolitical writing of the previous decade to a more individualistic, personal vision of reality. The thematic and ideological criteria that defined a literary work as Chicano (the yardstick being the author's loyalty to the political goals of the community) seemed increasingly anachronistic in view of the aesthetic and formal evolution in the cultural production that the writers wanted and achieved.

Toward the end of the 1970s, it appeared that Chicano literature was losing its focus. The ethnocultural clichés of the 1960s seemed exhausted, while researchers brought to light Mexican-American literary writings of the past, and some, like Juan Bruce-Novoa, tried to open up fresh perspectives for a more diversified cultural production. Indeed, as of 1977, with Nash Candelaria's *Memories of the Alhambra,* writers started contesting the validity of the movement's ideals and Chicanismo itself, a move that grew in the early 1980s.

The late 1970s brought one momentous literary event: Luis Valdez wrote and directed the immensely successful play *Zoot Suit,* later turned into a movie by Universal Studios. The protean playwright, who had already been criticized by "mainstream Chicano circles" for his *Mitos*'s lyricism and escapism, now came under attack for selling out to the American mainstream and its commercial theater. Valdez had creatively blended a historical episode, the 1942 Sleepy Lagoon incident, with the *pachuco* literary tradition, giving his musical docudrama a Brechtian touch.

The Chicano literary space was definitely expanding, yet, as Juan Bruce-Novoa has pointed out, in the late 1970s

[t]he most significant change was not generic, thematic nor stylistic, but much more fundamental and radical: it was sexual. . . . The questions that Zamora, Portillo and other Chicanas raised about the oppression women suffered at the hands of men within traditional Chicano culture brought cries of protest from Chicanos. (*Retrospace* 86)

Chicanas responded with more or less overt feminist works, proclaiming their solidarity with the Chicano movement's ideals of liberation but, by the same token, unmasking the traditional male-chauvinist attitudes that persisted in its ranks. In some of her poems written in the mid-1970s, Lorna Dee Cervantes, one of the most gifted Chicana poets, founder of the literary magazine *Mango* (1976), seemed to prefigure the creative potential soon to be released by so many Chicana writers.

THE 1980S—THE DECADE OF THE CHICANAS

If the Chicano renaissance works had foregrounded the issue of Mexican-American cultural identity (traditions, language, ethnic pride) in opposition with the Anglo world, on the whole, these writings, largely written by male writers, at best ascribed traditional roles to the feminine characters (cf. Anaya's *curandera* [woman healer] Ultima). More often they saw the woman as *la chingada* or altogether omitted her both from their works and from their political and ideological preoccupations. The monological stance of Chicano militantness allowed for no dialogue with the dominant Anglo-American society, let alone with the Chicanas, who started venting their frustration at being left out of the political debates of their *carnales* (brothers).

The official, static, and closed version of ethnicity proposed by the literature of the Chicano movement was bound to come under attack from other voices in the community that had been silenced for too long; first and foremost among them were the women writers who gave Chicano literature a new lease on life by opening it up to a dialogue both with itself and with the American mainstream and other ethnic writings. At first reluctant, Chicano critics are in the process of reconsidering Mexican-American literature, its past and present, which involves an acceptance of the dialogic nature of Chicano literature, whose textuality is characterized by an interplay of voices and perspectives.

Chicana writers themselves started out by reconsiderations of "four prefeminist icons of *herstory* and female identity—La Malinche, the Virgin of Guadalupe, Sor Juana and La Llorona—for each embodies important images of *la mujer* that have helped define and circumscribe the roles of Latin American women for at least five centuries" (Candelaria 143). This recuperation basically consists in seeking the Otherness of the figures, which the male tradition has not recognized. Thus, La Malinche, the Indian woman who became Cortéz's lover and interpreter, long denigrated for having betrayed her people, is being revised by Chicana writers (Lucha Corpi, Naomi Quinonez, Sandra Cisneros, and others) who see her as a distant alter ego, an ambivalent figure caught in the difficult but rewarding enterprise of mediating between cultures. Likewise, the emblematic figures of La Llorona and La Virgen are given multiple identities, again in contrast with the closed, binary vision of gender in male Chicano writing.

While Bernice Zamora (particularly with "So Not to Be Mottled") and Lucha Corpi (*Palabras de mediodia—Noon Words: Poems* 1977) had paved the way for a feminist liberating discourse, during the early 1980s, Chicana writers made their forceful appearance on the literary scene. The year 1981 saw the publication of two very different books that were to become works of reference, as it were, for future Chicana writing: Lorna Dee Cervantes's collection of poems *Emplumada* and *This Bridge Called My Back: Writings by Radical Women of Color,* edited by Cherrie Moraga and Gloria Anzaldua.

Cervantes's *Emplumada* signaled the presence of a complex poetic persona whose intersecting voices made up a multifaceted identity blending the motifs of the Chicana, attached to her family's feminine lineage ("Beneath the Shadow of the Freeway"), revolted by the racial injustice in her land ("Poem for the Young White Man"), and intent on acting as a mediator between Mexico's oral tradition and the U.S. literate world in which she was brought up. Likewise, in her more intimate poems, Cervantes transcends the apparent cultural dichotomy that defines her by blending her two linguistic consciousnesses into one utterance through a process of hybridization, as in "Astro-no-mia":

> But all I could remember was that man
> Orion, helplessly shooting his shaft
> into my lit house from the bow.
> Y Yo? Hay bow. Y ya voy. (*Americas Review* 15.3–4 [1987]: 44)

Cervantes's second collection of poems, *From the Cables of Genocide: Poems on Love and Hunger* (1991), dedicated to Sylvia Plath, Frida Kahlo, and Violeta Parra, confirmed the penetrating feminist and human vision of her poetic universe, which she now opened up to intertextual references beyond the Americas (Neruda, Kundera, Duras, Lorca).

During the 1980s, poets like Ana Castillo (*Women Are Not Roses,* 1984), Angela de Hoyos (*Woman, Woman,* 1985), Evangelina Vigil (*Thirty an' Seen a Lot,* 1982), Pat Mora (*Chants,* 1984; *Borders,* 1986), Sandra Cisneros (*My Wicked, Wicked Ways,* 1987) and others confirmed the literary breakthrough of Chicana poets as well as their crucial role in deconstructing the monologic character of the 1960s and 1970s Chicano literature.

By addressing the interrelated issues of ethnicity, gender, and class from a depolarized perspective, the new Chicana poetic discourse was beginning to undermine the ideological strategies of exclusion both within the ethnic group and in relation to the mainstream. Moreover, as Wilson Dominic Neate has suggested, "the articulation of the subject in Chicana poetry may be appropriated by the practice of Chicano literature which must define itself in such a way as to undermine the ideological strategies of exclusion of the national group." (61). In other words, the example of Chicana writing should carry over to, and benefit, Mexican-American literature as a whole.

This Bridge Called My Back, a collection of esays, poems, tales, and testimonials whose editors, Cherrie Moraga and Gloria Anzaldua, adhered to the ideology of Third World feminism, broke new ground in Chicano literature in that it viewed the woman of color's subjectivity as the locus of multiple, conflicting voicings in resistance to competing notions for self-identification. Gloria Anzaldua quips, "What am I? *A third world lesbian feminist with Marxist and mystic leanings.* They would chop me up into little fragments and tag each piece with a label" (*Bridge* 205).

In 1983 Cherrie Moraga published *Loving in the War Years: lo que nunca paso por sus labios,* an innovative autobiographical work made up of essays, poems, and stories that are meant, in Moraga's words, "to create a kind of emotional/political chronology" of the author's multivoiced consciousness; with remarkable honesty and insight, Moraga probes her Chicana lesbian self to reveal the instrumental role of Mexicano culture's view of the woman, originating in the myth of *la chingada, La Malinche.*

In *Borderlands—La Frontera: The New Mestiza* (1987), Gloria Anzaldua takes the race, class, and gender issues one step further by addressing their multiple intersections as well as the interrelations of post-colonialism, nationalism, and ethnicity. Her focus is on the exploration of Chicana identity within a specific localization, the United States/Mexico borderlands, a place of hybridity, struggle, and transgression. Through the uncanny mixture of genres (autobiography, historical document, political manifesto, poems) matched by the constant switching of languages (English, Spanish, Nahuatl), the literary text becomes itself a graphic expression of post-modernist *mestizaje.* The most original aspect of the book lies in the conceptualizing of the borderlands as an interstitial space, a painful but exhilarating collective experiment, possibly leading to the emergence of multiple, shifting, cross-cultural identities.

In the past few years, several Chicano writers have also focused their attention on the increasingly complex reality of the border(lands): Guillermo Gomez-Pena in his essay "Documented/Undocumented" (1988), Richard Rodriguez in *Days of Obligation* (1992), and Rubén Martinez in *The Other Side* (1993). In Chicana fiction two names have eventually made a breakthrough into major American publishing houses: Sandra Cisneros and Ana Castillo. In *The House on Mango Street* (1985), Cisneros's compelling series of vignettes makes up a kind of bildungsroman in which Esperanza Cordero, the author's alter ego, evokes her coming-of-age in a Chicago neighborhood and her gradual realization that she is meant to be a writer. The book has been compared to Galarza's *Barrio Boy* and to Rivera's . . . *Y no se lo trago la tierra,* although Cisneros's world is a heterogeneous one, devoid of the *pureza* ethic of her male predecessors. Renato Rosaldo's comment on *Mango Street* also holds true for Cisneros's second collection of short stories, *Woman Hollering Creek* (1991):

What culture is losing in coherence and in "pureza" it is gaining in range and engagement. The politics of culture found in these short story cycles moves toward terrain of borders, spaces that readily include African-Americans, Anglos, schools, workplaces, and heterogeneous changing neighborhoods. (93)

Neither Mexican nor American, the hybrid persona of the narrator (a *Merican*), this modern Malinche, taboo-free, open-minded, and resilient like her famous ancestor, is negotiating a modus vivendi between her deep-rooted affinity to her own people (Mexicans and Mexican Americans) and the everyday reality of the Anglo-American world in which she was born and is living.

In her epistolary novel *The Mixquiahuala Letters* (1986), dedicated to the memory of the Argentinian writer Julio Cortázar, Ana Castillo also crosses physical, spiritual, and sexual borders, observing and recording the limitations inherent to both the Anglo-American and the Mexican cultures. Combining the subjective and the objective narratives in a quasi-ethnographic manner, the writer keeps a certain aloofness from each of the two societies, as well as from the Chicano community, for that matter. More recently, Castillo published *So Far from God* (1993), a novel set in contemporary New Mexico that daringly combines the world of magical realism with the cruel reality of today's wars, environmental issues, and diseases. Both Cisneros and Castillo have received the Before Columbus American Book Award for *The House on Mango Street* and *The Mixquiahuala Letters,* respectively.

The unprecedented flourishing of Chicana literary production has prompted many a literary critic to test new approaches to their works. Besides authors like Castillo, Moraga, Cisneros, and Anzaldua, who are also engaged in literary criticism, a growing number of female scholars have published articles and/or edited magazines (e.g., Norma Alarcon and *Third Woman*), thus keeping up the dialogue within the Chicano/a literary community.

CONCLUSION

If the 1980s were primarily the decade of Chicana feminist writing, some Chicano writers of the previous generation continued to publish (Anaya, Hinojosa, Morales, Méndez), while a few new male voices emerged on the Chicano literary scene. One of the most promising was that of Arturo Islas, whose untimely death in 1991 left only two works, *The Rain God* (1984) and *Migrant Souls* (1990). In both books the narrator is, in many ways, the author's alter

ego—a homosexual, physically handicapped academic—who writes a fictionalized autobiography that becomes "an act of exorcism, a ritual within which
the writer is both confessor and collective sinner" (Sanchez, "Ideological Discourses" 119). Thus Islas, not unlike many a Chicana writer, resents the patriarchy of both Mexican and American society, with its gender roles, power
relations, and values.

Richard Rodriguez's *Hunger of Memory: The Education of Richard Rodriguez* (1982) has triggered heated ideological debates that continue to send ripples
in Chicano academic circles. The author's condemnation of bilingual education
and affirmative action programs precluded an unbiased reading of this autobiography, whose main thrust, clearly stated in the title, was to portray the anguish
of the immigrants' son, confronted with the passage from his native language
and culture to those of the host country and his deep-felt need to retrieve what
was so painfully lost in the process—the link to his family, to his Mexican
roots. In many ways *Days of Obligation: An Argument with My Mexican Father*
(1992) is an attempt by the estranged author to renew the dialogue with his
parents, with their Mexican culture whose traditions and values seem to outweigh those of the pragmatic United States. It would seem that the tension
between the self-made and the ancestral components of Rodriguez's identity is,
if not resolved, at least relieved by the descent into past, into memory. Here's
his confession in the closing chapter of his 1992 spiritual autobiography:

Ask me what it was like to have grown up a Mexican kid in Sacramento and I will think
of my father's smile, its sweetness, its introspection, its weight of sobriety. Mexico was
most powerfully my father's smile, and not, as you might otherwise imagine, not language, not pigment. My father's smile seemed older than anything around me. Older
than Sutter's Fort. (220)

Rodriguez's *Days of Obligation* features an important element that can also be
found in other recent Chicano/a writings: the numerous cross-ethnic references
in his book—to blacks, Japanese, Irish, Chinese, Italians, and others—seem to
indicate their relevance in the construction of a composite Mexican-American
identity within an increasingly multiethnic nation.

Thus, recent Chicano writing shows a marked inclination for the autobiographical mode (Gary Soto's *Lesser Evils: Ten Quartets,* Victor Villasenor's
Rain of Gold, Floyd Salas's *Buffalo Nickel,* or Luis Rodriguez's *Always Running*), often with a focus on the United States/Mexican border or on Los Angeles
as sites of encounter between the First World and the Third World (John Rechy's
latest novel, *The Miraculous Day of Amalia Gomez*). In *Days of Obligation,*
Rodriguez commutes between Tijuana and San Diego, where past and present
seem to have exchanged roles. An autobiographical narrative of a different kind,
Diary of an Undocumented Immigrant by Ramon "Tianguis" Pérez (1991) is
unique in that it reveals a highly perceptive, intelligent, and witty observer of

American life in the person of an undocumented immigrant who eventually prefers to cross the border again, this time legally, and return to Mexico. Guillermo Gomez-Pena, the performance artist and writer, clearly states his option for "borderness" as a state of mind and a way of life. More recently, with *The Other Side: Fault Lines, Guerrilla Saints, and the True Heart of Rock 'n Roll* (1993), Rubén Martinez has brought an internationalist, effervescent vision to the area.

Almost three decades after its renaissance, Mexican-American literature is certainly alive, probably in a more challenging way than ever. Echoing a heterogeneous community that lives in an increasingly complex society, the writers' response has been one of opening up to, acknowledging, the Other—be it the Anglo, the Mexican, or the Italian—and they have thus reached a truer knowledge of themselves. Together with other ethnic literatures—Native American, African-American, Asian-American—Chicano literature has successfully challenged and is revising the mainstream literary canon. *The Health Anthology of American Literature* displays a multiethnic perspective that acknowledges the Hispanic contribution to American literature from Cabeza de Vaca's *Relaciones* to contemporary writers like Tomas Rivera or Sandra Cisneros. In the past ten years Chicano literature has also made a considerable breakthrough overseas. Universities in Germany, France, Spain, and Austria have been organizing lectures and international conferences on Chicano and, more generally, on Hispanic literature in the United States.

If, according to Octavio Paz, the great Latin American writers have actually transgressed the Castillan idiom, it would seem that the best Mexican-American writings are the result of a double transgression—that of English and Spanish. By explicitly and implicitly using each or both languages, the Chicano author does more than invent: he or she uncovers the latent, virtual possibilities of an interlingual-intercultural idiom. The most valuable Mexican-American writings—and the best is yet to come—actually invalidate binary oppositions. Rather, their existential, cultural, and formal raison d'être lies in a search for inter-American complementary differences and areas of confluence.

NOTES

1. A cultural term that favorably describes the process of miscegenation, the mixture of different racial backgrounds. Chicanos in the 1960s started using the term with pride to refer to their mixed-blood heritage, European and Indian.

2. Following the *Harvard Encyclopedia of American Ethnic Groups,* the terms "Mexican-American" and "Chicano" will be used interchangeably without the nationalist connotation the latter acquired during the Chicano movement of the 1960s and 1970s.

3. Originally zoot-suited Chicano youths in Los Angeles during the 1940s, *pachucos* came to refer more generally to Chicano "dudes" from the barrios as characterized by their dress, invented language (*calo*), and socially marginal behavior.

SELECTED PRIMARY BIBLIOGRAPHY

Acosta, Oscar Zeta. *The Autobiography of a Brown Buffalo.* San Francisco: Straight Arrow Books, 1972.

———. *The Revolt of the Cockroach People.* San Francisco: Straight Arrow Books, 1973.

Alarcon, Norma, A. Castillo, and Charles Moraga, eds. *Third Woman: The Sexuality of Latinas.* Vol. 4. Berkeley: Third Woman Press, 1989.

Alurista (Alberto Urista) *Floricanto en Aztlan.* Los Angeles: Chicano Cultural Center, 1971.

———. *Nationchild Plumaroja.* San Diego: Toltecas on Aztlan, 1972.

———. *Return: Poems Collected and New.* Ypsilanti: Bilingual Review, 1982.

Anaya, Rudolfo. *Bless me, Ultima.* Berkeley: Quinto Sol, 1972.

———. *Albuquerque.* Albuquerque: University of New Mexico Press, 1992.

Anzaldua, Gloria. *Borderlands—La Frontera: The New Mestiza.* San Francisco: Spinsters/Aunt Lute, 1987.

———, ed. *Making Face, Making Soul. Haciendo Caras.* Creative and Critical Perspectives by Women of Color. San Francisco: Spinsters/Aunt Lute, 1990.

Arias, Ron. *The Road to Tamazunchale.* 1975. Tempe, AZ: Bilingual Press, 1987.

Arteaga, Alfred. *Cantos.* Los Angeles: Chusma House, 1991.

Barrio, Raymond. *The Plum Plum Pickers.* Sunnyvale, CA: Ventura Press, 1976.

Brito, Aristeo. *El diablo en Texas.* Tucson: Peregrinos, 1976.

Bruce-Novoa, Juan. *Inocencia Perversa.* Phoenix: Baleen Press, 1977.

Bus, Heiner, and Ana Castillo, eds. *Recent Chicano Poetry.* Bamberg: Universitäts Bibliothek. 1994.

Cabeza de Vaca, Alvar Nunez. *Adventures in the Unknown Interior of America.* Trans. Cyclone Covey. Albuquerque: University of New Mexico Press, 1983.

Candelaria, Nash. *Memories of the Alhambra.* Palo Alto, CA: Cibola, 1977.

Castillo, Ana. *Women Are Not Roses.* Houston: Arte Publico Press, 1984.

———. *The Mixquiahuala Letters.* Binghamton, NY: Bilingual Press, 1986.

———. *So Far from God.* New York: Norton, 1993.

Cervantes, Lorna Dee. *Emplumada.* Pittsburgh: University of Pittsburgh Press, 1981.

———. *From the Cables of Genocide: Poems on Love and Hunger.* Houston: Arte Público Press, 1991.

Chavez, Denise. *The Last of the Menu Girls.* Houston: Arte Público Press, 1986.

Cisneros, Sandra. *The House on Mango Street.* Houston: Arte Público Press, 1985.

———. *My Wicked, Wicked Ways.* Berkeley: Third Woman Press. 1987.

———. *Woman Hollering Creek.* New York: Random House, 1991.

———. *Loose Woman. Poems.* New York: Norton, 1994.

Corpi, Lucha. *Palabras de mediodia—Noon Words: Poems.* Berkeley: El Fuego de Aztlan, 1977.

de Hoyos, Angela, *Woman, Woman.* Houston: Arte Público Press, 1985.

Delgado, Abelardo. *Chicano: 25 Pieces of a Chicano Mind.* Denver: Barrio, 1969.

———. *It's Cold: 52 Cold-Thought Poems of Abelardo.* Salt Lake City: Barrio, 1977.

Fernandez, Roberta, ed. *In Other Words: Literature by Latinas of the United States.* Houston: Arte Público Press, 1994.

Galarza, Ernesto. *Barrio Boy: The Story of a Boy's Acculturation.* Notre Dame, IN: University of Notre Dame Press, 1971.

Gomez-Pena, Guillermo. "Documented/Undocumented." *Multi-Cultural Literacy.* Saint Paul: Graywolf Press, 1988.

Gonzales, Rodolfo "Corky." *Yo soy Joaquin.* Denver: Crusade for Justice, 1967.

Hinojosa, Rolando. *Estampas del Valle y otras obras.* Berkeley: Quinto Sol, 1973.

———. *Klail City y sus alrededores.* Havana: Casa de las Americas, 1976.

Islas, Arturo. *The Rain God.* Palo Alto, CA: Alexandrian Press, 1984.

———. *Migrant Souls.* New York: Morrow, 1990.

Martinez, Rubén. *The Other Side: Fault Lines, Guerrilla Saints, and the True Heart of Rock 'n Roll.* New York: Random House, 1993.

Méndez, Miguel. *Peregrinos de Aztlan.* Tucson: Editorial Peregrinos, 1974.

Montoya, José. "El Louie." *Rascatripas* 2 (1970): n.p.

Mora, Pat. *Chants.* Houston: Arte Público Press, 1984.

———. *Borders.* Houston: Arte Público Press, 1986.

———. *Communion.* Houston: Arte Público Press, 1991.

Moraga, Cherrie. *Loving in the War Years: Lo gue nunca paso pos sus Labios.* Boston: South End Press, 1983.

Moraga, Cherrie, and Gloria Anzaldua, eds. *This Bridge Called My Back: Writings by Radical Women of Color.* Watertown, MA: Persephone Press, 1981.

Morales, Alejandro. *Caras viejas y vino nuevo/Old Faces and New Wine.* 1975. Trans. Max Martinez. San Diego: Maize Press, 1981.

———. *Reto en el paraiso.* Ypsilanti, MI: Bilingual Press, 1983.

———. *Rag Doll Plagues.* Houston: Arte Público, 1992.

Pérez, Ramon "Tianguis." *Diary of an Undocumented Immigrant.* Houston: Arte Público Press, 1991.

Pineda, Cecile. *Face.* New York: Penguin, 1985.

Portillo Trambley, Estela. *Rain of Scorpions and Other Writings.* Berkeley: Tonatiuh International, 1975.

Quinonez, Naomi. *Sueno de colibri/Hummingbird Dream.* Albuquerque: West End Press, 1986.

Rechy, John. *City of Night.* New York: Grove Press, 1963.

———. *The Miraculous Day of Amalia Gomez.* New York: Little, Brown, 1991.

Rios, Isabella. *Victuum.* Ventura, CA: Diana-Etna, 1976.

Rivera, Tomas. *. . . Y no se lo trago la tierra.* Berkeley: Editorial Justa, 1971.

———. *The Harvest.* Houston: Arte Público Press, 1989.

Rodriguez, Luis. *Always Running—La Vida Loca: Gang Days in L.A.* New York: Simon and Schuster, 1993.

Rodriguez, Richard. *Hunger of Memory: The Education of Richard Rodriguez.* 1982. New York: Bantam Books, 1983.

———. "An American Writer." *The Invention of Ethnicity.* Ed. W. Sollors. New York: Oxford University Press, 1989. 3–13.

———. *Days of Obligation: An Argument with My Mexican Father.* New York: Viking, 1992.

Salas, Floyd. *Buffalo Nickel.* Houston: Arte Público Press, 1992.

Salinas, Raul. *Un Trip through the Mind Jail y Otras Excursions.* San Francisco: Editorial Pocho-Che, 1980.

Sanchez, Ricardo. *Canto y grito mi liberacion.* El Paso: Mictla, 1971.

———. *HechizoSpells.* Los Angeles: Chicano Studies Center, 1976.

Soto, Gary. *The Elements of San Joaquin.* Pittsburgh: University of Pittsburgh Press, 1977.

———. *Lesser Evils: Ten Quartets.* Houston: Arte Público Press, 1988.

Valdez, Luis, and El Teatro Campesino. *Actos.* San Juan Bautista: Cucaracha Press, 1971.

Valdez, Luis, and Stan Steiner, eds. *Aztlan—An Anthology of Mexican American Literature.* New York: Vintage Books, 1972.

Vigil, Evangelina. *Thirty an' Seen a Lot.* Houston: Arte Público Press, 1982.

Villanueva, Alma. *Bloodroot.* Austin: Place of Herons Press, 1982.

Villanueva, Tino. *Hay Otra Voz: Poems.* Madrid and New York: Mensaje, 1974.

———. *Shaking Off the Dark.* Houston: Arte Público Press, 1984.

Villarreal, José Antonio. *Pocho.* New York: Doubleday, 1959.

———. *The Fifth Horseman.* New York: Doubleday, 1974.

Villasenor, Victor. *Rain of Gold.* Houston: Arte Público Press, 1991.

Viramontes, Helena Maria. *The Moths and Other Stories.* Houston: Arte Público Press, 1985.

Zamora, Bernice. *Restless Serpents.* Berkeley: Disenos Literarios, 1976.

SELECTED SECONDARY BIBLIOGRAPHY

Alarcon, Norma. "The Theoretical Subjects(s) of *This Bridge Called My Back* and Anglo-American Feminism." *Criticism in the Borderlands: Studies in Chicano Literature, Culture and Ideology.* Ed. Hector Calderon and Jose D. Saldivar. Durham, NC: Duke University Press, 1991. 28–43.

Anaya, Rudolfo, and F. Lomeli, eds. *Aztlan: Essays on the Chicano Homeland.* Albuquerque, NM: Academia/El Norte Publications, 1989.

Bruce-Novoa, Juan. "The Space of Chicano Literature." *De Colores* 1.4 (1974): 22–42.

———. *Chicano Authors: Inquiry by Interview.* Austin: University of Texas Press, 1980.

———. *Chicano Poetry: A Response to Chaos.* Austin: University of Texas Press, 1982.

———. *Retrospace: Collected Essays on Chicano Literature.* Houston: Arte Público Press, 1990.

Bus, Heiner. "Gender Roles and the Emergence of a Writer in Denise Chavez's *The Last of the Menu Girls.*" *Missions in Conflict: Essays on U.S.–Mexican Relations and Chicano Culture.* Ed. Renate von Bardeleben. Tubingen: Gunter Narr Verlag, 1986. 277–287.

———. "The Establishment of Community in Zora Neal Hurston's *The Eatonville Anthology* (1926) and Rolando Hinojosa's *Estampas del Valle* (1973)." *European Perspectives on Hispanic Literature of the United States.* Ed. Geneviève Fabre. Houston: Arte Público Press, 1988. 66–81.

———. "Homosexuality and the Chicano Novel." *European Perspectives on Hispanic Literature in the U.S.* Ed. Geneviève Fabre. Houston: Arte Público Press, 1988. 98–106.

Buxo Rey, Maria Jesus, and T. Calvo Buezas, eds. *Culturas Hispanas de los Estados Unidos.* Madrid: Ediciones de Cultura Hispanica, 1990.

Calderon, Hector, and José D. Saldivar. *Criticism in the Borderlands: Studies in Chicano Literature, Culture, and Ideology.* Durham, NC: Duke University Press, 1991.

Candelaria, Cordelia. *Chicano Poetry: A Critical Introduction.* Westport, CT: Greenwood Press, 1986.

Fabre, Geneviève. "Dialectics of the Masks in El Teatro Campesino: From Images to Ritualized Events." *Missions in Conflict: Essays on U.S.–Mexican Relations and Chicano Culture.* Ed. Renate von Bardeleben. Tubingen: Gunter Narr Verlag, 1986. 93–101.

———, ed. *European Perspectives on Hispanic Literature of the United States.* Houston: Arte Público Press, 1988.

Fitz, Earl. *Rediscovering the New World: Inter-American Literature in a Comparative Context.* Iowa City: University of Iowa Press, 1991.

Fuentes, Carlos. *Myself with Others: Selected Essays.* London: Picador, 1989.

Grandjeat, Yves-Charles. "Doxy and Heterodoxy in the Emerging Chicano Critical Discourse: Metacritical Notes on Criticism in the Borderlands." *Annales du C.R.A.A.* 18 (1993): 313–323.

Gutierrez, Ramon, and Genaro Padilla, eds. *Recovering the U.S. Hispanic Heritage.* Houston: Arte Público Press, 1993.

Herrera-Sobek, Maria, ed. *Beyond Stereotypes: The Critical Analysis of Chicana Literature.* New York: Bilingual Press, 1985.

Huerta, Jorge. *Chicano Theater: Themes and Forms.* Ypsilanti: Bilingual Press, 1982.

Jiménez, Francisco, ed. *The Identification and Analysis of Chicano Literature.* New York: Bilingual Press, 1979.

Kanellos, Nicolas. *Hispanic Theater.* Austin: University of Texas Press, 1989.

Lattin, Vernon, ed. *Contemporary Chicano Fiction: A Critical Survey.* Binghamton, NY: Bilingual Press, 1986.

Leal, Luis, et al. *A Decade of Chicano Literature. 1970–1979: Critical Essays and Bibliography.* Santa Barbara: Editorial La Causa, 1982.

Lomeli, Francisco. "State of Siege in Alejandro Morales' *Old Faces and New Wine.*" *Missions in Conflict: Essays on U.S.–Mexican Relations and Chicano Culture.* Ed. Renate von Bardeleben. Tubingen: Gunter Narr Verlag, 1986. 185–195.

———, ed. *Handbook of Hispanic Cultures in the U.S.: Literature and Art.* Houston: Arte Público Press, 1993.

Lomeli, Francisco, and Carl Shirley. *Dictionary of Literary Biography Volume 82: Chicano Writers First Series.* Detroit: Gale Research, 1989.

Lomeli, Francisco, and D. Urioste. *Chicano Perspectives in Literature: A Critical and Annotated Bibliography.* Albuquerque: Pajarito, 1976.

Martinez, Julio, and F. Lomeli, eds. *Chicano Literature: A Reference Guide.* Westport, CT: Greenwood Press, 1985.

McWilliams, Carey. *North from Mexico: The Spanish-Speaking People of the United States.* New York: Greenwood Press, 1948.

Moncada, Alberto Lorenzo, et al. eds. *El Poder Hispano. Actas del V Congreso de Culturas Hispanas en los Estados Unidos.* Madrid: Universidad de Alcala, 1994.

Moquin, Walter, ed. *A Documentary History of the Mexican-Americans.* New York: Bantam Books, 1972.

Neate, Wilson Dominic. "Re-Writing/Re-Reading Ethnicity: The Lesson of Chicana Poetry." *Missions in Conflict: Essays on U.S.–Mexican Relations and Chicano Culture.* Ed. Renate von Bardeleben. Tubingen: Gunter Narr Verlag, 1986. 53–73.

Olivares, Julian, ed. *International Studies in Honor of Tomas Rivera.* Houston: Arte Público Press, 1986.

Padilla, Genaro. "The Recovery of Nineteenth-Century Chicano Autobiography." *European Perspectives* (1988): 44–54.

———. *My History, Not Yours: The Formation of Mexican American Autobiography.* Madison: University of Wisconsin Press, 1993.

Paredes, Américo. *With His Pistol in His Hand: A Border Ballad and Its Hero.* Austin: University of Texas Press, 1958.

Paz, Octavio. *The Labyrinth of Solitude: Life and Thought in Mexico.* New York: Grove Press, 1961.

———. *Nobel Lecture 1990.* The Nobel Foundation, 1990.

Pitt, Leonard. *The Decline of the Californios.* Berkeley: University of California Press, 1966.

Rocard, Marcienne. *Les fils du soleil: la minorité mexicaine à travers la littérature des Etats-Unis.* Paris: Maisonneuve et Larose, 1980. Trans. E. Brown, Jr. *The Children of the Sun: Mexican Americans in the Literature of the United States.* Tucson: University of Arizona Press, 1989.

Rosaldo, Renato. "Fables of the Fallen Guy." *Criticism in the Borderlands: Studies in Chicano Literature, Culture and Ideology.* Ed. Hector Calderon and Jose D. Saldivar. Durham, NC: Duke University Press, 1991. 84–97.

Saldivar, José David. *The Dialectics of Our America: Genealogy, Cultural Critique, and Literary History.* Durham, NC: Duke University Press, 1991.

Saldivar, Ramon. *Chicano Narrative: The Dialectics of Difference.* Madison: University of Wisconsin Press, 1990.

Sanchez, Martha. *Contemporary Chicana Poetry.* Berkeley: University of California Press, 1985.

Sanchez, Rosaura. "Ideological Discourses in Arturo Islas's *The Rain God.*" *Criticism in the Borderlands: Studies in Chicano Literature, Culture and Ideology.* Ed. Hector Calderon and Jose D. Saldivar. Durham, NC: Duke University Press, 1991. 114–127.

Savin, Ada. "Lorna Dee Cervantes: Portrait of the Woman as an Artist." *Missions in Conflict: Essays on U.S.–Mexican Relations and Chicano Culture.* Ed. Renate von Bardeleben. Tubingen: Gunter Narr Verlag, 1986. 123–131.

———. "Langue, identité et altérité dans *Hunger of Memory* de R. Rodriguez." *L'altérité dans la littérature et la culture du monde anglophone.* Le Mans: Presses Universitaires du Maine, 1991.

———. "Bilingualism and Dialogism: Another Reading of Lorna Dee Cervantes's Poetry." *An Other Tongue: Nation and Ethnicity in the Linguistic Borderlands.* Ed. A. Arteaga. Durham, NC: Duke University Press, 1994.

———. "Course and Discourse in G. Anzaldua's Borderlands—La Frontera." *Parcours identitaires.* Ed. G. Fabre. Paris: Presses de la Sorbonne Nouvelle, 1994. 110–120.

———. "Mexican-American Literature: A Bridge over the Americas." Binghamton, NY: Bilingual Press, forthcoming.

Sommers, Joseph. "From the Critical Premise to the Product: Critical Modes and Their Applications to a Chicano Literary Text." *New Directions in Chicano Scholarship.* Ed. R. Romo and R. Paredes. Santa Barbara: Center for Chicano Studies, 1984. 51–80.

Sommers, Joseph and Tomas Ybarra-Frausto, eds. *Modern Chicano Writers: A Collection of Critical Essays.* Englewood Cliffs, NJ: Prentice-Hall, 1979.

Tatum, Charles. *Mexican-American Literature*. Orlando: Harcourt Brace Jovanovich, 1990.

Todorov, Tzvetan. *La conquête de l'Amérique*. Trans. *The Conquest of the Americas*. New York: Harper and Row, 1984.

Villanueva, Tino. *Chicanos: Antologia historica y literaria*. México City: Fondo de Cultura Economica, 1980.

———. Introduction. *Imagine* 1.1 (1984): vii–xxxvii.

von Bardeleben, Renate, ed. *Missions in Conflict: Essays on U.S.–Mexican Relations and Chicano Culture*. Tubingen: Gunter Narr Verlag, 1986.

———. "Gender, Self, and Society." Proceedings of the Fourth International Conference on the Hispanic Cultures of the U.S. Frankfurt: Peter Lang, 1993.

Ybarra-Frausto, Tomas. "The Chicano Movement and the Emergence of a Chicano Poetic Consciousness." *New Directions in Chicano Scholarship*. Ed. Joseph Somers. Santa Barbara: Center for Chicano Studies, 1984. 81–110.

Selected Bibliography

Boelhower, William Q. "The Immigrant Novel as Genre." *MELUS* 8 (Spring 1981): 3–13.

Brown, Wesley, and Amy Ling. *Imagining America: Stories from the Promised Land.* New York: Persea Books, 1991.

Bryce, David L. *European Immigration and Ethnicity in the United States and Canada: A Historical Bibliography.* Santa Barbara: ABC-Clio Information Services, 1983.

Bryce-Laporte, Roy S., and Delores M. Mortimer, eds. *Caribbean Immigration to the United States.* Washington, DC: Smithsonian Institution, Research Institute on Immigration and Ethnic Studies, 1976.

Buelens, Gert. "Beyond Ethnicity?" *Journal of American Studies* 23 (August 1989): 315–320.

Cordasco, Francesco, ed. *Dictionary of American Immigration History.* Metuchen, NJ: Scarecrow P, 1990.

Cuddy, Dennis Laurence, ed. *Contemporary American Immigration: Interpretive Essays (Non-European).* Boston: Twayne, 1982.

Curran, Thomas J. *Xenophobia and Immigration, 1820–1930.* Boston: Twayne, 1975.

Daniels, Roger. *Coming to America: A History of Immigration and Ethnicity in American Life.* New York: HarperCollins, 1990.

Davis, Marilyn P. *Mexican Voices/American Dreams: An Oral History of Mexican Immigration to the United States.* New York: Henry Holt, 1990.

D'Innocenzo, Michael, and Josef P. Sirefman, eds. *Immigration and Ethnicity: American Society—"Melting Pot" or "Salad Bowl"?* Westport, CT: Greenwood P, 1992.

Di Pietro, Robert, and Edward Ifkovic, eds. *Ethnic Perspectives in American Literature: Selected Essays on the European Contribution, A Sourcebook.* New York: MLA, 1983.

Dinnerstein, Leonard, and David M. Reimers. *Ethnic Americans: A History of Immigration and Assimilation.* New York: Dodd, Mead, 1975.

Gennaro Lerda, Valeria, ed. *From "Melting Pot" to Multiculturalism: The Evolution of Ethnic Relations in the United States and Canada.* Rome: Bulzoni Editore, 1990.

Glazer, Nathan. *The New Immigration: A Challenge to American Society.* San Diego: San Diego State UP, 1988.

Glazer, Nathan, ed. *Clamor at the Gates: The New American Immigration.* San Francisco: ICS P, 1985.

Greenleaf, Barbara Kaye. *America Fever: The Story of American Immigration.* New York: Four Winds P, 1970.

Grenier, Guillermo J., and Alex Stepick, eds. *Miami Now!: Immigration, Ethnicity, and Social Change.* Gainesville: U Press of Florida, 1992.

Harap, Louis. *The Image of the Jew in American Literature: From Early Republic to Mass Immigration.* Philadelphia: Jewish Publication Society of America, 1974.

Holte, James Craig, ed. *The Ethnic I: A Sourcebook for Ethnic American Autobiography.* Westport, CT: Greenwood P, 1988.

Hondagneu-Sotelo, Pierrette. *Gendered Transitions: The Mexican Experience of Immigration.* Berkeley: U of California P, 1994.

Jones, Maldwyn Allen. *American Immigration.* Chicago: U of Chicago P, 1960.

Kelly, Gail Paradise. *From Vietnam to America: A Chronicle of the Vietnamese Immigration to the United States.* Boulder, CO: Westview P, 1977.

Kim, Hyung-chan, ed. *The Korean Diaspora: Historical and Sociological Studies of Korean Immigration and Assimilation in North America.* Santa Barbara: Clio Books, 1977.

Koszegi, Michael A., and J. Gordon Melton, eds. *Islam in North America: A Sourcebook.* New York: Garland, 1992.

Kulhanjian, Gary A. *The Historical and Sociological Aspects of Armenian Immigration to the United States.* San Francisco: R. and E. Research Associates, 1975.

Lasker, Bruno. *Filipino Immigration.* New York: Arno P, 1969.

Lee, Joann Faung Jean, ed. *Asian American Experiences in the United States: Oral Histories of First to Fourth Generation Americans from China, the Philippines, Japan, India, the Pacific Islands, Vietnam, and Cambodia.* Jefferson, NC: McFarland, 1991.

Luebke, Frederick C. *Germans in the New World: Essays in the History of Immigration.* Urbana: U of Illinois P, 1990.

Luedtke, Luther S., ed. *Making America: The Society and Culture of the United States.* Chapel Hill: U of North Carolina P, 1992.

Maidens, Melinda. *Immigration: New Americans, Old Questions.* New York: Facts on File, 1981.

Meister, Richard J., ed. *Race and Ethnicity in Modern America.* Lexington, MA: Heath, 1974.

Mills, Nicolaus, ed. *Arguing Immigration: Are New Immigrants a Wealth of Diversity . . . or a Crushing Burden?* New York: Touchstone, 1994.

Passel, Jeffrey S., and Barry Edmonston. *Immigration and Race in the United States: The Twentieth and Twenty-first Centuries.* Boston: UP of America, 1992.

Pozzetta, George F., ed. *Assimilation, Acculturation, and Social Mobility.* New York: Garland, 1991.

———. *Contemporary Immigration and American Society.* New York: Garland, 1991.

————. *Education and the Immigrant.* New York: Garland, 1991.

————. *Ethnicity and Gender: The Immigrant Woman.* New York: Garland, 1991.

————. *Nativism, Discrimination, and Images of Immigrants.* New York: Garland, 1991.

Skardal, Dorothy Burton. "Revising the American Literary Canon: The Case of Immigrant Literature." *American Studies in Transition.* Ed. D. Nye and C. Thomsen. Odense: Odense UP, 1985. 97–119.

Szeplaki, Joseph. *Hungarians in the United States and Canada: A Bibliography.* Minneapolis: Immigration History Research Center, U of Minnesota, 1977.

Tomasi, Lydio F., ed. *Italian Americans: New Perspectives in Italian Immigration and Ethnicity.* Staten Island: Center for Migration Studies of New York, 1985.

Index

About the Contributors

NERISSA BALCE-CORTES's publications include essays in the *Cultural Center of the Philippines Encyclopedia of Philippine Arts* and *Critical Mass,* fiction, and poetry. The discussion on Filipino American fiction will be part of a larger work on imagined homelands, culture, and imperialism.

CARRIE TIRADO BRAMEN wrote her dissertation on " 'An Innocent Way Out': The Literature and Politics of Cultural Pluralism, 1885–1925.'' She is currently an Assistant Professor of English at SUNY Buffalo.

DANIEL J. CASEY is President of Burlington College in Vermont. With Robert Rhodes, he has written and edited texts in Irish and Irish-American letters: *Views of the Irish Peasantry, 1800–1916; Irish-American Fiction: Essays in Criticism;* and *Modern Irish-American Fiction: A Reader.* He has authored more than 120 books, articles, and reviews. His *Critical Essays on John Millington Synge* was published in 1994.

FRED L. GARDAPHE is Professor of English at Columbia College in Chicago, where he teaches writing, American literature, and Italian/American culture. He is associate editor of *Fra Noi,* coeditor of *From the Margin: Writings in Italian Americana* and the journal *Voices in Italian Americana,* and editor of *New Chicago Stories* and *Italian American Ways.* He has published fiction, essays, and critical articles in local and national publications. His most recent book is *Italian Signs, American Streets: Reading Italian American Literature.*

JEAN VENGUA GIER is a poet and essayist. In 1995, her poetry appeared in the *Journal of American Culture, Proliferation,* and *Asian America.* Her essay, " ' . . . to have come from someplace': *October Light, America Is in the Heart,* and 'Flip' Writing after the Third World Strikes,'' is forthcoming in *Critical Mass: A Journal of Asian American Literary and Cultural Criticism.*

GURLEEN GREWAL is Assistant Professor of Women's Studies at the University of South Florida in Tampa, specializing in women's writing, feminist criticism, and post-colonial studies.

JAE-NAM HAN teaches composition and ESL courses at the University of Nebraska-Lincoln. He has also been an editor/translator for many publications both in the United States and South Korea.

SHAN QIANG HE is a doctoral student at the English Department of Simon Fraser University, British Columbia, Canada. His research area is post-colonial criticism and immigrant literature.

ANITA AUKEE JOHNSON teaches at Whatcom Community College in Bellingham, Washington, and plans continued study in culturally distinct and nature-centered literatures.

YIORGOS D. KALOGERAS is Associate Professor of American ethnic and minority literature in the English Department, Aristotle University of Thessaloniki, Greece. He has published critical essays in major American and Greek journals, compiled bibliographies of Greek-American literature, and is founder and chair of the Hellenic Association of American Studies and coeditor of *Gramma: A Journal of Theory and Criticism.* He is completing (in English) a book on Greek-American ethnicity entitled *Ethnic Geographies* and editing (in Greek) a collection of essays on Toni Morrison.

ALPANA SHARMA KNIPPLING teaches post-colonial literatures in the English Department, University of Nebraska–Lincoln. She has published on pedagogy and multiculturalism, Indian diasporic literature, and Indian literature in English in critical anthologies and journals. She is currently working on a book on Indian literature in English.

MARK KRUPNICK is Professor of religion and literature at the Divinity School of the University of Chicago. He edited *Displacement: Derrida and After* (1983) and is author of *Lionel Trilling and the Fate of Cultural Criticism* (1986). He is currently writing a book on the autobiographical impulse in Jewish-American writing. His reviews and essays have appeared in *Salmagundi, Forward, New York Times Book Review, New York Review of Books, New England Review,*

Contemporary Literature, and many other specialist journals and magazines of opinion.

DIANE MATZA is Professor of English at Utica College of Syracuse University, where she teaches writing and twentieth-century American literature. Her work on Sephardic Jewish culture and history in the United States has appeared in *American Jewish Archives, Immigration History Newsletter, MELUS, Midstream,* and *American Jewish History.* Her anthology *Writing the Culture: Sephardic American Literature* will be published in 1996. She is also working on a biography of Annie Nathan Meyer, playwright, publicist, and founder of Barnard College.

RICARDO L. ORTÍZ currently teaches critical and narrative theory at San Jose State University and, starting in Fall 1996, will teach at Dartmouth College in New Hampshire. He has published articles on Fielding's *Tom Jones* and on a number of gay Latino novelists, including John Rechy and Arturo Islas. He is currently working on a book on gay Latino novelists entitled *Pleasure's Exiles.*

NASRIN RAHIMIEH is Associate Professor in the Department of Comparative Literature and Film Studies of the University of Alberta. Her teaching and research focus on literatures of exile and displacement, contemporary Iranian women's writing, and gender studies.

ROBERT E. RHODES, now Professor Emeritus of Anglo-Irish literature at SUNY Cortland, has edited (with Daniel Casey) two books of Irish-American interest: *Irish-American Fiction: Essays in Criticism* and *Modern Irish-American Fiction: A Reader.* The author of numerous articles on Irish and Irish-American literature, he is a past president of the American Conference for Irish Studies and is a SUNY Faculty Exchange Scholar.

APARAJITA SAGAR teaches post-colonial literature in the English Department at Purdue University in West Lafayette. She has published on post-colonial studies and edited a special issue of *Modern Fiction Studies* on the fiction of the Indian subcontinent. She is working on a book on Caribbean women writers.

ADA SAVIN has been Associate Professor of American Studies at the University of Versailles since 1992. She has published numerous articles on Chicano authors in France, Germany, and Spain. She has contributed an essay on Lorna Dee Cervantes's poetry in *An Other Tongue: Nation and Ethnicity in the Linguistic Borderlands* (1994).

EVELYN SHAKIR is Associate Professor of English at Bentley College in Waltham, Massachusetts. Over the last decade, most of her research and publishing have centered on Arab-American literature. She is also nearing completion of a book on the history and experience of Arab (and Arab-American) women in the United States.

SUNIL SHARMA is a graduate student at the University of Chicago and studies Persian and Urdu literatures.

DAWN B. SOVA's sociohistorical study of the mistress, *The Encyclopedia of Mistresses,* was published in 1993, and she has a contract for a comprehensive guide to the works and life of Agatha Christie. She is also faculty consultant and mentor for the Enlightenment course for the directed, independent adult learning program (DIAL) of Thomas Edison State (New Jersey) College.

KHACHIG TOLOLYAN is Professor of English at Wesleyan University. He is the author of many articles on modern fiction, especially on the novels of Thomas Pynchon, as well as on ethnicity, diaspora, nationalism, and terrorism. He is coeditor of *Pynchon Notes* and editor of *Diaspora: A Journal of Transnational Studies.*

BENZI ZHANG teaches English and American literature at Carleton University and has published widely on ethnic/minority literature, modern and post-modern literature, and literary theory.